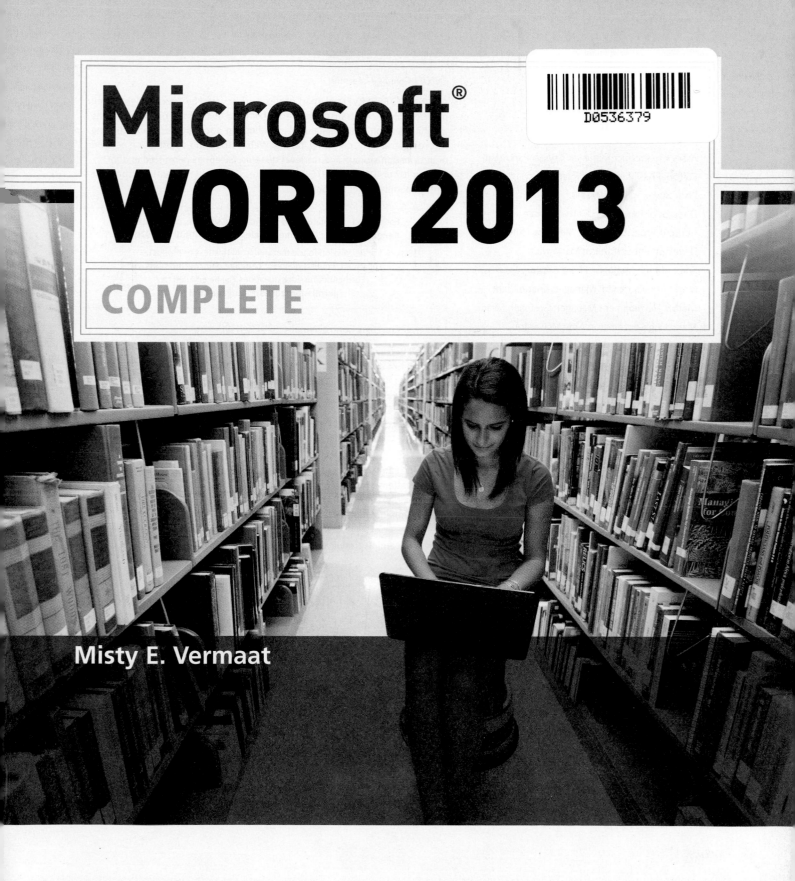

Microsoft® WORD 2013
COMPLETE

Misty E. Vermaat

CENGAGE Learning®

SHELLY CASHMAN SERIES®

Australia • Brazil • Japan • Korea • Mexico • Singapore • Spain • United Kingdom • United States

CENGAGE Learning

Microsoft® Word 2013: Complete
Misty E. Vermaat

Executive Editor: Kathleen McMahon

Product Manager: Jon Farnham

Associate Product Manager: Crystal Parenteau

Editorial Assistant: Sarah Ryan

Print Buyer: Julio Esperas

Director of Production: Patty Stephan

Content Project Manager: Matthew Hutchinson

Development Editor: Lyn Markowicz

Senior Brand Manager: Elinor Gregory

Market Development Manager: Kristie Clark

Market Development Manager: Gretchen Swann

Marketing Coordinator: Amy McGregor

QA Manuscript Reviewers: Jeffrey Schwartz,
John Freitas, Serge Palladino, Susan Pedicini,
Danielle Shaw, Susan Whalen

Art Director: GEX Publishing Services, Inc.

Text Design: Joel Sadagursky

Cover Design: Lisa Kuhn, Curio Press, LLC

Cover Photo: Tom Kates Photography

Compositor: PreMediaGlobal

Copyeditor: Harold Johnson

Proofreader: Foxxe Editorial

Indexer: Rich Carlson

For product information and technology assistance, contact us at
Cengage Learning Customer & Sales Support, 1-800-354-9706

For permission to use material from this text or product,
submit all requests online at **cengage.com/permissions**
Further permissions questions can be emailed to
permissionrequest@cengage.com

Library of Congress Control Number: 2013941390

ISBN-13: 978-1-285-16772-5
ISBN-10: 1-285-16772-4

Cengage Learning
20 Channel Center Street
Boston, MA 02210
USA

Cengage Learning is a leading provider of customized learning solutions with office locations around the globe, including Singapore, the United Kingdom, Australia, Mexico, Brazil, and Japan. Locate your local office at:
international.cengage.com/region

Cengage Learning products are represented in Canada by Nelson Education, Ltd.

To learn more about Cengage Learning, visit **www.cengage.com**

Purchase any of our products at your local college bookstore or at our preferred online store at **www.cengagebrain.com**

Printed in the United States of America
2 3 4 5 6 7 17 16 15 14

Microsoft® WORD 2013
COMPLETE

Contents

Microsoft **Office 365**

Microsoft **Word 2013**

The Shelly Cashman Series® offers the finest textbooks in computer education. We are proud that since Mircosoft Office 4.3, our series of Microsoft Office textbooks have been the most widely used books in education. With each new edition of our Office books, we make significant improvements based on the software and comments made by instructors and students. For this Microsoft Word 2013 text, the Shelly Cashman Series development team carefully reviewed our pedagogy and analyzed its effectiveness in teaching today's Office student. Students today read less, but need to retain more. They need not only to be able to perform skills, but to retain those skills and know how to apply them to different settings. Today's students need to be continually engaged and challenged to retain what they're learning.

With this Microsoft Word 2013 text, we continue our commitment to focusing on the users and how they learn best.

Objectives of This Textbook

Microsoft Word 2013: Complete is intended for a six- to nine-week period in a course that teaches Word 2013 in conjunction with another application or computer concepts. No experience with a computer is assumed and no mathematics beyond the high school freshman level is required. The objectives of this book are:

- To offer an in-depth presentation of Microsoft Word 2013

- To expose students to practical examples of the computer as a useful tool

- To acquaint students with the proper procedures to create documents suitable for coursework, professional purposes, and personal use

- To help students discover the underlying functionality of Word 2013 so they can become more productive

- To develop an exercise-oriented approach that allows learning by doing

The Shelly Cashman Approach

A Proven Pedagogy with an Emphasis on Project Planning

Each chapter presents a practical problem to be solved within a project planning framework. The project orientation is strengthened by the use of the Roadmap, which provides a visual framework for the project. Step-by-step instructions with supporting screens guide students through the steps. Instructional steps are supported by the Q&A, Experimental Step, and BTW features.

A Visually Engaging Book that Maintains Student Interest

The step-by-step tasks, with supporting figures, provide a rich visual experience for the student. Call-outs on the screens that present both explanatory and navigational information provide students with information they need when they need to know it.

Supporting Reference Materials (Quick Reference)

With the Quick Reference, students can quickly look up information about a single task, such as keyboard shortcuts, and find page references to where in the book the task is illustrated.

Integration of the World Wide Web

The World Wide Web is integrated into the Word 2013 learning experience with (1) BTW annotations; (2) BTW, Q&A, and Quick Reference Summary Web pages; and (3) the Learn Online resources for each chapter.

End-of-Chapter Student Activities

Extensive end-of-chapter activities provide a variety of reinforcement opportunities for students to apply and expand their skills through individual and group work. To complete some of these assignments, you will be required to use the Data Files for Students. Visit www.cengage.com/ct/studentdownload for detailed access instructions or contact your instructor for information about accessing the required files.

New to this Edition

Enhanced Coverage of Critical Thinking Skills

A new Consider This element poses thought-provoking questions throughout each chapter, providing an increased emphasis on critical thinking and problem-solving skills. Also, every task in the project now includes a reason *why* the students are performing the task and *why* the task is necessary.

Enhanced Retention and Transference

A new Roadmap element provides a visual framework for each project, showing students where they are in the process of creating each project, and reinforcing the context of smaller tasks by showing how they fit into the larger project.

Integration of Office with Cloud and Web Technologies

A new Lab focuses entirely on integrating cloud and web technologies with Word 2013, using technologies like Web Apps, online tools, and Google Docs.

More Personalization

Each chapter project includes an optional instruction for the student to personalize his or her solution, if required by an instructor, making each student's solution unique.

More Collaboration

A new Research and Collaboration project has been added to the Consider This: Your Turn assignment at the end of each chapter.

Instructor Resources

The Instructor Resources include both teaching and testing aids and can be accessed via CD-ROM or at www.cengage.com/login.

Instructor's Manual Includes lecture notes summarizing the chapter sections, figures and boxed elements found in every chapter, teacher tips, classroom activities, lab activities, and quick quizzes in Microsoft Word files.

Syllabus Easily customizable sample syllabi that cover policies, assignments, exams, and other course information.

Figure Files Illustrations for every figure in the textbook in electronic form.

Powerpoint Presentations A multimedia lecture presentation system that provides slides for each chapter. Presentations are based on chapter objectives.

Solutions to Exercises Includes solutions for all end-of-chapter and chapter reinforcement exercises.

Test Bank & Test Engine Test banks include 112 questions for every chapter, featuring objective-based and critical thinking question types, and including page number references and figure references, when appropriate. Also included is the test engine, ExamView, the ultimate tool for your objective-based testing needs.

Data Files for Students Includes all the files that are required by students to complete the exercises.

Additional Activities for Students Consists of Chapter Reinforcement Exercises, which are true/false, multiple-choice, and short answer questions that help students gain confidence in the material learned.

Learn Online

Cengagebrain.com is the premier destination for purchasing or renting Cengage Learning textbooks, eBooks, eChapters, and study tools at a significant discount (eBooks up to 50% off Print). In addition, cengagebrain.com provides direct access to all digital products, including eBooks, eChapters, and digital solutions, such as CourseMate and SAM, regardless of where purchased. The following are some examples of what is available for this product on www.cengagebrain.com.

Student Companion Site The Student Companion Site reinforces chapter terms and concepts using true/false questions, multiple choice questions, short answer questions, flash cards, practice tests, and learning games, all available for no additional cost at www.cengagebrain.com.

SAM: Skills Assessment Manager Get your students workplace-ready with SAM, the market-leading proficiency-based assessment and training solution for Microsoft Office! SAM's active, hands-on environment helps students master Microsoft Office skills and computer concepts that are essential to academic and career success, delivering the most comprehensive online learning solution for your course!

Through skill-based assessments, interactive trainings, business-centric projects, and comprehensive remediation, SAM engages students in mastering the latest Microsoft Office programs on their own, giving instructors more time to focus on teaching. Computer concepts labs supplement instruction of important technology-related topics and issues through engaging simulations and interactive, auto-graded assessments. With enhancements including streamlined course setup, more robust grading and reporting features, and the integration of fully interactive MindTap Readers containing Cengage Learning's premier textbook content, SAM provides the best teaching and learning solution for your course.

MindLinks MindLinks is a new Cengage Learning Service designed to provide the best possible user experience and facilitate the highest levels of learning retention and outcomes, enabled through a deep integration of Cengage Learning's digital suite into an instructor's Learning Management System (LMS). MindLinks works on any LMS that supports the IMS Basic LTI open standard. Advanced features, including grade-book exchange, are the result of active, enhanced LTI collaborations with industry-leading LMS partners to drive the evolving technology standards forward.

CourseNotes

Cengage Learning's CourseNotes are six-panel quick reference cards that reinforce the most important and widely used features of a software application in a visual and user-friendly format. CourseNotes serve as a great reference tool during and after the course. CourseNotes are available for software applications, such as Microsoft Office 2013. There are also topic-based CourseNotes available, such as Best Practices in Social Networking, Hot Topics in Technology, and Web 2.0. Visit www.cengagebrain.com to learn more!

course|notes™
quick reference guide

About Our Covers

The Shelly Cashman Series is continually updating our approach and content to reflect the way today's students learn and experience new technology. This focus on student success is reflected on our covers, which feature real students from The University of Rhode Island using the Shelly Cashman Series in their courses, and reflect the varied ages and backgrounds of the students learning with our books. When you use the Shelly Cashman Series, you can be assured that you are learning computer skills using the most effective courseware available.

Textbook Walk-Through

The Shelly Cashman Series Pedagogy: Project-Based — Step-by-Step — Variety of Assessments

Roadmaps provide a visual framework for each project, showing the students where they are in the process of creating each project.

Step-by-step instructions provide a context beyond the point-and-click. Each step provides information on why students are performing each task and what will occur as a result.

For an introduction to Windows and instruction about how to perform basic Windows tasks, read the Office and Windows chapter at the beginning of this book, where you can learn how to resize windows, change screen resolution, create folders, move and rename files, use Windows Help, and much more.

Roadmap

In this chapter, you will learn how to create the flyer shown in Figure 1–1. The following roadmap identifies general activities you will perform as you progress through this chapter:

1. **ENTER TEXT** in a new document.
2. **FORMAT** the **TEXT** in the flyer.
3. **INSERT** a **PICTURE**, called Mountain Trail, in the flyer.
4. **FORMAT** the **PICTURE** in the flyer.
5. **ENHANCE** the **PAGE** with a border and spacing.
6. **CORRECT** errors **AND REVISE** text in the flyer.
7. **PRINT OR READ** the flyer.

At the beginning of step instructions throughout the chapter, you will see an abbreviated form of this roadmap. The abbreviated roadmap uses colors to indicate chapter progress: gray means the chapter is beyond that activity, blue means the task being shown is covered in that activity, and black means that activity is yet to be covered. For example, the following abbreviated roadmap indicates the chapter would be showing a task in the 2 FORMAT TEXT activity.

| 1 ENTER TEXT | 2 FORMAT TEXT | 3 INSERT PICTURE | 4 FORMAT PICTURE |
| 5 ENHANCE PAGE | 6 CORRECT & REVISE | 7 PRINT OR READ |

Use the abbreviated roadmap as a progress guide while you read or step through the instructions in this chapter.

To Run Word and Create a Blank Document

If you are using a computer to step through the project in this chapter and you want your screens to match the figures in this book, you should change your resolution to 1366 × 768. For information about how to change a computer's resolution, refer to the Office and Windows chapter at the beginning of this book.

The following steps, which assume Windows 8 is running, use the Start screen or the Search box to run Word based on a typical installation. You may need to ask your instructor how to run Word on your computer. For a detailed example of the procedure summarized below, refer to the Office and Windows chapter.

Start screen for a Word 2013 tile. If your Start screen contains a Word 2013 tile, click it to run Word and then proceed to Step 5; if the Start screen does not contain the Word 2013 tile, proceed to the next step to search for the Word app.

From the right edge of the screen or point to the upper-right corner of the screen to display the Charms bar and then tap or click the Search charm on the Charms bar to display the Search menu.

Word as the search text in the Search box and watch the search results appear in the results list.

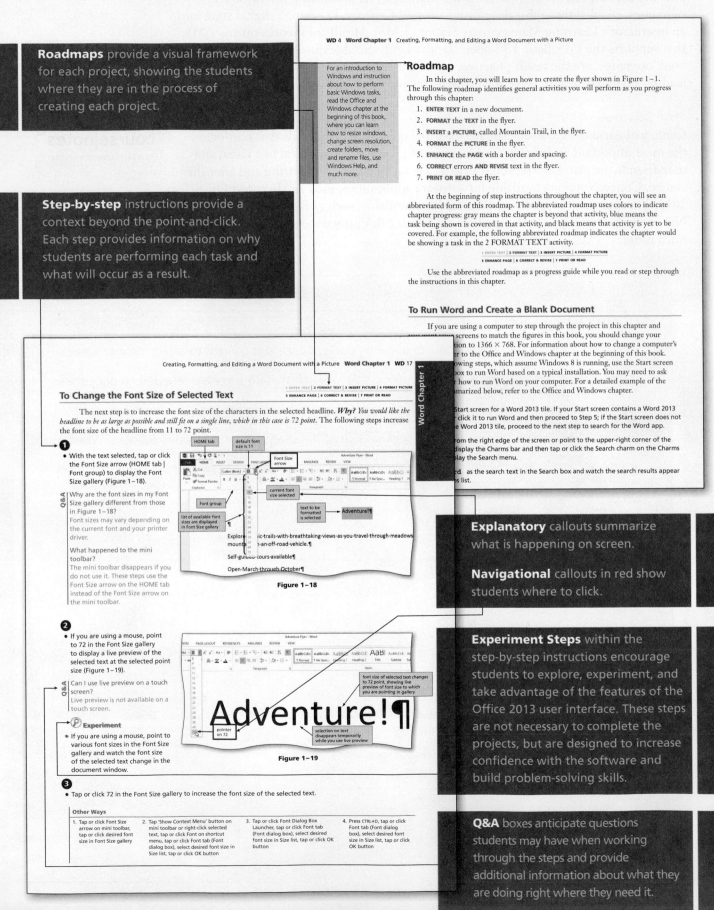

To Change the Font Size of Selected Text

| 1 ENTER TEXT | 2 FORMAT TEXT | 3 INSERT PICTURE | 4 FORMAT PICTURE |
| 5 ENHANCE PAGE | 6 CORRECT & REVISE | 7 PRINT OR READ |

The next step is to increase the font size of the characters in the selected headline. *Why? You would like the headline to be as large as possible and still fit on a single line, which in this case is 72 point.* The following steps increase the font size of the headline from 11 to 72 point.

1
- With the text selected, tap or click the Font Size arrow (HOME tab | Font group) to display the Font Size gallery (Figure 1–18).

Q&A Why are the font sizes in my Font Size gallery different from those in Figure 1–18?
Font sizes may vary depending on the current font and your printer driver.

What happened to the mini toolbar?
The mini toolbar disappears if you do not use it. These steps use the Font Size arrow on the HOME tab instead of the Font Size arrow on the mini toolbar.

Figure 1–18

2
- If you are using a mouse, point to 72 in the Font Size gallery to display a live preview of the selected text at the selected point size (Figure 1–19).

Q&A Can I use live preview on a touch screen?
Live preview is not available on a touch screen.

Experiment
- If you are using a mouse, point to various font sizes in the Font Size gallery and watch the font size of the selected text change in the document window.

Figure 1–19

3
- Tap or click 72 in the Font Size gallery to increase the font size of the selected text.

Other Ways

1. Tap or click Font Size arrow on mini toolbar, tap or click desired font size in Font Size gallery
2. Tap 'Show Context Menu' button on mini toolbar or right-click selected text, tap or click Font on shortcut menu, tap or click Font tab (Font dialog box), select desired font size in Size list, tap or click OK button
3. Tap or click Font Dialog Box Launcher, tap or click Font tab (Font dialog box), select desired font size in Size list, tap or click OK button
4. Press CTRL+D, tap or click Font tab (Font dialog box), select desired font size in Size list, tap or click OK button

Explanatory callouts summarize what is happening on screen.

Navigational callouts in red show students where to click.

Experiment Steps within the step-by-step instructions encourage students to explore, experiment, and take advantage of the features of the Office 2013 user interface. These steps are not necessary to complete the projects, but are designed to increase confidence with the software and build problem-solving skills.

Q&A boxes anticipate questions students may have when working through the steps and provide additional information about what they are doing right where they need it.

Consider This boxes pose thought-provoking questions with answers throughout each chapter, promoting critical thought along with immediate feedback.

Chapter Summary A listing of the tasks completed within the chapter, grouped into major task categories in an outline format.

Consider This: Plan Ahead box presents a single master planning guide that students can use as they create documents on their own.

---

flyer before formatting

Adventure!

Explore scenic trails with breathtaking views as you travel through meadows, forests, streams, and mountains in an off-road vehicle.

Self-guided tours available

Open March through October

All vehicles and gear provided

To book your adventure, call 555-8928!

flyer after formatting

ADVENTURE!

Explore scenic trails with *breathtaking* views as you travel through meadows, forests, streams, and mountains in an **off-road** vehicle.

- Self-guided tours available
- All vehicles and gear provided
- Open March through October

To book your adventure, call 555-8928!

(a) Unformatted Flyer

(b) Formatted Flyer

Figure 1–13

Font, Font Sizes, and Themes

Characters that appear on the screen are a specific shape and size. The **font**, or typeface, defines the appearance and shape of the letters, numbers, and special characters. In Word, the default font usually is Calibri (shown in Figure 1–14 on page WD 15). You can leave characters in the default font or change them to a different font. **Font size** specifies the size of the characters and is determined by a measurement system called points. A single point is about 1/72 of one inch in height. The default font size in Word typically is 11 (Figure 1–14). Thus, a character with a font size of 11 is about 11/72 or a little less than 1/6 of one inch in height. You can increase or decrease the font size of characters in a document.

A document **theme** is a set of unified formats for fonts, colors, and graphics. Word includes a variety of document themes to assist you with coordinating these visual elements in a document. The default theme fonts are Calibri Light for headings and Calibri for body text. By changing the document theme, you quickly can give your document a new look. You also can define your own document themes.

BTW

Formatting Marks
With some fonts, the formatting marks will not be displayed properly on the screen. For example, the raised dot that signifies a blank space between words may be displayed behind a character instead of in the blank space, causing the characters to look incorrect.

CONSIDER THIS

How do I know which formats to use in a flyer?
In a flyer, consider the following formatting suggestions.

- **Increase the font size of characters.** Flyers usually are posted on a bulletin board or in a window. Thus, the font size should be as large as possible so that passersby easily can read the flyer. To give the headline more impact, its font size should be larger than the font size of the text in the body copy. If possible, make the font size of the signature line larger than the body copy but smaller than the headline.

- **Change the font of characters.** Use fonts that are easy to read. Try to use only two different fonts in a flyer; for example, use one for the headline and the other for all other text. Too many fonts can make the flyer visually confusing.

- **Change the paragraph alignment.** The default alignment for paragraphs in a document is **left-aligned**, that is, flush at the left margin of the document with uneven right edges. Consider changing the alignment of some of the paragraphs to add interest and variety to the flyer.

- **Highlight key paragraphs with bullets.** A bulleted paragraph is a paragraph that begins with a dot or other symbol. Use bulleted paragraphs to highlight important points in a flyer.

- **Emphasize important words.** To call attention to certain words or lines, you can underline them, italicize them, or bold them. Use these formats sparingly, however, because overuse will minimize their effect and make the flyer look too busy.

- **Use color.** Use colors that complement each other and convey the meaning of the flyer. Vary colors in terms of hue and brightness. Headline colors, for example, can be bold and bright. Signature lines should stand out more than body copy but less than headlines. Keep in mind that too many colors can detract from the flyer and make it difficult to read.

Chapter Summary

In this chapter, you have learned how to enter text in a document, form page border, adjust paragraph and page spacing, and print and read a d all the new Word skills you have learned in this chapter, with the tasks

Enter and Edit Text
Type Text (WD 5)
Insert a Blank Line (WD 7)
Wordwrap Text as You Type (WD 9)
Check Spelling and Grammar as You Type (WD 10)
Insert Text in an Existing Document (WD 48)
Delete Text (WD 48)
Move Text (WD 49)

File Management
Run Word (WD 46)
Save a Document (WD 12)
Save an Existing Document with the Same File Name (WD 33)
Exit Word (WD 46)
Change Document Properties (WD 44)
Open a Document from Word (WD 47)
Print a Document (WD 51)

Format a Page
Change Theme Colors (WD 31)
Add a Page Border (WD 41)
Center Page Contents Vertically (WD 43)

Format Text
Center a Paragraph (WD 15)
Change the Font Size of Selected Text (WD 17)
Change the Font of Selected Text (WD 18)
Change the Case of Selected Text (WD 19)
Apply a Text Effect to Selected Text (WD 20)

Shade a Pa
Bullet a Li
Undo and
Italicize Te
Color Text
Use the M
Underline
Bold Text
Change Sp
    Paragra

Select Text
Select a Li
Select Mul
Select a G

Word Settings
Display Formatting Marks (WD 6)
Zoom Page Width (WD 7)
Zoom One Page (WD 30)
Zoom the Document (WD 35)
Zoom 100% (WD 37)
Switch to Read Mode (WD 52)
Switch to Print Layout View (WD 53)

Work with Graphics (Pictures)
Insert a Picture (WD 34)
Resize a Graphic (WD 36)
Apply a Picture Style (WD 38)
Apply Picture Effects (WD 39)

CONSIDER THIS

What decisions will you need to make when creating your next flyer?
Use these guidelines as you complete the assignments in this chapter and create your own flyers outside of this class.

1. Choose the text for the headline, body copy, and signature line—using as few words as possible to make a point.

2. Format various elements of the text.

   a) Select appropriate font sizes for text in the headline, body copy, and signature line.

   b) Select appropriate fonts for text in the headline, body copy, and signature line.

   c) Adjust paragraph alignment, as appropriate.

   d) Highlight key paragraphs with bullets.

   e) Emphasize important words.

   f) Use color to convey meaning and add appeal.

3. Find an eye-catching graphic(s) that conveys the overall message and meaning of the flyer.

4. Establish where to position and how to format the graphical image(s) so that the image grabs the attention of passersby and draws them into reading the flyer.

5. Determine whether the flyer needs enhancements such as a graphical, color-coordinated border or spacing adjustments to improve readability or overall appearance.

6. Correct errors and revise the document as necessary.

   a) Post the flyer on a wall and make sure all text and images are legible from a distance.

   b) Ask someone else to read the flyer and give you suggestions for improvements.

7. Determine the best method for distributing the document such as printing, sending via email, or posting on the web.

Textbook Walk-Through

Apply Your Knowledge This exercise usually requires students to open and manipulate a file that parallels the activities learned in the chapter.

How should you submit solutions to questions in the assignments identified with a ✳ symbol?
Every assignment in this book contains one or more questions identified with a ✳ symbol. These questions require you to think beyond the assigned document. Present your solutions to the questions in the format required by your instructor. Possible formats may include one or more of these options: write the answer; create a document that contains the answer; present your answer to the class; discuss your answer in a group; record the answer as audio or video using a webcam, smartphone, or portable media player; or post answers on a blog, wiki, or website.

Apply Your Knowledge

Reinforce the skills and apply the concepts you learned in this chapter.

Modifying Text and Formatting a Document

Note: To complete this assignment, you will be required to use the Data Files for Students. Visit www.cengage.com/ct/studentdownload for detailed instructions or contact your instructor for information about accessing the required files.

Instructions: Run Word. Open the document, Apply 1-1 County Park Flyer Unformatted, from the Data Files for Students. The document you open is an unformatted flyer. You are to modify text, format paragraphs and characters, and insert a picture in the flyer to create the flyer shown in Figure 1–74.

Perform the following tasks:

1. Delete the word, below, in the sentence below the headline.
2. Insert the word, Valley, between the words, Green County, in the second to last line of the flyer.
3. Change the period to an exclamation point in the last line so the text reads: Thank You!
4. If requested by your instructor, change the phone number in the flyer to your phone number.
5. Center the headline and the last two paragraphs of the flyer.
6. Select the third, fourth, and fifth paragraphs in the flyer and add bullets to the selected paragraphs.
7. Change the theme colors to the Red Orange color scheme.
8. Change the font and font size of the headline to 48-point Franklin Gothic Heavy, or a similar font. Change the case of the headline text to uppercase letters. Apply the text effect called Fill - Black, Text 1, Outline - Background 1, Hard Shadow - Background 1 to the headline. Change the font color of the headline text to Dark Red, Accent 6.

PLEASE DO NOT FEED THE WILDLIFE!

Follow these guidelines to keep our wildlife healthy and our environment clean.

- Do **not** feed the wildlife.
- Never leave food unattended.
- Discard *all* trash in provided containers.

Questions? Call Green Valley County Park at 329-555-1020.

Thank You!

Courtesy of Misty Vermaat

headline

bulleted list

Figure 1–74

Continued >

Apply Your Knowledge continued

9. Change the font size of the sentence below the h... flyer to 26 point.
10. Use the mini toolbar to change the font size of t...
11. Select the words, Follow these guidelines, in the pa...
12. Bold the word, not, in the first bulleted paragraph... Dark Red, Accent 6.
13. Italicize the word, all, in the second bulleted item...
14. Switch the last two bulleted paragraphs. That is, ... and move it so that it is the second bulleted para...
15. Bold the text, Thank You!, in the last line of the f... Accent 6, Darker 25%. If the font color does not ... change its color to White, Background 1.
16. Change the zoom so that the entire page is visibl...
17. Insert the picture of the squirrel eating the sucke... headline. The picture is called Squirrel and is av... the Soft Edge Oval picture style to the inserted picture.
18. Change the spacing before the first bulleted paragraph to 12 point and the spacing after the last bulleted paragraph to 24 point.
19. The entire flyer should fit on a single page. If it flows to two pages, resize the picture or decrease spacing before and after paragraphs until the entire flyer text fits on a single page.
20. Change the zoom to text width, then page width, then 100% and notice the differences.
21. If requested by your instructor, enter the text, Green Valley, as the keywords in the document properties. Change the other document properties, as specified by your instructor.
22. Click FILE on the ribbon and then click Save As. Save the document using the file name, Apply 1-1 County Park Flyer Formatted.
23. Print the document. Switch to Read Mode and browse pages through the document. Switch to Print Layout view.
24. Submit the revised document, shown in Figure 1–74, in the format specified by your instructor.
25. Exit Word.
26. ✳ If this flyer were announcing the park reopening instead of including a warning, which color scheme would you apply and why?

Extend Your Knowledge

Extend Your Knowledge projects at the end of each chapter allow students to extend and expand on the skills learned within the chapter. Students use critical thinking to experiment with new skills to complete each project.

Extend the skills you learned in this chapter and experiment with new skills. You may need to use Help to complete the assignment.

Modifying Text and Picture Formats and Adding Page Borders

Note: To complete this assignment, you will be required to use the Data Files for Students. Visit www.cengage.com/ct/studentdownload for detailed instructions or contact your instructor for information about accessing the required files.

Instructions: Run Word. Open the document, Extend 1-1 Baseball Tryouts Flyer Draft, from the Data Files for Students. You will enhance the look of the flyer shown in Figure 1–75.
Hint: Remember, if you make a mistake while formatting the picture, you can reset it by using the Reset Picture button or Reset Picture arrow (PICTURE TOOLS FORMAT tab | Adjust group).

12. If requested by your instructor, print a single mailing label for the letter and then a full page of mailing labels, each containing the address shown in Figure 3–78.

13. 🌐 Answer the questions posed in #2 and #6. Why would you group objects? Which picture bullet did you use and why?

Analyze, Correct, Improve

Analyze a document, correct all errors, and improve it.

Formatting a Business Letter

Note: To complete this assignment, you will be required to use the Data Files for Students. Visit www.cengage.com/ct/studentdownload for detailed instructions or contact your instructor for information about accessing the required files.

Instructions: Run Word. Open the document, Analyze 3-1 Recommendation Letter Draft, located on the Data Files for Students. The document is a business letter that is missing elements and is formatted poorly or incorrectly (Figure 3–79). You are to change the color of the text, insert symbols, remove a hyperlink, change the letter style from block to modified block, insert and format clip art, and format the table.

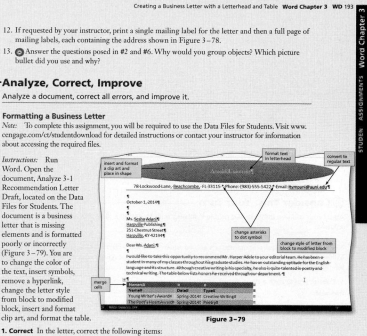

Figure 3–79

1. Correct In the letter, correct the following items:

  a. Increase the font size of the text in the letterhead. Change the color of the text in the letterhead so that the text is readable.

  b. Change the asterisks in the contact information to the dot symbol.

  c. Convert the email address hyperlink to regular text.

  d. The letter currently is the block letter style. It should be the modified block letter style. Format the appropriate paragraphs by setting custom tab stops and then positioning those paragraphs at the tab stops. Be sure to position the insertion point in the paragraph before setting the tab stop.

  e. Merge the three cells in the first row of the table into one cell and then center the title in the cell. Center the entire table between the page margins.

2. Improve Enhance the letterhead by changing the theme to one you prefer. Then, locate and insert at least one appropriate clip art image in the letterhead. If necessary, resize the graphic(s). Change the text wrapping of the clip art to In Front of Text and move the graphic(s) into the shape. Change the color of the graphic to match the color of the text or shape. Adjust the brightness and contrast of the graphic. Format one color in the graphic as transparent. Change the picture border color. If requested by your instructor, change the name in the signature block to your name. Save the modified document with the file name, Analyze 3-1 Recommendation Letter Modified, and then submit it in the format specified by your instructor.

3. 🌐 In this assignment, you located and inserted clip art. What image did you select and why?

In the Labs

Design and/or create a document using the guidelin[es]... in this chapter. Labs 1 and 2, which increase in diffic[ulty] based on what you learned in the chapter; Lab 3 re[quires] uses cloud and web technologies, by learning and i[n]... general guidance.

Lab 1: Creating a Letter with a Le...

Problem: As office manager for a fitness club, you send [letters].... One letter you prepare is shown in Figure 3–80.

shape style: Moderate Effect - Orange, Accent 1

BUGBY'S FITNESS CLUB

centered

35 Lake Street, Donner, OH 44772 • Phone: 677-555-9023 • Email: info@bugby.com

September 9, 2014

Mr. Timo Perez
404 Runway Road
Ponrolet, OH 44770

Dear Mr. Perez:

Your membership at Bugby's Fitness Club will expire at the end of next month. We hope you choose to continue to take advantage of our state-of-the-art fitness equipment and facilities.

The longer your term of renewal, the more you save! Current members can guarantee their membership rates as follows:

- Six-month renewal: $185
- One-year renewal: $350
- Two-year renewal: $675

You can renew your membership in one of three ways: online at www.bugby.com, by phone at 677-555-9023, or in person at the registration desk. We look forward to seeing you soon!

Sincerely,

Jonathon White
Office Manager

Figure 3–80

Textbook Walk-Through

5. Insert the picture called Bean Bag Toss, which is located on the Data Files for Students.

6. Use the features available in the Word Web App, along with the concepts and techniques presented in this chapter, to format this flyer. Be sure to change the font and font size of text, center a paragraph(s), italicize text, color text, underline text, and apply a picture style. Adjust spacing above and below paragraphs as necessary. Resize the picture, if necessary.

7. If requested by your instructor, replace the contact name in the flyer with your name.

8. Save the document again. Tap or click the button to open the document in the Word desktop app. If necessary, sign in to your Microsoft account when prompted. Notice how the document appears in the Word desktop app.

9. Using either the Word Web App or Word desktop app, submit the document in the format requested by your instructor. Exit the Word Web App (FILE tab | Exit). Sign out of your SkyDrive account. Sign out of the Microsoft account in Word.

10. ✪ What is the Word Web App? Which features that are covered in this chapter are not available in the Word Web App? Do you prefer using the Word Web App or the Word desktop app? Why?

✸ Consider This: Your Turn

Apply your creative thinking and problem solving skills to design and implement a solution.

Note: To complete these assignments, you may be required to use the Data Files for Students. Visit www.cengage.com/ct/studentdownload for detailed instructions or contact your instructor for information about accessing the required files.

1: Design and Create a Photography Club Flyer

Personal

Part 1:   As secretary of your school's Photography Club, you are responsible for creating and distributing flyers announcing the club. The flyer should contain two digital pictures appropriately resized; the Data Files for Students contains two pictures called Photography 1 and Photography 2, or you can use your own digital pictures if they are appropriate for the topic of the flyer. The flyer should contain the headline, Photography Club, and this signature line: Questions? Call Emily at (883) 555-0901. The body copy consists of the following text, in any order: Do you love photography? This is the club for you! All skill levels are welcome. Meetings every Tuesday at 5:00 p.m. in the Student Center (room 232). Bring your camera. We look forward to seeing you at our next meeting!

Use the concepts and techniques presented in this chapter to create and format this flyer. Be sure to check spelling and grammar. Submit your assignment and answers to the critical thinking questions in the format specified by your instructor.

Part 2:   ✪ You made several decisions while creating the flyer in this assignment: where to place text, how to format the text (i.e., font, font size, paragraph alignment, bulleted paragraphs, underlines, italics, bold, color, etc.), which graphics to use, where to position the graphics, how to format the graphics (i.e., borders and spacing). What was the rationale behind each of these decisions? When you proofread the document, what further revisions did you make and why? How would you recommend distributing this flyer?

2: Design and Create a Hot Air Balloon Rides Flyer

Professional

Part 1:   As a part-time employee at Galaxy Recreations, your boss has asked you to create and distribute flyers announcing hot air balloon rides. The flyer should contain two digital pictures appropriately resized; the Data Files for Students contains two pictures called Hot Air Balloon 1

Continued >

Consider This: Your Turn exercises call on students to apply creative thinking and problem solving skills to design and implement a solution.

Office 2013 and Windows 8: Essential Concepts and Skills

Microsoft product screen shots used with permission from Microsoft Corporation.

Objectives

You will have mastered the material in this chapter when you can:

- Use a touch screen
- Perform basic mouse operations
- Start Windows and sign in to an account
- Identify the objects in the Windows 8 desktop
- Identify the apps in and versions of Microsoft Office 2013
- Run an app
- Identify the components of the Microsoft Office ribbon

- Create folders
- Save files
- Change screen resolution
- Perform basic tasks in Microsoft Office apps
- Manage files
- Use Microsoft Office Help and Windows Help

Office 2013 and Windows 8: Essential Concepts and Skills

This introductory chapter uses Word 2013 to cover features and functions common to Office 2013 apps, as well as the basics of Windows 8.

Roadmap

In this chapter, you will learn how to perform basic tasks in Windows and Word. The following roadmap identifies general activities you will perform as you progress through this chapter:

1. SIGN IN to an account
2. USE WINDOWS
3. USE Features in Word that are Common across Office APPS
4. FILE and Folder MANAGEMENT
5. SWITCH between APPS
6. SAVE and Manage FILES
7. CHANGE SCREEN RESOLUTION
8. EXIT APPS
9. USE ADDITIONAL Office APP FEATURES
10. USE Office and Windows HELP

At the beginning of the step instructions throughout the chapter, you will see an abbreviated form of this roadmap. The abbreviated roadmap uses colors to indicate chapter progress: gray means the chapter is beyond that activity, blue means the task being shown is covered in that activity, and black means that activity is yet to be covered. For example, the following abbreviated roadmap indicates the chapter would be showing a task in the 2 USE APPS activity.

1 SIGN IN | 2 USE WINDOWS | 3 USE APPS | 4 FILE MANAGEMENT | 5 SWITCH APPS | 6 SAVE FILES
7 CHANGE SCREEN RESOLUTION | 8 EXIT APPS | 9 USE ADDITIONAL APP FEATURES | 10 USE HELP

Use the abbreviated roadmap as a progress guide while you read or step through the instructions in this chapter.

Introduction to the Windows 8 Operating System

Windows 8 is the newest version of Microsoft Windows, which is a popular and widely used operating system. An **operating system** is a computer program (set of computer instructions) that coordinates all the activities of computer hardware, such as memory, storage devices, and printers, and provides the capability for you to communicate with the computer.

The Windows operating system simplifies the process of working with documents and apps by organizing the manner in which you interact with the computer. Windows is used to run apps. An **app** (short for application) consists of programs designed to make users more productive and/or assist them with personal tasks, such as word processing or browsing the web.

The Windows 8 interface begins with the **Start screen**, which shows tiles (Figure 1). A **tile** is a shortcut to an app or other content. The tiles on the Start screen include installed apps that you use regularly. From the Start screen, you can choose which apps to run using a touch screen, mouse, or other input device.

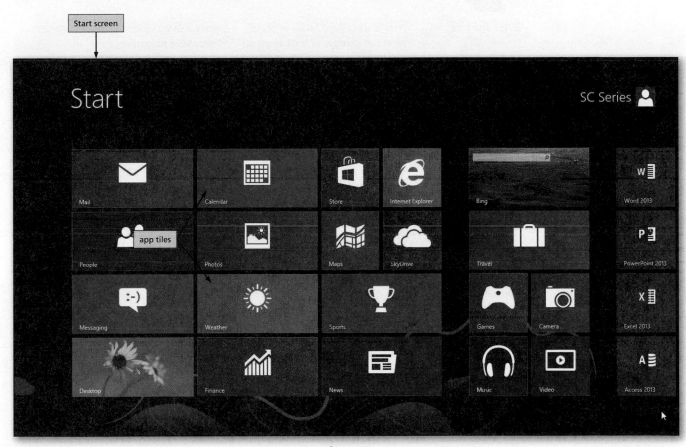

Figure 1

Using a Touch Screen and a Mouse

Windows users who have computers or devices with touch screen capability can interact with the screen using gestures. A **gesture** is a motion you make on a touch screen with the tip of one or more fingers or your hand. Touch screens are convenient because they do not require a separate device for input. Table 1 on the next page presents common ways to interact with a touch screen.

If you are using your finger on a touch screen and are having difficulty completing the steps in this chapter, consider using a stylus. Many people find it easier to be precise with a stylus than with a finger. In addition, with a stylus you see the pointer. If you still are having trouble completing the steps with a stylus, try using a mouse.

Table 1 Touch Screen Gestures

Motion	Description	Common Uses
Tap	Quickly touch and release one finger one time.	Activate a link (built-in connection) Press a button Run a program or an app
Double-tap	Quickly touch and release one finger two times.	Run a program or an app Zoom in (show a smaller area on the screen, so that contents appear larger) at the location of the double-tap
Press and hold	Press and hold one finger to cause an action to occur, or until an action occurs.	Display a shortcut menu (immediate access to allowable actions) Activate a mode enabling you to move an item with one finger to a new location
Drag, or slide	Press and hold one finger on an object and then move the finger to the new location.	Move an item around the screen Scroll
Swipe	Press and hold one finger and then move the finger horizontally or vertically on the screen.	Select an object Swipe from edge to display a bar such as the Charms bar, Apps bar, and Navigation bar (all discussed later)
Stretch	Move two fingers apart.	Zoom in (show a smaller area on the screen, so that contents appear larger)
Pinch	Move two fingers together.	Zoom out (show a larger area on the screen, so that contents appear smaller)

© 2014 Cengage Learning

BTW

BTWs

For a complete list of the BTWs found in the margins of this book, visit the BTW resource on the Student Companion Site located on www.cengagebrain.com. For detailed instructions about accessing available resources, visit www.cengage.com/ct/studentdownload or contact your instructor for information about accessing the required files.

BTW

Touch Screen Differences

The Office and Windows interfaces may vary if you are using a touch screen. For this reason, you might notice that the function or appearance of your touch screen differs slightly from this chapter's presentation.

CONSIDER THIS

Will your screen look different if you are using a touch screen?

The Windows and Microsoft Office interface varies slightly if you are using a touch screen. For this reason, you might notice that your Windows or Word screens look slightly different from the screens in this book.

Windows users who do not have touch screen capabilities typically work with a mouse that usually has at least two buttons. For a right-handed user, the left button usually is the primary mouse button, and the right mouse button is the secondary mouse button. Left-handed people, however, can reverse the function of these buttons.

Table 2 explains how to perform a variety of mouse operations. Some apps also use keys in combination with the mouse to perform certain actions. For example, when you hold down the CTRL key while rolling the mouse wheel, text on the screen may become larger or smaller based on the direction you roll the wheel. The function of the mouse buttons and the wheel varies depending on the app.

Table 2 Mouse Operations

Operation	Mouse Action	Example
Point	Move the mouse until the pointer on the desktop is positioned on the item of choice.	Position the pointer on the screen.
Click	Press and release the primary mouse button, which usually is the left mouse button.	Select or deselect items on the screen or run an app or app feature.
Right-click	Press and release the secondary mouse button, which usually is the right mouse button.	Display a shortcut menu.
Double-click	Quickly press and release the primary mouse button twice without moving the mouse.	Run an app or app feature.
Triple-click	Quickly press and release the primary mouse button three times without moving the mouse.	Select a paragraph.
Drag	Point to an item, hold down the primary mouse button, move the item to the desired location on the screen, and then release the mouse button.	Move an object from one location to another or draw pictures.
Right-drag	Point to an item, hold down the right mouse button, move the item to the desired location on the screen, and then release the right mouse button.	Display a shortcut menu after moving an object from one location to another.
Rotate wheel	Roll the wheel forward or backward.	Scroll vertically (up and down).
Free-spin wheel	Whirl the wheel forward or backward so that it spins freely on its own.	Scroll through many pages in seconds.
Press wheel	Press the wheel button while moving the mouse.	Scroll continuously.
Tilt wheel	Press the wheel toward the right or left.	Scroll horizontally (left and right).
Press thumb button	Press the button on the side of the mouse with your thumb.	Move forward or backward through webpages and/or control media, games, etc.

© 2014 Cengage Learning

Scrolling

A **scroll bar** is a horizontal or vertical bar that appears when the contents of an area may not be visible completely on the screen (Figure 2). A scroll bar contains **scroll arrows** and a **scroll box** that enable you to view areas that currently cannot be seen on the screen. Tapping or clicking the up and down scroll arrows moves the screen content up or down one line. You also can tap or click above or below the scroll box to move up or down a section, or drag the scroll box up or down to move to a specific location.

scroll arrows

scroll bar

scroll box

Figure 2

BTW
Pointer
If you are using a touch screen, the pointer may not appear on the screen as you perform touch gestures. The pointer will reappear when you begin using the mouse.

BTW
Minimize Wrist Injury
Computer users frequently switch between the keyboard and the mouse during a word processing session; such switching strains the wrist. To help prevent wrist injury, minimize switching. For instance, if your fingers already are on the keyboard, use keyboard keys to scroll. If your hand already is on the mouse, use the mouse to scroll. If your hand is on the touch screen, use touch gestures to scroll.

What should you do if you are running Windows 7 instead of Windows 8?

Although Windows 8 includes several user interface and feature enhancements, many of the steps in this book work in both Windows 7 and Windows 8. If you have any questions about differences between the two operating systems or how to perform tasks in an earlier version of Windows, contact your instructor.

CONSIDER THIS

Keyboard Shortcuts

In many cases, you can use the keyboard instead of the mouse to accomplish a task. To perform tasks using the keyboard, you press one or more keyboard keys, sometimes identified as a **keyboard shortcut**. Some keyboard shortcuts consist of a single key, such as the F1 key. For example, to obtain help in many apps, you can press the F1 key. Other keyboard shortcuts consist of multiple keys, in which case a plus sign separates the key names, such as CTRL+ESC. This notation means to press and hold down the first key listed, press one or more additional keys, and then release all keys. For example, to display the Start screen, press CTRL+ESC, that is, hold down the CTRL key, press the ESC key, and then release both keys.

Starting Windows

It is not unusual for multiple people to use the same computer in a work, educational, recreational, or home setting. Windows enables each user to establish a **user account**, which identifies to Windows the resources, such as apps and storage locations, a user can access when working with the computer.

Each user account has a user name and may have a password and an icon, as well. A **user name** is a unique combination of letters or numbers that identifies a specific user to Windows. A **password** is a private combination of letters, numbers, and special characters associated with the user name that allows access to a user's account resources. An icon is a small image that represents an object, thus a **user icon** is a picture associated with a user name.

When you turn on a computer, Windows starts and displays a **lock screen** consisting of the time and date (Figure 3a). To unlock the screen, swipe up or click the lock screen. Depending on your computer's settings, Windows may or may not display a sign-in screen that shows the user names and user icons for users who have accounts on the computer (Figure 3b). This **sign-in screen** enables you to sign in to your user account and makes the computer available for use. Tapping or clicking the user icon begins the process of signing in, also called logging on, to your user account.

At the bottom of the sign-in screen is the 'Ease of access' button and a Shut down button. Tapping or clicking the 'Ease of access' button displays the Ease of access menu, which provides tools to optimize a computer to accommodate the needs of the mobility, hearing, and vision impaired users. Tapping or clicking the Shut down

Figure 3a

SC Series user icon

Note: To help you locate screen elements that are referenced in the step instructions, such as buttons and commands, this book uses red boxes to point to these screen elements.

Figure 3b

button displays a menu containing commands related to restarting the computer, putting it in a low-power state, and shutting it down. The commands available on your computer may differ.

- The Sleep command saves your work, turns off the computer fans and hard disk, and places the computer in a lower-power state. To wake the computer from sleep mode, press the power button or lift a laptop's cover, and sign in to your account.
- The Shut down command exits running apps, shuts down Windows, and then turns off the computer.
- The Restart command exits running apps, shuts down Windows, and then restarts Windows.

BTW

Q&As

For a complete list of the Q&As found in many of the step-by-step sequences in this book, visit the Q&A resource on the Student Companion Site located on www.cengagebrain.com. For detailed instructions about accessing available resources, visit www.cengage.com/ct/studentdownload or contact your instructor for information about accessing the required files.

To Sign In to an Account

1 SIGN IN | 2 USE WINDOWS | 3 USE APPS | 4 FILE MANAGEMENT | 5 SWITCH APPS | 6 SAVE FILES
7 CHANGE SCREEN RESOLUTION | 8 EXIT APPS | 9 USE ADDITIONAL APP FEATURES | 10 USE HELP

The following steps, which use SC Series as the user name, sign in to an account based on a typical Windows installation. *Why? After starting Windows, you might be required to sign in to an account to access the computer's resources.* You may need to ask your instructor how to sign in to your account. If you are using Windows 7, skip these steps and instead perform the steps in the yellow box that immediately follows these Windows 8 steps.

 1

- Swipe up or click the lock screen (shown in Figure 3a) to display a sign-in screen (shown in Figure 3b).
- Tap or click the user icon (for SC Series, in this case) on the sign-in screen, which depending on settings, either will display a second sign-in screen that contains a Password text box (Figure 4) or will display the Windows Start screen (shown in Figure 5 on the next page).

Q&A Why do I not see a user icon?
Your computer may require you to type a user name instead of tapping or clicking an icon.

What is a text box?
A text box is a rectangular box in which you type text.

Why does my screen not show a Password text box?
Your account does not require a password.

password text box

SC Series

Password

Submit button

'Ease of access' button

Shut down button

Figure 4

- If Windows displays a sign-in screen with a Password text box, type your password in the text box.

2

- Tap or click the Submit button (shown in Figure 4 on the previous page) to sign in to your account and display the Windows Start screen (Figure 5).

Q&A | Why does my Start screen look different from the one in Figure 5? The Windows Start screen is customizable, and your school or employer may have modified the screen to meet its needs. Also, your screen resolution, which affects the size of the elements on the screen, may differ from the screen resolution used in this book. Later in this chapter, you learn how to change screen resolution.

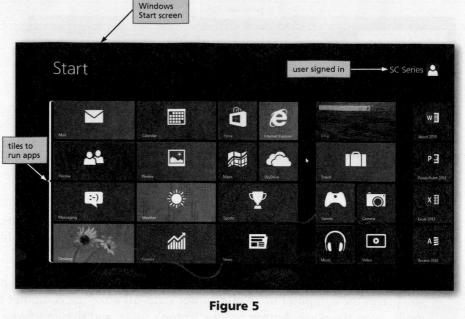

Figure 5

How do I type if my tablet has no keyboard?
You can use your fingers to press keys on a keyboard that appears on the screen, called an on-screen keyboard, or you can purchase a separate physical keyboard that attaches to or wirelessly communicates with the tablet.

TO SIGN IN TO AN ACCOUNT USING WINDOWS 7

If you are using Windows 7, perform these steps to sign in to an account instead of the previous steps that use Windows 8.

1. Click the user icon on the Welcome screen; depending on settings, this either will display a password text box or will sign in to the account and display the Windows 7 desktop.

2. If Windows 7 displays a password text box, type your password in the text box and then click the arrow button to sign in to the account and display the Windows 7 desktop.

The Windows Start Screen

BTW
Modern UI
The new Windows 8 user interface also is referred to as the Modern UI (user interface).

The Windows Start screen provides a scrollable space for you to access apps that have been pinned to the Start screen (shown in Figure 5). Pinned apps appear as tiles on the Start screen. In addition to running apps, you can perform tasks such as pinning apps (placing tiles) on the Start screen, moving the tiles around the Start screen, and unpinning apps (removing tiles) from the Start screen.

If you swipe up from the bottom of or right-click an open space on the Start screen, the App bar will appear. The **App bar** includes a button that enables you to display all of your apps. When working with tiles, the App bar also provides options for manipulating the tiles, such as resizing them.

CONSIDER THIS

How do you pin apps, move tiles, and unpin apps?

- To pin an app, swipe up from the bottom of the Start screen or right-click an open space on the Start screen to display the App bar, tap or click the All apps button on the App bar to display the Apps list, swipe down on or right-click the app you want to pin, and then tap or click the 'Pin to Start' button on the App bar. One way to return to the Start screen is to swipe up from the bottom or right-click an open space in the Apps list and then tap or click the All apps button again.

- To move a tile, drag the tile to the desired location.

- To unpin an app, swipe down on or right-click the app to display the App bar and then tap or click the 'Unpin from Start' button on the App bar.

Introduction to Microsoft Office 2013

Microsoft Office 2013 is the newest version of Microsoft Office, offering features that provide users with better functionality and easier ways to work with the various files they create. These features include enhanced design tools, such as improved picture formatting tools and new themes, shared notebooks for working in groups, mobile versions of Office apps, broadcast presentations for the web, and a digital notebook for managing and sharing multimedia information.

Microsoft Office 2013 Apps

Microsoft Office 2013 includes a wide variety of apps such as Word, PowerPoint, Excel, Access, Outlook, Publisher, OneNote, InfoPath, SharePoint Workspace, and Lync:

- **Microsoft Word 2013**, or Word, is a full-featured word processing app that allows you to create professional-looking documents and revise them easily.

- **Microsoft PowerPoint 2013**, or PowerPoint, is a complete presentation app that enables you to produce professional-looking presentations and then deliver them to an audience.

- **Microsoft Excel 2013**, or Excel, is a powerful spreadsheet app that allows you to organize data, complete calculations, make decisions, graph data, develop professional-looking reports, publish organized data to the web, and access real-time data from websites.

- **Microsoft Access 2013**, or Access, is a database management system that enables you to create a database; add, change, and delete data in the database; ask questions concerning the data in the database; and create forms and reports using the data in the database.

- **Microsoft Outlook 2013**, or Outlook, is a communications and scheduling app that allows you to manage email accounts, calendars, contacts, and access to other Internet content.

- **Microsoft Publisher 2013**, or Publisher, is a desktop publishing app that helps you create professional-quality publications and marketing materials that can be shared easily.

- **Microsoft OneNote 2013**, or OneNote, is a note taking app that allows you to store and share information in notebooks with other people.

- **Microsoft InfoPath Designer 2013**, or InfoPath, is a form development app that helps you create forms for use on the web and gather data from these forms.

- **Microsoft SharePoint Workspace 2013**, or SharePoint, is a collaboration app that allows you to access and revise files stored on your computer from other locations.

- **Microsoft Lync 2013** is a communications app that allows you to use various modes of communications such as instant messaging, videoconferencing, and sharing files and apps.

Microsoft Office 2013 Suites

A **suite** is a collection of individual apps available together as a unit. Microsoft offers a variety of Office suites, including a stand-alone desktop app (boxed software), Microsoft Office 365, and Microsoft Office Web Apps. **Microsoft Office 365**, or Office 365, provides plans that allow organizations to use Office in a mobile setting while also being able to communicate and share files, depending upon the type of plan selected by the organization. **Microsoft Office Web Apps**, or Web Apps, are apps that allow you to edit and share files on the web using the familiar Office interface. Table 3 on the next page outlines the differences among these Office suites.

Table 3 Office Suites

Apps/ Licenses	Office 365 Home Premium	Office 365 Small Business Premium	Office Home & Student	Office Home & Business	Office Professional
Word	✔	✔	✔	✔	✔
PowerPoint	✔	✔	✔	✔	✔
Excel	✔	✔	✔	✔	✔
Access	✔	✔			✔
Outlook	✔	✔		✔	✔
Publisher	✔	✔			✔
Lync		✔			
OneNote			✔	✔	✔
InfoPath		✔			
Licenses	5	5	1	1	1

© 2014 Cengage Learning

During the Office 365 installation, you select a plan, and depending on your plan, you receive different apps and services. Office Web Apps do not require a local installation and are accessed through SkyDrive and your browser. **SkyDrive** is a cloud storage service that provides storage and other services, such as Office Web Apps, to computer users.

CONSIDER THIS

How do you sign up for a SkyDrive account?

• Use your browser to navigate to skydrive.live.com.

• Create a Microsoft account by tapping or clicking the 'Sign up now' link (or a similar link) and then entering your information to create the account.

• Sign in to SkyDrive using your new account or use it in Word to save your files on SkyDrive.

Apps in a suite, such as Microsoft Office, typically use a similar interface and share features. Once you are comfortable working with the elements and the interface and performing tasks in one app, the similarity can help you apply the knowledge and skills you have learned to another app(s) in the suite. For example, the process for saving a file in Word is the same in PowerPoint, Excel, and the other Office apps. While briefly showing how to use Word, this chapter illustrates some of the common functions across the Office apps and identifies the characteristics unique to Word.

Running and Using an App

To use an app, such as Word, you must instruct the operating system to run the app. Windows provides many different ways to run an app, one of which is presented in this section (other ways to run an app are presented throughout this chapter). After an app is running, you can use it to perform a variety of tasks. The following pages use Word to discuss some elements of the Office interface and to perform tasks that are common to other Office apps.

Word

Word is a full-featured word processing app that allows you to create many types of personal and business documents, including flyers, letters, memos, resumes, reports, fax cover sheets, mailing labels, and newsletters. Word also provides tools that enable you to create webpages and save these webpages directly on a web server. Word has many features designed to simplify the production of documents and add visual appeal. Using Word, you easily can change the shape, size, and color of text. You also can include borders, shading, tables, images, pictures, charts, and web addresses in documents.

To Run an App from the Start Screen

The Start screen contains tiles that allow you to run apps, some of which may be stored on your computer. *Why? When you install an app, for example, tiles are added to the Start screen for the various Office apps included in the suite.*

The following steps, which assume Windows is running, use the Start screen to run Word based on a typical installation. You may need to ask your instructor how to run Word on your computer. Although the steps illustrate running the Word app, the steps to run any Office app are similar. If you are using Windows 7, skip these steps and instead perform the steps in the yellow box that immediately follows these Windows 8 steps.

1

• If necessary, scroll to display the Word tile on the Start screen (Figure 6).

Q&A Why does my Start screen look different?
It may look different because of your computer's configuration. The Start screen may be customized for several reasons, such as usage requirements or security restrictions.

What if the app I want to run is not on the Start screen?
You can display all installed apps by swiping up from the bottom of the Start screen or right-clicking an open space on the Start screen and then tapping or clicking the All apps button on the App bar.

How do I scroll on a touch screen?
Use the slide gesture; that is, press and hold your finger on the screen and then move your finger in the direction you wish to scroll.

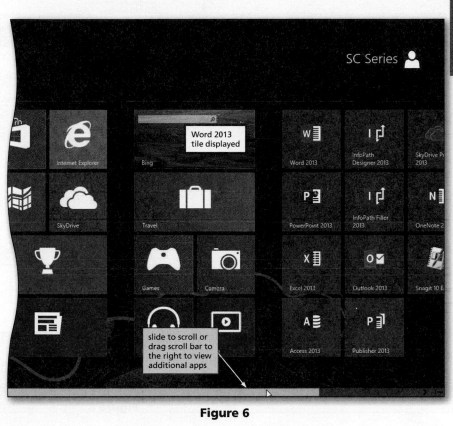

Figure 6

2

• Tap or click the Word 2013 tile to run the Word app and display the Word start screen (Figure 7).

Figure 7

❸

- Tap or click the Blank document thumbnail on the Word start screen to create a blank Word document in the Word window (Figure 8).

Q&A | What happens when you run an app?

Some apps provide a means for you to create a blank document, as shown in Figure 7 on the previous page; others immediately display a blank document in an app window, such as the Word window shown in Figure 8. A **window** is a rectangular area that displays data and information. The top of a window has a **title bar**, which is a horizontal space that contains the window's name.

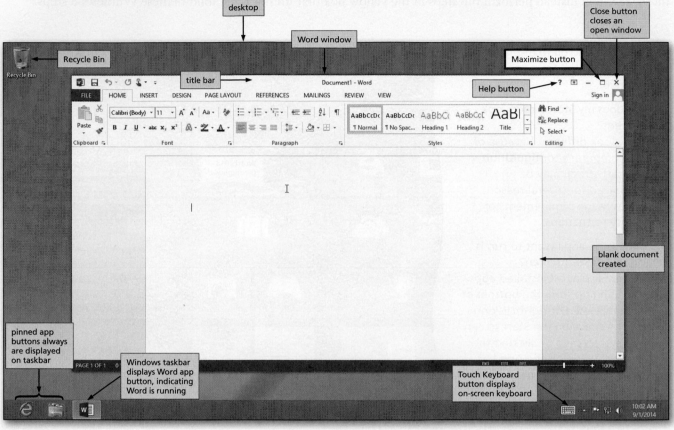

Figure 8

Other Ways

1. Tap or click Search charm on Charms bar, type app name in search box, tap or click app name in results list

2. Double-tap or double-click file created in app you want to run

BTW

Touch Keyboard

To display the on-screen touch keyboard, tap the Touch Keyboard button on the Windows taskbar. When finished using the touch keyboard, tap the X button on the touch keyboard to close the keyboard.

TO RUN AN APP USING THE START MENU IN WINDOWS 7

If you are using Windows 7, perform these steps to run Word using the Start menu instead of the previous steps that use Windows 8.

1. Click the Start button on the Windows 7 taskbar to display the Start menu.

2. Click All Programs at the bottom of the left pane on the Start menu to display the All Programs list.

3. If the Word app is located in a folder, click, or scroll to and then click, the folder in the All Programs list to display a list of the folder's contents.

4. Click, or scroll to and then click, the app name (Word, in this case) in the list to run the selected app.

Windows Desktop

When you run an app in Windows, it may appear in an on-screen work area app, called the **desktop** (shown in Figure 8). You can perform tasks such as placing objects in the desktop, moving the objects around the desktop, and removing items from the desktop.

Some icons also may be displayed in the desktop. For instance, the icon for the **Recycle Bin**, the location of files that have been deleted, appears in the desktop by default. A **file** is a named unit of storage. Files can contain text, images, audio, and video. You can customize your desktop so that icons representing apps and files you use often appear in the desktop.

To Switch between an App and the Start Screen

1 SIGN IN | 2 USE WINDOWS | 3 USE APPS | 4 FILE MANAGEMENT | 5 SWITCH APPS | 6 SAVE FILES
7 CHANGE SCREEN RESOLUTION | 8 EXIT APPS | 9 USE ADDITIONAL APP FEATURES | 10 USE HELP

While working with an app, such as Word, or in the desktop, you easily can return to the Start screen. The following steps switch from the Word app to the Start screen. *Why? Returning to the Start screen allows you to run any of your other apps.* If you are using Windows 7, read these steps without performing them because Windows 7 does not have a Start screen.

❶

- Swipe in from the left edge of the screen and then back to the left, or point to the lower-left corner of the desktop to display a thumbnail of the Start screen (Figure 9).

Figure 9

❷

- Tap or click the thumbnail of the Start screen to display the Start screen (Figure 10).

❸

- Tap or click the Desktop tile to redisplay the Word app in the desktop (shown in Figure 8).

Figure 10

Other Ways

1. Press WINDOWS key to display Start screen

To Maximize a Window

Sometimes content is not visible completely in a window. One method of displaying the entire contents of a window is to **maximize** it, or enlarge the window so that it fills the entire screen. The following step maximizes the Word window; however, any Office app's window can be maximized using this step. *Why? A maximized window provides the most space available for using the app.*

1

- If the Word window is not maximized already, tap or click the Maximize button (shown in Figure 8 on page OFF 12) next to the Close button on the window's title bar to maximize the window (Figure 11).

Q&A

What happened to the Maximize button?
It changed to a Restore Down button, which you can use to return a window to its size and location before you maximized it.

How do I know whether a window is maximized?
A window is maximized if it fills the entire display area and the Restore Down button is displayed on the title bar.

Figure 11

Other Ways

1. Double-tap or double-click title bar	2. Drag title bar to top of screen

Word Document Window, Ribbon, and Elements Common to Office Apps

The Word window consists of a variety of components to make your work more efficient and documents more professional. These include the document window, ribbon, mini toolbar, shortcut menus, Quick Access Toolbar, and Microsoft Account area. Most of these components are common to other Microsoft Office apps; others are unique to Word.

You view a portion of a document on the screen through a **document window** (Figure 12). The default (preset) view is **Print Layout view**, which shows the document on a mock sheet of paper in the document window.

Scroll Bars   You use a scroll bar to display different portions of a document in the document window. At the right edge of the document window is a vertical scroll bar. If a document is too wide to fit in the document window, a horizontal scroll bar also appears at the bottom of the document window. On a scroll bar, the position of the scroll box reflects the location of the portion of the document that is displayed in the document window.

Status Bar   The **status bar**, located at the bottom of the document window above the Windows taskbar, presents information about the document, the progress of current tasks, and the status of certain commands and keys; it also provides controls for viewing the document. As you type text or perform certain tasks, various indicators and buttons may appear on the status bar.

Figure 12

The left side of the status bar in Figure 12 shows the current page followed by the total number of pages in the document, the number of words in the document, and an icon to check spelling and grammar. The right side of the status bar includes buttons and controls you can use to change the view of a document and adjust the size of the displayed document.

Ribbon   The ribbon, located near the top of the window below the title bar, is the control center in Word and other Office apps (Figure 13). The ribbon provides easy, central access to the tasks you perform while creating a document. The ribbon consists of tabs, groups, and commands. Each **tab** contains a collection of groups, and each **group** contains related commands. When you run an Office app, such as Word, it initially displays several main tabs, also called default or top-level tabs. All Office apps have a HOME tab, which contains the more frequently used commands.

Figure 13

In addition to the main tabs, the Office apps display **tool tabs**, also called contextual tabs (Figure 14), when you perform certain tasks or work with objects such as pictures or tables. If you insert a picture in a Word document, for example, the PICTURE TOOLS tab and its related subordinate FORMAT tab appear, collectively referred to as the PICTURE TOOLS FORMAT tab. When you are finished working with the picture, the PICTURE TOOLS FORMAT tab disappears from the ribbon. Word and other Office apps determine when tool tabs should appear and disappear based on tasks you perform. Some tool tabs, such as the TABLE TOOLS tab, have more than one related subordinate tab.

Figure 14

SEE THE ELEPHANT HABITAT

Figure 15

Items on the ribbon include buttons, boxes, and galleries (shown in Figure 13 on the previous page). A **gallery** is a set of choices, often graphical, arranged in a grid or in a list. You can scroll through choices in an in-ribbon gallery by tapping or clicking the gallery's scroll arrows. Or, you can tap or click a gallery's More button to view more gallery options on the screen at a time.

Some buttons and boxes have arrows that, when tapped or clicked, also display a gallery; others always cause a gallery to be displayed when tapped or clicked. Most galleries support **live preview**, which is a feature that allows you to point to a gallery choice and see its effect in the document — without actually selecting the choice (Figure 15). Live preview works only if you are using a mouse; if you are using a touch screen, you will not be able to view live previews.

Some commands on the ribbon display an image to help you remember their function. When you point to a command on the ribbon, all or part of the command glows in a shade of blue, and a ScreenTip appears on the screen. A **ScreenTip** is an on-screen note that provides the name of the command, available keyboard shortcut(s), a description of the command, and sometimes instructions for how to obtain help about the command (Figure 16).

Figure 16

Some groups on the ribbon have a small arrow in the lower-right corner, called a **Dialog Box Launcher**, that when tapped or clicked, displays a dialog box or a task pane with additional options for the group (Figure 17). When presented with a dialog box, you make selections and must close the dialog box before returning to the document. A **task pane**, in contrast to a dialog box, is a window that can remain open and visible while you work in the document.

BTW

Touch Mode

The Office and Windows interfaces may vary if you are using Touch mode. For this reason, you might notice that the function or appearance of your touch screen in Word differs slightly from this book's presentation.

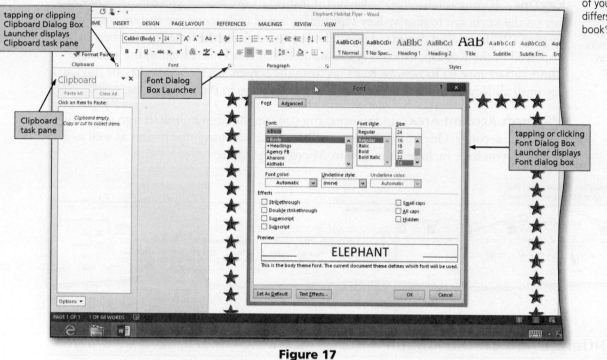

Figure 17

Mini Toolbar   The **mini toolbar**, which appears automatically based on tasks you perform, contains commands related to changing the appearance of text in a document (Figure 18). If you do not use the mini toolbar, it disappears from the screen. The buttons, arrows, and boxes on the mini toolbar vary, depending on whether you are using Touch mode versus Mouse mode. If you press and hold or right-click an item in the document window, Word displays both the mini toolbar and a shortcut menu, which is discussed in a later section in this chapter.

All commands on the mini toolbar also exist on the ribbon. The purpose of the mini toolbar is to minimize hand or mouse movement.

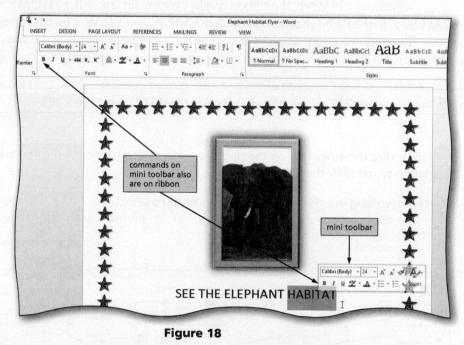

Figure 18

Quick Access Toolbar   The **Quick Access Toolbar**, located initially (by default) above the ribbon at the left edge of the title bar, provides convenient, one-tap or one-click access to frequently used commands (shown in Figure 16). The commands on the Quick Access Toolbar always are available, regardless of the task you are performing. The Touch/Mouse Mode button on the Quick Access Toolbar allows you to switch between Touch mode and Mouse mode. If you primarily are using touch gestures, Touch mode will add more

BTW

Turning Off the Mini Toolbar

If you do not want the mini toolbar to appear, tap or click FILE on the ribbon to open the Backstage view, tap or click Options in the Backstage view, tap or click General (Options dialog box), remove the check mark from the 'Show Mini Toolbar on selection' check box, and then tap or click the OK button.

space between commands on menus and on the ribbon so that they are easier to tap. While touch gestures are convenient ways to interact with Office apps, not all features are supported when you are using Touch mode. If you are using a mouse, Mouse mode will not add the extra space between buttons and commands. The Quick Access Toolbar is discussed in more depth later in the chapter.

KeyTips If you prefer using the keyboard instead of the mouse, you can press the ALT key on the keyboard to display **KeyTips**, or keyboard code icons, for certain commands (Figure 19). To select a command using the keyboard, press the letter or number displayed in the KeyTip, which may cause additional KeyTips related to the selected command to appear. To remove KeyTips from the screen, press the ALT key or the ESC key until all KeyTips disappear, or tap or click anywhere in the app window.

Microsoft Account Area In this area, you can use the Sign in link to sign in to your Microsoft account. Once signed in, you will see your account information as well as a picture if you have included one in your Microsoft account.

Figure 19

To Display a Different Tab on the Ribbon

1 SIGN IN | 2 USE WINDOWS | 3 USE APPS | 4 FILE MANAGEMENT | 5 SWITCH APPS | 6 SAVE FILES
7 CHANGE SCREEN RESOLUTION | 8 EXIT APPS | 9 USE ADDITIONAL APP FEATURES | 10 USE HELP

When you run Word, the ribbon displays nine main tabs: FILE, HOME, INSERT, DESIGN, PAGE LAYOUT, REFERENCES, MAILINGS, REVIEW, and VIEW. The tab currently displayed is called the **active tab**.

The following step displays the INSERT tab, that is, makes it the active tab. *Why? When working with an Office app, you may need to switch tabs to access other options for working with a document.*

1

- Tap or click INSERT on the ribbon to display the INSERT tab (Figure 20).

🔎 **Experiment**

- Tap or click the other tabs on the ribbon to view their contents. When you are finished, tap or click INSERT on the ribbon to redisplay the INSERT tab.

Q&A If I am working in a different Office app, such as PowerPoint or Access, how do I display a different tab on the ribbon?
Follow this same procedure; that is, tap or click the desired tab on the ribbon.

Figure 20

To Collapse and Expand the Ribbon and Use Full Screen Mode

1 SIGN IN | 2 USE WINDOWS | 3 USE APPS | 4 FILE MANAGEMENT | 5 SWITCH APPS | 6 SAVE FILES
7 CHANGE SCREEN RESOLUTION | 8 EXIT APPS | 9 USE ADDITIONAL APP FEATURES | 10 USE HELP

To display more of a document or other item in the window of an Office app, some users prefer to collapse the ribbon, which hides the groups on the ribbon and displays only the main tabs, or to use **Full Screen mode**, which hides all the commands and just displays the document. Each time you run an Office app, such as Word, the ribbon appears the same way it did the last time you used that Office app. The chapters in this book, however, begin with the ribbon appearing as it did at the initial installation of Office or Word.

The following steps collapse, expand, and restore the ribbon in Word and then switch to Full Screen mode. *Why? If you need more space on the screen to work with your document, you may consider collapsing the ribbon or switching to Full Screen mode to gain additional workspace.*

1

- Tap or click the 'Collapse the Ribbon' button on the ribbon (shown in Figure 20) to collapse the ribbon (Figure 21).

Q&A What happened to the groups on the ribbon?
When you collapse the ribbon, the groups disappear so that the ribbon does not take up as much space on the screen.

What happened to the 'Collapse the Ribbon' button?
The 'Pin the ribbon' button replaces the 'Collapse the Ribbon' button when the ribbon is collapsed. You will see the 'Pin the ribbon' button only when you expand a ribbon by tapping or clicking a tab.

Figure 21

2

- Tap or click HOME on the ribbon to expand the HOME tab (Figure 22).

Q&A Why would I click the HOME tab?
If you want to use a command on a collapsed ribbon, tap or click the main tab to display the groups for that tab. After you select a command on the ribbon, the groups will be collapsed once again.
If you decide not to use a command on the ribbon, you can collapse the groups by tapping or clicking the same main tab or tapping or clicking in the app window.

Figure 22

Experiment

- Tap or click HOME on the ribbon to collapse the groups again. Tap or click HOME on the ribbon to expand the HOME tab.

3

- Tap or click the 'Pin the ribbon' button on the expanded HOME tab to restore the ribbon.

- Tap or click the 'Ribbon Display Options' button to display the Ribbon Display Options menu (Figure 23).

Figure 23

4

- Tap or click Auto-hide Ribbon to use Full Screen mode, which hides all the commands from the screen (Figure 24).

- Tap or click the ellipsis to display the ribbon temporarily.

- Tap or click the 'Ribbon Display Options' button to display the Ribbon Display Options menu (shown in Figure 23 on the previous page).

- Tap or click 'Show Tabs and Commands' to exit Full Screen mode.

Figure 24

Other Ways

1. Double-tap or double-click a main tab on the ribbon   2. Press CTRL+F1

To Use a Shortcut Menu to Relocate the Quick Access Toolbar

1 SIGN IN | 2 USE WINDOWS | 3 USE APPS | 4 FILE MANAGEMENT | 5 SWITCH APPS | 6 SAVE FILES
7 CHANGE SCREEN RESOLUTION | 8 EXIT APPS | 9 USE ADDITIONAL APP FEATURES | 10 USE HELP

When you press and hold or right-click certain areas of the Word and other Office app windows, a shortcut menu will appear. A **shortcut menu** is a list of frequently used commands that relate to an object. *Why? You can use shortcut menus to access common commands quickly.* When you press and hold or right-click the status bar, for example, a shortcut menu appears with commands related to the status bar. When you press and hold or right-click the Quick Access Toolbar, a shortcut menu appears with commands related to the Quick Access Toolbar. The following steps use a shortcut menu to move the Quick Access Toolbar, which by default is located on the title bar.

1

- Press and hold or right-click the Quick Access Toolbar to display a shortcut menu that presents a list of commands related to the Quick Access Toolbar (Figure 25).

Q&A What if I cannot make the shortcut menu appear using the touch instruction?
When you use the press and hold technique, be sure to release your finger when the circle appears on the screen to display the shortcut menu. If the technique still does not work, you might need to add more space around objects on the screen, making it easier for you to press or tap them. Click the 'Customize Quick Access Toolbar' button and then click Touch/Mouse Mode on the menu. Another option is to use the stylus.

Figure 25

2

- Tap or click 'Show Quick Access Toolbar Below the Ribbon' on the shortcut menu to display the Quick Access Toolbar below the ribbon (Figure 26).

3

- Press and hold or right-click the Quick Access Toolbar to display a shortcut menu (Figure 27).

4

- Tap or click 'Show Quick Access Toolbar Above the Ribbon' on the shortcut menu to return the Quick Access Toolbar to its original position (shown in Figure 25).

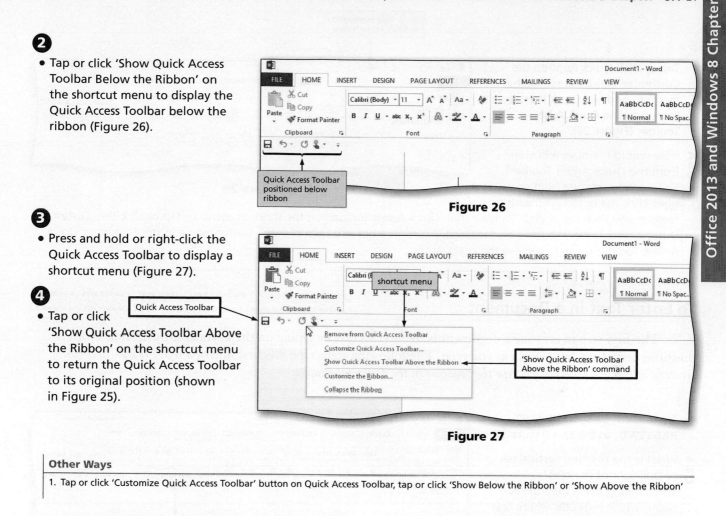

Figure 26

Figure 27

Other Ways
1. Tap or click 'Customize Quick Access Toolbar' button on Quick Access Toolbar, tap or click 'Show Below the Ribbon' or 'Show Above the Ribbon'

To Customize the Quick Access Toolbar

1 SIGN IN | 2 USE WINDOWS | 3 USE APPS | 4 FILE MANAGEMENT | 5 SWITCH APPS | 6 SAVE FILES
7 CHANGE SCREEN RESOLUTION | 8 EXIT APPS | 9 USE ADDITIONAL APP FEATURES | 10 USE HELP

The Quick Access Toolbar provides easy access to some of the more frequently used commands in the Office apps. By default, the Quick Access Toolbar contains buttons for the Save, Undo, and Redo commands. You can customize the Quick Access Toolbar by changing its location in the window, as shown in the previous steps, and by adding more buttons to reflect commands you would like to access easily. The following steps add the Quick Print button to the Quick Access Toolbar in the Word window. *Why? Adding the Quick Print button to the Quick Access Toolbar speeds up the process of printing.*

1

- Tap or click the 'Customize Quick Access Toolbar' button to display the Customize Quick Access Toolbar menu (Figure 28).

Q&A

Which commands are listed on the Customize Quick Access Toolbar menu?
It lists commands that commonly are added to the Quick Access Toolbar.

What do the check marks next to some commands signify?
Check marks appear next to commands that already are on the Quick Access Toolbar. When you add a button to the Quick Access Toolbar, a check mark will be displayed next to its command name.

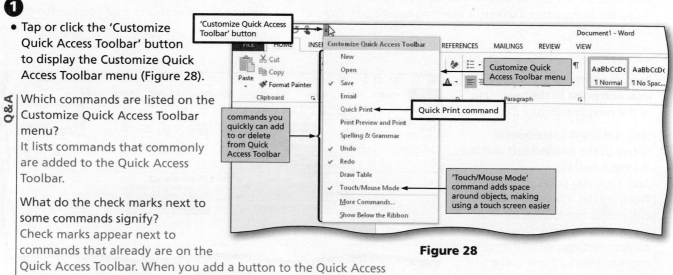

Figure 28

2

• Tap or click Quick Print on the Customize Quick Access Toolbar menu to add the Quick Print button to the Quick Access Toolbar (Figure 29).

Q&A How would I remove a button from the Quick Access Toolbar?
You would press and hold or right-click the button you wish to remove and then tap or click 'Remove from Quick Access Toolbar' on the shortcut menu or tap or click the 'Customize Quick Access Toolbar' button on the Quick Access Toolbar and then click the button name in the Customize Quick Access Toolbar menu to remove the check mark.

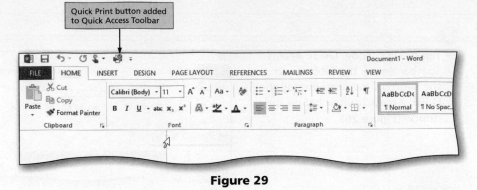

Quick Print button added to Quick Access Toolbar

Figure 29

To Enter Text in a Document

1 SIGN IN | 2 USE WINDOWS | 3 USE APPS | 4 FILE MANAGEMENT | 5 SWITCH APPS | 6 SAVE FILES
7 CHANGE SCREEN RESOLUTION | 8 EXIT APPS | 9 USE ADDITIONAL APP FEATURES | 10 USE HELP

The first step in creating a document is to enter its text by typing on the keyboard. By default, Word positions text at the left margin as you type. The following steps type this first line of a flyer. *Why? To begin creating a flyer, for example, you type the headline in the document window.*

1

• Type **SEE THE ELEPHANT HABITAT** as the text (Figure 30).

Q&A What is the blinking vertical bar to the right of the text?
The blinking bar is the insertion point, which indicates where text, graphics, and other items will be inserted in the document. As you type, the insertion point moves to the right, and when you reach the end of a line, it moves down to the beginning of the next line.

What if I make an error while typing?
You can press the BACKSPACE key until you have deleted the text in error and then retype the text correctly.

Why does a circle appear below the insertion point?
If you are using a touch screen, a selection handle (small circle) may appear below the text so that you can format the text easily.

insertion point

SEE THE ELEPHANT HABITAT

text typed

Figure 30

2

• Press the ENTER key to move the insertion point to the beginning of the next line (Figure 31).

Q&A Why did blank space appear between the entered text and the insertion point?
Each time you press the ENTER key, Word creates a new paragraph and inserts blank space between the two paragraphs. Depending on your settings, Word may or may not insert a blank space between the two paragraphs.

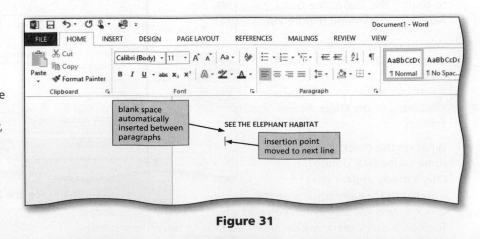

blank space automatically inserted between paragraphs

SEE THE ELEPHANT HABITAT

insertion point moved to next line

Figure 31

Saving and Organizing Files

While you are creating a document, the computer stores it in memory. When you save a document, the computer places it on a storage medium such as a hard disk, solid-state drive (SSD), USB flash drive, or optical disc. The storage medium can be permanent in your computer, may be portable where you remove it from your computer, or may be on a web server you access through a network or the Internet.

A saved document is referred to as a file. A **file name** is the name assigned to a file when it is saved. When saving files, you should organize them so that you easily can find them later. Windows provides tools to help you organize files.

How often should you save a document?

It is important to save a document frequently for the following reasons:

• The document in memory might be lost if the computer is turned off or you lose electrical power while an app is running.

• If you run out of time before completing a project, you may finish it at a future time without starting over.

Organizing Files and Folders

A file contains data. This data can range from a research paper to an accounting spreadsheet to an electronic math quiz. You should organize and store files in folders to avoid misplacing a file and to help you find a file quickly.

If you are taking an introductory computer class (CIS 101, for example), you may want to design a series of folders for the different subjects covered in the class. To accomplish this, you can arrange the folders in a hierarchy for the class, as shown in Figure 32.

The hierarchy contains three levels. The first level contains the storage medium, such as a hard disk. The second level contains the class folder (CIS 101, in this case), and the third level contains seven folders, one each for a different Office app that will be covered in the class (Word, PowerPoint, Excel, Access, Outlook, Publisher, and OneNote).

When the hierarchy in Figure 32 is created, the storage medium is said to contain the CIS 101 folder, and the CIS 101 folder is said to contain the separate Office folders (i.e., Word, PowerPoint, Excel, etc.). In addition, this hierarchy easily can be expanded to include folders from other classes taken during additional semesters.

The vertical and horizontal lines in Figure 32 form a pathway that allows you to navigate to a drive or folder on a computer or network. A **path** consists of a drive letter (preceded by a drive name when necessary) and colon, to identify the storage device, and one or more folder names. A hard disk typically has a drive letter of C. Each drive or folder in the hierarchy has a corresponding path.

By default, Windows saves documents in the Documents library, music in the Music library, pictures in the Pictures library, and videos in the Videos library. A **library**

BTW

File Type
Depending on your Windows settings, the file type .docx may be displayed immediately to the right of the file name after you save the file. The file type .docx is a Word 2013 document.

© 2014 Cengage Learning

Figure 32

helps you manage multiple folders stored in various locations on a computer and devices. It does not store the folder contents; rather, it keeps track of their locations so that you can access the folders and their contents quickly. For example, you can save pictures from a digital camera in any folder on any storage location on a computer. Normally, this would make organizing the different folders difficult. If you add the folders to a library, however, you can access all the pictures from one location regardless of where they are stored.

The following pages illustrate the steps to organize the folders for this class and save a file in a folder:

1. Create the folder identifying your class.
2. Create the Word folder in the folder identifying your class.
3. Save a file in the Word folder.
4. Verify the location of the saved file.

To Create a Folder

1 SIGN IN | 2 USE WINDOWS | 3 USE APPS | 4 FILE MANAGEMENT | 5 SWITCH APPS | 6 SAVE FILES
7 CHANGE SCREEN RESOLUTION | 8 EXIT APPS | 9 USE ADDITIONAL APP FEATURES | 10 USE HELP

When you create a folder, such as the CIS 101 folder shown in Figure 32 on the previous page, you must name the folder. A folder name should describe the folder and its contents. A folder name can contain spaces and any uppercase or lowercase characters, except a backslash (\), slash (/), colon (:), asterisk (*), question mark (?), quotation marks ("), less than symbol (<), greater than symbol (>), or vertical bar (|). Folder names cannot be CON, AUX, COM1, COM2, COM3, COM4, LPT1, LPT2, LPT3, PRN, or NUL. The same rules for naming folders also apply to naming files.

The following steps create a class folder (CIS 101, in this case) in the Documents library. *Why? When storing files, you should organize the files so that it will be easier to find them later.* If you are using Windows 7, skip these steps and instead perform the steps in the yellow box that immediately follows these Windows 8 steps.

1
- Tap or click the File Explorer app button on the taskbar to run the File Explorer app (Figure 33).

Q&A | Why does the title bar say Libraries?
| File Explorer, by default, displays the name of the selected library or folder on the title bar.

Figure 33

2

- Tap or click the Documents library in the navigation pane to display the contents of the Documents library in the file list (Figure 34).

Q&A What if my screen does not show the Documents, Music, Pictures, and Videos libraries?
Double-tap or double-click Libraries in the navigation pane to expand the list.

Figure 34

3

- Tap or click the New folder button on the Quick Access Toolbar to create a new folder with the name, New folder, selected in a text box (Figure 35).

Q&A Why is the folder icon displayed differently on my computer?
Windows might be configured to display contents differently on your computer.

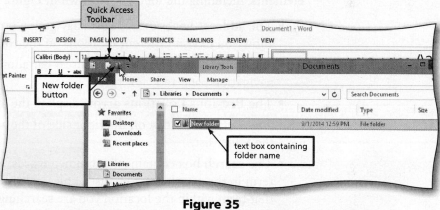

Figure 35

4

- Type **CIS 101** (or your class code) in the text box as the new folder name.
  If requested by your instructor, add your last name to the end of the folder name.

- Press the ENTER key to change the folder name from New folder to a folder name identifying your class (Figure 36).

Q&A What happens when I press the ENTER key?
The class folder (CIS 101, in this case) is displayed in the file list, which contains the folder name, date modified, type, and size.

Figure 36

Other Ways

1. Press CTRL+SHIFT+N   2. Tap or click the New folder button (Home tab | New group)

TO CREATE A FOLDER USING WINDOWS 7

If you are using Windows 7, perform these steps to create a folder instead of the previous steps that use Windows 8.

1. Click the Windows Explorer button on the taskbar to run Windows Explorer.
2. Click the Documents library in the navigation pane to display the contents of the Documents library in the file list.
3. Click the New folder button on the toolbar to display a new folder icon with the name, New folder, selected in a text box.
4. Type `CIS 101` (or your class code) in the text box to name the folder.
5. Press the ENTER key to create the folder.

Folder Windows

The Documents window (shown in Figure 36 on the previous page) is called a folder window. Recall that a folder is a specific named location on a storage medium that contains related files. Most users rely on **folder windows** for finding, viewing, and managing information on their computers. Folder windows have common design elements, including the following (shown in Figure 36).

- The **address bar** provides quick navigation options. The arrows on the address bar allow you to visit different locations on the computer.
- The buttons to the left of the address bar allow you to navigate the contents of the navigation pane and view recent pages.
- The **Previous Locations arrow** displays the locations you have visited.
- The **Refresh button** on the right side of the address bar refreshes the contents of the folder list.
- The **search box** contains the dimmed words, Search Documents. You can type a term in the search box for a list of files, folders, shortcuts, and elements containing that term within the location you are searching. A **shortcut** is an icon on the desktop that provides a user with immediate access to an app or file.
- The **ribbon** contains five tabs used to accomplish various tasks on the computer related to organizing and managing the contents of the open window. This ribbon works similarly to the ribbon in the Office apps.
- The **navigation pane** on the left contains the Favorites area, Libraries area, Homegroup area, Computer area, and Network area.
- The **Favorites area** shows your favorite locations. By default, this list contains only links to your Desktop, Downloads, and Recent places.
- The **Libraries area** shows folders included in a library.

To Create a Folder within a Folder

1 SIGN IN | 2 USE WINDOWS | 3 USE APPS | 4 FILE MANAGEMENT | 5 SWITCH APPS | 6 SAVE FILES
7 CHANGE SCREEN RESOLUTION | 8 EXIT APPS | 9 USE ADDITIONAL APP FEATURES | 10 USE HELP

With the class folder created, you can create folders that will store the files you create using Word. The following steps create a Word folder in the CIS 101 folder (or the folder identifying your class). *Why? To be able to organize your files, you should create a folder structure.* If you are using Windows 7, skip these steps and instead perform the steps in the yellow box that immediately follows these Windows 8 steps.

1

- Double-tap or double-click the icon or folder name for the CIS 101 folder (or the folder identifying your class) in the file list to open the folder (Figure 37).

Figure 37

2

- Tap or click the New folder button on the Quick Access Toolbar to create a new folder with the name, New folder, selected in a text box folder.

- Type `Word` in the text box as the new folder name.

- Press the ENTER key to rename the folder (Figure 38).

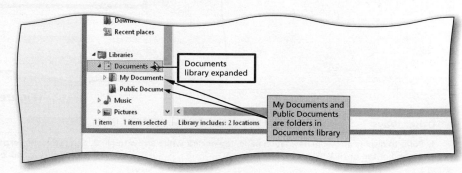

Figure 38

Other Ways

1. Press CTRL+SHIFT+N   2. Tap or click the New folder button (Home tab | New group)

TO CREATE A FOLDER WITHIN A FOLDER USING WINDOWS 7

If you are using Windows 7, perform these steps to create a folder within a folder instead of the previous steps that use Windows 8.

1. Double-click the icon or folder name for the CIS 101 folder (or the folder identifying your class) in the file list to open the folder.

2. Click the New folder button on the toolbar to display a new folder icon and text box for the folder.

3. Type `Word` in the text box to name the folder.

4. Press the ENTER key to create the folder.

To Expand a Folder, Scroll through Folder Contents, and Collapse a Folder

1 SIGN IN | 2 USE WINDOWS | 3 USE APPS | 4 FILE MANAGEMENT | 5 SWITCH APPS | 6 SAVE FILES

7 CHANGE SCREEN RESOLUTION | 8 EXIT APPS | 9 USE ADDITIONAL APP FEATURES | 10 USE HELP

Folder windows display the hierarchy of items and the contents of drives and folders in the file list. You might want to expand a library or folder in the navigation pane to view its contents, slide or scroll through its contents, and collapse it when you are finished viewing its contents. *Why? When a folder is expanded, you can see all the folders it contains. By contrast, a collapsed folder hides the folders it contains.* The following steps expand, slide or scroll through, and then collapse the folder identifying your class (CIS 101, in this case).

1

- Double-tap or double-click the Documents library in the navigation pane, which expands the library to display its contents and displays a black arrow to the left of the Documents library icon (Figure 39).

Figure 39

2

• Double-tap or double-click the My Documents folder, which expands the folder to display its contents and displays a black arrow to the left of the My Documents folder icon.

Q&A What is the My Documents folder?
When you save files on your hard disk, the My Documents folder is the default save location.

• Double-tap or double-click the CIS 101 folder, which expands the folder to display its contents and displays a black arrow to the left of the folder icon (Figure 40).

🔍 **Experiment**

• Slide the scroll bar down or click the down scroll arrow on the vertical scroll bar to display additional folders at the bottom of the navigation pane. Slide the scroll bar up or click the scroll bar above the scroll box to move the scroll box to the top of the navigation pane. Drag the scroll box down the scroll bar until the scroll box is halfway down the scroll bar.

Figure 40

3

• Double-tap or double-click the folder identifying your class (CIS 101, in this case) to collapse the folder (Figure 41).

Q&A Why are some folders indented below others?
A folder contains the indented folders below it.

Figure 41

Other Ways

1. Point to display arrows in navigation pane, tap or click white arrow to expand or tap or click black arrow to collapse

2. Select folder to expand or collapse using arrow keys, press RIGHT ARROW to expand; press LEFT ARROW to collapse.

To Switch from One App to Another

The next step is to save the Word file containing the headline you typed earlier. Word, however, currently is not the active window. You can use the app button on the taskbar and live preview to switch to Word and then save the document in the Word document window.

Why? *By clicking the appropriate app button on the taskbar, you can switch to the open app you want to use.* The following steps switch to the Word window; however, the steps are the same for any active Office app currently displayed as an app button on the taskbar.

1

- If you are using a mouse, point to the Word app button on the taskbar to see a live preview of the open document(s) or the window title(s) of the open document(s), depending on your computer's configuration (Figure 42).

Figure 42

2

- Tap or click the Word app button or the live preview to make the app associated with the app button the active window (Figure 43).

Q&A

What if multiple documents are open in an app?

Tap or click the desired live preview to switch to the window you want to use.

Figure 43

To Save a File in a Folder

With the Word folder created, you can save the Word document shown in the document window in the Word folder. **Why?** *Without saving a file, you may lose all the work you have completed and will be unable to reuse or share it with others later.* The following steps save a file in the Word folder contained in your class folder (CIS 101, in this case) using the file name, Elephant Habitat.

1

- Tap or click the Save button (shown in Figure 43) on the Quick Access Toolbar, which depending on settings, will display either the Save As gallery in the Backstage view (Figure 44) or the Save As dialog box (Figure 45 on the next page).

Q&A

What is the Backstage view?

The **Backstage view** contains a set of commands that enable you to manage documents and data about the documents.

What if the Save As gallery is not displayed in the Backstage view?

Tap or click the Save As tab to display the Save As gallery.

How do I close the Backstage view?

Tap or click the Back button in the upper-left corner of the Backstage view to return to the Word window.

Figure 44

2

- If your screen displays the Backstage view, tap or click Computer, if necessary, to display options in the right pane related to saving on your computer; if your screen already displays the Save As dialog box, proceed to Step 3.

Q&A What if I wanted to save on SkyDrive instead?
You would tap or click SkyDrive. Saving on SkyDrive is discussed in a later section in this chapter.

- Tap or click the Browse button in the right pane to display the Save As dialog box (Figure 45).

Q&A Why does a file name already appear in the File name box?
Word automatically suggests a file name the first time you save a document. The file name normally consists of the first few words contained in the document. Because the suggested file name is selected, you do not need to delete it; as soon as you begin typing, the new file name replaces the selected text.

Figure 45

3

- Type **Elephant Habitat** in the File name box (Save As dialog box) to change the file name. Do not press the ENTER key after typing the file name because you do not want to close the dialog box at this time (Figure 46).

Q&A What characters can I use in a file name?
The only invalid characters are the backslash (\), slash (/), colon (:), asterisk (*), question mark (?), quotation mark ("), less than symbol (<), greater than symbol (>), and vertical bar (|).

Figure 46

4

- Navigate to the desired save location (in this case, the Word folder in the CIS 101 folder [or your class folder] in the My Documents folder in the Documents library) by performing the tasks in Steps 4a and 4b.

4a

- If the Documents library is not displayed in the navigation pane, slide to scroll or drag the scroll bar in the navigation pane until Documents appears.

- If the Documents library is not expanded in the navigation pane, double-tap or double-click Documents to display its folders in the navigation pane.

- If the My Documents folder is not expanded in the navigation pane, double-tap or double-click My Documents to display its folders in the navigation pane.

- If your class folder (CIS 101, in this case) is not expanded, double-tap or double-click the CIS 101 folder to select the folder and display its contents in the navigation pane (Figure 47).

Q&A What if I do not want to save in a folder?
Although storing files in folders is an effective technique for organizing files, some users prefer not to store files in folders. If you prefer not to save this file in a folder, select the storage device on which you wish to save the file and then proceed to Step 5.

Figure 47

4b

• Tap or click the Word folder in the navigation pane to select it as the new save location and display its contents in the file list (Figure 48).

Figure 48

Figure 48

5

• Tap or click the Save button (Save As dialog box) to save the document in the selected folder in the selected location with the entered file name (Figure 49).

Q&A How do I know that the file is saved?

While an Office app such as Word is saving a file, it briefly displays a message on the status bar indicating the amount of the file saved. In addition, the file name appears on the title bar.

Figure 49

Other Ways

1. Tap or click FILE on ribbon, tap or click Save As in Backstage view, tap or click Computer, tap or click Browse button, type file name (Save As dialog box), navigate to desired save location, tap or click Save button

2. Press F12, type file name (Save As dialog box), navigate to desired save location, tap or click Save button

Navigating in Dialog Boxes

Navigating is the process of finding a location on a storage device. While saving the Elephant Habitat file, for example, Steps 4a and 4b in the previous set of steps navigated to the Word folder located in the CIS 101 folder in the My Documents folder in the Documents library. When performing certain functions in Windows apps, such as saving a file, opening a file, or inserting a picture in an existing document, you most likely will have to navigate to the location where you want to save the file or to the folder containing the file you want to open or insert. Most dialog boxes in Windows apps requiring navigation follow a similar procedure; that is, the way you navigate to a folder in one dialog box, such as the Save As dialog box, is similar to how you might navigate in another dialog box, such as the Open dialog box. If you chose to navigate to a specific location in a dialog box, you would follow the instructions in Steps 4a and 4b.

To Minimize and Restore a Window

Before continuing, you can verify that the Word file was saved properly. To do this, you will minimize the Word window and then open the CIS 101 window so that you can verify the file is stored in the CIS 101 folder on the hard disk. A **minimized window** is an open window that is hidden from view but can be displayed quickly by clicking the window's app button on the taskbar.

In the following example, Word is used to illustrate minimizing and restoring windows; however, you would follow the same steps regardless of the Office app you are using. *Why? Before closing an app, you should make sure your file saved correctly so that you can find it later.*

The following steps minimize the Word window, verify that the file is saved, and then restore the minimized window. If you are using Windows 7, skip these steps and instead perform the steps in the yellow box that immediately follows these Windows 8 steps.

①

- Tap or click the Minimize button on the Word window title bar (shown in Figure 49) to minimize the window (Figure 50).

Q&A Is the minimized window still available?
The minimized window, Word in this case, remains available but no longer is the active window. It is minimized as an app button on the taskbar.

- If the File Explorer window is not open on the screen, tap or click the File Explorer app button on the taskbar to make the File folder window the active window.

Figure 50

②

- Double-tap or double-click the Word folder in the file list to select the folder and display its contents (Figure 51).

Q&A Why does the File Explorer app button on the taskbar change?
A selected app button indicates that the app is active on the screen. When the button is not selected, the app is running but not active.

③

- After viewing the contents of the selected folder, tap or click the Word app button on the taskbar to restore the minimized window (as shown in Figure 49 on the previous page).

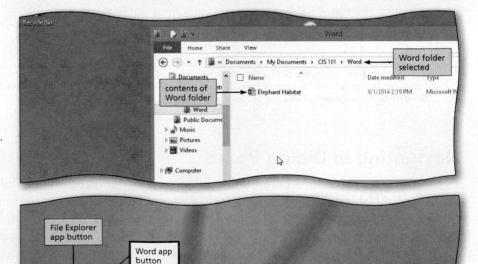

Figure 51

Other Ways

1. Press and hold or right-click title bar, tap or click Minimize on shortcut menu, tap or click taskbar button in taskbar button area

2. Press WINDOWS+M, press WINDOWS+SHIFT+M

TO MINIMIZE AND RESTORE A WINDOW USING WINDOWS 7

If you are using Windows 7, perform these steps to minimize and restore a window instead of the previous steps that use Windows 8.

1. Click the Minimize button on the app's title bar to minimize the window.

2. If the Windows Explorer window is not open on the screen, click the Windows Explorer button on the taskbar to make the Windows Explorer window the active window.

3. Double-click the Word folder in the file list to select the folder and display its contents.

4. After viewing the contents of the selected folder, click the Word button on the taskbar to restore the minimized window.

To Save a File on SkyDrive

1 SIGN IN | 2 USE WINDOWS | 3 USE APPS | 4 FILE MANAGEMENT | 5 SWITCH APPS | **6 SAVE FILES**
7 CHANGE SCREEN RESOLUTION | 8 EXIT APPS | 9 USE ADDITIONAL APP FEATURES | 10 USE HELP

One of the features of Office is the capability to save files on SkyDrive so that you can use the files on multiple computers without having to use external storage devices such as a USB flash drive. Storing files on SkyDrive also enables you to share files more efficiently with others, such as when using Office Web Apps and Office 365.

In the following example, Word is used to save a file to SkyDrive. *Why? Storing files on SkyDrive provides more portability options than are available from storing files in the Documents library.*

You can save files directly to SkyDrive from within Word, PowerPoint, and Excel. The following steps save the current Word file to the SkyDrive. These steps require you have a Microsoft account and an Internet connection.

1

• Tap or click FILE on the ribbon to open the Backstage view (Figure 52).

Q&A What is the purpose of the FILE tab?
The FILE tab opens the Backstage view for each Office app, including Word.

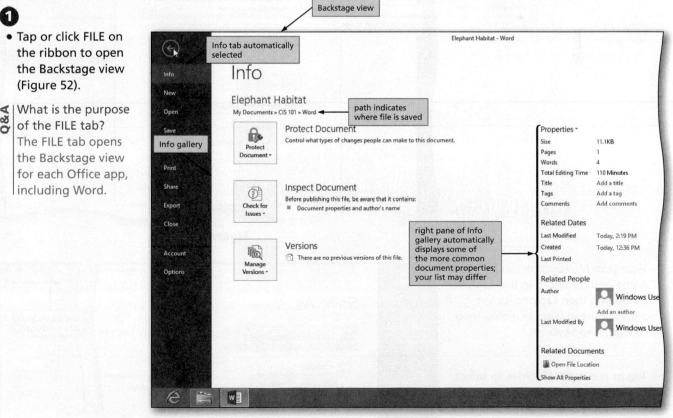

Figure 52

2

- Tap or click the Save As tab in the Backstage view to display the Save As gallery.

- Tap or click SkyDrive to display SkyDrive saving options or a Sign In button, if you are not signed in already to your Microsoft account (Figure 53).

Q&A What if my Save As gallery does not display SkyDrive as a save location?
Tap or click 'Add a Place' and proceed to Step 3.

Figure 53

3

- If your screen displays a Sign In button, tap or click it to display the Sign in dialog box (Figure 54).

Q&A What if the Sign In button does not appear?
If you already are signed into your Microsoft account, the Sign In button will not be displayed. In this case, proceed to Step 5.

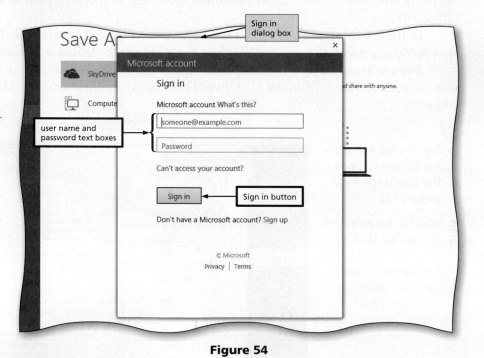

Figure 54

4

- Type your Microsoft account user name and password in the text boxes and then tap or click the Sign in button (Sign in dialog box) to sign in to SkyDrive.

5

- Tap or click your SkyDrive to select your SkyDrive as the storage location (Figure 55).

Figure 55

6

- Tap or click the Browse button to contact the SkyDrive server (which may take some time, depending on the speed of your Internet connection) and then display the Save As dialog box (Figure 56).

Q&A
Why does the path in the address bar contain various letters and numbers?
The letters and numbers in the address bar uniquely identify the location of your SkyDrive files and folders.

7

- Tap or click the Save button (Save As dialog box) to save the file on SkyDrive.

Save As dialog box

folder name refers to location on SkyDrive

default file name

Save button

Figure 56

To Sign Out of a Microsoft Account

If you are using a public computer or otherwise wish to sign out of your Microsoft account, you should sign out of the account from the Accounts gallery in the Backstage view. Signing out of the account is the safest way to make sure that nobody else can access online files or settings stored in your Microsoft account. For security reasons, you should sign out of your Microsoft account when you are finished using a public or shared computer. Staying signed in to your Microsoft account might enable others to access your files.

The following steps sign out of a Microsoft account from Word. You would use the same steps in any Office app. If you do not wish to sign out of your Microsoft account, read these steps without performing them.

1 Tap or click FILE on the ribbon to open the Backstage view.

2 Tap or click the Account tab to display the Account gallery (Figure 57 on the next page).

3 Tap or click the Sign out link, which displays the Remove Account dialog box. If a Can't remove Windows accounts dialog box appears instead of the Remove Account dialog box, click the OK button and skip the remaining steps.

Q&A
Why does a Can't remove Windows accounts dialog box appear?
If you signed in to Windows using your Microsoft account, then you also must sign out from Windows, rather than signing out from within Word. When you are finished using Windows, be sure to sign out at that time.

4 Tap or click the Yes button (Remove Account dialog box) to sign out of your Microsoft account on this computer.

Q&A
Should I sign out of Windows after removing my Microsoft account?
When you are finished using the computer, you should sign out of Windows for maximum security.

5 Tap or click the Back button in the upper-left corner of the Backstage view to return to the document.

Figure 57

Screen Resolution

Screen resolution indicates the number of pixels (dots) that the computer uses to display the letters, numbers, graphics, and background you see on the screen. When you increase the screen resolution, Windows displays more information on the screen, but the information decreases in size. The reverse also is true: as you decrease the screen resolution, Windows displays less information on the screen, but the information increases in size.

Screen resolution usually is stated as the product of two numbers, such as 1366 × 768 (pronounced "thirteen sixty-six by seven sixty-eight"). A 1366 × 768 screen resolution results in a display of 1366 distinct pixels on each of 768 lines, or about 1,050,624 pixels. Changing the screen resolution affects how the ribbon appears in Office apps and some Windows dialog boxes. Figure 58, for example, shows the Word ribbon at screen resolutions of 1366 × 768 and 1024 × 768. All of the same commands are available regardless of screen resolution. The app (Word, in this case), however, makes changes to the groups and the buttons within the groups to accommodate the various screen resolutions. The result is that certain commands may need to be accessed differently depending on the resolution chosen. A command that is visible on the ribbon and available by tapping or clicking a button at one resolution may not be visible and may need to be accessed using its Dialog Box Launcher at a different resolution.

Comparing the two ribbons in Figure 58, notice the changes in content and layout of the groups and galleries. In some cases, the content of a group is the same in each resolution, but the layout of the group differs. For example, the same gallery and buttons appear in the Styles groups in the two resolutions, but the layouts differ. In other cases, the content and layout are the same across the resolution, but the level of detail differs with the resolution.

(a) Ribbon at 1366 X 768 Resolution

Figure 58 (continued)

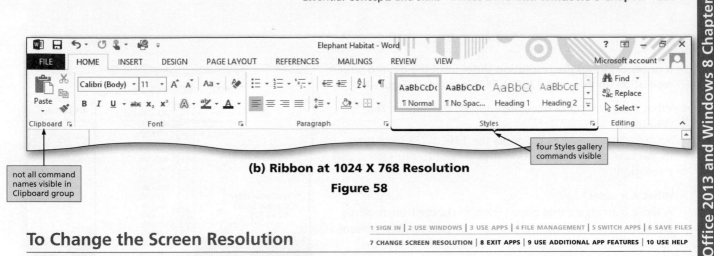

(b) Ribbon at 1024 X 768 Resolution

Figure 58

not all command names visible in Clipboard group

four Styles gallery commands visible

To Change the Screen Resolution

1 SIGN IN | 2 USE WINDOWS | 3 USE APPS | 4 FILE MANAGEMENT | 5 SWITCH APPS | 6 SAVE FILES

7 CHANGE SCREEN RESOLUTION | 8 EXIT APPS | 9 USE ADDITIONAL APP FEATURES | 10 USE HELP

If you are using a computer to step through the chapters in this book and you want your screen to match the figures, you may need to change your screen's resolution. *Why? The figures in this book use a screen resolution of 1366 × 768.* The following steps change the screen resolution to 1366 × 768. Your computer already may be set to 1366 × 768. Keep in mind that many computer labs prevent users from changing the screen resolution; in that case, read the following steps for illustration purposes.

1

• Tap or click the Show desktop button, which is located at the far-right edge of the taskbar, to display the Windows desktop.

Q&A I cannot see the Show desktop button. Why not?
When you point to the far-right edge of the taskbar, a small outline appears to mark the Show desktop button.

• Press and hold or right-click an empty area on the Windows desktop to display a shortcut menu that contains a list of commands related to the desktop (Figure 59).

shortcut menu

Screen resolution command

Show desktop button

Figure 59

Q&A Why does my shortcut menu display different commands?
Depending on your computer's hardware and configuration, different commands might appear on the shortcut menu.

2

• Tap or click Screen resolution on the shortcut menu to open the Screen Resolution window (Figure 60).

3

• Tap or click the Resolution button in the Screen Resolution window to display the resolution slider.

Screen Resolution window

Change the appearance of your display

name of current display device

tapping or clicking link displays advanced settings

Display: 1. Generic Non-PnP Monitor

Resolution: 1366 × 768

Resolution button

Advanced settings

Make text and other items larger or smaller

What display settings should I choose?

OK   Cancel   Apply

Figure 60

• If necessary, drag the resolution slider until the desired screen resolution (in this case, 1366 × 768) is selected (Figure 61).

Q&A

What if my computer does not support the 1366 × 768 resolution?

Some computers do not support the 1366 ×768 resolution. In this case, select a resolution that is close to the 1366 × 768 resolution.

What is a slider?

A **slider** is an object that allows users to choose from multiple predetermined options. In most cases, these options represent some type of numeric value. In most cases, one end of the slider (usually the left or bottom) represents the lowest of available values, and the opposite end (usually the right or top) represents the highest available value.

Figure 61

⑤

• Tap or click an empty area of the Screen Resolution window to close the resolution slider.

• Tap or click the OK button to change the screen resolution and display the Display Settings dialog box (Figure 62).

• Tap or click the Keep changes button (Display Settings dialog box) to accept the new screen resolution.

Q&A

Why does a message display stating that the image quality can be improved?

Some computer monitors or screens are designed to display contents better at a certain screen resolution, sometimes referred to as an optimal resolution.

Figure 62

To Exit an App with One Document Open

1 SIGN IN | 2 USE WINDOWS | 3 USE APPS | 4 FILE MANAGEMENT | 5 SWITCH APPS | 6 SAVE FILES
7 CHANGE SCREEN RESOLUTION | 8 EXIT APPS | 9 USE ADDITIONAL APP FEATURES | 10 USE HELP

When you exit an Office app, such as Word, if you have made changes to a file since the last time the file was saved, the app displays a dialog box asking if you want to save the changes you made to the file before it closes the app window. *Why? The dialog box contains three buttons with these resulting actions: the Save button saves the changes and then exits the Office app, the Don't Save button exits the Office app without saving changes, and the Cancel button closes the dialog box and redisplays the file without saving the changes.*

If no changes have been made to an open document since the last time the file was saved, the Office app will close the window without displaying a dialog box.

The following steps exit Word. You would follow similar steps in other Office apps.

❶

• If necessary, tap or click the Word app button on the taskbar (shown in Figure 62) to display the Word window on the desktop.

• If you are using a mouse, point to the Close button on the right side of the Word window title bar (Figure 63).

Figure 63

2

- Tap or click the Close button to close the document and exit Word.

Q&A | What if I have more than one document open in Word?
You could click the Close button for each open document. When you click the last open document's Close button, you also exit Word. As an alternative that is more efficient, you could press and hold or right-click the Word app button on the taskbar and then tap or click 'Close all windows' on the shortcut menu to close all open documents and exit Word.

3

- If a Microsoft Word dialog box appears, tap or click the Save button to save any changes made to the document since the last save.

Other Ways

1. Press and hold or right-click the Word app button on Windows taskbar, click 'Close all windows' on shortcut menu
2. Press ALT+F4

To Copy a Folder to a USB Flash Drive

1 SIGN IN | 2 USE WINDOWS | 3 USE APPS | **4 FILE MANAGEMENT** | 5 SWITCH APPS | 6 SAVE FILES
7 CHANGE SCREEN RESOLUTION | 8 EXIT APPS | **9 USE ADDITIONAL APP FEATURES** | 10 USE HELP

To store files and folders on a USB flash drive, you must connect the USB flash drive to an available USB port on a computer. The following steps copy your CIS 101 folder to a USB flash drive. *Why? It often is good practice to have a backup of your files. Besides SkyDrive, you can save files to a portable storage device, such as a USB flash drive.* If you are using Windows 7, skip these steps and instead perform the steps in the yellow box that immediately follows these Windows 8 steps.

1

- Insert a USB flash drive in an available USB port on the computer to connect the USB flash drive.

Q&A | How can I ensure the USB flash drive is connected?
In File Explorer, you can use the navigation bar to find the USB flash drive. If it is not showing, then it is not connected properly.

2

- Tap or click the File Explorer app button on the taskbar to make the folder window the active window.

- If necessary, navigate to the CIS 101 folder in the File Explorer window (see Step 4a on page OFF 30 for instructions about navigating to a folder location).

- Press and hold or right-click the CIS 101 folder to display a shortcut menu (Figure 64).

Figure 64

3

- Tap or point to Send to, which causes a submenu to appear (Figure 65).

Figure 65

4

• Tap or click the USB flash drive to copy the folder to the USB flash drive (Figure 66).

Q&A

Why does the drive letter of my USB flash drive differ?
Windows assigns the next available drive letter to your USB flash drive when you connect it. The next available drive letter may vary by computer, depending on the number of storage devices that currently are connected.

Figure 66

TO COPY A FOLDER TO A USB FLASH DRIVE USING WINDOWS 7

If you are using Windows 7, perform these steps to copy a folder to a USB flash drive instead of the previous steps that use Windows 8.

1. Insert a USB flash drive in an available USB port on the computer to open the AutoPlay window.
2. Click the 'Open folder to view files' link in the AutoPlay window to open the Windows Explorer window.
3. Navigate to the Documents library.
4. Right-click the CIS 101 folder to display a shortcut menu.
5. Point to Send to, which causes a submenu to appear.
6. Click the USB flash drive to copy the folder to the USB flash drive.

Break Point: If you wish to take a break, this is a good place to do so. To resume at a later time, continue to follow the steps from this location forward.

Additional Common Features of Office Apps

The previous section used Word to illustrate common features of Office and some basic elements unique to Word. The following sections continue to use Word to present additional common features of Office.

In the following pages, you will learn how to do the following:

1. Run Word using the Search box.
2. Open a document in Word.
3. Close the document.
4. Reopen the document just closed.
5. Create a blank Word document from Windows Explorer and then open the file.
6. Save a document with a new file name.

To Run an App Using the Search Box

1 SIGN IN | 2 USE WINDOWS | 3 USE APPS | 4 FILE MANAGEMENT | 5 SWITCH APPS | 6 SAVE FILES
7 CHANGE SCREEN RESOLUTION | 8 EXIT APPS | 9 USE ADDITIONAL APP FEATURES | 10 USE HELP

The following steps, which assume Windows is running, use the search box to run Word based on a typical installation; however, you would follow similar steps to run any app. *Why? Sometimes an app does not appear on the Start screen, so you can find it quickly by searching.* You may need to ask your instructor how to run apps for your computer. If you are using Windows 7, skip these steps and instead perform the steps in the yellow box that immediately follows these Windows 8 steps.

1

- Swipe in from the right edge of the screen or point to the upper-right corner of the screen to display the Charms bar (Figure 67).

Figure 67

2

- Tap or click the Search charm on the Charms bar to display the Search menu (Figure 68).

Figure 68

3

- Type **Word 2013** as the search text in the Search box and watch the search results appear in the Apps list (Figure 69).

Q&A Do I need to type the complete app name or use correct capitalization?

No, you need to type just enough characters of the app name for it to appear in the Apps list. For example, you may be able to type Word or word, instead of Word 2013.

Figure 69

4

- Tap or click Word 2013 in the search results to run Word.

- Tap or click the Blank document thumbnail to create a blank document and display it in the Word window.

- If the Word window is not maximized, tap or click the Maximize button on its title bar to maximize the window (Figure 70).

Figure 70

TO RUN AN APP USING THE SEARCH BOX USING WINDOWS 7

If you are using Windows 7, perform these steps to run an app using the search box instead of the previous steps that use Windows 8.

1. Click the Start button on the Windows 7 taskbar to display the Start menu.

2. Type **Word 2013** as the search text in the 'Search programs and files' text box and watch the search results appear on the Start menu.

3. Click Word 2013 in the search results on the Start menu to run Word.

4. Click the Blank document thumbnail to create a blank document and display it in the Word window.

5. If the Word window is not maximized, click the Maximize button on its title bar to maximize the window.

To Open an Existing File

1 SIGN IN | 2 USE WINDOWS | 3 USE APPS | 4 FILE MANAGEMENT | 5 SWITCH APPS | 6 SAVE FILES
7 CHANGE SCREEN RESOLUTION | 8 EXIT APPS | 9 USE ADDITIONAL APP FEATURES | 10 USE HELP

As discussed earlier, the Backstage view contains a set of commands that enable you to manage documents and data about the documents. *Why? From the Backstage view in Word, for example, you can create, open, print, and save documents. You also can share documents, manage versions, set permissions, and modify document properties. In other Office 2013 apps, the Backstage view may contain features specific to those apps.* The following steps open a saved file, specifically the Elephant Habitat file, that recently was saved.

1

- Tap or click FILE on the ribbon to open the Backstage view and then tap or click Open in the Backstage view to display the Open gallery in the Backstage view.

- Tap or click Computer to display recent folders accessed on your computer.

- Tap or click the Browse button to display the Open dialog box.

- If necessary, navigate to the location of the file to open as described in Steps 4a and 4b on pages OFF 30–31.

- Tap or click the file to open, Elephant Habitat in this case, to select the file (Figure 71).

Office 2013 and Windows 8 Chapter

Figure 71

2

- Tap or click the Open button (Open dialog box) to open the file (shown in Figure 49 on page OFF 31).

Other Ways	
1. Press CTRL+O	2. Navigate to file in File Explorer window, double-tap or double-click file

To Create a New Document from the Backstage View

1 SIGN IN | 2 USE WINDOWS | 3 USE APPS | 4 FILE MANAGEMENT | 5 SWITCH APPS | 6 SAVE FILES
7 CHANGE SCREEN RESOLUTION | 8 EXIT APPS | 9 USE ADDITIONAL APP FEATURES | 10 USE HELP

You can open multiple documents in an Office program, such as Word, so that you can work on the documents at the same time. The following steps create a file, a blank document in this case, from the Backstage view. *Why? You want to create a new document while keeping the current document open.*

1

- Tap or click FILE on the ribbon to open the Backstage view.

- Tap or click the New tab in the Backstage view to display the New gallery (Figure 72).

Q&A Can I create documents through the Backstage view in other Office apps?
Yes. If the Office app has a New tab in the Backstage view, the New gallery displays various options for creating a new file.

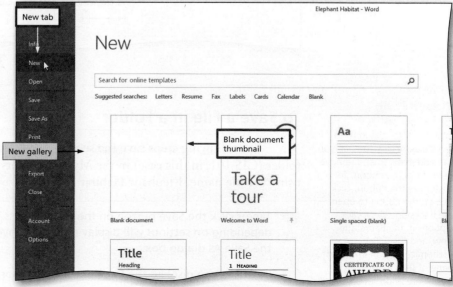

Figure 72

2

- Tap or click the Blank document thumbnail in the New gallery to create a new document (Figure 73).

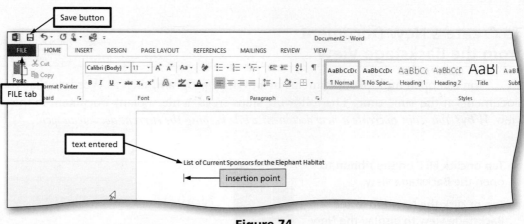

Figure 73

Other Ways
1. Press CTRL+N

To Enter Text in a Document

The next Word document identifies the names of the Elephant Habitat sponsors. The following step enters text in a document.

1 Type `List of Current Sponsors for the Elephant Habitat` and then press the ENTER key to move the insertion point to the beginning of the next line (Figure 74).

Figure 74

BTW

Customizing the Ribbon

In addition to customizing the Quick Access Toolbar, you can add items to and remove items from the ribbon. To customize the ribbon, click FILE on the ribbon to open the Backstage view, click Options in the Backstage view, and then click Customize Ribbon in the left pane of the Options dialog box. More information about customizing the ribbon is presented in a later chapter.

To Save a File in a Folder

The following steps save the second document in the Word folder in the class folder (CIS 101, in this case) in the My Documents folder in the Documents library using the file name, Elephant Habitat Sponsors.

1 Tap or click the Save button on the Quick Access Toolbar (shown in Figure 74), which depending on settings will display either the Save As gallery in the Backstage view or the Save As dialog box.

2 If your screen displays the Backstage view, tap or click Computer, if necessary, to display options in the right pane related to saving on your computer; if your screen already displays the Save As dialog box, proceed to Step 4.

3 Tap or click the Browse button in the right pane to display the Save As dialog box.

4 If necessary, type **Elephant Habitat Sponsors** in the File name box (Save As dialog box) to change the file name. Do not press the ENTER key after typing the file name because you do not want to close the dialog box at this time.

5 If necessary, navigate to the desired save location (in this case, the Word folder in the CIS 101 folder [or your class folder] in the My Documents folder in the Documents library). For specific instructions, perform the tasks in Steps 4a and 4b on pages OFF 30–31.

6 Tap or click the Save button (Save As dialog box) to save the document in the selected folder on the selected drive with the entered file name.

To Close a File
Using the Backstage View

1 SIGN IN | 2 USE WINDOWS | 3 USE APPS | 4 FILE MANAGEMENT | 5 SWITCH APPS | 6 SAVE FILES
7 CHANGE SCREEN RESOLUTION | 8 EXIT APPS | **9 USE ADDITIONAL APP FEATURES** | **10 USE HELP**

Sometimes, you may want to close an Office file, such as a Word document, entirely and start over with a new file. *Why else would I close a file? You also may want to close a file when you are finished working with it so that you can begin a new file.* The following steps close the current active Word file, that is, the Elephant Habitat Sponsors document, without exiting Word.

1
- Tap or click FILE on the ribbon (shown in Figure 74) to open the Backstage view (Figure 75).

2
- Tap or click Close in the Backstage view to close the open file (Elephant Habitat Sponsors, in this case) without exiting the active app.

Q&A

What if Word displays a dialog box about saving?

Tap or click the Save button if you want to save the changes, tap or click the Don't Save button if you want to ignore the changes since the last time you saved, and tap or click the Cancel button if you do not want to close the document.

Can I use the Backstage view to close an open file in other Office apps, such as PowerPoint and Excel?
Yes.

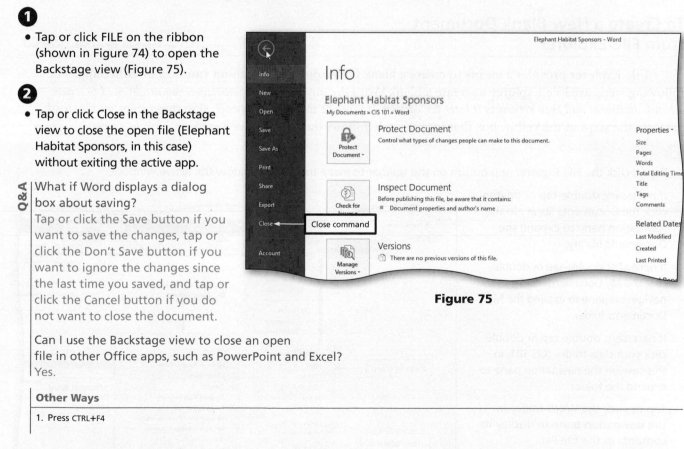

Figure 75

Other Ways

1. Press CTRL+F4

To Open a Recent File
Using the Backstage View

1 SIGN IN | 2 USE WINDOWS | 3 USE APPS | 4 FILE MANAGEMENT | 5 SWITCH APPS | 6 SAVE FILES
7 CHANGE SCREEN RESOLUTION | 8 EXIT APPS | **9 USE ADDITIONAL APP FEATURES** | **10 USE HELP**

You sometimes need to open a file that you recently modified. *Why? You may have more changes to make, such as adding more content or correcting errors.* The Backstage view allows you to access recent files easily. The steps on the next page reopen the Elephant Habitat Sponsors file just closed.

1

- Tap or click FILE on the ribbon to open the Backstage view.
- Tap or click the Open tab in the Backstage view to display the Open gallery (Figure 76).

2

- Tap or click the desired file name in the Recent Documents list, Elephant Habitat Sponsors in this case, to open the file (shown in Figure 74 on page OFF 44).

Figure 76

Q&A Can I use the Backstage view to open a recent file in other Office apps, such as PowerPoint and Excel?
Yes, as long as the file name appears in the list of recent files.

Other Ways
1. Tap or click FILE on ribbon, tap or click Open in Backstage view, tap or click Computer, tap or click Browse, navigate to file (Open dialog box), tap or click Open button

To Create a New Blank Document from File Explorer

1 SIGN IN | 2 USE WINDOWS | 3 USE APPS | 4 FILE MANAGEMENT | 5 SWITCH APPS | 6 SAVE FILES
7 CHANGE SCREEN RESOLUTION | 8 EXIT APPS | 9 USE ADDITIONAL APP FEATURES | 10 USE HELP

File Explorer provides a means to create a blank Office document without running an Office app. The following steps use File Explorer to create a blank Word document. *Why? Sometimes you might need to create a blank document and then return to it later for editing.* If you are using Windows 7, skip these steps and instead perform the steps in the yellow box that immediately follows these Windows 8 steps.

1

- Tap or click the File Explorer app button on the taskbar to make the folder window the active window.
- If necessary, double-tap or double-click the Documents library in the navigation pane to expand the Documents library.
- If necessary, double-tap or double-click the My Documents folder in the navigation pane to expand the My Documents folder.
- If necessary, double-tap or double-click your class folder (CIS 101, in this case) in the navigation pane to expand the folder.
- Tap or click the Word folder in the navigation pane to display its contents in the file list.
- With the Word folder selected, press and hold or right-click an open area in the file list to display a shortcut menu.
- Tap or point to New on the shortcut menu to display the New submenu (Figure 77).

Figure 77

2

• Tap or click 'Microsoft Word Document' on the New submenu to display an icon and text box for a new file in the current folder window with the file name, New Microsoft Word Document, selected (Figure 78).

Figure 78

3

• Type **Elephant Habitat Volunteers** in the text box and then press the ENTER key to assign a new name to the new file in the current folder (Figure 79).

Figure 79

TO CREATE A NEW BLANK DOCUMENT FROM WINDOWS EXPLORER USING WINDOWS 7

If you are using Windows 7, perform these steps to create a new blank Office document from Windows Explorer instead of the previous steps that use Windows 8.

1. If necessary, click the Windows Explorer button on the taskbar to make the folder window the active window.

2. If necessary, double-click the Documents library in the navigation pane to expand the Documents library.

3. If necessary, double-click the My Documents folder in the navigation pane to expand the My Documents folder.

4. If necessary, double-click your class folder (CIS 101, in this case) in the navigation pane to expand the folder.

5. Click the Word folder in the navigation pane to display its contents in the file list.

6. With the Word folder selected, right-click an open area in the file list to display a shortcut menu.

7. Point to New on the shortcut menu to display the New submenu.

8. Click 'Microsoft Word Document' on the New submenu to display an icon and text box for a new file in the current folder window with the name, New Microsoft Word Document, selected.

9. Type **Elephant Habitat Volunteers** in the text box and then press the ENTER key to assign a new name to the new file in the current folder.

To Run an App from File Explorer and Open a File

1 SIGN IN | 2 USE WINDOWS | 3 USE APPS | 4 FILE MANAGEMENT | 5 SWITCH APPS | 6 SAVE FILES
7 CHANGE SCREEN RESOLUTION | 8 EXIT APPS | 9 USE ADDITIONAL APP FEATURES | 10 USE HELP

Previously, you learned how to run Word using the Start screen and the Search charm. The steps on the next page, which assume Windows is running, use File Explorer to run Word based on a typical installation. *Why? Another way to run an Office app is to open an existing file from File Explorer, which causes the app in which the file was created to run and then open the selected file.* You may need to ask your instructor how to run Word for your computer. If you are using Windows 7, follow the steps in the yellow box that immediately follows these Windows 8 steps.

1

- If necessary, display the file to open in the folder window in File Explorer (shown in Figure 79 on the previous page).

- Press and hold or right-click the file icon or file name (Elephant Habitat Volunteers, in this case) to display a shortcut menu (Figure 80).

Figure 80

2

- Tap or click Open on the shortcut menu to open the selected file in the app used to create the file, Word in this case (Figure 81).

- If the Word window is not maximized, tap or click the Maximize button on the title bar to maximize the window.

Figure 81

TO RUN AN APP FROM WINDOWS EXPLORER AND OPEN A FILE USING WINDOWS 7

If you are using Windows 7, perform these steps to run an app from Windows Explorer and open a file instead of the previous steps that use Windows 8.

1. Display the file to open in the folder window in Windows Explorer.

2. Right-click the file icon or file name (Elephant Habitat Volunteers, in this case) to display a shortcut menu.

3. Click Open on the shortcut menu to open the selected file in the app used to create the file, Word in this case.

4. If the Word window is not maximized, click the Maximize button on the title bar to maximize the window.

To Enter Text in a Document

The next step is to enter text in this blank Word document. The following step enters a line of text.

1 Type `Elephant Habitat Staff and Volunteers` and then press the ENTER key to move the insertion point to the beginning of the next line (shown in Figure 82).

To Save an Existing File with the Same File Name

1 SIGN IN | 2 USE WINDOWS | 3 USE APPS | 4 FILE MANAGEMENT | 5 SWITCH APPS | 6 SAVE FILES
7 CHANGE SCREEN RESOLUTION | 8 EXIT APPS | 9 USE ADDITIONAL APP FEATURES | 10 USE HELP

Saving frequently cannot be overemphasized. *Why? You have made modifications to the file (document) since you created it. Thus, you should save again. Similarly, you should continue saving files frequently so that you do not lose the changes you have made since the time you last saved the file.* You can use the same file name, such as Elephant Habitat Volunteers, to save the changes made to the document. The next step saves a file again with the same file name.

- Tap or click the Save button on the Quick Access Toolbar to overwrite the previously saved file (Elephant Habitat Volunteers, in this case) in the Word folder (Figure 82).

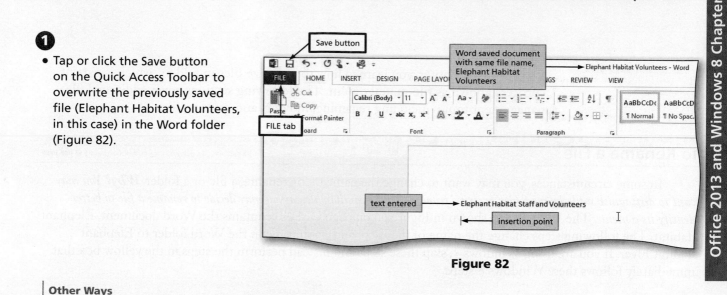

Figure 82

Other Ways

1. Press CTRL+S or press SHIFT+F12

To Save a File with a New File Name

You might want to save a file with a different name or to a different location. For example, you might start a homework assignment with a data file and then save it with a final file name for submission to your instructor, saving it to a location designated by your instructor. The following steps save a file with a different file name.

1 Tap or click the FILE tab to open the Backstage view.

2 Tap or click the Save As tab to display the Save As gallery.

3 If necessary, tap or click Computer to display options in the right pane related to saving on your computer.

4 Tap or click the Browse button in the right pane to display the Save As dialog box.

5 Type **Elephant Habitat Staff and Volunteers** in the File name box (Save As dialog box) to change the file name. Do not press the ENTER key after typing the file name because you do not want to close the dialog box at this time.

6 If necessary, navigate to the desired save location (in this case, the Word folder in the CIS 101 folder [or your class folder] in the My Documents folder in the Documents library). For specific instructions, perform the tasks in Steps 4a and 4b on pages OFF 30–31.

7 Tap or click the Save button (Save As dialog box) to save the document in the selected folder on the selected drive with the entered file name.

To Exit an Office App

You are finished using Word. The following steps exit Word. You would use similar steps to exit other Office apps.

1 Because you have multiple Word documents open, press and hold or right-click the app button on the taskbar and then tap or click 'Close all windows' on the shortcut menu to close all open documents and exit Word.

2 If a dialog box appears, tap or click the Save button to save any changes made to the file since the last save.

Renaming, Moving, and Deleting Files

Earlier in this chapter, you learned how to organize files in folders, which is part of a process known as **file management**. The following sections cover additional file management topics including renaming, moving, and deleting files.

To Rename a File

In some circumstances, you may want to change the name of, or rename, a file or a folder. *Why? You may want to distinguish a file in one folder or drive from a copy of a similar file, or you may decide to rename a file to better identify its contents.* The Word folder shown in Figure 66 on page OFF 40 contains the Word document, Elephant Habitat. The following steps change the name of the Elephant Habitat file in the Word folder to Elephant Habitat Flyer. If you are using Windows 7, skip these steps and instead perform the steps in the yellow box that immediately follows these Windows 8 steps.

1
- If necessary, tap or click the File Explorer app button on the taskbar to make the folder window the active window.
- If necessary, navigate to the location of the file to be renamed (in this case, the Word folder in the CIS 101 [or your class folder] folder in the My Documents folder in the Documents library) to display the file(s) it contains in the file list.
- Press and hold or right-click the Elephant Habitat icon or file name in the file list to select the Elephant Habitat file and display a shortcut menu that presents a list of commands related to files (Figure 83).

Figure 83

2
- Tap or click Rename on the shortcut menu to place the current file name in a text box.
- Type **Elephant Habitat Flyer** in the text box and then press the ENTER key (Figure 84).

Q&A Are any risks involved in renaming files that are located on a hard disk?
If you inadvertently rename a file that is associated with certain apps, the apps may not be able to find the file and, therefore, may not run properly. Always use caution when renaming files.

Can I rename a file when it is open?
No, a file must be closed to change the file name.

Figure 84

Other Ways

1. Select file, press F2, type new file name, press ENTER   2. Select file, tap or click Rename (Home tab | Organize group), type new file name, press ENTER

TO RENAME A FILE USING WINDOWS 7

If you are using Windows 7, perform these steps to rename a file instead of the previous steps that use Windows 8.

1. If necessary, click the Windows Explorer app button on the taskbar to make the folder window the active window.

2. Navigate to the location of the file to be renamed (in this case, the Word folder in the CIS 101 [or your class folder] folder in the My Documents folder in the Documents library) to display the file(s) it contains in the file list.

3. Right-click the Elephant Habitat icon or file name in the file list to select the Elephant Habitat file and display a shortcut menu that presents a list of commands related to files.

4. Click Rename on the shortcut menu to place the current file name in a text box.

5. Type `Elephant Habitat Flyer` in the text box and then press the ENTER key.

To Move a File

1 SIGN IN | 2 USE WINDOWS | 3 USE APPS | 4 FILE MANAGEMENT | 5 SWITCH APPS | 6 SAVE FILES
7 CHANGE SCREEN RESOLUTION | 8 EXIT APPS | 9 USE ADDITIONAL APP FEATURES | 10 USE HELP

Why? *At some time, you may want to move a file from one folder, called the source folder, to another, called the destination folder.* When you move a file, it no longer appears in the original folder. If the destination and the source folders are on the same media, you can move a file by dragging it. If the folders are on different media, then you will need to press and hold and then drag, or right-drag the file, and then click Move here on the shortcut menu. The following step moves the Elephant Habitat Volunteers file from the Word folder to the CIS 101 folder. If you are using Windows 7, skip these steps and instead perform the steps in the yellow box that immediately follows these Windows 8 steps.

1

- In File Explorer, if necessary, navigate to the location of the file to be moved (in this case, the Word folder in the CIS 101 folder [or your class folder] in the Documents library).

- If necessary, tap or click the Word folder in the navigation pane to display the files it contains in the right pane.

- Drag the Elephant Habitat Volunteers file in the right pane to the CIS 101 folder in the navigation pane and notice the ScreenTip as you drag the mouse (Figure 85).

 Experiment

- Click the CIS 101 folder in the navigation pane to verify that the file was moved.

Figure 85

Other Ways

1. Press and hold or right-click file to move, tap or click Cut on shortcut menu, press and hold or right-click destination folder, tap or click Paste on shortcut menu

2. Select file to move, press CTRL+X, select destination folder, press CTRL+V

1 SIGN IN | 2 USE WINDOWS | 3 USE APPS | **4 FILE MANAGEMENT** | 5 SWITCH APPS | 6 SAVE FILES
7 CHANGE SCREEN RESOLUTION | 8 EXIT APPS | 9 USE ADDITIONAL APP FEATURES | **10 USE HELP**

TO MOVE A FILE USING WINDOWS 7

If you are using Windows 7, perform these steps to move a file instead of the previous steps that use Windows 8.

1. In Windows Explorer, navigate to the location of the file to be moved (in this case, the Word folder in the CIS 101 folder [or your class folder] in the Documents library).

2. Click the Word folder in the navigation pane to display the files it contains in the right pane.

3. Drag the Elephant Habitat Volunteers file in the right pane to the CIS 101 folder in the navigation pane.

To Delete a File

A final task you may want to perform is to delete a file. Exercise extreme caution when deleting a file or files. When you delete a file from a hard disk, the deleted file is stored in the Recycle Bin where you can recover it until you empty the Recycle Bin. If you delete a file from removable media, such as a USB flash drive, the file is deleted permanently. The next steps delete the Elephant Habitat Volunteers file from the CIS 101 folder. *Why?* *When a file no longer is needed, you can delete it to conserve space in your storage location.* If you are using Windows 7, skip these steps and instead perform the steps in the yellow box that immediately follows these Windows 8 steps.

❶

- In File Explorer, navigate to the location of the file to be deleted (in this case, the CIS 101 folder [or your class folder] in the Documents library).

- Press and hold or right-click the Elephant Habitat Volunteers icon or file name in the right pane to select the file and display a shortcut menu (Figure 86).

❷

- Tap or click Delete on the shortcut menu to delete the file.

- If a dialog box appears, tap or click the Yes button to delete the file.

Q&A
Can I use this same technique to delete a folder?
Yes. Right-click the folder and then click Delete on the shortcut menu. When you delete a folder, all of the files and folders contained in the folder you are deleting, together with any files and folders on lower hierarchical levels, are deleted as well.

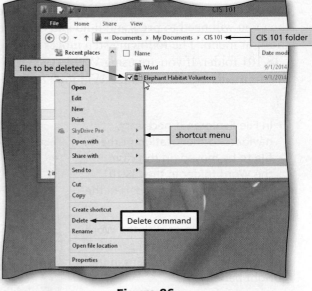

Figure 86

Other Ways

1. Select icon, press DELETE

TO DELETE A FILE USING WINDOWS 7

If you are using Windows 7, perform these steps to delete a file instead of the previous steps that use Windows 8.

1. In Windows Explorer, navigate to the location of the file to be deleted (in this case, the CIS 101 folder [or your class folder] in the Documents library).

2. Right-click the Elephant Habitat Volunteers icon or file name in the right pane to select the file and display a shortcut menu.

3. Click Delete on the shortcut menu to delete the file.

4. If a dialog box appears, click the Yes button to delete the file.

Microsoft Office and Windows Help

At any time while you are using one of the Office apps, such as Word, you can use Office Help to display information about all topics associated with the app. This section illustrates the use of Word Help. Help in other Office apps operates in a similar fashion.

In Office, Help is presented in a window that has browser-style navigation buttons. Each Office app has its own Help home page, which is the starting Help page that is displayed in the Help window. If your computer is connected to the Internet, the contents of the Help page reflect both the local help files installed on the computer and material from Microsoft's website.

To Open the Help Window in an Office App

1 SIGN IN | 2 USE WINDOWS | 3 USE APPS | 4 FILE MANAGEMENT | 5 SWITCH APPS | 6 SAVE FILES
7 CHANGE SCREEN RESOLUTION | 8 EXIT APPS | 9 USE ADDITIONAL APP FEATURES | **10 USE HELP**

The following step opens the Word Help window. *Why? You might not understand how certain commands or operations work in Word, so you can obtain the necessary information using help.* The step to open a Help window in other Office programs is similar.

1

- Run Word.

- Tap or click the Microsoft Word Help button near the upper-right corner of the app window to open the Word Help window (Figure 87).

Figure 87

Other Ways

1. Press F1

Moving and Resizing Windows

At times, it is useful, or even necessary, to have more than one window open and visible on the screen at the same time. You can resize and move these open windows so that you can view different areas of and elements in the window. In the case of the Help window, for example, it could be covering document text in the Word window that you need to see.

To Move a Window by Dragging

1 SIGN IN | 2 USE WINDOWS | 3 USE APPS | 4 FILE MANAGEMENT | 5 SWITCH APPS | 6 SAVE FILES
7 CHANGE SCREEN RESOLUTION | 8 EXIT APPS | 9 USE ADDITIONAL APP FEATURES | **10 USE HELP**

You can move any open window that is not maximized to another location on the desktop by dragging the title bar of the window. *Why? You might want to have a better view of what is behind the window or just want to move the window so that you can see it better.* The step on the next page drags the Word Help window to the upper-left corner of the desktop.

1

- Drag the window title bar (the Word Help window title bar, in this case) so that the window moves to the upper-left corner of the desktop, as shown in Figure 88.

Figure 88

To Resize a Window by Dragging

1 SIGN IN | 2 USE WINDOWS | 3 USE APPS | 4 FILE MANAGEMENT | 5 SWITCH APPS | 6 SAVE FILES
7 CHANGE SCREEN RESOLUTION | 8 EXIT APPS | 9 USE ADDITIONAL APP FEATURES | 10 USE HELP

A method used to change the size of the window is to drag the window borders. The following step changes the size of the Word Help window by dragging its borders. *Why? Sometimes, information is not visible completely in a window, and you want to increase the size of the window.*

1

- If you are using a mouse, point to the lower-right corner of the window (the Word Help window, in this case) until the pointer changes to a two-headed arrow.

- Drag the bottom border downward to display more of the active window (Figure 89).

Q&A

Can I drag other borders on the window to enlarge or shrink the window?
Yes, you can drag the left, right, and top borders and any window corner to resize a window.

Will Windows remember the new size of the window after I close it?
Yes. When you reopen the window, Windows will display it at the same size it was when you closed it.

Figure 89

Using Office Help

Once an Office app's Help window is open, several methods exist for navigating Help. You can search for help by using any of the three following methods from the Help window:

1. Enter search text in the 'Search online help' text box.
2. Click the links in the Help window.
3. Use the Table of Contents.

To Obtain Help Using the 'Search online help' Text Box

1 SIGN IN | 2 USE WINDOWS | 3 USE APPS | 4 FILE MANAGEMENT | 5 SWITCH APPS | 6 SAVE FILES
7 CHANGE SCREEN RESOLUTION | 8 EXIT APPS | 9 USE ADDITIONAL APP FEATURES | 10 USE HELP

Assume for the following example that you want to know more about fonts. The following steps use the 'Search online help' text box to obtain useful information about fonts by entering the word, fonts, as search text. *Why? You may not know the exact help topic you are looking to find, so using keywords can help narrow your search.*

1

- Type **fonts** in the 'Search online help' text box at the top of the Word Help window to enter the search text.

- Tap or click the 'Search online help' button to display the search results (Figure 90).

Q&A

Why do my search results differ?
If you do not have an Internet connection, your results will reflect only the content of the Help files on your computer. When searching for help online, results also can change as material is added, deleted, and updated on the online Help webpages maintained by Microsoft.

Why were my search results not very helpful?
When initiating a search, be sure to check the spelling of the search text; also, keep your search specific to return the most accurate results.

Figure 90

2

- Tap or click the 'Change the default font' link to display the Help information associated with the selected topic (Figure 91).

Figure 91

③

- Tap or click the Home button in the Help window to clear the search results and redisplay the Help home page (Figure 92).

Figure 92

To Obtain Help Using Help Links

1 SIGN IN | 2 USE WINDOWS | 3 USE APPS | 4 FILE MANAGEMENT | 5 SWITCH APPS | 6 SAVE FILES
7 CHANGE SCREEN RESOLUTION | 8 EXIT APPS | 9 USE ADDITIONAL APP FEATURES | 10 USE HELP

If your topic of interest is listed in the Help window, you can click the link to begin browsing the Help categories instead of entering search text. *Why? You browse Help just as you would browse a website. If you know which category contains your Help information, you may wish to use these links.* The following step finds the Resume information using the Resume link from the Word Help home page.

❶

- Tap or click the Resume link on the Help home page (shown in Figure 92) to display the Resume help links (Figure 93).

❷

- After reviewing the page, tap or click the Close button to close the Help window.

- Tap or click Word's Close button to exit Word.

Q&A

Why does my Help window display different links?

The content of your Help window may differ because Microsoft continually updates its Help information.

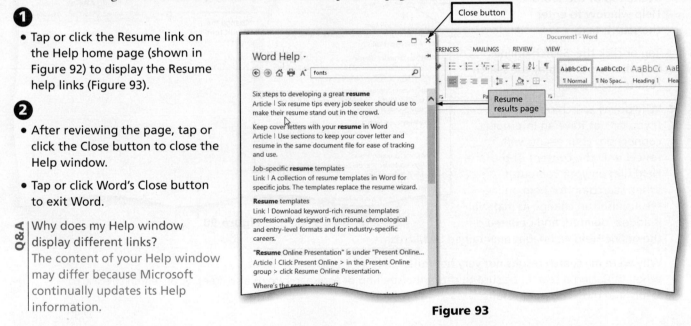

Figure 93

Obtaining Help while Working in an Office App

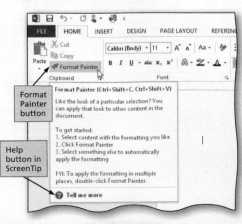

Figure 94

Help in the Office apps, such as Word, provides you with the ability to obtain help directly, without opening the Help window and initiating a search. For example, you may be unsure about how a particular command works, or you may be presented with a dialog box that you are not sure how to use.

Figure 94 shows one option for obtaining help while working in an Office app. If you want to learn more about a command, point to its button and wait for the ScreenTip to appear. If the Help icon appears in the ScreenTip, press the F1 key while pointing to the button to open the Help window associated with that command.

Figure 95 shows a dialog box that contains a Help button. Pressing the F1 key while the dialog box is displayed opens a Help window. The Help window contains help about that dialog box, if available. If no help file is available for that particular dialog box, then the main Help window opens.

Using Windows Help and Support

One of the more powerful Windows features is Windows Help and Support. **Windows Help and Support** is available when using Windows or when using any Microsoft app running in Windows. The same methods used for searching Microsoft Office Help can be used in Windows Help and Support. The difference is that Windows Help and Support displays help for Windows, instead of for Microsoft Office.

Figure 95

To Use Windows Help and Support

1 SIGN IN | 2 USE WINDOWS | 3 USE APPS | 4 FILE MANAGEMENT | 5 SWITCH APPS | 6 SAVE FILES
7 CHANGE SCREEN RESOLUTION | 8 EXIT APPS | 9 USE ADDITIONAL APP FEATURES | 10 USE HELP

The following steps use Windows Help and Support and open the Windows Help and Support window, which contains links to more information about Windows. *Why? This feature is designed to assist you in using Windows or the various apps.* If you are using Windows 7, skip these steps and instead perform the steps in the yellow box that immediately follows these Windows 8 steps.

1

- Swipe in from the right edge of the screen or point to the upper-right corner of the screen to display the Charms bar (Figure 96).

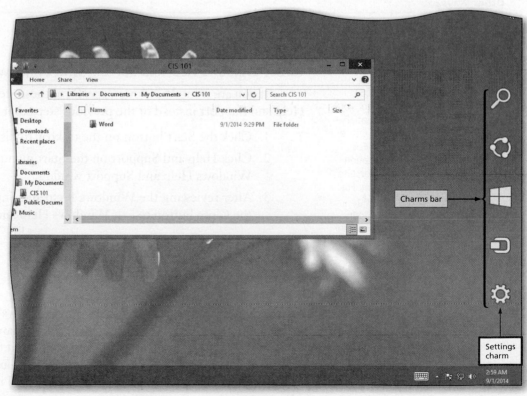

Figure 96

2

- Tap or click the Settings charm on the Charms bar to display the Settings menu (Figure 97).

Settings menu

Settings

Desktop

Control Panel

Personalization

PC info

Help   Help command

Figure 97

3

- Tap or click Help to open the Windows Help and Support window (Figure 98).

4

- After reviewing the Windows Help and Support window, tap or click the Close button to close the Windows Help and Support window.

Windows Help and Support window

Close button

Windows Help and Support

You're not connected to online Help, where the latest help content is available. Get online Help now.

Search

Help home | Browse help | Contact support

→ Getting started

Learn what's new, install apps, connect your devices, and more.

More to explore
Check out what's possible through the videos and articles on the Windows website.

Figure 98

Other Ways

1. Press WINDOWS + F1

BTW

Certification
The Microsoft Office Specialist (MOS) program provides an opportunity for you to obtain a valuable industry credential — proof that you have the Microsoft Office 2013 skills required by employers. For more information, visit the Certification resource on the Student Companion Site located on www.cengagebrain.com. For detailed instructions about accessing available resources, visit www.cengage .com/ct/studentdownload or contact your instructor for information about accessing the required files.

BTW

Quick Reference
For a table that lists how to complete the tasks covered in this book using touch gestures, the mouse, ribbon, shortcut menu, and keyboard, see the Quick Reference Summary at the back of this book, or visit the Quick Reference resource on the Student Companion Site located on www .cengagebrain.com. For detailed instructions about accessing available resources, visit www.cengage.com/ct/studentdownload or contact your instructor for information about accessing the required files.

TO USE WINDOWS HELP AND SUPPORT WITH WINDOWS 7

If you are using Windows 7, perform these steps to start Windows Help and Support instead of the previous steps that use Windows 8.

1. Click the Start button on the taskbar to display the Start menu.
2. Click Help and Support on the Start menu to open the Windows Help and Support window.
3. After reviewing the Windows Help and Support window, click the Close button to exit Windows Help and Support.

Chapter Summary

In this chapter, you learned how to use the Windows interface, several touch screen and mouse operations, and file and folder management. You also learned some basic features of Word and discovered the common elements that exist among Microsoft Office apps. The following items include all of the new Windows and Word skills you have learned in this chapter, with the tasks grouped by activity.

File Management
Create a Folder (OFF 24)
Create a Folder within a Folder (OFF 26)
Expand a Folder, Scroll through Folder Contents, and Collapse a Folder (OFF 27)
Copy a Folder to a USB Flash Drive (OFF 39)
Rename a File (OFF 50)
Move a File (OFF 51)
Delete a File (OFF 52)

Use Help
Open the Help Window in an Office App (OFF 53)
Obtain Help Using the 'Search online help' Text Box (OFF 55)
Obtain Help Using Help Links (OFF 56)
Use Windows Help and Support (OFF 57)

Use Windows
Sign In to an Account (OFF 7)
Run an App from the Start Screen (OFF 11)
Switch between an App and the Start Screen (OFF 13)
Maximize a Window (OFF 14)
Switch from One App to Another (OFF 29)
Minimize and Restore a Window (OFF 32)
Change the Screen Resolution (OFF 37)
Run an App Using the Search Box (OFF 40)

Run an App from File Explorer and Open a File (OFF 47)
Move a Window by Dragging (OFF 53)
Resize a Window by Dragging (OFF 54)

Use Word
Display a Different Tab on the Ribbon (OFF 18)
Collapse and Expand the Ribbon and Use Full Screen Mode (OFF 19)
Use a Shortcut Menu to Relocate the Quick Access Toolbar (OFF 20)
Customize the Quick Access Toolbar (OFF 21)
Enter Text in a Document (OFF 22)
Save a File in a Folder (OFF 29)
Save a File on SkyDrive (OFF 33)
Sign Out of a Microsoft Account (OFF 35)
Exit an App with One Document Open (OFF 38)
Open an Existing File (OFF 42)
Create a New Document from the Backstage View (OFF 43)
Close a File Using the Backstage View (OFF 45)
Open a Recent File Using the Backstage View (OFF 45)
Create a New Blank Document from File Explorer (OFF 46)
Save an Existing File with the Same File Name (OFF 48)

CONSIDER THIS: PLAN AHEAD

What guidelines should you follow to plan your projects?
The process of communicating specific information is a learned, rational skill. Computers and software, especially Microsoft Office 2013, can help you develop ideas and present detailed information to a particular audience and minimize much of the laborious work of drafting and revising projects. No matter what method you use to plan a project, it is beneficial to follow some specific guidelines from the onset to arrive at a final product that is informative, relevant, and effective. Use some aspects of these guidelines every time you undertake a project, and others as needed in specific instances.

1. Determine the project's purpose.
   a) Clearly define why you are undertaking this assignment.
   b) Begin to draft ideas of how best to communicate information by handwriting ideas on paper; composing directly on a laptop, tablet, or mobile device; or developing a strategy that fits your particular thinking and writing style.

2. Analyze your audience.
   a) Learn about the people who will read, analyze, or view your work.
   b) Determine their interests and needs so that you can present the information they need to know and omit the information they already possess.
   c) Form a mental picture of these people or find photos of people who fit this profile so that you can develop a project with the audience in mind.

3. Gather possible content.
   a) Locate existing information that may reside in spreadsheets, databases, or other files.
   b) Conduct a web search to find relevant websites.
   c) Read pamphlets, magazine and newspaper articles, and books to gain insights of how others have approached your topic.
   d) Conduct personal interviews to obtain perspectives not available by any other means.
   e) Consider video and audio clips as potential sources for material that might complement or support the factual data you uncover.

Continued >

CONSIDER THIS: PLAN AHEAD *continued*

4. Determine what content to present to your audience.
   a) Write three or four major ideas you want an audience member to remember after reading or viewing your project.
   b) Envision your project's endpoint, the key fact you wish to emphasize, so that all project elements lead to this final element.
   c) Determine relevant time factors, such as the length of time to develop the project, how long readers will spend reviewing your project, or the amount of time allocated for your speaking engagement.
   d) Decide whether a graph, photo, or artistic element can express or enhance a particular concept.
   e) Be mindful of the order in which you plan to present the content, and place the most important material at the top or bottom of the page, because readers and audience members generally remember the first and last pieces of information they see and hear.

CONSIDER THIS

How should you submit solutions to questions in the assignments identified with a ✸ symbol?
Every assignment in this book contains one or more questions identified with a ✸ symbol. These questions require you to think beyond the assigned file. Present your solutions to the questions in the format required by your instructor. Possible formats may include one or more of these options: write the answer; create a document that contains the answer; present your answer to the class; discuss your answer in a group; record the answer as audio or video using a webcam, smartphone, or portable media player; or post answers on a blog, wiki, or website.

Apply Your Knowledge

Reinforce the skills and apply the concepts you learned in this chapter.

Creating a Folder and a Document

Instructions: You will create a Word folder and then create a Word document and save it in the folder.

Perform the following tasks:

1. Open the File Explorer window and then double-tap or double-click to open the Documents library.

2. Tap or click the New folder button on the Quick Access Toolbar to display a new folder icon and text box for the folder name.

3. Type **Word** in the text box to name the folder. Press the ENTER key to create the folder in the Documents library.

Figure 99

4. Run Word.

5. Enter the text shown in Figure 99 in a new blank document.

6. If requested by your instructor, enter your name in the Word document.

7. Tap or click the Save button on the Quick Access Toolbar. Navigate to the Word folder in the Documents library and then save the document using the file name, Apply 1 Class List.

8. If your Quick Access Toolbar does not show the Quick Print button, add the Quick Print button to the Quick Access Toolbar. Print the document using the Quick Print button on the Quick Access Toolbar. When you are finished printing, remove the Quick Print button from the Quick Access Toolbar.

9. Submit the printout to your instructor.

10. Exit Word.

11. ✸ What other commands might you find useful to include on the Quick Access Toolbar?

Extend Your Knowledge

Extend the skills you learned in this chapter and experiment with new skills. You will use Help to complete the assignment.

Using Help
Instructions: Use Word Help to perform the following tasks.

Perform the following tasks:
1. Run Word.
2. Tap or click the Microsoft Word Help button to open the Word Help window (Figure 100).
3. Search Word Help to answer the following questions.

   a) What are three features new to Word 2013?
   b) What type of training courses are available through Help?
   c) What are the steps to add a new group to the ribbon?
   d) What are Quick Parts?
   e) How do you insert clip art?
   f) What is a template?
   g) How do you use Read mode?
   h) What is a SmartArt graphic?
   i) What is cropping?
   j) What is the purpose of the Navigation Pane?

Figure 100

4. Type the answers from your searches in a new blank Word document. Save the document with a new file name and then submit it in the format specified by your instructor.
5. If requested by your instructor, enter your name in the Word document.
6. Exit Word.
7. ❋ What search text did you use to perform the searches above? Did it take multiple attempts to search and locate the exact information for which you were searching?

Analyze, Correct, Improve

Analyze a file structure, correct all errors, and improve the design.

Organizing Vacation Photos
Note: To complete this assignment, you will be required to use the Data Files for Students. Visit www.cengage.com/ct/studentdownload for detailed instructions or contact your instructor for information about accessing the required files.

Instructions: Traditionally, you have stored photos from past vacations together in one folder. The photos are becoming difficult to manage, and you now want to store them in appropriate folders. You will create the folder structure shown in Figure 101. You then will move the photos to the folders so that they will be organized properly.

1. Correct Create the folder structure in Figure 101 so that you are able to store the photos in an organized manner. If requested by your instructor, add another folder using your last name as the folder name.

Figure 101

© 2014 Cengage Learning

2. Improve View each photo and drag it to the appropriate folder to improve the organization. Submit the assignment in the format specified by your instructor.

3. ❋ In which folder did you place each photo? Think about the files you have stored on your computer. What folder hierarchy would be best to manage your files?

In the Labs

Use the guidelines, concepts, and skills presented in this chapter to increase your knowledge of Windows 8 and Word 2013. Labs 1 and 2, which increase in difficulty, require you to create solutions based on what you learned in the chapter; Lab 3 requires you to create a solution, which uses cloud and web technologies, by learning and investigating on your own from general guidance.

Lab 1: Creating Folders for a Video Store

Problem: Your friend works for Ebaird Video. He would like to organize his files in relation to the types of videos available in the store. He has six main categories: drama, action, romance, foreign, biographical, and comedy. You are to create a folder structure similar to Figure 102.

Instructions: Perform the following tasks:

1. Insert a USB flash drive in an available USB port and then open the USB flash drive window.

2. Create the main folder for Ebaird Video.

3. Navigate to the Ebaird Video folder.

4. Within the Ebaird Video folder, create a folder for each of the following: Drama, Action, Romance, Foreign, Biographical, and Comedy.

© 2014 Cengage Learning

Figure 102

5. Within the Action folder, create two additional folders, one for Science Fiction and the second for Western.

6. If requested by your instructor, add another folder using your last name as the folder name.

7. Submit the assignment in the format specified by your instructor.

8. ✸ Think about how you use your computer for various tasks (consider personal, professional, and academic reasons). What folders do you think will be required on your computer to store the files you save?

Lab 2: Saving Files in Folders

Problem: You are taking a class that requires you to complete three Word chapters. You will save the work completed in each chapter in a different folder (Figure 103).

Instructions: Create the folders shown in Figure 103. Then, using Word, create three small files to save in each folder.

1. Create a Word document containing the text, First Word Chapter.

2. In the Backstage view, tap or click Save As and then tap or click Computer.

© 2014 Cengage Learning

Figure 103

3. Tap or click the Browse button to display the Save As dialog box.

4. Tap or click Documents to open the Documents library. Next, create the folder structure shown in Figure 103 using the New folder button.

5. Navigate to the Chapter 1 folder and then save the file in the Chapter 1 folder using the file name, Word Chapter 1 Document.

6. Create another Word document containing the text, Second Word Chapter, and then save it in the Chapter 2 folder using the file name, Word Chapter 2 Document.

7. Create a third Word document containing the text, Third Word Chapter, and then save it in the Chapter 3 folder using the file name, Word Chapter 3 Document.

8. If requested by your instructor, add your name to each of the three Word files.

9. Submit the assignment in the format specified by your instructor.

10. ❀ Based on your current knowledge of Windows and Word, how will you organize folders for assignments in this class? Why?

Lab 3: Expand Your World: Cloud and Web Technologies
Creating Folders on SkyDrive and Using the Word Web App

Problem: You are taking a class that requires you to create folders on SkyDrive, use the Word Web App to create a document, and then save the document in a folder on SkyDrive (Figure 104).

Instructions: Perform the following tasks:

1. Sign in to SkyDrive in your browser.

2. Use the Create button to create the folder structure shown in Figure 104.

3. In the Notes folder, use the Create button to create a Word document with the file name, Notes, and containing the text, Important Test on Tuesday.

4. If requested by your instructor, add your name to the Word document.

5. Save the document in the Notes folder and then exit the app.

6. Submit the assignment in the format specified by your instructor.

7. ❀ Based on your current knowledge of SkyDrive, do you think you will use it? What about the Word Web App?

Figure 104

❀ Consider This: Your Turn

Apply your creative thinking and problem solving skills to design and implement a solution.

1: Creating Beginning Files for Classes

Personal

Part 1: You are taking the following classes: Introduction to Sociology, Chemistry, Calculus, and Marketing. Create folders for each of the classes. Create a folder structure that will store the documents for each of these classes. Use Word to create a separate Word document for each class. Each document should contain the name of each class and the class meeting locations and times: Introduction to Sociology meets on Mondays and Wednesdays from 8:00 a.m. to 10:00 a.m.; Chemistry meets on Tuesdays and Thursdays from 11:00 a.m. to 1:00 p.m.; Calculus meets on Mondays, Wednesdays, and Fridays from 1:30 p.m. to 3:00 p.m.; and Marketing meets on Tuesdays from 5:00 p.m. to 8:00 p.m. If requested by your instructor, add your name to each of the Word

Continued >

Consider This: Your Turn *continued*

documents. Use the concepts and techniques presented in this chapter to create the folders and files, and store the files in their respective locations. Submit your assignment in the format specified by your instructor.

Part 2:   ✸ You made several decisions while determining the folder structure in this assignment. What was the rationale behind these decisions? Are there any other decisions that also might have worked?

2: Creating Folders
Professional

Part 1:   Your boss at the media store where you work part-time has asked for help with organizing his files. After looking through the files, you decided upon a file structure for her to use, including the following folders: CDs, DVDs, and general merchandise. Use Word to create separate Word documents that list examples in each category. For example, CDs include music [blues, rock, country, new age, pop, and soundtracks], blank discs, books, and games; DVDs include movies [action, documentary, music videos, mystery, and drama], television series, and blank discs; and general merchandise includes clothing, portable media players, cases, earbuds, chargers, and cables. If requested by your instructor, add your name to each of the Word documents. Use the concepts and techniques presented in this chapter to create the folders. Submit your assignment in the format specified by your instructor.

Part 2:   ✸ You made several decisions while determining the folder structure in this assignment. What was the rationale behind these decisions? Justify why you feel this folder structure will help your boss organize her files.

3: Using Help
Research and Collaboration

Part 1:   You have just installed a new computer with the Windows operating system and want to be sure that it is protected from the threat of viruses. You ask two of your friends to help research computer viruses, virus prevention, and virus removal. In a team of three people, each person should choose a topic (computer viruses, virus prevention, and virus removal) to research. Use the concepts and techniques presented in this chapter to use Help to find information regarding these topics. Create a Word document that contains steps to properly safeguard a computer from viruses, ways to prevent viruses, as well as the different ways to remove a virus should your computer become infected. Submit your assignment in the format specified by your instructor.

Part 2:   ✸ You made several decisions while searching Windows Help and Support for this assignment. What decisions did you make? What was the rationale behind these decisions? How did you locate the required information about viruses in help?

Learn Online

Reinforce what you learned in this chapter with games, exercises, training, and many other online activities and resources.

Student Companion Site   Reinforcement activities and resources are available at no additional cost on www.cengagebrain.com. Visit www.cengage.com/ct/studentdownload for detailed instructions about accessing the resources available at the Student Companion Site.

 SAM   Put your skills into practice with SAM Projects! If you have a SAM account, go to www.cengage.com/sam2013 to access SAM assignments for this chapter.

Office 365 Essentials

Microsoft product screen shots used with permission from Microsoft Corporation.

Objectives

You will have mastered the material in this chapter when you can:

- Describe the components of Office 365
- Compare Office 2013 to Office 365 subscription plans
- Understand the productivity tools of Office 365
- Sync multiple devices using Office 365

- Describe how business teams collaborate using SharePoint
- Describe how to use a SharePoint template to design a public website
- Describe how to conduct an online meeting with Lync

Explore Office 365

Introduction to Office 365

Microsoft Office 365 uses the cloud to deliver a subscription-based service offering the newest Office suite and much more. The Microsoft cloud provides Office software and information stored on remote servers all over the world. Your documents are located online or on the cloud, which provides you access to your information anywhere using a PC, Mac, tablet, mobile phone, or other device with an Internet connection. For businesses and students alike, Office 365 offers significant cost savings compared to the traditional cost of purchasing Microsoft Office 2013. In addition to the core desktop Office suite, Office 365 provides access to email, calendars, conferencing, file sharing, and website design, which sync across multiple devices.

Cloud Computing

Cloud computing refers to a collection of computer servers that house resources users access through the Internet (Figure 1). These resources include email messages, schedules, music, photos, videos, games, websites, programs, apps, servers, storage, and more. Instead of accessing these resources on your computer or mobile device, you access them on the cloud.

Figure 1

Cloud computing can help businesses be more efficient and save them money by shifting usage and the consumption of resources, such as servers and programs, from a local environment to the Internet. For example, an employee working during the day in California could use computing resources located in an office in London that is closed for the evening. When the company in California uses the computing resources, it pays a fee that is based on the amount of computing time and other resources it consumes, much in the same way that consumers pay utility companies for the amount of electricity they use.

Cloud computing is changing how users access and pay for software applications. Fading fast are the days when software packages were sold in boxes at a physical store location with a one-time purchase software license fee. Instead, the new pricing structure is a subscription-based model, where users pay a monthly or annual fee for the software that you can use on multiple devices. The cloud-based Office 365 offers the Office suite with added features that allow you to communicate and collaborate with others in real time.

When you create a free Microsoft account, do you get free cloud storage space?
Yes, when you create a free Microsoft account at Outlook.com, you have access to 7 GB of cloud storage for any type of files.

CONSIDER THIS

What Is Office 365?

Office 365 (Office365.com) is a collection of programs and services, which includes the Microsoft Office 2013 suite, file storage, online collaboration, and file synchronization, as shown in Figure 2 on the next page. You can access these services using your computer, browser, or supported mobile device. For example, a business has two options for providing Office to their employees. A business could purchase Office 2013 and install the software on company computers and servers; however, this traditional Office 2013 package with perpetual licensing does not include the communication and collaboration tools. Employees could not access the Office software if they were not using their work computers. In contrast, if the business purchases a monthly subscription to Office 365, each employee has access to the Office suite on up to five different computers, whether at home or work; company-wide email; web conferencing; website creation capabilities; cloud storage; and shared files. For a lower price, Office 365 provides many more features. In addition, a business may prefer a subscription plan with predictable monthly costs and no up-front infrastructure costs.

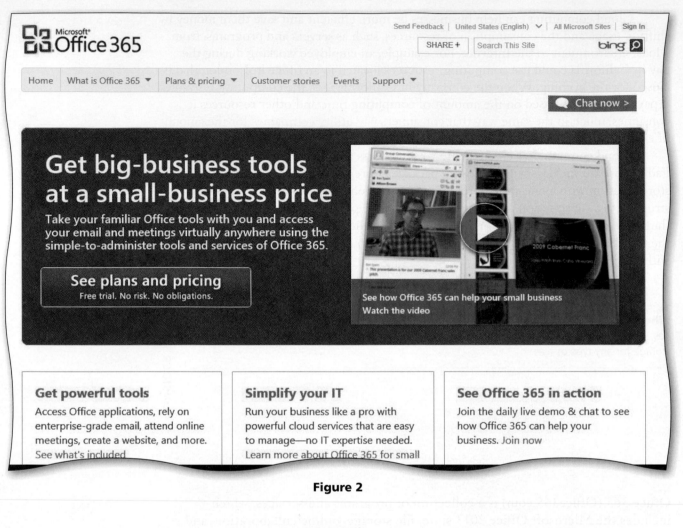

Figure 2

Office 2013 and Office 365 Features Comparison

Office 2013 is the name of the perpetual software package that includes individual applications that can be installed on a single computer. An Office 365 subscription comes with a license to install the software on multiple PCs or Macs at the same time, giving you more flexibility to use your Office products in your home, school, or workplace, whether on a computer or a mobile device. Office 365 provides the Office 2013 programs as part of a subscription service that includes online storage, sharing, and syncing via Microsoft cloud services as shown in Table 1.

Office 365 is available in business, consumer, education, and government editions. Office 365 combines the full version of the Microsoft Office desktop suite with cloud-based versions of Microsoft's communications and collaboration services. The subscription package includes:

- Microsoft Exchange online for shared email and calendars
- Microsoft SharePoint Online for shared file access and public website creation
- Microsoft Office Web apps for browser viewing
- Microsoft Lync Online for communication services

Table 1 Office 2013 and Office 365 Feature Comparison

Office 2013 Professional (Installed on a single device)	Office 365 Subscription (Installed on 2 to 5 devices)
Microsoft Word	Microsoft Word
Microsoft Excel	Microsoft Excel
Microsoft PowerPoint	Microsoft PowerPoint
Microsoft Access	Microsoft Access
Microsoft Outlook	Microsoft Outlook
Microsoft Publisher	Microsoft Publisher
Microsoft OneNote	Microsoft OneNote
	email and calendars (Exchange Online)
	file sharing (SharePoint Online)
	public website design and publishing (SharePoint Online)
	browser-based Office Web Apps
	instant messaging (Lync Online)
	audio and video web conferencing (Lync Online)
	screen sharing with shared control (Lync Online)
	technical support

© 2014 Cengage Learning

Subscription-Based Office 365 Plans

Microsoft provides various subscription plans for Office 365 with different benefits for each individual or organization. Subscription plans include Office 365 Home Premium for home users, Office 365 University for students, Office 365 Small Business, Office 365 Small Business Premium, Office 365 Midsize Business, and Office 365 Enterprise and Government. During the Office 365 sign-up process, you create a Microsoft email address and password to use on your multiple devices. A single subscription to an Office 365 Home Premium account can cover an entire household. The Office 365 Home Premium subscription allows up to five concurrent installations by using the same email address and password combination. This means that your mother could be on the main family computer while you use your tablet and smartphone at the same time. You each can sign in with your individual Microsoft accounts using your settings and accessing your own documents using a single Office 365 subscription.

The Office 365 University subscription plan is designed for higher-education full-time and part-time students, faculty, and staff. By submitting the proper credentials, such as a school email address, students and faculty can purchase Office 365 University, including Word, PowerPoint, Excel, Access, Outlook, Publisher, and OneNote. A one-time payment covers a four-year subscription. In addition, Office 365 University provides users with 27 GB of SkyDrive cloud storage rather than the free 7 GB provided by a Microsoft account, and 60 Skype world minutes per month for videoconferencing. Students have the option of renewing for another four years, for a total of eight years. The Office 365 University edition is limited to two computers (PC or Mac).

The Microsoft Office 365 Business Plans can provide full support for employees to work from any location, whether they are in their traditional business office, commuting to and from work across the country, or working from a home office. Office 365 small business plans (Small Business and Small Business Premium) are best for companies with up to 10 employees, but can accommodate up to 25 users. Office 365 Midsize Business accommodates from 11 to 300 users. Office 365 Enterprise Plan fits organizations ranging in size from a single employee to 50,000-plus users. Each employee can install Microsoft Office 365 on five different computers.

First Look at Office 365

Microsoft Office 365 subscription plans offer all the same applications that are available in the Microsoft Office Professional 2013 suite in addition to multiple communication and collaboration tools. With Office 365 you can retrieve, edit, and save Office documents on the Office 365 cloud, coauthor documents in real time with others, and quickly initiate computer-based calls, instant messages, and web conferences with others.

Productivity Tools

Whether you are inserting audio and video into a Word document to create a high-impact business plan proposal or utilizing the visualization tools in Excel to chart the return on investment of a new mobile marketing program, Office 365 premium plans deliver the full Office product with the same features as the latest version of Microsoft Office. Office 365 uses a quick-start installation technology, called **Click-to-Run**, that downloads and installs the basics within minutes, so that users are able to start working almost immediately. It also includes **Office on Demand**, which streams Office to Windows 7- and Windows 8-based PCs for work performed on public computers. The single-use copy that is installed temporarily on the Windows computer does not count toward the device limit. No installation is necessary when using Office on Demand, and the applications disappear from the computer once you are finished using them. If you have a document on a USB drive or on SkyDrive that you need to edit on another PC, you can use Office on Demand to get the full version of Word in just a few minutes.

In effect, the Office 365 subscription provides access to the full Office applications wherever you are working. When you access your Office 365 account management panel, three choices are listed: 32- and 64-bit versions of Office 2013, and Office for Mac. Selecting the third option will initiate a download of an installer that must be run in the standard OS X fashion. When you install Office 365 on a Mac, the most current Mac version of Office is installed.

CONSIDER THIS

Unlike Google, which offers online documents, spreadsheets, and presentations called Google Docs, Microsoft Office 365 installs locally on your computer in addition to being available online. Google Docs is entirely browser based, which means if you are not connected to the Internet, you cannot access your Google Docs files.

Email and Calendars

In business, sharing information is essential to meeting the needs of your customers and staff. Office 365 offers shared access to business email, calendars, and contacts using **Exchange Online** from a computer, tablet, phone, and browser. The cloud-based Exchange Online enables business people to access Outlook information from anywhere at any time, while eliminating the cost of purchasing and maintaining servers to store data. If you need to meet with a colleague about a new project, you can compare calendars to view availability, confirm conference room availability, share project contacts, search email messages related to the project, and send email invitations to the project meeting. Exchange Online also allows you to search and access your company's address list.

Online Meetings

When you are working with a team on a project that requires interaction, email and text communications can slow the communications process. Microsoft Lync connects you with others by facilitating real-time, interactive presentations and meetings over the Internet using both video and audio calling. As shown in Figure 3, you can conduct an online meeting with a team member or customer that includes an instant messaging conversation, audio, high-definition video, virtual whiteboards, and screen sharing. If the customer does not have an Office 365 subscription, they still can join the meeting through the invitation link, which runs the Lync Web App.

Skype is another tool in the Office 365 subscription, which enables users to place video calls to computers and smartphones and voice calls to landlines. Skype also supports instant message and file sharing to computers and mobile devices. While Skype may be adequate for simple communication, Lync provides for more robust, comprehensive communications. These robust features include high-definition (HD) videoconferencing capabilities, a whiteboard, and a larger audience. Using Lync, meeting attendees simultaneously can view up to five participants' video, identify the active speaker, and associate names with faces. Lync supports up to 250 attendees per meeting. Unlike Skype, Lync meetings can be recorded for replaying at a later time. This enables businesses and schools to schedule meetings or organize online classes using Lync capabilities.

File Sharing

Office 365 includes a team site, which is a password-protected portal that supports sharing of large, difficult-to-email files and provides a single location for the latest versions of documents. In business, for example, colleagues working on common projects can save valuable time by being able to access instantly the latest master copy of each document. Security can be managed through different

Lync communications program

Figure 3

levels of user access so that users see only what they are supposed to see. Office 365 provides access to shared files using the cloud, making writing, editing, and sharing documents easier. If a construction company creates a commercial bid for a building project, the customers can be invited to view an Excel spreadsheet bid, construction timetable with a shared calendar, and an Access database of all the materials needed using the file sharing feature online.

Website Creation

Office 365 business plan subscriptions include a built-in hosted public website, where customers and clients can find an online storefront of a company. This public website, called the Website, can be customized to market a company by using various templates within the Office 365 cloud. The website creation tools include those for adding a theme, graphics, fonts, maps, directions, blogs, stock tickers, slide shows, PayPal, weather, and videos to interact with the website's visitors.

Synchronization

Office 365 subscription plans provide a central place to store and access your documents and business information. A feature of Office 365 ensures the original and backup computer files in two or more locations are identical through a process called **Active Directory Synchronization**. For example, if you open a PowerPoint presentation on your smartphone while you are riding a city bus and then add a new slide as you head to school, the PowerPoint presentation automatically is synced with Office 365. When you arrive on campus and open the PowerPoint presentation on a school computer, your new slide already is part of the finished slide show. By storing your files in Office 365, you can access your files on another computer if your home computer fails, with no loss of time or important information. When using your mobile phone's data plan, you do not need to search for a Wi-Fi hot spot to connect to the Office 365 cloud. Computer labs in schools can be configured to synchronize automatically all student files to Office 365 online.

Multiple Device Access to Office 365

With a single sign-in process, Office 365 provides access to multiple computers and mobile devices, including Android smartphones and tablets, Apple iPhones and iPads, Windows phones, and Blackberry phones. After you configure your devices' email settings, you can view your Microsoft account calendar, contacts, and email. Your personalized settings, preferences, and documents can be synchronized among all the different devices included in your Office 365 premium subscription. With the mobility of Office 365, students and employees can work anywhere, accessing information and responding to email requests immediately. If you lose your phone, Office 365 includes a feature that allows you to remotely wipe your phone clean of any data. By wiping your phone's data, you can prevent any unauthorized access to sensitive information, such as your banking information, passwords, and contacts, as well as discourage identity theft. Because your phone contacts and other information are stored on the Microsoft cloud, damaged or lost equipment is never a problem.

A thief can be quite resourceful if he or she steals your phone. Before you can alert your parents or spouse to the theft, they might receive a text from "you" asking for your ATM or credit card PIN number. Your parents or spouse might then reply with the PIN number. Your bank account could be emptied in minutes.

Teams Using Office 365 in Business

In the business world, rarely does an employee work in isolation. Companies need their employees to collaborate, whether they work in the same office or in locations around the world. Telecommuters working from home can communicate as if they were on-site by using a common team website and conferencing software. SharePoint Online and Lync Online provide seamless communication.

Small business subscription plans as low as $6.00 per user per month allow employees to create and store Word documents, Excel spreadsheets, and PowerPoint presentations online and communicate with one another via email, instant messaging, or video chat as they work on projects together. As shown in Figure 4, a team portal page is shown when you subscribe at https://portal.microsoftonline.com. Larger companies and those requiring more features can take advantage of the Office 365 business premium package, which, in addition to the features listed above, provides access to the Office 365 portal website and eliminates the effort and cost of the users maintaining their own costly computer servers.

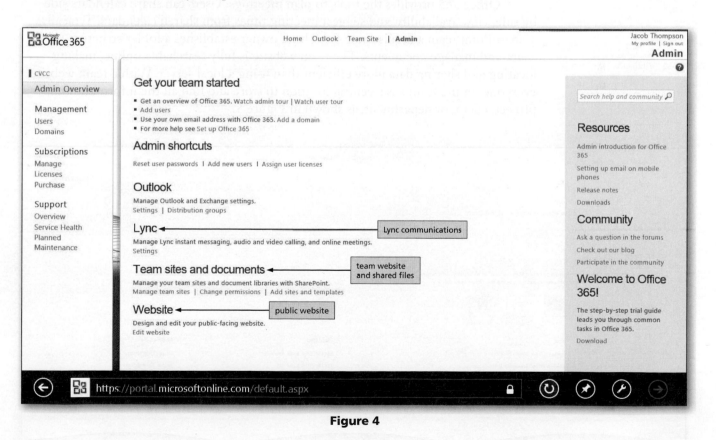

Figure 4

Email Communication Using Exchange

Office 365 includes Exchange Online, an email-based collaborative communications server for business. Exchange enables employees to be more productive by effectively managing email across multiple devices and facilitating teamwork.

Collaboration Using SharePoint

SharePoint Online, a part of Office 365 subscription plans, allows employees to collaborate with one another, share documents, post announcements, and track tasks, as shown in Table 2.

Table 2 Office 365 SharePoint Features	
Team Site Feature	**Description**
Calendar	Track important dates
Shared Document Library	Store related documents according to topic; picture, report, and slide libraries often are included
Task List	Track team tasks according to who is responsible for completion
Team Discussion Board	Discuss the topics at hand in an open forum
Contacts List	Share contact lists of employees, customers, contractors, and suppliers

© 2014 Cengage Learning

Office 365 provides the tools to plan meetings. Users can share calendars side by side, view availability, and suggest meeting times from shared calendars. Typically, a SharePoint team administrator or website owner establishes a folder structure to share and manage documents. The team website is fully searchable online, making locating and sharing data more efficient than using a local server. With a team website, everyone on the team has a central location to store and find all the information for a project, client, or department, as shown in Figure 5.

Figure 5

Website Design Using SharePoint

SharePoint provides templates to create a professional looking, public website for an online presence to market your business. As shown in Figure 6, a local pet sitting business is setting up a business website by customizing a SharePoint template. SharePoint Public Website includes features within the Design Manager that you use to customize and design your website by adding your own images, forms, style sheets, maps, themes, and social networking tools. When you finish customizing your business site, you can apply your own domain name to the site. A **domain** is a unique web address that identifies where your website can be found. Office 365 SharePoint hosts your website as part of your subscription. Your customers easily can find your business online and learn about your services.

BTW

Creating SharePoint Intranet Sites
A SharePoint website also can be customized to serve as an internal company website for private communications within the company.

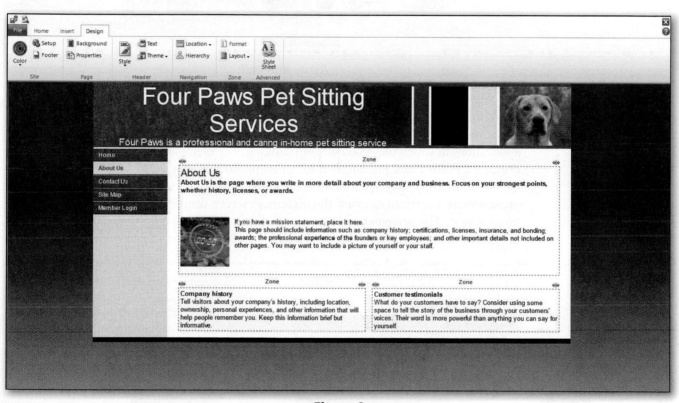

Figure 6

Real-Time Communications Using Lync

Lync Online is Microsoft's server platform for online team communications and comes bundled with Office 365 business subscriptions. As shown in Figure 7, Lync connects in real time to allow instant messaging, videoconferencing, and voice communications; it also integrates with email and Microsoft Office applications.

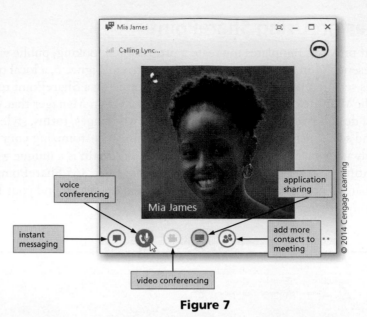

Figure 7

Lync allows you to connect with staff at remote locations using instant messaging capabilities, desktop sharing, videoconferencing, and shared agendas or documents. Lync is integrated into Office 365, which allows staff to start communicating from within the applications in which they currently are working. For example, while an employee is creating a PowerPoint presentation for a new product line, as shown in Figure 8, Lync enables him or her to collaborate with the entire team about the details of the product presentation. The team can view the presenter's screen displaying the PowerPoint presentation. The presenter can share control with any member of the team and can share his or her screen at any time during the Lync meeting.

Figure 8

Users can send a Lync meeting request to schedule a team meeting, or an impromptu conversation can be started immediately using the Meet Now feature. Participants receive a Lync meeting request link via an email message, and when they click the meeting request link, Lync automatically connects them to the online conference. If the participant does not have Lync installed, the Lync Web App automatically connects to the Lync meeting through the user's PC or Mac OS X browser. If a participant is away from his or her computer, he or she still can participate using the Lync Mobile apps for Windows Phone, iOS, and Android. As shown in Figure 9, Lync utilizes **instant messaging** (IM), allowing two or more people to share text messages. They can communicate in real time, similar to a voice conversation. In addition to a simple instant message, Lync provides a feature called **persistent chat**, which allows end-users to participate in a working session of instant messages that is persistent or sustained over a specified amount of time in a moderated chat room. Consider having an instant messaging session with a group of colleagues in different parts of your organization, regardless of geographic region, where you all are working on the same project. Over the course of the project, different people post questions and concerns, and others are able to respond to all those who have subscribed to your topic or been admitted to the chat room. Instead of a long trail of email messages, a team can keep information in a controlled environment with a full history of the discussion in one location.

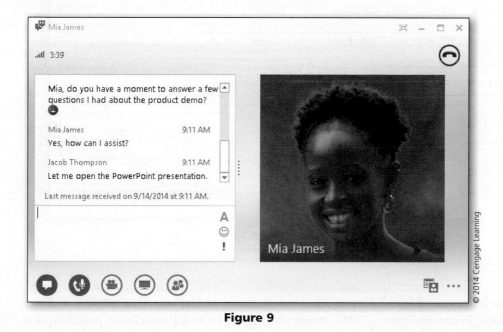

Figure 9

Lync also delivers support for full high-definition (HD) videoconferencing, so that a team can have a clear view of the participants, products, and demos. Before you join the video feed, you can preview your video feed to make sure your video camera is at the correct angle, your image is centered within the video frame, and that your room lighting provides for a clear image. The Lync preview option is important in creating a positive first impression over video. Your audio devices can be tested for clarity to make sure your headset, microphone, and speakers are functioning properly.

Lync provides a polling feature that presenters can use to ask the participants' opinions during a meeting (Figure 10). The poll question can consist of up to seven possible choices. The presenter has the option to view the results privately or share the results with the entire group.

Figure 10

Finally, by enabling the recording feature, Lync meetings and conversations can be captured for viewing at a later time. For instance, you can capture the audio, video, instant messaging (IM), screen sharing, Microsoft PowerPoint presentations, whiteboard, and polling portions of the Lync session and then play them back just as they transpired during the live Lync event. The meeting recordings can be made available to others so that they can view all or part of the Lync event. Instructors can record Lync online class sessions for students who were unable to attend the original presentation. The recording starts in Microsoft Lync; recordings then can be viewed within the Recording Manager feature.

Chapter Summary

In this chapter, you have learned how to subscribe to Office 365, which provides local and online access to Office applications, email, document sharing, web conferencing, and business websites. You also learned how a business can utilize Office 365 features on the cloud to facilitate teamwork. Finally, you learned about the features of SharePoint and Lync, which provide collaboration and communications for business teams using Office 365.

✸ Consider This: Your Turn

Apply your creative thinking and problem solving skills to design and implement a solution.

1: Comparing Office 365 Personal Plans

Personal

Part 1: You are a freshman in college living at home with your family. You are considering if it would be a better value to subscribe to Office 365 University or Office 365 Home Premium. Write a one-page document comparing the pros and cons of the two subscription plans. Research the different subscriptions in detail at Office365.com. Submit your assignment in the format specified by your instructor.

Part 2: ✸ Which type of computer and/or devices would you use with your Office 365 subscription? If you are at a friend's home that does not have Office 365, how could you access your Office files if you do not have your computer or mobile device with you?

2: Upgrading a Local Business to Office 365

Professional

Part 1: You are an employee at Impact Digital Marketing, a small marketing firm with 12 employees. The firm is setting up an Office 365 Small Business subscription next week, and you need to compose an email message with multiple paragraphs to explain the features of this new subscription plan to the members of your firm. Research the Office 365 Small Business subscription plan in detail at Office365.com, and compile your findings in an email message. Submit your assignment in the format specified by your instructor.

Part 2: ✸ Give three examples of how a marketing firm could use Lync. How could a marketing firm use the SharePoint Websites feature?

3: Conducting a Lync Meeting

Research and Collaboration

* Students need an Office 365 subscription to complete the following assignment.

Part 1: Using your Office 365 subscription, conduct a meeting using Lync. Working with a partner, use your Office 365 subscription to research how to use Lync. Then, conduct a 15-minute Lync meeting, including instant messaging, to discuss the features of Lync. Use the concepts and techniques presented in this chapter to create the Lync meeting. Submit your assignment in the format specified by your instructor.

Part 2: ✸ When using Lync in business, when would the video feature best be utilized?

1 Creating, Formatting, and Editing a Word Document with a Picture

Microsoft product screen shots used with permission from Microsoft Corporation.

Objectives

You will have mastered the material in this chapter when you can:

- Enter text in a Word document
- Check spelling as you type
- Format paragraphs
- Format text
- Undo and redo commands or actions
- Change theme colors
- Insert digital pictures in a Word document

- Format pictures
- Add a page border
- Adjust spacing
- Change document properties
- Correct errors and revise a document
- Print and read a document

1 | Creating, Formatting, and Editing a Word Document with a Picture

Introduction

To advertise a sale, promote a business, publicize an event, or convey a message to the community, you may want to create a flyer and hand it out in person or post it in a public location. Libraries, schools, religious organizations, grocery stores, coffee shops, and other places often provide bulletin boards or windows for flyers. You also see flyers posted on webpages or as email messages.

Flyers announce personal items for sale or rent (car, boat, apartment); garage or block sales; services being offered (animal care, housecleaning, lessons, tours); membership, sponsorship, or donation requests (club, religious organization, charity); and other messages, such as a lost or found pet.

Project — Flyer with a Picture

Individuals and businesses create flyers to gain public attention. Flyers, which usually are a single page in length, are an inexpensive means of reaching the community. Many flyers, however, go unnoticed because they are designed poorly.

The project in this chapter follows general guidelines and uses Word to create the flyer shown in Figure 1–1. This colorful, eye-catching flyer announces tour adventures. The picture of the tour group on the mountain trail, taken with a digital camera, entices passersby or viewers to stop and look at the flyer. The headline on the flyer is large and colorful to draw attention into the text. The body copy below the picture briefly describes the tours, along with a bulleted list that concisely highlights important tour information. The signature line of the flyer calls attention to the contact phone number. The word, breathtaking, and the signature line are in a different color so that they stand apart from the rest of the text on the flyer. Finally, the graphical page border nicely frames and complements the contents of the flyer.

For an introduction to Office and instruction about how to perform basic tasks in Office apps, read the Office and Windows chapter at the beginning of this book, where you can learn how to run an application, use the ribbon, save a file, open a file, exit an application, use Help, and much more.

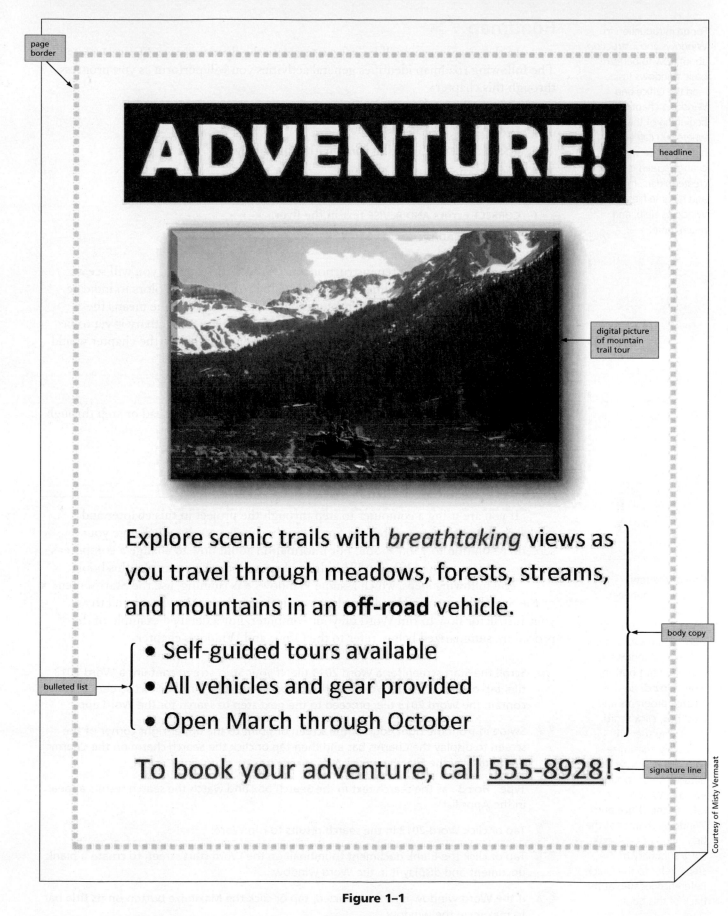

Figure 1–1

For an introduction to Windows and instruction about how to perform basic Windows tasks, read the Office and Windows chapter at the beginning of this book, where you can learn how to resize windows, change screen resolution, create folders, move and rename files, use Windows Help, and much more.

Roadmap

In this chapter, you will learn how to create the flyer shown in Figure 1–1. The following roadmap identifies general activities you will perform as you progress through this chapter:

1. ENTER TEXT in a new document.
2. FORMAT the TEXT in the flyer.
3. INSERT a PICTURE, called Mountain Trail, in the flyer.
4. FORMAT the PICTURE in the flyer.
5. ENHANCE the PAGE with a border and spacing.
6. CORRECT errors AND REVISE text in the flyer.
7. PRINT OR READ the flyer.

At the beginning of step instructions throughout the chapter, you will see an abbreviated form of this roadmap. The abbreviated roadmap uses colors to indicate chapter progress: gray means the chapter is beyond that activity, blue means the task being shown is covered in that activity, and black means that activity is yet to be covered. For example, the following abbreviated roadmap indicates the chapter would be showing a task in the 2 FORMAT TEXT activity.

1 ENTER TEXT | 2 FORMAT TEXT | 3 INSERT PICTURE | 4 FORMAT PICTURE
5 ENHANCE PAGE | 6 CORRECT & REVISE | 7 PRINT OR READ

Use the abbreviated roadmap as a progress guide while you read or step through the instructions in this chapter.

To Run Word and Create a Blank Document

If you are using a computer to step through the project in this chapter and you want your screens to match the figures in this book, you should change your screen's resolution to 1366 × 768. For information about how to change a computer's resolution, refer to the Office and Windows chapter at the beginning of this book.

The following steps, which assume Windows 8 is running, use the Start screen or the Search box to run Word based on a typical installation. You may need to ask your instructor how to run Word on your computer. For a detailed example of the procedure summarized below, refer to the Office and Windows chapter.

One of the few differences between Windows 7 and Windows 8 occurs in the steps to run Word. If you are using Windows 7, click the Start button, type **Word** in the 'Search programs and files' box, click Word 2013, and then, if necessary, maximize the Word window. For detailed steps to run Word in Windows 7, refer to the Office and Windows chapter at the beginning of this book. For a summary of the steps, refer to the Quick Reference located at the back of this book.

1 Scroll the Start screen for a Word 2013 tile. If your Start screen contains a Word 2013 tile, tap or click it to run Word and then proceed to Step 5; if the Start screen does not contain the Word 2013 tile, proceed to the next step to search for the Word app.

2 Swipe in from the right edge of the screen or point to the upper-right corner of the screen to display the Charms bar and then tap or click the Search charm on the Charms bar to display the Search menu.

3 Type **Word** as the search text in the Search box and watch the search results appear in the Apps list.

4 Tap or click Word 2013 in the search results to run Word.

5 Tap or click the Blank document thumbnail on the Word start screen to create a blank document and display it in the Word window.

6 If the Word window is not maximized, tap or click the Maximize button on its title bar to maximize the window.

7 If the Print Layout button on the status bar is not selected (shown in Figure 1–2), tap or click it so that your screen is in Print Layout view.

Q&A What is Print Layout view?
The default (preset) view in Word is **Print Layout view**, which shows the document on a mock sheet of paper in the document window.

8 If Normal (HOME tab | Styles group) is not selected in the Styles gallery (shown in Figure 1–2), tap or click it so that your document uses the Normal style.

Q&A What is the Normal style?
When you create a document, Word formats the text using a particular style. The default style in Word is called the **Normal style**, which is discussed later in this book.

What if rulers appear on my screen?
Tap or click VIEW on the ribbon to display the VIEW tab and then remove the check mark from the View Ruler check box (VIEW tab | Show group).

Entering Text

The first step in creating a document is to enter its text. With the projects in this book, you enter text by typing on the keyboard. By default, Word positions text you type at the left margin. In a later section of this chapter, you will learn how to format, or change the appearance of, the entered text.

BTW
The Word Window
The chapters in this book begin with the Word window appearing as it did at the initial installation of the software. Your Word window may look different depending on your screen resolution and other Word settings.

To Type Text

1 ENTER TEXT | 2 FORMAT TEXT | 3 INSERT PICTURE | 4 FORMAT PICTURE
5 ENHANCE PAGE | 6 CORRECT & REVISE | 7 PRINT OR READ

To begin creating the flyer in this chapter, type the headline in the document window. *Why? The headline is the first line of text in the Adventure Flyer.* The following steps type the first line of text in the document.

1
- Type **Adventure!** as the headline (Figure 1–2).

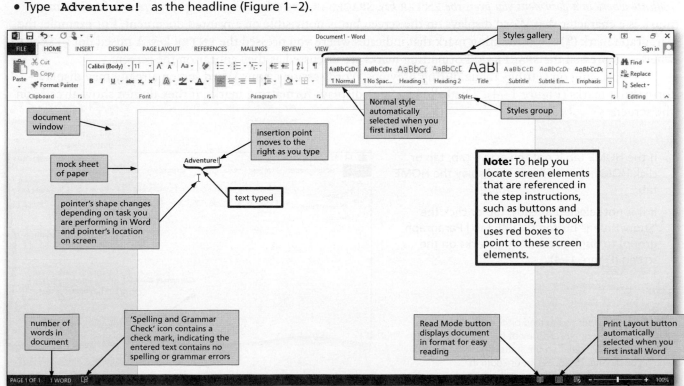

Figure 1–2

Q&A

What if I make an error while typing?

You can press the BACKSPACE key until you have deleted the text in error and then retype the text correctly.

What is the purpose of the Spelling and Grammar Check icon on the status bar?

The **Spelling and Grammar Check icon** displays either a check mark to indicate the entered text contains no spelling or grammar errors, or an X to indicate that it found potential errors. Word flags potential errors in the document with a red, green, or blue wavy underline. Later in this chapter, you will learn how to fix flagged errors.

2

- Press the ENTER key to move the insertion point to the beginning of the next line (Figure 1–3).

Q&A

Why did blank space appear between the headline and the insertion point?

Each time you press the ENTER key, Word creates a new paragraph and inserts blank space between the two paragraphs. Later in this chapter, you will learn how to increase and decrease the spacing between paragraphs.

blank space automatically inserted between paragraphs

Adventure!

insertion point moved to next line

Figure 1–3

CONSIDER THIS

How do you use the touch keyboard with a touch screen?

To display the on-screen touch keyboard, tap the Touch Keyboard button on the Windows taskbar. When finished using the touch keyboard, tap the X button on the touch keyboard to close the keyboard.

To Display Formatting Marks

1 ENTER TEXT | 2 FORMAT TEXT | 3 INSERT PICTURE | 4 FORMAT PICTURE
5 ENHANCE PAGE | 6 CORRECT & REVISE | 7 PRINT OR READ

You may find it helpful to display formatting marks while working in a document. ***Why?*** *Formatting marks indicate where in a document you press the* ENTER *key,* SPACEBAR, *and other nonprinting characters.* A **formatting mark** is a character that Word displays on the screen but is not visible on a printed document. For example, the paragraph mark (¶) is a formatting mark that indicates where you pressed the ENTER key. A raised dot (·) shows where you pressed the SPACEBAR. Formatting marks are discussed as they appear on the screen.

Depending on settings made during previous Word sessions, your Word screen already may display formatting marks (Figure 1–4). The following step displays formatting marks, if they do not show already on the screen.

1

- If the HOME tab is not the active tab, tap or click HOME on the ribbon to display the HOME tab.

- If it is not selected already, tap or click the 'Show/Hide ¶' button (HOME tab | Paragraph group) to display formatting marks on the screen (Figure 1–4).

BTW

Zooming

If text is too small for you to read on the screen, you can zoom the document by dragging the Zoom slider on the status bar or tapping or clicking the Zoom Out or Zoom In buttons on the status bar. Changing the zoom has no effect on the printed document.

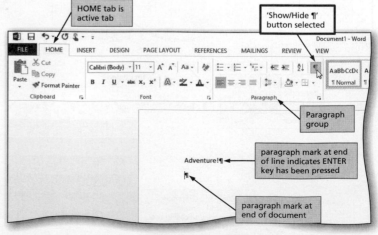

HOME tab is active tab

'Show/Hide ¶' button selected

Paragraph group

paragraph mark at end of line indicates ENTER key has been pressed

Adventure!¶

paragraph mark at end of document

Figure 1–4

Q&A What if I do not want formatting marks to show on the screen?

You can hide them by tapping or clicking the 'Show/Hide ¶' button (HOME tab | Paragraph group) again. It is recommended that you display formatting marks so that you visually can identify when you press the ENTER key, SPACEBAR, and other keys associated with nonprinting characters. Most of the document windows presented in this book, therefore, show formatting marks.

Other Ways

1. Press CTRL+SHIFT+*

To Insert a Blank Line

1 ENTER TEXT | 2 FORMAT TEXT | 3 INSERT PICTURE | 4 FORMAT PICTURE
5 ENHANCE PAGE | 6 CORRECT & REVISE | 7 PRINT OR READ

In the flyer, the digital picture of the mountain trail appears between the headline and body copy. You will not insert this picture, however, until after you enter and format all text. *Why? Although you can format text and insert pictures in any order, for illustration purposes, this chapter formats all text first before inserting the picture. Thus, you leave a blank line in the document as a placeholder for the picture.*

To enter a blank line in a document, press the ENTER key without typing any text on the line. The following step inserts one blank line below the headline.

1

• Press the ENTER key to insert a blank line in the document (Figure 1–5).

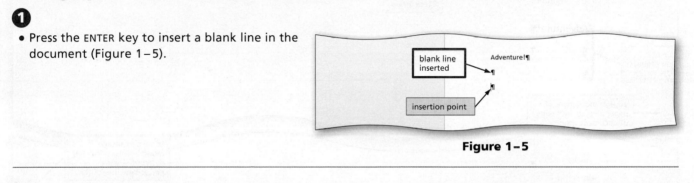

Figure 1–5

To Zoom Page Width

1 ENTER TEXT | 2 FORMAT TEXT | 3 INSERT PICTURE | 4 FORMAT PICTURE
5 ENHANCE PAGE | 6 CORRECT & REVISE | 7 PRINT OR READ

The next step in creating this flyer is to enlarge the contents that appear on the screen. *Why? You would like the text on the screen to be larger so that it is easier to read.* The document currently displays at 100% (shown in Figure 1–6). With Word, you can zoom page width, which zooms (enlarges or shrinks) the mock sheet of paper on the screen so that it is the width of the Word window. The following steps zoom page width.

1

• Tap or click VIEW on the ribbon to display the VIEW tab.

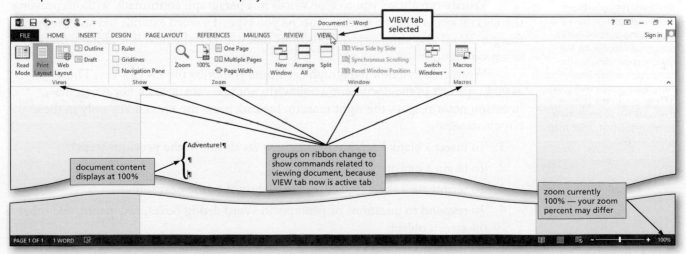

Figure 1–6

2

- Tap or click the Page Width button (VIEW tab | Zoom group) to display the page the same width as the document window (Figure 1–7).

Q&A

If I change the zoom, will the document print differently?
Changing the zoom has no effect on the printed document.

What are the other predefined zoom options?
Through the VIEW tab | Zoom group or the Zoom dialog box (Zoom button in Zoom group), you can zoom to one page (an entire single page appears in the document window), many pages (multiple pages appear at once in the document window), page width, text width, and a variety of set percentages. Whereas page width zoom places the edges of the page at the edges of the document window, text width zoom places the document contents at the edges of the document window.

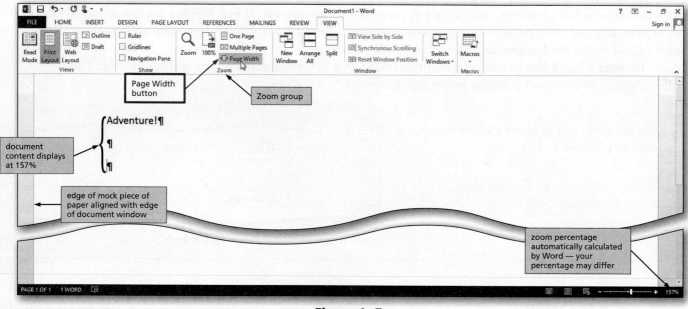

Figure 1–7

Other Ways

1. Tap or click Zoom button (VIEW tab | Zoom group), tap or click Page width (Zoom dialog box), tap or click OK button

Wordwrap

Wordwrap allows you to type words in a paragraph continually without pressing the ENTER key at the end of each line. As you type, if a word extends beyond the right margin, Word also automatically positions that word on the next line along with the insertion point.

Word creates a new paragraph each time you press the ENTER key. Thus, as you type text in the document window, do not press the ENTER key when the insertion point reaches the right margin. Instead, press the ENTER key only in these circumstances:

1. To insert a blank line(s) in a document (as shown in the previous steps)

2. To begin a new paragraph

3. To terminate a short line of text and advance to the next line

4. To respond to questions or prompts in Word dialog boxes, task panes, and other on-screen objects

To Wordwrap Text as You Type

The next step in creating the flyer is to type the body copy. *Why? In many flyers, the body copy text appears below the headline.* The following steps illustrate how the body copy text wordwraps as you enter it in the document.

1

- Type the first sentence of the body copy: `Explore scenic trails with breathtaking views as you travel through meadows, forests, streams, and mountains in an off-road vehicle.`

Q&A

Why does my document wrap on different words?

The printer connected to a computer is one factor that can control where wordwrap occurs for each line in a document. Thus, it is possible that the same document could wordwrap differently if printed on different printers.

2

- Press the ENTER key to position the insertion point on the next line in the document (Figure 1–8).

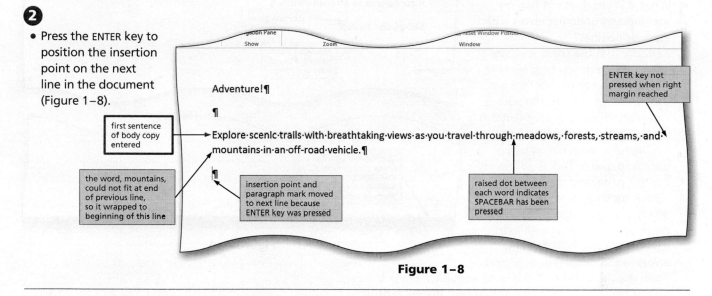

Figure 1–8

Spelling and Grammar Check

As you type text in a document, Word checks your typing for possible spelling and grammar errors. If all of the words you have typed are in Word's dictionary and your grammar is correct, as mentioned earlier, the Spelling and Grammar Check icon on the status bar displays a check mark. Otherwise, the icon shows an X. In this case, Word flags the potential error in the document window with a red, green, or blue wavy underline. A red wavy underline means the flagged text is not in Word's dictionary (because it is a proper name or misspelled). A green wavy underline indicates the text may be incorrect grammatically. A blue wavy underline indicates the text may contain a contextual spelling error, such as the misuse of homophones (words that are pronounced the same but that have different spellings or meanings, such as one and won). Although you can check the entire document for spelling and grammar errors at once, you also can check flagged errors as they appear on the screen.

A flagged word is not necessarily misspelled. For example, many names, abbreviations, and specialized terms are not in Word's main dictionary. In these cases, you can instruct Word to ignore the flagged word. As you type, Word also detects duplicate words while checking for spelling errors. For example, if your document contains the phrase, to the the store, Word places a red wavy underline below the second occurrence of the word, the.

BTW

Automatic Spelling Correction

As you type, Word automatically corrects some misspelled words. For example, if you type recieve, Word automatically corrects the misspelling and displays the word, receive, when you press the SPACEBAR or type a punctuation mark. To see a complete list of automatically corrected words, click FILE on the ribbon to open the Backstage view, click Options in the Backstage view, click Proofing in the left pane (Word Options dialog box), click the AutoCorrect Options button, and then scroll through the list near the bottom of the dialog box.

To Check Spelling and Grammar as You Type

In the following steps, the word, tours, has been misspelled intentionally as tuors. *Why? These steps illustrate Word's check spelling as you type feature. If you are completing this project on a computer, your flyer may contain different or no misspelled words, depending on the accuracy of your typing.*

1

- Type **Self-guided tuors** and then press the SPACEBAR, so that a red wavy line appears below the misspelled word (Figure 1–9).

Q&A What if Word does not flag my spelling and grammar errors with wavy underlines?
To verify that the check spelling and grammar as you type features are enabled, tap or click FILE on the ribbon to open the Backstage view and then tap or click Options in the Backstage view. When the Word Options dialog box is displayed, tap or click Proofing in the left pane, and then ensure the 'Check spelling as you type' and 'Mark grammar errors as you type' check boxes contain check marks. Also ensure the 'Hide spelling errors in this document only' and 'Hide grammar errors in this document only' check boxes do not contain check marks. Tap or click the OK button.

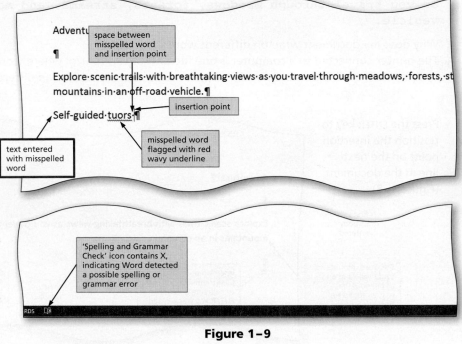

Figure 1–9

2

- Press and hold or right-click the flagged word (tuors, in this case) to display a shortcut menu that presents a list of suggested spelling corrections for the flagged word (Figure 1–10).

Q&A What if, when I press and hold or right-click the misspelled word, my desired correction is not in the list on the shortcut menu?
You can tap or click outside the shortcut menu to close the shortcut menu and then retype the correct word.

What if a flagged word actually is, for example, a proper name and spelled correctly?
Press and hold or right-click it and then tap or click Ignore All on the shortcut menu to instruct Word not to flag future occurrences of the same word in this document.

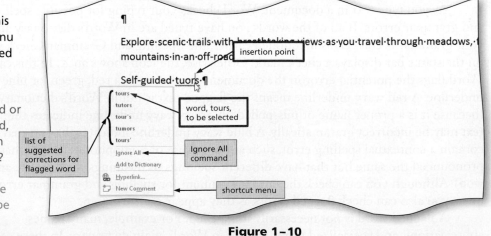

Figure 1–10

3

- Tap or click tours on the shortcut menu to replace the misspelled word in the document with a correctly spelled word (Figure 1–11).

Explore·scenic·trails·with·breathtaking·views·as·you·travel·through·meadows,·forests,·streams,·and mountains·in·an·off-road·vehicle.¶

Self-guided·tours¶

flagged word replaced with word selected on shortcut menu

'Spelling and Grammar Check' icon now shows check mark because no errors are flagged in document

22 WORDS

Figure 1–11

Other Ways

1. Tap or click 'Spelling and Grammar Check' icon on status bar, tap or click desired word in Spelling pane, tap or click Change button, tap or click OK button

To Enter More Text

In the flyer, the text yet to be entered includes the remainder of the body copy, which will be formatted as a bulleted list, and the signature line. The next steps enter the remainder of text in the flyer.

1 Press the END key to move the insertion point to the end of the current line.

2 Type **available** and then press the ENTER key.

3 Type **Open March through October** and then press the ENTER key.

4 Type **All vehicles and gear provided** and then press the ENTER key.

5 Type the signature line in the flyer (Figure 1–12): **To book your adventure, call 555-8928!**

If requested by your instructor, enter your phone number instead of 555-8928 in the signature line.

BTW
Character Widths
Many word processing documents use variable character fonts, where some characters are wider than others; for example, the letter w is wider than the letter i.

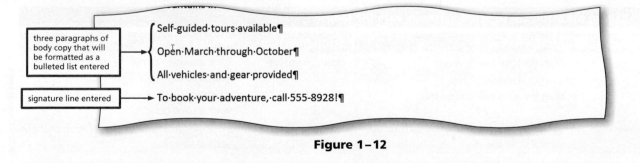

three paragraphs of body copy that will be formatted as a bulleted list entered

Self-guided·tours·available¶

Open·March·through·October¶

All·vehicles·and·gear·provided¶

signature line entered

To·book·your·adventure,·call·555-8928!¶

Figure 1–12

How should you organize text in a flyer?

The text in a flyer typically is organized into three areas: headline, body copy, and signature line.

- The **headline** is the first line of text on the flyer. It conveys the product or service being offered, such as a car for sale, personal lessons, or sightseeing tours, or the benefit that will be gained, such as a convenience, better performance, greater security, higher earnings, or more comfort, or it can contain a message, such as a lost or found pet.

- The **body copy** consists of text between the headline and the signature line. This text highlights the key points of the message in as few words as possible. It should be easy to read and follow. While emphasizing the positive, the body copy must be realistic, truthful, and believable.

- The **signature line**, which is the last line of text on the flyer, contains contact information or identifies a call to action.

CONSIDER THIS

Navigating a Document

You view only a portion of a document on the screen through the document window. At some point when you type text or insert graphics, Word probably will **scroll** the top or bottom portion of the document off the screen. Although you cannot see the text and graphics once they scroll off the screen, they remain in the document.

You can use touch gestures, the keyboard, or a mouse to scroll to a different location in a document and/or move the insertion point around a document. If you are using a touch screen, simply use your finger to slide the document up or down to display a different location in the document and then tap to move the insertion point to a new location. When you use the keyboard, the insertion point automatically moves when you press the desired keys. For example, the previous steps used the END key to move the insertion point to the end of the current line. Table 1–1 outlines various techniques to navigate a document using the keyboard.

With the mouse, you can use the scroll arrows or the scroll box on the scroll bar to display a different portion of the document in the document window and then click the mouse to move the insertion point to that location. Table 1–2 explains various techniques for using the scroll bar to scroll vertically with the mouse.

Table 1–1 Moving the Insertion Point with the Keyboard

Insertion Point Direction	Key(s) to Press	Insertion Point Direction	Key(s) to Press
Left one character	LEFT ARROW	Up one paragraph	CTRL+UP ARROW
Right one character	RIGHT ARROW	Down one paragraph	CTRL+DOWN ARROW
Left one word	CTRL+LEFT ARROW	Up one screen	PAGE UP
Right one word	CTRL+RIGHT ARROW	Down one screen	PAGE DOWN
Up one line	UP ARROW	To top of document window	ALT+CTRL+PAGE UP
Down one line	DOWN ARROW	To bottom of document window	ALT+CTRL+PAGE DOWN
To end of line	END	To beginning of document	CTRL+HOME
To beginning of line	HOME	To end of document	CTRL+END

Table 1–2 Using the Scroll Bar to Scroll Vertically with the Mouse

Scroll Direction	Mouse Action	Scroll Direction	Mouse Action
Up	Drag the scroll box upward.	Down one screen	Click anywhere below the scroll box on the vertical scroll bar.
Down	Drag the scroll box downward.	Up one line	Click the scroll arrow at the top of the vertical scroll bar.
Up one screen	Click anywhere above the scroll box on the vertical scroll bar.	Down one line	Click the scroll arrow at the bottom of the vertical scroll bar.

To Save a Document

You have performed many tasks while creating this document and do not want to risk losing work completed thus far. Accordingly, you should save the document on your hard disk, SkyDrive, or a location that is most appropriate to your situation.

The following steps assume you already have created folders for storing your files, for example, a CIS 101 folder (for your class) that contains a Word folder (for your assignments). Thus, these steps save the document in the Word folder in the

CIS 101 folder on your desired save location. For a detailed example of the procedure for saving a file in a folder or saving a file on SkyDrive, refer to the Office and Windows chapter at the beginning of this book.

BTW
Organizing Files and Folders
You should organize and store files in folders so that you easily can find the files later. For example, if you are taking an introductory computer class called CIS 101, a good practice would be to save all Word files in a Word folder in a CIS 101 folder. For a discussion of folders and detailed examples of creating folders, refer to the Office and Windows chapter at the beginning of this book.

1 Tap or click the Save button on the Quick Access Toolbar, which depending on settings, will display either the Save As gallery in the Backstage view or the Save As dialog box.

2 To save on a hard disk or other storage media on your computer, proceed to Step 2a. To save on SkyDrive, proceed to Step 2b.

2a If your screen opens the Backstage view and you want to save on storage media on your computer, tap or click Computer in the left pane, if necessary, to display options in the right pane related to saving on your computer. If your screen already displays the Save As dialog box, proceed to Step 4.

2b If your screen opens the Backstage view and you want to save on SkyDrive, tap or click SkyDrive in the left pane to display SkyDrive saving options or a Sign In button. If your screen displays a Sign In button, tap or click it and then sign in to SkyDrive.

3 Tap or click the Browse button in the right pane to display the Save As dialog box associated with the selected save location (i.e., Computer or SkyDrive).

4 Type `Adventure Flyer` in the File name box to change the file name. Do not press the ENTER key after typing the file name because you do not want to close the dialog box at this time.

5 Navigate to the desired save location (in this case, the Word folder in the CIS 101 folder [or your class folder] on your computer or SkyDrive).

6 Tap or click the Save button (Save As dialog box) to save the document in the selected folder on the selected save location with the entered file name.

Formatting Paragraphs and Characters

With the text for the flyer entered, the next step is to **format**, or change the appearance of, its text. A paragraph encompasses the text from the first character in the paragraph up to and including its paragraph mark (¶). **Paragraph formatting** is the process of changing the appearance of a paragraph. For example, you can center or add bullets to a paragraph. Characters include letters, numbers, punctuation marks, and symbols. **Character formatting** is the process of changing the way characters appear on the screen and in print. You use character formatting to emphasize certain words and improve readability of a document. For example, you can color, italicize, or underline characters. Often, you apply both paragraph and character formatting to the same text. For example, you may center a paragraph (paragraph formatting) and underline some of the characters in the same paragraph (character formatting).

Although you can format paragraphs and characters before you type, many Word users enter text first and then format the existing text. Figure 1–13a on the next page shows the flyer in this chapter before formatting its paragraphs and characters. Figure 1–13b on the next page shows the flyer after formatting. As you can see from the two figures, a document that is formatted is easier to read and looks more professional. The following pages discuss how to format the flyer so that it looks like Figure 1–13b.

If you are using your finger on a touch screen and are having difficulty completing the steps in this chapter, consider using a stylus. Many people find it easier to be precise with a stylus than with a finger. In addition, with a stylus you see the pointer. If you still are having trouble completing the steps with a stylus, try using a mouse.

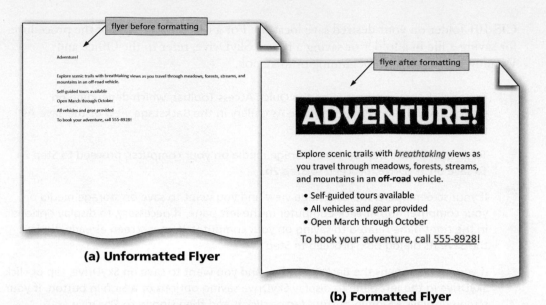

(a) Unformatted Flyer

(b) Formatted Flyer

Figure 1–13

Font, Font Sizes, and Themes

Characters that appear on the screen are a specific shape and size. The **font**, or typeface, defines the appearance and shape of the letters, numbers, and special characters. In Word, the default font usually is Calibri (shown in Figure 1–14). You can leave characters in the default font or change them to a different font. **Font size** specifies the size of the characters and is determined by a measurement system called points. A single **point** is about 1/72 of one inch in height. The default font size in Word typically is 11 (Figure 1–14). Thus, a character with a font size of 11 is about 11/72 or a little less than 1/6 of one inch in height. You can increase or decrease the font size of characters in a document.

A document **theme** is a set of unified formats for fonts, colors, and graphics. Word includes a variety of document themes to assist you with coordinating these visual elements in a document. The default theme fonts are Calibri Light for headings and Calibri for body text. By changing the document theme, you quickly can give your document a new look. You also can define your own document themes.

CONSIDER THIS

How do I know which formats to use in a flyer?

In a flyer, consider the following formatting suggestions.

- **Increase the font size of characters.** Flyers usually are posted on a bulletin board or in a window. Thus, the font size should be as large as possible so that passersby easily can read the flyer. To give the headline more impact, its font size should be larger than the font size of the text in the body copy. If possible, make the font size of the signature line larger than the body copy but smaller than the headline.

- **Change the font of characters.** Use fonts that are easy to read. Try to use only two different fonts in a flyer; for example, use one for the headline and the other for all other text. Too many fonts can make the flyer visually confusing.

- **Change the paragraph alignment.** The default alignment for paragraphs in a document is **left-aligned**, that is, flush at the left margin of the document with uneven right edges. Consider changing the alignment of some of the paragraphs to add interest and variety to the flyer.

- **Highlight key paragraphs with bullets.** A bulleted paragraph is a paragraph that begins with a dot or other symbol. Use bulleted paragraphs to highlight important points in a flyer.

- **Emphasize important words.** To call attention to certain words or lines, you can underline them, italicize them, or bold them. Use these formats sparingly, however, because overuse will minimize their effect and make the flyer look too busy.

- **Use color.** Use colors that complement each other and convey the meaning of the flyer. Vary colors in terms of hue and brightness. Headline colors, for example, can be bold and bright. Signature lines should stand out more than body copy but less than headlines. Keep in mind that too many colors can detract from the flyer and make it difficult to read.

To Center a Paragraph

The headline in the flyer currently is left-aligned (Figure 1–14). *Why? Word, by default left-aligns text, unless you specifically change the alignment.* You want the headline to be **centered**, that is, positioned horizontally between the left and right margins on the page. Recall that Word considers a single short line of text, such as the one-word headline, a paragraph. Thus, you will center the paragraph containing the headline. The following steps center a paragraph.

1
- Tap or click HOME on the ribbon to display the HOME tab.
- Tap or click somewhere in the paragraph to be centered (in this case, the headline) to position the insertion point in the paragraph to be formatted (Figure 1–14).

Figure 1–14

2
- Tap or click the Center button (HOME tab | Paragraph group) to center the paragraph containing the insertion point (Figure 1–15).

Q&A What if I want to return the paragraph to left-aligned?
You would tap or click the Center button again or tap or click the Align Left button (HOME tab | Paragraph group).

Figure 1–15

Other Ways

1. Tap 'Show Context Menu' button on mini toolbar or right-click paragraph, tap or click Paragraph on shortcut menu, tap or click Indents and Spacing tab (Paragraph dialog box), tap or click Alignment arrow, tap or click Centered, tap or click OK button

2. Tap or click Paragraph Settings Dialog Box Launcher (HOME tab or PAGE LAYOUT tab | Paragraph group), tap or click Indents and Spacing tab (Paragraph dialog box), tap or click Alignment arrow, tap or click Centered, tap or click OK button

3. Press CTRL+E

To Center Another Paragraph

In the flyer, the signature line is to be centered to match the paragraph alignment of the headline. The following steps center the signature line.

1 Tap or click somewhere in the paragraph to be centered (in this case, the signature line) to position the insertion point in the paragraph to be formatted.

2 Tap or click the Center button (HOME tab | Paragraph group) to center the paragraph containing the insertion point (shown in Figure 1–16 on the next page).

BTW
File Type
Depending on your Windows settings, the file type .docx may be displayed on the title bar immediately to the right of the file name after you save the file. The file type .docx identifies a Word 2013 document.

BTW
Touch Screen Differences
The Office and Windows interfaces may vary if you are using a touch screen. For this reason, you might notice that the function or appearance of your touch screen differs slightly from this chapter's presentation.

Formatting Single versus Multiple Paragraphs and Characters

As shown on the previous pages, to format a single paragraph, simply move the insertion point in the paragraph to make it the current paragraph, and then format the paragraph. Similarly, to format a single word, position the insertion point in the word to make it the current word, and then format the word.

To format multiple paragraphs or words, however, you first must select the paragraphs or words you want to format and then format the selection.

To Select a Line

1 ENTER TEXT | 2 FORMAT TEXT | 3 INSERT PICTURE | 4 FORMAT PICTURE
5 ENHANCE PAGE | 6 CORRECT & REVISE | 7 PRINT OR READ

The default font size of 11 point is too small for a headline in a flyer. To increase the font size of the characters in the headline, you first must select the line of text containing the headline. *Why? If you increase font size of text without selecting any text, Word will increase the font size only of the word containing the insertion point.* The following steps select a line.

1

- If you are using a mouse, move the pointer to the left of the line to be selected (in this case, the headline) until the pointer changes to a right-pointing block arrow (Figure 1–16).

Figure 1–16

2

- If you are using a touch screen, double-tap to the left of the line to be selected to select the line; if you are using a mouse, while the pointer is a right-pointing block arrow, click the mouse to select the entire line to the right of the pointer (Figure 1–17).

Q&A Why is the selected text shaded gray?

If your screen normally displays dark letters on a light background, which is the default setting in Word, then selected text displays with a light shading color, such as gray, on the dark letters. Note that the selection that appears on the text does not print.

Figure 1–17

Other Ways

1. Drag pointer through line

2. With insertion point at beginning of desired line, press SHIFT+DOWN ARROW

To Change the Font Size of Selected Text

The next step is to increase the font size of the characters in the selected headline. *Why? You would like the headline to be as large as possible and still fit on a single line, which in this case is 72 point.* The following steps increase the font size of the headline from 11 to 72 point.

1

- With the text selected, tap or click the Font Size arrow (HOME tab | Font group) to display the Font Size gallery (Figure 1–18).

Q&A

Why are the font sizes in my Font Size gallery different from those in Figure 1–18?
Font sizes may vary depending on the current font and your printer driver.

What happened to the mini toolbar?
The mini toolbar disappears if you do not use it. These steps use the Font Size arrow on the HOME tab instead of the Font Size arrow on the mini toolbar.

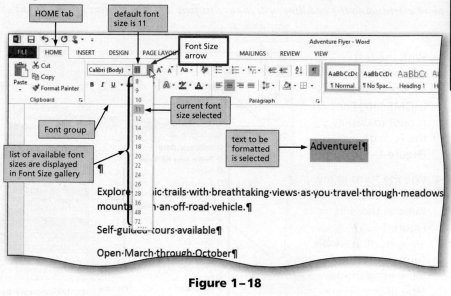

Figure 1–18

2

- If you are using a mouse, point to 72 in the Font Size gallery to display a live preview of the selected text at the selected point size (Figure 1–19).

Q&A

Can I use live preview on a touch screen?
Live preview is not available on a touch screen.

Experiment

- If you are using a mouse, point to various font sizes in the Font Size gallery and watch the font size of the selected text change in the document window.

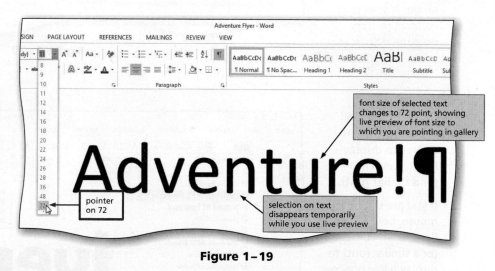

Figure 1–19

3

- Tap or click 72 in the Font Size gallery to increase the font size of the selected text.

Other Ways

1. Tap or click Font Size arrow on mini toolbar, tap or click desired font size in Font Size gallery	2. Tap 'Show Context Menu' button on mini toolbar or right-click selected text, tap or click Font on shortcut menu, tap or click Font tab (Font dialog box), select desired font size in Size list, tap or click OK button	3. Tap or click Font Dialog Box Launcher, tap or click Font tab (Font dialog box), select desired font size in Size list, tap or click OK button	4. Press CTRL+D, tap or click Font tab (Font dialog box), select desired font size in Size list, tap or click OK button

To Change the Font of Selected Text

The default theme font for headings is Calibri Light and for all other text, called body text in Word, is Calibri. Many other fonts are available, however, so that you can add variety to documents.

The following steps change the font of the headline from Calibri to Berlin Sans FB Demi. *Why? To draw more attention to the headline, you change its font so that it differs from the font of other text in the flyer.*

1

- With the text selected, tap or click the Font arrow (HOME tab | Font group) to display the Font gallery (Figure 1–20).

Q&A

Will the fonts in my Font gallery be the same as those in Figure 1–20?
Your list of available fonts may differ, depending on the type of printer you are using and other settings.

What if the text no longer is selected? Follow the steps on page WD 16 to select a line.

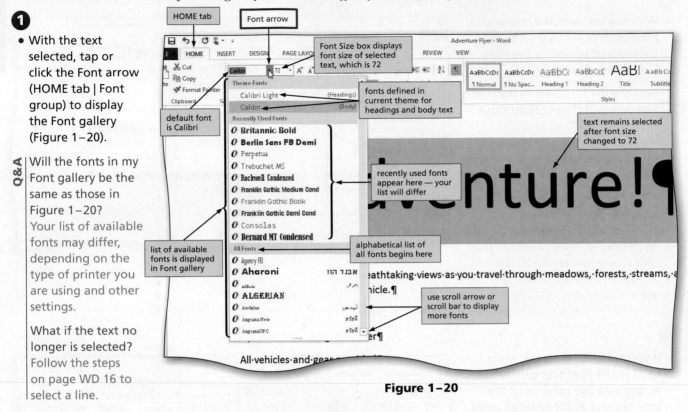

Figure 1–20

2

- If necessary, scroll through the Font gallery to display Berlin Sans FB Demi (or a similar font).

- If you are using a mouse, point to Berlin Sans FB Demi (or a similar font) to display a live preview of the selected text in the selected font (Figure 1–21).

Experiment

- If you are using a mouse, point to various fonts in the Font gallery and watch the font of the selected text change in the document window.

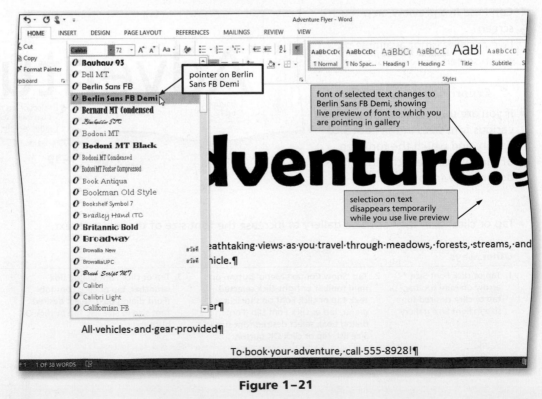

Figure 1–21

3

- Tap or click Berlin Sans FB Demi (or a similar font) to change the font of the selected text.

Q&A If the font I want to use appears in the Recently Used Fonts list in the Font gallery, could I tap or click it there instead?
Yes.

Other Ways

1. Tap or click Font arrow on mini toolbar, tap or click desired font in Font gallery	2. Tap 'Show Context Menu' button on mini toolbar or right-click selected text, tap or click Font on shortcut menu, tap or click Font tab (Font dialog box), select desired font in Font list, tap or click OK button	3. Tap or click Font Dialog Box Launcher (HOME tab | Font group), tap or click Font tab (Font dialog box), select desired font in Font list, tap or click OK button	4. Press CTRL+D, tap or click Font tab (Font dialog box), select desired font in Font list, tap or click OK button

---

To Change the Case of Selected Text

1 ENTER TEXT | 2 FORMAT TEXT | 3 INSERT PICTURE | 4 FORMAT PICTURE
5 ENHANCE PAGE | 6 CORRECT & REVISE | 7 PRINT OR READ

The headline currently shows the first letter in each word capitalized, which sometimes is referred to as initial cap. The following steps change the headline to uppercase. *Why? To draw more attention to the headline, you would like the entire line of text to be capitalized, or in uppercase letters.*

1

- With the text selected, tap or click the Change Case button (HOME tab | Font group) to display the Change Case gallery (Figure 1–22).

Figure 1–22

2

- Tap or click UPPERCASE in the Change Case gallery to change the case of the selected text (Figure 1–23).

Q&A What if a ruler appears on the screen or the pointer shape changes?
If you are using a mouse, depending on the position of your pointer and locations you click on the screen, a ruler may automatically appear or the pointer's shape may change. Simply move the mouse and the ruler should disappear and/or the pointer shape will change.

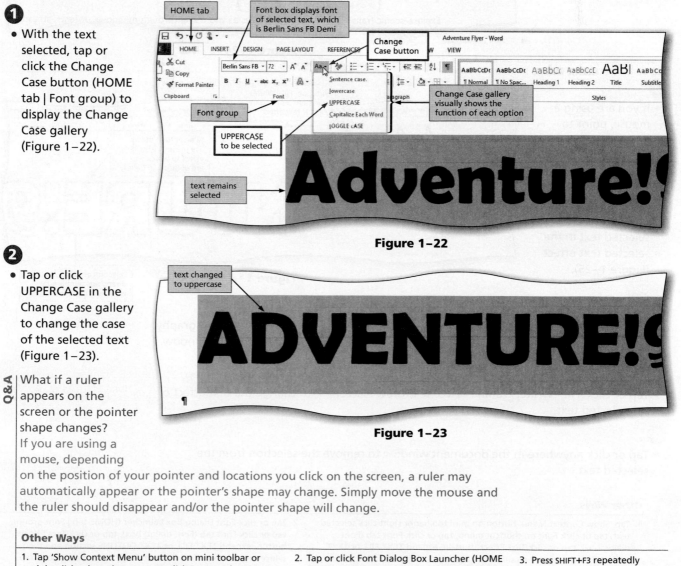

Figure 1–23

Other Ways

1. Tap 'Show Context Menu' button on mini toolbar or right-click selected text, tap or click Font on shortcut menu, tap or click Font tab (Font dialog box), select All caps in Effects area, tap or click OK button	2. Tap or click Font Dialog Box Launcher (HOME tab | Font group), tap or click Font tab (Font dialog box), select All caps in Effects area, tap or click OK button	3. Press SHIFT+F3 repeatedly until text is desired case

To Apply a Text Effect to Selected Text

Word provides many text effects to add interest and variety to text. The following steps apply a text effect to the headline. **Why?** *You would like the text in the headline to be even more noticeable.*

1

• With the text selected, tap or click the 'Text Effects and Typography' button (HOME tab | Font group) to display the Text Effects and Typography gallery (Figure 1–24).

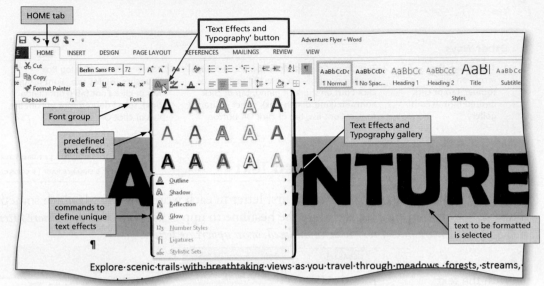

Figure 1–24

2

• If you are using a mouse, point to 'Fill - White, Outline - Accent 1, Glow - Accent 1' (fourth text effect in second row) to display a live preview of the selected text in the selected text effect (Figure 1–25).

Figure 1–25

🔍 **Experiment**

• If you are using a mouse, point to various text effects in the Text Effects and Typography gallery and watch the text effects of the selected text change in the document window.

3

• Tap or click 'Fill - White, Outline - Accent 1, Glow - Accent 1' to change the text effect of the selected text.

4

• Tap or click anywhere in the document window to remove the selection from the selected text.

Other Ways

1. Tap 'Show Context Menu' button on mini toolbar or right-click selected text, tap or click Font on shortcut menu, tap or click Font tab (Font dialog box), tap or click Text Effects button, expand TEXT FILL or TEXT OUTLINE section and then select the desired text effect(s) (Format Text Effects dialog box), tap or click OK button, tap or click OK button

2. Tap or click Font Dialog Box Launcher (HOME tab | Font group), tap or click Font tab (Font dialog box), tap or click Text Effects button, expand TEXT FILL or TEXT OUTLINE section and then select desired text effect (Format Text Effects dialog box), tap or click OK button, tap or click OK button

To Shade a Paragraph

When you **shade** text, Word colors the rectangular area behind any text or graphics. If the text to shade is a paragraph, Word shades the area from the left margin to the right margin of the current paragraph. To shade a paragraph, place the insertion point in the paragraph. To shade any other text, you must first select the text to be shaded.

This flyer uses green as the shading color for the headline. *Why? To make the headline of the flyer more eye-catching, you shade it.* The following steps shade a paragraph.

1

- Tap or click somewhere in the paragraph to be shaded (in this case, the headline) to position the insertion point in the paragraph to be formatted.

- Tap or click the Shading arrow (HOME tab | Paragraph group) to display the Shading gallery (Figure 1–26).

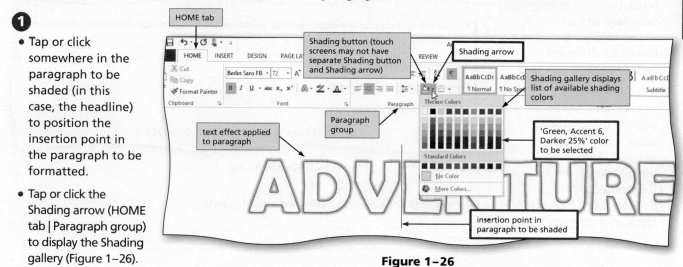

Figure 1–26

Q&A If I am using a mouse, what if I click the Shading button by mistake?
Click the Shading arrow and proceed with Step 2. If you are using a touch screen, you may not have a separate Shading button.

Experiment

- If you are using a mouse, point to various colors in the Shading gallery and watch the shading color of the current paragraph change.

2

- Tap or click 'Green, Accent 6, Darker 25%' (rightmost color in fifth row) to shade the current paragraph (Figure 1–27).

Q&A What if I apply a dark shading color to dark text?
When the font color of text is Automatic, it usually is black. If you select a dark shading color, Word automatically may change the text color to white so that the shaded text is easier to read.

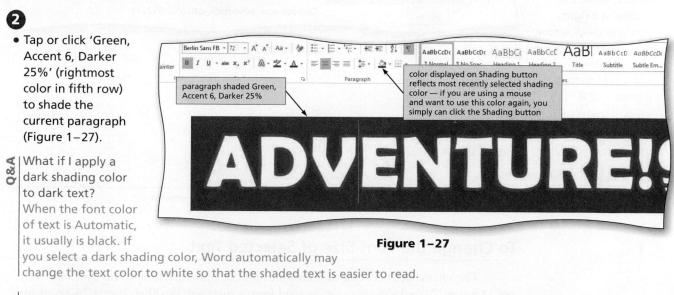

Figure 1–27

Other Ways

1. Tap or click Borders arrow (HOME tab | Paragraph group), tap or click Borders and Shading, tap or click Shading tab (Borders and Shading dialog box), tap or click Fill arrow, select desired color, tap or click OK button

To Select Multiple Lines

The next formatting step for the flyer is to increase the font size of the characters between the headline and the signature line. *Why? You want this text to be easier to read from a distance.*

To change the font size of the characters in multiple lines, you first must select all the lines to be formatted. The following steps select multiple lines.

1

- Scroll, if necessary, so that all text below the headline is displayed on the screen.

- If you are using a touch screen, tap to position the insertion point in the text to select; if you are using a mouse, move the pointer to the left of the first paragraph to be selected until the pointer changes to a right-pointing block arrow (Figure 1–28).

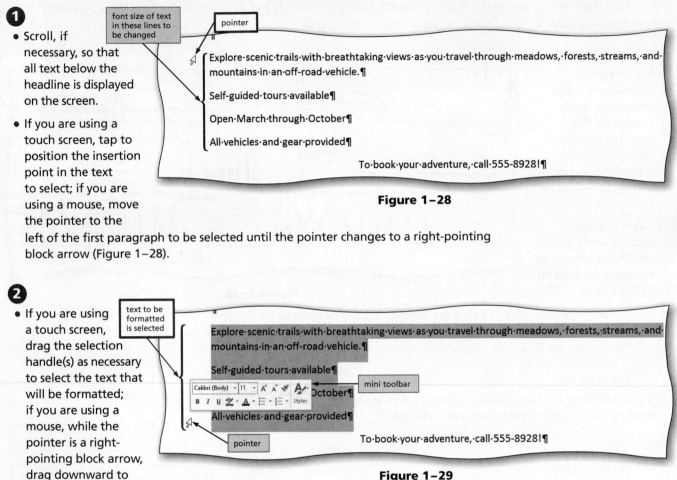

Figure 1–28

2

- If you are using a touch screen, drag the selection handle(s) as necessary to select the text that will be formatted; if you are using a mouse, while the pointer is a right-pointing block arrow, drag downward to select all lines that will be formatted (Figure 1–29).

Figure 1–29

Q&A What is a selection handle?

When working on a touch screen, a **selection handle** (small circle) appears below the insertion point. Using a fingertip, you drag a selection handle to select text.

Other Ways

1. With insertion point at beginning of desired line, press SHIFT+DOWN ARROW repeatedly until all lines are selected

To Change the Font Size of Selected Text

The characters between the headline and the signature line in the flyer currently are 11 point. To make them easier to read from a distance, this flyer uses a 24-point font size for these characters. The following steps change the font size of the selected text.

 With the text selected, tap or click the Font Size arrow (HOME tab | Font group) to display the Font Size gallery.

 Tap or click 24 in the Font Size gallery to increase the font size of the selected text.

3 Tap or click anywhere in the document window to remove the selection from the text.

4 If necessary, scroll so that you can see all the resized text on the screen (Figure 1–30).

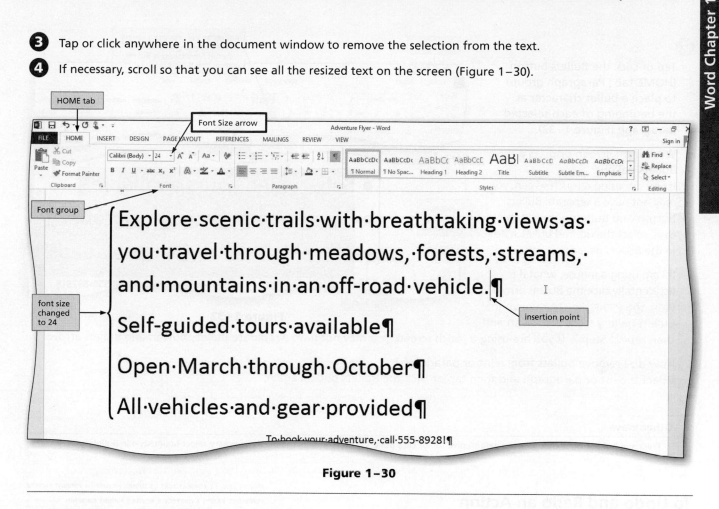

Figure 1–30

To Bullet a List of Paragraphs

1 ENTER TEXT | 2 FORMAT TEXT | 3 INSERT PICTURE | 4 FORMAT PICTURE
5 ENHANCE PAGE | 6 CORRECT & REVISE | 7 PRINT OR READ

A **bulleted list** is a series of paragraphs, each beginning with a bullet character. The next step is to format the three paragraphs about the tours that are above the signature line in the flyer as a bulleted list.

To format a list of paragraphs with bullets, you first must select all the lines in the paragraphs. ***Why?*** *If you do not select all paragraphs, Word will place a bullet only in the paragraph containing the insertion point.* The following steps bullet a list of paragraphs.

1

• If you are using a touch screen, tap to position the insertion point in the text to select; if you are using a mouse, move the pointer to the left of the first paragraph to be selected until the pointer changes to a right-pointing block arrow.

Figure 1–31

• If you are using a touch screen, drag the selection handle(s) as necessary to select the text that will be formatted; if you are using a mouse, drag downward until all paragraphs that word be formatted with a bullet character are selected (Figure 1–31).

2

- Tap or click the Bullets button (HOME tab | Paragraph group) to place a bullet character at the beginning of each selected paragraph (Figure 1–32).

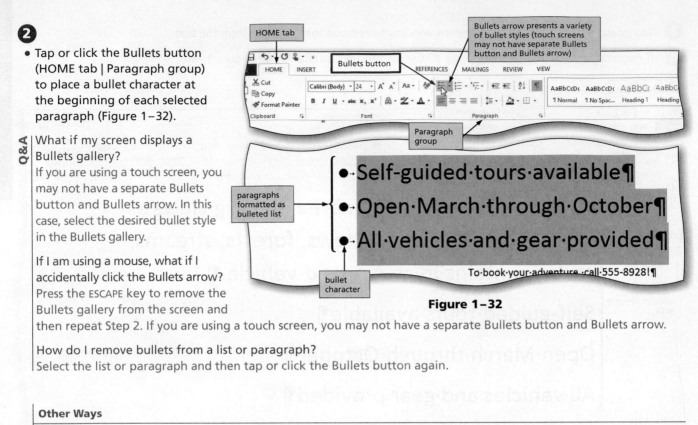

Q&A

What if my screen displays a Bullets gallery?
If you are using a touch screen, you may not have a separate Bullets button and Bullets arrow. In this case, select the desired bullet style in the Bullets gallery.

If I am using a mouse, what if I accidentally click the Bullets arrow?
Press the ESCAPE key to remove the Bullets gallery from the screen and then repeat Step 2. If you are using a touch screen, you may not have a separate Bullets button and Bullets arrow.

How do I remove bullets from a list or paragraph?
Select the list or paragraph and then tap or click the Bullets button again.

Figure 1–32

Other Ways

1. Press and hold or right-click selected paragraphs, tap or click Bullets button on mini toolbar, if necessary select bullet style in Bullets gallery

---

To Undo and Redo an Action

1 ENTER TEXT | 2 FORMAT TEXT | 3 INSERT PICTURE | 4 FORMAT PICTURE
5 ENHANCE PAGE | 6 CORRECT & REVISE | 7 PRINT OR READ

Word provides a means of canceling your recent command(s) or action(s). For example, if you format text incorrectly, you can undo the format and try it again. When you point to the Undo button, Word displays the action you can undo as part of a ScreenTip.

If, after you undo an action, you decide you did not want to perform the undo, you can redo the undone action. Word does not allow you to undo or redo some actions, such as saving or printing a document. The following steps undo the bullet format just applied and then redo the bullet format. *Why? These steps illustrate the undo and redo actions.*

1

- Tap or click the Undo button on the Quick Access Toolbar to reverse your most recent action (in this case, remove the bullets from the paragraphs) (Figure 1–33).

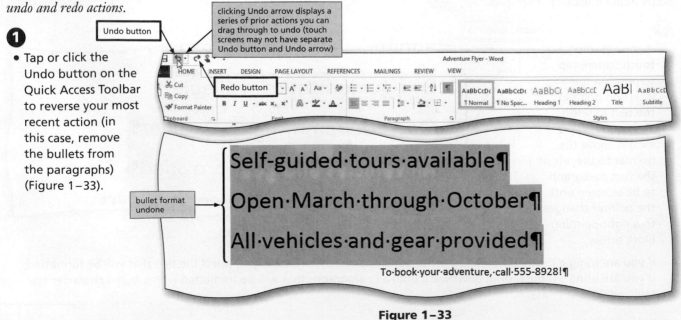

Figure 1–33

2

- Tap or click the Redo button on the Quick Access Toolbar to reverse your most recent undo (in this case, place a bullet character on the paragraphs again) (shown in Figure 1–32).

Other Ways

1. Press CTRL+Z to undo; press CTRL+Y to redo

To Italicize Text

1 ENTER TEXT | 2 FORMAT TEXT | 3 INSERT PICTURE | 4 FORMAT PICTURE
5 ENHANCE PAGE | 6 CORRECT & REVISE | 7 PRINT OR READ

Italic text has a slanted appearance. The next step is to italicize the word, breathtaking, in the flyer to further emphasize it. As with a single paragraph, if you want to format a single word, you do not need to select it. *Why? To format a single word, you simply position the insertion point somewhere in the word and apply the desired format.* The following step italicizes a word.

1

- Tap or click somewhere in the word to be italicized (breathtaking, in this case) to position the insertion point in the word to be formatted.

- Tap or click the Italic button (HOME tab | Font group) to italicize the word containing the insertion point (Figure 1–34).

Q&A How would I remove an italic format? You would tap or click the Italic button a second time, or you immediately could tap or click the Undo button on the Quick Access Toolbar or press CTRL+Z.

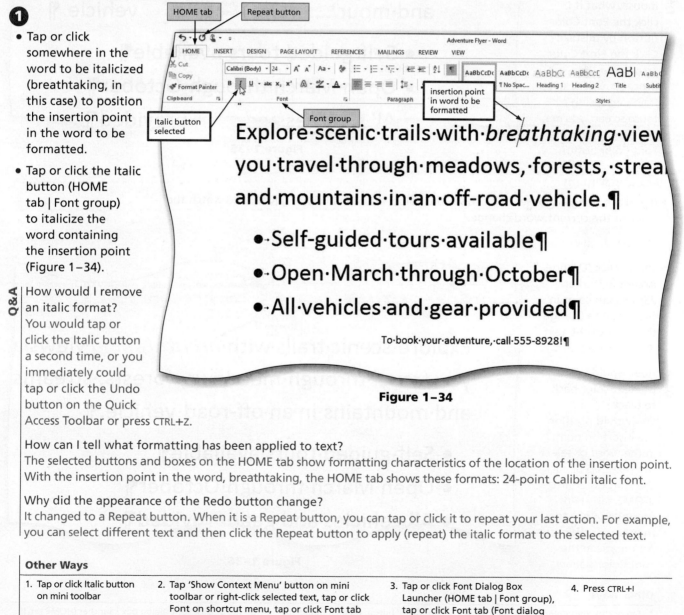

Figure 1–34

How can I tell what formatting has been applied to text?
The selected buttons and boxes on the HOME tab show formatting characteristics of the location of the insertion point. With the insertion point in the word, breathtaking, the HOME tab shows these formats: 24-point Calibri italic font.

Why did the appearance of the Redo button change?
It changed to a Repeat button. When it is a Repeat button, you can tap or click it to repeat your last action. For example, you can select different text and then click the Repeat button to apply (repeat) the italic format to the selected text.

Other Ways

| 1. Tap or click Italic button on mini toolbar | 2. Tap 'Show Context Menu' button on mini toolbar or right-click selected text, tap or click Font on shortcut menu, tap or click Font tab (Font dialog box), tap or click Italic in Font style list, tap or click OK button | 3. Tap or click Font Dialog Box Launcher (HOME tab | Font group), tap or click Font tab (Font dialog box), tap or click Italic in Font style list, tap or click OK button | 4. Press CTRL+I |

To Color Text

The following steps change the color of the word, breathtaking. **Why?** *To emphasize the word even more, you change its color to a shade of orange.*

1

- With the insertion point in the word to format, tap or click the Font Color arrow (HOME tab | Font group) to display the Font Color gallery (Figure 1–35).

Q&A If I am using a mouse, what if I click the Font Color button by mistake? Click the Font Color arrow and then proceed with Step 2. If you are using a touch screen, you may not have a separate Font Color button.

Figure 1–35

Experiment

- If you are using a mouse, point to various colors in the Font Color gallery and watch the color of the current word change.

2

- Tap or click 'Orange, Accent 2, Darker 25%' (sixth color in fifth row) to change the color of the text (Figure 1–36).

Q&A How would I change the text color back to black? You would position the insertion point in the word or select the text, tap or click the Font Color arrow (HOME tab | Font group) again, and then tap or click Automatic in the Font Color gallery.

Figure 1–36

Other Ways

1. Tap or click Font Color arrow on mini toolbar, tap or click desired color

2. Tap 'Show Context Menu' button on mini toolbar or right-click selected text, tap or click Font on shortcut menu, tap or click Font tab (Font dialog box), tap or click Font color arrow, tap or click desired color, tap or click OK button

3. Tap or click Font Dialog Box Launcher (HOME tab | Font group), tap or click Font tab (Font dialog box), tap or click Font color arrow, tap or click desired color, tap or click OK button

To Use the Mini Toolbar to Format Text

Recall from the Office and Windows chapter at the beginning of this book that the mini toolbar automatically appears based on certain tasks you perform. *Why? Word places commonly used buttons and boxes on the mini toolbar for your convenience. If you do not use the mini toolbar, it disappears from the screen.* All commands on the mini toolbar also exist on the ribbon.

The following steps use the mini toolbar to change the color and font size of text in the signature line of the flyer.

1

- If you are using a touch screen, double-tap to the left of the line to be selected to select the line, and then tap the selection to display the mini toolbar; if you are using a mouse, move the pointer to the left of the line to be selected until the pointer changes to a right-pointing block arrow and then click to select the line and display the mini toolbar (Figure 1–37).

Figure 1–37

Q&A

Why does my mini toolbar look different than the one in Figure 1–37?

If you are using a touch screen, the buttons and boxes on the mini toolbar differ. For example, it contains a 'Show Context Menu' button at the far-right edge, which you tap to display a shortcut menu.

2

- Tap or click the Font Size arrow on the mini toolbar to display the Font Size gallery.

- If you are using a mouse, point to 28 in the Font Size gallery to display a live preview of the selected font size (Figure 1–38).

3

- Tap or click 28 in the Font Size gallery to increase the font size of the selected text.

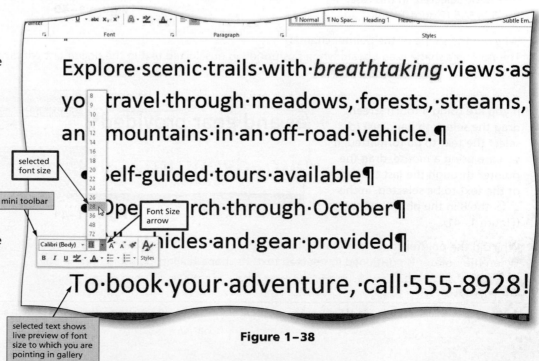

Figure 1–38

4

- With the text still selected and the mini toolbar still displayed, tap or click the Font Color arrow on the mini toolbar to display the Font Color gallery.

- If you are using a mouse, point to 'Orange, Accent 2, Darker 25%' (sixth color in the fifth row) to display a live preview of the selected font color (Figure 1–39).

5

- Tap or click 'Orange, Accent 2, Darker 25%' to change the color of the selected text.

- Tap or click anywhere in the document window to remove the selection from the text.

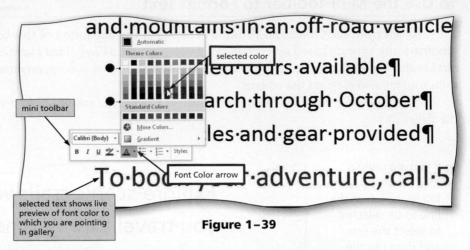

Figure 1–39

To Select a Group of Words

1 ENTER TEXT | 2 FORMAT TEXT | 3 INSERT PICTURE | 4 FORMAT PICTURE
5 ENHANCE PAGE | 6 CORRECT & REVISE | 7 PRINT OR READ

To emphasize the contact phone number (555-8928), this text is underlined in the flyer. Because the phone number is separated with a hyphen, Word considers it a group of words. To format a group of words, you first must select them. *Why? If you underline text without selecting any text first, Word will underline only the word containing the insertion point.* The following steps select a group of words.

1

- If you are using a touch screen, tap to position the insertion point in the text you want to select; if you are using a mouse, position the pointer immediately to the left of the first character of the text to be selected, in this case, the 5 in 555 (Figure 1–40).

Q&A Why did the shape of the pointer change?
The pointer's shape is an I-beam when positioned in unselected text in the document window.

2

- If you are using a touch screen, drag the selection handle(s) to select the text to be formatted; if you are using a mouse, drag the pointer through the last character of the text to be selected, in this case, the 8 in the phone number (Figure 1–41).

Q&A Why did the pointer shape change again?
When the pointer is positioned in selected text, its shape is a left-pointing block arrow.

Figure 1–40

Figure 1–41

Other Ways

1. With insertion point at beginning of first word in group, press CTRL+SHIFT+RIGHT ARROW repeatedly until all words are selected

To Underline Text

Underlined text prints with an underscore (_) below each character. In the flyer, the contact phone number, 555-8928, in the signature line is underlined. *Why? Underlines are used to emphasize or draw attention to specific text.* The following step formats selected text with an underline.

1

- With the text selected, tap or click the Underline button (HOME tab | Font group) to underline the selected text (Figure 1–42).

Q&A

What if my screen displays an Underline gallery?
If you are using a touch screen, you may not have a separate Underline button and Underline arrow. In this case, select the desired underline style in the Underline gallery.

If a button exists on the mini toolbar, can I tap or click that instead of using the ribbon?
Yes.

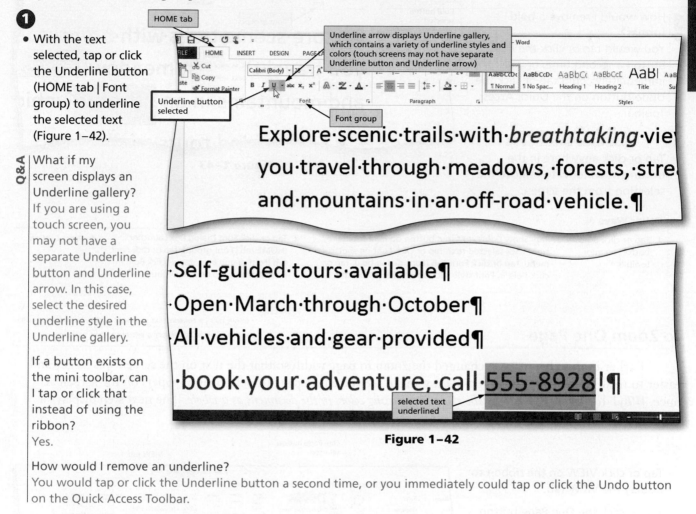

Figure 1–42

How would I remove an underline?
You would tap or click the Underline button a second time, or you immediately could tap or click the Undo button on the Quick Access Toolbar.

Other Ways

1. Tap or click Underline button on mini toolbar	2. Tap 'Show Context Menu' button on mini toolbar or right-click text, tap or click Font on shortcut menu, tap or click Font tab (Font dialog box), tap or click Underline style box arrow, tap or click desired underline style, tap or click OK button	3. Tap or click Font Dialog Box Launcher (HOME tab | Font group), tap or click Font tab (Font dialog box), tap or click Underline style arrow, tap or click desired underline style, tap or click OK button	4. Press CTRL+U

To Bold Text

Bold characters appear somewhat thicker and darker than those that are not bold. The steps on the next page format the text, off-road, in bold characters. *Why? To further emphasize this text, it is bold in the flyer.* Recall that if you want to format a single word, you simply position the insertion point in the word and then format the word. To format text that consists of more than one word, as you have learned previously, you select the text first.

1

- Select the text to be formatted (the text, off-road, in this case); that is, if you are using a touch screen, tap to position the insertion point in the text you want to select and then drag the selection handle(s) to select the text to be formatted; if you are using a mouse, position the pointer immediately to the left of the first character of the text to be selected and then drag the pointer through the last character of the text to be selected.

2

- With the text selected, tap or click the Bold button (HOME tab | Font group) to bold the selected text (Figure 1–43).

Q&A

How would I remove a bold format?

You would tap or click the Bold button a second time, or you immediately could tap or click the Undo button on the Quick Access Toolbar.

3

- Tap or click anywhere in the document window to remove the selection from the screen.

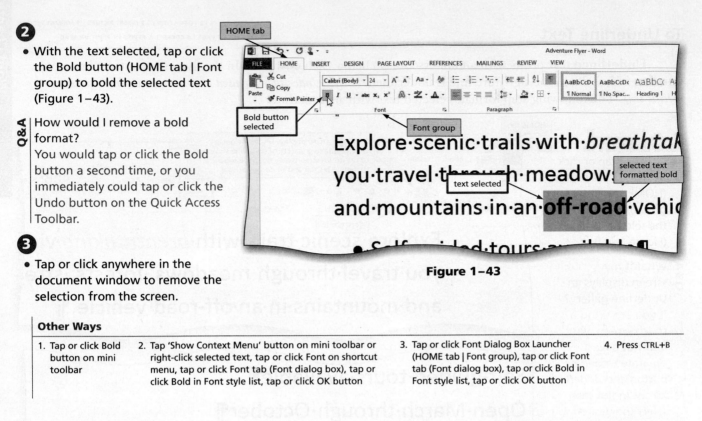

Figure 1–43

Other Ways

1. Tap or click Bold button on mini toolbar	2. Tap 'Show Context Menu' button on mini toolbar or right-click selected text, tap or click Font on shortcut menu, tap or click Font tab (Font dialog box), tap or click Bold in Font style list, tap or click OK button	3. Tap or click Font Dialog Box Launcher (HOME tab | Font group), tap or click Font tab (Font dialog box), tap or click Bold in Font style list, tap or click OK button	4. Press CTRL+B

To Zoom One Page

1 ENTER TEXT | 2 FORMAT TEXT | 3 INSERT PICTURE | 4 FORMAT PICTURE
5 ENHANCE PAGE | 6 CORRECT & REVISE | 7 PRINT OR READ

Earlier in this chapter, you changed the zoom to page width so that the text on the screen was larger and easier to read. In the next set of steps, you want to see the entire page (mock sheet of paper) on the screen at once. *Why? You want be able to see the effect of adjusting colors in the document as a whole.* The next step displays a single page in its entirety in the document window as large as possible.

1

- Tap or click VIEW on the ribbon to display the VIEW tab.

- Tap or click the One Page button (VIEW tab | Zoom group) to display the entire page in the document window as large as possible (Figure 1–44).

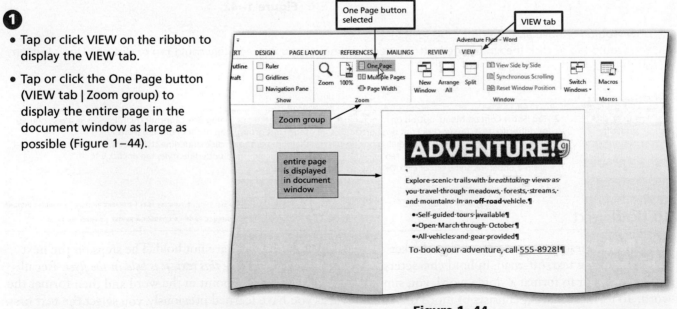

Figure 1–44

Other Ways

1. Tap or click Zoom button (VIEW tab | Zoom group), tap or click Whole page (Zoom dialog box), tap or click OK button

What colors should I choose when creating documents?

When choosing color, associate the meaning of the color with your message:

- Red expresses danger, power, or energy and often is associated with sports or physical exertion.

- Brown represents simplicity, honesty, and dependability.

- Orange denotes success, victory, creativity, and enthusiasm.

- Yellow suggests sunshine, happiness, hope, liveliness, and intelligence.

- Green symbolizes growth, healthiness, harmony, blooming, and healing and often is associated with safety or money.

- Blue indicates integrity, trust, importance, confidence, and stability.

- Purple represents wealth, power, comfort, extravagance, magic, mystery, and spirituality.

- White stands for purity, goodness, cleanliness, precision, and perfection.

- Black suggests authority, strength, elegance, power, and prestige.

- Gray conveys neutrality and, thus, often is found in backgrounds and other effects.

To Change Theme Colors

1 ENTER TEXT | 2 FORMAT TEXT | 3 INSERT PICTURE | 4 FORMAT PICTURE
5 ENHANCE PAGE | 6 CORRECT & REVISE | 7 PRINT OR READ

A **color scheme** in Word is a document theme that identifies 12 complementary colors for text, background, accents, and links in a document. With more than 20 predefined color schemes, Word provides a simple way to coordinate colors in a document.

The default color scheme is called Office. In the flyer, you will change the color scheme from Office to Green. *Why? You want the colors in the flyer to suggest growth, harmony, blooming, trust, and stability, which are conveyed by shades of greens and blues. In Word, the Green color scheme uses these colors.* The following steps change theme colors.

1

- Tap or click DESIGN on the ribbon to display the DESIGN tab.

- Tap or click the Theme Colors button (DESIGN tab | Document Formatting group) to display the Theme Colors gallery.

- If you are using a mouse, point to Green in the Theme Colors gallery to display a live preview of the selected theme color (Figure 1–45).

Figure 1–45

Experiment

- If you are using a mouse, point to various color schemes in the Theme Colors gallery and watch the colors change in the document.

- Tap or click Green in the Colors gallery to change the document theme colors.

Q&A What if I want to return to the original color scheme?
You would tap or click the Theme Colors button again and then tap or click Office in the Theme Colors gallery.

BTW
Selecting Nonadjacent Items
In Word, you can use keyboard keys to select nonadjacent items, that is, items not next to each other. This is helpful when you are applying the same formatting to multiple items. To select nonadjacent items (text or graphics), select the first item, such as a word or paragraph, as usual; then, press and hold down the CTRL key. While holding down the CTRL key, select additional items.

To Zoom Page Width

Because the document contents are small when displayed at one page, the next steps zoom page width again.

1 Tap or click VIEW on the ribbon to display the VIEW tab.

2 Tap or click the Page Width button (VIEW tab | Zoom group) to display the page the same width as the document window (shown in Figure 1–46 on page WD 34).

Selecting Text

In many of the previous steps, you have selected text. Table 1–3 summarizes the techniques used to select various items.

Table 1–3 Techniques for Selecting Text			
Item to Select	**Touch**	**Mouse**	**Keyboard (where applicable)**
Block of text	Tap to position insertion point in text to select and then drag selection handle(s) to select text.	Click at beginning of selection, scroll to end of selection, position pointer at end of selection, hold down SHIFT key, and then click; or drag through text.	
Character(s)	Tap to position insertion point in text to select and then drag selection handle(s) to select text.	Drag through character(s).	SHIFT+RIGHT ARROW or SHIFT+LEFT ARROW
Document		Move pointer to left of text until pointer changes to right-pointing block arrow and then triple-click.	CTRL+A
Graphic	Tap the graphic.	Click the graphic.	
Line	Double-tap to left of line to be selected.	Move pointer to left of line until pointer changes to right-pointing block arrow and then click.	HOME, then SHIFT+END or END, then SHIFT+HOME
Lines	Tap to position insertion point in text to select and then drag selection handle(s) to select text.	Move pointer to left of first line until pointer changes to right-pointing block arrow and then drag up or down.	HOME, then SHIFT+DOWN ARROW or END, then SHIFT+UP ARROW
Paragraph	Tap to position insertion point in text to select and then drag selection handle(s) to select text.	Triple-click paragraph; or move pointer to left of paragraph until pointer changes to right-pointing block arrow and then double-click.	CTRL+SHIFT+DOWN ARROW or CTRL+SHIFT+UP ARROW
Paragraphs	Tap to position insertion point in text to select and then drag selection handle(s) to select text.	Move pointer to left of paragraph until pointer changes to right-pointing block arrow, double-click, and then drag up or down.	CTRL+SHIFT+DOWN ARROW or CTRL+SHIFT+UP ARROW repeatedly
Sentence	Tap to position insertion point in text to select and then drag selection handle(s) to select text.	Press and hold down CTRL key and then click sentence.	
Word	Double-tap word.	Double-click word.	CTRL+SHIFT+RIGHT ARROW or CTRL+SHIFT+LEFT ARROW
Words	Tap to position insertion point in text to select and then drag selection handle(s) to select text.	Drag through words.	CTRL+SHIFT+RIGHT ARROW or CTRL+SHIFT+LEFT ARROW repeatedly

To Save an Existing Document with the Same File Name

You have made several modifications to the document since you last saved it. Thus, you should save it again. The following step saves the document again. For an example of the step listed below, refer to the Office and Windows chapter at the beginning of this book.

 Tap or click the Save button on the Quick Access Toolbar to overwrite the previously saved file.

Break Point: If you wish to take a break, this is a good place to do so. You can exit Word now (refer to page WD 46 for instructions). To resume at a later time, run Word (refer to pages WD 46 to WD 47 for instructions), open the file called Adventure Flyer (refer to page WD 47 for instructions), and continue following the steps from this location forward.

Inserting and Formatting a Picture in a Word Document

With the text formatted in the flyer, the next step is to insert a digital picture in the flyer and format the picture. Flyers usually contain a graphical image(s), such as a picture, to attract the attention of passersby. In the following pages, you will perform these tasks:

1. Insert a digital picture into the flyer and then reduce its size.
2. Enlarge the size of the picture.
3. Change the look of the picture.

CONSIDER THIS

How do I locate a graphic file to use in a document?
To use a graphic in a Word document, the image must be stored digitally in a file. Files containing graphics are available from a variety of sources:

• Microsoft has free digital images on the web for use in a document. Other websites also have images available, some of which are free, while others require a fee.

• You can take a picture with a digital camera or camera phone and **download** it, which is the process of copying the digital picture from the camera or phone to your computer.

• With a scanner, you can convert a printed picture, drawing, or diagram to a digital file.

If you receive a picture from a source other than yourself, do not use the file until you are certain it does not contain a virus. A **virus** is a computer program that can damage files and programs on your computer. Use an antivirus program to verify that any files you use are virus free.

To Center Another Paragraph

In the flyer, the digital picture of a mountain trail tour group should be centered on the blank line below the headline. The blank paragraph below the headline currently is left-aligned. The following steps center this paragraph.

 Tap or click HOME on the ribbon to display the HOME tab.

❷ Tap or click somewhere in the paragraph to be centered (in this case, the blank line below the headline) to position the insertion point in the paragraph to be formatted.

❸ Tap or click the Center button (HOME tab | Paragraph group) to center the paragraph containing the insertion point (shown in Figure 1–46 on the next page).

BTW
BTWs
For a complete list of the BTWs found in the margins of this book, visit the BTW resource on the Student Companion Site located on www.cengagebrain.com. For detailed instructions about accessing available resources, visit www.cengage.com/ct/studentdownload or contact your instructor for information about accessing the required files.

To Insert a Picture

The next step in creating the flyer is to insert a digital picture of a mountain trail tour group in the flyer on the blank line below the headline. The picture, which was taken with a digital camera, is available on the Data Files for Students. Visit www.cengage.com/ct/studentdownload for detailed instructions or contact your instructor for information about accessing the required files.

The following steps insert a picture, which, in this example, is located in the Chapter 01 folder in the Word folder in the Data Files for Students folder. *Why? It is good practice to organize and store files in folders so that you easily can find the files at a later date.*

1
- If necessary, position the insertion point at the location where you want to insert the picture (in this case, on the centered blank paragraph below the headline).

- Tap or click INSERT on the ribbon to display the INSERT tab (Figure 1–46).

2
- Tap or click the From File button (INSERT tab | Illustrations group) (shown in Figure 1–46) to display the Insert Picture dialog box (shown in Figure 1–47).

3
- Navigate to the desired picture location (in this case, the Chapter 01 folder in the Word folder in the Data Files for Students folder). For a detailed example of this procedure, refer to Steps 4a and 4b in the To Save a File in a Folder section in the Office and Windows chapter at the beginning of this book.

- Tap or click Mountain Trail to select the file (Figure 1–47).

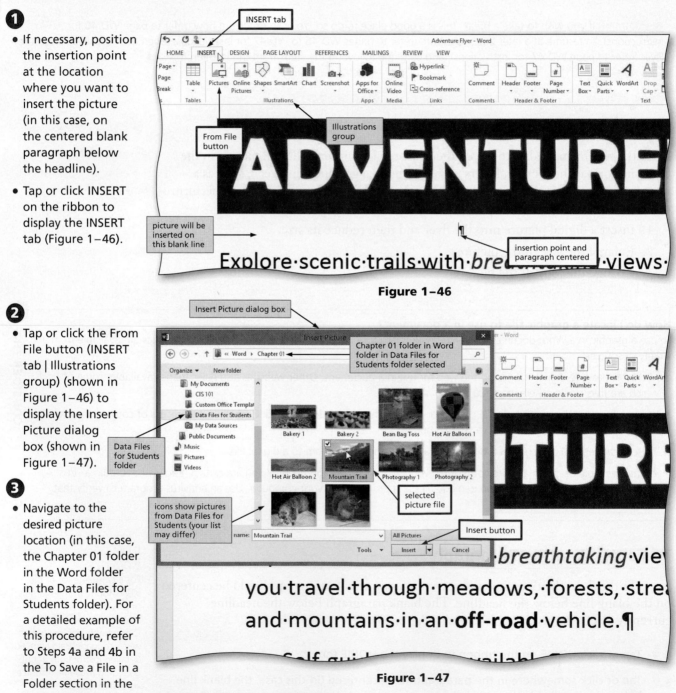

Figure 1–46

Figure 1–47

4

- Tap or click the Insert button (Insert Picture dialog box) to insert the picture at the location of the insertion point in the document (Figure 1–48).

Q&A

What are the symbols around the picture?

A selected graphic appears surrounded by a **selection rectangle**, which has small squares and circles, called **sizing handles**, at each corner and middle location.

What is the purpose of the Layout Options button?

When you tap or click the Layout Options button, Word provides options for changing how the graphic is positioned with text in the document.

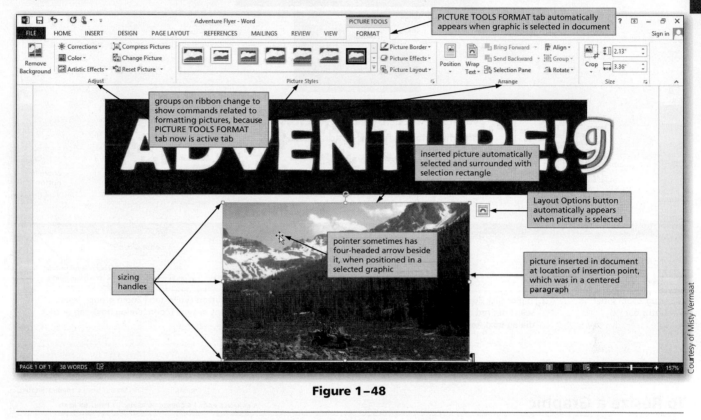

Figure 1–48

Courtesy of Misty Vermaat

How do you know where to position a graphic on a flyer?

The content, size, shape, position, and format of a graphic should capture the interest of passersby, enticing them to stop and read the flyer. Often, the graphic is the center of attention and visually the largest element on a flyer. If you use colors in the graphical image, be sure they are part of the document's color scheme.

CONSIDER THIS

1 ENTER TEXT | 2 FORMAT TEXT | 3 INSERT PICTURE | 4 FORMAT PICTURE
5 ENHANCE PAGE | 6 CORRECT & REVISE | 7 PRINT OR READ

To Zoom the Document

In the steps on the following pages, you will work with the picture just inserted. The next task is to adjust the zoom percentage. *Why? Currently, you can see only a small amount of text with the picture. Seeing more of the document at once helps you determine the appropriate size for the picture.* The following step zooms the document.

1

Experiment

- If you are using a mouse, repeatedly click the Zoom Out and Zoom In buttons on the status bar and watch the size of the document change in the document window.

- If you are using a touch screen, repeatedly pinch (move two fingers together) and stretch (move two fingers apart) and watch the size of the document change in the document window.

• Pinch and stretch or click the Zoom Out or Zoom In button as many times as necessary until the Zoom button on the status bar displays 80% on its face (Figure 1–49).

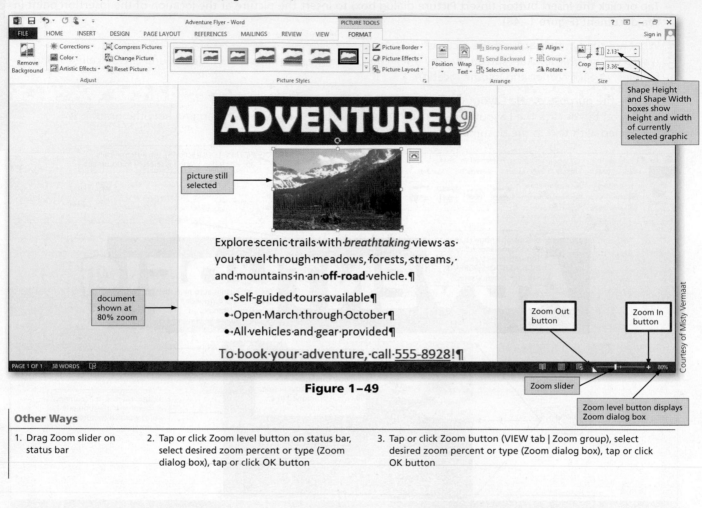

Figure 1–49

Other Ways

1. Drag Zoom slider on status bar

2. Tap or click Zoom level button on status bar, select desired zoom percent or type (Zoom dialog box), tap or click OK button

3. Tap or click Zoom button (VIEW tab | Zoom group), select desired zoom percent or type (Zoom dialog box), tap or click OK button

To Resize a Graphic

1 ENTER TEXT | 2 FORMAT TEXT | 3 INSERT PICTURE | **4 FORMAT PICTURE**
5 ENHANCE PAGE | 6 CORRECT & REVISE | 7 PRINT OR READ

Resizing includes both increasing and reducing the size of a graphic. The next step is to resize the picture so that it is larger in the flyer. **Why?** *You want the graphic as large as possible on a single page flyer to draw the attention of passersby.* The following steps resize a selected graphic.

1

• Be sure the graphic still is selected.

Q&A What if my graphic (picture) is not selected?
To select a graphic, tap or click it.

• If you are using a mouse, point to the lower-left corner sizing handle on the picture so that the pointer shape changes to a two-headed arrow (Figure 1–50).

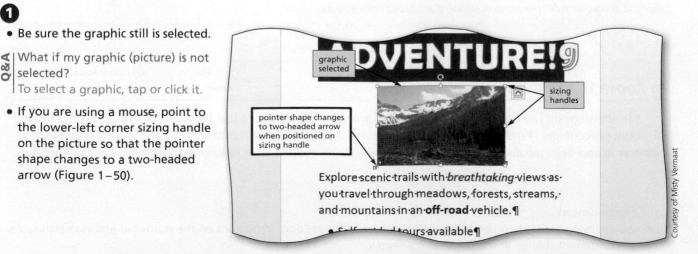

Figure 1–50

2

- Drag the sizing handle diagonally outward until the lower-left corner of the picture is positioned approximately as shown in Figure 1–51. Do not lift your finger or release the mouse button at this point.

3

- Release your finger or the mouse button to resize the graphic, which in this case, should have a height of about 3.26" and a width of about 5.04".

Q&A

How can I see the height and width measurements?
Look in the Size group on the PICTURE TOOLS FORMAT tab to see the height and width measurements of the currently selected graphic (shown in Figure 1–49).

What if the graphic is the wrong size?
Repeat Steps 1, 2, and 3, or enter the desired height and width values in the Shape Height and Shape Width boxes (PICTURE TOOLS FORMAT tab | Size group).

What if I want to return a graphic to its original size and start again?
With the graphic selected, tap or click the Size Dialog Box Launcher (PICTURE TOOLS FORMAT tab | Size group), tap or click the Size tab (Layout dialog box), tap or click the Reset button, and then tap or click the OK button.

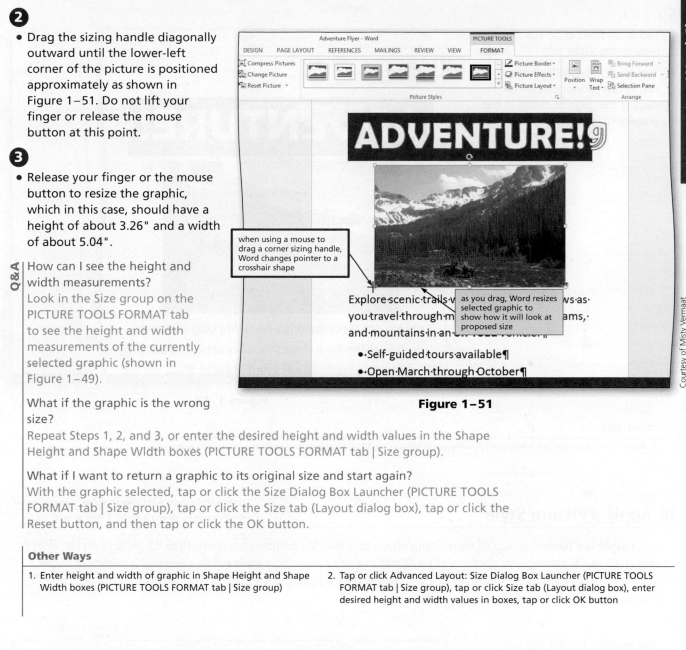

when using a mouse to drag a corner sizing handle, Word changes pointer to a crosshair shape

as you drag, Word resizes selected graphic to show how it will look at proposed size

Figure 1–51

Courtesy of Misty Vermaat

Other Ways

1. Enter height and width of graphic in Shape Height and Shape Width boxes (PICTURE TOOLS FORMAT tab | Size group)

2. Tap or click Advanced Layout: Size Dialog Box Launcher (PICTURE TOOLS FORMAT tab | Size group), tap or click Size tab (Layout dialog box), enter desired height and width values in boxes, tap or click OK button

---

To Zoom 100%

1 ENTER TEXT | 2 FORMAT TEXT | 3 INSERT PICTURE | **4 FORMAT PICTURE**
5 ENHANCE PAGE | 6 CORRECT & REVISE | 7 PRINT OR READ

In the next series of steps, you will format the picture. Earlier in this chapter, you changed the zoom to 80% so that you could see more of the page while resizing the graphic. The step on the next page zooms the screen to 100%. *Why? You want the contents of the image to be enlarged a bit, while still seeing some of the text in the document.*

1

- Tap or click VIEW on the ribbon to display the VIEW tab.

- Tap or click the 100% button (VIEW tab | Zoom group) to display the page at 100% in the document window (Figure 1–52).

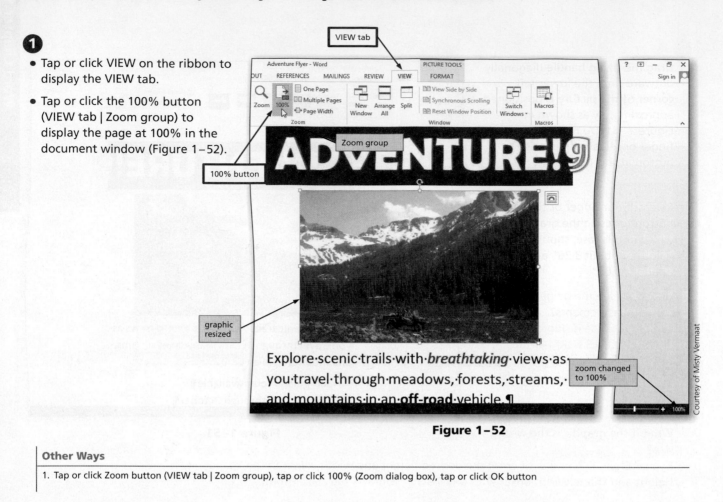

Figure 1–52

Other Ways

1. Tap or click Zoom button (VIEW tab | Zoom group), tap or click 100% (Zoom dialog box), tap or click OK button

To Apply a Picture Style

1 ENTER TEXT | 2 FORMAT TEXT | 3 INSERT PICTURE | 4 FORMAT PICTURE
5 ENHANCE PAGE | 6 CORRECT & REVISE | 7 PRINT OR READ

A **style** is a named group of formatting characteristics. Word provides more than 25 picture styles. *Why? Picture styles enable you easily to change a picture's look to a more visually appealing style, including a variety of shapes, angles, borders, and reflections.* The flyer in this chapter uses a style that applies a drop shadow to the picture. The following steps apply a picture style to a picture.

1

- Tap or click PICTURE TOOLS FORMAT on the ribbon to display the PICTURE TOOLS FORMAT tab.

- Be sure the graphic still is selected (Figure 1–53).

Q&A What if my graphic (picture) is not selected?
To select a graphic, tap or click it.

What is the white circle attached to top of the selected graphic?
It is called a rotate handle. When you drag a graphic's **rotate handle**, the graphic moves in either a clockwise or counterclockwise direction.

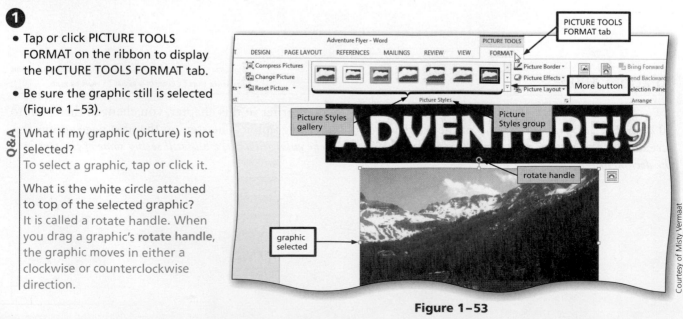

Figure 1–53

2

- Tap or click the More button in the Picture Styles gallery (PICTURE TOOLS FORMAT tab | Picture Styles group) (shown in Figure 1–53) to expand the gallery.

- If you are using a mouse, point to 'Drop Shadow Rectangle' in the Picture Styles gallery to display a live preview of that style applied to the picture in the document (Figure 1–54).

Experiment

- If you are using a mouse, point to various picture styles in the Picture Styles gallery and watch the style of the picture change in the document window.

3

- Tap or click 'Drop Shadow Rectangle' in the Picture Styles gallery (fourth style in first row) to apply the style to the selected picture.

Figure 1–54

Other Ways

1. Press and hold or right-click picture, tap or click 'Picture Quick Styles' on mini toolbar, select desired style

To Apply Picture Effects

1 ENTER TEXT | 2 FORMAT TEXT | 3 INSERT PICTURE | **4 FORMAT PICTURE**
5 ENHANCE PAGE | 6 CORRECT & REVISE | 7 PRINT OR READ

Word provides a variety of picture effects, such as shadows, reflections, glow, soft edges, bevel, and 3-D rotation. The difference between the effects and the styles is that each effect has several options, providing you with more control over the exact look of the image.

In this flyer, the picture has a slight green glow effect and beveled edges. The following steps apply picture effects to the selected picture. *Why? Picture effects enable you to further customize the a picture.*

1

- With the picture still selected, tap or click the Picture Effects button (PICTURE TOOLS FORMAT tab | Picture Styles group) to display the Picture Effects menu.

- Tap or point to Glow on the Picture Effects menu to display the Glow gallery.

- If you are using a mouse, point to 'Turquoise, 5 pt glow, Accent color 6' in the Glow Variations area (rightmost glow in first row) to display a live preview of the selected glow effect applied to the picture in the document window (Figure 1–55).

Experiment

- If you are using a mouse, point to various glow effects in the Glow gallery and watch the picture change in the document window

Figure 1–55

2

- Tap or click 'Turquoise, 5 pt glow, Accent color 6' in the Glow gallery to apply the selected picture effect.

Q&A What if I wanted to discard formatting applied to a picture?

You would tap or click the Reset Picture button (PICTURE TOOLS FORMAT tab | Adjust group). To reset formatting and size, you would tap or click the Reset Picture arrow (PICTURE TOOLS FORMAT tab | Adjust group) and then tap or click 'Reset Picture & Size' on the Reset Picture menu.

3

- Tap or click the Picture Effects button (PICTURE TOOLS FORMAT tab | Picture Styles group) to display the Picture Effects menu again.

- Tap or point to Bevel on the Picture Effects menu to display the Bevel gallery.

- If you are using a mouse, point to Angle in the Bevel area (first effect in second row) to display a live preview of the selected bevel effect applied to the picture in the document window (Figure 1–56).

Experiment

- If you are using a mouse, point to various bevel effects in the Bevel gallery and watch the picture change in the document window.

4

- Tap or click Angle in the Bevel gallery to apply the selected picture effect.

Figure 1–56

Courtesy of Misty Vermaat

Other Ways

1. Tap 'Show Context Menu' button on mini toolbar or right-click picture, tap or click Format Object or Format Picture on shortcut menu, tap or click Effects button (Format Picture task pane), select desired options, tap or click Close button

2. Tap or click Format Shape Dialog Box Launcher (PICTURE TOOLS FORMAT tab | Picture Styles group), tap or click Effects button (Format Picture task pane), select desired options, tap or click Close button

Enhancing the Page

BTW

Word Help

At any time while using Word, you can find answers to questions and display information about various topics through Word Help. Used properly, this form of assistance can increase your productivity and reduce your frustrations by minimizing the time you spend learning how to use Word. For instruction about Word Help and exercises that will help you gain confidence in using it, read the Office and Windows chapter at the beginning of this book.

With the text and graphics entered and formatted, the next step is to look at the page as a whole and determine if it looks finished in its current state. As you review the page, answer these questions:

- Does it need a page border to frame its contents, or would a page border make it look too busy?

- Is the spacing between paragraphs and graphics on the page adequate? Do any sections of text or graphics look as if they are positioned too closely to the items above or below them?

- Does the flyer have too much space at the top or bottom? Should the contents be centered vertically?

You determine that a graphical, color-coordinated border would enhance the flyer. You also notice that the flyer would look better proportioned if it had a little more space above and below the picture. You also want to ensure that the contents are centered vertically. The following pages make these enhancements to the flyer.

To Add a Page Border

1 ENTER TEXT | 2 FORMAT TEXT | 3 INSERT PICTURE | 4 FORMAT PICTURE
5 ENHANCE PAGE | 6 CORRECT & REVISE | 7 PRINT OR READ

In Word, you can add a border around the perimeter of an entire page. The flyer in this chapter has a light green border. *Why? This border color complements the color of the flyer contents.* The following steps add a page border.

1
- Tap or click DESIGN on the ribbon to display the DESIGN tab.
- Tap or click the 'Borders and Shading' button (DESIGN tab | Page Background group) to display the Borders and Shading dialog box (Figure 1–57).

Figure 1–57

Courtesy of Misty Vermaat

2
- Tap or click the second border style in the Style list (Borders and Shading dialog box) to select the style.
- Tap or click the Color arrow to display a Color palette (Figure 1–58).

Figure 1–58

Courtesy of Misty Vermaat

③

- Tap or click 'Lime, Accent 2, Lighter 80%' (sixth color in second row) in the Color palette to select the color for the page border.

- Tap or click the Width arrow to display the Width list and then tap or click 4 ½ pt to select the thickness of the page border (Figure 1–59).

④

- Tap or click the OK button to add the border to the page (shown in Figure 1–60).

Q&A What if I wanted to remove the border?
You would tap or click None in the Setting list in the Borders and Shading dialog box.

Figure 1–59

To Zoom One Page

1 ENTER TEXT | 2 FORMAT TEXT | 3 INSERT PICTURE | 4 FORMAT PICTURE
5 ENHANCE PAGE | 6 CORRECT & REVISE | 7 PRINT OR READ

The next steps zoom one page so that you can see the entire page on the screen at once.

① Tap or click VIEW on the ribbon to display the VIEW tab.

② Tap or click the One Page button (VIEW tab | Zoom group) to display the entire page in the document window as large as possible.

To Change Spacing before and after Paragraphs

1 ENTER TEXT | 2 FORMAT TEXT | 3 INSERT PICTURE | 4 FORMAT PICTURE
5 ENHANCE PAGE | 6 CORRECT & REVISE | 7 PRINT OR READ

The default spacing above (before) a paragraph in Word is 0 points and below (after) is 8 points. In the flyer, you want to increase the spacing below the paragraph containing the headline and above the signature line. *Why? The flyer spacing will look more balanced with spacing increased above and below these paragraphs.* The following steps change the spacing above and below a paragraph.

①

- Position the insertion point in the paragraph to be adjusted, in this case, the paragraph containing the headline.

Q&A What happened to the PICTURE TOOLS FORMAT tab?
When you tap or click outside of a graphic or press a key to scroll through a document, Word deselects the graphic and removes the PICTURE TOOLS FORMAT tab from the screen. That is, this tab appears only when a graphic is selected.

- Tap or click PAGE LAYOUT on the ribbon to display the PAGE LAYOUT tab.

- If you are using a touch screen, tap the Spacing After box (PAGE LAYOUT tab | Paragraph group) and then type 12 to change the spacing below the paragraph; if you are using a mouse, click the Spacing After up arrow (PAGE LAYOUT tab | Paragraph group) so that 12 pt is displayed in the Spacing After box to increase the space below the current paragraph (Figure 1–60).

Figure 1–60

2

- Position the insertion point in the paragraph to be adjusted, in this case, the paragraph containing the signature line.

- If you are using a touch screen, tap the Spacing Before box (PAGE LAYOUT tab | Paragraph group) and then type 12 to change the spacing above the paragraph; if you are using a mouse, click the Spacing Before up arrow (PAGE LAYOUT tab | Paragraph group) as many times as necessary so that 12 pt is displayed in the Spacing Before box to increase the space above the current paragraph (Figure 1–61).

- If the text flows to two pages, reduce the spacing above and below paragraphs as necessary.

Figure 1–61

Courtesy of Misty Vermaat

Other Ways

1. Tap 'Show Context Menu' button on mini toolbar or right-click paragraph, tap or click Paragraph on shortcut menu, tap or click Indents and Spacing tab (Paragraph dialog box), enter spacing before and after values, tap or click OK button

2. Tap or click Paragraph Settings Dialog Box Launcher (HOME tab or PAGE LAYOUT tab | Paragraph group), tap or click Indents and Spacing tab (Paragraph dialog box), enter spacing before and after values, tap or click OK button

---

To Center Page Contents Vertically

1 ENTER TEXT | 2 FORMAT TEXT | 3 INSERT PICTURE | 4 FORMAT PICTURE
5 ENHANCE PAGE | 6 CORRECT & REVISE | 7 PRINT OR READ

In Word, you can center the page contents vertically. *Why? This places the same amount of space at the top and bottom of the page.* The following steps center page contents vertically.

1

- If necessary, tap or click PAGE LAYOUT on the ribbon to display the PAGE LAYOUT tab.

- Tap or click the Page Setup Dialog Box Launcher (PAGE LAYOUT tab | Page Setup group) to display the Page Setup dialog box.

- Tap or click the Layout tab (Page Setup dialog box) to display the Layout sheet (Figure 1–62).

Figure 1–62

2

- Tap or click the Vertical alignment arrow (Page Setup dialog box) to display the list of alignment options and then tap or click Center in the list (Figure 1–63).

3

- Tap or click the OK button to center the page contents vertically on the screen (shown in Figure 1–1 on page WD 3).

Q&A What if I wanted to change the alignment back?
You would select the Top vertical alignment from the Vertical alignment list in the Layout sheet (Page Setup dialog box).

Figure 1–63

To Save an Existing Document with the Same File Name

You have made several modifications to the document since you last saved it. Thus, you should save it again. The following step saves the document again. For an example of the step listed below, refer to the Office and Windows chapter at the beginning of this book.

1 Tap or click the Save button on the Quick Access Toolbar to overwrite the previously saved file.

Document Properties

Word helps you organize and identify your files by using **document properties**, which are the details about a file such as the project author, title, and subject. For example, a class name or document topic can describe the file's purpose or content.

The more common document properties are standard and automatically updated properties. **Standard properties** are associated with all Microsoft Office files and include author, title, and subject. **Automatically updated properties** include file system properties, such as the date you create or change a file, and statistics, such as the file size.

TO CHANGE DOCUMENT PROPERTIES

To change document properties, you would follow these steps.

1. Tap or click FILE on the ribbon to open the Backstage view and then, if necessary, tap or click the Info tab in the Backstage view to display the Info gallery.

2. If the property you wish to change is displayed in the Properties list in the right pane of the Info gallery, try to tap or click to the right of the property. If a text box appears to the right of the property, type the text for the property in the text box, and then tap or click the Back button in the upper-left corner of the Backstage view to return to the Word window. Skip the remaining steps.

3. If the property you wish to change is not displayed in the Properties list in the right pane of the Info gallery or you cannot change it in the Info gallery, tap or click the Properties button in the right pane to display the Properties menu, and then tap or click 'Show Document Panel' on the Properties menu to close the Backstage view and display the Document Information Panel in the Word document window.

Q&A Why are some of the document properties in my Document Information Panel already filled in?
The person who installed Office 2013 on your computer or network may have set or customized the properties.

4. Type the desired text in the appropriate property text boxes.

Q&A What if the property I want to change is not displayed in the Document Information Panel?
Tap or click the Document Properties button in the Document Information Panel and then tap or click Advanced Properties on the menu to display the Properties dialog box. If necessary, tap or click the Summary tab (Properties dialog box) to display the Summary sheet, fill in the appropriate text boxes, and then tap or click the OK button.

5. Tap or click the 'Close the Document Information Panel' button at the right edge of the Document Information Panel so that the panel no longer appears in the Word document window.

To Sign Out of a Microsoft Account

If you are signed in to a Microsoft account and are using a public computer or otherwise wish to sign out of your Microsoft account, you should sign out of the account from the Account gallery in the Backstage view before exiting Word. Signing out of the account is the safest way to make sure that nobody else can access SkyDrive files or settings stored in your Microsoft account. The following steps sign out of a Microsoft account from Word. For a detailed example of the procedure summarized below, refer to the Office and Windows chapter at the beginning of this book.

1 If you wish to sign out of your Microsoft account, tap or click FILE on the ribbon to open the Backstage view and then tap or click the Account tab to display the Account gallery.

2 Tap or click the Sign out link, which displays the Remove Account dialog box. If a Can't remove Windows accounts dialog box appears instead of the Remove Account dialog box, tap or click the OK button and skip the remaining steps.

Q&A Why does a Can't remove Windows accounts dialog box appear?
If you signed in to Windows using your Microsoft account, then you also must sign out from Windows, rather than signing out from within the Word. When you are finished using Windows, be sure to sign out at that time.

3 Tap or click the Yes button (Remove Account dialog box) to sign out of your Microsoft account on this computer.

Q&A Should I sign out of Windows after signing out of my Microsoft account?
When you are finished using the computer, you should sign out of your account for maximum security.

4 Tap or click the Back button in the upper-left corner of the Backstage view to return to the document.

To Exit Word

Although you still need to make some edits to this document, you want to exit Word and resume working on the project at a later time. Thus, the following steps exit Word. For a detailed example of the procedure summarized below, refer to the Office and Windows chapter at the beginning of this book.

1a If you have one Word document open, tap or click the Close button on the right side of the title bar to close the open document and exit Word.

1b If you have multiple Word documents open, press and hold or right-click the Word app button on the taskbar and then tap or click 'Close all windows' on the shortcut menu to close all open documents and exit Word.

Q&A Could I press and hold or repeatedly click the Close button to close all open documents and exit Word?
Yes.

2 If a Microsoft Word dialog box appears, tap or click the Save button to save any changes made to the document since the last save.

Break Point: If you wish to take a break, this is a good place to do so. To resume at a later time, continue following the steps from this location forward.

Correcting Errors and Revising a Document

After creating a document, you may need to change it. For example, the document may contain an error, or new circumstances may require you to add text to the document.

Types of Changes Made to Documents

The types of changes made to documents normally fall into one of the three following categories: additions, deletions, or modifications.

Additions Additional words, sentences, or paragraphs may be required in a document. Additions occur when you omit text from a document and want to insert it later. For example, you may want to add your email address to the flyer.

Deletions Sometimes, text in a document is incorrect or no longer is needed. For example, you may discover that the tours no longer provide gear. In this case, you would delete the words, and gear, from the flyer.

Modifications If an error is made in a document or changes take place that affect the document, you might have to revise a word(s) in the text. For example, the tours may start in April instead of March.

To Run Word

Once you have created and saved a document, you may need to retrieve it from your storage medium. For example, you might want to revise the document or print it. The following steps, which assume Windows 8 is running, use the Start screen or the Search box to run Word based on a typical installation. You may need to ask your instructor how to run Word on your computer. For a detailed example of the procedure summarized below, refer to the Office and Windows chapter.

BTW
Certification
The Microsoft Office Specialist (MOS) program provides an opportunity for you to obtain a valuable industry credential — proof that you have the Word 2013 skills required by employers. For more information, visit the Certification resource on the Student Companion Site located on www.cengagebrain.com. For detailed instructions about accessing available resources, visit www.cengage.com/ct/studentdownload or contact your instructor for information about accessing the required files.

1 Scroll the Start screen for a Word 2013 tile. If your Start screen contains a Word 2013 tile, tap or click it to run Word and then proceed to Step 5; if the Start screen does not contain the Word 2013 tile, proceed to the next step to search for the Word app.

2 Swipe in from the right edge of the screen or point to the upper-right corner of the screen to display the Charms bar and then tap or click the Search charm on the Charms bar to display the Search menu.

3 Type `Word` as the search text in the Search box and watch the search results appear in the Apps list.

4 Tap or click Word 2013 in the search results to run Word.

5 Tap or click the Blank document thumbnail on the Word start screen to create a blank document and display it in the Word window.

6 If the Word window is not maximized, tap or click the Maximize button on its title bar to maximize the window.

To Open a Document from Word

Earlier in this chapter you saved your flyer using the file name, Adventure Flyer. The following steps open the Adventure Flyer file from the Word folder in the CIS 101 folder. For a detailed example of the procedure summarized below, refer to the Office and Windows chapter at the beginning of this book.

1 Tap or click FILE on the ribbon to open the Backstage view and then tap or click the Open tab in the Backstage view to display the Open gallery.

2 If the file you wish to open is displayed in the Recent Documents list, tap or click the file name to open the file and display the opened document in the Word window; then, skip the remaining steps. If the file you wish to open is not displayed in the Recent Documents list, proceed to the next step to locate the file.

3 Tap or click Computer, SkyDrive, or another location in the left pane, tap or click the Browse button, and then navigate to the location of the file to be opened (in this case the Word folder in the CIS 101 folder).

4 Tap or click Adventure Flyer to select the file to be opened.

5 Tap or click the Open button (Open dialog box) to open the selected file and display the opened document in the Word window.

To Zoom the Document

While modifying the document, you prefer the document at 100% so that it is easier to read. Thus, the following step changes the zoom back to 100%.

1 Tap or click VIEW on the ribbon to display the VIEW tab.

2 Tap or click the 100% button (VIEW tab | Zoom group) to display the page at 100% in the document window.

BTW

Quick Reference

For a table that lists how to complete the tasks covered in this book using touch gestures, the mouse, ribbon, shortcut menu, and keyboard, see the Quick Reference Summary at the back of this book, or visit the Quick Reference resource on the Student Companion Site located on www.cengagebrain.com. For detailed instructions about accessing available resources, visit www.cengage.com/ct/studentdownload or contact your instructor for information about accessing the required files.

To Insert Text in an Existing Document

1 ENTER TEXT | 2 FORMAT TEXT | 3 INSERT PICTURE | 4 FORMAT PICTURE
5 ENHANCE PAGE | 6 CORRECT & REVISE | 7 PRINT OR READ

Word inserts text to the left of the insertion point. The text to the right of the insertion point moves to the right and downward to fit the new text. The following steps insert the word, today, to the left of the word, with, in the flyer. **Why?** *These steps illustrate the process of inserting text.*

1

- Scroll through the document and then tap or click to the left of the location of text to be inserted (in this case, the w in with) to position the insertion point where text should be inserted (Figure 1–64).

2

- Type **today** and then press the SPACEBAR to insert the word to the left of the insertion point (Figure 1–65).

Q&A

Why did the text move to the right as I typed?

In Word, the default typing mode is **insert mode**, which means as you type a character, Word moves all the characters to the right of the typed character one position to the right.

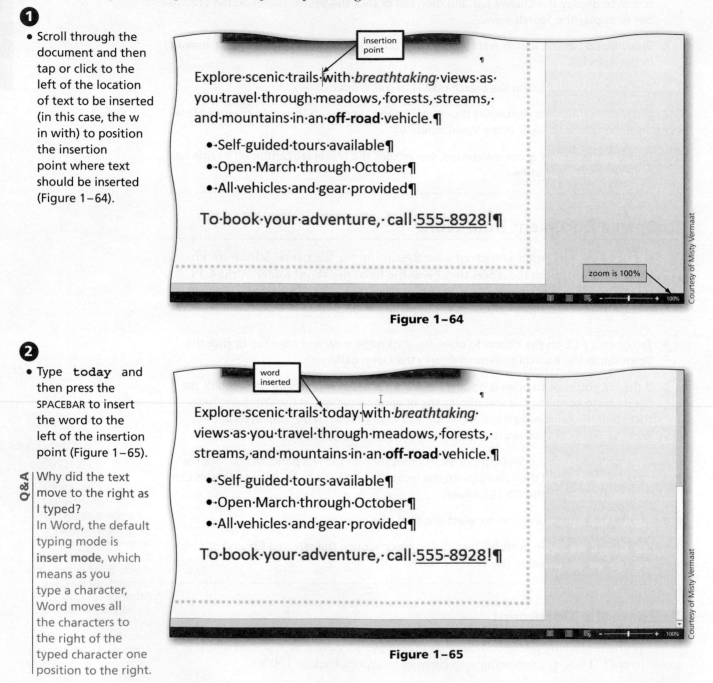

Figure 1–64

Figure 1–65

To Delete Text

1 ENTER TEXT | 2 FORMAT TEXT | 3 INSERT PICTURE | 4 FORMAT PICTURE
5 ENHANCE PAGE | 6 CORRECT & REVISE | 7 PRINT OR READ

It is not unusual to type incorrect characters or words in a document. As discussed earlier in this chapter, you can tap or click the Undo button on the Quick Access Toolbar to undo a command or action immediately — this includes typing. Word also provides other methods of correcting typing errors.

To delete an incorrect character in a document, simply tap or click next to the incorrect character and then press the BACKSPACE key to erase to the left of the insertion point, or press the DELETE key to erase to the right of the insertion point.

To delete a word or phrase, you first must select the word or phrase. The following steps select the word, today, which was just added in the previous steps and then delete the selection. *Why? These steps illustrate the process of selecting a word and then deleting selected text.*

1

- Double-tap or double-click the word to be selected (in this case, today) to select the word (Figure 1–66).

2

- If you are using a touch screen, tap the selected text to display the mini toolbar and then tap the Cut button on the mini toolbar to delete the selected text; if you are using a keyboard, with the text selected, press the DELETE key to delete the selected text.

text to be deleted is selected

mini toolbar appears because text is selected

Calibri (Body) 24

B I U

Explore·scenic·trails·today·with·*breathtaking*·
views·as·you·travel·through·meadows,·forests,·
streams,·and·mountains·in·an·off-road·vehicle.¶

pointer

- • Self-guided·tours·available¶
- • Open·March·through·October¶
- • All·vehicles·and·gear·provided¶

Courtesy of Misty Vermaat

Figure 1–66

Other Ways

1. Press and hold or right-click selected item, tap Cut on mini toolbar or click Cut on shortcut menu
2. Select item, press BACKSPACE to delete to left of insertion point or press DELETE to delete to right of insertion point
3. Select item, press CTRL+X

To Move Text

1 ENTER TEXT | 2 FORMAT TEXT | 3 INSERT PICTURE | 4 FORMAT PICTURE
5 ENHANCE PAGE | 6 CORRECT & REVISE | 7 PRINT OR READ

An efficient way to move text a short distance is drag-and-drop editing. With **drag-and-drop editing**, you select the item to be moved, drag the selected item to the new location, and then drop, or insert, it in the new location. Another technique for moving text is the cut-and-paste technique, which is discussed in the next chapter.

The following steps use drag-and-drop editing to move text. *Why? While proofreading the flyer, you realize that the body copy would read better if the last two bulleted paragraphs were reversed.*

1

- If you are using a mouse, position the pointer in the paragraph to be moved (in this case, the last bulleted item) and then triple-click to select the paragraph.

- If you are using a mouse, with the pointer in the selected text, press and hold down the mouse button, which displays a small dotted box with the pointer (Figure 1–67).

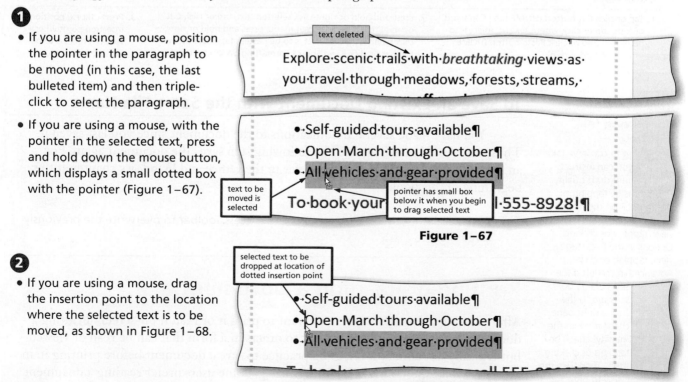

text deleted

Explore·scenic·trails·with·*breathtaking*·views·as·
you·travel·through·meadows,·forests,·streams,·

- • Self-guided·tours·available¶
- • Open·March·through·October¶
- • All·vehicles·and·gear·provided¶

text to be moved is selected

pointer has small box below it when you begin to drag selected text

To·book·your   555-8928!¶

Figure 1–67

2

- If you are using a mouse, drag the insertion point to the location where the selected text is to be moved, as shown in Figure 1–68.

selected text to be dropped at location of dotted insertion point

- • Self-guided·tours·available¶
- • Open·March·through·October¶
- • All·vehicles·and·gear·provided¶

Figure 1–68

3

- If you are using a mouse, release the mouse button to move the selected text to the location of the dotted insertion point (Figure 1–69).

Q&A What if I accidentally drag text to the wrong location?
Tap or click the Undo button on the Quick Access Toolbar and try again.

Can I use drag-and-drop editing to move any selected item?
Yes, you can select words, sentences, phrases, and graphics and then use drag-and-drop editing to move them.

What is the purpose of the Paste Options button?
If you are using a mouse and click the Paste Options button, a menu appears that allows you to change the format of the item that was moved. The next chapter discusses the Paste Options menu.

- Tap or click anywhere in the document window to remove the selection from the bulleted item.

Q&A What if I am using a touch screen?
If you have a stylus, you can follow Steps 1 through 3 using the stylus. If you are using your finger, you will need to use the cut-and-paste technique: tap to position the insertion point in the text to be moved and then drag the selection handles as necessary to select the text that you want to move; tap the selection to display the mini toolbar and then tap the Cut button on the mini toolbar to remove the text; tap to position the insertion point at the location where you want to move the text; display the HOME tab and then tap the Paste button on the HOME tab to place the text at the location of the insertion point. The next chapter discusses this procedure in more depth.

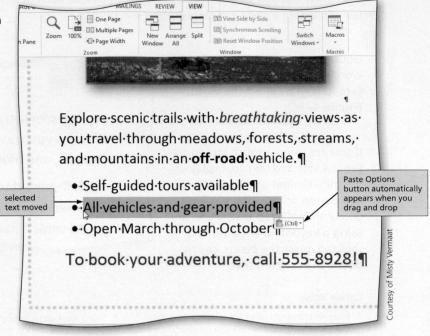

Explore·scenic·trails·with·*breathtaking*·views·as·you·travel·through·meadows,·forests,·streams,·and·mountains·in·an·**off-road**·vehicle.¶

- •·Self-guided·tours·available¶
- •·All·vehicles·and·gear·provided¶
- •·Open·March·through·October¶

To·book·your·adventure,·call·555-8928!¶

selected text moved

Paste Options button automatically appears when you drag and drop

Courtesy of Misty Vermaat

Figure 1–69

Other Ways

1. Tap or click Cut button (HOME tab | Clipboard group), tap or click where text or object is to be pasted, tap or click Paste button (HOME tab | Clipboard group)

2. Press and hold or right-click selected text, tap or click Cut on mini toolbar or shortcut menu, press and hold or right-click where text or object is to be pasted, tap Paste on mini toolbar or click Keep Source Formatting on shortcut menu

3. Press CTRL+X, position insertion point where text or object is to be pasted, press CTRL+V

To Save an Existing Document with the Same File Name

You have made several modifications to the document since you last saved it. Thus, you should save it again. The following step saves the document again. For an example of the step listed below, refer to the Office and Windows chapter at the beginning of this book.

1 Tap or click the Save button on the Quick Access Toolbar to overwrite the previously saved file.

Printing or Reading a Document

After creating a document, you may want to print it or read it on-screen. Printing a document enables you to distribute it to others in a form that can be read or viewed but typically not edited. It is a good practice to save a document before printing it, in the event you experience difficulties printing. Some users prefer reading a document on-screen instead of on paper.

What is the best method for distributing a document?

The traditional method of distributing a document uses a printer to produce a hard copy. A **hard copy** or **printout** is information that exists on a physical medium such as paper. Hard copies can be useful for the following reasons:

- Some people prefer proofreading a hard copy of a document rather than viewing it on the screen to check for errors and readability.

- Hard copies can serve as a backup reference if your storage medium is lost or becomes corrupted and you need to recreate the document.

Instead of distributing a hard copy of a document, users can distribute the document as an electronic image that mirrors the original document's appearance. The electronic image of the document can be sent as an email attachment, posted on a website, or copied to a portable storage medium such as a USB flash drive. Two popular electronic image formats, sometimes called fixed formats, are PDF by Adobe Systems and XPS by Microsoft. In Word, you can create electronic image files through the Save As dialog box and the Export, Share, and Print tabs in the Backstage view. Electronic images of documents, such as PDF and XPS, can be useful for the following reasons:

- Users can view electronic images of documents without the software that created the original document (e.g., Word). Specifically, to view a PDF file, you use a program called Adobe Reader, which can be downloaded free from Adobe's website. Similarly, to view an XPS file, you use a program called XPS Viewer, which is included in the latest versions of Windows and Internet Explorer.

- Sending electronic documents saves paper and printer supplies. Society encourages users to contribute to **green computing**, which involves reducing the electricity consumed and environmental waste generated when using computers, mobile devices, and related technologies.

To Print a Document

With the completed document saved, you may want to print it. *Why? Because this flyer is being posted, you will print a hard copy on a printer.* The following steps print a hard copy of the contents of the saved Adventure Flyer document.

1

- Tap or click FILE on the ribbon to open the Backstage view.

- Tap or click the Print tab in the Backstage view to display the Print gallery (Figure 1–70).

Q&A How can I print multiple copies of my document?
Increase the number in the Copies box in the Print gallery.

What if I decide not to print the document at this time?
Tap or click the Back button in the upper-left corner of the Backstage view to return to the document window.

2

- Verify that the printer listed on the Printer Status button will print a hard copy of the document. If necessary, click the Printer Status button to display a list of available printer options and then click the desired printer to change the currently selected printer.

Figure 1–70

3

- Tap or click the Print button in the Print gallery to print the document on the currently selected printer.

- When the printer stops, retrieve the hard copy (Figure 1–71).

Q&A Do I have to wait until my document is complete to print it?
No, you can follow these steps to print a document at any time while you are creating it.

What if I want to print an electronic image of a document instead of a hard copy?
You would click the Printer Status button in the Print gallery and then select the desired electronic image option, such as Microsoft XPS Document Writer, which would create an XPS file.

What if one or more of my borders do not print?
Tap or click the Page Borders button (DESIGN tab | Page Background group), tap or click the Options button (Borders and Shading dialog box), tap or click the Measure from arrow and click Text, change the four text boxes to 15 pt, and then tap or click the OK button in each dialog box. Try printing the document again. If the borders still do not print, adjust the boxes in the dialog box to a number smaller than 15 point.

Figure 1–71

To Switch to Read Mode

1 ENTER TEXT | 2 FORMAT TEXT | 3 INSERT PICTURE | 4 FORMAT PICTURE
5 ENHANCE PAGE | 6 CORRECT & REVISE | **7 PRINT OR READ**

The next steps switch from Print Layout view to Read mode. *Why? If you are not composing a document, you can switch to **Read mode**, which hides the ribbon and other writing tools so that more content fits on the screen. Read mode is intended to make it easier to read a document.* The following step switches to Read mode.

1

- Tap or click the Read Mode button on the status bar to switch to Read mode (Figure 1–72).

Experiment

- Tap or click the arrows to advance forward and then move backward through the document.

Q&A Besides reading, what can I do in Read mode?
You can zoom, copy text, highlight text, search, add comments, and more.

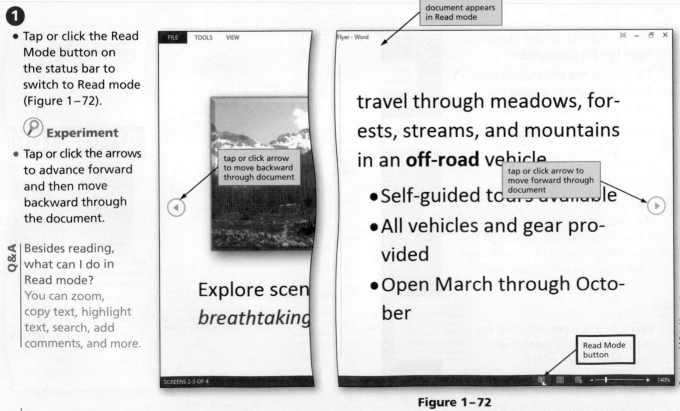

Figure 1–72

Other Ways

1. Tap or click Read Mode button (VIEW tab | Views group)   2. Tap or click VIEW on the ribbon, tap or click Edit Document

To Switch to Print Layout View

The next steps switch back to Print Layout view. *Why? If you want to show the document on a mock sheet of paper in the document window, along with the ribbon and other writing tools, you should switch to Print Layout view.* The following step switches to Print Layout view.

• Tap or click the Print Layout button on the status bar to switch to Print Layout view (Figure 1–73).

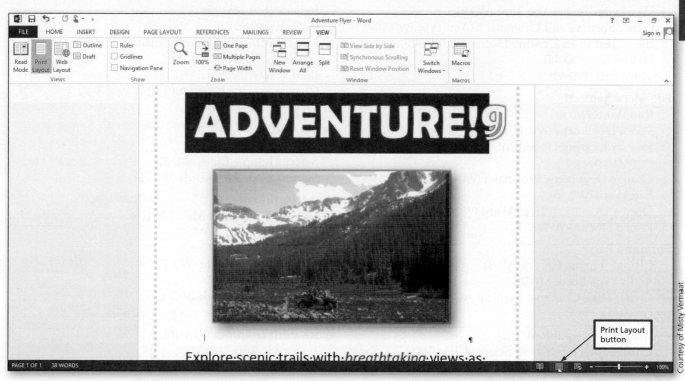

Figure 1–73

Other Ways

1. Tap or click Print Layout button (VIEW tab | Views group)

To Exit Word

This project now is complete. The following steps exit Word. For a detailed example of the procedure summarized below, refer to the Office and Windows chapter at the beginning of this book.

1a If you have one Word document open, tap or click the Close button on the right side of the title bar to close the open document and exit Word.

1b If you have multiple Word documents open, press and hold or right-click the Word app button on the taskbar and then tap or click 'Close all windows' on the shortcut menu to close all open documents and exit Word.

2 If a Microsoft Word dialog box appears, tap or click the Save button to save any changes made to the document since the last save.

BTW

Printing Document Properties

To print document properties, tap or click FILE on the ribbon to open the Backstage view, tap or click the Print tab in the Backstage view to display the Print gallery, tap or click the first button in the Settings area to display a list of options specifying what you can print, tap or click Document Info in the list to specify you want to print the document properties instead of the actual document, and then tap or click the Print button in the Print gallery to print the document properties on the currently selected printer.

Chapter Summary

In this chapter, you have learned how to enter text in a document, format text, insert and format a picture, add a page border, adjust paragraph and page spacing, and print and read a document. The items listed below include all the new Word skills you have learned in this chapter, with the tasks grouped by activity.

Enter and Edit Text
Type Text (WD 5)
Insert a Blank Line (WD 7)
Wordwrap Text as You Type (WD 9)
Check Spelling and Grammar as You Type (WD 10)
Insert Text in an Existing Document (WD 48)
Delete Text (WD 48)
Move Text (WD 49)

File Management
Run Word (WD 4)
Save a Document (WD 12)
Save an Existing Document with the Same File Name (WD 33)
Change Document Properties (WD 44)
Exit Word (WD 46)
Open a Document from Word (WD 47)
Print a Document (WD 51)

Format a Page
Change Theme Colors (WD 31)
Add a Page Border (WD 41)
Center Page Contents Vertically (WD 43)

Format Text
Center a Paragraph (WD 15)
Change the Font Size of Selected Text (WD 17)
Change the Font of Selected Text (WD 18)
Change the Case of Selected Text (WD 19)
Apply a Text Effect to Selected Text (WD 20)

Shade a Paragraph (WD 21)
Bullet a List of Paragraphs (WD 23)
Undo and Redo an Action (WD 24)
Italicize Text (WD 25)
Color Text (WD 26)
Use the Mini Toolbar to Format Text (WD 27)
Underline Text (WD 29)
Bold Text (WD 29)
Change Spacing before and after Paragraphs (WD 42)

Select Text
Select a Line (WD 16)
Select Multiple Lines (WD 22)
Select a Group of Words (WD 28)

Word Settings
Display Formatting Marks (WD 6)
Zoom Page Width (WD 7)
Zoom One Page (WD 30)
Zoom the Document (WD 35)
Zoom 100% (WD 37)
Switch to Read Mode (WD 52)
Switch to Print Layout View (WD 53)

Work with Graphics (Pictures)
Insert a Picture (WD 34)
Resize a Graphic (WD 36)
Apply a Picture Style (WD 38)
Apply Picture Effects (WD 39)

CONSIDER THIS: PLAN AHEAD

What decisions will you need to make when creating your next flyer?
Use these guidelines as you complete the assignments in this chapter and create your own flyers outside of this class.

1. Choose the text for the headline, body copy, and signature line — using as few words as possible to make a point.

2. Format various elements of the text.

   a) Select appropriate font sizes for text in the headline, body copy, and signature line.
   b) Select appropriate fonts for text in the headline, body copy, and signature line.
   c) Adjust paragraph alignment, as appropriate.
   d) Highlight key paragraphs with bullets.
   e) Emphasize important words.
   f) Use color to convey meaning and add appeal.

3. Find an eye-catching graphic(s) that conveys the overall message and meaning of the flyer.

4. Establish where to position and how to format the graphical image(s) so that the image grabs the attention of passersby and draws them into reading the flyer.

5. Determine whether the flyer needs enhancements such as a graphical, color-coordinated border or spacing adjustments to improve readability or overall appearance.

6. Correct errors and revise the document as necessary.

   a) Post the flyer on a wall and make sure all text word images are legible from a distance.
   b) Ask someone else to read the flyer and give you suggestions for improvements.

7. Determine the best method for distributing the document such as printing, sending via email, or posting on the web.

How should you submit solutions to questions in the assignments identified with a ✸ symbol?
Every assignment in this book contains one or more questions identified with a ✸ symbol. These questions require you to think beyond the assigned document. Present your solutions to the questions in the format required by your instructor. Possible formats may include one or more of these options: write the answer; create a document that contains the answer; present your answer to the class; discuss your answer in a group; record the answer as audio or video using a webcam, smartphone, or portable media player; or post answers on a blog, wiki, or website.

Apply Your Knowledge

Reinforce the skills and apply the concepts you learned in this chapter.

Modifying Text and Formatting a Document

Note: To complete this assignment, you will be required to use the Data Files for Students. Visit www.cengage.com/ct/studentdownload for detailed instructions or contact your instructor for information about accessing the required files.

Instructions: Run Word. Open the document, Apply 1-1 County Park Flyer Unformatted, from the Data Files for Students. The document you open is an unformatted flyer. You are to modify text, format paragraphs and characters, and insert a picture in the flyer to create the flyer shown in Figure 1–74.

Perform the following tasks:

1. Delete the word, below, in the sentence below the headline.

2. Insert the word, Valley, between the words, Green County, in the second to last line of the flyer.

3. Change the period to an exclamation point in the last line so that the text reads: Thank You!

4. If requested by your instructor, change the phone number in the flyer to your phone number.

5. Center the headline and the last two paragraphs of the flyer.

6. Select the third, fourth, and fifth paragraphs in the flyer and add bullets to the selected paragraphs.

7. Change the theme colors to the Red Orange color scheme.

8. Change the font and font size of the headline to 48-point Franklin Gothic Heavy, or a similar font. Change the case of the headline text to uppercase letters. Apply the text effect called Fill - Black, Text 1, Outline - Background 1, Hard Shadow - Background 1 to the headline. Change the font color of the headline text to Dark Red, Accent 6.

headline →

PLEASE DO NOT FEED THE WILDLIFE!

bulleted list →

<u>Follow these guidelines</u> to keep our wildlife healthy and our environment clean.

- Do **not** feed the wildlife.
- Never leave food unattended.
- Discard *all* trash in provided containers.

Questions? Call Green Valley County Park at 329-555-1020.

Thank You!

Courtesy of Misty Vermaat

Figure 1–74

Continued >

Apply Your Knowledge *continued*

9. Change the font size of the sentence below the headline, the bulleted list, and the last line of flyer to 26 point.

10. Use the mini toolbar to change the font size of the sentence below the bulleted list to 18 point.

11. Select the words, Follow these guidelines, in the paragraph below the headline and underline them.

12. Bold the word, not, in the first bulleted paragraph. Change the font color of this same word to Dark Red, Accent 6.

13. Italicize the word, all, in the second bulleted item. Undo this change and then redo the change.

14. Switch the last two bulleted paragraphs. That is, select the 'Never leave food unattended' bullet and move it so that it is the second bulleted paragraph.

15. Bold the text, Thank You!, in the last line of the flyer. Shade this same paragraph Dark Red, Accent 6, Darker 25%. If the font color does not automatically change to a lighter color, change its color to White, Background 1.

16. Change the zoom so that the entire page is visible in the document window.

17. Insert the picture of the squirrel eating the sucker centered on the blank line below the headline. The picture is called Squirrel and is available on the Data Files for Students. Apply the Soft Edge Oval picture style to the inserted picture.

18. Change the spacing before the first bulleted paragraph to 12 point and the spacing after the last bulleted paragraph to 24 point.

19. The entire flyer should fit on a single page. If it flows to two pages, resize the picture or decrease spacing before and after paragraphs until the entire flyer text fits on a single page.

20. Change the zoom to text width, then page width, then 100% and notice the differences.

21. If requested by your instructor, enter the text, Green Valley, as the keywords in the document properties. Change the other document properties, as specified by your instructor.

22. Click FILE on the ribbon and then click Save As. Save the document using the file name, Apply 1-1 County Park Flyer Formatted.

23. Print the document. Switch to Read Mode and browse pages through the document. Switch to Print Layout view.

24. Submit the revised document, shown in Figure 1–74, in the format specified by your instructor.

25. Exit Word.

26. ✸ If this flyer were announcing the park reopening instead of including a warning, which color scheme would you apply and why?

Extend Your Knowledge

Extend the skills you learned in this chapter and experiment with new skills. You may need to use Help to complete the assignment.

Modifying Text and Picture Formats and Adding Page Borders

Note: To complete this assignment, you will be required to use the Data Files for Students. Visit www.cengage.com/ct/studentdownload for detailed instructions or contact your instructor for information about accessing the required files.

Instructions: Run Word. Open the document, Extend 1-1 Baseball Tryouts Flyer Draft, from the Data Files for Students. You will enhance the look of the flyer shown in Figure 1–75.
Hint: Remember, if you make a mistake while formatting the picture, you can reset it by using the Reset Picture button or Reset Picture arrow (PICTURE TOOLS FORMAT tab | Adjust group).

Perform the following tasks:

1. Use Help to learn about the following: remove bullets, grow font, shrink font, art page borders, decorative underline(s), picture bullets, picture border shading, picture border color, shadow picture effects, and color saturation and tone.

2. Remove the bullet from the last line of the flyer.

3. Select the text, August 30, and use the 'Increase Font Size' button (HOME tab | Font group) to increase its font size.

4. Add an art page border to the flyer. If the border is not in color, add color to it.

5. Change the solid underline below the word, Travel, to a decorative underline. Change the color of the underline.

6. Change the style of the bullets to picture bullet(s). Adjust the hanging indent, if necessary, to align the text in bulleted list.

7. Change the color of the picture border. Add the Perspective Right 3-D Rotation picture effect to the picture.

8. Change the color saturation and color tone of the picture.

9. If requested by your instructor, change the name of the field (High Crop) to your last name.

10. Save the revised document with the file name, Extend 1-1 Baseball Tryouts Flyer Final, and then submit it in the format specified by your instructor.

11. ✳ In this assignment you added an art page border to the flyer. Which border did you select and why?

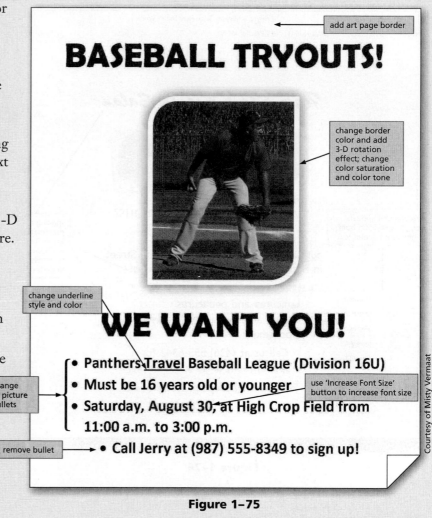

Figure 1–75

Analyze, Correct, Improve

Analyze a document, correct all errors, and improve it.

Correcting Spelling and Grammar Errors and Adding Color

Note: To complete this assignment, you will be required to use the Data Files for Students. Visit www.cengage.com/ct/studentdownload for detailed instructions or contact your instructor for information about accessing the required files.

Instructions: Run Word. Open the document, Analyze 1-1 Beauty Salon Flyer Draft, from the Data Files for Students. The document is a flyer that contains spelling and grammar errors, as shown in Figure 1–76 on the next page. It also could include color to make it more visually appealing.

Continued >

STUDENT ASSIGNMENTS

Analyze, Correct, Improve *continued*

1. Correct You are to correct each spelling (red wavy underline) and grammar (green and blue wavy underlines) error by pressing and holding or right-clicking the flagged text and then clicking the appropriate correction on the shortcut menu.

    If your screen does not display the wavy underlines, tap or click FILE on the ribbon and then tap or click Options in the Backstage view. When the Word Options dialog box is displayed, tap or click Proofing in the left pane, be sure the 'Hide spelling errors in this document only' and 'Hide grammar errors in this document only' check boxes do not contain check marks, and then tap or click the OK button. If your screen still does not display the wavy underlines, redisplay the Word Options dialog box, tap or click Proofing, and then tap or click the Recheck Document button.

2. Improve Enhance the flyer by (a) adding a shading color to the first and last lines (paragraphs) on the flyer, (b) changing the color of the text in the first line and last line of the flyer, and (c) adding a color glow effect to the three pictures in the flyer.

    If requested by your instructor, change the street name in the flyer to your first name. Save the revised document with the file name, Extend 1-1 Beauty Salon Flyer Final, and then submit it in the format specified by your instructor.

3. ✻ In this assignment, you selected color to add to the flyer. Which color(s) did you select and why?

Courtesy of Misty Vermaat

Figure 1–76

In the Labs

Design and/or create a document using the guidelines, concepts, and skills presented in this chapter. Labs 1 and 2, which increase in difficulty, require you to create solutions based on what you learned in the chapter; Lab 3 requires you to create a solution, which uses cloud and web technologies, by learning and investigating on your own from general guidance.

Lab 1: Creating a Flyer with a Picture

Problem: Your friend asked you to prepare a flyer that advertises the puppy she has for sale. First, you prepare the unformatted flyer shown in Figure 1–77a, and then you format it so that it looks like Figure 1–77b on page WD 60. *Hint:* Remember, if you make a mistake while formatting the flyer, you can use the Undo button on the Quick Access Toolbar to undo your last action.

Note: To complete this assignment, you will be required to use the Data Files for Students. Visit www.cengage.com/ct/studentdownload for detailed instructions or contact your instructor for information about accessing the required files.

Instructions: Perform the following tasks:

1. Run Word. Display formatting marks on the screen.

2. Type the flyer text, unformatted, as shown in Figure 1–77a, inserting a blank line between the headline and the body copy. If Word flags any misspelled words as you type, check their spelling and correct them.

3. Save the document using the file name, Lab 1-1 Puppy for Sale Flyer.

4. Center the headline and the signature line.

5. Change the theme colors to Aspect.

6. Change the font size of the headline to 72 point and the font to Gil Sans Ultra Bold Condensed, or a similar font. Apply the text effect called Fill - Dark Purple, Accent 1, Outline - Background, Hard Shadow - Accent 1.

7. Change the font size of body copy between the headline and the signature line to 22 point.

8. Change the font size of the signature line to 20 point.

9. Change the font of the body copy and signature line to Comic Sans MS.

10. Bullet the three lines (paragraphs) of text above the signature line.

11. Change the color of the words, purebred American Cocker Spaniel, to Dark Green, Accent 4, Darker 50%.

12. Italicize the word, and, in the third bulleted paragraph.

13. Bold the text in the signature line. Shade this paragraph containing the signature line in Dark Purple, Accent 5, Lighter 80%.

14. Underline the phone number in the signature line.

15. Change the zoom so that the entire page is visible in the document window.

16. Insert the picture centered on a blank line below the headline. The picture is called Puppy and is available on the Data Files for Students.

17. Apply the Rotated, White picture style to the inserted picture. Apply the glow effect called Dark Purple, 5 pt glow, Accent color 5 to the picture.

Puppy for Sale

blank line →

Own this six-month-old male, potty-trained, purebred American Cocker Spaniel puppy.

Fun, smart, cuddly, and playful

Needs a loving home

Knows these commands: sit, down, stay, heel, and leave it

If interested, call Vivian at (356) 555-7733.

(a) Unformatted Text
Figure 1–77 (Continued)

Continued >

STUDENT ASSIGNMENTS

In the Labs *continued*

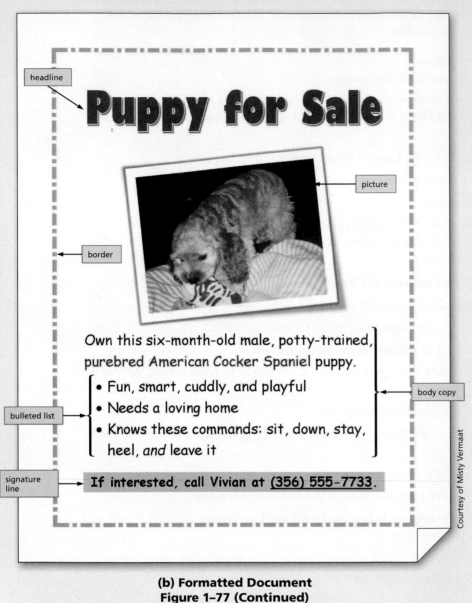

(b) Formatted Document
Figure 1–77 (Continued)

18. Change the spacing after the paragraph containing the headline to 0 pt. Change the spacing above (before) the signature line to 18 pt. The entire flyer should fit on a single page. If it flows to two pages, resize the picture or decrease spacing before and after paragraphs until the entire flyer text fits on a single page.

19. Add a 6-pt Dark Green, Accent 4, Lighter 60% page border, as shown in Figure 1–77b.

20. If requested by your instructor, change the contact name in the flyer to your first name.

21. Save the flyer again with the same file name. Submit the document, shown in Figure 1–77b, in the format specified by your instructor.

22. ✸ Why do you think this flyer used shades of purple and green?

Lab 2: **Creating a Flyer with a Resized Pictures**

Problem: Your boss at Junior's Wedding Bakery has asked you to prepare a flyer that promotes its business. You prepare the flyer shown in Figure 1–78. *Hint:* Remember, if you make a mistake while formatting the flyer, you can use the Undo button on the Quick Access Toolbar to undo your last action.

Note: To complete this assignment, you will be required to use the Data Files for Students. Visit www.cengage.com/ct/studentdownload for detailed instructions or contact your instructor for information about accessing the required files.

Instructions: Perform the following tasks:
1. Run Word. Type the flyer text, unformatted. If Word flags any misspelled words as you type, check their spelling and correct them.

2. Save the document using the file name, Lab 1-2 Wedding Bakery Flyer.

3. Change the theme colors to the Marquee color scheme.

4. Add bullets to the three paragraphs shown in the figure. Center all paragraphs, except the paragraphs containing the bulleted list.

5. Change the font size of the headline to 36 point and the font to Franklin Gothic Heavy, or a similar font. Apply the text effect called Fill - Orange, Accent 3, Sharp Bevel.

6. Change the font size of body copy between the headline and signature line to 20 point, except for line above the bulleted list, which is 24 point.

7. Change the font size of the signature line to 22 point. Bold the text in the signature line. Change the font color of the text in the signature line to Orange, Accent 3.

8. Italicize the word, personalize.

9. Bold the text above the bulleted list.

10. Underline the text, Junior's Wedding Bakery.

11. Shade the line above the bulleted list to the Orange, Accent 3 color. If the font color does not automatically change to a lighter color, change it to White, Background 1.

12. Change the zoom so that the entire page is visible in the document window.

13. Insert the first picture on a blank line below the headline and the second picture on a blank line below the bulleted list. The pictures are called Bakery 1 and Bakery 2, respectively, and are available on the Data Files for Students.

14. Resize the top picture so that it is approximately 2.8" × 5.39". Apply the Soft Edge Oval picture style to the top inserted picture. Apply the Offset Right Shadow picture effect to the top picture. Resize the bottom picture so that it is approximately 1.5" × 4.05". Apply the Simple Frame, Black picture style to the bottom inserted picture.

15. Change the spacing after the paragraph containing the bakery name to 0 pt and the spacing after the last bulleted paragraph to 12 pt. The entire flyer should fit on a single page. If it flows to two pages, resize the picture or decrease spacing before and after paragraphs until the entire flyer text fits on a single page.

16. Add the page border shown in Figure 1–78, using the color Gold, Accent 5.

17. Center the page contents vertically.

18. If requested by your instructor, change the bakery name to your last name.

19. Save the flyer again with the same file name. Submit the document, shown in Figure 1–78, in the format specified by your instructor.

20. ✸ Why do you think this flyer used shades of orange and yellow?

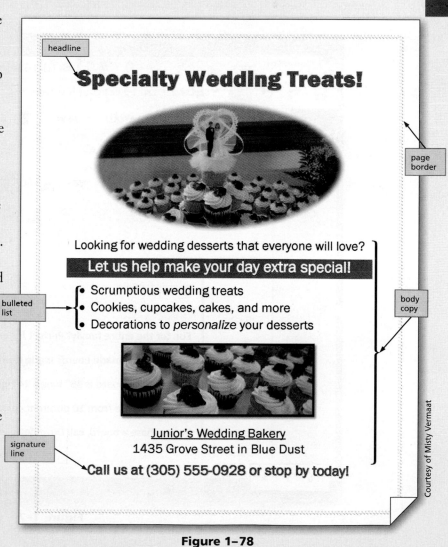

Figure 1–78

Courtesy of Misty Vermaat

Lab 3: Expand Your World: Cloud and Web Technologies
Using the Word Web App to Create a Flyer with a Picture

Problem: You have a side business where you build bean bag toss boards. You would like to create a flyer that promotes this business. You will use the Word Web App to prepare a flyer. The text for the unformatted flyer is shown in Figure 1–79.

Note: To complete this assignment, you will be required to use the Data Files for Students. Visit www.cengage.com/ct/studentdownload for detailed instructions or contact your instructor for information about accessing the required files.

Instructions: Perform the following tasks:

1. Run a browser. Search for the text, Word Web App, using a search engine. Visit several websites to learn about the Word Web App. Navigate to the Office Web Apps website. You will need to sign in to your SkyDrive account.

2. Use the Create button to begin creating a Word document using the Word Web App. Name the document Lab 1-3 Bean Bag Toss Flyer.

3. Notice the differences between the Word Web App and the Word desktop app you used to create the project in this chapter.

4. Enter the text in the flyer, shown in Figure 1–79, checking spelling as you type.

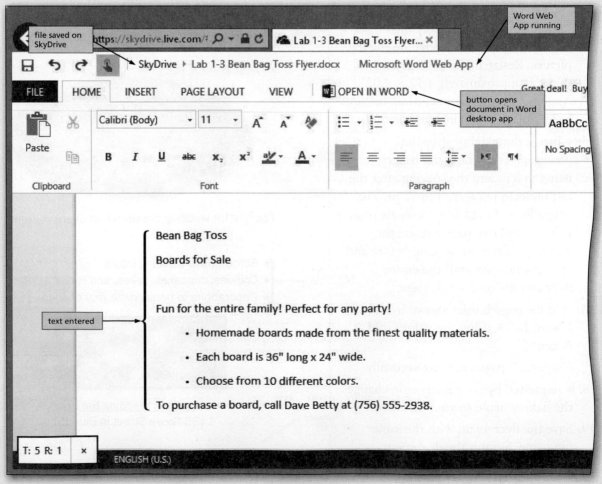

Figure 1–79

5. Insert the picture called Bean Bag Toss, which is located on the Data Files for Students.

6. Use the features available in the Word Web App, along with the concepts and techniques presented in this chapter, to format this flyer. Be sure to change the font and font size of text, center a paragraph(s), italicize text, color text, underline text, and apply a picture style. Adjust spacing above and below paragraphs as necessary. Resize the picture, if necessary.

7. If requested by your instructor, replace the contact name in the flyer with your name.

8. Save the document again. Tap or click the button to open the document in the Word desktop app. If necessary, sign in to your Microsoft account when prompted. Notice how the document appears in the Word desktop app.

9. Using either the Word Web App or Word desktop app, submit the document in the format requested by your instructor. Exit the Word Web App (FILE tab | Exit). Sign out of your SkyDrive account. Sign out of the Microsoft account in Word.

10. ✺ What is the Word Web App? Which features that are covered in this chapter are not available in the Word Web App? Do you prefer using the Word Web App or the Word desktop app? Why?

✺ Consider This: Your Turn

Apply your creative thinking and problem solving skills to design and implement a solution.

Note: To complete these assignments, you may be required to use the Data Files for Students. Visit www.cengage.com/ct/studentdownload for detailed instructions or contact your instructor for information about accessing the required files.

1: Design and Create a Photography Club Flyer

Personal

Part 1: As secretary of your school's Photography Club, you are responsible for creating and distributing flyers announcing the club. The flyer should contain two digital pictures appropriately resized; the Data Files for Students contains two pictures called Photography 1 and Photography 2, or you can use your own digital pictures if they are appropriate for the topic of the flyer. The flyer should contain the headline, Photography Club, and this signature line: Questions? Call Emily at (883) 555-0901. The body copy consists of the following text, in any order: Do you love photography? This is the club for you! All skill levels are welcome. Meetings every Tuesday at 5:00 p.m. in the Student Center (room 232). Bring your camera. We look forward to seeing you at our next meeting!

Use the concepts and techniques presented in this chapter to create and format this flyer. Be sure to check spelling and grammar. Submit your assignment and answers to the critical thinking questions in the format specified by your instructor.

Part 2: ✺ You made several decisions while creating the flyer in this assignment: where to place text, how to format the text (i.e., font, font size, paragraph alignment, bulleted paragraphs, underlines, italics, bold, color, etc.), which graphics to use, where to position the graphics, how to format the graphics, and which page enhancements to add (i.e., borders and spacing). What was the rationale behind each of these decisions? When you proofread the document, what further revisions did you make and why? How would you recommend distributing this flyer?

2: Design and Create a Hot Air Balloon Rides Flyer

Professional

Part 1: As a part-time employee at Galaxy Recreations, your boss has asked you to create and distribute flyers announcing hot air balloon rides. The flyer should contain two digital pictures appropriately resized; the Data Files for Students contains two pictures called Hot Air Balloon 1

Continued >

Consider This: Your Turn *continued*

and Hot Air Balloon 2, or you can use your own digital pictures if they are appropriate for the topic of the flyer. The flyer should contain the headline, Hot Air Balloon Rides, and this signature line: For reservations, call (485) 555-2295. The body copy consists of the following text, in any order: Amazing sights from incredible heights! The experience of a lifetime. Fun for the whole family. No pets. Bring your camera. Open seven days a week from 10:00 a.m. to 4:00 p.m. Book your private tour with Galaxy Recreations today!

Use the concepts and techniques presented in this chapter to create and format this flyer. Be sure to check spelling and grammar. Submit your assignment in the format specified by your instructor.

Part 2: ✹ You made several decisions while creating the flyer in this assignment: where to place text, how to format the text (i.e., font, font size, paragraph alignment, bulleted paragraphs, underlines, italics, bold, color, etc.), which graphics to use, where to position the graphics, how to format the graphics, and which page enhancements to add (i.e., borders and spacing). What was the rationale behind each of these decisions? When you proofread the document, what further revisions did you make and why? How would you recommend distributing this flyer?

3: Design and Create a Water Park Flyer
Research and Collaboration

Part 1: As a part-time employee at a local water park, your boss has asked you and two other employees to create and distribute flyers for the upcoming water park season. Form a three-member team to compose and create this flyer. Research a local water park: its location, hours, prices, rules, specials, etc. As a group, determine the text for the flyer's headline, body copy, and signature line. Your team also will need to obtain at least two digital pictures appropriate for the content of this flyer. You could take the pictures with a digital camera or search for public-domain images on the web.

Use the concepts and techniques presented in this chapter to create and format this flyer. Be sure to check spelling and grammar. Submit your team assignment in the format specified by your instructor.

Part 2: ✹ You made several decisions while creating the flyer in this assignment: text to use, where to place text, how to format the text (i.e., font, font size, paragraph alignment, bulleted paragraphs, underlines, italics, bold, color, etc.), which graphics to use, where to position the graphics, how to format the graphics, and which page enhancements to add (i.e., borders and spacing). What was the rationale behind each of these decisions? When you proofread the document, what further revisions did you make and why? What research methods did you use to create the flyer? Where did you obtain your pictures? How would you recommend distributing this flyer?

Learn Online

Reinforce what you learned in this chapter with games, exercises, training, and many other online activities and resources.

Student Companion Site Reinforcement activities and resources are available at no additional cost on www.cengagebrain.com. Visit www.cengage.com/ct/studentdownload for detailed instructions about accessing the resources available at the Student Companion Site.

SAM Put your skills into practice with SAM Projects! If you have a SAM account, go to www.cengage.com/sam2013 to access SAM assignments for this chapter.

2 Creating a Research Paper with References and Sources

Microsoft product screen shots used with permission from Microsoft Corporation.

Objectives

You will have mastered the material in this chapter when you can:

- Describe the MLA documentation style for research papers
- Modify a style
- Change line and paragraph spacing in a document
- Use a header to number pages of a document
- Apply formatting using keyboard shortcuts
- Modify paragraph indentation
- Insert and edit citations and their sources

- Add a footnote to a document
- Insert a manual page break
- Create a bibliographical list of sources
- Cut, copy, and paste text
- Find text and replace text
- Find a synonym
- Check spelling and grammar at once
- Look up information

2 | Creating a Research Paper with References and Sources

Introduction

In both academic and business environments, you will be asked to write reports. Business reports range from proposals to cost justifications to five-year plans to research findings. Academic reports focus mostly on research findings.

A **research paper** is a document you can use to communicate the results of research findings. To write a research paper, you learn about a particular topic from a variety of sources (research), organize your ideas from the research results, and then present relevant facts and/or opinions that support the topic. Your final research paper combines properly credited outside information along with personal insights. Thus, no two research papers — even if they are about the same topic — will or should be the same.

Project — Research Paper

When preparing a research paper, you should follow a standard documentation style that defines the rules for creating the paper and crediting sources. A variety of documentation styles exists, depending on the nature of the research paper. Each style requires the same basic information; the differences in styles relate to requirements for presenting the information. For example, one documentation style uses the term bibliography for the list of sources, whereas another uses references, and yet a third prefers the title works cited. Two popular documentation styles for research papers are the **Modern Language Association of America (MLA)** and **American Psychological Association (APA)** styles. This chapter uses the MLA documentation style because it is used in a wide range of disciplines.

The project in this chapter follows research paper guidelines and uses Word to create the short research paper shown in Figure 2–1. This paper, which discusses biometric devices, follows the MLA documentation style. Each page contains a page number. The first two pages present the name and course information (student name, instructor name, course name, and paper due date), paper title, an introduction with a thesis statement, details that support the thesis, and a conclusion. This section of the paper also includes references to research sources and a footnote. The third page contains a detailed, alphabetical list of the sources referenced in the research paper. All pages include a header at the upper-right edge of the page.

BTW

APA Appendix
If your version of this book includes the Word APA Appendix and you are required to create a research paper using the APA documentation style instead of the MLA documentation style, the appendix shows the steps required to create the research paper in this chapter using following APA guidelines. If your version of this book does not include the Word APA Appendix, see online or print publications for the APA guidelines or see your instructor.

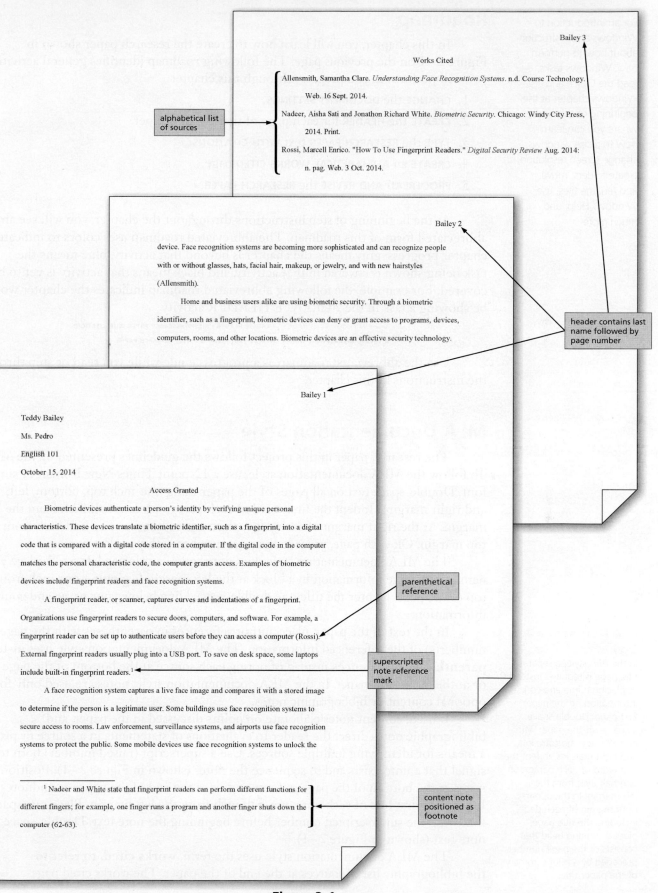

Bailey 3

Works Cited

Allensmith, Samantha Clare. *Understanding Face Recognition Systems*. n.d. Course Technology.

Web. 16 Sept. 2014.

Nadeer, Aisha Sati and Jonathon Richard White. *Biometric Security*. Chicago: Windy City Press,

2014. Print.

Rossi, Marcell Enrico. "How To Use Fingerprint Readers." *Digital Security Review* Aug. 2014:

n. pag. Web. 3 Oct. 2014.

alphabetical list of sources

Bailey 2

device. Face recognition systems are becoming more sophisticated and can recognize people

with or without glasses, hats, facial hair, makeup, or jewelry, and with new hairstyles

(Allensmith).

Home and business users alike are using biometric security. Through a biometric

identifier, such as a fingerprint, biometric devices can deny or grant access to programs, devices,

computers, rooms, and other locations. Biometric devices are an effective security technology.

header contains last name followed by page number

Bailey 1

Teddy Bailey

Ms. Pedro

English 101

October 15, 2014

Access Granted

Biometric devices authenticate a person's identity by verifying unique personal

characteristics. These devices translate a biometric identifier, such as a fingerprint, into a digital

code that is compared with a digital code stored in a computer. If the digital code in the computer

matches the personal characteristic code, the computer grants access. Examples of biometric

devices include fingerprint readers and face recognition systems.

A fingerprint reader, or scanner, captures curves and indentations of a fingerprint.

Organizations use fingerprint readers to secure doors, computers, and software. For example, a

fingerprint reader can be set up to authenticate users before they can access a computer (Rossi).

External fingerprint readers usually plug into a USB port. To save on desk space, some laptops

include built-in fingerprint readers.[1]

A face recognition system captures a live face image and compares it with a stored image

to determine if the person is a legitimate user. Some buildings use face recognition systems to

secure access to rooms. Law enforcement, surveillance systems, and airports use face recognition

systems to protect the public. Some mobile devices use face recognition systems to unlock the

parenthetical reference

superscripted note reference mark

[1] Nadeer and White state that fingerprint readers can perform different functions for

different fingers; for example, one finger runs a program and another finger shuts down the

computer (62-63).

content note positioned as footnote

Figure 2–1

For an introduction to Windows and instruction about how to perform basic Windows tasks, read the Office and Windows chapter at the beginning of this book, where you can learn how to resize windows, change screen resolution, create folders, move and rename files, use Windows Help, and much more.

Roadmap

In this chapter, you will learn how to create the research paper shown in Figure 2–1 on the previous page. The following roadmap identifies general activities you will perform as you progress through this chapter:

1. CHANGE the DOCUMENT SETTINGS.
2. CREATE the HEADER for each page of the research paper.
3. TYPE the RESEARCH PAPER text WITH CITATIONS.
4. CREATE an ALPHABETICAL WORKS CITED page.
5. PROOFREAD AND REVISE the RESEARCH PAPER.

At the beginning of step instructions throughout the chapter, you will see an abbreviated form of this roadmap. The abbreviated roadmap uses colors to indicate chapter progress: gray means the chapter is beyond that activity, blue means the task being shown is covered in that activity, and black means that activity is yet to be covered. For example, the following abbreviated roadmap indicates the chapter would be showing a task in the 2 CREATE HEADER activity.

1 CHANGE DOCUMENT SETTINGS | 2 CREATE HEADER | 3 TYPE RESEARCH PAPER WITH CITATIONS
4 CREATE ALPHABETICAL WORKS CITED | 5 PROOFREAD & REVISE RESEARCH PAPER

Use the abbreviated roadmap as a progress guide while you read or step through the instructions in this chapter.

MLA Documentation Style

The research paper in this project follows the guidelines presented by the MLA. To follow the MLA documentation style, use a 12-point Times New Roman or similar font. Double-space text on all pages of the paper using one-inch top, bottom, left, and right margins. Indent the first word of each paragraph one-half inch from the left margin. At the right margin of each page, place a page number one-half inch from the top margin. On each page, precede the page number with your last name.

The MLA documentation style does not require a title page. Instead, place your name and course information in a block at the left margin beginning one inch from the top of the page. Center the title one double-spaced line below your name and course information.

In the text of the paper, place author references in parentheses with the page number(s) of the referenced information. The MLA documentation style uses in-text **parenthetical references** instead of noting each source at the bottom of the page or at the end of the paper. In the MLA documentation style, notes are used only for optional content or bibliographic notes.

If used, content notes elaborate on points discussed in the paper, and bibliographic notes direct the reader to evaluations of statements in a source or provide a means for identifying multiple sources. Use a superscript (raised number) both to signal that a note exists and to sequence the notes (shown in Figure 2–1). Position notes at the bottom of the page as footnotes or at the end of the paper as endnotes. Indent the first line of each note one-half inch from the left margin. Place one space following the superscripted number before beginning the note text. Double-space the note text (shown in Figure 2–1).

The MLA documentation style uses the term, **works cited,** to refer to the bibliographic list of sources at the end of the paper. The works cited page

BTW

APA Documentation Style

In the APA style, a separate title page is required instead of placing name and course information on the paper's first page. Double-space all pages of the paper with one-inch top, bottom, left, and right margins. Indent the first word of each paragraph one-half inch from the left margin. In the upper-right margin of each page, including the title page, place a running head that consists of the page number preceded by a brief summary of the paper title.

alphabetically lists sources that are referenced directly in the paper. Place the list of sources on a separate numbered page. Center the title, Works Cited, one inch from the top margin. Double-space all lines. Begin the first line of each source at the left margin, indenting subsequent lines of the same source one-half inch from the left margin. List each source by the author's last name, or, if the author's name is not available, by the title of the source.

Changing Document Settings

The MLA documentation style defines some global formats that apply to the entire research paper. Some of these formats are the default in Word. For example, the default left, right, top, and bottom margin settings in Word are one inch, which meets the MLA documentation style. You will modify, however, the font, font size, and line and paragraph spacing.

To Run Word and Create a Blank Document

If you are using a computer to step through the project in this chapter and you want your screens to match the figures in this book, you should change your screen's resolution to 1366 × 768. For information about how to change a computer's resolution, refer to the Office and Windows chapter at the beginning of this book.

The following steps, which assume Windows 8 is running, use the Start screen or the Search box to run Word based on a typical installation. You may need to ask your instructor how to run Word on your computer. For a detailed example of the procedure summarized below, refer to the Office and Windows chapter.

 Scroll the Start screen for a Word 2013 tile. If your Start screen contains a Word 2013 tile, tap or click it to run Word and then proceed to Step 5; if the Start screen does not contain the Word 2013 tile, proceed to the next step to search for the Word app.

❷ Swipe in from the right edge of the screen or point to the upper-right corner of the screen to display the Charms bar and then tap or click the Search charm on the Charms bar to display the Search menu.

❸ Type **Word** as the search text in the Search box and watch the search results appear in the Apps list.

❹ Tap or click Word 2013 in the search results to run Word.

❺ Tap or click the Blank document thumbnail on the Word start screen to create a blank document and display it in the Word window.

❻ If the Word window is not maximized, tap or click the Maximize button on its title bar to maximize the window.

❼ If the Print Layout button on the status bar is not selected (shown in Figure 2–2 on the next page), tap or click it so that your screen is in Print Layout view.

❽ If Normal (HOME tab | Styles group) is not selected in the Styles gallery (shown in Figure 2–2), tap or click it so that your document uses the Normal style.

 To display the page the same width as the document window, if necessary, tap or click the Page Width button (VIEW tab | Zoom group).

For an introduction to Office and instruction about how to perform basic tasks in Office apps, read the Office and Windows chapter at the beginning of this book, where you can learn how to run an application, use the ribbon, save a file, open a file, exit an application, use Help, and much more.

One of the few differences between Windows 7 and Windows 8 occurs in the steps to run Word. If you are using Windows 7, click the Start button, type **Word** in the 'Search programs and files' box, click Word 2013, and then, if necessary, maximize the Word window. For detailed steps to run Word in Windows 7, refer to the Office and Windows chapter at the beginning of this book. For a summary of the steps, refer to the Quick Reference located at the back of this book.

To Display Formatting Marks

BTW
Style Formats
To see the formats assigned to a particular style in a document, tap or click the Styles Dialog Box Launcher (HOME tab | Styles group) and then tap or click the Style Inspector button in the Styles task pane. Position the insertion point in the style in the document and then point to the Paragraph formatting or Text level formatting areas in the Style Inspector task pane to display a ScreenTip describing formats assigned to the location of the insertion point. You also can tap or click the Reveal Formatting button in the Style Inspector task pane or press SHIFT+F1 to display the Reveal Formatting task pane.

As discussed in Chapter 1, it is helpful to display formatting marks that indicate where in the document you press the ENTER key, SPACEBAR, and other keys. The following steps display formatting marks.

1 If the HOME tab is not the active tab, tap or click HOME on the ribbon to display the HOME tab.

2 If the 'Show/Hide ¶' button (HOME tab | Paragraph group) is not selected already, tap or click it to display formatting marks on the screen.

Styles

When you create a document, Word formats the text using a particular style. A **style** is a named group of formatting characteristics, including font and font size. The default style in Word is called the **Normal style**, which most likely uses an 11-point Calibri font. If you do not specify a style for text you type, Word applies the Normal style to the text. In addition to the Normal style, Word has many other built-in, or predefined, styles that you can use to format text. Styles make it easy to apply many formats at once to text. You can modify existing styles and create your own styles. Styles are discussed as they are used in this book.

To Modify a Style

1 CHANGE DOCUMENT SETTINGS | 2 CREATE HEADER | 3 TYPE RESEARCH PAPER WITH CITATIONS
4 CREATE ALPHABETICAL WORKS CITED | 5 PROOFREAD & REVISE RESEARCH PAPER

The MLA documentation style requires that all text in the research paper use a 12-point Times New Roman or similar font. If you change the font and font size using buttons on the ribbon, you will need to make the change many times during the course of creating the paper. *Why? Word formats various areas of a document based on the Normal style, which uses an 11-point Calibri font. For example, body text, headers, and bibliographies all display text based on the Normal style.*

Thus, instead of changing the font and font size for various document elements, a more efficient technique is to change the Normal style for this document to use a 12-point Times New Roman font. *Why? By changing the Normal style, you ensure that all text in the document will use the format required by the MLA.* The following steps change the Normal style.

1

- Press and hold or right-click Normal in the Styles gallery (HOME tab | Styles group) to display a shortcut menu related to styles (Figure 2–2).

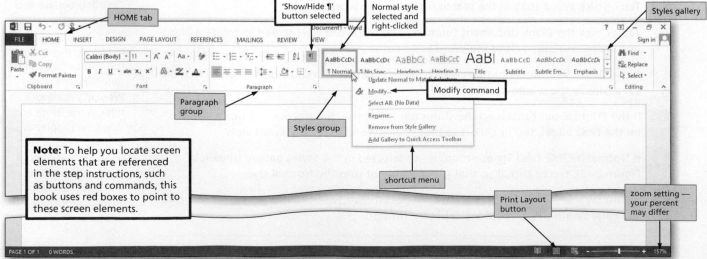

Figure 2–2

2

- Tap or click Modify on the shortcut menu to display the Modify Style dialog box (Figure 2–3).

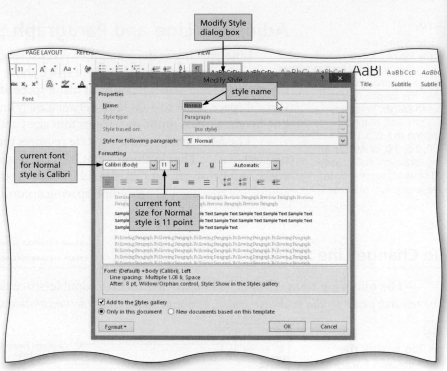

Figure 2–3

3

- Tap or click the Font arrow (Modify Style dialog box) to display the Font list. Scroll to and then click Times New Roman in the list to change the font for the style being modified.

- Tap or click the Font Size arrow (Modify Style dialog box) and then tap or click 12 in the Font Size list to change the font size for the style being modified.

- Ensure that the 'Only in this document' option button is selected (Figure 2–4).

Q&A
Will all future documents use the new font and font size?
No, because the 'Only in this document' option button is selected. If you wanted all future documents to use a new setting, you would select the 'New documents based on this template' option button.

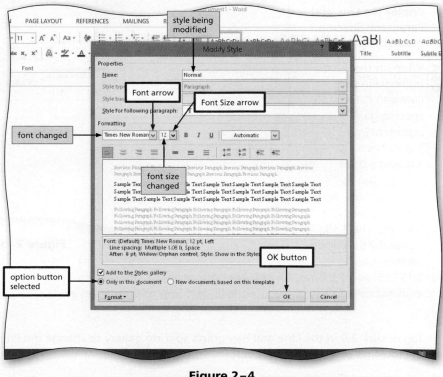

Figure 2–4

4

- Tap or click the OK button (Modify Style dialog box) to update the Normal style to the specified settings.

Other Ways

1. Tap or click Styles Dialog Box Launcher, tap or click arrow next to style name, tap or click Modify on menu, change settings (Modify Style dialog box), tap or click OK button

2. Press ALT+CTRL+SHIFT+S, tap or click arrow next to style name, tap or click Modify on menu, change settings (Modify Style dialog box), tap or click OK button

BTW
Line Spacing
If the top of a set of characters or a graphical image is chopped off, then line spacing may be set to Exactly. To remedy the problem, change line spacing to 1.0, 1.15, 1.5, 2.0, 2.5, 3.0, or At least (in the Paragraph dialog box), all of which accommodate the largest font or image.

Adjusting Line and Paragraph Spacing

Line spacing is the amount of vertical space between lines of text in a paragraph. **Paragraph spacing** is the amount of space above and below a paragraph. By default, the Normal style places 8 points of blank space after each paragraph and inserts a vertical space equal to 1.08 lines between each line of text. It also automatically adjusts line height to accommodate various font sizes and graphics.

The MLA documentation style requires that you **double-space** the entire research paper. That is, the amount of vertical space between each line of text and above and below paragraphs should be equal to one blank line. The next sets of steps adjust line spacing and paragraph spacing according to the MLA documentation style.

To Change Line Spacing

1 CHANGE DOCUMENT SETTINGS | 2 CREATE HEADER | 3 TYPE RESEARCH PAPER WITH CITATIONS
4 CREATE ALPHABETICAL WORKS CITED | 5 PROOFREAD & REVISE RESEARCH PAPER

The following steps change the line spacing to 2.0 to double-space lines in a paragraph. *Why? The lines of the research paper should be double-spaced, according to the MLA documentation style.*

1

• Tap or click the 'Line and Paragraph Spacing' button (HOME tab | Paragraph group) to display the Line and Paragraph Spacing gallery (Figure 2–5).

Q&A
What do the numbers in the Line and Paragraph Spacing gallery represent?
The options 1.0, 2.0, and 3.0 set line spacing to single, double, and triple, respectively. Similarly, the 1.15, 1.5, and 2.5 options set line spacing to 1.15, 1.5, and 2.5 lines. All of these options adjust line spacing automatically to accommodate the largest font or graphic on a line.

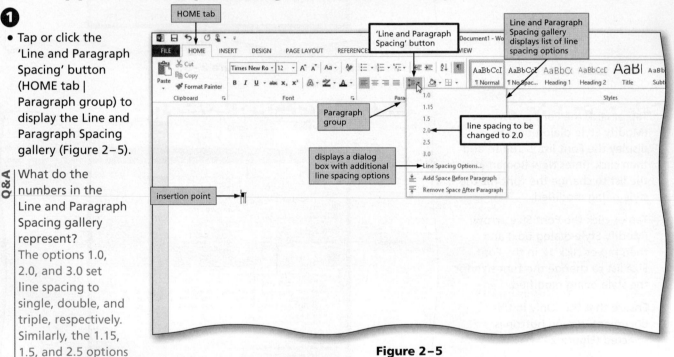

Figure 2–5

2

• Tap or click 2.0 in the Line and Paragraph Spacing gallery to change the line spacing at the location of the insertion point.

Q&A
Can I change the line spacing of existing text?
Yes. Select the text first and then change the line spacing as described in these steps.

Other Ways

1. Tap 'Show Context Menu' on mini toolbar or right-click paragraph, tap or click Paragraph on shortcut menu, tap or click Indents and Spacing tab (Paragraph dialog box), tap or click Line spacing arrow, select desired spacing, tap or click OK button

2. Tap or click Paragraph Settings Dialog Box Launcher (HOME tab or PAGE LAYOUT tab | Paragraph group), tap or click Indents and Spacing tab (Paragraph dialog box), tap or click Line spacing arrow, select desired spacing, tap or click OK button

3. Press CTRL+2 for double-spacing

To Remove Space after a Paragraph

The following steps remove space after a paragraph. *Why? The research paper should not have additional blank space after each paragraph, according to the MLA documentation style.*

1

- Tap or click the 'Line and Paragraph Spacing' button (HOME tab | Paragraph group) to display the Line and Paragraph Spacing gallery (Figure 2–6).

Q&A Why is there a check mark to the left of 2.0 in the gallery?
The check mark indicates the currently selected line spacing.

2

- Tap or click 'Remove Space After Paragraph' in the Line and Paragraph Spacing gallery so that no blank space appears after paragraphs.

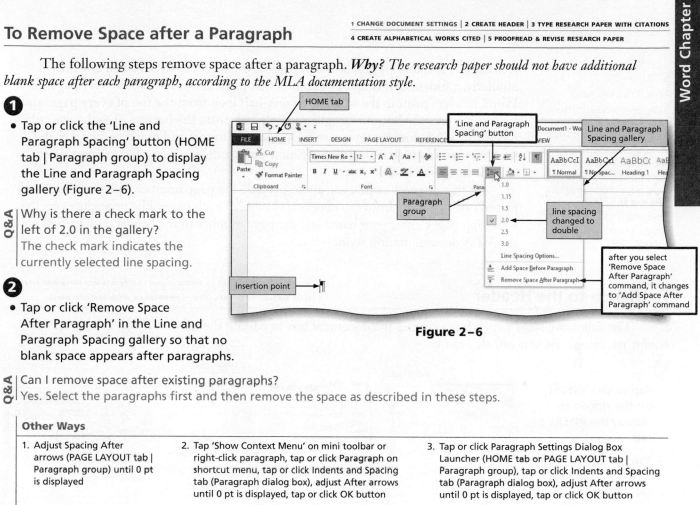

Figure 2–6

Q&A Can I remove space after existing paragraphs?
Yes. Select the paragraphs first and then remove the space as described in these steps.

Other Ways

1. Adjust Spacing After arrows (PAGE LAYOUT tab | Paragraph group) until 0 pt is displayed

2. Tap 'Show Context Menu' on mini toolbar or right-click paragraph, tap or click Paragraph on shortcut menu, tap or click Indents and Spacing tab (Paragraph dialog box), adjust After arrows until 0 pt is displayed, tap or click OK button

3. Tap or click Paragraph Settings Dialog Box Launcher (HOME tab or PAGE LAYOUT tab | Paragraph group), tap or click Indents and Spacing tab (Paragraph dialog box), adjust After arrows until 0 pt is displayed, tap or click OK button

To Update a Style to Match a Selection

To ensure that all paragraphs in the paper will be double-spaced and do not have space after the paragraphs, you want the Normal style to include the line and paragraph spacing changes made in the previous two sets of steps. The following steps update the Normal style. *Why? You can update a style to reflect the settings of the location of the insertion point or selected text. Because no text has yet been typed in the research paper, you do not need to select text prior to updating the Normal style.*

1

- Press and hold or right-click Normal in the Styles gallery (HOME tab | Styles group) to display a shortcut menu (Figure 2–7).

2

- Tap or click 'Update Normal to Match Selection' on the shortcut menu to update the selected (or current) style to reflect the settings at the location of the insertion point.

Figure 2–7

Other Ways

1. Tap or click Styles Dialog Box Launcher, tap or click arrow next to style name, tap or click 'Update Normal to Match Selection'

2. Press ALT+CTRL+SHIFT+S, tap or click arrow next to style name, tap or click 'Update Normal to Match Selection'

Creating a Header

A **header** is text and/or graphics that print at the top of each page in a document. Similarly, a **footer** is text and/or graphics that print at the bottom of every page. In Word, headers print in the top margin one-half inch from the top of every page, and footers print in the bottom margin one-half inch from the bottom of each page, which meets the MLA documentation style. In addition to text and graphics, headers and footers can include document information such as the page number, current date, current time, and author's name.

In this research paper, you are to precede the page number with your last name placed one-half inch from the upper-right edge of each page. The procedures on the following pages enter your name and the page number in the header, as specified by the MLA documentation style.

To Switch to the Header

1 CHANGE DOCUMENT SETTINGS | 2 CREATE HEADER | 3 TYPE RESEARCH PAPER WITH CITATIONS
4 CREATE ALPHABETICAL WORKS CITED | 5 PROOFREAD & REVISE RESEARCH PAPER

The following steps switch from editing the document text to editing the header. *Why? To enter text in the header, you instruct Word to edit the header.*

1
- Tap or click INSERT on the ribbon to display the INSERT tab.

- Tap or click the 'Add a Header' button (INSERT tab | Header & Footer group) to display the Add a Header gallery (Figure 2–8).

🔍 **Experiment**
- Tap or click the down scroll arrow in the Add a Header gallery to see the available built-in headers.

Q&A Can I use a built-in header for this research paper?
None of the built-in headers adheres to the MLA documentation style. Thus, you enter your own header content instead of using a built-in header for this research paper.

How would I remove a header from a document?
You would tap or click Remove Header in the Add a Header gallery. Similarly, to remove a footer, you would tap or click Remove Footer in the Add a Footer gallery.

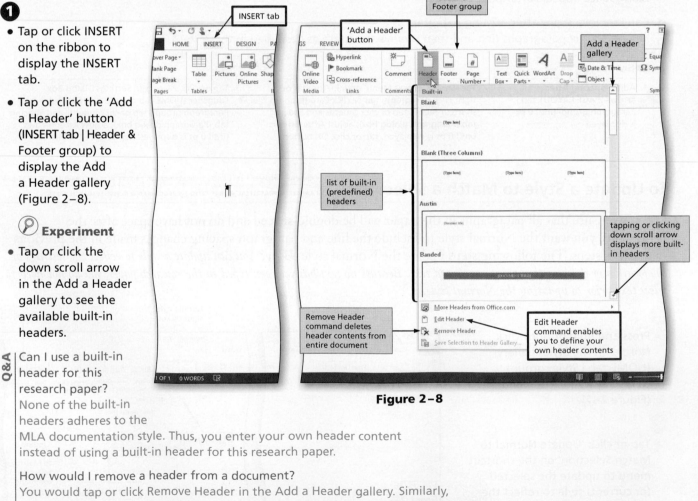

Figure 2–8

2

• Tap or click Edit Header in the Add a Header gallery to switch from the document text to the header, which allows you to edit the contents of the header (Figure 2–9).

Q&A How do I remove the HEADER & FOOTER TOOLS DESIGN tab from the ribbon? When you are finished editing the header, you will close it, which removes the HEADER & FOOTER TOOLS DESIGN tab.

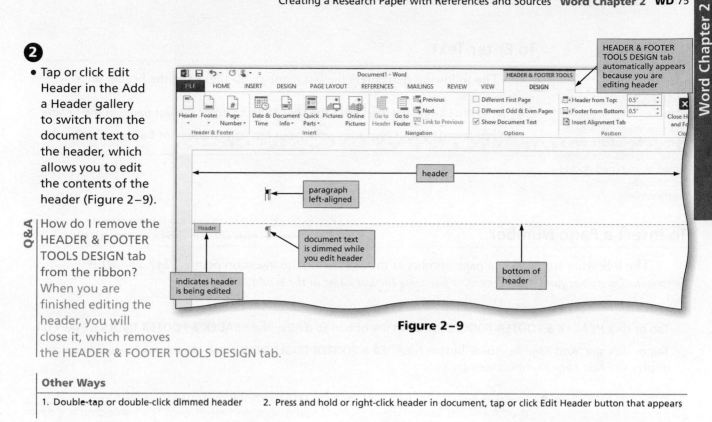

Figure 2–9

Other Ways

1. Double-tap or double-click dimmed header   2. Press and hold or right-click header in document, tap or click Edit Header button that appears

To Right-Align a Paragraph

1 CHANGE DOCUMENT SETTINGS | 2 CREATE HEADER | 3 TYPE RESEARCH PAPER WITH CITATIONS
4 CREATE ALPHABETICAL WORKS CITED | 5 PROOFREAD & REVISE RESEARCH PAPER

The paragraph in the header currently is left-aligned (Figure 2–9). The following steps right-align this paragraph. *Why? Your last name and the page number should print **right-aligned**; that is, they should print at the right margin, according to the MLA documentation style.*

1

• Tap or click HOME on the ribbon to display the HOME tab.

2

• Tap or click the Align Right button (HOME tab | Paragraph group) to right-align the current paragraph (Figure 2–10).

Q&A What if I wanted to return the paragraph to left-aligned? Tap or click the Align Right button again, or tap or click the Align Left button (HOME tab | Paragraph group).

Figure 2–10

Other Ways

1. Tap 'Show Context Menu' button on mini toolbar or right-click paragraph, tap or click Paragraph on shortcut menu, tap or click Indents and Spacing tab (Paragraph dialog box), tap or click Alignment arrow, tap or click Right, tap or click OK button

2. Tap or click Paragraph Settings Dialog Box Launcher (HOME tab or PAGE LAYOUT tab | Paragraph group), tap or click Indents and Spacing tab (Paragraph dialog box), tap or click Alignment arrow, tap or click Right, tap or click OK button

3. Press CTRL+R

BTW
Footers
If you wanted to create a footer, you would click the Footer button (INSERT tab | Header & Footer group) and then select the desired built-in footer or click Edit Footer to create a customized footer; or, you could double-tap or double-click the dimmed footer.

To Enter Text

The following step enters the last name right-aligned in the header area.

1 Type **Bailey** and then press the SPACEBAR to enter the last name in the header.

If requested by your instructor, enter your last name instead of Bailey in the header.

To Insert a Page Number

1 CHANGE DOCUMENT SETTINGS | 2 CREATE HEADER | 3 TYPE RESEARCH PAPER WITH CITATIONS
4 CREATE ALPHABETICAL WORKS CITED | 5 PROOFREAD & REVISE RESEARCH PAPER

The following steps insert a page number at the location of the insertion point. *Why? The MLA documentation style requires a page number following the last name in the header.*

1
- Tap or click HEADER & FOOTER TOOLS DESIGN on the ribbon to display the HEADER & FOOTER TOOLS DESIGN tab.
- Tap or click the 'Add Page Numbers' button (HEADER & FOOTER TOOLS DESIGN tab | Header & Footer group) to display the Add Page Numbers menu.

Q&A Why does the button name in the step differ from the name on the face of the button in the figure?
The text that appears on the face of the button may vary, depending on screen resolution. The name that appears in the ScreenTip (when you point to the button), however, never changes. For this reason, this book uses the name that appears in the ScreenTip to identify buttons, boxes, and other on-screen elements.

- Tap or point to Current Position on the Add Page Numbers menu to display the Current Position gallery (Figure 2–11).

 Experiment
- Tap or click the down scroll arrow in the Current Position gallery to see the available page number formats.

Figure 2–11

2

- If necessary, scroll to the top of the Current Position gallery.

- Tap or click Plain Number in the Current Position gallery to insert an unformatted page number at the location of the insertion point (Figure 2–12).

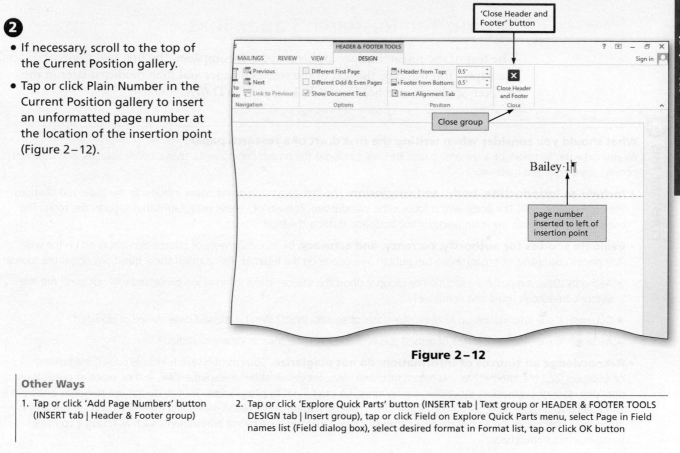

Figure 2–12

To Close the Header

1 CHANGE DOCUMENT SETTINGS | 2 CREATE HEADER | 3 TYPE RESEARCH PAPER WITH CITATIONS
4 CREATE ALPHABETICAL WORKS CITED | 5 PROOFREAD & REVISE RESEARCH PAPER

The next task is to switch back to the document text. *Why? You are finished entering text in the header.* The following step closes the header.

1

- Tap or click the 'Close Header and Footer' button (HEADER & FOOTER TOOLS DESIGN tab | Close group) (shown in Figure 2–12) to close the header and switch back to the document text (Figure 2–13).

Q&A

How do I make changes to existing header text?
Switch to the header using the steps described on page WD 74, edit the header as you would edit text in the document window, and then switch back to the document text.

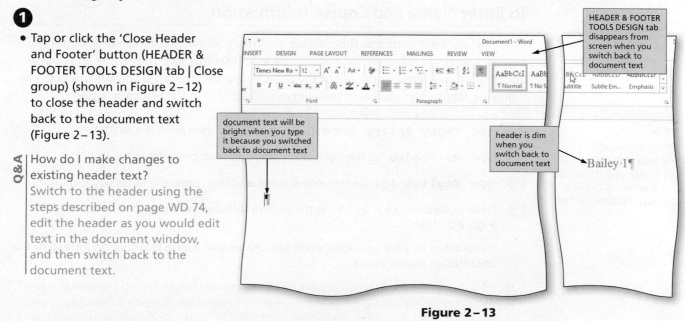

Figure 2–13

Typing the Research Paper Text

The text of the research paper in this chapter encompasses the first two pages of the paper. You will type the text of the research paper and then modify it later in the chapter, so that it matches Figure 2–1 on page WD 67.

CONSIDER THIS

What should you consider when writing the first draft of a research paper?
As you write the first draft of a research paper, be sure it includes the proper components, uses credible sources, and does not contain any plagiarized material.

- **Include an introduction, body, and conclusion.** The first paragraph of the paper introduces the topic and captures the reader's attention. The body, which follows the introduction, consists of several paragraphs that support the topic. The conclusion summarizes the main points in the body and restates the topic.

- **Evaluate sources for authority, currency, and accuracy.** Be especially wary of information obtained on the web. Any person, company, or organization can publish a webpage on the Internet. Ask yourself these questions about the source:

  - Authority: Does a reputable institution or group support the source? Is the information presented without bias? Are the author's credentials listed and verifiable?

  - Currency: Is the information up to date? Are dates of sources listed? What is the last date revised or updated?

  - Accuracy: Is the information free of errors? Is it verifiable? Are the sources clearly identified?

- **Acknowledge all sources of information; do not plagiarize.** Sources of research include books, magazines, newspapers, and the Internet. As you record facts and ideas, list details about the source: title, author, place of publication, publisher, date of publication, etc. When taking notes, be careful not to **plagiarize**. That is, do not use someone else's work and claim it to be your own. If you copy information directly, place it in quotation marks and identify its source. Not only is plagiarism unethical, but it is considered an academic crime that can have severe punishments such as failing a course or being expelled from school.

When you summarize, paraphrase (rewrite information in your own words), present facts, give statistics, quote exact words, or show a map, chart, or other graphic, you must acknowledge the source. Information that commonly is known or accessible to the audience constitutes common knowledge and does not need to be acknowledged. If, however, you question whether certain information is common knowledge, you should document it — just to be safe.

To Enter Name and Course Information

As discussed earlier in this chapter, the MLA documentation style does not require a separate title page for research papers. Instead, place your name and course information in a block at the top of the page, below the header, at the left margin. The following steps enter the name and course information in the research paper.

BTW

Date Formats
The MLA style prefers the day-month-year (15 October 2014) or month-day-year (October 15, 2014) format.

1 Type **Teddy Bailey** as the student name and then press the ENTER key.

2 Type **Ms. Pedro** as the instructor name and then press the ENTER key.

3 Type **English 101** as the course name and then press the ENTER key.

4 Type **October 15, 2014** as the paper's due date and then press the ENTER key (Figure 2–14).

If requested by your instructor, enter your name and course information instead of the information shown above.

Q&A Why did the word, October, appear on the screen as I began typing the month name?
Word has an AutoComplete feature, where it predicts some words or phrases as you are typing and displays its prediction in a ScreenTip. If the AutoComplete prediction is correct, you can tap the ScreenTip or press the ENTER key to instruct Word to finish your typing with the word or phrase that appears in the ScreenTip.

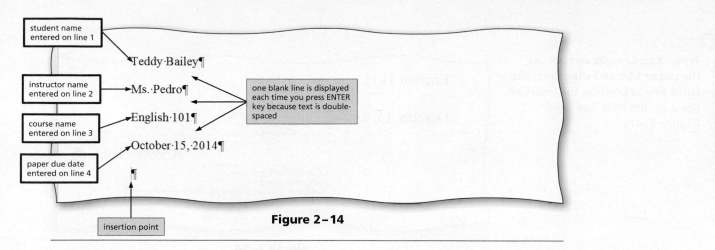

Figure 2–14

To Click and Type

1 CHANGE DOCUMENT SETTINGS | 2 CREATE HEADER | **3 TYPE RESEARCH PAPER WITH CITATIONS**
4 CREATE ALPHABETICAL WORKS CITED | 5 PROOFREAD & REVISE RESEARCH PAPER

The next task is to enter the title of the research paper centered between the page margins. In Chapter 1, you used the Center button (HOME tab | Paragraph group) to center text and graphics. As an alternative, if you are using a mouse, you can use Word's Click and Type feature to format and enter text, graphics, and other items. *Why? With **Click and Type**, you can double-click a blank area of the document window and Word automatically formats the item you type or insert according to the location where you double-clicked.* If you are using a mouse, the following steps use Click and Type to center and then type the title of the research paper. If you are using a touch screen, you will use a different method.

1

- If you are using a touch screen, tap the Center button (HOME tab | Paragraph group) and then proceed to Step 3 because the Click and Type feature does not work with a touch screen.

🔎 **Experiment**

- If you are using a mouse, move the pointer around the document below the entered name and course information and observe the various icons that appear with the I-beam.

- If you are using a mouse, position the pointer in the center of the document at the approximate location for the research paper title until a center icon appears below the I-beam (Figure 2–15).

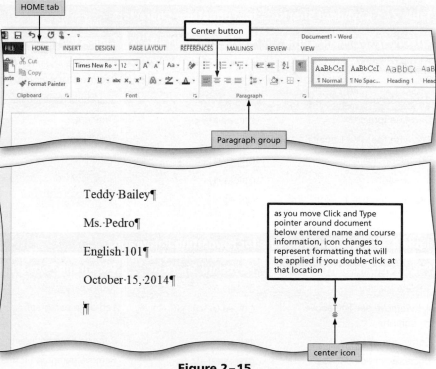

Figure 2–15

Q&A What are the other icons that appear in the Click and Type pointer?
A left-align icon appears to the right of the I-beam when the Click and Type pointer is in certain locations on the left side of the document window. A right-align icon appears to the left of the I-beam when the Click and Type pointer is in certain locations on the right side of the document window.

2

- If you are using a mouse, double-click to center the paragraph mark and insertion point between the left and right margins.

3

- Type `Access Granted` as the paper title and then press the ENTER key to position the insertion point on the next line (Figure 2–16).

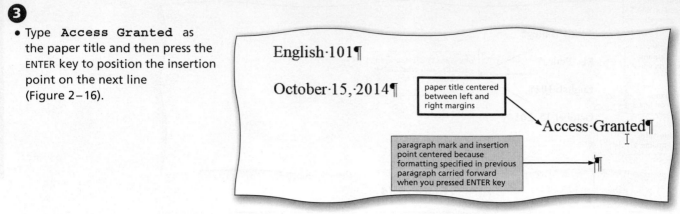

English·101¶

October·15,·2014¶

paper title centered between left and right margins

Access·Granted¶

paragraph mark and insertion point centered because formatting specified in previous paragraph carried forward when you pressed ENTER key

Figure 2–16

Keyboard Shortcuts

Word has many **keyboard shortcuts**, sometimes called shortcut keys or keyboard key combinations, for your convenience while typing. Table 2–1 lists the common keyboard shortcuts for formatting characters. Table 2–2 lists common keyboard shortcuts for formatting paragraphs.

Table 2–1 Keyboard Shortcuts for Formatting Characters

Character Formatting Task	Keyboard Shortcut	Character Formatting Task	Keyboard Shortcut
All capital letters	CTRL+SHIFT+A	Italic	CTRL+I
Bold	CTRL+B	Remove character formatting (plain text)	CTRL+SPACEBAR
Case of letters	SHIFT+F3	Small uppercase letters	CTRL+SHIFT+K
Decrease font size	CTRL+SHIFT+<	Subscript	CTRL+EQUAL SIGN
Decrease font size 1 point	CTRL+[	Superscript	CTRL+SHIFT+PLUS SIGN
Double-underline	CTRL+SHIFT+D	Underline	CTRL+U
Increase font size	CTRL+SHIFT+>	Underline words, not spaces	CTRL+SHIFT+W
Increase font size 1 point	CTRL+]		

Table 2–2 Keyboard Shortcuts for Formatting Paragraphs

Paragraph Formatting	Keyboard Shortcut	Paragraph Formatting	Keyboard Shortcut
1.5 line spacing	CTRL+5	Justify paragraph	CTRL+J
Add/remove one line above paragraph	CTRL+0 (ZERO)	Left-align paragraph	CTRL+L
Center paragraph	CTRL+E	Remove hanging indent	CTRL+SHIFT+T
Decrease paragraph indent	CTRL+SHIFT+M	Remove paragraph formatting	CTRL+Q
Double-space lines	CTRL+2	Right-align paragraph	CTRL+R
Hanging indent	CTRL+T	Single-space lines	CTRL+1
Increase paragraph indent	CTRL+M		

To Format Text Using a Keyboard Shortcut

The paragraphs below the paper title should be left-aligned, instead of centered. Thus, the next step is to left-align the paragraph below the paper title. When your fingers are already on the keyboard, you may prefer using keyboard shortcuts to format text as you type it.

The following step left-aligns a paragraph using the keyboard shortcut CTRL+L. (Recall from Chapter 1 that a notation such as CTRL+L means to press the letter L on the keyboard while holding down the CTRL key.)

1 Press CTRL+L to left-align the current paragraph, that is, the paragraph containing the insertion point (shown in Figure 2–17 on the next page).

Q&A Why would I use a keyboard shortcut instead of the ribbon to format text?
Switching between the mouse and the keyboard takes time. If your hands are already on the keyboard, use a keyboard shortcut. If your hand is on the mouse, use the ribbon.

To Save a Document

You have performed many tasks while creating this research paper and do not want to risk losing work completed thus far. Accordingly, you should save the document. The following steps assume you already have created folders for storing your files, for example, a CIS 101 folder (for your class) that contains a Word folder (for your assignments). Thus, these steps save the document in the Word folder in the CIS 101 folder using the file name, Biometric Devices Paper.

1 Tap or click the Save button on the Quick Access Toolbar, which depending on settings, will display either the Save As gallery in the Backstage view or the Save As dialog box.

2 To save on a hard disk or other storage media on your computer, proceed to Step 2a. To save on SkyDrive, proceed to Step 2b.

2a If your screen opens the Backstage view and you want to save on storage media on your computer, tap or click Computer in the left pane, if necessary, to display options in the right pane related to saving on your computer. If your screen already displays the Save As dialog box, proceed to Step 4.

2b If your screen opens the Backstage view and you want to save on SkyDrive, tap or click SkyDrive in the left pane to display SkyDrive saving options or a Sign In button. If your screen displays a Sign In button, tap or click it and then sign in to SkyDrive.

3 Tap or click the Browse button in the right pane to display the Save As dialog box associated with the selected save location (i.e., Computer or SkyDrive).

4 Type **Biometric Devices Paper** in the File name box to change the file name. Do not press the ENTER key after typing the file name because you do not want to close the dialog box at this time.

5 Navigate to the desired save location (in this case, the Word folder in the CIS 101 folder [or your class folder] on your computer or SkyDrive).

6 Tap or click the Save button (Save As dialog box) to save the research paper in the selected folder on the selected save location with the entered file name.

To Display the Rulers

According to the MLA documentation style, the first line of each paragraph in the research paper is to be indented one-half inch from the left margin. Although you can use a dialog box to indent paragraphs, Word provides a quicker way through the **horizontal ruler**. This ruler is displayed at the top edge of the document window just below the ribbon. Word also provides a **vertical ruler** that is displayed along the left edge of the Word window. The following step displays the rulers. *Why? You want to use the horizontal ruler to indent paragraphs.*

1

- If necessary, scroll the document so that the research paper title is at the top of the document window.

- Tap or click VIEW on the ribbon to display the VIEW tab.

- If the rulers are not displayed, tap or click the View Ruler check box (VIEW tab | Show group) to place a check mark in the check box and display the horizontal and vertical rulers on the screen (Figure 2–17).

Q&A What tasks can I accomplish using the rulers?
You can use the rulers to indent paragraphs, set tab stops, change page margins, and adjust column widths.

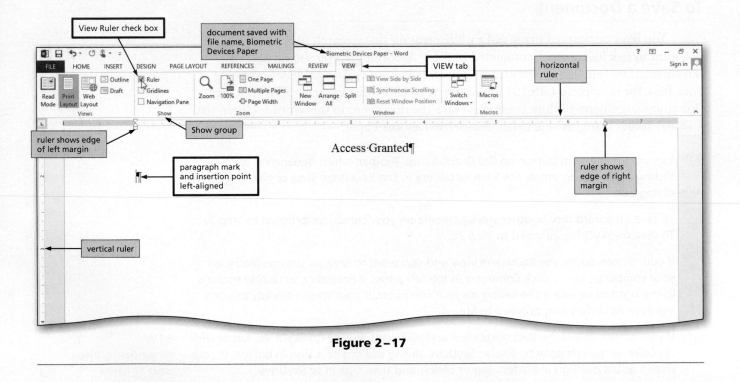

Figure 2–17

To First-Line Indent Paragraphs

If you are using a mouse, you can use the horizontal ruler, usually simply called the **ruler**, to indent just the first line of a paragraph, which is called a **first-line indent**. The left margin on the ruler contains two triangles above a square. The **'First Line Indent' marker** is the top triangle at the 0" mark on the ruler (Figure 2–18). The bottom triangle is discussed later in this chapter. The small square at the 0" mark is the Left Indent marker. The **Left Indent marker** allows you to change the entire left margin, whereas the 'First Line Indent' marker indents only the first line of the paragraph.

The next steps first-line indent paragraphs in the research paper. *Why? The first line of each paragraph in the research paper is to be indented one-half inch from the left margin, according to the MLA documentation style.*

1

- If you are using a mouse, with the insertion point on the paragraph mark below the research paper title, point to the 'First Line Indent' marker on the ruler (Figure 2–18).

Figure 2–18

2

- If you are using a mouse, drag the 'First Line Indent' marker to the .5" mark on the ruler to display a vertical dotted line in the document window, which indicates the proposed indent location of the first line of the paragraph (Figure 2–19).

Figure 2–19

3

- If you are using a mouse, release the mouse button to place the 'First Line Indent' marker at the .5" mark on the ruler, or one-half inch from the left margin (Figure 2–20).

- If you are using a touch screen, you cannot drag the 'First Line Indent' marker and must follow these steps instead: tap the Paragraph Settings Dialog Box Launcher (HOME tab or PAGE LAYOUT tab | Paragraph group) to display the Paragraph dialog box, tap the Indents and Spacing tab (Paragraph dialog box), tap the Special arrow, tap First line, and then tap the OK button.

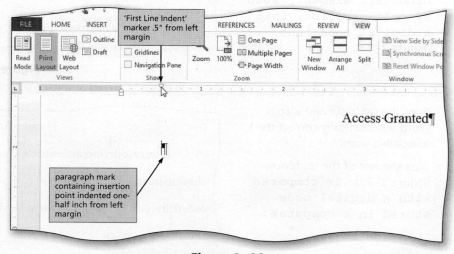

Figure 2–20

4

- Type `Biometric devices authenticate a person's identity by verifying unique personal characteristics.` and notice that Word automatically indented the first line of the paragraph by one-half inch (Figure 2–21).

Q&A

Will I have to set a first-line indent for each paragraph in the paper?

No. Each time you press the ENTER key, paragraph formatting in the previous paragraph carries forward to the next paragraph. Thus, once you set the first-line indent, its format carries forward automatically to each subsequent paragraph you type.

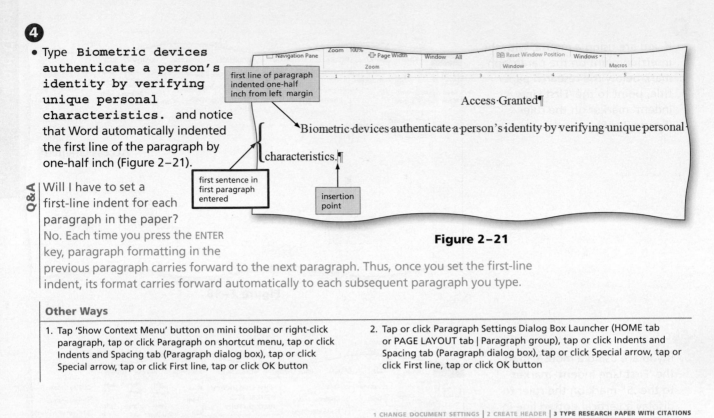

Figure 2–21

Other Ways

1. Tap 'Show Context Menu' button on mini toolbar or right-click paragraph, tap or click Paragraph on shortcut menu, tap or click Indents and Spacing tab (Paragraph dialog box), tap or click Special arrow, tap or click First line, tap or click OK button

2. Tap or click Paragraph Settings Dialog Box Launcher (HOME tab or PAGE LAYOUT tab | Paragraph group), tap or click Indents and Spacing tab (Paragraph dialog box), tap or click Special arrow, tap or click First line, tap or click OK button

To AutoCorrect as You Type

1 CHANGE DOCUMENT SETTINGS | 2 CREATE HEADER | 3 TYPE RESEARCH PAPER WITH CITATIONS
4 CREATE ALPHABETICAL WORKS CITED | 5 PROOFREAD & REVISE RESEARCH PAPER

Word has predefined many commonly misspelled words, which it automatically corrects for you. *Why?* *As you type, you may make typing, spelling, capitalization, or grammar errors. Word's **AutoCorrect** feature automatically corrects these kinds of errors as you type them in the document. For example, if you type ahve, Word automatically changes it to the correct spelling, have, when you press the SPACEBAR or a punctuation mark key such as a period or comma.*

The following steps intentionally misspell the word, that, as taht to illustrate the AutoCorrect feature.

1

- Press the SPACEBAR.

- Type the beginning of the next sentence, misspelling the word, that, as follows: `These devices translate a biometric element, such as a fingerprint, into a digital code taht` (Figure 2–22).

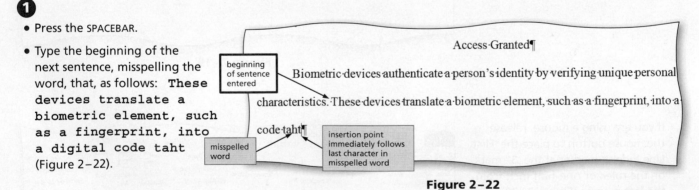

Figure 2–22

2

- Press the SPACEBAR and watch Word automatically correct the misspelled word.

- Type the rest of the sentence (Figure 2–23): `is compared with a digital code stored in a computer.`

Figure 2–23

To Use the AutoCorrect Options Button

The following steps illustrate the AutoCorrect Options button and menu. *Why? If you are using a mouse, when you position the pointer on text that Word automatically corrected, a small blue box appears below the text. If you point to the small blue box, Word displays the AutoCorrect Options button. When you tap or click the* **AutoCorrect Options button***, Word displays a menu that allows you to undo a correction or change how Word handles future automatic corrections of this type.* If you are using a touch screen, read these steps without performing them.

1
- If you are using a mouse, position the pointer in the text automatically corrected by Word (the word, that, in this case) to display a small blue box below the automatically corrected word (Figure 2–24).

2
- Point to the small blue box to display the AutoCorrect Options button.
- Click the AutoCorrect Options button to display the AutoCorrect Options menu (Figure 2–25).
- Press the ESCAPE key to remove the AutoCorrect Options menu from the screen.

Q&A Do I need to remove the AutoCorrect Options button from the screen?
No. When you move the pointer, the AutoCorrect Options button will disappear from the screen. If, for some reason, you wanted to remove the AutoCorrect Options button from the screen, you could press the ESCAPE key a second time.

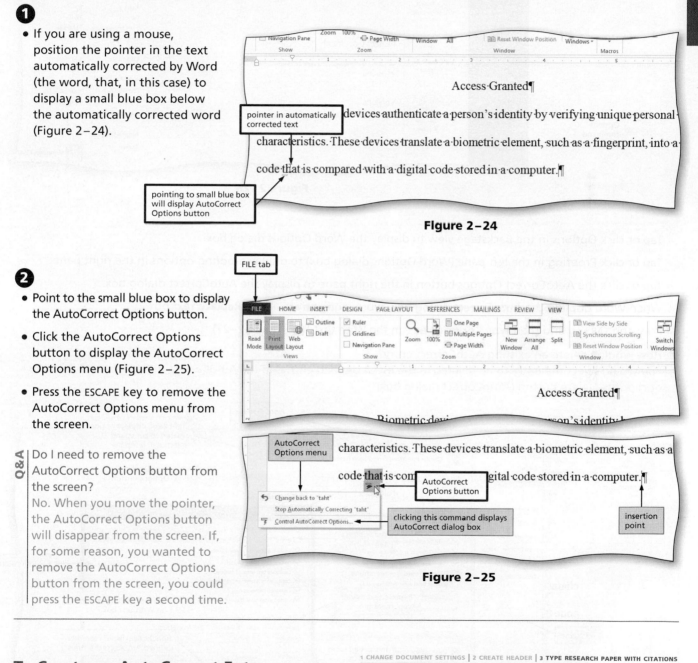

Figure 2–24

Figure 2–25

To Create an AutoCorrect Entry

The next steps create an AutoCorrect entry. *Why? In addition to the predefined list of AutoCorrect spelling, capitalization, and grammar errors, you can create your own AutoCorrect entries to add to the list. For example, if you tend to mistype the word computer as comptuer, you should create an AutoCorrect entry for it.*

1

- Tap or click FILE on the ribbon (shown in Figure 2–25 on the previous page) to open the Backstage view (Figure 2–26).

Figure 2–26

2

- Tap or click Options in the Backstage view to display the Word Options dialog box.

- Tap or click Proofing in the left pane (Word Options dialog box) to display proofing options in the right pane.

- Tap or click the AutoCorrect Options button in the right pane to display the AutoCorrect dialog box.

- When Word displays the AutoCorrect dialog box, type **comptuer** in the Replace text box.

- Press the TAB key and then type **computer** in the With text box (Figure 2–27).

Q&A How would I delete an existing AutoCorrect entry?
You would select the entry to be deleted in the list of defined entries in the AutoCorrect dialog box and then tap or click the Delete button (AutoCorrect dialog box).

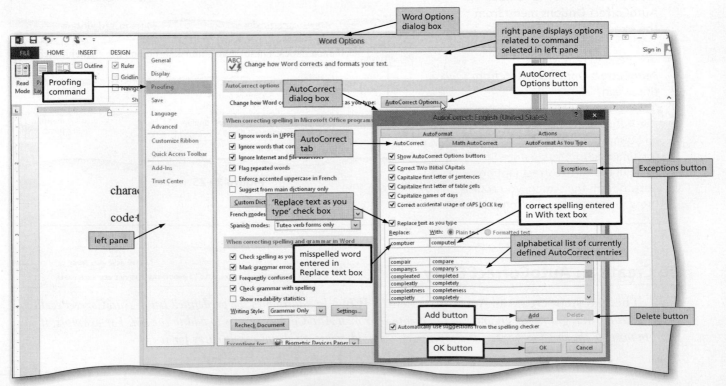

Figure 2–27

❸

- Tap or click the Add button (AutoCorrect dialog box) to add the entry alphabetically to the list of words to correct automatically as you type. (If your dialog box displays a Replace button instead, tap or click it and then tap or click the Yes button in the Microsoft Word dialog box to replace the previously defined entry.)

- Tap or click the OK button (AutoCorrect dialog box) to close the dialog box.

- Tap or click the OK button (Word Options dialog box) to close the dialog box.

The AutoCorrect Dialog Box

In addition to creating AutoCorrect entries for words you commonly misspell or mistype, you can create entries for abbreviations, codes, and so on. For example, you could create an AutoCorrect entry for asap, indicating that Word should replace this text with the phrase, as soon as possible.

If, for some reason, you do not want Word to correct automatically as you type, you can turn off the Replace text as you type feature by tapping or clicking Options in the Backstage view, tapping or clicking Proofing in the left pane (Word Options dialog box), tapping or clicking the AutoCorrect Options button in the right pane (Figure 2–27), removing the check mark from the 'Replace text as you type' check box, and then tapping or clicking the OK button in each open dialog box.

The AutoCorrect sheet in the AutoCorrect dialog box (Figure 2–27) contains other check boxes that correct capitalization errors if the check boxes are selected:

- If you type two capital letters in a row, such as TH, Word makes the second letter lowercase, Th.

- If you begin a sentence with a lowercase letter, Word capitalizes the first letter of the sentence.

- If you type the name of a day in lowercase letters, such as tuesday, Word capitalizes the first letter in the name of the day, Tuesday.

- If you leave the CAPS LOCK key on and begin a new sentence, such as aFTER, Word corrects the typing, After, and turns off the CAPS LOCK key.

If you do not want Word to automatically perform any of these corrections, simply remove the check mark from the appropriate check box in the AutoCorrect dialog box.

Sometimes you do not want Word to AutoCorrect a particular word or phrase. For example, you may use the code WD. in your documents. Because Word automatically capitalizes the first letter of a sentence, the character you enter following the period will be capitalized (in the previous sentence, it would capitalize the letter i in the word, in). To allow the code WD. to be entered into a document and still leave the AutoCorrect feature turned on, you would set an exception. To set an exception to an AutoCorrect rule, tap or click Options in the Backstage view, tap or click Proofing in the left pane (Word Options dialog box), tap or click the AutoCorrect Options button in the right pane, tap or click the Exceptions button (Figure 2–27), tap or click the appropriate tab in the AutoCorrect Exceptions dialog box, type the exception entry in the text box, tap or click the Add button, tap or click the Close button (AutoCorrect Exceptions dialog box), and then tap or click the OK button in each of the remaining dialog boxes.

BTW

Automatic Corrections
If you do not want to keep a change automatically made by Word and you immediately notice the automatic correction, you can undo the change by clicking the Undo button on the Quick Access Toolbar or pressing CTRL+Z. You also can undo a correction through the AutoCorrect Options button, which was shown on page WD 85.

BTW

Touch Screen Differences
The Office and Windows interfaces may vary if you are using a touch screen. For this reason, you might notice that the function or appearance of your touch screen differs slightly from this chapter's presentation.

To Enter More Text

The next task is to continue typing text in the research paper up to the location of the in-text parenthetical reference. The following steps enter this text.

BTW

Spacing after Punctuation
Because word processing documents use variable character fonts, it often is difficult to determine in a printed document how many times someone has pressed the SPACEBAR between sentences. Thus, the rule is to press the SPACEBAR only once after periods, colons, and other punctuation marks.

1 With the insertion point positioned at the end of the first paragraph in the paper, as shown in Figure 2–25 on page WD 85, press the SPACEBAR and then type these two sentences, intentionally misspelling the word readers as raders: `If the digital code in the computer matches the personal characteristic code, the computer grants access. Examples of biometric devices include fingerprint raders and face recognition systems.`

Q&A Why is the word, readers, misspelled?
Later in this chapter, you will use Word's check spelling and grammar at once feature to check the entire document for errors.

2 Press the ENTER key to start a new paragraph.

3 Type `A fingerprint reader, or scanner, captures curves and indentations of a fingerprint. Organizations use fingerprint readers to secure doors, computers, and software. For example, a fingerprint reader can be set up to authenticate users before they can access a computer` and then press the SPACEBAR (Figure 2–28).

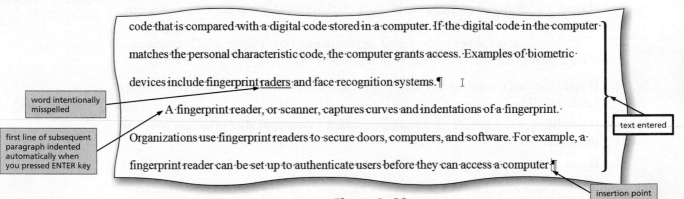

code that is compared with a digital code stored in a computer. If the digital code in the computer matches the personal characteristic code, the computer grants access. Examples of biometric devices include fingerprint raders and face recognition systems.¶

A fingerprint reader, or scanner, captures curves and indentations of a fingerprint. Organizations use fingerprint readers to secure doors, computers, and software. For example, a fingerprint reader can be set up to authenticate users before they can access a computer¶

word intentionally misspelled

first line of subsequent paragraph indented automatically when you pressed ENTER key

text entered

insertion point

Figure 2–28

Citations

Both the MLA and APA guidelines suggest the use of in-text parenthetical references (placed at the end of a sentence), instead of footnoting each source of material in a paper. These parenthetical references, called citations in Word, guide the reader to the end of the paper for complete information about the source.

BTW

BTWs
For a complete list of the BTWs found in the margins of this book, visit the BTW resource on the Student Companion Site located on www.cengagebrain.com. For detailed instructions about accessing available resources, visit www.cengage.com/ct/studentdownload or contact your instructor for information about accessing the required files.

Word provides tools to assist you with inserting citations in a paper and later generating a list of sources from the citations. With a documentation style selected, Word automatically formats the citations and list of sources according to that style. The process for adding citations in Word is as follows:

1. Modify the documentation style, if necessary.

2. Insert a citation placeholder.

3. Enter the source information for the citation.

You can combine Steps 2 and 3, where you insert the citation placeholder and enter the source information at once. Or, you can insert the citation placeholder as you write and then enter the source information for the citation at a later time. While creating the research paper in this chapter, you will use both methods.

To Change the Bibliography Style

The first step in inserting a citation is to be sure the citations and sources will be formatted using the correct documentation style, called the bibliography style in Word. *Why? You want to ensure that Word is using the MLA documentation style for this paper.* The following steps change the specified documentation style.

1

- Tap or click REFERENCES on the ribbon to display the REFERENCES tab.

- Tap or click the Bibliography Style arrow (REFERENCES tab | Citations & Bibliography group) to display the Bibliography Style gallery, which lists predefined documentation styles (Figure 2–29).

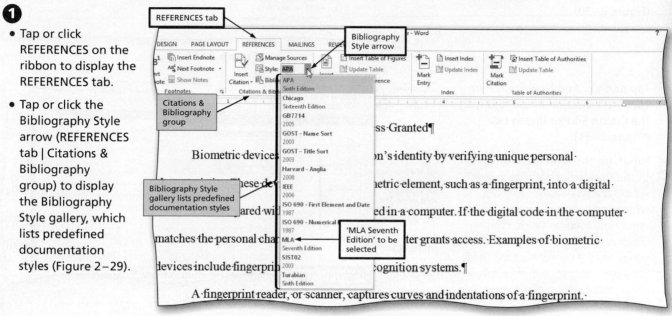

Figure 2–29

2

- Tap or click 'MLA Seventh Edition' in the Bibliography Style gallery to change the documentation style to MLA.

Q&A What if I am using a different edition of a documentation style shown in the Bibliography Style gallery?
Select the closest one and then, if necessary, perform necessary edits before submitting the paper.

CONSIDER THIS

What details are required for sources?
During your research, be sure to record essential publication information about each of your sources. Following is a sample list of types of required information for the MLA documentation style.

- Book: full name of author(s), complete title of book, edition (if available), volume (if available), publication city, publisher name, publication year, and publication medium

- Magazine: full name of author(s), complete title of article, magazine title, issue number (if available), date of magazine, page numbers of article, publication medium, and date viewed (if medium is a website)

- Website: full name of author(s), title of website, website publisher or sponsor (if none, write N.p.), publication date (if none, write n.d.), publication medium, and date viewed

---

To Insert a Citation and Create Its Source

With the documentation style selected, the next task is to insert a citation at the location of the insertion point and enter the source information for the citation. You can accomplish these steps at once by instructing Word to add a new source. The steps on the next page add a new source for a magazine (periodical) article on the web. *Why? The material preceding the insertion point was summarized from an online magazine article.*

1

• Tap or click the Insert Citation button (REFERENCES tab | Citations & Bibliography group) to display the Insert Citation menu (Figure 2–30).

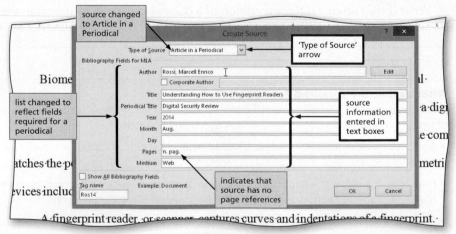

Figure 2–30

2

• Tap or click 'Add New Source' on the Insert Citation menu to display the Create Source dialog box (Figure 2–31).

Q&A | What are the Bibliography Fields in the Create Source dialog box?
A **field** is a placeholder for data whose contents can change. You enter data in some fields; Word supplies data for others. In this case, you enter the contents of the fields for a particular source, for example, the author name in the Author field.

Figure 2–31

🔍 **Experiment**

• Tap or click the 'Type of Source' arrow and then tap or click one of the source types in the list, so that you can see how the list of fields changes to reflect the type of source you selected.

3

• If necessary, tap or click the 'Type of Source' arrow (Create Source dialog box) and then tap or click 'Article in a Periodical', so that the list shows fields required for a magazine (periodical).

• Tap or click the Author text box. Type **Rossi, Marcell Enrico** as the author.

• Tap or click the Title text box. Type **Understanding How to Use Fingerprint Readers** as the article title.

• Press the TAB key and then type **Digital Security Review** as the periodical title.

Figure 2–32

• Press the TAB key and then type **2014** as the year.

• Press the TAB key and then type **Aug.** as the month.

• Press the TAB key twice and then type **n. pag.** as the number of pages.

• Press the TAB key and then type **Web** as the medium (Figure 2–32).

Q&A | Why is the month abbreviated?
The MLA documentation style abbreviates all months, except May, June, and July, when they appear in a source.

What does the n. pag. entry mean in the Pages text box?
The MLA documentation style uses the abbreviation n. pag. for no pagination, which indicates the source has no page references. This is common for web sources.

4

- Place a check mark in the 'Show All Bibliography Fields' check box so that Word displays all fields available for the selected source, including the date viewed (accessed) fields.

- If necessary, scroll to the bottom of the Bibliography Fields list to display the date viewed (accessed) fields.

- Tap or click the Year Accessed text box. Type **2014** as the year.

- Press the TAB key and then type **Oct.** as the month accessed.

- Press the TAB key and then type **3** as the day accessed (Figure 2–33).

Figure 2–33

Q&A What if some of the text boxes disappear as I enter the fields?

With the 'Show All Bibliography Fields' check box selected, the dialog box may not be able to display all fields at the same time. In this case, some may scroll up off the screen.

5

- Tap or click the OK button to close the dialog box, create the source, and insert the citation in the document at the location of the insertion point.

- Press the END key to move the insertion point to the end of the line, which also deselects the citation.

- Press the PERIOD key to end the sentence (Figure 2–34).

…de fingerprint raders and face recognition systems.¶

…gerprint reader, or scanner, captures curves and indentations of a fingerprint. ·

…s use fingerprint readers to secure doors, computers, and software. For example, a ·

…ader can be set up to authenticate users before they can access a computer (Rossi).¶

insertion point

citation inserted in text

Figure 2–34

To Enter More Text

The next task is to continue typing text in the research paper up to the location of the footnote. The following steps enter this text.

1 Press the SPACEBAR.

2 Type the next sentences (Figure 2–35): **External fingerprint readers usually plug into a USB port. To save on desk space, some laptops include built-in fingerprint readers.**

fingerprint reader can be set up to authenticate users before they can access a computer (Rossi). ·

External fingerprint readers usually plug into a USB port. To save on desk space, some laptops ·

include built-in fingerprint readers.¶

text entered

insertion point

Figure 2–35

BTW
Word Help
At any time while using Word, you can find answers to questions and display information about various topics through Word Help. Used properly, this form of assistance can increase your productivity and reduce your frustrations by minimizing the time you spend learning how to use Word. For instruction about Word Help and exercises that will help you gain confidence in using it, read the Office and Windows chapter at the beginning of this book.

To Save an Existing Document with the Same File Name

You have made several modifications to the document since you last saved it. Thus, you should save it again. The following step saves the document again. For an example of the step listed below, refer to the Office and Windows chapter at the beginning of this book.

1 Tap or click the Save button on the Quick Access Toolbar to overwrite the previously saved file.

Footnotes

As discussed earlier in this chapter, notes are optional in the MLA documentation style. If used, content notes elaborate on points discussed in the paper, and bibliographic notes direct the reader to evaluations of statements in a source or provide a means for identifying multiple sources. The MLA documentation style specifies that a superscript (raised number) be used for a **note reference mark** to signal that a note exists either at the bottom of the page as a **footnote** or at the end of the document as an **endnote**.

In Word, **note text** can be any length and format. Word automatically numbers notes sequentially by placing a note reference mark both in the body of the document and to the left of the note text. If you insert, rearrange, or remove notes, Word renumbers any subsequent note reference marks according to their new sequence in the document.

To Insert a Footnote Reference Mark

1 CHANGE DOCUMENT SETTINGS | 2 CREATE HEADER | **3 TYPE RESEARCH PAPER WITH CITATIONS**
4 CREATE ALPHABETICAL WORKS CITED | **5 PROOFREAD & REVISE RESEARCH PAPER**

The following step inserts a footnote reference mark in the document at the location of the insertion point and at the location where the footnote text will be typed. *Why? You will insert a content note elaborating on fingerprint reader functions, which you want to position as a footnote.*

1
- With the insertion point positioned as shown in Figure 2–35 on the previous page, tap or click the Insert Footnote button (REFERENCES tab | Footnotes group) to display a note reference mark (a superscripted 1) in two places: (1) in the document window at the location of the insertion point and (2) at the bottom of the page where the footnote will be positioned, just below a separator line (Figure 2–36).

Figure 2–36

Q&A | What if I wanted notes to be positioned as endnotes instead of as footnotes?
You would tap or click the Insert Endnote button (REFERENCES tab | Footnotes group), which places the separator line and the endnote text at the end of the document, instead of at the bottom of the page containing the reference.

Other Ways

1. Press ALT+CTRL+F

To Enter Footnote Text

The following step types the footnote text to the right of the note reference mark below the separator line.

1 Type the footnote text up to the citation (shown in Figure 2–37): **Nadeer and White state that fingerprint readers can perform different functions for different fingers; for example, one finger runs a program and another finger shuts down the computer** and then press the SPACEBAR.

To Insert a Citation Placeholder

1 CHANGE DOCUMENT SETTINGS | 2 CREATE HEADER | **3 TYPE RESEARCH PAPER WITH CITATIONS**
4 CREATE ALPHABETICAL WORKS CITED | 5 PROOFREAD & REVISE RESEARCH PAPER

Earlier in this chapter, you inserted a citation and its source at once. In Word, you also can insert a citation without entering the source information. *Why? Sometimes, you may not have the source information readily available and would prefer to enter it at a later time.*

The following steps insert a citation placeholder in the footnote, so that you can enter the source information later.

1

- With the insertion point positioned as shown in Figure 2–37, tap or click the Insert Citation button (REFERENCES tab | Citations & Bibliography group) to display the Insert Citation menu (Figure 2–37).

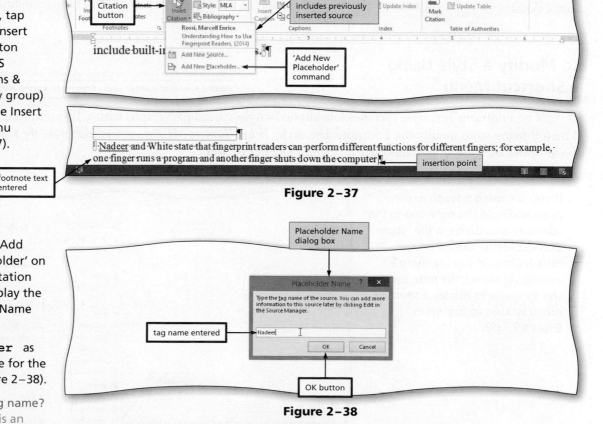

Figure 2–37

2

- Tap or click 'Add New Placeholder' on the Insert Citation menu to display the Placeholder Name dialog box.

- Type **Nadeer** as the tag name for the source (Figure 2–38).

Figure 2–38

Q&A What is a tag name?
A tag name is an identifier that links a citation to a source. Word automatically creates a tag name when you enter a source. When you create a citation placeholder, enter a meaningful tag name, which will appear in the citation placeholder until you edit the source.

3

- Tap or click the OK button (Placeholder Name dialog box) to close the dialog box and insert the entered tag name in the citation placeholder in the document (shown in Figure 2–39).

- Press the PERIOD key to end the sentence.

Q&A What if the citation is in the wrong location?
Tap or click the citation to select it and then drag the citation tab (on the upper-left corner of the selected citation) to any location in the document.

If you are using your finger on a touch screen and are having difficulty completing the steps in this chapter, consider using a stylus. Many people find it easier to be precise with a stylus than with a finger. In addition, with a stylus you see the pointer. If you still are having trouble completing the steps with a stylus, try using a mouse.

Footnote Text Style

When you insert a footnote, Word formats it using the Footnote Text style, which does not adhere to the MLA documentation style. For example, notice in Figure 2–37 on the previous page that the footnote text is single-spaced, left-aligned, and a smaller font size than the text in the research paper. According to the MLA documentation style, notes should be formatted like all other paragraphs in the paper.

You could change the paragraph formatting of the footnote text to first-line indent and double-spacing and then change the font size from 10 to 12 point. If you use this technique, however, you will need to change the format of the footnote text for each footnote you enter into the document.

A more efficient technique is to modify the format of the Footnote Text style so that every footnote you enter in the document will use the formats defined in this style.

To Modify a Style Using a Shortcut Menu

1 CHANGE DOCUMENT SETTINGS | 2 CREATE HEADER | 3 TYPE RESEARCH PAPER WITH CITATIONS
4 CREATE ALPHABETICAL WORKS CITED | 5 PROOFREAD & REVISE RESEARCH PAPER

The Footnote Text style specifies left-aligned single-spaced paragraphs with a 10-point font size for text. The following steps modify the Footnote Text style. *Why?* *To meet MLA documentation style, the footnotes should be double-spaced with a first line indent and a 12-point font size for text.*

1

- If you are using a touch screen, press and hold the note text in the footnote and then tap the 'Show Context Menu' button on the mini toolbar; if you are using a mouse, right-click the note text in the footnote to display a shortcut menu related to footnotes (Figure 2–39).

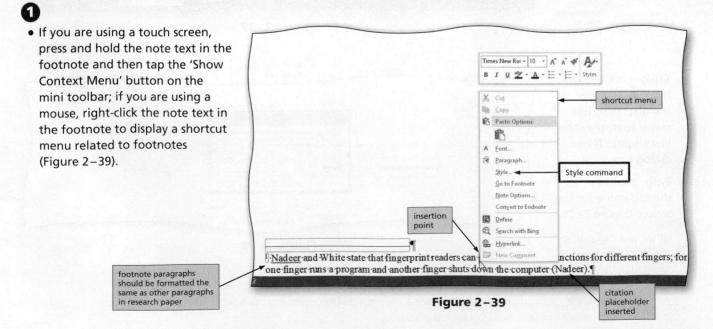

footnote paragraphs should be formatted the same as other paragraphs in research paper

shortcut menu

Style command

insertion point

citation placeholder inserted

¹ Nadeer and White state that fingerprint readers can functions for different fingers; for one finger runs a program and another finger shuts down the computer (Nadeer).¶

Figure 2–39

2

- Tap or click Style on the shortcut menu to display the Style dialog box. If necessary, tap or click the Category arrow, tap or click All styles in the Category list, and then tap or click Footnote Text in the Styles list to select the style to modify.

- Tap or click the Modify button (Style dialog box) to display the Modify Style dialog box.

- Tap or click the Font Size arrow (Modify Style dialog box) to display the Font Size list and then tap or click 12 in the Font Size list to change the font size.

- Tap or click the Double Space button to change the line spacing.

- Tap or click the Format button to display the Format menu (Figure 2–40).

Figure 2–40

3

- Tap or click Paragraph on the Format menu (Modify Style dialog box) to display the Paragraph dialog box.

- Tap or click the Special arrow (Paragraph dialog box) and then tap or click First line (Figure 2–41).

Figure 2–41

4

- Tap or click the OK button (Paragraph dialog box) to close the dialog box.

- Tap or click the OK button (Modify Style dialog box) to close the dialog box.

- Tap or click the Apply button (Style dialog box) to apply the style changes to the footnote text (Figure 2–42).

Q&A Will all footnotes use this modified style?
Yes. Any future footnotes entered in the document will use a 12-point font with the paragraphs first-line indented and double-spaced.

include-built-in-fingerprint-readers.¶

> Footnote Text style modified to match research paper paragraphs

Nadeer and White state that fingerprint readers can perform different functions for different fingers; for example, one finger runs a program and another finger shuts down the computer (Nadeer).¶

164 WORDS

Figure 2–42

Other Ways

1. Tap or click Styles Dialog Box Launcher (HOME tab | Styles group), tap or point to style name in list, tap or click style name arrow, tap or click Modify, change settings (Modify Style dialog box), tap or click OK button

2. Tap or click Styles Dialog Box Launcher (HOME tab | Styles group), tap or click Manage Styles button in task pane, select style name in list, tap or click Modify button (Manage Styles dialog box), change settings (Modify Style dialog box), tap or click OK button in each dialog box

---

To Edit a Source

1 CHANGE DOCUMENT SETTINGS | 2 CREATE HEADER | 3 TYPE RESEARCH PAPER WITH CITATIONS
4 CREATE ALPHABETICAL WORKS CITED | 5 PROOFREAD & REVISE RESEARCH PAPER

When you typed the footnote text for this research paper, you inserted a citation placeholder for the source. The following steps edit a source. *Why? Assume you now have the source information and are ready to enter it.*

1

- Tap or click somewhere in the citation placeholder to be edited, in this case (Nadeer), to select the citation placeholder.

- Tap or click the Citation Options arrow to display the Citation Options menu (Figure 2–43).

Q&A What is the purpose of the tab to the left of the selected citation?
If, for some reason, you wanted to move a citation to a different location in the document, you would select the citation and then drag the citation tab to the desired location.

> Citation Options menu

Edit Citation
Edit Source
Convert citation to static text
Update Citations and Bibliography

> Edit Source command

Nadeer and White state that fingerprint readers can perform different functions for e, one finger runs a program and another finger shuts down the computer (Nadeer).

> citation tab is used to move citation to different location in document

> citation placeholder selected

> Citation Options arrow

Figure 2–43

2

- Tap or click Edit Source on the Citation Options menu to display the Edit Source dialog box.

- If necessary, tap or click the 'Type of Source' arrow (Edit Source dialog box) and then tap or click Book, so that the list shows fields required for a book.

- Because this source has two authors, tap or click the Edit button to display the Edit Name dialog box, which assists you with entering multiple author names.

- Type **Nadeer** as the first author's last name; press the TAB key and then type **Aisha** as the first name; press the TAB key and then type **Sati** as the middle name (Figure 2–44).

Q&A What if I already know how to punctuate the author entry properly?
You can enter the name directly in the Author box.

Figure 2–44

3

- Tap or click the Add button (Edit Name dialog box) to add the first author name to the Names list.

- Type **White** as the second author's last name; press the TAB key and then type **Jonathon** as the first name; press the TAB key and then type **Richard** as the middle name.

- Tap or click the Add button to add the second author name to the Names list (Figure 2–45).

Figure 2–45

4

- Tap or click the OK button (Edit Name dialog box) to add the author names that appear in the Names list to the Author box in the Edit Source dialog box.

- Tap or click the Title text box (Edit Source dialog box). Type **Biometric Security** as the book title.

- Press the TAB key and then type **2014** as the year.

- Press the TAB key and then type **Chicago** as the city.

- Press the TAB key and then type **Windy City Press** as the publisher.

- Press the TAB key and then type **Print** as the medium (Figure 2–46).

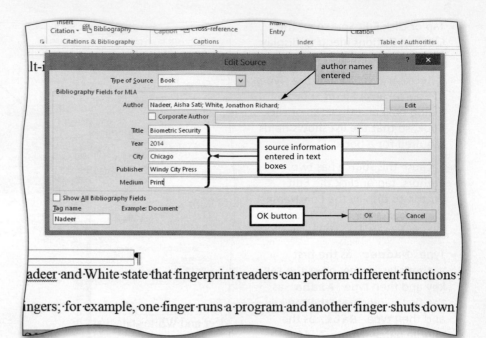

Figure 2–46

5

- Tap or click the OK button to close the dialog box, create the source, and update the citation to display both author last names (shown in Figure 2–47).

Other Ways

1. Tap or click Manage Sources button (REFERENCES tab | Citations & Bibliography group), tap or click placeholder source in Current List, tap or click Edit button (Source Manager dialog box)

To Edit a Citation

1 CHANGE DOCUMENT SETTINGS | 2 CREATE HEADER | 3 TYPE RESEARCH PAPER WITH CITATIONS
4 CREATE ALPHABETICAL WORKS CITED | 5 PROOFREAD & REVISE RESEARCH PAPER

In the MLA documentation style, if a source has page numbers, you should include them in the citation. Thus, Word provides a means to enter the page numbers to be displayed in the citation. Also, if you reference the author's name in the text, you should not list it again in the parenthetical citation. Instead, just list the page number(s) in the citation. To do this, you instruct Word to suppress author and title. *Why? If you suppress the author, Word automatically displays the title, so you need to suppress both the author and title if you want just the page number(s) to be displayed.* The following steps edit the citation, suppressing the author and title but displaying the page numbers.

1

- If necessary, tap or click somewhere in the citation to be edited, in this case somewhere in (Nadeer and White), which selects the citation and displays the Citation Options arrow.

- Tap or click the Citation Options arrow to display the Citation Options menu (Figure 2–47).

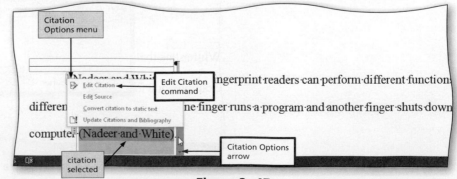

Figure 2–47

2

- Tap or click Edit Citation on the Citation Options menu to display the Edit Citation dialog box.

- Type **62–63** in the Pages text box (Edit Citation dialog box).

- Tap or click the Author check box to place a check mark in it.

- Tap or click the Title check box to place a check mark in it (Figure 2–48).

Edit Citation dialog box

check boxes selected so that author name and title do not appear in citation

pages entered

OK button

Figure 2–48

3

- Tap or click the OK button to close the dialog box, remove the author names from the citation in the footnote, suppress the title from showing, and add page numbers to the citation.

- Press the END key to move the insertion point to the end of the line, which also deselects the citation (Figure 2–49).

Nadeer and White state that fingerprint readers can perform different fingers; for example, one finger runs a program and anothe computer (62-63).

author names removed from citation and page numbers added

Figure 2–49

Working with Footnotes and Endnotes

You edit footnote text just as you edit any other text in the document. To delete or move a note reference mark, however, the insertion point must be in the document text (not in the footnote text).

To delete a note, select the note reference mark in the document text (not in the footnote text) by dragging through the note reference mark and then tap or click the Cut button (HOME tab | Clipboard group). Or, tap or click immediately to the right of the note reference mark in the document text and then press the BACKSPACE key twice, or tap or click immediately to the left of the note reference mark in the document text and then press the DELETE key twice.

To move a note to a different location in a document, select the note reference mark in the document text (not in the footnote text), tap or click the Cut button (HOME tab | Clipboard group), tap or click the location where you want to move the note, and then tap or click the Paste button (HOME tab | Clipboard group). When you move or delete notes, Word automatically renumbers any remaining notes in the correct sequence.

If you are using a mouse and position the pointer on the note reference mark in the document text, the note text is displayed above the note reference mark as a ScreenTip. To remove the ScreenTip, move the pointer.

If, for some reason, you wanted to change the format of note reference marks in footnotes or endnotes (i.e., from 1, 2, 3, to A, B, C), you would tap or click the Footnote & Endnote Dialog Box Launcher (REFERENCES tab | Footnotes group) to display the Footnote and Endnote dialog box, tap or click the Number format arrow (Footnote and Endnote dialog box), tap or click the desired number format in the list, and then tap or click the Apply button.

If, for some reason, you wanted to change a footnote number, you would tap or click the Footnote & Endnote Dialog Box Launcher (REFERENCES tab | Footnotes group) to display the Footnote and Endnote dialog box, enter the desired number in the Start at box, and then tap or click the Apply button (Footnote and Endnote dialog box).

If, for some reason, you wanted to convert footnotes to endnotes, you would tap or click the Footnote & Endnote Dialog Box Launcher (REFERENCES tab | Footnotes group) to display the Footnote and Endnote dialog box, tap or click the

BTW

Footnote and Endnote Location
You can change the location of footnotes from the bottom of the page to the end of the text by tapping or clicking the Footnote & Endnote Dialog Box Launcher (REFERENCES tab | Footnotes group), tapping or clicking the Footnotes arrow (Footnote and Endnote dialog box), and then tapping or clicking Below text. Similarly, tapping or clicking the Endnotes arrow (Footnote and Endnote dialog box) enables you to change the location of endnotes from the end of the document to the end of a section.

Convert button (Footnote and Endnote dialog box), select the 'Convert all footnotes to endnotes' option button, tap or click the OK button, and then tap or click the Close button (Footnote and Endnote dialog box).

To Enter More Text

The next task is to continue typing text in the body of the research paper. The following steps enter this text.

1 Position the insertion point after the note reference mark in the document and then press the ENTER key.

2 Type the first three sentences in the third paragraph of the research paper (shown in Figure 2–50): `A face recognition system captures a live face image and compares it with a stored image to determine if the person is a legitimate user. Some buildings use face recognition systems to secure access to rooms. Law enforcement, surveillance systems, and airports use face recognition systems to protect the public.`

To Count Words

1 CHANGE DOCUMENT SETTINGS | 2 CREATE HEADER | **3 TYPE RESEARCH PAPER WITH CITATIONS**
4 CREATE ALPHABETICAL WORKS CITED | 5 PROOFREAD & REVISE RESEARCH PAPER

Often when you write papers, you are required to compose the papers with a minimum number of words. The minimum requirement for the research paper in this chapter is 275 words. You can look on the status bar and see the total number of words thus far in a document. For example, Figure 2–50 shows the research paper has 214 words, but you are not sure if that count includes the words in your footnote. The following steps display the Word Count dialog box. *Why? You want to verify that the footnote text is included in the count.*

1

• Tap or click the Word Count indicator on the status bar to display the Word Count dialog box.

• If necessary, place a check mark in the 'Include textboxes, footnotes and endnotes' check box (Word Count dialog box) (Figure 2–50).

Q&A Why do the statistics in my Word Count dialog box differ from those in Figure 2–50?
Depending on the accuracy of your typing, your statistics may differ.

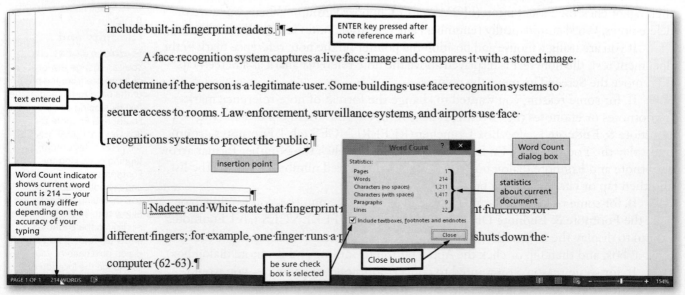

Figure 2–50

2

• Tap or click the Close button to close the dialog box.

Q&A
Can I display statistics for just a section of the document?
Yes. Select the section and then click the Word Count indicator on the status bar to display statistics about the selected text.

Other Ways

1. Tap or click Word Count button (REVIEW tab | Proofing group) 2. Press CTRL+SHIFT+G

Automatic Page Breaks

As you type documents that exceed one page, Word automatically inserts page breaks, called **automatic page breaks** or **soft page breaks**, when it determines the text has filled one page according to paper size, margin settings, line spacing, and other settings. If you add text, delete text, or modify text on a page, Word recalculates the location of automatic page breaks and adjusts them accordingly.

Word performs page recalculation between the keystrokes, that is, in between the pauses in your typing. Thus, Word refers to the automatic page break task as **background repagination**. An automatic page break will occur in the next set of steps.

To Enter More Text and Insert a Citation Placeholder

The next task is to type the remainder of the third paragraph in the body of the research paper. The following steps enter this text and a citation placeholder at the end of the paragraph.

1 With the insertion point positioned at the end of the third sentence in the third paragraph, as shown in Figure 2–50, press the SPACEBAR.

2 Type the rest of the third paragraph: **Some mobile devices use face recognition systems to unlock the device. Face recognition systems are becoming more sophisticated and can recognize people with or without glasses, hats, facial hair, makeup, or jewelry, and with new hairstyles** and then press the SPACEBAR.

Q&A
Why does the text move from the second page to the first page as I am typing?
Word, by default, will not allow the first line of a paragraph to be by itself at the bottom of a page (an **orphan**) or the last line of a paragraph to be by itself at the top of a page (a **widow**). As you type, Word adjusts the placement of the paragraph to avoid orphans and widows.

3 Tap or click the Insert Citation button (REFERENCES tab | Citations & Bibliography group) to display the Insert Citation menu. Tap or click 'Add New Placeholder' on the Insert Citation menu to display the Placeholder Name dialog box.

4 Type **Allensmith** as the tag name for the source.

5 Tap or click the OK button to close the dialog box and insert the tag name in the citation placeholder.

6 Press the PERIOD key to end the sentence.

BTW
Page Break Locations
As you type, your page break may occur at different locations depending on Word settings and the type of printer connected to the computer.

To Hide and Show White Space

With the page break and header, it is difficult to see the entire third paragraph at once on the screen. With the screen in Print Layout view, you can hide white space, which is the space that is displayed at the top and bottom of pages (including headers and footers) and also the space between pages. The following steps hide white space, if your screen displays it, and then shows white space. *Why? You want to see the as much of the third paragraph as possible at once, which spans the bottom of the first page and the top of the second page.*

1

- If you are using a mouse, position the pointer in the document window in the space between pages so that the pointer changes to a 'Hide White Space' button (Figure 2–51).

2

- If you are using a touch screen, double-tap in the space between pages; if you are using a mouse, double-click while the pointer is a 'Hide White Space' button to hide white space.

computer (62-63).¶

footnote remains at bottom of first page

page break

'Hide White Space' button

Double-click to hide white space

correct page number automatically appears in header

Bailey 2¶

device. Face recognition systems are becoming more sophisticated and can recognize people with or without glasses, hats, facial hair, makeup, or jewelry, and with new hairstyles (Allensmith).¶

placeholder citation entered

Figure 2–51

Q&A Does hiding white space have any effect on the printed document?
No.

3

- If you are using a mouse, position the pointer in the document window on the page break between pages so that the pointer changes to a 'Show White Space' button (Figure 2–52).

4

- If you are using a touch screen, double-tap the page break; if you are using a mouse, double-click while the pointer is a 'Show White Space' button to show white space.

to determine if the person is a legitimate user. Some buildings use face recognition systems to secure access to rooms. Law enforcement, surveillance systems, and airports use face recognition systems to protect the public. Some mobile devices use face recognition systems to unlock the

entered paragraph spans two pages

Nadeer and White state that fingerprint readers can perform different functions for different fingers; for example, in finger runs a program and another finger shuts down the computer (62-63).¶

page break

'Show White Space' button

Double-click to sh

device. Face recognition systems are becoming more sophisticated and can recognize people with or without glasses, hats, facial hair, makeup, or jewelry, and with new hairstyles

Figure 2–52

Other Ways

1. Tap or click FILE on ribbon, tap or click Options in Backstage view, tap or click Display in left pane (Word Options dialog box), remove or select check mark from 'Show white space between pages in Print Layout view' check box, tap or click OK button

To Edit a Source

When you typed the third paragraph of the research paper, you inserted a citation placeholder, Allensmith, for the source. You now have the source information, which is for a website, and are ready to enter it. The following steps edit the source for the Allensmith citation placeholder.

1 Tap or click somewhere in the citation placeholder to be edited, in this case (Allensmith), to select the citation placeholder.

2 Tap or click the Citation Options arrow to display the Citation Options menu.

3 Tap or click Edit Source on the Citation Options menu to display the Edit Source dialog box.

4 If necessary, tap or click the Type of Source arrow (Edit Source dialog box); scroll to and then click Web site, so that the list shows fields required for a Web site.

5 Place a check mark in the 'Show All Bibliography Fields' check box to display more fields related to Web sites.

6 Tap or click the Author text box. Type `Allensmith, Samantha Clare` as the author.

7 Tap or click the Name of Web Page text box. Type `Understanding Face Recognition Systems` as the webpage name.

8 Tap or click the Production Company text box. Type `Course Technology` as the production company.

9 Tap or click the Year Accessed text box. Type `2014` as the year accessed (Figure 2–53).

10 Press the TAB key and then type `Sept.` as the month accessed.

11 Press the TAB key and then type `16` as the day accessed.

12 Press the TAB key and then type `Web` as the Medium.

Q&A Do I need to enter a web address (URL)?
The latest MLA documentation style update does not require the web address in the source.

13 Tap or click the OK button to close the dialog box and create the source.

BTW
Q&As
For a complete list of the Q&As found in many of the step-by-step sequences in this book, visit the Q&A resource on the Student Companion Site located on www.cengagebrain.com. For detailed instructions about accessing available resources, visit www.cengage.com/ct/studentdownload or contact your instructor for information about accessing the required files.

Figure 2–53

To Enter More Text

The next task is to type the last paragraph of text in the research paper. The following steps enter this text.

1 Press the END key to position the insertion point at the end of the third paragraph and then press the ENTER key.

2 Type the last paragraph of the research paper (Figure 2–54): `Home and occupational users alike are using biometric security. Through a biometric element, such as a fingerprint, devices can deny or grant access to programs, devices, computers, rooms, and other locations. Biometric devices are an effective security technology.`

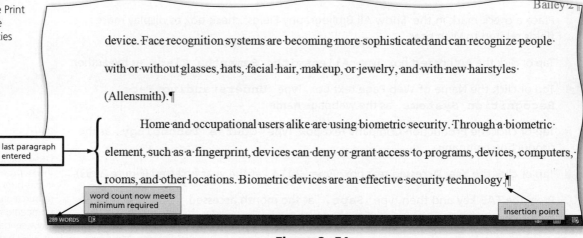

Bailey 2

device. Face recognition systems are becoming more sophisticated and can recognize people with or without glasses, hats, facial hair, makeup, or jewelry, and with new hairstyles (Allensmith).¶

Home and occupational users alike are using biometric security. Through a biometric element, such as a fingerprint, devices can deny or grant access to programs, devices, computers, rooms, and other locations. Biometric devices are an effective security technology.¶

last paragraph entered

word count now meets minimum required

insertion point

289 WORDS

Figure 2–54

To Save an Existing Document with the Same File Name

You have made several modifications to the document since you last saved it. Thus, you should save it again. The following step saves the document again.

1 Tap or click the Save button on the Quick Access Toolbar to overwrite the previously saved file.

Break Point: If you wish to take a break, this is a good place to do so. You can exit Word now (refer to page WD 46 for instructions). To resume at a later time, run Word (refer to page WD 46 for instructions), open the file called Biometric Devices Paper (refer to page WD 47 for instructions), and continue following the steps from this location forward.

Creating an Alphabetical Works Cited Page

According to the MLA documentation style, the **works cited page** is a list of sources that are referenced directly in a research paper. You place the list on a separate numbered page with the title, Works Cited, centered one inch from the top margin. The works are to be alphabetized by the author's last name or, if the work has no author, by the work's title. The first line of each entry begins at the left margin. Indent subsequent lines of the same entry one-half inch from the left margin.

What is a bibliography?

A **bibliography** is an alphabetical list of sources referenced in a paper. Whereas the text of the research paper contains brief references to the source (the citations), the bibliography lists all publication information about the source. Documentation styles differ significantly in their guidelines for preparing a bibliography. Each style identifies formats for various sources, including books, magazines, pamphlets, newspapers, websites, television programs, paintings, maps, advertisements, letters, memos, and much more. You can find information about various styles and their guidelines in printed style guides and on the web.

To Page Break Manually

1 CHANGE DOCUMENT SETTINGS | 2 CREATE HEADER | 3 TYPE RESEARCH PAPER WITH CITATIONS
4 CREATE ALPHABETICAL WORKS CITED | 5 PROOFREAD & REVISE RESEARCH PAPER

The next step is to insert a manual page break following the body of the research paper. *Why? According to the MLA documentation style, the works cited are to be displayed on a separate numbered page.*

A **manual page break**, or **hard page break**, is one that you force into the document at a specific location. Word never moves or adjusts manual page breaks. Word, however, does adjust any automatic page breaks that follow a manual page break. Word inserts manual page breaks immediately above or to the left of the location of the insertion point. The following step inserts a manual page break after the text of the research paper.

1

- Verify that the insertion point is positioned at the end of the text of the research paper, as shown in Figure 2–54.

- Tap or click INSERT on the ribbon to display the INSERT tab.

- Tap or click the 'Insert a Page Break' button (INSERT tab | Pages group) to insert a manual page break immediately to the left of the insertion point and position the insertion point immediately below the manual page break (Figure 2–55).

Figure 2–55

Other Ways

1. Press CTRL+ENTER

To Apply a Style

1 CHANGE DOCUMENT SETTINGS | 2 CREATE HEADER | 3 TYPE RESEARCH PAPER WITH CITATIONS
4 CREATE ALPHABETICAL WORKS CITED | 5 PROOFREAD & REVISE RESEARCH PAPER

The works cited title is to be centered between the margins of the paper. If you simply issue the Center command, the title will not be centered properly. *Why? It will be to the right of the center point because earlier you set the first-line indent for paragraphs to one-half inch.*

To properly center the title of the works cited page, you could drag the 'First Line Indent' marker back to the left margin before centering the paragraph, or you could apply the Normal style to the location of the insertion point. Recall that you modified the Normal style for this document to 12-point Times New Roman with double-spaced, left-aligned paragraphs that have no space after the paragraphs.

To apply a style to a paragraph, first position the insertion point in the paragraph and then apply the style. The step on the next page applies the modified Normal style to the location of the insertion point.

1

- Tap or click HOME on the ribbon to display the HOME tab.

- With the insertion point on the paragraph mark at the top of page 3 (as shown in Figure 2–55 on the previous page) even if Normal is selected, tap or click Normal in the Styles gallery (HOME tab | Styles group) to apply the Normal style to the paragraph containing the insertion point (Figure 2–56).

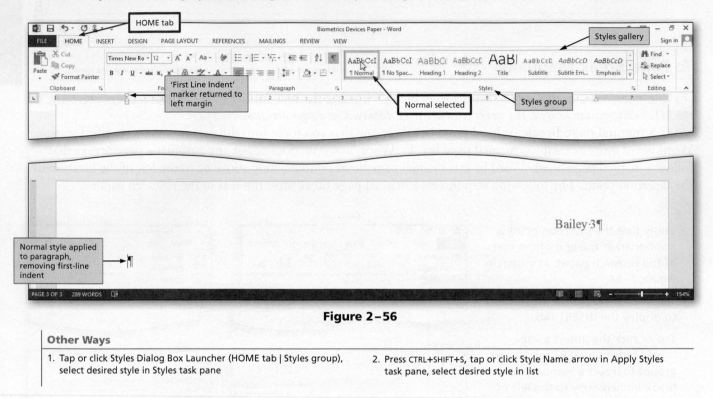

Figure 2–56

Other Ways

1. Tap or click Styles Dialog Box Launcher (HOME tab | Styles group), select desired style in Styles task pane

2. Press CTRL+SHIFT+S, tap or click Style Name arrow in Apply Styles task pane, select desired style in list

To Center Text

The next task is to enter the title, Works Cited, centered between the margins of the paper. The following steps use a keyboard shortcut to format the title.

1 Press CTRL+E to center the paragraph mark.

2 Type **Works Cited** as the title.

3 Press the ENTER key.

4 Press CTRL+L to left-align the paragraph mark (shown in Figure 2–57).

To Create a Bibliographical List

1 CHANGE DOCUMENT SETTINGS | 2 CREATE HEADER | 3 TYPE RESEARCH PAPER WITH CITATIONS
4 CREATE ALPHABETICAL WORKS CITED | 5 PROOFREAD & REVISE RESEARCH PAPER

While typing the research paper, you created several citations and their sources. The next task is to use Word to format the list of sources and alphabetize them in a **bibliographical list**. *Why? Word can create a bibliographical list with each element of the source placed in its correct position with proper punctuation, according to the specified style, saving you time looking up style guidelines. For example, in this research paper, the book source will list, in this order, the author name(s), book title, publisher city, publishing company name, and publication year with the correct punctuation between each element according to the MLA documentation style.* The next steps create an MLA-styled bibliographical list from the sources previously entered.

1

- Tap or click REFERENCES on the ribbon to display the References tab.

- With the insertion point positioned as shown in Figure 2–56, tap or click the Bibliography button (REFERENCES tab | Citations & Bibliography group) to display the Bibliography gallery (Figure 2–57).

Q&A Will I select the Works Cited option from the Bibliography gallery?
No. The title it inserts is not formatted according to the MLA documentation style. Thus, you will use the Insert Bibliography command instead.

REFERENCES tab

Biometric Devices Paper - Word

HOME INSERT DESIGN PAGE LAYOUT REFERENCES MAILINGS REVIEW VIEW

Bibliography button

Citations & Bibliography group

Bibliography gallery

Insert Bibliography command

title centered and typed

Works·Cited¶

insertion point

Figure 2–57

2

- Tap or click Insert Bibliography in the Bibliography gallery to insert a list of sources at the location of the insertion point.

- If necessary, scroll to display the entire list of sources in the document window (Figure 2–58).

Q&A What is the n.d. in the first work?
The MLA documentation style uses the abbreviation n.d. for no date (for example, no date appears on the webpage).

Hanging Indent marker

Bailey·3¶

stands for no date

Works·Cited¶

Allensmith,·Samantha·Clare.·*Understanding·Face·Recognition·Systems*.·n.d.·Course·Technology.·

Web.·16·Sept.·2014.¶

second line in paragraphs indented one-half inch from left margin, called a hanging indent

Nadeer,·Aisha·Sati·and·Jonathon·Richard·White.·*Biometric·Security*.·Chicago:·Windy·City·Press,·

2014.·Print.¶

alphabetical list of sources automatically generated by Word

Rossi,·Marcell·Enrico.·"Understanding·How·to·Use·Fingerprint·Readers."·*Digital·Security·*

Review·Aug.·2014:·n.·pag.·Web.·3·Oct.·2014.¶

Figure 2–58

To Format Paragraphs with a Hanging Indent

Notice in Figure 2–58 on the previous page that the first line of each source entry begins at the left margin, and subsequent lines in the same paragraph are indented one-half inch from the left margin. In essence, the first line hangs to the left of the rest of the paragraph; thus, this type of paragraph formatting is called a **hanging indent**. The Bibliography style in Word automatically formats the works cited paragraphs with a hanging indent.

If you wanted to format paragraphs with a hanging indent, you would use one of the following techniques.

- With the insertion point in the paragraph to format, drag the **Hanging Indent marker** (the bottom triangle) on the ruler to the desired mark on the ruler (i.e., .5") to set the hanging indent at that location from the left margin.

or

- Tap the 'Show Context Menu' button on the mini toolbar or right-click the paragraph to format, tap or click Paragraph on shortcut menu, tap or click the Indents and Spacing tab (Paragraph dialog box), tap or click the Special arrow, tap or click Hanging, and then tap or click the OK button.

or

- Tap or click the Paragraph Dialog Box Launcher (HOME tab or PAGE LAYOUT tab | Paragraph group), tap or click the Indents and Spacing tab (Paragraph dialog box), tap or click the Special arrow, tap or click Hanging, and then tap or click the OK button.

or

- With the insertion point in the paragraph to format, press CTRL+T.

To Save an Existing Document with the Same File Name

You have made several modifications to the document since you last saved it. Thus, you should save it again. The following step saves the document again. For an example of the step listed below, refer to the Office and Windows chapter at the beginning of this book.

1 Tap or click the Save button on the Quick Access Toolbar to overwrite the previously saved file.

Proofreading and Revising the Research Paper

As discussed in Chapter 1, once you complete a document, you might find it necessary to make changes to it. Before submitting a paper to be graded, you should proofread it. While **proofreading**, ensure all the source information is correct and look for grammatical errors and spelling errors. Also ensure that transitions between sentences flow smoothly and the sentences themselves make sense.

To assist you with the proofreading effort, Word provides several tools. You can go to a page, copy text, find text, replace text, insert a synonym, check spelling and grammar, and look up information. The following pages discuss these tools.

What should you consider when proofreading and revising a paper?

As you proofread the paper, look for ways to improve it. Check all grammar, spelling, and punctuation. Be sure the text is logical and transitions are smooth. Where necessary, add text, delete text, reword text, and move text to different locations. Ask yourself these questions:

- Does the title suggest the topic?
- Is the thesis clear?
- Is the purpose of the paper clear?
- Does the paper have an introduction, body, and conclusion?
- Does each paragraph in the body relate to the thesis?
- Is the conclusion effective?
- Are sources acknowledged correctly?
- Are all sources acknowledged?

To Modify a Source

1 CHANGE DOCUMENT SETTINGS | 2 CREATE HEADER | 3 TYPE RESEARCH PAPER WITH CITATIONS
4 CREATE ALPHABETICAL WORKS CITED | **5 PROOFREAD & REVISE RESEARCH PAPER**

While proofreading the paper, you notice an error in the magazine title; specifically, the first word (Understanding) should be removed. If you modify the contents of any source, the list of sources automatically updates. *Why? Word automatically updates the contents of fields, and the bibliography is a field.* The following steps delete a word from the title of the magazine article.

1

- Tap or click the Manage Sources button (REFERENCES tab | Citations & Bibliography group) to display the Source Manager dialog box.

- Tap or click the source you wish to edit in the Current List, in this case the article by Rossi, to select the source.

- Tap or click the Edit button (Source Manager dialog box) to display the Edit Source dialog box.

- In the Title text box, delete the word, Understanding, from the beginning of the title (Figure 2–59).

Figure 2–59

2

- Tap or click the OK button (Edit Source dialog box) to close the dialog box.

- If a Microsoft Word dialog box appears, tap or click its Yes button to update all occurrences of the source.

- Tap or click the Close button (Source Manager dialog box) to update the list of sources and close the dialog box.

To Update a Field

Depending on settings, the bibliography field may not automatically reflect the edited magazine title. Thus, the following steps update the bibliography field. **Why?** *Because the bibliography is a field, you may need to instruct Word to update its contents.*

1

- If you are using a touch screen, press and hold anywhere in the bibliography text and then tap the 'Show Context Menu' button on the mini toolbar; if you are using a mouse, right-click anywhere in the bibliography text to display a shortcut menu related to fields (Figure 2–60).

Q&A | Why are all the words in the bibliography shaded gray?
By default, Word shades selected fields gray.

What if the bibliography field is not shaded gray?
Tap or click FILE on the ribbon to open the Backstage view, tap or click Options in the Backstage view, tap or click Advanced in the left pane (Word Options dialog box), scroll to the 'Show document content' area, tap or click the Field shading arrow, tap or click When selected, and then tap or click the OK button.

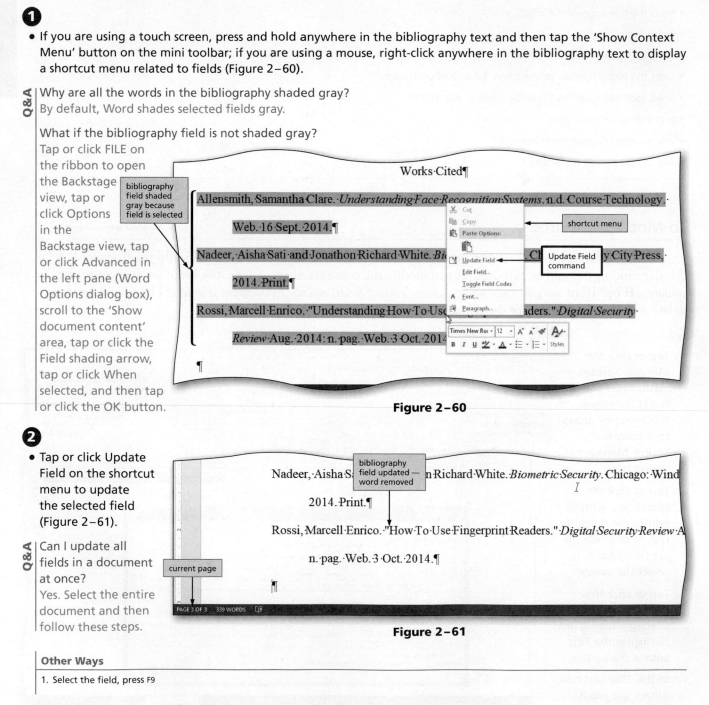

Figure 2–60

Figure 2–61

2

- Tap or click Update Field on the shortcut menu to update the selected field (Figure 2–61).

Q&A | Can I update all fields in a document at once?
Yes. Select the entire document and then follow these steps.

Other Ways

1. Select the field, press F9

TO CONVERT A FIELD TO REGULAR TEXT

If, for some reason, you wanted to convert a field, such as the bibliography field, to regular text, you would perform the following steps. Keep in mind, though, once you convert the field to regular text, it no longer is a field that can be updated.

1. Tap or click somewhere in the field to select it, in this case, somewhere in the bibliography.

2. Press CTRL+SHIFT+F9 to convert the selected field to regular text.

To Go to a Page

The next task in revising the paper is to modify text on the second page of the document. *Why? You want to copy text from one location to another on the second page.* You could scroll to the desired location in the document, or you can use the Navigation Pane to browse through pages in a document. The following steps display the top of the second page in the document window and position the insertion point at the beginning of that page.

1

- Tap or click VIEW on the ribbon to display the VIEW tab.

- Place a check mark in the 'Open the Navigation Pane' check box (VIEW tab | Show group) to open the Navigation Pane on the left side of the Word window.

- If necessary, tap or click the PAGES tab in the Navigation Pane to display thumbnails of the pages in the document.

- Scroll to and then tap or click the thumbnail of the second page to display the top of the selected page in the top of the document window (Figure 2–62).

Q&A What is the Navigation Pane?
The **Navigation Pane** is a window that enables you to browse through headings in a document, browse through pages in a document, or search for text in a document.

Figure 2–62

2

- Tap or click the Close button in the Navigation Pane to close the pane.

Other Ways

1. Tap or click Find arrow (HOME tab | Editing group), tap or click Go To on Find menu, tap or click Go To tab (Find and Replace dialog box), enter page number, tap or click Go To button

2. Tap or click Page Number indicator on status bar, tap or click PAGES tab in Navigation Pane, tap or click thumbnail of desired page (Navigation Pane)

3. Press CTRL+G, enter page number, tap or click Go To button

Copying, Cutting, and Pasting

While proofreading the research paper, you decide it would read better if the word, biometric, in the second sentence of the last paragraph also appeared in front of the word, devices, in the same sentence. You could type the word at the desired location, but because this is a difficult word to spell and type, you decide to use the Office Clipboard. The **Office Clipboard** is a temporary storage area that holds up to 24 items (text or graphics) copied from any Office program. The Office Clipboard works with the copy, cut, and paste commands:

- **Copying** is the process of placing items on the Office Clipboard, leaving the item in the document.

- **Cutting** removes the item from the document before placing it on the Office Clipboard.

- **Pasting** is the process of copying an item from the Office Clipboard into the document at the location of the insertion point.

BTW

Quick Reference
For a table that lists how to complete the tasks covered in this book using touch gestures, the mouse, ribbon, shortcut menu, and keyboard, see the Quick Reference Summary at the back of this book, or visit the Quick Reference resource on the Student Companion Site located on www.cengagebrain .com. For detailed instructions about accessing available resources, visit www.cengage.com/ct/ studentdownload or contact your instructor for information about accessing the required files.

To Copy and Paste

In the research paper, you copy a word from one location to another. *Why? The sentence reads better with the word, biometric, inserted before the word, devices.* The following steps copy and paste a word.

1

- Select the item to be copied (the word, biometric, in this case).

- Tap or click HOME on the ribbon to display the HOME tab.

- Tap or click the Copy button (HOME tab | Clipboard group) to copy the selected item in the document to the Office Clipboard (Figure 2–63).

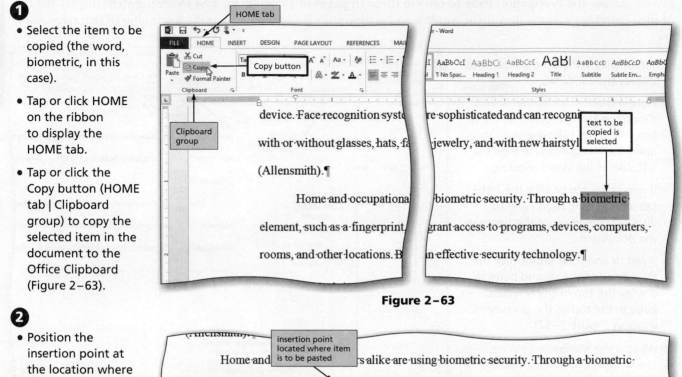

Figure 2–63

2

- Position the insertion point at the location where the item should be pasted (immediately to the left of the word, devices, in this case) (Figure 2–64).

Figure 2–64

3

- Tap or click the Paste button (HOME tab | Clipboard group) to paste the copied item in the document at the location of the insertion point (Figure 2–65).

Q&A
What if I click the Paste arrow by mistake?
Click the Paste arrow again to remove the Paste menu and repeat Step 3.

Figure 2–65

Other Ways

1. Press and hold or right-click selected item, tap Copy on mini toolbar or click Copy on shortcut menu, press and hold or right-click where item is to be pasted, tap Paste on mini toolbar or click Keep Source Formatting in Paste Options area on shortcut menu

2. Select item, press CTRL+C, position insertion point at paste location, press CTRL+V

To Display the Paste Options Menu

When you paste an item or move an item using drag-and-drop editing, which was discussed in the previous chapter, Word automatically displays a Paste Options button near the pasted or moved text (Figure 2–65). *Why? The Paste Options button allows you to change the format of a pasted item. For example, you can instruct Word to format the pasted item the same way as where it was copied (the source), or format it the same way as where it is being pasted (the destination).* The following steps display the Paste Options menu.

1

- Tap or click the Paste Options button to display the Paste Options menu (Figure 2–66).

Q&A What are the functions of the buttons on the Paste Options menu?
In general, the left button indicates the pasted item should look the same as it did in its original location (the source). The second button formats the pasted text to match the rest of the item where it was pasted (the destination). The third button removes all formatting from the pasted item. The Set Default Paste command displays the Word Options dialog box. Keep in mind that the buttons shown on a Paste Options menu will vary, depending on the item being pasted.

Figure 2–66

2

- Tap or click anywhere to remove the Paste Options menu from the window.

Other Ways

1. CTRL (to remove the Paste Options menu)

To Find Text

While proofreading the paper, you would like to locate all occurrences of the word, element. *Why? You are contemplating changing occurrences of this word to the word, identifier.* The following steps find all occurrences of specific text in a document.

1

- If you are using a touch screen, tap the Find button (HOME tab | Editing group) and then tap Find on the menu; if you are using a mouse, click the Find button (HOME tab | Editing group) to display the Navigation Pane.

- If necessary, tap or click the RESULTS tab in the Navigation Pane, which displays a Search box where you can type text for which you want to search (Figure 2–67).

Figure 2–67

2

- Type **element** in the Navigation Pane Search box to display all occurrences of the typed text, called the search text, in the Navigation Pane and to highlight the occurrences of the search text in the document window (Figure 2–68).

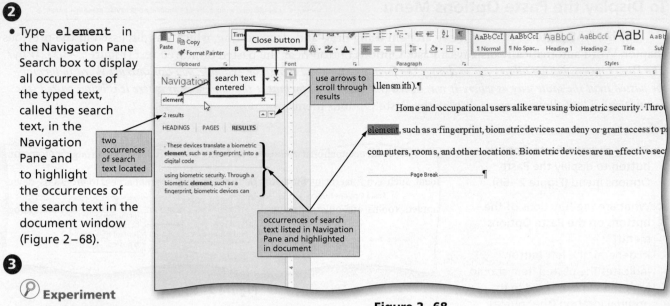

Figure 2–68

3

Experiment

- Tap or click both occurrences in the Navigation Pane and watch Word display the associated text in the document window.

- Type various search text in the Navigation Pane Search box, and watch Word both list matches in the Navigation Pane and highlight matches in the document window.

- Tap or click the Close button in the Navigation Pane to close the pane.

Other Ways
1. Tap or click Find arrow (HOME tab | Editing group), tap or click Find on Find menu, enter search text in Navigation Pane   2. Tap or click Page Number indicator on status bar, enter search text in Navigation Pane   3. Press CTRL+F, enter search text in Navigation Pane

To Replace Text

1 CHANGE DOCUMENT SETTINGS | 2 CREATE HEADER | 3 TYPE RESEARCH PAPER WITH CITATIONS
4 CREATE ALPHABETICAL WORKS CITED | **5 PROOFREAD & REVISE RESEARCH PAPER**

You decide to change all occurrences of element to identifier. **Why?** *The text, biometric identifier, is a better description than biometric element.* Word's find and replace feature locates each occurrence of a word or phrase and then replaces it with text you specify. The following steps find and replace text.

1

- Tap or click the Replace button (HOME tab | Editing group) to display the Replace sheet in the Find and Replace dialog box.

- If necessary, type **element** in the Find what box (Find and Replace dialog box).

- Type **identifier** in the Replace with box (Figure 2–69).

Figure 2–69

2

- Tap or click the Replace All button to instruct Word to replace all occurrences of the Find what text with the Replace with text (Figure 2–70). If Word displays a dialog box asking if you want to continue searching from the beginning of the document, tap or click the Yes button.

Q&A

Does Word search the entire document?

If the insertion point is at the beginning of the document, Word searches the entire document; otherwise, Word searches from the location of the insertion point to the end of the document and then displays a dialog box asking if you want to continue searching from the beginning. You also can search a section of text by selecting the text before tapping or clicking the Replace button.

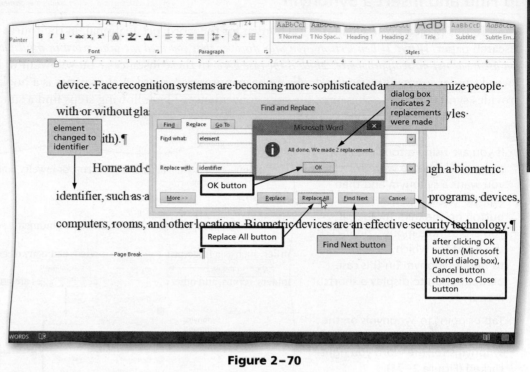

Figure 2–70

3

- Tap or click the OK button (Microsoft Word dialog box) to close the dialog box.
- Tap or click the Close button (Find and Replace dialog box) to close the dialog box.

Other Ways

1. Press CTRL+H

Find and Replace Dialog Box

The Replace All button (Find and Replace dialog box) replaces all occurrences of the Find what text with the Replace with text. In some cases, you may want to replace only certain occurrences of a word or phrase, not all of them. To instruct Word to confirm each change, tap or click the Find Next button (Find and Replace dialog box) (Figure 2–70), instead of the Replace All button. When Word locates an occurrence of the text, it pauses and waits for you to tap or click either the Replace button or the Find Next button. Tapping or clicking the Replace button changes the text; tapping or clicking the Find Next button instructs Word to disregard the replacement and look for the next occurrence of the Find what text.

If you accidentally replace the wrong text, you can undo a replacement by tapping or clicking the Undo button on the Quick Access Toolbar. If you used the Replace All button, Word undoes all replacements. If you used the Replace button, Word undoes only the most recent replacement.

BTW

Finding Formatting
To search for formatting or a special character, tap or click the More button in the Find and Replace dialog box (shown in Figure 2–69). To find formatting, use the Format button in the Find dialog box. To find a special character, use the Special button.

To Find and Insert a Synonym

In this project, you would like a synonym for the word, occupational, in the fourth paragraph of the research paper. *Why? When writing, you may discover that you used the same word in multiple locations or that a word you used was not quite appropriate, which is the case here.* In these instances, you will want to look up a **synonym**, or a word similar in meaning, to the duplicate or inappropriate word. A **thesaurus** is a book of synonyms. Word provides synonyms and a thesaurus for your convenience. The following steps find a suitable synonym.

- If you are using a touch screen, press and hold the word for which you want a synonym and then tap the 'Show Context Menu' button on the mini toolbar; if you are using a mouse, right-click the word for which you want to find a synonym (in this case, occupational) to display a shortcut menu.

- Tap or point to Synonyms on the shortcut menu to display a list of synonyms for the word you right-clicked (Figure 2–71).

Figure 2–71

- Tap or click the synonym you want (in this case, business) on the Synonyms submenu to replace the selected word in the document with the selected synonym (Figure 2–72).

Q&A

What if the synonyms list on the shortcut menu does not display a suitable word?

You can display the thesaurus in the Thesaurus task pane by tapping or clicking Thesaurus on the Synonyms submenu. The Thesaurus task pane displays a complete thesaurus, in which you can look up synonyms for various meanings of a word. You also can look up an **antonym,** or word with an opposite meaning.

Figure 2–72

Other Ways

1. Click Thesaurus button (REVIEW tab | Proofing group)   2. Press SHIFT+F7

To Check Spelling and Grammar at Once

As discussed in Chapter 1, Word checks spelling and grammar as you type and places a wavy underline below possible spelling or grammar errors. Chapter 1 illustrated how to check these flagged words immediately. The next steps check spelling and grammar at once. *Why? Some users prefer to wait and check their entire document for spelling and grammar errors at once.*

Note: In the following steps, the word, readers, has been misspelled intentionally as raders to illustrate the use of Word's check spelling and grammar at once feature. If you are completing this project on a personal computer, your research paper may contain different misspelled words, depending on the accuracy of your typing.

1

- Press CTRL+HOME because you want the spelling and grammar check to begin from the top of the document.

- Tap or click REVIEW on the ribbon to display the REVIEW tab.

- Tap or click the Spelling & Grammar button (REVIEW tab | Proofing group) to begin the spelling and grammar check at the location of the insertion point, which, in this case, is at the beginning of the document.

- Tap or click the desired word in the list of suggestions in the Spelling pane (readers, in this case) (Figure 2–73).

Figure 2–73

2

- With the word, reader, selected in the list of suggestions, tap or click the Change button (Spelling task pane) to change the flagged word to the selected suggestion and then continue the spelling and grammar check until the next error is identified or the end of the document is reached (Figure 2–74).

3

- Because the flagged word is a proper noun and spelled correctly, tap or click the Ignore All button (Spelling task pane) to ignore this and future occurrences of the flagged proper noun and then continue the spelling and grammar check until the next error is identified or the end of the document is reached.

Figure 2–74

4

- When the spelling and grammar check is finished and Word displays a dialog box, tap or click its OK button.

Q&A | Can I check spelling of just a section of a document?
Yes, select the text before starting the spelling and grammar check.

Other Ways

1. Tap or click 'Spelling and Grammar Check' icon on status bar   2. Press F7

The Main and Custom Dictionaries

As shown in the previous steps, Word may flag a proper noun as an error because the proper noun is not in its main dictionary. To prevent Word from flagging proper nouns as errors, you can add the proper nouns to the custom dictionary. To add a correctly spelled word to the custom dictionary, tap or click the Add button (Spelling task pane) or press and hold and then tap 'Show Context Menu' button on mini toolbar or right-click the flagged word and then tap or click Add to Dictionary on the shortcut menu. Once you have added a word to the custom dictionary, Word no longer will flag it as an error.

TO VIEW OR MODIFY ENTRIES IN A CUSTOM DICTIONARY

To view or modify the list of words in a custom dictionary, you would follow these steps.

1. Tap or click FILE on the ribbon and then tap or click Options in the Backstage view.
2. Tap or click Proofing in the left pane (Word Options dialog box).
3. Tap or click the Custom Dictionaries button.
4. When Word displays the Custom Dictionaries dialog box, place a check mark next to the dictionary name to view or modify. Tap or click the 'Edit Word List' button (Custom Dictionaries dialog box). (In this dialog box, you can add or delete entries to and from the selected custom dictionary.)
5. When finished viewing and/or modifying the list, tap or click the OK button in the dialog box.
6. Tap or click the OK button (Custom Dictionaries dialog box).
7. If the 'Suggest from main dictionary only' check box is selected in the Word Options dialog box, remove the check mark. Tap or click the OK button (Word Options dialog box).

TO SET THE DEFAULT CUSTOM DICTIONARY

If you have multiple custom dictionaries, you can specify which one Word should use when checking spelling. To set the default custom dictionary, you would follow these steps.

1. Tap or click FILE on the ribbon and then tap or click Options in the Backstage view.
2. Tap or click Proofing in the left pane (Word Options dialog box).
3. Tap or click the Custom Dictionaries button.
4. When the Custom Dictionaries dialog box is displayed, place a check mark next to the desired dictionary name. Tap or click the Change Default button (Custom Dictionaries dialog box).
5. Tap or click the OK button (Custom Dictionaries dialog box).
6. If the 'Suggest from main dictionary only' check box is selected in the Word Options dialog box, remove the check mark. Tap or click the OK button (Word Options dialog box).

To Look Up Information

If you are signed in to your Microsoft account, you can look up a definition by tapping or clicking the Define button (REVIEW tab | Proofing group). If you are not signed in to your Microsoft account but are connected to the Internet, you can use the Research task pane to search through various forms of reference information on the web. The following steps use the Research task pane to look up a definition of a word. *Why?* *Assume you want to know more about the word, legitimate, but are not signed in to your Microsoft account.*

1

• While holding down the ALT key, tap or click the word you want to look up (in this case, legitimate) to open the Research task pane and display a dictionary entry for the ALT+clicked word (Figure 2–75). Release the ALT key.

Q&A Why does my Research task pane look different?
Depending on your settings and Microsoft's website search settings, your Research task pane may appear different from the figures shown here.

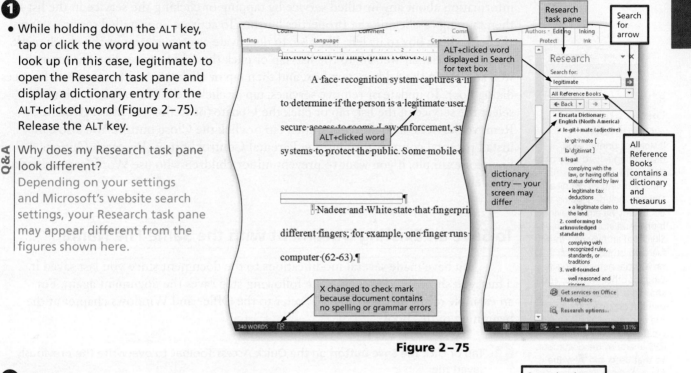

Figure 2–75

2

• Tap or click the Source arrow in the Research task pane to display a list of search locations and then tap or click 'All Research Sites' in the list (Figure 2–76).

Q&A Can I copy information from the Research task pane into my document?
Yes, you can use the Copy and Paste commands. When using Word to insert material from the Research task pane or any other online reference, however, be careful not to plagiarize.

3

• Tap or click the Close button in the Research task pane.

Figure 2–76

Other Ways

1. Press ALT+SHIFT+F7

Research Task Pane Options

When you install Word, it selects a series of services (reference books and websites) that it searches through when you use the Research task pane. You can view, modify, and update the list of services at any time.

Tapping or clicking the Research options link at the bottom of the Research task pane (shown in Figure 2–76 on the previous page) displays the Research Options dialog box, where you can view or modify the list of installed services. You can view information about any installed service by tapping or clicking the service in the list and then tapping or clicking the Properties button. To activate an installed service, tap or click the check box to its left; likewise, to deactivate a service, remove the check mark. To add a particular website to the list, tap or click the Add Services button, enter the web address in the Address text box, and then tap or click the Add button (Add Services dialog box). To update or remove services, tap or click the Update/Remove button, select the service in the list, tap or click the Update (or Remove) button (Update or Remove Services dialog box), and then tap or click the Close button. You also can install parental controls through the Parental Control button (Research Options dialog box), for example, if you want to prevent minor children who use Word from accessing the web.

To Save an Existing Document with the Same File Name

You have made several modifications to the document since you last saved it. Thus, you should save it again. The following step saves the document again. For an example of the step listed below, refer to the Office and Windows chapter at the beginning of this book.

 Tap or click the Save button on the Quick Access Toolbar to overwrite the previously saved file.

To Zoom Multiple Pages

1 CHANGE DOCUMENT SETTINGS | 2 CREATE HEADER | 3 TYPE RESEARCH PAPER WITH CITATIONS
4 CREATE ALPHABETICAL WORKS CITED | **5 PROOFREAD & REVISE RESEARCH PAPER**

The next steps display multiple pages in the document window at once. *Why? You want be able to see all pages in the research paper on the screen at the same time. You also hide formatting marks and the rulers so that the display is easier to view.*

- Tap or click HOME on the ribbon to display the HOME tab.
- If the 'Show/Hide ¶' button (HOME tab | Paragraph group) is selected, tap or click it to hide formatting marks.
- Tap or click VIEW on the ribbon to display the VIEW tab.
- If the rulers are displayed, tap or click the View Ruler check box (VIEW tab | Show group) to remove the check mark from the check box and remove the horizontal and vertical rulers from the screen.
- Tap or click the Multiple Pages button (VIEW tab | Zoom group) to display the all three pages at once in the document window (Figure 2–77).

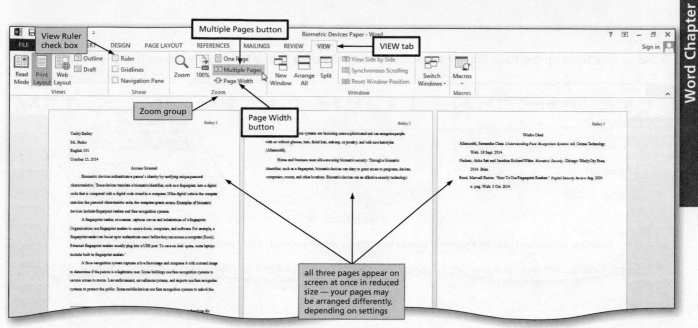

Figure 2–77

2

- When finished, tap or click the Page Width button (VIEW tab | Zoom group) to return to the page width zoom.

To Change Read Mode Color

1 CHANGE DOCUMENT SETTINGS | 2 CREATE HEADER | 3 TYPE RESEARCH PAPER WITH CITATIONS
4 CREATE ALPHABETICAL WORKS CITED | 5 PROOFREAD & REVISE RESEARCH PAPER

You would like to read the entire research paper using Read mode but would like to change the background color of the Read mode screen. *Why? You prefer a background that is easier on your eyes when reading on the screen.* The following steps change the color of the screen in Read mode.

1

- Tap or click the Read Mode button on the status bar to switch to Read mode.
- Tap or click the VIEW tab to display the VIEW menu.
- Tap or point to Page Color on the VIEW menu to display the Page Color menu (Figure 2–78).

Figure 2–78

2

- Tap or click Sepia on the Page Color submenu to change the color of the Read mode screen to sepia (Figure 2–79).

FILE   TOOLS   VIEW   Biometric Devices Paper - Word

Teddy Bailey

Ms. Pedro

English 101

October 15, 2014

> Read mode page color changed to sepia

Access Granted

Biometric devices authenticate a person's identity by verifying unique personal characteristics. These devices translate a bio-

metric identifier, such as a fingerprint, into a digital code that is compared with a digital code stored in a computer. If the digital code

Figure 2–79

3

- When finished, tap or click the Print Layout button (shown in Figure 2–78 on the previous page) on the status bar to return to Print Layout view.

To Print a Document

If you want a hard copy of the research paper, perform the following steps.

1 Tap or click FILE on the ribbon to open the Backstage view.

2 Tap or click the Print tab in the Backstage view to display the Print gallery.

3 Verify that the printer listed on the Printer Status button will print a hard copy of the document. If necessary, tap or click the Printer Status button to display a list of available printer options and then tap or click the desired printer to change the currently selected printer.

4 Tap or click the Print button in the Print gallery to print the document on the currently selected printer.

5 When the printer stops, retrieve the hard copy (shown in Figure 2–1 on page WD 67).

To Exit Word

This project now is complete. The following steps exit Word. For a detailed example of the procedure summarized below, refer to the Office and Windows chapter at the beginning of this book.

1a If you have one Word document open, tap or click the Close button on the right side of the title bar to close the open document and exit Word.

1b If you have multiple Word documents open, press and hold or right-click the Word app button on the taskbar and then tap or click 'Close all windows' on the shortcut menu to close all open documents and exit Word.

2 If a Microsoft Word dialog box appears, tap or click the Save button to save any changes made to the document since the last save.

Chapter Summary

In this chapter, you have learned how to change document settings, use headers to number pages, modify a style, insert and edit citations and their sources, add footnotes, create a bibliographical list of sources, and use proofreading tools. The items listed below include all the new Word skills you have learned in this chapter, with the tasks grouped by activity.

Enter and Edit Text
AutoCorrect as You Type (WD 84)
Use the AutoCorrect Options Button (WD 85)
Create an AutoCorrect Entry (WD 85)
Count Words (WD 100)
Update a Field (WD 110)
Copy and Paste (WD 112)
Find Text (WD 113)
Replace Text (WD 114)
Find and Insert a Synonym (WD 115)
Check Spelling and Grammar at Once (WD 116)
View or Modify Entries in a Custom Dictionary (WD 118)
Set the Default Custom Dictionary (WD 118)

Format a Page
Switch to the Header (WD 74)
Insert a Page Number (WD 76)
Close the Header (WD 77)
Page Break Manually (WD 105)

Format Text
Modify a Style (WD 70)
Change Line Spacing (WD 72)
Remove Space after a Paragraph (WD 73)
Update a Style to Match a Selection (WD 73)

Right-Align a Paragraph (WD 75)
Click and Type (WD 79)
First-Line Indent Paragraphs (WD 82)
Modify a Style Using a Shortcut Menu (WD 94)
Apply a Style (WD 105)
Format Paragraphs with a Hanging Indent (WD 108)
Convert a Field to Regular Text (WD 110)
Display the Paste Options Menu (WD 113)

Word Settings
Display the Rulers (WD 82)
Hide and Show White Space (WD 102)
Go to a Page (WD 111)
Look Up Information (WD 119)
Zoom Multiple Pages (WD 120)
Change Read Mode Color (WD 121)

Work with Citations, Sources, and Footnotes
Change the Bibliography Style (WD 89)
Insert a Citation and Create Its Source (WD 89)
Insert a Footnote Reference Mark (WD 92)
Insert a Citation Placeholder (WD 93)
Edit a Source (WD 96)
Edit a Citation (WD 98)
Create a Bibliographical List (WD 106)
Modify a Source (WD 109)

What decisions will you need to make when creating your next research paper?
Use these guidelines as you complete the assignments in this chapter and create your own research papers outside of this class.

1. Select a topic.

    a) Spend time brainstorming ideas for a topic.

    b) Choose a topic you find interesting.

    c) For shorter papers, narrow the scope of the topic; for longer papers, broaden the scope.

    d) Identify a tentative thesis statement, which is a sentence describing the paper's subject matter.

2. Research the topic and take notes, being careful not to plagiarize.

3. Organize your notes into related concepts, identifying all main ideas and supporting details in an outline.

4. Write the first draft from the outline, referencing all sources of information and following the guidelines identified in the required documentation style.

5. Create the list of sources, using the formats specified in the required documentation style.

6. Proofread and revise the paper.

CONSIDER THIS: PLAN AHEAD

How should you submit solutions to questions in the assignments identified with a ✳ symbol?
Every assignment in this book contains one or more questions identified with a ✳ symbol. These questions require you to think beyond the assigned document. Present your solutions to the questions in the format required by your instructor. Possible formats may include one or more of these options: write the answer; create a document that contains the answer; present your answer to the class; discuss your answer in a group; record the answer as audio or video using a webcam, smartphone, or portable media player; or post answers on a blog, wiki, or website.

Apply Your Knowledge

Reinforce the skills and apply the concepts you learned in this chapter.

Revising Text and Paragraphs in a Document

Note: To complete this assignment, you will be required to use the Data Files for Students. Visit www.cengage.com/ct/studentdownload for detailed instructions or contact your instructor for information about accessing the required files.

Instructions: Run Word. Open the document, Apply 2 - 1 Virtual Reality Paragraph Draft, from the Data Files for Students. The document you open contains a paragraph of text. You are to revise the document as follows: move a word, move another word and change the format of the moved word, change paragraph indentation, change line spacing, find all occurrences of a word, replace all occurrences of a word with another word, locate a synonym, and edit the header.

Perform the following tasks:
1. Copy the text, VR, from the first sentence and paste it in the last sentence after the underlined word, potential.

2. Select the underlined word, potential, in the paragraph. If you are using a mouse, use drag-and-drop editing to move the selected word, potential, so that it is before the word, buyers, in the same sentence. If you are using a touch screen, use the cut and paste commands to move the word. Tap or click the Paste Options button that displays to the right of the moved word, potential. Remove the underline format from the moved sentence by tapping or clicking 'Keep Text Only' on the Paste Options menu.

3. Display the ruler, if necessary. If you are using a mouse, use the ruler to indent the first line of the paragraph one-half inch; otherwise, use the Paragraph dialog box.

4. Change the line spacing of the paragraph to double.

5. Use the Navigation Pane to find all occurrences of the word, VR. How many are there?

6. Use the Find and Replace dialog box to replace all occurrences of the word, 3D, with the word, 3-D. How many replacements were made?

7. Use the Navigation Pane to find the word, endless. Use Word's thesaurus to change the word, endless, to the word, infinite. What other words are in the list of synonyms?

8. Switch to the header so that you can edit it. In the first line of the header, change the word, Draft, to the word, Modified, so that it reads: VR Paragraph Modified.

9. In the second line of the header, insert the page number (with no formatting) one space after the word, Page.

10. Change the alignment of both lines of text in the header from left-aligned to right-aligned. Switch back to the document text.

11. If requested by your instructor, enter your first and last name on a separate line below the page number in the header.

12. Tap or click FILE on the ribbon and then tap or click Save As. Save the document using the file name, Apply 2 - 1 Virtual Reality Paragraph Modified.

13. Submit the modified document, shown in Figure 2–80, in the format specified by your instructor.

14. Use the Research task pane to look up the definition of the word, simulate, in the paragraph. Which dictionary was used? If you have a Microsoft account and are signed into it, use the Define button (REVIEW tab | Proofing group) to look up a definition of the word.

15. Change the search location to All Research Sites. Submit an article from one of the sites.

16. Display the Research Options dialog box. How many currently active Reference Books and Research Sites are in the list? If your instructor approves, activate one of the services.

17. ❀ Answer the questions posed in #5, #6, #7, #14, and #16. How would you find and replace a special character, such as a paragraph mark?

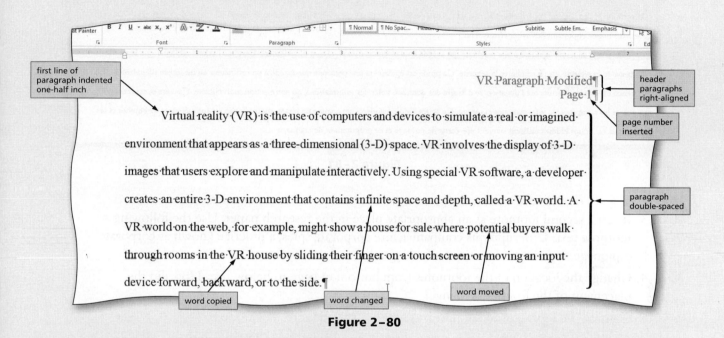

Figure 2–80

Extend Your Knowledge

Extend the skills you learned in this chapter and experiment with new skills. You may need to use Help to complete the assignment.

Working with References and Proofing Tools

Note: To complete this assignment, you will be required to use the Data Files for Students. Visit www.cengage.com/ct/studentdownload for detailed instructions or contact your instructor for information about accessing the required files.

Instructions: Run Word. Open the document, Extend 2-1 Cybercrime Paper Draft, from the Data Files for Students. You will add another footnote to the paper, convert the footnotes to endnotes, modify the Endnote Text style, change the format of the note reference marks, use Word's readability statistics, translate the document to another language (Figure 2–81 on the next page), and convert the document from MLA to APA documentation style.

Perform the following tasks:

1. Use Help to learn more about footers, footnotes and endnotes, readability statistics, bibliography styles, AutoCorrect, and the Mini Translator.

2. Delete the footer from the document.

Continued >

Extend Your Knowledge *continued*

© Microsoft	Translator Privacy	Logo		Microsoft®	Translator
Translator Help			Powered by

Translate URL http://

English ▼ ⇒ French ▼ → Views

Translated 100%   Mouse over text to see original

Mme Humphries

106 Français

> research paper translated
> from English to French

30 Octobre 2014

Le monde de la cybercriminalité

    Une infraction prévue à la sécurité numérique implique souvent un acte délibéré qui est contraire à la Loi.La cybercriminalité [A] fait

référence à en ligne ou illégal sur Internet des actes tels que la distribution de logiciels malveillants ou d'avoir commis le vol d'identité. Auteurs de la

cybercriminalité en général appartiennent à l'une de ces catégories : hacker, pirate, script kiddie, espionne, employé contraires à l'éthique,

cyberextortionist et potentielles cyberterroriste ont.

    Le pirate de terme se réfère à une personne qui accède à un ordinateur ou un réseau illégalement. Certains hackers réclamer que leurs

violations de la sécurité vise à améliorer la sécurité. Un pirate est également une personne qui accède à un ordinateur ou un réseau illégalement. La

différence est que les biscuits ont l'intention de détruire des données, voler des informations, ou autre action malveillante. Hackers et crackers ont fait

progresser les compétences informatiques et réseau. Un script kiddie est identique comme un pirate, mais n'a pas les compétences techniques et les

connaissances. Script kiddies utilisent souvent pré-écrite de piratage et de programmes de craquage.

Figure 2–81

3. Insert a second footnote at an appropriate place in the research paper. Use the following footnote text: Unscrupulous companies hire corporate spies, a practice known as corporate espionage, to gain a competitive advantage.

4. Change the location of the footnotes from bottom of page to below text. How did the placement of the footnotes change?

5. Convert the footnotes to endnotes. Where are the endnotes positioned?

6. Modify the Endnote Text style to 12-point Times New Roman font, double-spaced text with a hanging-line indent.

7. Change the format of the note reference marks to capital letters (A, B, etc.).

8. Add an AutoCorrect entry that replaces the word, perpetraters, with the word, perpetrators. Add this sentence as the last sentence in the paper, misspelling the word perpetrators to test the AutoCorrect entry: These perpetraters present a growing threat to society. Delete the AutoCorrect entry that replaces perpetraters with the word, perpetrators.

9. Display the Word Count dialog box. How many words, characters without spaces, characters with spaces, paragraphs, and lines are in the document? Be sure to include footnote and endnote text in the statistics.

10. Check spelling of the document, displaying readability statistics. What are the Flesch-Kincaid Grade Level, the Flesch Reading Ease score, and the percent of passive sentences? Modify the paper to lower the grade level, increase the reading ease score, and lower the percent of passive sentences. How did you modify the paper? What are the new statistics?

11. If requested by your instructor, change the student name at the top of the paper to your name, including the last name in the header.

12. Save the revised document with the file name, Extend 2-1 Cybercrime Paper Modified, and then submit it in the format specified by your instructor.

13. If you have an Internet connection, translate the research paper into a language of your choice using the Translate button (REVIEW tab | Language group). Submit the translated document in the format specified by your instructor. Use the Mini Translator to hear how to pronounce three words in your paper.

14. Select the entire document and then change the documentation style from MLA to APA. Save the APA version of the document with a new file name. Compare the APA version to the MLA version. If you have a hard copy of each and your instructor requests it, circle the differences between the two documents.

15. ✳ Answer the questions posed in #4, #5, #9, and #10. Where did you insert the second footnote and why?

Analyze, Correct, Improve

Analyze a document, correct all errors, and improve it.

Inserting Missing Elements in an MLA-Styled Research Paper

Note: To complete this assignment, you will be required to use the Data Files for Students. Visit www.cengage.com/ct/studentdownload for detailed instructions or contact your instructor for information about accessing the required files.

Instructions: Run Word. Open the document, Analyze 2 - 1 Internet Filters Paper Draft, from the Data Files for Students. The document is a research paper that is missing several elements. You are to insert these missing elements, all formatted according to the MLA documentation style: header with a page number, name and course information, paper title, footnote, and source information for a citation.

1. Correct In the research paper, correct the following items:

(a) Insert a header with a your own last name and page number and then type the course information (your name, your instructor's name, your course name, and today's date), and an appropriate paper title, all formatted according to the MLA documentation style.

(b) The Clark citation placeholder is missing its source information (shown in Figure 2–82 on the next page). Use the following information to edit the source: book titled *Internet Protection*, written by Addison Lee Clark, publication year is 2014, publication city is New York, publisher is Journey Press, medium is Print. Edit the citation so that it displays the author name and the page numbers of 35–37 for this reference.

(c) Modify the website author name to include his middle name: Robert Timothy Lane. Also, change the medium in this same source from Print to Web.

(d) Use the Navigation Pane to display page 2. Insert a page break before the Works Cited heading. Use Word to insert the bibliographical list (bibliography) below the Works Cited heading.

2. Improve Enhance the paper by inserting a footnote with the note reference at an appropriate place in the paper, formatted according to the MLA documentation style, that gives a statistic about spam. (You will need to do research to obtain this statistic.) Change the Footnote Text style to 12-point Times New Roman, double-spaced paragraphs with a first-line indent. Add a citation and source for your new footnote. Be sure to update the works cited page after you add the citation and source. Save the modified document with the file name, Analyze 2 - 1 Internet Filters Paper Modified, and then submit it in the format specified by your instructor.

3. ✳ In this assignment you inserted a statistic from a web source. Why did you select that website?

Continued >

Analyze, Correct, Improve *continued*

Figure 2–82

In the Labs

Design and/or create a document using the guidelines, concepts, and skills presented in this chapter. Labs 1 and 2, which increase in difficulty, require you to create solutions based on what you learned in the chapter; Lab 3 requires you to create a solution, which uses cloud and web technologies, by learning and investigating on your own from general guidance.

Lab 1: Preparing a Short Research Paper

Problem: You are a college student currently enrolled in an introductory English class. Your assignment is to prepare a short research paper (350–450 words) in any area of interest to you. The requirements are that the paper be presented according to the MLA documentation style and have three references. At least one of the three references must be from the web. You prepare the paper shown in Figure 2–83, which discusses health risks associated with technology.

Instructions: Perform the following tasks:

1. Run Word. If necessary, display formatting marks on the screen.

2. Modify the Normal style to the 12-point Times New Roman font.

3. Adjust line spacing to double.

4. Remove space below (after) paragraphs.

5. Update the Normal style to reflect the adjusted line and paragraph spacing.

6. Create a header to number pages.

7. Type the name and course information at the left margin. If requested by your instructor, use your name and course information instead of the information shown in Figure 2–83a. Center and type the title.

8. Set a first-line indent to one-half inch for paragraphs in the body of the research paper.

Delhi 1

Rajesh Delhi

Ms. June

English 102

November 9, 2014

Health Risks Associated with Technology

The widespread use of technology has led to some important user health concerns. Some of the more common physical health risks are repetitive strain injuries, computer vision syndrome, and muscular pain. These injuries are on the rise for users of technology.

A repetitive strain injury (RSI) is an injury or disorder of the muscles, nerves, tendons, ligaments, and joints. Technology-related RSIs include tendonitis and carpal tunnel syndrome (CTS). Tendonitis is inflammation of a tendon due to repeated motion or stress on that tendon. CTS is inflammation of the nerve that connects the forearm to the palm. Repeated or forceful bending of the wrist can cause tendonitis or CTS of the wrist. Factors that cause these disorders include prolonged typing or mouse usage and continual shifting between a mouse and keyboard (Jones 45-48). If untreated, these disorders can lead to permanent physical damage.

Computer vision syndrome (CVS) affects eyesight. Symptoms of CVS are sore, tired, burning, itching, or dry eyes; blurred or double vision; distance blurred vision after prolonged staring at a display device; headache or sore neck; difficulty shifting focus between a display device and documents; difficulty focusing on a screen image; color fringes or afterimages when looking away from a display device; and increased sensitivity to light. Eyestrain associated with CVS is not thought to have serious or long-term consequences (Anderson and Dean).

People who spend their workday using the computer sometimes complain of lower back pain, muscle fatigue, and emotional fatigue. Lower back pain sometimes is caused from poor

(a) Page 1

Figure 2–83

Continued >

In the Labs *continued*

Delhi 2

posture. It is advisable to sit properly in a chair while working and take periodic breaks. Users

also should be sure their workplace is designed ergonomically. Ergonomic studies have shown

that using the correct type and configuration of chair, keyboard, display device, and work surface

helps users work comfortably and efficiently and helps protect their health (Sanchez).

Many physical health risks are associated with using technology. These risks include

repetitive strain injuries, computer vision syndrome, and muscular pain. Users should take as

many preventive measures as possible to avoid these risks.

(b) Page 2
Figure 2–83 (Continued)

9. Type the research paper as shown in Figures 2–83a and 2–83b. Change the bibliography style to MLA. As you insert citations, enter their source information (shown in Figure 2–83c). Edit the citations so that they are displayed according to Figures 2–83a and 2–83b.

10. At the end of the research paper text, press the ENTER key and then insert a manual page break so that the Works Cited page begins on a new page. Enter and format the works cited title (Figure 2–83c). Use Word to insert the bibliographical list (bibliography).

11. Check the spelling and grammar of the paper at once.

12. Save the document using Lab 2-1 Technology Health Risks Paper as the file name. Submit the document, shown in Figure 2–83, in the format specified by your instructor.

13. ✷ Read the paper in Print Layout view. Switch to Read mode and scroll through the pages. Do you prefer reading in Print Layout view or Read mode. Why? In Read mode, which of the page colors do you like best and why?

Delhi 3

Works Cited

Anderson, Cricket Finley and Stacey Anne Dean. "Computer Pains." *The Medical Update* Aug.

2014: n. pag. Web. 2 October 2014.

Jones, Jacob Lee. *Medical Concerns of the 21st Century*. Chicago: Smiley Incorporated, 2014.

Print.

Sanchez, Jorge Mario. *Aches and Pains*. 30 Sept. 2014. Course Technology. Web. 5 Aug. 2014.

(c) Page 3
Figure 2–83 (Continued)

Lab 2: Preparing a Research Report with a Footnote

Problem: You are a college student enrolled in an introductory technology class. Your assignment is to prepare a short research paper (350–450 words) in any area of interest to you. The requirements are that the paper be presented according to the MLA documentation style, contain at least one note positioned as a footnote, and have three references. At least one ne of the three references must be from the Internet. You prepare a paper about protecting mobile devices (Figure 2–84).

Instructions: Perform the following tasks:
1. Run Word. Modify the Normal style to the 12-point Times New Roman font. Adjust line spacing to double and remove space below (after) paragraphs. Update the Normal style to include the adjusted line and paragraph spacing. Create a header to number pages. Type the name and course information at the left margin. If requested by your instructor, use your name and course information instead of the information shown in Figure 2–84a on the next page. Center and type the title. Set a first-line indent for paragraphs in the body of the research paper.   *Continued >*

In the Labs *continued*

Tanner 1

Camryn Tanner

Dr. Bai

Technology 101

October 16, 2014

Mobile Device Protection

The consequences of losing a smartphone or other mobile device are significant because these devices store personal and business data. The goal, therefore, for mobile device users is to make their data as secure as possible. Techniques include avoiding unsafe links, using caution when downloading apps, turning off GPS tracking, and installing mobile security software.

A high percentage of users follow unknown links, which can lead to a malicious website. Malicious links can inject malware on a mobile device. The malware may steal personal information or create toll fraud, which secretly contacts wireless messaging services that impose steep fees on a monthly bill (Bao). Users should avoid tapping or clicking unknown links.

Any device that connects to the Internet is susceptible to mobile malware.[1] Popular games are likely candidates to house malware, and it often is difficult to distinguish the legitimate apps from the fake apps. Users should check the reliability of the seller, the descriptions and reviews of the app, and the requested permissions before downloading.

GPS technology can track the mobile device's location as long as it is transmitting and receiving signals to and from satellites. Although this feature may be helpful, serious privacy concerns can arise when the technology is used in malicious ways, such as to stalk individuals or trace their whereabouts (Fields). It is best to keep this feature disabled until needed.

---

[1] According to Jameson and Bennett, cyberthieves target apps on popular devices (72).

(a) Page 1

Figure 2–84

2. Type the research paper as shown in Figures 2–84a and 2–84b. Insert the footnote as shown in Figure 2–84a. Change the Footnote Text style to the format specified in the MLA documentation style. Change the bibliography style to MLA. As you insert citations, use the following source information, entering it according to the MLA style:

a. Type of Source: Article in a Periodical
   Author: He Gao Bao
   Article Title: Securing Mobile Devices
   Periodical Title: Technology Today
   Year: 2014
   Month: Sept.
   Pages: no pages used
   Medium: Web
   Year Accessed: 2014
   Month Accessed: Oct.
   Day Accessed: 1

b. Type of Source: Web site
   Author: Charlotte Fields
   Name of webpage: Secure Your Mobile Device
   Year/Month/Date: none given
   Medium: Web
   Year Accessed: 2014
   Month Accessed: Sept.
   Day Accessed: 22

c. Type of Source: Book
   Author: Lewis Taylor Jameson and Kathryn Leona Bennett
   Title: Mobile Technologies
   Year: 2014
   City: New York
   Publisher: Maxwell Press
   Medium: Print

3. At the end of the research paper text, press the ENTER key once and insert a manual page break so that the Works Cited page begins on a new page. Enter and format the works cited title. Use Word to insert the bibliographical list.

4. Check the spelling and grammar of the paper.

5. Save the document using Lab 2-2 Mobile Devices Protection Paper as the file name. Submit the document, shown in Figure 2–84, in the format specified by your instructor.

6. ✳ This paper uses web sources. What factors should you consider when selecting web sources?

Tanner 2

Users can enable the password feature on their mobile device as the first step in stopping prying eyes from viewing contents. More protection is necessary, however, to stop viruses and spyware and to safeguard personal and business data. Mobile security apps can lock a mobile device remotely, erase its memory, and activate its GPS function (Bao).

Some techniques users can take to protect their mobile devices include avoiding unsafe links, using caution when downloading, turning off GPS tracking, and using mobile security software. Users should take these measures to protect their mobile devices.

(b) Page 2

Figure 2–84 (Continued)

Continued >

Lab 3: Expand Your World: Cloud and Web Technologies
Using an Online Bibliography Tool to Create a List of Sources

Problem: Assume you are using a mobile device or computer that does not have Word but has Internet access. To make use of time between classes, you will use an online bibliography tool to create a list of sources that you can copy and paste into the Works Cited pages of a research paper due tomorrow.

Instructions: Perform the following tasks:

1. Run a browser. Search for the text, online bibliography tool, using a search engine. Visit several of the online bibliography tools and determine which you would like to use to create a list of sources. Navigate to the desired online bibliography tool.

2. Use the online bibliography tool to enter list of sources shown below (Figure 2–85):

Dayton, Lacey Marie and Sally Louise Walsh. *The Wireless Revolution*. New York: New Artists Press, 2014. Print.

Dover, Guy Sean. *Communications of Today*. Los Angeles: Sunshine Works, 2014. Print.

Figure 2–85

Howard, Timothy James. "The Wireless Era." *Computers and Networks* Aug. 2014. Web. 29 Aug. 2014.

Matthews, Carl James. *Wireless Trends*. Aug. 2014. Course Technology. Web. 8 Sept. 2014.

Newby, Trisha Lynn and Howard Lou Hopper. "Wireless Communications." *Communications News* Aug. 2014. Web. 4 Oct. 2014.

Newman, William Jared. *The Amazing Wireless World*. Sept. 2014. Course Technology. Web. 28 Sept. 2014.

3. If requested by your instructor, replace the name in one of the sources above with your name.

4. Search for another source that discusses wireless communications. Add that source.

5. Copy and paste the list of sources into a Word document.

6. Save the document with the name Lab 1-3 Wireless Communications Sources. Submit the document in the format specified by your instructor.

7. ✺ Which online bibliography tools did you evaluate? Which one did you select to use and why? Do you prefer using the online bibliography tool or Word to create sources? Why? What differences, if any, did you notice between the list of sources created with the online bibliography tool and the lists created when you use Word?

✺ Consider This: Your Turn

Apply your creative thinking and problem solving skills to design and implement a solution.

Note: To complete these assignments, you may be required to use the Data Files for Students. Visit www.cengage.com/ct/studentdownload for detailed instructions or contact your instructor for information about accessing the required files.

1: Create a Research Paper about Laptops, Tablets, and Desktops

Personal

Part 1: As a student in an introductory computer class, your instructor has assigned a brief research paper that discusses types of computers. The source for the text in your research paper is in a file called Your Turn 2 - 1 Computer Notes, which is located on the Data Files for Students. If your instructor requests, use the Research task pane to obtain information from another source and include that information as a note positioned as a footnote in the paper, along with entering its corresponding source information as appropriate. Add an AutoCorrect entry to correct a word you commonly mistype. If necessary, set the default dictionary. Add one of the source last names to the dictionary.

Using the concepts and techniques presented in this chapter, organize the notes in the text in the file on the Data Files for Students, rewording as necessary, and then create and format this research paper according to the MLA documentation style. Be sure to check spelling and grammar of the finished paper. Submit your assignment and answers to the critical thinking questions in the format specified by your instructor.

Part 2: ✺ You made several decisions while creating the research paper in this assignment: how to organize the notes, where to place citations, how to format sources, and which source on the web to use for the footnote text (if requested by your instructor). What was the rationale behind each of these decisions? When you proofread the document, what further revisions did you make and why?

Continued >

STUDENT ASSIGNMENTS

Consider This: Your Turn *continued*

2: Create a Research Paper about POS Terminals, ATMs, and Self-Service Kiosks
Professional

Part 1: As a part-time employee at an advertising firm that specializes in marketing for technology, your boss has asked you to write a brief research paper that discusses types of terminals. The source for the text in your research paper is in a file called Your Turn 2-2 Terminals Notes, which is located on the Data Files for Students. If your instructor requests, use the Research task pane to obtain information from another source and include that information as a note positioned as a footnote in the paper, and enter its corresponding source information as appropriate. Add an AutoCorrect entry to correct a word you commonly mistype. If necessary, set the default dictionary. Add one of the source last names to the dictionary.

Using the concepts and techniques presented in this chapter, organize the notes in the file on the Data Files for Students, rewording as necessary, and then create and format this research paper according to the MLA documentation style. Be sure to check spelling and grammar of the finished paper. Submit your assignment and answers to the critical thinking questions in the format specified by your instructor.

Part 2: ✺ You made several decisions while creating the research paper in this assignment: how to organize the notes, where to place citations, how to format sources, and which source on the web to use for the footnote text (if requested by your instructor). What was the rationale behind each of these decisions? When you proofread the document, what further revisions did you make and why?

3: Create a Research Paper about Social Media Sites
Research and Collaboration

Part 1: Because all local youth groups will be creating a page on a social media site, you and two other leaders of local youth groups have been asked to prepare a research paper comparing and contrasting three different social media sites. Form a three-member team to research, compose, and create this paper. Research three separate social media sites: features, capabilities, typical uses, privacy settings, etc. Each team member should write the supporting paragraphs for the social media site he or she researched, including all citations and sources. As a group, write the introduction and conclusion. Be sure to include your team's recommendation in the conclusion.

Use the concepts and techniques presented in this chapter to create and format this paper according to the MLA documentation style. Be sure to check spelling and grammar of the finished paper. Submit your team notes and research paper in the format specified by your instructor.

Part 2: ✺ You made several decisions while creating the research paper in this assignment: the sources to use, which notes to take from the sources, how to organize the notes, how to organize each team member's submissions, what text to write for the introduction and conclusion, where to place citations, and how to format sources. What was the rationale behind each of these decisions? When you proofread the document, what further revisions did you make and why?

Learn Online

Reinforce what you learned in this chapter with games, exercises, training, and many other online activities and resources.

Student Companion Site Reinforcement activities and resources are available at no additional cost on www.cengagebrain.com. Visit www.cengage.com/ct/studentdownload for detailed instructions about accessing the resources available at the Student Companion Site.

 SAM Put your skills into practice with SAM! If you have a SAM account, go to www.cengage.com/sam2013 to access SAM assignments for this chapter.

3 Creating a Business Letter with a Letterhead and Table

Microsoft product screen shots used with permission from Microsoft Corporation.

Objectives

You will have mastered the material in this chapter when you can:

- Change margins
- Insert and format a shape
- Change text wrapping
- Insert and format a clip art image
- Insert a symbol
- Add a border to a paragraph
- Clear formatting
- Convert a hyperlink to regular text

- Apply a style
- Set and use tab stops
- Insert the current date
- Create, modify, and insert a building block
- Insert a Word table, enter data in the table, and format the table
- Address and print an envelope

3 | Creating a Business Letter with a Letterhead and Table

Introduction

In a business environment, people use documents to communicate with others. Business documents can include letters, memos, newsletters, proposals, and resumes. An effective business document clearly and concisely conveys its message and has a professional, organized appearance. You can use your own creative skills to design and compose business documents. Using Word, for example, you can develop the content and decide on the location of each item in a business document.

Project — Business Letter with a Letterhead and Table

At some time, you more than likely will prepare a business letter. Contents of business letters include requests, inquiries, confirmations, acknowledgements, recommendations, notifications, responses, thank you letters, invitations, offers, referrals, complaints, and more.

The project in this chapter follows generally accepted guidelines for writing letters and uses Word to create the business letter shown in Figure 3–1. This business letter is a thank you letter from a volunteer applicant to a volunteer organization (Washington Volunteer Foundation). The letter includes a custom letterhead, as well as all essential business letter components: date line, inside address, salutation, body, complimentary close, and signature block. To easily present his volunteer service background, the candidate presents this information in a table. His availability appears in a bulleted list.

For an introduction to Office and instruction about how to perform basic tasks in Office apps, read the Office and Windows chapter at the beginning of this book, where you can learn how to run an application, use the ribbon, save a file, open a file, exit an application, use Help, and much more.

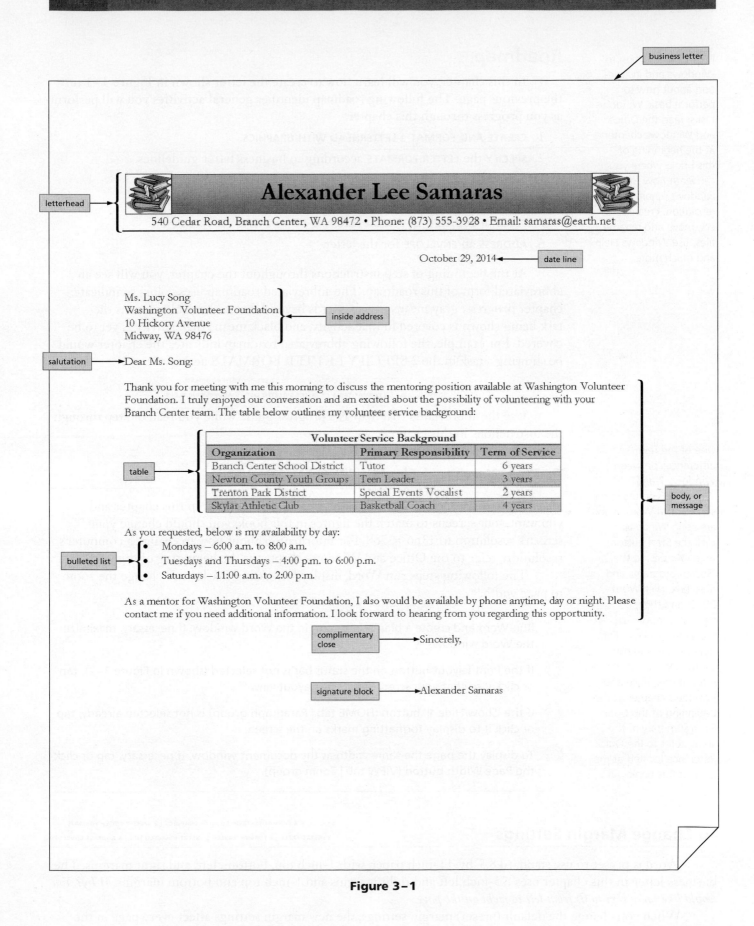

business letter

letterhead

Alexander Lee Samaras

540 Cedar Road, Branch Center, WA 98472 • Phone: (873) 555-3928 • Email: samaras@earth.net

October 29, 2014 ◄ date line

inside address

Ms. Lucy Song
Washington Volunteer Foundation
10 Hickory Avenue
Midway, WA 98476

salutation → Dear Ms. Song:

Thank you for meeting with me this morning to discuss the mentoring position available at Washington Volunteer Foundation. I truly enjoyed our conversation and am excited about the possibility of volunteering with your Branch Center team. The table below outlines my volunteer service background:

table →

Volunteer Service Background		
Organization	Primary Responsibility	Term of Service
Branch Center School District	Tutor	6 years
Newton County Youth Groups	Teen Leader	3 years
Trenton Park District	Special Events Vocalist	2 years
Skylar Athletic Club	Basketball Coach	4 years

body, or message

As you requested, below is my availability by day:

bulleted list →
- Mondays – 6:00 a.m. to 8:00 a.m.
- Tuesdays and Thursdays – 4:00 p.m. to 6:00 p.m.
- Saturdays – 11:00 a.m. to 2:00 p.m.

As a mentor for Washington Volunteer Foundation, I also would be available by phone anytime, day or night. Please contact me if you need additional information. I look forward to hearing from you regarding this opportunity.

complimentary close → Sincerely,

signature block → Alexander Samaras

Figure 3–1

For an introduction to Windows and instruction about how to perform basic Windows tasks, read the Office and Windows chapter at the beginning of this book, where you can learn how to resize windows, change screen resolution, create folders, move and rename files, use Windows Help, and much more.

Roadmap

In this chapter, you will learn how to create the letter shown in Figure 3–1 on the previous page. The following roadmap identifies general activities you will perform as you progress through this chapter:

1. **CREATE AND FORMAT** a **LETTERHEAD WITH GRAPHICS.**
2. **SPECIFY** the **LETTER FORMATS** according to business letter guidelines.
3. **INSERT** a **TABLE** in the letter.
4. **FORMAT** the **TABLE** in the letter.
5. **INSERT** a **BULLETED LIST** in the letter.
6. **ADDRESS** an **ENVELOPE** for the letter.

At the beginning of step instructions throughout the chapter, you will see an abbreviated form of this roadmap. The abbreviated roadmap uses colors to indicate chapter progress: gray means the chapter is beyond that activity, blue means the task being shown is covered in that activity, and black means that activity is yet to be covered. For example, the following abbreviated roadmap indicates the chapter would be showing a task in the 2 SPECIFY LETTER FORMATS activity.

| 1 CREATE & FORMAT LETTERHEAD WITH GRAPHICS | 2 SPECIFY LETTER FORMATS |
| 3 INSERT TABLE | 4 FORMAT TABLE | 5 INSERT BULLETED LIST | 6 ADDRESS ENVELOPE |

Use the abbreviated roadmap as a progress guide while you read or step through the instructions in this chapter.

To Run Word and Change Word Settings

One of the few differences between Windows 7 and Windows 8 occurs in the steps to run Word. If you are using Windows 7, click the Start button, type **Word** in the 'Search programs and files' box, click Word 2013, and then, if necessary, maximize the Word window. For detailed steps to run Word in Windows 7, refer to the Office and Windows chapter at the beginning of this book. For a summary of the steps, refer to the Quick Reference located at the back of this book.

If you are using a computer to step through the project in this chapter and you want your screens to match the figures in this book, you should change your screen's resolution to 1366×768. For information about how to change a computer's resolution, refer to the Office and Windows chapter at the beginning of this book.

The following steps run Word, display formatting marks, and change the zoom to page width.

1. Run Word and create a blank document in the Word window. If necessary, maximize the Word window.

2. If the Print Layout button on the status bar is not selected (shown in Figure 3–2), tap or click it so that your screen is in Print Layout view.

3. If the 'Show/Hide ¶' button (HOME tab | Paragraph group) is not selected already, tap or click it to display formatting marks on the screen.

4. To display the page the same width as the document window, if necessary, tap or click the Page Width button (VIEW tab | Zoom group).

To Change Margin Settings

| 1 CREATE & FORMAT LETTERHEAD WITH GRAPHICS | 2 SPECIFY LETTER FORMATS |
| 3 INSERT TABLE | 4 FORMAT TABLE | 5 INSERT BULLETED LIST | 6 ADDRESS ENVELOPE |

Word is preset to use standard 8.5-by-11-inch paper, with 1-inch top, bottom, left, and right margins. The business letter in this chapter uses .75-inch left and right margins and 1-inch top and bottom margins. *Why? You would like more text to fit from left to right on the page.*

When you change the default (preset) margin settings, the new margin settings affect every page in the document. If you wanted the margins to affect just a portion of the document, you would divide the document into sections (discussed in a later chapter), which enables you to specify different margin settings for each section. The next steps change margin settings.

1

- Display the PAGE LAYOUT tab.

- Tap or click the Adjust Margins button (PAGE LAYOUT tab | Page Setup group) to display the Adjust Margins gallery (Figure 3–2).

2

- Tap or click Moderate in the Adjust Margins gallery to change the margins to the specified settings.

Q&A What if the margin settings I want are not in the Adjust Margins gallery?

You can tap or click Custom Margins in the Adjust Margins gallery and then enter your desired margin values in the top, bottom, left, and right boxes in the Page Setup dialog box.

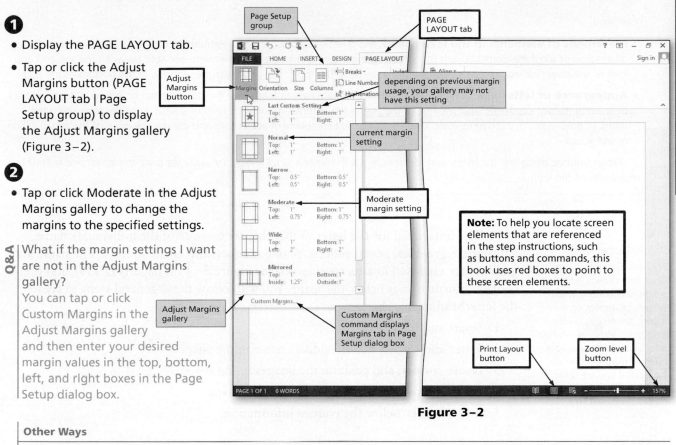

Figure 3–2

Other Ways

1. If you are using a mouse, position pointer on margin boundary on ruler; when pointer changes to two-headed arrow, drag margin boundary on ruler

---

Creating a Letterhead

The cost of preprinted letterhead can be high. An alternative is to create your own letterhead and save it in a file. When you want to create a letter at a later time, you can start by using the letterhead file. The following pages create a letterhead and then save it in a file for future use.

What is a letterhead?

A **letterhead** is the section of a letter that identifies an organization or individual. Often, the letterhead appears at the top of a letter. Although you can design and print a letterhead yourself, many businesses pay an outside firm to design and print their letterhead, usually on higher-quality paper. They then use the professionally preprinted paper for external business communications.

If you do not have preprinted letterhead paper, you can design a creative letterhead. It is important the letterhead appropriately reflect the essence of the organization or individual (i.e., formal, technical, creative, etc.). That is, it should use text, graphics, formats, and colors that reflect the organization or individual. The letterhead should leave ample room for the contents of the letter.

When designing a letterhead, consider its contents, placement, and appearance.

- **Contents of letterhead.** A letterhead should contain these elements:

  – Complete legal name of the individual, group, or company

  – Complete mailing address: street address including building, room, suite number, or post office box, along with city, state, and postal code

  – Phone number(s) and fax number, if applicable

  – Email address

  – Web address, if applicable

  – Many letterheads also include a logo or other image; if an image is used, it should express the organization or individual's personality or goals

Continued

Continued

- **Placement of elements in the letterhead.** Many letterheads center their elements across the top of the page. Others align some or all of the elements with the left or right margins. Sometimes, the elements are split between the top and bottom of the page. For example, a name and logo may be at the top of the page with the address at the bottom of the page.

- **Appearance of letterhead elements.** Use fonts that are easy to read. Give the organization or individual name impact by making its font size larger than the rest of the text in the letterhead. For additional emphasis, consider formatting the name in bold, italic, or a different color. Choose colors that complement each other and convey the goals of the organization or individual.

When finished designing the letterhead, determine if a divider line would help to visually separate the letterhead from the remainder of the letter.

BTW

The Ribbon and Screen Resolution
Word may change how the groups and buttons within the groups appear on the ribbon, depending on the computer's screen resolution. Thus, your ribbon may look different from the ones in this book if you are using a screen resolution other than 1366 × 768.

The letterhead for the letter in this chapter consists of the individual's name, appropriate graphics, postal address, phone number, and email address. The name and graphics are enclosed in a rectangular shape (Figure 3–1 on page WD 139), and the contact information is below the shape. You will follow these general steps to create the letterhead in this chapter:

1. Insert and format a shape.
2. Enter and format the individual's name in the shape.
3. Insert, format, and position the images in the shape.
4. Enter the contact information below the shape.
5. Add a border below the contact information.

To Insert a Shape

1 CREATE & FORMAT LETTERHEAD WITH GRAPHICS | 2 SPECIFY LETTER FORMATS
3 INSERT TABLE | 4 FORMAT TABLE | 5 INSERT BULLETED LIST | 6 ADDRESS ENVELOPE

Word has a variety of predefined shapes, which are a type of drawing object, that you can insert in documents. A **drawing object** is a graphic that you create using Word. Examples of shape drawing objects include rectangles, circles, triangles, arrows, flowcharting symbols, stars, banners, and callouts. The following steps insert a rectangle shape in the letterhead. *Why? The individual's name is placed in a rectangle for emphasis and visual appeal.*

1

- Display the INSERT tab.

- Tap or click the 'Draw a Shape' button (INSERT tab | Illustrations group) to display the Draw a Shape gallery (Figure 3–3).

Figure 3–3

2

- Tap or click the Rectangle shape in the Rectangles area of the Draw a Shape gallery, which removes the gallery. If you are using a touch screen, the shape is inserted in the document window; if you are using a mouse, the pointer changes to the shape of a crosshair in the document window.

- If you are using a mouse, position the pointer (a crosshair) in the approximate location for the upper-left corner of the desired shape (Figure 3–4).

Q&A What is the purpose of the crosshair pointer?
With a mouse, you drag the crosshair pointer from the upper-left corner to the lower-right corner to form the desired location and size of the shape.

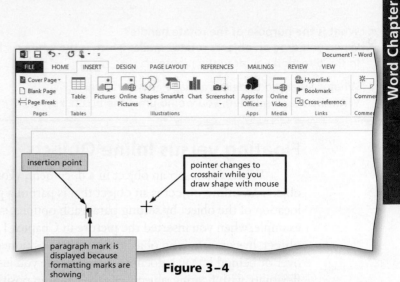

Figure 3–4

3

- Drag the mouse to the right and downward to form the boundaries of the shape, as shown in Figure 3–5. Do not release the mouse button.

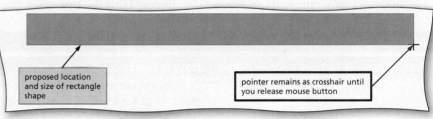

Figure 3–5

4

- Release the mouse button so that Word draws the shape according to your drawing in the document window.

5

- If you are using a touch screen, change the values in the Shape Height and Shape Width boxes (DRAWING TOOLS FORMAT tab | Size group) to 0.53" and 5.7" by typing each value in the respective box and then pressing the ENTER key; if you are using a mouse, verify your shape is the same approximate height and width as the one in this project by reviewing, and if necessary changing, the values in the Shape Height box and Shape Width boxes to 0.53" and 5.7" by typing each value in the respective box and then pressing the ENTER key (Figure 3–6).

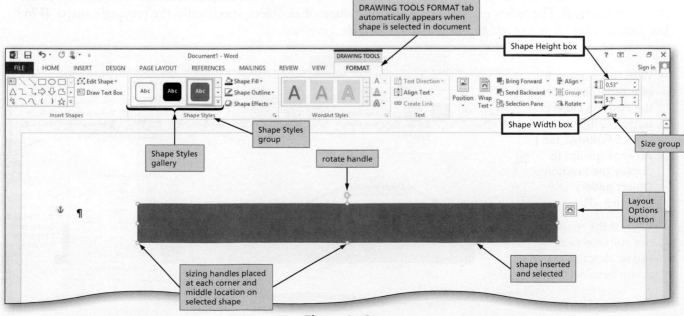

Figure 3–6

© 2014 Cengage Learning

Q&A What is the purpose of the rotate handle?

When you drag an object's **rotate handle**, which is the white circle on the top of the object, Word rotates the object in the direction you drag the mouse.

What if I wanted to delete a shape and start over?

With the shape selected, you would press the DELETE key.

Floating versus Inline Objects

When you insert an object in a document, Word inserts it as either an inline object or a floating object. An **inline object** is an object that is part of a paragraph. With inline objects, you change the location of the object by setting paragraph options, such as centered, right-aligned, and so on. For example, when you inserted the picture in Chapter 1, Word inserted it as an inline object. A **floating object**, by contrast, is an object that can be positioned at a specific location in a document or in a layer over or behind text in a document. The shape you just inserted is a floating object. You have more flexibility with floating objects because you can position a floating object anywhere on the page.

In addition to changing an object from inline to floating and vice versa, Word provides several floating options, which along with inline, are called text wrapping options because they affect how text wraps with or around the object. Table 3–1 presents the various text wrapping options.

Table 3–1 Text Wrapping Options

Text Wrapping Option	Object Type	How It Works
In Line with Text	Inline	Object positioned according to paragraph formatting; for example, if paragraph is centered, object will be centered with any text in the paragraph.
Square	Floating	Text wraps around object, with text forming a box around the object.
Tight	Floating	Text wraps around object, with text forming to shape of the object.
Through	Floating	Object appears at beginning, middle, or end of text. Moving object changes location of text.
Top and Bottom	Floating	Object appears above or below text. Moving object changes location of text.
Behind Text	Floating	Object appears behind text.
In Front of Text	Floating	Object appears in front of text and may cover the text.

To Change an Object's Position

1 CREATE & FORMAT LETTERHEAD WITH GRAPHICS | 2 SPECIFY LETTER FORMATS
3 INSERT TABLE | 4 FORMAT TABLE | 5 INSERT BULLETED LIST | 6 ADDRESS ENVELOPE

You can specify that an object's vertical position on a page (top, middle, bottom) and its horizontal position (left, center, right). The following steps change the position of an object, specifically, the rectangle shape. *Why? You want the shape to be centered at the top of the page in the letterhead.*

1

- With the shape still selected, tap or click the Position Object button (DRAWING TOOLS FORMAT tab | Arrange group) to display the Position Object gallery (Figure 3–7).

Q&A What if the shape is not still selected?

Tap or click the shape to select it.

Figure 3–7

- If you are using a mouse, point to various text options in the Position Object gallery and watch the shape move to the selected position option.

2

- Tap or click 'Position in Top Center with Square Text Wrapping' in the Position Object gallery so that the object does not cover the document and is centered at the top of the document.

Other Ways

1. Tap or click Layout Options button attached to graphic, tap or click See more link in Layout Options gallery, tap or click Horizontal Alignment arrow and select alignment (Layout dialog box), tap or click Vertical Alignment arrow and select alignment, tap or click OK button

2. Tap or click Advanced Layout: Size Dialog Box Launcher (DRAWING TOOLS FORMAT tab | Size group), tap or click Position tab (Layout dialog box), tap or click Horizontal Alignment arrow and select alignment, tap or click Vertical Alignment arrow and select alignment, tap or click OK button

To Change an Object's Text Wrapping

1 CREATE & FORMAT LETTERHEAD WITH GRAPHICS | 2 SPECIFY LETTER FORMATS
3 INSERT TABLE | 4 FORMAT TABLE | 5 INSERT BULLETED LIST | 6 ADDRESS ENVELOPE

When you insert a shape in a Word document, the default text wrapping is In Front of Text, which means the object will cover any text behind it. The previous steps, which changed the shape's position, changed the text wrapping to Square. In the letterhead, you want the shape's text wrapping to be Top and Bottom. *Why? You want the letterhead above the contents of the letter when you type it, instead of covering the contents of the letter.* The following steps change an object's text wrapping.

1

- With the shape still selected, tap or click the Layout Options button attached to the graphic to display the Layout Options gallery (Figure 3–8).

2

- Tap or click 'Top and Bottom' in the Layout Options gallery so that the object does not cover the document text (shown in Figure 3–9 on the next page).

Q&A How can I tell that the text wrapping has changed? Because the letter has no text, you need to look at the paragraph mark, which now is positioned below the shape instead of to its left.

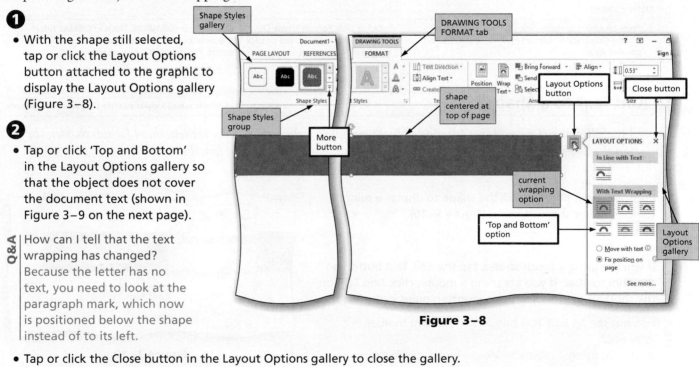

Figure 3–8

- Tap or click the Close button in the Layout Options gallery to close the gallery.

Other Ways

1. Tap 'Show Context Menu' button on mini toolbar or right-click object, tap or point to Wrap Text on shortcut menu, tap or click desired wrapping option

2. Tap or click Wrap Text button (DRAWING TOOLS FORMAT tab | Arrange group), select desired wrapping option

To Apply a Shape Style

1 CREATE & FORMAT LETTERHEAD WITH GRAPHICS | 2 SPECIFY LETTER FORMATS
3 INSERT TABLE | 4 FORMAT TABLE | 5 INSERT BULLETED LIST | 6 ADDRESS ENVELOPE

Why apply a shape style? Word provides a Shape Styles gallery so that you easily can change the appearance of the shape. The steps on the next page apply a shape style to the rectangle shape.

1

- With the shape still selected, tap or click the More button (shown in Figure 3–8 on the previous page) in the Shape Styles gallery (DRAWING TOOLS FORMAT tab | Shape Styles group) to expand the gallery.

Q&A What if the shape is no longer selected?
Tap or click the shape to select it.

- If you are using a mouse, point to 'Subtle Effect - Blue, Accent 1' (second effect in fourth row) in the Shape Styles gallery to display a live preview of that style applied to the shape in the document (Figure 3–9).

Experiment

- If you are using a mouse, point to various styles in the Shape Styles gallery and watch the style of the shape change in the document.

Figure 3–9

2

- Tap or click 'Subtle Effect - Blue, Accent 1' in the Shape Styles gallery to apply the selected style to the shape.

Other Ways

1. Press and hold or right-click shape, tap or click 'Shape Quick Styles' button on mini toolbar, select desired style

2. Tap or click Format Shape Dialog Box Launcher (DRAWING TOOLS FORMAT tab | Shape Styles group), tap or click 'Fill & Line' button (Format Shape task pane), expand FILL section, select desired colors, tap or click Close button

To Add Text to a Shape

1 CREATE & FORMAT LETTERHEAD WITH GRAPHICS | 2 SPECIFY LETTER FORMATS
3 INSERT TABLE | 4 FORMAT TABLE | 5 INSERT BULLETED LIST | 6 ADDRESS ENVELOPE

The following steps add text (the individual's name) to a shape. *Why? In the letterhead for this chapter, the name is in the shape. Similarly, an organization could put its name in a shape on a letterhead.*

1

- Press and hold or right-click the shape to display a mini toolbar and/or shortcut menu (Figure 3–10).

2

- If you are using a touch screen, tap the Edit Text button on the mini toolbar; if you are using a mouse, click Add Text on the shortcut menu to place an insertion point in the shape.

Q&A I do not see an Edit Text button on the mini toolbar. Why not?
If you are using a mouse in Mouse mode, the buttons on your mini toolbar will differ from those that appear when you use a touch screen in Touch mode.

- If the insertion point and paragraph mark are not centered in the shape, tap or click the Center button (HOME tab | Paragraph group) to center them.

- Type **Alexander Lee Samaras** as the name in the shape (Figure 3–11).

If requested by your instructor, enter your name instead of the name shown in Figure 3–11.

Figure 3–10

Figure 3–11

To Use the 'Increase Font Size' Button

In previous chapters, you used the Font Size arrow (HOME tab | Font group) to change the font size of text. Word also provides an 'Increase Font Size' button (HOME tab | Font group), which increases the font size of selected text each time you tap or click the button. The following steps use the 'Increase Font Size' button to increase the font size of the name in the shape to 24 point. *Why? You want the name to be as large as possible in the shape.*

1

• Drag through the text to be formatted (in this case, the name in the shape).

2

• If necessary, display the HOME tab.

• Repeatedly tap or click the 'Increase Font Size' button (HOME tab | Font group) until the Font Size box displays 24 to increase the font size of the selected text (Figure 3–12).

Q&A What if I tap or click the 'Increase Font Size' button (HOME tab | Font group) too many times, causing the font size to be too big?
Tap or click the 'Decrease Font Size' button (HOME tab | Font group) until the desired font size is displayed.

Experiment

• Repeatedly tap or click the 'Increase Font Size' and 'Decrease Font Size' buttons (HOME tab | Font group) and watch the font size of the selected name change in the document window. When you are finished experimenting with these two buttons, set the font size to 24.

Alexander·Lee·Samaras¶

Figure 3–12

Other Ways

1. Press CTRL+SHIFT+>

To Bold Selected Text

To make the name stand out even more, bold it. The following steps bold the selected text.

1 With the text selected, tap or click the Bold button (HOME tab | Font group) to bold the selected text.

2 Tap or click anywhere in the text in the shape to remove the selection and place the insertion point in the shape.

BTW
Touch Screen Differences
The Office and Windows interfaces may vary if you are using a touch screen. For this reason, you might notice that the function or appearance of your touch screen differs slightly from this chapter's presentation.

To Change the Document Theme

A **document theme** is a coordinated combination of colors, fonts, and effects. The current default document theme is Office, which uses Calibri and Calibri Light as its font and shades of grays and blues primarily. The following steps change the document theme to Organic for the letter in this chapter. *Why? You want to use shades of greens, browns, and blues in the letterhead because those colors are associated with growth, honesty, dependability, and integrity. You also want to use a serif font, which is a font that has short decorative lines on some characters. The Organic theme meets both of these requirements.*

❶

- Display the DESIGN tab.

- Tap or click the Themes button (DESIGN tab | Document Formatting group) to display the Themes gallery.

- If you are using a mouse, point to Organic in the Themes gallery to display a live preview of that theme applied to the document (Figure 3–13).

🔍 **Experiment**

- If you are using a mouse, point to various themes in the Themes gallery and watch the color scheme and font set change in the document window.

Figure 3–13

❷

- Tap or click Organic in the Themes gallery to change the document theme.

To Insert Clip Art

Files containing graphics are available from a variety of sources. In the Chapter 1 flyer, you inserted a digital picture taken with a camera phone. In this project, you insert **clip art**, which is a predefined graphic. Microsoft Office applications can access a collection of royalty-free clip art, photos, and animations.

The letterhead in this project contains clip art of books (Figure 3–1 on page WD 139). *Why? Because the writer of the letter enjoys reading and teaching, he selects an image of books for his letterhead.* The following steps insert clip art in the document.

❶

- If necessary, tap or click the paragraph mark below the shape to position the insertion point where you want to insert the clip art.

- Display the INSERT tab.

- Tap or click the Online Pictures button (INSERT tab | Illustrations group) to display the Insert Pictures dialog box.

- Type **books** in the Search box (Insert Pictures dialog box) to specify the search text, which indicates the type of image you want to locate (Figure 3–14).

Figure 3–14

2

- Tap or click the Search button to display a list of clip art that matches the entered search text.

- Scroll through the list of clip art to locate the one shown in Figure 3–15 (or a similar image) and then tap or click the clip art to select it.

Q&A Why is my list of clip art different from Figure 3–15?
Microsoft continually updates the online images.

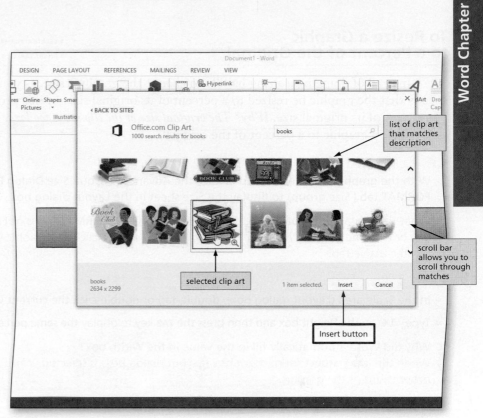

Figure 3–15

3

- Tap or click the Insert button to insert the selected clip art in the document at the location of the insertion point (Figure 3–16).

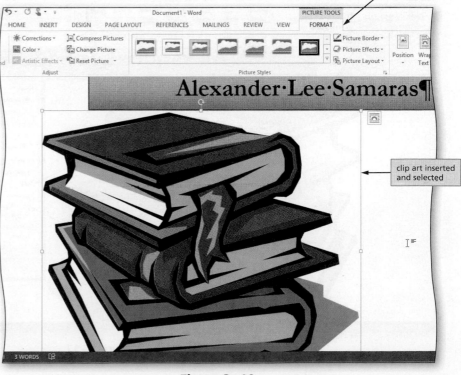

Figure 3–16

To Resize a Graphic
to a Percent of the Original

Instead of dragging a sizing handle to change the graphic's size, as you learned in Chapter 1, you can specify that the graphic be resized to a percent of its original size. In this project, the graphic is resized to 14 percent of its original size. *Why? The original size of the clip art is too large for the letterhead.* The following steps resize a graphic to a percent of the original.

1

• With the graphic still selected, tap or click the Advanced Layout: Size Dialog Box Launcher (PICTURE TOOLS FORMAT tab | Size group) to display the Size sheet in the Layout dialog box.

Q&A What if the graphic is not selected or the PICTURE TOOLS FORMAT tab is not on the ribbon?
Tap or click the graphic to select it or double-tap or double-click the graphic to make the PICTURE TOOLS FORMAT tab the active tab.

2

• In the Scale area (Layout dialog box), double-tap or double-click the current value in the Height box to select it.

• Type **14** in the Height box and then press the TAB key to display the same percent value in the Width box (Figure 3–17).

Q&A Why did Word automatically fill in the value in the Width box?
When the 'Lock aspect ratio' check box (Layout dialog box) is selected, Word automatically maintains the size proportions of the graphic.

How do I know to use 14 percent for the resized graphic?
The larger graphic consumed too much room on the page. Try various percentages to determine the size that works best in the letterhead design.

Figure 3–17

3

- Tap or click the OK button to close the dialog box and resize the selected graphic.

- If necessary, scroll to display the top of the document (Figure 3–18).

graphic selected and resized to 14% of its original size

Figure 3–18

Other Ways

1. Tap or click Layout Options button attached to graphic, tap or click See more link in the Layout Options gallery, tap or click Size tab (Layout dialog box), enter height and width values, tap or click OK button

2. If you are using a mouse, right-click graphic, click 'Size and Position' on shortcut menu, enter height and width values (Layout dialog box), click OK button

To Change the Color of a Graphic

1 CREATE & FORMAT LETTERHEAD WITH GRAPHICS | 2 SPECIFY LETTER FORMATS
3 INSERT TABLE | 4 FORMAT TABLE | 5 INSERT BULLETED LIST | 6 ADDRESS ENVELOPE

In Word, you can change the color of a graphic. The clip art currently uses a variety of colors including red, orange, and blue. The following steps change the color of the clip art (graphic). *Why? Because the clip art in this project will be placed beside the rectangle shape, you prefer to use colors that blend better with the current color scheme.*

1

- With the graphic still selected (shown in Figure 3–18), tap or click the Color button (PICTURE TOOLS FORMAT tab | Adjust group) to display the Color gallery.

- If you are using a mouse, point to 'Green, Accent color 1 Dark' in the Color gallery (second color in second row) to display a live preview of that color applied to the selected graphic in the document (Figure 3–19).

Experiment

- If you are using a mouse, point to various colors in the Color gallery and watch the color of the graphic change in the document.

Color button

Color gallery

PICTURE TOOLS FORMAT tab

Adjust group

More Variations displays additional color choices

'Green, Accent color 1 Dark' to be selected

color changes to Green, Accent color 1 Dark, showing live preview of color to which you are pointing in gallery

Figure 3–19

2

- Tap or click 'Green, Accent color 1 Dark' in the Color gallery to change the color of the selected graphic.

Q&A How would I change a graphic back to its original colors?
With the graphic selected, you would tap or click No Recolor, which is the upper-left color in the Color gallery.

Other Ways

1. Tap or click Format Shape Dialog Box Launcher (PICTURE TOOLS FORMAT tab | Picture Styles group), tap or click Picture button (Format Picture task pane), expand PICTURE COLOR section, select desired options

2. Tap 'Show Context Menu' button on mini toolbar or right-click graphic, tap Format Object or click Format Picture on shortcut menu, tap or click Picture button (Format Picture task pane), expand PICTURE COLOR section, select desired options

To Set a Transparent Color in a Graphic

In Word, you can make one color in a graphic transparent, that is, remove the color. You would make a color transparent if you wanted to remove part of a graphic or see text or colors behind a graphic. The following steps set part of the bookmark in the books graphic in a transparent color. *Why? Instead of its current dark green color, the bookmark will be easier to see if it is transparent.*

1
- Increase the zoom percent enough so that you easily can see the bookmark in the graphic.
- With the graphic still selected, tap or click the Color button (PICTURE TOOLS FORMAT tab | Adjust group) to display the Color gallery (Figure 3–20).

Figure 3–20

2
- Tap or click 'Set Transparent Color' in the Color gallery to display a pen pointer in the document window.
- If you are using a mouse, position the pen pointer in the graphic where you want to make the color transparent (Figure 3–21).

Q&A Can I make multiple colors in a graphic transparent?
No, you can make only one color transparent.

Figure 3–21

3
- Tap or click the location in the graphic where you want the color to be transparent (Figure 3–22).

Q&A What if this step does not work on a touch screen?
You may need to use a stylus or mouse to perform these steps.

What if I make the wrong color transparent?
Tap or click the Undo button on the Quick Access Toolbar, or press CTRL+Z, and then repeat these steps.

- Change the zoom back to page width.

Figure 3–22

To Adjust the Brightness and Contrast of a Graphic

In Word, you can adjust the brightness, or lightness, of a graphic and also the contrast, or the difference between the lightest and darkest areas of the graphic. The following steps increase the brightness and contrast of the books graphic, each by 20%. *Why? You want to lighten the graphic slightly to decrease its emphasis on the page and, at the same time, increase the difference between the light and dark areas of the graphic.*

1

- Display the PICTURE TOOLS FORMAT tab.

- With the graphic still selected (shown in Figure 3–22), tap or click the Corrections button (PICTURE TOOLS FORMAT tab | Adjust group) to display the Corrections gallery.

- If you are using a mouse, point to 'Brightness: +20% Contrast: +20%' (fourth image in fourth row) in the Corrections gallery to display a live preview of that correction applied to the graphic in the document (Figure 3–23).

Experiment

- If you are using a mouse, point to various corrections in the Corrections gallery and watch the brightness and contrast of the graphic change in the document.

Figure 3–23

2

- Tap or click 'Brightness: +20% Contrast: +20%' in the Corrections gallery (fourth image in fourth row) to change the brightness and contrast of the selected graphic.

Other Ways

1. Tap or click Format Shape Dialog Box Launcher (PICTURE TOOLS FORMAT tab | Picture Styles group), tap or click Picture button (Format Picture task pane), expand PICTURE CORRECTIONS section, select desired options

2. Tap 'Show Context Menu' button on mini toolbar or right-click graphic, tap Format Object or click Format Picture on shortcut menu, tap or click Picture button (Format Picture task pane), expand PICTURE CORRECTIONS section, select desired options

---

If you are using your finger on a touch screen and are having difficulty completing the steps in this chapter, consider using a stylus. Many people find it easier to be precise with a stylus than with a finger. In addition, with a stylus you see the pointer. If you still are having trouble completing the steps with a stylus, try using a mouse.

To Change the Border Color on a Graphic

The books graphic currently has no border (outline). The following steps change the border color on the graphic. **Why?** *You would like the graphic to have a green border so that it matches the border on the shape.*

1

- Tap or click the Picture Border arrow (PICTURE TOOLS FORMAT tab | Picture Styles group) to display the Picture Border gallery.

- If you are using a mouse, point to 'Green, Accent 1' (fifth theme color from left in the first row) in the Picture Border gallery to display a live preview of that border color around the picture (Figure 3–24).

Q&A If I am using a mouse, what if I click the Picture Border button by mistake?
Click the Picture Border arrow and proceed with Step 2. If you are using a touch screen, you may not have a separate Picture Border button.

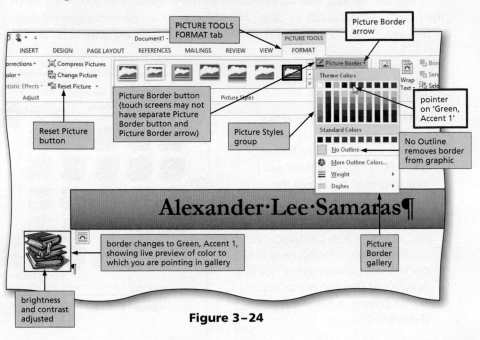

Figure 3–24

Experiment

- If you are using a mouse, point to various colors in the Picture Border gallery and watch the border color on the graphic change in the document window.

2

- Tap or click 'Green, Accent 1' in the Picture Border gallery to change the picture border color.

Q&A How would I remove a border from a graphic?
With the graphic selected, you would tap or click the No Outline in the Picture Border gallery.

Can I remove all formatting applied to a graphic and start over?
Yes. With the graphic selected, you would tap or click the Reset Picture button (PICTURE TOOLS FORMAT tab | Adjust group).

To Change an Object's Text Wrapping

The books graphic is to be positioned to the right of the shape. Clip art, by default, is formatted as an inline graphic, which cannot be moved to a precise location on a page. Recall that inline graphics are part of a paragraph and, thus, can be positioned according to paragraph formatting, such as centered or left-aligned. To move the graphic to the right of a shape, you format it as a floating object with 'In Front of Text' wrapping. The following steps change a graphic's text wrapping.

BTW

Q&As
For a complete list of the Q&As found in many of the step-by-step sequences in this book, visit the Q&A resource on the Student Companion Site located on www.cengagebrain.com. For detailed instructions about accessing available resources, visit www.cengage.com/ct/studentdownload or contact your instructor for information about accessing the required files.

1 If necessary, tap or click the graphic to select it.

2 Tap or click the Layout Options button attached to the graphic to display the Layout Options gallery.

3 Tap or click 'In Front of Text' in the Layout Options gallery so that you can position the object on top of any item in the document, in this case, on top of the rectangular shape.

4 Tap or click the Close button to close the gallery.

To Move a Graphic

The following steps move a graphic. *Why?* *In this letterhead, the books graphic is positioned to the right of the shape.*

1

- If you are using a mouse, position the pointer in the graphic so that the pointer has a four-headed arrow attached to it (Figure 3–25).

> when pointer has four-headed arrow attached to it, you can drag floating graphic to any location in document

Figure 3–25

2

- Drag the graphic to the right of the shape, as shown in Figure 3–26.

Q&A

What if I moved the graphic to the wrong location?
Repeat these steps. You can drag a floating graphic to any location in a document.

Why do green lines appear on my screen as I drag a graphic?
You have alignment guides set, which help you line up graphics. To set alignment guides, tap or click the Align Objects button (PICTURE TOOLS FORMAT tab | Arrange group) and then tap or click 'Use Alignment Guides'.

> graphic moved to right of the shape

Figure 3–26

To Copy a Graphic

In this project, the same books graphic is to be placed to the left of the shape. Instead of performing the same steps to insert and format another books graphic, you can copy the graphic to the Office Clipboard, paste the graphic from the Office Clipboard, and then move the graphic to the desired location.

You use the same steps to copy a graphic as you used in Chapter 2 to copy text. The following steps copy a graphic.

1 If necessary, tap or click the graphic to select it.

2 Display the HOME tab.

3 Tap or click the Copy button, shown in Figure 3–27 on the next page (HOME tab | Clipboard group), to copy the selected item to the Office Clipboard.

To Use Paste Options

The following steps paste a graphic using the Paste Options gallery. *Why? Recall from Chapter 2 that you can specify the format of a pasted item using Paste Options.*

1

- Tap or click the Paste arrow (HOME tab | Clipboard group) to display the Paste gallery.

Q&A If I am using a mouse, what if I accidentally click the Paste button?
Click the Paste Options button below the graphic pasted in the document to display a Paste Options gallery. If you are using a touch screen, you may not have a separate Paste button.

- If you are using a mouse, point to the 'Keep Source Formatting' button in the Paste gallery to display a live preview of that paste option (Figure 3–27).

Experiment

- Point to the two buttons in the Paste gallery and watch the appearance of the pasted graphic change.

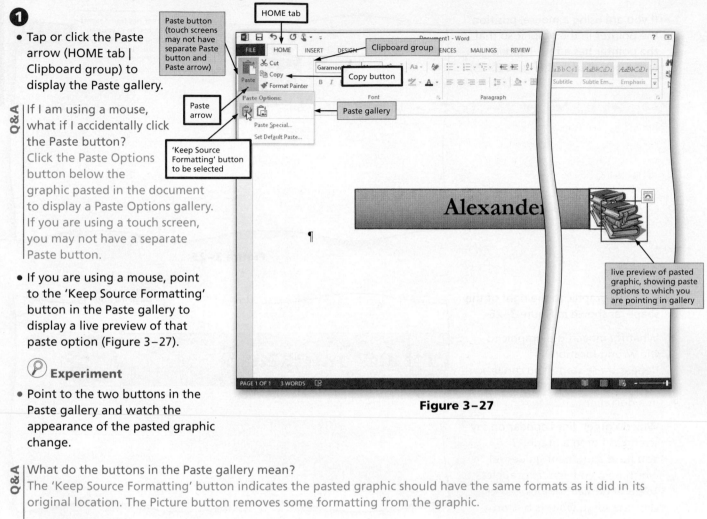

Figure 3–27

Q&A What do the buttons in the Paste gallery mean?
The 'Keep Source Formatting' button indicates the pasted graphic should have the same formats as it did in its original location. The Picture button removes some formatting from the graphic.

Why are these paste buttons different from the ones in Chapter 2?
The buttons that appear in the Paste gallery differ depending on the item you are pasting. Use live preview to see how the pasted object will look in the document.

2

- Tap or click the 'Keep Source Formatting' button in the Paste gallery to paste the object using the same formatting as the original.

To Move a Graphic

The next step is to move the second books graphic so that it is positioned to the left of the rectangle shape. The following steps move a graphic.

1 If you are using a mouse, position the pointer in the graphic so that the pointer has a four-headed arrow attached to it.

2 Drag the graphic to the location shown in Figure 3–28.

To Flip a Graphic

The following steps flip a graphic horizontally. *Why? In this letterhead, you want the books graphics to face each other.*

1

- If necessary, display the PICTURE TOOLS FORMAT tab.

2

- With the graphic still selected, tap or click the Rotate Objects button (PICTURE TOOLS FORMAT tab | Arrange group) to display the Rotate Objects gallery (Figure 3–28).

🔍 **Experiment**

- If you are using a mouse, point to the various rotate options in the Rotate Options gallery and watch the picture rotate in the document window.

Figure 3–28

3

- Tap or click Flip Horizontal in the Rotate Options gallery, so that Word flips the graphic to display its mirror image.

Q&A Can I flip a graphic vertically?

Yes, you would tap or click Flip Vertical in the Rotate Options gallery. You also can rotate a graphic clockwise or counterclockwise by tapping or clicking the 'Rotate Right 90°' and 'Rotate Left 90°' commands, respectively, in the Rotate Options gallery.

To Save a Document

You have performed many tasks while creating this letterhead and do not want to risk losing work completed thus far. Accordingly, you should save the document. The following steps assume you already have created folders for storing your files, for example, a CIS 101 folder (for your class) that contains a Word folder (for your assignments). Thus, these steps save the document in the Word folder in the CIS 101 folder using the file name, Samaras Letterhead.

1 Tap or click the Save button on the Quick Access Toolbar, which depending on settings, will display either the Save As gallery in the Backstage view or the Save As dialog box.

2 To save on a hard disk or other storage media on your computer, proceed to Step 2a. To save on SkyDrive, proceed to Step 2b.

2a If your screen opens the Backstage view and you want to save on storage media on your computer, tap or click Computer in the left pane, if necessary, to display options in the right pane related to saving on your computer. If your screen already displays the Save As dialog box, proceed to Step 4.

2b If your screen opens the Backstage view and you want to save on SkyDrive, tap or click SkyDrive in the left pane to display SkyDrive saving options or a Sign In button. If your screen displays a Sign In button, tap or click it and then sign in to SkyDrive.

3 Tap or click the Browse button in the right pane to display the Save As dialog box associated with the selected save location (i.e., Computer or SkyDrive).

4 Type **Samaras Letterhead** in the File name box to change the file name. Do not press the ENTER key after typing the file name because you do not want to close the dialog box at this time.

BTW

Organizing Files and Folders
You should organize and store files in folders so that you easily can find the files later. For example, if you are taking an introductory computer class called CIS 101, a good practice would be to save all Word files in a Word folder in a CIS 101 folder. For a discussion of folders and detailed examples of creating folders, refer to the Office and Windows chapter at the beginning of this book.

5 Navigate to the desired save location (in this case, the Word folder in the CIS 101 folder [or your class folder] on your computer or SkyDrive).

6 Tap or click the Save button (Save As dialog box) to save the letterhead in the selected folder on the selected save location with the entered file name.

To Format and Enter Text

The contact information for the letterhead in this project is located on the line below the shape containing the name. The following steps format and then enter the postal address in the letterhead.

1 Position the insertion point on the line below the shape containing the name.

2 If necessary, display the HOME tab. Tap or click the Center button (HOME tab | Paragraph group) to center the paragraph.

3 Tap or click the 'Increase Font Size' button (HOME tab | Font group) to increase the font size to 12 point.

4 Type `540 Cedar Road, Branch Center, WA 98472` and then press the SPACEBAR (shown in Figure 3–29).

To Insert a Symbol
from the Symbol Dialog Box

1 CREATE & FORMAT LETTERHEAD WITH GRAPHICS | 2 SPECIFY LETTER FORMATS
3 INSERT TABLE | 4 FORMAT TABLE | 5 INSERT BULLETED LIST | 6 ADDRESS ENVELOPE

Word provides a method of inserting dots and other symbols, such as letters in the Greek alphabet and mathematical characters, that are not on the keyboard. The following steps insert a dot symbol, sometimes called a bullet symbol, in the letterhead. *Why? You want a visual separator between the postal address and phone number in the letterhead, and also between the phone number and email address.*

1
- If necessary, position the insertion point as shown in Figure 3–29.
- Display the INSERT tab.
- Tap or click the 'Insert a Symbol' button (INSERT tab | Symbols group) to display the Insert a Symbol gallery (Figure 3–29).

Q&A What if the symbol I want to insert already appears in the Insert a Symbol gallery?

You can tap or click any symbol shown in the Insert a Symbol gallery to insert it in the document.

Figure 3–29

2

- Tap or click More Symbols in the Insert a Symbol gallery to display the Symbol dialog box.

- If the font in the Font box is not (normal text), tap or click the Font arrow (Symbol dialog box) and then scroll to and tap or click (normal text) to select this font.

- If the subset in the Subset box is not General Punctuation, tap or click the Subset arrow and then scroll and tap or click General Punctuation to select this subset.

- In the list of symbols, if necessary, scroll to the dot symbol shown in Figure 3–30 and then tap or click the symbol to select it.

Figure 3–30

- Tap or click the Insert button (Symbol dialog box) to place the selected symbol in the document to the left of the insertion point (Figure 3–30).

Q&A | Why is the Symbol dialog box still open?
The Symbol dialog box remains open, allowing you to insert additional symbols.

3

- Tap or click the Close button (Symbol dialog box) to close the dialog box.

To Insert a Symbol from the Insert a Symbol Gallery

1 CREATE & FORMAT LETTERHEAD WITH GRAPHICS | 2 SPECIFY LETTER FORMATS
3 INSERT TABLE | 4 FORMAT TABLE | 5 INSERT BULLETED LIST | 6 ADDRESS ENVELOPE

In the letterhead, another dot symbol separates the phone number from the email address. The following steps use the Insert a Symbol gallery to insert a dot symbol between the phone number and email address. *Why? Once you insert a symbol using the Symbol dialog box, Word adds that symbol to the Insert a Symbol gallery so that it is more readily available.*

1

- Press the SPACEBAR, type **Phone: (873) 555-3928** and then press the SPACEBAR.

2

- Tap or click the 'Insert a Symbol' button (INSERT tab | Symbols group) to display the Insert a Symbol gallery (Figure 3–31).

Q&A | Why is the dot symbol now in the Insert a Symbol gallery?
When you insert a symbol from the Symbol dialog box, Word automatically adds the symbol to the Insert a Symbol gallery.

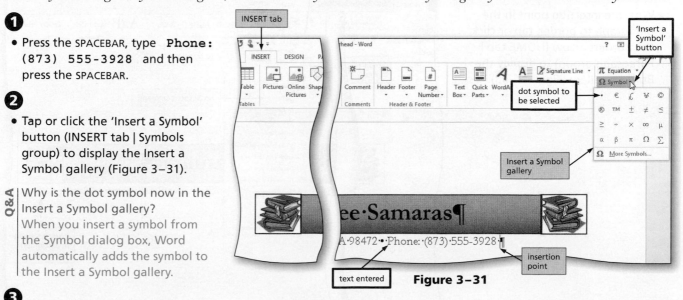

Figure 3–31

3

- Tap or click the dot symbol in the Insert a Symbol gallery to insert the symbol at the location of the insertion point (shown in Figure 3–32 on the next page).

To Enter Text

The following steps enter the email address in the letterhead.

1 Press the SPACEBAR.

2 Type `Email: samaras@earth.net` to finish the text in the letterhead (Figure 3–32).

Figure 3–32

To Bottom Border a Paragraph

1 CREATE & FORMAT LETTERHEAD WITH GRAPHICS | 2 SPECIFY LETTER FORMATS
3 INSERT TABLE | 4 FORMAT TABLE | 5 INSERT BULLETED LIST | 6 ADDRESS ENVELOPE

In Word, you can draw a solid line, called a **border**, at any edge of a paragraph. That is, borders may be added above or below a paragraph, to the left or right of a paragraph, or in any combination of these sides.

The letterhead in this project has a border that extends from the left margin to the right margin immediately below the address, phone, and email address information. *Why? The horizontal line separates the letterhead from the rest of the letter.* The following steps add a bottom border to a paragraph.

1

• Display the HOME tab.

• With the insertion point in the paragraph to border, tap or click the Borders arrow (HOME tab | Paragraph group) to display the Borders gallery (Figure 3–33).

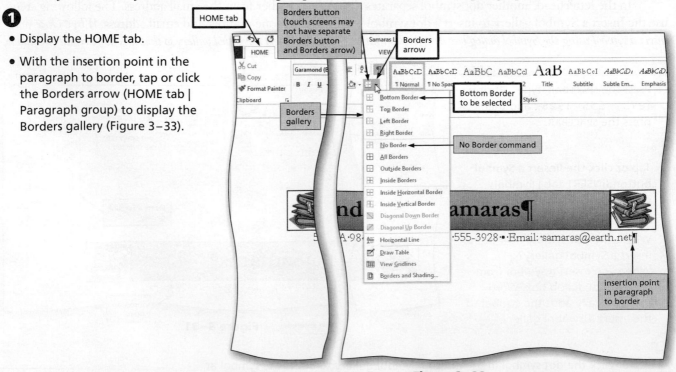

Figure 3–33

❷

- Tap or click Bottom Border in the Borders gallery to place a border below the paragraph containing the insertion point (Figure 3–34).

Q&A

If the face of the Borders button displays the border icon I want to use and if I am using a mouse, can I click the Borders button instead of using the Borders arrow?
Yes.

How would I remove an existing border from a paragraph?
If, for some reason, you wanted to remove a border from a paragraph, you would position the insertion point in the paragraph, tap or click the Borders arrow (HOME tab | Paragraph group), and then tap or click No Border in the Borders gallery.

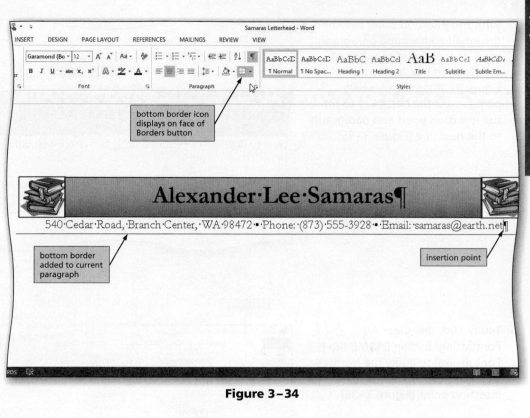

Figure 3–34

Other Ways

1. Tap or click 'Borders and Shading' button (DESIGN tab | Page Background group), tap or click Borders tab (Borders and Shading dialog box), select desired border options, tap or click OK button

To Clear Formatting

1 CREATE & FORMAT LETTERHEAD WITH GRAPHICS | 2 SPECIFY LETTER FORMATS
3 INSERT TABLE | 4 FORMAT TABLE | 5 INSERT BULLETED LIST | 6 ADDRESS ENVELOPE

The next step is to position the insertion point below the letterhead, so that you can type the contents of the letter. When you press the ENTER key at the end of a paragraph containing a border, Word moves the border forward to the next paragraph. The paragraph also retains all current settings, such as the center format. Instead, you want the paragraph and characters on the new line to use the Normal style: black font with no border.

Word uses the term, **clear formatting**, to refer to returning the formats to the Normal style. The following steps clear formatting at the location of the insertion point. *Why? You do not want to retain the current formatting in the new paragraph.*

1

- With the insertion point between the email address and paragraph mark at the end of the contact information line (as shown in Figure 3–34 on the previous page), press the ENTER key to move the insertion point and paragraph to the next line (Figure 3–35).

Figure 3–35

2

- Tap or click the 'Clear All Formatting' button (HOME tab | Font group) to apply the Normal style to the location of the insertion point (Figure 3–36).

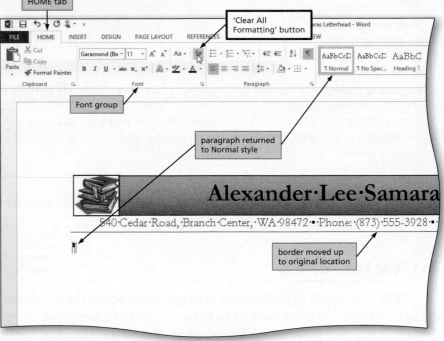

Figure 3–36

Other Ways

1. Tap or click More button in Styles gallery (HOME tab | Styles group), tap or click Clear Formatting
2. Tap or click Styles Dialog Box Launcher (HOME tab | Styles group), tap or click Clear All in Styles task pane
3. Select text, press CTRL+SPACEBAR, press CTRL+Q

AutoFormat as You Type

As you type text in a document, Word automatically formats some of it for you. For example, when you press the ENTER key or SPACEBAR after typing an email address or web address, Word automatically formats the address as a hyperlink, that is, in a different color and underlined. In Figure 3–35, for example, Word formatted the email address as a hyperlink because you pressed the ENTER key at the end of the line. Table 3–2 outlines commonly used AutoFormat As You Type options and their results.

Table 3–2 Commonly Used AutoFormat As You Type Options

Typed Text	AutoFormat Feature	Example
Quotation marks or apostrophes	Changes straight quotation marks or apostrophes to curly ones	"the" becomes "the"
Text, a space, one hyphen, one or no spaces, text, space	Changes the hyphen to an en dash	ages 20 - 45 becomes ages 20–45
Text, two hyphens, text, space	Changes the two hyphens to an em dash	Two types--yellow and red becomes Two types—yellow and red
Web or email address followed by SPACEBAR or ENTER key	Formats web or email address as a hyperlink	www.cengagebrain.com becomes www.cengagebrain.com

Number followed by a period, hyphen, right parenthesis, or greater than sign and then a space or tab followed by text	Creates a numbered list	1. Word
		2. PowerPoint
		
		becomes
		
		  1. Word
		  2. PowerPoint

Asterisk, hyphen, or greater than sign and then a space or tab followed by text	Creates a bulleted list	* HOME tab
		* INSERT tab
		
		becomes
		
		  • HOME tab
		  • INSERT tab

Fraction and then a space or hyphen	Condenses the fraction entry so that it consumes one space instead of three	1/2 becomes ½
Ordinal and then a space or hyphen	Makes part of the ordinal a superscript	3rd becomes 3rd

© 2014 Cengage Learning

To Convert a Hyperlink to Regular Text

1 CREATE & FORMAT LETTERHEAD WITH GRAPHICS | 2 SPECIFY LETTER FORMATS
3 INSERT TABLE | 4 FORMAT TABLE | 5 INSERT BULLETED LIST | 6 ADDRESS ENVELOPE

The email address in the letterhead should be formatted as regular text; that is, it should not be a different color or underlined. *Why? Hyperlinks are useful only in online documents, and this letter will be printed instead of distributed electronically.* The following steps remove a hyperlink format.

1

- If you are using a touch screen, press and hold the hyperlink and then tap the 'Show Context Menu' button on the mini toolbar; if you are using a mouse, right-click the hyperlink (in this case, the email address) to display a shortcut menu (Figure 3–37).

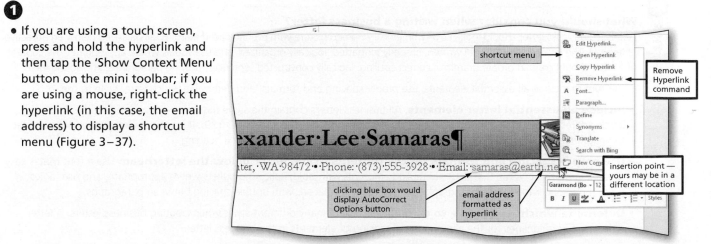

Figure 3–37

2

- Tap or click Remove Hyperlink on the shortcut menu to remove the hyperlink format from the text.

- Position the insertion point on the paragraph mark below the border because you are finished with the letterhead (Figure 3–38).

Q&A

Could I have used the AutoCorrect Options button instead of the Remove Hyperlink command?

Yes. Alternatively, if you are using a mouse, you could have pointed to the small blue box at the beginning of the hyperlink, clicked the AutoCorrect Options button, and then clicked Undo Hyperlink on the AutoCorrect Options menu.

Alexander·Lee·Samaras¶

540·Cedar·Road,·Branch·Center,·WA·98472·•·Phone:·(873)·555-3928·•·Email:·samaras@earth.net¶

insertion point

hyperlink format removed from email address

Figure 3–38

Other Ways

1. With insertion point in hyperlink, tap or click 'Add a Hyperlink' button (INSERT tab | Links group), tap or click Remove Link button

To Save an Existing Document with the Same File Name

You have made several modifications to the letterhead since you last saved it. Thus, you should save it again. The following step saves the document again. For an example of the step listed below, refer to the Office and Windows chapter at the beginning of this book.

1 Tap or click the Save button on the Quick Access Toolbar to overwrite the previously saved file.

Break Point: If you wish to take a break, this is a good place to do so. You can exit Word now. To resume at a later time, run Word, open the file called Samaras Letterhead, and continue following the steps from this location forward.

Creating a Business Letter

With the letterhead for the business letter complete, the next task is to create the remainder of the content in the letter. The following pages use Word to create a business letter that contains a table and a bulleted list.

CONSIDER THIS

What should you consider when writing a business letter?

A finished business letter should look like a symmetrically framed picture with evenly spaced margins, all balanced below an attractive letterhead. The letter should be well written, properly formatted, logically organized, and use visuals where appropriate. The content of a letter should contain proper grammar, correct spelling, logically constructed sentences, flowing paragraphs, and sound ideas.

Be sure to include all essential elements, use proper spacing and formats, and determine which letter style to use.

- **Include all essential letter elements.** All business letters contain the same basic elements, including the date line, inside address, message, and signature block (shown in Figure 3–1 on page WD 139). If a business letter does not use a letterhead, then the top of the letter should include return address information in a heading.

- **Use proper spacing and formats for the contents of the letter below the letterhead.** Use a font that is easy to read, in a size between 8 and 12 point. Add emphasis with bold, italic, and bullets where appropriate, and use tables to present numeric information. Paragraphs should be single-spaced, with double-spacing between paragraphs.

- **Determine which letter style to use.** You can follow many different styles when creating business letters. A letter style specifies guidelines for the alignment and spacing of elements in the business letter.

If possible, keep the length of a business letter to one page. Be sure to proofread the finished letter carefully.

To Save a Document with a New File Name

The current open file has the name Samaras Letterhead, which is the name of the personal letterhead. Because you want the letterhead file to remain intact so that you can reuse it, you save the document with a new name. The following steps save a document with a new name.

 Tap or click FILE on the ribbon to open the Backstage view and then tap or click the Save As tab in the Backstage view, which depending on settings, will display either the Save As gallery in the Backstage view or the Save As dialog box.

2 To save on a hard disk or other storage media on your computer, proceed to Step 2a. To save on SkyDrive, proceed to Step 2b.

2a If your screen opens the Backstage view and you want to save on storage media on your computer, tap or click Computer in the left pane, if necessary, to display options in the right pane related to saving on your computer. If your screen already displays the Save As dialog box, proceed to Step 4.

2b If your screen opens the Backstage view and you want to save on SkyDrive, tap or click SkyDrive in the left pane to display SkyDrive saving options or a Sign In button. If your screen displays a Sign In button, tap or click it and then sign in to SkyDrive.

3 Tap or click the Browse button in the right pane to display the Save As dialog box associated with the selected save location (i.e., Computer or SkyDrive).

4 Type `Samaras Thank You Letter` in the File name box to change the file name. Do not press the ENTER key after typing the file name because you do not want to close the dialog box at this time.

5 Navigate to the desired save location (in this case, the Word folder In the CIS 101 folder [or your class folder] on your computer or SkyDrive).

6 Tap or click the Save button (Save As dialog box) to save the letter in the selected folder on the selected save location with the entered file name.

BTW

Saving a Template

As an alternative to saving the letterhead as a Word document, you could save it as a template. To do so, tap or click FILE on the ribbon to open the Backstage view, tap or click the Export tab to display the Export gallery, tap or click 'Change File Type', tap or click Template in the right pane, tap or click the Save As button, enter the template name (Save As dialog box), if necessary select the Templates folder, and then tap or click the Save button in the dialog box. To use the template, tap or click FILE on the ribbon to open the Backstage view, tap or click the New tab to display the New gallery, tap or click the Personal tab in the New gallery, and then tap or click the template icon or name.

To Apply a Style

1 CREATE & FORMAT LETTERHEAD WITH GRAPHICS | 2 SPECIFY LETTER FORMATS
3 INSERT TABLE | 4 FORMAT TABLE | 5 INSERT BULLETED LIST | 6 ADDRESS ENVELOPE

Recall that the Normal style in Word places 8 points of blank space after each paragraph and inserts a vertical space equal to 1.08 lines between each line of text. You will need to modify the spacing used for the paragraphs in the business letter. *Why? Business letters should use single spacing for paragraphs and double spacing between paragraphs.*

Word has many built-in, or predefined, styles that you can use to format text. The No Spacing style, for example, defines line spacing as single and does not insert any additional blank space between lines when you press the ENTER key. To apply a style to a paragraph, you first position the insertion point in the paragraph. The following step applies the No Spacing style to a paragraph.

1

- With the insertion point positioned in the paragraph to be formatted, tap or click No Spacing in the Styles gallery (HOME tab | Styles group) to apply the selected style to the current paragraph (Figure 3–39).

Figure 3–39

Q&A

Will this style be used in the rest of the document?

Yes. The paragraph formatting, which includes the style, will carry forward to subsequent paragraphs each time you press the ENTER key.

Other Ways

1. Tap or click Styles Dialog Box Launcher (HOME tab | Styles group), tap or click desired style in Styles task pane

2. Press CTRL+SHIFT+S, tap or click Style Name arrow in Apply Styles task pane, tap or click desired style in list

CONSIDER THIS

What elements should a business letter contain?

Be sure to include all essential business letter elements, properly spaced, in your letter:

• The **date line**, which consists of the month, day, and year, is positioned two to six lines below the letterhead.

• The **inside address**, placed three to eight lines below the date line, usually contains the addressee's courtesy title plus full name, job title, business affiliation, and full geographical address.

• The **salutation**, if present, begins two lines below the last line of the inside address. If you do not know the recipient's name, avoid using the salutation "To whom it may concern" — it is impersonal. Instead, use the recipient's title in the salutation, e.g., Dear Personnel Director. In a business letter, use a colon (:) at the end of the salutation; in a personal letter, use a comma.

• The body of the letter, the **message**, begins two lines below the salutation. Within the message, paragraphs are single-spaced with one blank line between paragraphs.

• Two lines below the last line of the message, the **complimentary close** is displayed. Capitalize only the first word in a complimentary close.

• Type the **signature block** at least four blank lines below the complimentary close, allowing room for the author to sign his or her name.

CONSIDER THIS

What are the common styles of business letters?

Three common business letter styles are the block, the modified block, and the modified semi-block. Each style specifies different alignments and indentations.

• In the block letter style, all components of the letter begin flush with the left margin.

• In the modified block letter style, the date, complimentary close, and signature block are positioned approximately one-half inch to the right of center or at the right margin. All other components of the letter begin flush with the left margin.

• In the modified semi-block letter style, the date, complimentary close, and signature block are centered, positioned approximately one-half inch to the right of center or at the right margin. The first line of each paragraph in the body of the letter is indented one-half to one inch from the left margin. All other components of the letter begin flush with the left margin.

The business letter in this project follows the modified block style.

Using Tab Stops to Align Text

A **tab stop** is a location on the horizontal ruler that tells Word where to position the insertion point when you press the TAB key on the keyboard. Word, by default, places a tab stop at every one-half inch mark on the ruler. You also can set your own custom tab stops. Tab settings are a paragraph format. Thus, each time you press the ENTER key, any custom tab stops are carried forward to the next paragraph.

To move the insertion point from one tab stop to another, press the TAB key on the keyboard. When you press the TAB key, a **tab character** formatting mark appears in the empty space between the tab stops.

When you set a custom tab stop, you specify how the text will align at a tab stop. The tab marker on the ruler reflects the alignment of the characters at the location of the tab stop. Table 3–3 shows types of tab stop alignments in Word and their corresponding tab markers.

Table 3–3 Types of Tab Stop Alignments			
Tab Stop Alignment	**Tab Marker**	**Result of Pressing TAB Key**	**Example**
Left Tab		Left-aligns text at the location of the tab stop	toolbar ruler
Center Tab		Centers text at the location of the tab stop	toolbar ruler
Right Tab		Right-aligns text at the location of the tab stop	toolbar ruler
Decimal Tab		Aligns text on decimal point at the location of the tab stop	45.72 223.75
Bar Tab		Aligns text at a bar character at the location of the tab stop	toolbar ruler

© 2014 Cengage Learning

To Display the Ruler

If you are using a mouse, one way to set custom tab stops is by using the horizontal ruler. Thus, the following steps display the ruler in the document window.

1 If the rulers are not showing, display the VIEW tab.

2 Tap or click the View Ruler check box (VIEW tab | Show group) to place a check mark in the check box and display the horizontal and vertical rulers on the screen (shown in Figure 3–40).

To Set Custom Tab Stops

1 CREATE & FORMAT LETTERHEAD WITH GRAPHICS | 2 SPECIFY LETTER FORMATS
3 INSERT TABLE | 4 FORMAT TABLE | 5 INSERT BULLETED LIST | 6 ADDRESS ENVELOPE

The first required element of the business letter is the date line, which in this letter is positioned two lines below the letterhead. The date line contains the month, day, and year, and begins four inches from the left margin. *Why? Business letter guidelines specify to begin the date line approximately one-half inch to the right of center. Thus, you should set a custom tab stop at the 4" mark on the ruler.* The following steps set a left-aligned tab stop.

1

- With the insertion point on the paragraph mark below the border (shown in Figure 3–39 on page WD 165), press the ENTER key so that a blank line appears above the insertion point.

- If you are using a touch screen, proceed to Step 3 on the next page because you have to use a different method to set custom tabs.

- If you are using a mouse, if necessary, click the tab selector at the left edge of the horizontal ruler until it displays the type of tab you wish to use, which is the Left Tab icon in this case.

- If you are using a mouse, position the pointer on the 4" mark on the ruler, which is the location of the desired custom tab stop (Figure 3–40).

Q&A
What is the purpose of the tab selector?
Before using the ruler to set a tab stop, ensure the correct tab stop icon appears in the tab selector. Each time you click the tab selector, its icon changes. The Left Tab icon is the default. For a list of the types of tab stops, see Table 3–3.

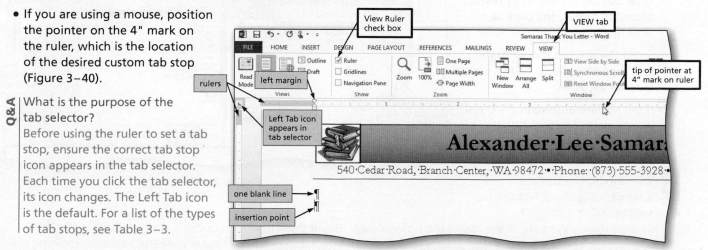

Figure 3–40

2

- If you are using a mouse, click the 4" mark on the ruler to place a tab marker at that location (Figure 3–41).

Q&A

What if I click the wrong location on the ruler?

You can move a custom tab stop by dragging the tab marker to the desired location on the ruler. Or, you can remove an existing custom tab stop by pointing to the tab marker on the ruler and then dragging the tab marker down and out of the ruler.

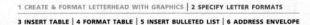

Figure 3–41

3

- If you are using a touch screen, display the HOME tab, tap the Paragraph Settings Dialog Box Launcher (HOME tab | Paragraph group), tap the Tabs button (Paragraph dialog box), type 4 in the Tab stop position box (Tabs dialog box), tap the Set button, and then tap the OK button to set a custom tab stop and place a corresponding tab marker on the ruler.

Other Ways

1. Tap or click Paragraph Dialog Box Launcher (HOME tab or PAGE LAYOUT tab | Paragraph group), tap or click Tabs button (Paragraph dialog box), type tab stop position (Tabs dialog box), tap or click Set button, tap or click OK button

To Insert the Current Date in a Document

1 CREATE & FORMAT LETTERHEAD WITH GRAPHICS | 2 SPECIFY LETTER FORMATS
3 INSERT TABLE | 4 FORMAT TABLE | 5 INSERT BULLETED LIST | 6 ADDRESS ENVELOPE

The next step is to enter the current date at the 4" tab stop in the document. *Why? The date in this letter will be positioned according to the guidelines for a modified block style letter.* In Word, you can insert a computer's system date in a document. The following steps insert the current date in the letter.

1

- Press the TAB key to position the insertion point at the location of the tab stop in the current paragraph.

- Display the INSERT tab.

- Tap or click the 'Insert Date and Time' button (INSERT tab | Text group) to display the Date and Time dialog box.

- Select the desired format (Date and Time dialog box), in this case October 29, 2014.

- If the Update automatically check box is selected, tap or click the check box to remove the check mark (Figure 3–42).

Q&A

Why should the Update automatically check box not be selected?

In this project, the date at the top of the letter always should show today's date (for example, October 29, 2014). If, however, you wanted the date always to change to reflect the current computer date (for example, showing the date you open or print the letter), then you would place a check mark in this check box.

Figure 3–42

2

- Tap or click the OK button to insert the current date at the location of the insertion point (Figure 3–43).

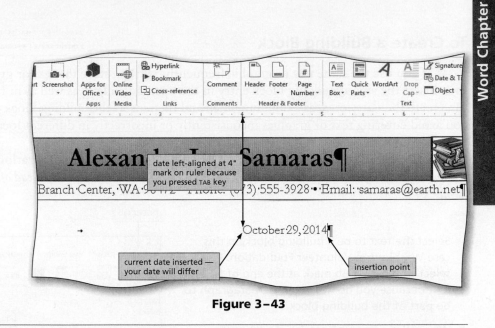

date left-aligned at 4" mark on ruler because you pressed TAB key

Alexan   **Samaras¶**

Branch·Center,·WA·98472 Phone:·(873)·555-3928·• ·Email:·samaras@earth.net¶

October·29,·2014¶

current date inserted — your date will differ

insertion point

Figure 3–43

To Enter the Inside Address and Salutation

The next step in composing the business letter is to type the inside address and salutation. The following steps enter this text.

1 With the insertion point at the end of the date (shown in Figure 3–43), press the ENTER key three times.

2 Type **Ms. Lucy Song** and then press the ENTER key.

3 Type **Washington Volunteer Foundation** and then press the ENTER key.

4 Type **10 Hickory Avenue** and then press the ENTER key.

5 Type **Midway, WA 98476** and then press the ENTER key twice.

6 Type **Dear Ms. Song:** to complete the inside address and salutation entries (Figure 3–44).

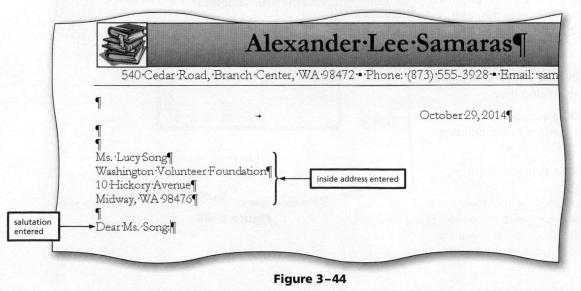

Alexander·Lee·Samaras¶

540·Cedar·Road,·Branch·Center,·WA·98472·• ·Phone:·(873)·555-3928·• ·Email:·sam

¶

¶   October·29,·2014¶

¶

Ms.·Lucy·Song¶
Washington·Volunteer·Foundation¶   inside address entered
10·Hickory·Avenue¶
Midway,·WA·98476¶

¶

salutation entered → Dear·Ms.·Song:¶

Figure 3–44

To Create a Building Block

If you use the same text or graphic frequently, you can store the text or graphic as a **building block** and then insert the stored building block entry in the open document, as well as in future documents. That is, you can create the entry once as a building block and then insert the building block when you need it. In this way, you avoid entering text or graphics inconsistently or incorrectly in different locations throughout the same or multiple documents.

The following steps create a building block for the volunteer organization name, Washington Volunteer Foundation. *Why? Later, you will insert the building block in the document instead of typing the volunteer organization name.*

1

- Select the text to be a building block, in this case Washington Volunteer Foundation. Do not select the paragraph mark at the end of the text because you do not want the paragraph to be part of the building block.

Q&A
Why is the paragraph mark not part of the building block?
Select the paragraph mark only if you want to store paragraph formatting, such as indentation and line spacing, as part of the building block.

- Tap or click the 'Explore Quick Parts' button (INSERT tab | Text group) to display the Explore Quick Parts gallery (Figure 3–45).

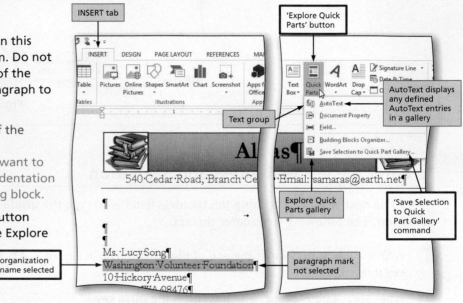

Figure 3–45

2

- Tap or click 'Save Selection to Quick Part Gallery' in the Explore Quick Parts gallery to display the Create New Building Block dialog box.

- Type **wvf** in the Name text box (Create New Building Block dialog box) to replace the proposed building block name (Washington, in this case) with a shorter building block name (Figure 3–46).

3

- Tap or click the OK button to store the building block entry and close the dialog box.

- If Word displays another dialog box, tap or click the Yes button to save changes to the building blocks.

Q&A
Will this building block be available in future documents?
When you exit Word, a dialog box may appear asking if you want to save changes to the building blocks. Tap or click the Save button if you want to use the new building block in future documents.

Figure 3–46

Other Ways

1. Select text, press ALT+F3

To Modify a Building Block

When you save a building block in the Explore Quick Parts gallery, the building block is displayed at the top of the Explore Quick Parts gallery. When you point to the building block in the Explore Quick Parts gallery, a ScreenTip displays the building block name. If you want to display more information when the user points to the building block, you can include a description in the ScreenTip.

The following steps modify a building block to include a description and change its category to AutoText. **Why?** *Because you want to reuse this text, you place it in the AutoText gallery, which also is accessible through the Explore Quick Parts gallery.*

1

- Tap or click the 'Explore Quick Parts' button (INSERT tab | Text group) to display the Explore Quick Parts gallery.

- Press and hold or right-click the Washington Volunteer Foundation building block to display a shortcut menu (Figure 3–47).

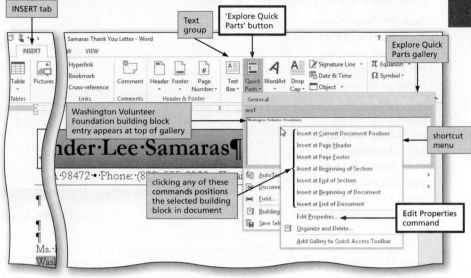

Figure 3–47

2

- Tap or click Edit Properties on the shortcut menu to display the Modify Building Block dialog box, filled in with information related to the selected building block.

- Tap or click the Gallery arrow (Modify Building Block dialog box) and then tap or click AutoText to change the gallery in which the building block will be placed.

- Type **Potential Volunteer Opportunity** in the Description text box (Figure 3–48).

3

- Tap or click the OK button to store the building block entry and close the dialog box.

- Tap or click the Yes button when asked if you want to redefine the building block entry.

Figure 3–48

To Insert a Building Block

The prospective volunteer organization, Washington Volunteer Foundation, appears in the first sentence in the body of the letter. You will type the building block name, wvf, and then instruct Word to replace this building block name with the stored building block entry, Washington Volunteer Foundation. The following steps insert a building block. **Why?** *Instead of typing the name, you will insert the stored building block.*

1

- Tap or click to the right of the colon in the salutation and then press the ENTER key twice to position the insertion point one blank line below the salutation.

- Type the beginning of the first sentence as follows, entering the building block name as shown: **Thank you for meeting with me this morning to discuss the mentoring position available at wvf** (Figure 3–49).

Figure 3–49

2

- Press the F3 key to instruct Word to replace the building block name (wvf) with the stored building block entry (Washington Volunteer Foundation).

- Press the PERIOD key (Figure 3–50).

Figure 3–50

Other Ways

1. Tap or click 'Explore Quick Parts' button (INSERT tab | Text group), if necessary point to AutoText, select desired building block

2. Tap or click 'Explore Quick Parts' button (INSERT tab | Text group), tap or click Building Blocks Organizer, select desired building block, tap or click Insert button

BTW

Certification
The Microsoft Office Specialist (MOS) program provides an opportunity for you to obtain a valuable industry credential — proof that you have the Word 2013 skills required by employers. For more information, visit the Certification resource on the Student Companion Site located on www.cengagebrain .com. For detailed instructions about accessing available resources, visit www.cengage .com/ct/studentdownload or contact your instructor for information about accessing the required files.

Building Blocks versus AutoCorrect

In Chapter 2, you learned how to use the AutoCorrect feature, which enables you to insert and create AutoCorrect entries, similarly to how you created and inserted building blocks in this chapter. The difference between an AutoCorrect entry and a building block entry is that the AutoCorrect feature makes corrections for you automatically as soon as you press the SPACEBAR or type a punctuation mark, whereas you must instruct Word to insert a building block. That is, you enter the building block name and then press the F3 key, or tap or click the Explore Quick Parts button and select the building block from one of the galleries or the Building Blocks Organizer.

To Insert a Nonbreaking Space

Some compound words, such as proper nouns, dates, units of time and measure, abbreviations, and geographic destinations, should not be divided at the end of a line. These words either should fit as a unit at the end of a line or be wrapped together to the next line.

Word provides two special characters to assist with this task: the nonbreaking space and the nonbreaking hyphen. A **nonbreaking space** is a special space character that prevents two words from splitting if the first word falls at the end of a line. Similarly, a **nonbreaking hyphen** is a special type of hyphen that prevents two words separated by a hyphen from splitting at the end of a line.

The following steps insert a nonbreaking space between the two words in the city name, Branch Center. *Why? You want these two words in the city name to appear on the same physical line.*

❶

- With the insertion point at the end of the first sentence in the body of the letter (as shown in Figure 3–50), press the SPACEBAR.

- Type **I truly enjoyed our conversation and am excited about the possibility of volunteering with your Branch** and then press CTRL+SHIFT+SPACEBAR to insert a nonbreaking space after the entered word (Figure 3–51).

Figure 3–51

❷

- Type **Center team** and then press PERIOD key (Figure 3–52).

Figure 3–52

Other Ways

1. Tap or click 'Insert a Symbol' button (INSERT tab | Symbols group), tap or click More Symbols, tap or click Special Characters tab (Symbol dialog box), tap or click Nonbreaking Space in Character list, tap or click Insert button, tap or click Close button

To Enter Text

The next step in creating the letter is to enter the rest of the text in the first paragraph. The following steps enter this text.

❶ Press the SPACEBAR.

❷ Type this sentence: **The table below outlines my volunteer service background:**

❸ Press the ENTER key twice to place a blank line between paragraphs (shown in Figure 3–53 on the next page).

Q&A Why does my document wrap on different words?
Differences in wordwrap may relate to the printer connected to your computer. Thus, it is possible that the same document could wordwrap differently if associated with a different printer.

BTW

Nonbreaking Hyphen
If you wanted to insert a nonbreaking hyphen, you would press CTRL+SHIFT+HYPHEN.

To Save an Existing Document with the Same File Name

You have made several modifications to the document since you last saved it. Thus, you should save it again. The following step saves the document again.

1 Tap or click the Save button on the Quick Access Toolbar to overwrite the previously saved file.

Break Point: If you wish to take a break, this is a good place to do so. You can exit Word now. To resume at a later time, run Word, open the file called Samaras Thank You Letter, and continue following the steps from this location forward.

Tables

The next step in composing the business letter is to place a table listing the volunteer service background (shown in Figure 3–1 on page WD 139). A Word **table** is a collection of rows and columns. The intersection of a row and a column is called a **cell**, and cells are filled with data.

The first step in creating a table is to insert an empty table in the document. When inserting a table, you must specify the total number of rows and columns required, which is called the **dimension** of the table. The table in this project has three columns. You often do not know the total number of rows in a table. Thus, many Word users create one row initially and then add more rows as needed. In Word, the first number in a dimension is the number of columns, and the second is the number of rows. For example, in Word, a 3 × 1 (pronounced "three by one") table consists of three columns and one row.

To Insert an Empty Table

1 CREATE & FORMAT LETTERHEAD WITH GRAPHICS | 2 SPECIFY LETTER FORMATS
3 INSERT TABLE | 4 FORMAT TABLE | 5 INSERT BULLETED LIST | 6 ADDRESS ENVELOPE

The next step is to insert an empty table in the letter. The following steps insert a table with three columns and one row at the location of the insertion point. *Why? The first column will identify the organization, the second will identify the primary responsibility, and the third will identify the term of service in years. You will start with one row and add them as needed.*

1

- Scroll the document so that you will be able to see the table in the document window.

- Display the INSERT tab.

- With the insertion point positioned as shown in Figure 3–53, tap or click the 'Add a Table' button (INSERT tab | Tables group) to display the Add a Table gallery (Figure 3–53).

Experiment

- If you are using a mouse, point to various cells on the grid to see a preview of various table dimensions in the document window.

Figure 3–53

2

- If you are using a mouse, position the pointer on the cell in the first row and third column of the grid to preview the desired table dimension in the document (Figure 3–54).

Figure 3–54

3

- Tap or click the cell in the first row and third column of the grid to insert an empty table with one row and three columns in the document.

- If necessary, scroll the document so that the table is visible (Figure 3–55).

Q&A What are the small circles in the table cells?
Each table cell has an **end-of-cell mark**, which is a formatting mark that assists you with selecting and formatting cells. Similarly, each row has an **end-of-row mark**, which you can use to add columns to the right of a table. Recall that formatting marks do not print on a hard copy. The end-of-cell marks currently are left-aligned, that is, positioned at the left edge of each cell.

Figure 3–55

Other Ways

1. Tap or click 'Add a Table' button (INSERT tab | Tables group), tap or click Insert Table in Add a Table gallery, enter number of columns and rows (Insert Table dialog box), tap or click OK button

To Enter Data in a Table

1 CREATE & FORMAT LETTERHEAD WITH GRAPHICS | 2 SPECIFY LETTER FORMATS
3 INSERT TABLE | 4 FORMAT TABLE | 5 INSERT BULLETED LIST | 6 ADDRESS ENVELOPE

The next step is to enter data in the cells of the empty table. The data you enter in a cell wordwraps just as text wordwraps between the margins of a document. To place data in a cell, you tap or click the cell and then type.

To advance rightward from one cell to the next, press the TAB key. When you are at the rightmost cell in a row, press the TAB key to move to the first cell in the next row; do not press the ENTER key. *Why? The* ENTER *key is used to begin a new paragraph within a cell.* One way to add new rows to a table is to press the TAB key when the insertion point is positioned in the bottom-right corner cell of the table. The step on the next page enters data in the first row of the table and then inserts a blank second row.

1

- With the insertion point in the left cell of the table, type `Organization` and then press the TAB key to advance the insertion point to the next cell.

- Type `Primary Responsibility` and then press the TAB key to advance the insertion point to the next cell.

- Type `Term of Service` and then press the TAB key to add a second row at the end of the table and position the insertion point in the first column of the new row (Figure 3–56).

Figure 3–56

Q&A How do I edit cell contents if I make a mistake?
Tap or click in the cell and then correct the entry.

BTW

Tables

For simple tables, such as the one just created, Word users often select the table dimension in the Add a Table gallery to create the table. For a more complex table, such as one with a varying number of columns per row, Word has a Draw Table feature that allows users to draw a table in the document using a pencil pointer. To use this feature, click the 'Add a Table' button (INSERT tab | Tables group) and then click Draw Table on the Add a Table menu.

To Enter More Data in a Table

The following steps enter the remaining data in the table.

1 Type `Branch Center School District` and then press the TAB key to advance the insertion point to the next cell. Type `Tutor` and then press the TAB key to advance the insertion point to the next cell. Type `6 years` and then press the TAB key to add a row at the end of the table and position the insertion point in the first column of the new row.

2 In the third row, type `Newton County Youth Groups` in the first column, `Teen Leader` in the second column, and `3 years` in the third column. Press the TAB key to position the insertion point in the first column of a new row.

3 In the fourth row, type `Trenton Park District` in the first column, `Special Events Vocalist` in the second column, and `2 years` in the third column. Press the TAB key.

4 In the fifth row, type `Skylar Athletic Club` in the first column, `Basketball Coach` in the second column, and `4 years` in the third column (Figure 3–57).

Figure 3–57

To Apply a Table Style

Word provides a gallery of more than 90 table styles, which include a variety of colors and shading. *Why? Table styles allow you to change the basic table format to a more visually appealing style.* The following steps apply a table style to the table in the letter.

1

- If the First Column check box in the Table Style Options group (TABLE TOOLS DESIGN tab) contains a check mark, tap or click the check box to remove the check mark. Be sure the remaining check marks match those in the Table Style Options group (TABLE TOOLS DESIGN tab) as shown in Figure 3–58.

Q&A

What if the TABLE TOOLS DESIGN tab no longer is the active tab?
Tap or click in the table and then display the TABLE TOOLS DESIGN tab.

What do the options in the Table Style Options group mean?
When you apply table styles, if you want the top row of the table (header row), a row containing totals (total row), first column, or last column to be formatted differently, select those check boxes. If you want the rows or columns to alternate with colors, select Banded Rows or Banded Columns, respectively.

2

- With the insertion point in the table, tap or click the More button in the Table Styles gallery (TABLE TOOLS DESIGN tab | Table Styles group), shown in Figure 3–57, to expand the gallery.

- If you are using a mouse, scroll and then point to 'Grid Table 6 Colorful - Accent 1' In the Table Styles gallery to display a live preview of that style applied to the table in the document (Figure 3–58).

Experiment

- If you are using a mouse, point to various styles in the Table Styles gallery and watch the format of the table change in the document window.

Figure 3–58

3

- Tap or click 'Grid Table 6 Colorful - Accent 1' in the Table Styles gallery to apply the selected style to the table (Figure 3–59).

Experiment

- Select and remove check marks from various check boxes in the Table Style Options group and watch the format of the table change in the document window. When finished experimenting, be sure the check marks match those shown in Figure 3–58.

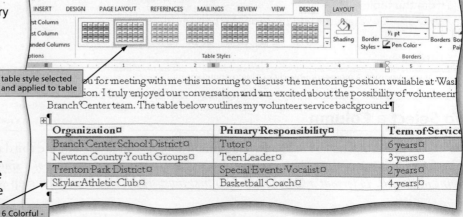

Figure 3–59

To Resize Table Columns to Fit Table Contents

The table in this project currently extends from the left margin to the right margin of the document. The following steps instruct Word to fit the width of the columns to the contents of the table automatically. *Why?* *You want each column to be only as wide as the longest entry in the table. That is, the first column must be wide enough to accommodate the words, Newton County Youth Groups, and the second column should be only as wide as the title, Special Events Vocalist, and so on.*

1

- With the insertion point in the table, display the TABLE TOOLS LAYOUT tab.

- Tap or click the AutoFit button (TABLE TOOLS LAYOUT tab | Cell Size group) to display the AutoFit menu (Figure 3–60).

Figure 3–60

2

- Tap or click AutoFit Contents on the AutoFit menu, so that Word automatically adjusts the widths of the columns based on the text in the table (Figure 3–61).

Figure 3–61

Q&A

Can I resize columns manually?
Yes, you can drag a **column boundary**, the border to the right of a column, until the column is the desired width. Similarly, you can resize a row by dragging the **row boundary**, the border at the bottom of a row, until the row is the desired height. You also can resize the entire table by dragging the **table resize handle**, which is a small square that appears when you point to a corner of the table.

What causes the table move handle and table resize handle to appear and disappear from the table?
They appear whenever you position the pointer in the table.

Other Ways

1. If you are using a mouse, double-click column boundary

To Select a Column

The next task is to change the alignment of the data in cells in the third column of the table. To do this, you first must select the column. *Why?* *If you want to format the contents of a single cell, simply position the insertion point in the cell. To format a series of cells, you first must select them.* The next step selects a column.

1

- If you are using a mouse, position the pointer at the boundary above the column to be selected, the third column in this case, so that the pointer changes to a downward pointing arrow and then click to select the column (Figure 3–62).

- If you are using a touch screen, position the insertion point in the third column, tap the Select Table button (TABLE TOOLS LAYOUT tab | Table group), and then tap Select Column on the Select Table menu.

Figure 3–62

Other Ways

1. Tap or click Select Table button (TABLE TOOLS LAYOUT tab | Table group), tap or click Select Column In Select Table gallery

Selecting Table Contents

When working with tables, you may need to select the contents of cells, rows, columns, or the entire table. Table 3–4 identifies ways to select various items in a table.

Table 3–4 Selecting Items in a Table	
Item to Select	**Action**
Cell	If you are using a mouse, point to left edge of cell and then click when the pointer changes to a small solid upward angled pointing arrow.
	Or, position insertion point in cell, click Select Table button (TABLE TOOLS LAYOUT tab | Table group), and then click Select Cell on the Select Table menu.
Column	If you are using a mouse, point to border at top of column and then click when the pointer changes to a small solid downward-pointing arrow.
	Or, position insertion point in column, click Select Table button (TABLE TOOLS LAYOUT tab | Table group), and then click Select Column on the Select Table menu.
Row	If you are using a mouse, point to the left of the row and then click when pointer changes to a right-pointing block arrow.
	Or, position insertion point in row, click Select Table button (TABLE TOOLS LAYOUT tab | Table group), and then click Select Row on the Select Table menu.
Multiple cells, rows, or columns adjacent to one another	Drag through cells, rows, or columns.
Multiple cells, rows, or columns not adjacent to one another	Select first cell, row, or column (as described above) and then hold down CTRL key while selecting next cell, row, or column.
Next cell	Press TAB key.
Previous cell	Press SHIFT+TAB.
Table	If you are using a mouse, point somewhere in table and then click table move handle that appears in upper-left corner of table.
	Or, position insertion point in table, click Select Table button (TABLE TOOLS LAYOUT tab | Table group), and then click Select Table on the Select Table menu.

To Align Data in Cells

The next step is to change the alignment of the data in cells in the third column of the table. In addition to aligning text horizontally in a cell (left, center, or right), you can align it vertically within a cell (top, center, bottom). When the height of the cell is close to the same height as the text, however, differences in vertical alignment are not readily apparent, which is the case for this table. The following step centers data in cells. *Why? The column containing the term of service would look better if its contents are centered.*

1

- With the cells selected, as shown in Figure 3–62 on the previous page, tap or click the desired alignment, in this case the 'Align Top Center' button (TABLE TOOLS LAYOUT tab | Alignment group) to center the contents of the selected cells (Figure 3–63).

Figure 3–63

To Center a Table

When you first create a table, it is left-aligned; that is, it is flush with the left margin. In this letter, the table should be centered between the margins. To center a table, you first select the entire table. The following steps select and center a table using the mini toolbar. *Why? Recall that you can use buttons and boxes on the mini toolbar instead of those on the ribbon.*

1

- If you are using a mouse, position the pointer in the table so that the table move handle appears (shown in Figure 3–63).

Q&A What if the table move handle does not appear?
You also can select a table by clicking the Select Table button (TABLE TOOLS LAYOUT tab | Table group) and then clicking Select Table on the menu.

2

- If you are using a mouse, click the table move handle to select the entire table (Figure 3–64).

- If you are using a touch screen, tap the Select Table button (TABLE TOOLS LAYOUT tab | Table group) and then tap Select Table on the Select Table menu to select the table.

Figure 3–64

3

- If you are using a mouse, click the Center button on the mini toolbar to center the selected table between the left and right margins (Figure 3–65).

Thank you for meeting with me this morning to discuss the mentoring position available at Washing... ...versation and am excited about the possibility of volunteering with you... ...w outlines my volunteer service background:¶

Organization¤	Primary·Responsibility¤	Term·of·Service¤
Branch·Center·School·District¤	Tutor¤	6·years¤
Newton·County·Youth·Groups¤	Teen·Leader¤	3·years¤
Trenton·Park·District¤	Special·Events·Vocalist¤	2·years¤

mini toolbar

Center button selected

table centered between page margins

Figure 3–65

Q&A

Could I have clicked the Center button on the HOME tab?

Yes. If the command you want to use is not on the currently displayed tab on the ribbon and it is available on the mini toolbar, use the mini toolbar instead of switching to a different tab. This technique minimizes mouse movement.

- If you are using a touch screen, display the HOME tab and then tap the Center button (HOME tab | Paragraph group) to center the table.

To Insert a Row in a Table

1 CREATE & FORMAT LETTERHEAD WITH GRAPHICS | 2 SPECIFY LETTER FORMATS
3 INSERT TABLE | 4 FORMAT TABLE | 5 INSERT BULLETED LIST | 6 ADDRESS ENVELOPE

The next step is to insert a row at the top of the table. *Why? You want to place a title on the table.* As discussed earlier, you can insert a row at the end of a table by positioning the insertion point in the bottom-right corner cell and then pressing the TAB key. You cannot use the TAB key to insert a row at the beginning or middle of a table. Instead, you use the 'Insert Rows Above' or 'Insert Rows Below' command or the Insert Control (shown in Figure 3–70 on page WD 183). The following steps insert a row to the top of a table.

1

- Position the insertion point somewhere in the first row of the table because you want to insert a row above this row (Figure 3–66).

insertion point in first row

Organization¤ I	Primary·Responsibility¤	Term·of·Service¤
Branch·Center·School·District¤	Tutor¤	6·years¤

Figure 3–66

2

- Tap or click the 'Insert Rows Above' button (TABLE TOOLS LAYOUT tab | Rows & Columns group) to insert a row above the row containing the insertion point and then select the newly inserted row (Figure 3–67).

'Insert Rows Above' button

'Insert Rows Below' button

Delete Table button contains commands for deleting table elements

TABLE TOOLS LAYOUT tab

'Insert Columns to the Right' button

Rows & Columns group

'Insert Columns to the Left' button

...for meeting with me this morning to discuss the mentoring position available at Washington·Volunteer· Foundation. I truly enjoyed ...nd am excited about the possibility of volunteering with your· Branch·Center team. The ta... ...my volunteer service background:¶

row with three columns inserted and selected

Organization¤	Primary·Responsibility¤	Term·of·Service¤

column headings no longer are bold because they no longer are in first row of table

Figure 3–67

Q&A

Do I have to insert rows above the row containing the insertion point?

No. You can insert below the row containing the insertion point by tapping or clicking the 'Insert Rows Below' button (TABLE TOOLS LAYOUT tab | Rows & Columns group).

Why did the colors in the second row change?

The table style specifies to format the Header row differently, which is the first row.

Other Ways

1. If you are using a mouse, point to the left of the table and click the desired Insert Control

2. Press and hold or right-click row, tap Insert Table button on mini toolbar or point to Insert on shortcut menu, tap or click desired command on Insert submenu

BTW
Resizing Table Columns and Rows
To change the width of a column or height of a row to an exact measurement, hold down the ALT key while dragging markers on the ruler. Or, enter values in the 'Table Column Width' or 'Table Row Height' boxes (TABLE TOOLS LAYOUT tab | Cell Size group).

To INSERT A COLUMN IN A TABLE

If you wanted to insert a column in a table, instead of inserting rows, you would perform the following steps.

1. If you are using a mouse, point above the table and then click the desired Insert Control.

or

1. Position the insertion point in the column to the left or right of where you want to insert the column.

2. Tap or click the 'Insert Columns to the Left' button (TABLE TOOLS LAYOUT tab | Rows & Columns group) to insert a column to the left of the current column, or tap or click the 'Insert Columns to the Right' button (TABLE TOOLS LAYOUT tab | Rows & Columns group) to insert a column to the right of the current column.

or

1. Press and hold or right-click the table, tap Insert Table button on mini toolbar or point to Insert on the shortcut menu, and then tap Insert Left or Insert Right or click 'Insert Columns to the Left' or 'Insert Columns to the Right' on the Insert submenu.

To Merge Cells

1 CREATE & FORMAT LETTERHEAD WITH GRAPHICS | 2 SPECIFY LETTER FORMATS
3 INSERT TABLE | 4 FORMAT TABLE | 5 INSERT BULLETED LIST | 6 ADDRESS ENVELOPE

The row just inserted has one cell for each column, in this case, three cells (shown in Figure 3–67). The top row of the table, however, is to be a single cell that spans all rows. **Why?** *The top row contains the table title, which should be centered above the columns of the table.* Thus, the following steps merge the three cells into a single cell.

1
- With the cells to merge selected (as shown in Figure 3–67 on the previous page), tap or click the Merge Cells button (TABLE TOOLS LAYOUT tab | Merge group) to merge the selected cells into a single cell (Figure 3–68).

Figure 3–68

2
- Position the insertion point in the first row and then type **Volunteer Service Background** as the table title (Figure 3–69).

Figure 3–69

Other Ways

1. Tap 'Show Context Menu' button on mini toolbar or right-click selected cells, tap or click Merge Cells on shortcut menu

BTW
Moving Tables
If you wanted to move a table to a new location, you would point to the upper-left corner of the table until the table move handle appears (shown in Figure 3–69), point to the table move handle, and then drag it to move the entire table to a new location.

To Split Table Cells

Instead of merging multiple cells into a single cell, sometimes you want to split a single cell into multiple cells. If you wanted to split cells, you would perform the following steps.

1. Position the insertion point in the cell to split.
2. Tap or click the Split Cells button (TABLE TOOLS LAYOUT tab | Merge group); or tap 'Show Context Menu' button on mini toolbar or right-click the cell and then tap or click Split Cells on the shortcut menu to display the Split Cells dialog box.
3. Enter the number of columns and rows into which you want the cell split (Split Cells dialog box).
4. Tap or click the OK button.

To Split a Table

Instead of splitting table cells into multiple cells, sometimes you want to split a single table into multiple cells. If you wanted to split a table, you would perform the following steps.

1. Position the insertion point in the cell where you want the table to be split.
2. Tap or click the Split Table button (TABLE TOOLS LAYOUT tab | Merge group) to split the table into two tables at the location of the insertion point.

To Change the Font of Text in a Table Row

When you added a row to the top of the table for the title, Word moved the bold format from the column headings (which originally were in the first row of the table) to the title row (which now is the first row). Because you would like the columns headings bold also, the following steps select a table row and bold its contents.

① Select the row containing the column headings (Figure 3–70).

② With the text selected, tap or click the Bold button (HOME tab | Font group) to bold the selected text.

Q&A What is the symbol that appeared to the left of the table?
When you use a mouse to select a row or column in a table, Word displays an Insert Control. You can click the **Insert Control** to add a row or column to the table at that location.

Figure 3–70

BTW
Tab Character in Tables
In a table, the TAB key advances the insertion point from one cell to the next. To insert a tab character in a cell, you must press CTRL+TAB.

Deleting Table Data

If you want to delete row(s) or delete column(s) from a table, position the insertion point in the row(s) or column(s) to delete, tap or click the Delete Table button (TABLE TOOLS LAYOUT tab | Rows & Columns group), and then tap or click Delete Rows or Delete Columns on the Delete Table menu. Or, select the row or column to delete, press and hold or right-click the selection, and then tap or click Delete Rows or Delete Columns on the mini toolbar or shortcut menu.

To delete the contents of a cell, select the cell contents and then press the DELETE or BACKSPACE key. You also can drag and drop or cut and paste the contents of cells. To delete an entire table, select the table, tap or click the Delete Table button (TABLE TOOLS LAYOUT tab | Rows & Columns group), and then tap or click Delete Table on the Delete menu. To delete the contents of a table and leave an empty table, you would select the table and then press the DELETE key.

BTW

AutoFormat Settings
Before you can use them, AutoFormat options must be enabled. To check if an AutoFormat option is enabled, tap or click FILE on the ribbon to open the Backstage view, tap or click Options in the Backstage view, tap or click Proofing in the left pane (Word Options dialog box), tap or click the AutoCorrect Options button, tap or click the AutoFormat As You Type tab, select the appropriate check boxes, and then tap or click the OK button in each open dialog box.

To Add More Text

The table now is complete. The next step is to enter text below the table. The following steps enter text.

1 Position the insertion point on the paragraph mark below the table and then press the ENTER key.

2 Type **As you requested, below is my availability by day:** and then press the ENTER key (shown in Figure 3–71).

1 CREATE & FORMAT LETTERHEAD WITH GRAPHICS | 2 SPECIFY LETTER FORMATS
3 INSERT TABLE | 4 FORMAT TABLE | 5 INSERT BULLETED LIST | 6 ADDRESS ENVELOPE

To Bullet a List As You Type

In Chapter 1, you learned how to apply bullets to existing paragraphs. If you know before you type that a list should be bulleted, you can use Word's AutoFormat As You Type feature to bullet the paragraphs as you type them (see Table 3–2 on page WD 163). *Why? The AutoFormat As You Type feature saves you time because it applies formats automatically.* The following steps add bullets to a list as you type.

1
• Press the ASTERISK key (*) as the first character on the line (Figure 3–71).

2
• Press the SPACEBAR to convert the asterisk to a bullet character.

Q&A
What if I did not want the asterisk converted to a bullet character?
You could undo the AutoFormat by tapping or clicking the Undo button; pressing CTRL+Z; tapping or clicking the AutoCorrect Options button that appears to the left of the bullet character as soon as you press the SPACEBAR and then tapping or clicking Undo Automatic Bullets on the AutoCorrect Options menu; or tapping or clicking the Bullets button (HOME tab | Paragraph group).

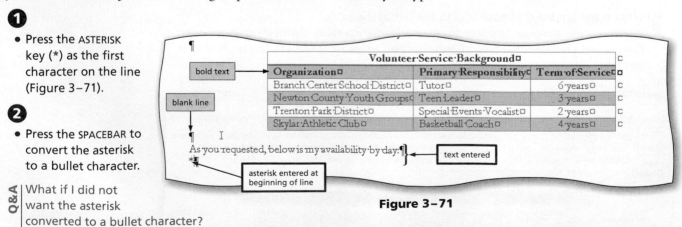

Figure 3–71

3

- Type `Mondays - 6:00 a.m. to 8:00 a.m.` as the first bulleted item.

- Press the ENTER key to place another bullet character at the beginning of the next line (Figure 3–72).

asterisk converted to bullet automatically

bullet automatically inserted when you press ENTER key

text entered

Figure 3–72

4

- Type `Tuesdays and Thursdays - 4:00 p.m. to 6:00 p.m.` and then press the ENTER key.

- Type `Saturdays - 11:00 a.m. to 2:00 p.m.` and then press the ENTER key.

- Press the ENTER key to turn off automatic bullets as you type (Figure 3–73).

Q&A Why did automatic bullets stop? When you press the ENTER key without entering any text after the automatic bullet character, Word turns off the automatic bullets feature.

Bullets button no longer selected

bulleted list

automatic bullets turned off

insertion point

text entered

Figure 3–73

Other Ways

1. Tap or click Bullets button (HOME tab | Paragraph group)

2. Press and hold or right-click paragraph to be bulleted, tap or click Bullets button on mini toolbar, tap or click desired bullet style, if necessary

To Enter More Text

The following steps enter the remainder of text in the letter.

1 With the insertion point positioned on the paragraph below the bulleted list, press the ENTER key and then type the paragraph shown in Figure 3–74 on the next page, making certain you use the building block name, wvf, to insert the organization name.

2 Press the ENTER key twice. Press the TAB key to position the insertion point at the tab stop set at the 4" mark on the ruler. Type `Sincerely,` and then press the ENTER key four times.

3 Press the TAB key to position the insertion point at the tab stop set at the 4" mark on the ruler. Type `Alexander Samaras` and then press the ENTER key (Figure 3–74).

If requested by your instructor, enter your name instead of the name shown above.

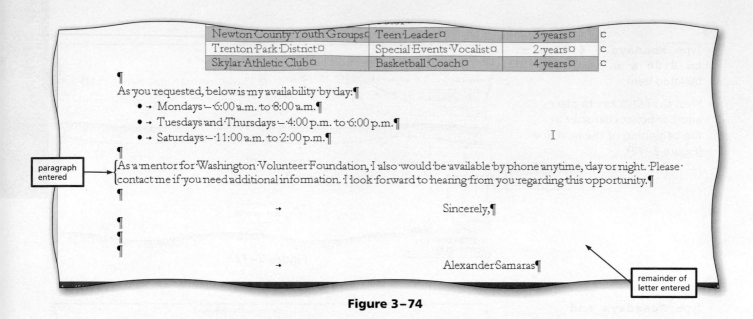

Figure 3–74

To Save an Existing Document with the Same File Name

You have made several modifications to the document since you last saved it. Thus, you should save it again. The following step saves the document again. For an example of the step listed below, refer to the Office and Windows chapter at the beginning of this book.

1 Tap or click the Save button on the Quick Access Toolbar to overwrite the previously saved file.

BTW

Conserving Ink and Toner

If you want to conserve ink or toner, you can instruct Word to print draft quality documents by tapping or clicking FILE on the ribbon to open the Backstage view, tapping or clicking Options in the Backstage view to display the Word Options dialog box, tapping or clicking Advanced in the left pane (Word Options dialog box), sliding or scrolling to the Print area in the right pane, placing a check mark in the 'Use draft quality' check box, and then tapping or clicking the OK button. Then, use the Backstage view to print the document as usual.

To Print a Document

If you want a hard copy of the letter, perform the following steps.

1 Tap or click FILE on the ribbon to open the Backstage view.

2 Tap or click the Print tab in the Backstage view to display the Print gallery.

3 Verify that the printer listed on the Printer Status button will print a hard copy of the document. If necessary, tap or click the Printer Status button to display a list of available printer options and then tap or click the desired printer to change the currently selected printer.

4 Tap or click the Print button in the Print gallery to print the document on the currently selected printer.

5 When the printer stops, retrieve the hard copy (shown in Figure 3–1 on page WD 139).

Addressing and Printing Envelopes and Mailing Labels

With Word, you can print address information on an envelope or on a mailing label. Computer-printed addresses look more professional than handwritten ones.

Creating a Business Letter with a Letterhead and Table **Word Chapter 3**

1 CREATE & FORMAT LETTERHEAD WITH GRAPHICS | 2 SPECIFY LETTE...
3 INSERT TABLE | 4 FORMAT TABLE | 5 INSERT BULLETED LIST | 6 ADDRESS EN...

Word C

To Address and Print an Envelope

The following steps address and print an envelope. If you are in a lab environment, check with your instructor before performing these steps. *Why? Some printers may not accommodate printing envelopes; others may stop printing until an envelope is inserted.*

1

- Scroll through the letter to display the inside address in the document window.

- Drag through the inside address to select it (Figure 3–75).

Figure 3–75

2

- Display the MAILINGS tab.

- Tap or click the Create Envelopes button (MAILINGS tab | Create group) to display the Envelopes and Labels dialog box.

- If necessary, tap or click the Envelopes tab (Envelopes and Labels dialog box), which automatically displays the selected delivery address in the dialog box.

- Type the return address as shown in Figure 3–76.

3

- Insert an envelope in your printer, as shown in the Feed area of the dialog box (your Feed area may be different depending on your printer).

- If your printer can print envelopes, tap or click the Print button (Envelopes and Labels dialog box) to print the envelope.

Figure 3–76

Envelopes and Labels

Instead of printing the envelope immediately, you can add it to the document by tapping or clicking the 'Add to Document' button (Envelopes and Labels dialog box). To specify a different envelope or label type (identified by a number on the box of envelopes or labels), tap or click the Options button (Envelopes and Labels dialog box).

Instead of printing an envelope, you can print a mailing label. To do this, tap or click the Labels button (MAILINGS tab | Create group) (shown in Figure 3–76) and then type the delivery address in the Delivery address box. To print the same address on all labels on the page, tap or click 'Full page of the same label' in the Print area. Tap or click the Print button (Envelopes and Labels dialog box) to print the label(s).

To Sign Out of a Microsoft Account

If you are signed in to a Microsoft account and are using a public computer or otherwise wish to sign out of your Microsoft account, you should sign out of the account from the Account gallery in the Backstage view before exiting Word. Signing out of the account is the safest way to make sure that nobody else can access SkyDrive files or settings stored in your Microsoft account. The following steps sign out of a Microsoft account from Word. For a detailed example of the procedure summarized below, refer to the Office and Windows chapter at the beginning of this book.

1 If you wish to sign out of your Microsoft account, tap or click FILE on the ribbon to open the Backstage view and then tap or click the Account tab to display the Account gallery.

2 Tap or click the Sign out link, which displays the Remove Account dialog box. If a Can't remove Windows accounts dialog box appears instead of the Remove Account dialog box, tap or click the OK button and skip the remaining steps.

Q&A Why does a Can't remove Windows accounts dialog box appear?
If you signed in to Windows using your Microsoft account, then you also must sign out from Windows, rather than signing out from within Word. When you are finished using Windows, be sure to sign out at that time.

3 Tap or click the Yes button (Remove Account dialog box) to sign out of your Microsoft account on this computer.

Q&A Should I sign out of Windows after signing out of my Microsoft account?
When you are finished using the computer, you should sign out of your account for maximum security.

4 Tap or click the Back button in the upper-left corner of the Backstage view to return to the document.

To Exit Word

This project now is complete. The following steps exit Word. For a detailed example of the procedure summarized below, refer to the Office and Windows chapter at the beginning of this book.

1a If you have one Word document open, tap or click the Close button on the right side of the title bar to close the open document and exit Word.

1b If you have multiple Word documents open, press and hold or right-click the Word app button on the taskbar and then tap or click 'Close all windows' on the shortcut menu to close all open documents and exit Word.

2 If a Microsoft Word dialog box appears, tap or click the Save button to save any changes made to the document since the last save.

Chapter Summary

In this chapter, you have learned how to use Word to change margins, insert and format a shape, change text wrapping, insert and format clip art, move and copy graphics, insert symbols, add a border, clear formatting, convert a hyperlink to regular text, set and use tab stops, insert the current date, create and insert building blocks, insert and format tables, and address and print envelopes and mailing labels. The items listed below include all the new Word skills you have learned in this chapter, with the tasks grouped by activity.

Enter and Edit Text
Insert a Symbol from the Symbol Dialog Box (WD 158)
Insert a Symbol from the Insert a Symbol Gallery (WD 159)
Set Custom Tab Stops (WD 167)
Insert the Current Date in a Document (WD 168)
Create a Building Block (WD 170)
Modify a Building Block (WD 171)
Insert a Building Block (WD 172)
Insert a Nonbreaking Space (WD 173)
Bullet a List as You Type (WD 184)
Address and Print an Envelope (WD 187)

Format a Page
Change Margin Settings (WD 140)
Change the Document Theme (WD 148)

Format Text
Use the 'Increase Font Size' Button (WD 147)
Bottom Border a Paragraph (WD 160)
Clear Formatting (WD 161)
Convert a Hyperlink to Regular Text (WD 163)
Apply a Style (WD 165)

Work with Graphics
Insert a Shape (WD 142)
Change an Object's Position (WD 144)
Change an Object's Text Wrapping (WD 145)

Apply a Shape Style (WD 145)
Add Text to a Shape (WD 146)
Insert Clip Art (WD 148)
Resize a Graphic to a Percent of the Original (WD 150)
Change the Color of a Graphic (WD 151)
Set a Transparent Color in a Graphic (WD 152)
Adjust the Brightness and Contrast of a Graphic (WD 153)
Change the Border Color on a Graphic (WD 154)
Move a Graphic (WD 155)
Copy a Graphic (WD 155)
Use Paste Options (WD 156)
Flip a Graphic (WD 157)

Work with Tables
Insert an Empty Table (WD 174)
Enter Data in a Table (WD 175)
Apply a Table Style (WD 177)
Resize Table Columns to Fit Table Contents (WD 178)
Select a Column (WD 178)
Align Data in Cells (WD 180)
Center a Table (WD 180)
Insert a Row in a Table (WD 181)
Insert a Column in a Table (WD 182)
Merge Cells (WD 182)
Split Table Cells (WD 183)
Split a Table (WD 183)

What decisions will you need to make when creating your next business letter?
Use these guidelines as you complete the assignments in this chapter and create your own business letters outside of this class.

1. Create a letterhead.

   a) Ensure that the letterhead contains a complete legal name, mailing address, phone number, and if applicable, fax number, email address, web address, logo, or other image.

   b) Place elements in the letterhead in a visually appealing location.

   c) Format the letterhead with appropriate fonts, font sizes, font styles, and color.

2. Compose an effective business letter.

   a) Include date line, inside address, message, and signature block.

   b) Use proper spacing and formats for letter contents.

   c) Follow the alignment and spacing guidelines based on the letter style used (i.e., block, modified block, or modified semi-block).

   d) Ensure the message is well written, properly formatted, and logically organized.

CONSIDER THIS: PLAN AHEAD

How should you submit solutions to questions in the assignments identified with a ✳ symbol?
Every assignment in this book contains one or more questions identified with a ✳ symbol. These questions require you to think beyond the assigned document. Present your solutions to the questions in the format required by your instructor. Possible formats may include one or more of these options: write the answer; create a document that contains the answer; present your answer to the class; discuss your answer in a group; record the answer as audio or video using a webcam, smartphone, or portable media player; or post answers on a blog, wiki, or website.

Apply Your Knowledge

Reinforce the skills and apply the concepts you learned in this chapter.

Working with Tabs and a Table

Note: To complete this assignment, you will be required to use the Data Files for Students. Visit www.cengage.com/ct/studentdownload for detailed instructions or contact your instructor for information about accessing the required files.

Instructions: Run Word. Open the document called Apply 3-1 October Work Schedule Draft located on the Data Files for Students. The document is a Word table that you are to edit and format. The revised table is shown in Figure 3–77.

October Work Schedule							
Shift	Sunday	Monday	Tuesday	Wednesday	Thursday	Friday	Saturday
6:00 a.m. to 9:00 a.m.	R. Punjap S. Dent	A. Garcia S. Dent	R. Punjap D. Owens	A. Garcia S. Dent	R. Punjap P. Carter	A. Garcia D. Owens	B. Knott P. Carter
9:00 a.m. to Noon	C. Odell H. Ottawa	T. Amra J. Long	C. Odell H. Ottawa	B. Knott D. Owens	C. Odell H. Ottawa	T. Amra J. Long	A. Kim H. Chai
Noon to 3:00 p.m.	W. Starr T. Amra	L. Simon B. Knott	W. Starr G. Vicario	L. Simon T. Hopp	W. Starr G. Vicario	L. Marvin T. Hopp	L. Simon T. Hopp
3:00 p.m. to 6:00 p.m.	J. Long T. Malley	P. Carter J. Reese	L. Marvin Y. Tanya	J. Long J. Reese	L. Marvin Y. Tanya	J. Long J. Reese	H. Fox Y. Tanya
6:00 p.m. to 9:00 p.m.	V. Sade G. Vicario	V. Sade T. Malley	V. Sade T. Malley	R. Dean O. Wayne	R. Dean O. Wayne	A. Kim H. Chai	R. Dean O. Wayne

Figure 3–77

Perform the following tasks:

1. Change the document theme to Metropolitan.
2. In the line containing the table title, October Work Schedule, remove the tab stop at the 1" mark on the ruler.
3. Set a centered tab at the 3" mark on the ruler. Move the centered tab stop to the 3.5" mark on the ruler.
4. Bold the characters in the title. Use the 'Increase Font Size' button to increase their font size to 14. Change their color to Blue-Gray, Accent 4.
5. In the table, delete the row containing the 1:00 p.m. to 4:00 p.m. shift.
6. Insert a column between the Monday and Wednesday columns. Fill in the column as follows, pressing the ENTER key between each name so that each name appears on a separate line:
   Column Title – Tuesday
   6:00 a.m. to 9:00 a.m. – R. Punjap D. Owens
   9:00 a.m. to Noon – C. Odell H. Ottawa
   Noon to 3:00 p.m. – W. Starr G. Vicario
   3:00 p.m. to 6:00 p.m. – L. Marvin Y. Tanya
   If the column heading, Tuesday, is not bold, apply the bold format to the text in this cell.

7. Insert a new row at the bottom of the table. In the first cell of the new row, enter 6:00 p.m. to 9:00 p.m. in the cell, pressing the ENTER key before the word, to, so that the text appears on two separate lines. (*Hint: You can use the AutoCorrect Options button to turn off the automatic capitalization of the first letter of the sentence, which will stop capitalizing the T in to each time you type it.*) If this cell's contents are bold, remove the bold format. Fill in the cells in the remainder of the row as follows, pressing the ENTER key between each name so that each name appears on a separate line:

   Sunday – V. Sade G. Vicario

   Monday – V. Sade T. Malley

   Tuesday – V. Sade T. Malley

   Wednesday – R. Dean O. Wayne

   Thursday – R. Dean O. Wayne

   Friday – A. Kim H. Chai

   Saturday – R. Dean O. Wayne

8. In the Table Style Options group (TABLE TOOLS DESIGN tab), ensure that these check boxes have check marks: Header Row, Banded Rows, and First Column. The Total Row, Last Column, and Banded Columns check boxes should not be selected.

9. Apply the Grid Table 5 Dark - Accent 4 style to the table.

10. Make all columns as wide as their contents (AutoFit Contents).

11. Align center left all cells in the first column.

12. Align center the column headings containing the weekday names and also all cells containing employee names in the table.

13. Center the table between the left and right margins of the page.

14. If requested by your instructor, change O. Wayne in the bottom-right cell of the table to your first initial and last name.

15. Save the document using the file name, Apply 3-1 October Work Schedule Modified, and submit it (shown in Figure 3–77) in the format specified by your instructor.

16. ✹ If you wanted the employee names to appear on the same line in each cell with a comma between each name, how would you modify the data in the table?

Extend Your Knowledge

Extend the skills you learned in this chapter and experiment with new skills. You may need to use Help to complete the assignment.

Working with Formulas, Graphics, Sorting, Picture Bullets, and Mailing Labels

Note: To complete this assignment, you will be required to use the Data Files for Students. Visit www.cengage.com/ct/studentdownload for detailed instructions or contact your instructor for information about accessing the required files.

Instructions: Run Word. Open the document called Extend 3-1 Sponsor Letter Draft located on the Data Files for Students. You will enter formulas in the table, use the Format Picture task pane, group objects, change the table style, sort paragraphs, use picture bullets, move tabs, and print mailing labels.

Perform the following tasks:

1. Use Help to learn about entering formulas, grouping objects, sorting, picture bullets, and printing mailing labels.

Continued >

Extend Your Knowledge *continued*

2. Add a row to the bottom of the table. Insert the word, Total, in the first column of the new row. In the last cell of the new row, use the Formula dialog box to insert a formula that adds the cells in the column so that the total approximate cost is displayed; in the dialog box, select a number format and then modify it in the dialog box so that the total displays with dollar signs and no cents. Which formula did you use? What number format?

3. Select the graphic of the tiger head and then click the Format Shape Dialog Box Launcher (PICTURE TOOLS FORMAT tab | Picture Styles group) to display the Format Picture task pane (Figure 3–78). Experiment with all the buttons in the task pane and modify the look of the graphic to your preferences.

Figure 3–78

4. Select the shape around the WILDCATS title and then use the Edit Shape button (DRAWING TOOLS FORMAT tab | Insert Shapes group) to change the shape to your preference. Position the tiger head graphic in the desired location to the right of the shape.

5. Copy and paste the modified tiger head graphic, flip it horizontally, and then position it on the opposite site of the shape. Group the two tiger head graphics with the shape at the top of the letterhead. Change the text wrapping of the grouped shape to Top and Bottom.

6. Position the insertion point in the table and one at a time, select and deselect each check box in the Table Style Options group. What are the functions of each check box: Header Row, Total Row, Banded Rows, First Column, Last Column, and Banded Columns? Select the check boxes you prefer for the table.

7. Sort the paragraphs in the bulleted list.

8. Change the bullets in the bulleted list to picture bullets.

9. Move the tab stops in the date line, complimentary close, and signature block from the 3.5" mark to the 4" mark on the ruler.

10. If requested by your instructor, change the name in the signature block to your name.

11. Save the revised document using the file name, Extend 3-1 Sponsor Letter Modified, and then submit it in the format specified by your instructor.

12. If requested by your instructor, print a single mailing label for the letter and then a full page of mailing labels, each containing the address shown in Figure 3–78.

13. ✸ Answer the questions posed in #2 and #6. Why would you group objects? Which picture bullet did you use and why?

Analyze, Correct, Improve

Analyze a document, correct all errors, and improve it.

Formatting a Business Letter

Note: To complete this assignment, you will be required to use the Data Files for Students. Visit www.cengage.com/ct/studentdownload for detailed instructions or contact your instructor for information about accessing the required files.

Instructions: Run Word. Open the document, Analyze 3-1 Recommendation Letter Draft, located on the Data Files for Students. The document is a business letter that is missing elements and is formatted poorly or incorrectly (Figure 3–79). You are to change the color of the text, insert symbols, remove a hyperlink, change the letter style from block to modified block, insert and format clip art, and format the table.

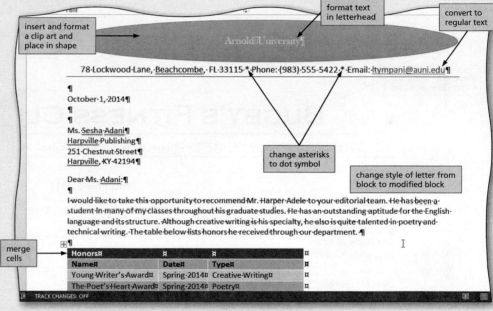

Figure 3–79

1. Correct In the letter, correct the following items:

    a. Increase the font size of the text in the letterhead. Change the color of the text in the letterhead so that the text is readable.

    b. Change the asterisks in the contact information to the dot symbol.

    c. Convert the email address hyperlink to regular text.

    d. The letter currently is the block letter style. It should be the modified block letter style. Format the appropriate paragraphs by setting custom tab stops and then positioning those paragraphs at the tab stops. Be sure to position the insertion point in the paragraph before setting the tab stop.

    e. Merge the three cells in the first row of the table into one cell and then center the title in the cell. Center the entire table between the page margins.

2. Improve Enhance the letterhead by changing the theme to one you prefer. Then, locate and insert at least one appropriate clip art image in the letterhead. If necessary, resize the graphic(s). Change the text wrapping of the clip art to In Front of Text and move the graphic(s) into the shape. Change the color of the graphic to match the color of the text or shape. Adjust the brightness and contrast of the graphic. Format one color in the graphic as transparent. Change the picture border color. If requested by your instructor, change the name in the signature block to your name. Save the modified document with the file name, Analyze 3-1 Recommendation Letter Modified, and then submit it in the format specified by your instructor.

3. ✸ In this assignment, you located and inserted clip art. What image did you select and why?

In the Labs

Design and/or create a document using the guidelines, concepts, and skills presented in this chapter. Labs 1 and 2, which increase in difficulty, require you to create solutions based on what you learned in the chapter; Lab 3 requires you to create a solution, which uses cloud and web technologies, by learning and investigating on your own from general guidance.

Lab 1: Creating a Letter with a Letterhead

Problem: As office manager for a fitness club, you send membership renewal letters to members. One letter you prepare is shown in Figure 3–80.

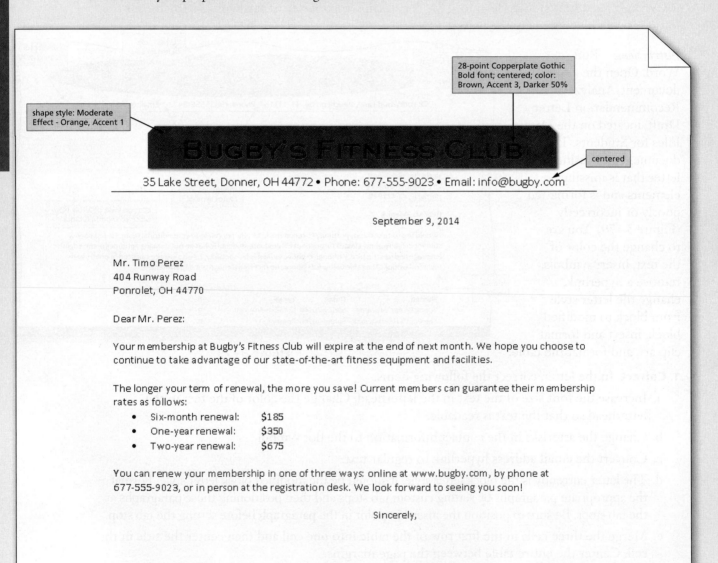

shape style: Moderate Effect - Orange, Accent 1

28-point Copperplate Gothic Bold font; centered; color: Brown, Accent 3, Darker 50%

centered

BUGBY'S FITNESS CLUB

35 Lake Street, Donner, OH 44772 • Phone: 677-555-9023 • Email: info@bugby.com

September 9, 2014

Mr. Timo Perez
404 Runway Road
Ponrolet, OH 44770

Dear Mr. Perez:

Your membership at Bugby's Fitness Club will expire at the end of next month. We hope you choose to continue to take advantage of our state-of-the-art fitness equipment and facilities.

The longer your term of renewal, the more you save! Current members can guarantee their membership rates as follows:

- Six-month renewal: $185
- One-year renewal: $350
- Two-year renewal: $675

You can renew your membership in one of three ways: online at www.bugby.com, by phone at 677-555-9023, or in person at the registration desk. We look forward to seeing you soon!

Sincerely,

Jonathon White
Office Manager

Figure 3–80

Perform the following tasks:

1. Change the theme to Retrospect.

2. Create the letterhead shown at the top of Figure 3–80, following these guidelines:

   a. Insert the Snip Same Side Corner Rectangle shape at an approximate height of 0.56" and width of 5.5". Change position of the shape to 'Position in Top Center with Square Text Wrapping'. Change the text wrapping for the shape to Top and Bottom. Add the company name, Bugby's Fitness Club, to the shape. Format the shape and its text as indicated in the figure.

   b. Insert the dot symbols as shown in the contact information. Remove the hyperlink format from the email address. If necessary, clear formatting after entering the bottom border.

   c. Save the letterhead with the file name, Lab 3-1 Fitness Club Letterhead.

3. Create the letter shown in Figure 3–80 using the modified block letter style, following these guidelines:

   a. Apply the No Spacing Quick Style to the document text (below the letterhead).

   b. Set a left-aligned tab stop at the 3.5" mark on the ruler for the date line, complimentary close, and signature block. Insert the current date.

   c. Bullet the list as you type it.

   d. Set a left-aligned tab stop at the 2" mark for the dollar amounts in the bulleted list.

   e. Convert the web address to regular text.

   f. Enter nonbreaking hyphens in the phone number.

   g. If requested by your instructor, change the name in the signature block to your name.

   h. Check the spelling of the letter. Save the letter with Lab 3-1 Fitness Club Letter as the file name and then submit it in the format specified by your instructor.

4. If your instructor permits, address and print an envelope or a mailing label for the letter.

5. ✹ What is the purpose of the nonbreaking hyphens in this letter? The letter in this assignment uses the modified block letter style. If you wanted to use the modified semi-block letter style, what changes would you make to this letter?

Lab 2: **Creating a Letter with a Letterhead and Table**

Problem: As a junior at your school, you are seeking an internship for the upcoming summer break. You prepare the letter shown in Figure 3–81 on the next page.

Perform the following tasks:

1. Change the theme to Celestial. Change the margins to 1" top and bottom and .75" left and right (Moderate).

2. Create the letterhead shown at the top of Figure 3–81, following these guidelines:

   a. Insert the Up Ribbon shape at an approximate height of 0.7" and width of 6". Change the position of the shape to 'Position in Top Center with Square Text Wrapping'. Change the text wrapping for the shape to Top and Bottom. Add the name to the shape. If requested by your instructor, place your name in the shape instead of the name shown in the figure. Format the shape and its text as indicated in the figure.

Continued >

In the Labs *continued*

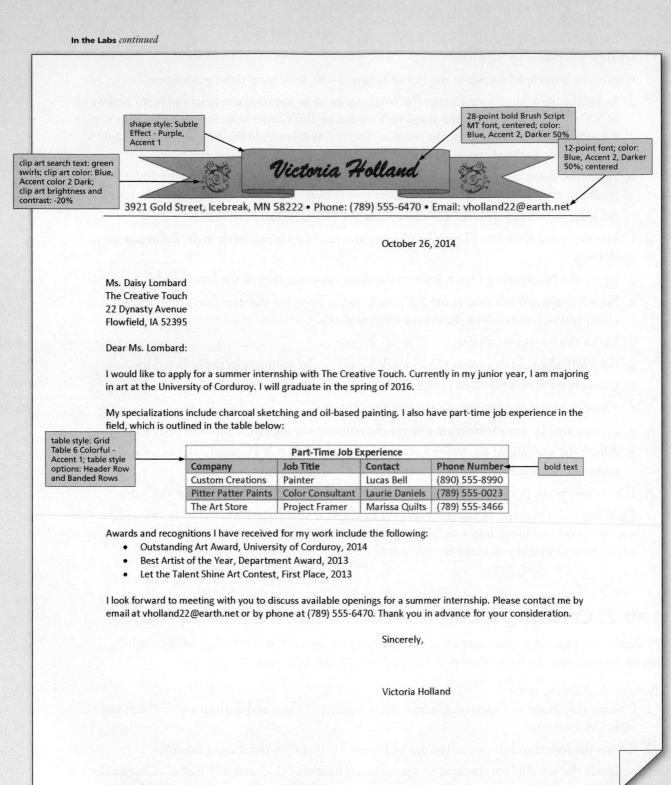

clip art search text: green swirls; clip art color: Blue, Accent color 2 Dark; clip art brightness and contrast: -20%

shape style: Subtle Effect - Purple, Accent 1

28-point bold Brush Script MT font, centered; color: Blue, Accent 2, Darker 50%

12-point font; color: Blue, Accent 2, Darker 50%; centered

Victoria Holland

3921 Gold Street, Icebreak, MN 58222 • Phone: (789) 555-6470 • Email: vholland22@earth.net

October 26, 2014

Ms. Daisy Lombard
The Creative Touch
22 Dynasty Avenue
Flowfield, IA 52395

Dear Ms. Lombard:

I would like to apply for a summer internship with The Creative Touch. Currently in my junior year, I am majoring in art at the University of Corduroy. I will graduate in the spring of 2016.

My specializations include charcoal sketching and oil-based painting. I also have part-time job experience in the field, which is outlined in the table below:

table style: Grid Table 6 Colorful - Accent 1; table style options: Header Row and Banded Rows

bold text

Part-Time Job Experience			
Company	Job Title	Contact	Phone Number
Custom Creations	Painter	Lucas Bell	(890) 555-8990
Pitter Patter Paints	Color Consultant	Laurie Daniels	(789) 555-0023
The Art Store	Project Framer	Marissa Quilts	(789) 555-3466

Awards and recognitions I have received for my work include the following:
- Outstanding Art Award, University of Corduroy, 2014
- Best Artist of the Year, Department Award, 2013
- Let the Talent Shine Art Contest, First Place, 2013

I look forward to meeting with you to discuss available openings for a summer internship. Please contact me by email at vholland22@earth.net or by phone at (789) 555-6470. Thank you in advance for your consideration.

Sincerely,

Victoria Holland

Figure 3–81

b. Insert the clip art, resize it, change text wrapping to In Front of Text, move it to the left on the shape, and format it as indicated in the figure. Copy the clip art and move the copy of the image to the right on the shape, as shown in the figure. Flip the copied image horizontally.

c. Insert the small dot symbols as shown in the contact information. Remove the hyperlink format from the email address. If necessary, clear formatting after entering the bottom border.

d. Save the letterhead with the file name, Lab 3-2 Internship Letterhead.

3. Create the letter shown in Figure 3–81, following these guidelines:

   a. Apply the No Spacing Quick Style to the document text (below the letterhead).

   b. Set a left-aligned tab stop at the 4" mark on the ruler for the date line, complimentary close, and signature block. Insert the current date.

   c. Insert and center the table. Format the table as specified in the figure. Make all columns as wide as their contents (AutoFit Contents).

   d. Bullet the list as you type it.

   e. Convert the email address to regular text.

   f. Check the spelling of the letter. Save the letter with Lab 3-2 Internship Letter as the file name, and then submit it in the format specified by your instructor.

4. If your instructor permits, address and print an envelope or a mailing label for the letter.

5. ❈ Why do you think the clip art in this letter used a text wrapping of In Front of Text? If the table used banded columns instead of banded rows, how would its appearance change?

Lab 3: Expand Your World: Cloud and Web Technologies
Using Google Docs to Upload and Edit Files

Problem: You have created a letter in Word at work and want to proofread and edit it at home. The problem is that you do not have Word at home. You do, however, have an Internet connection at home. Because you have a Google account, you upload your Word document to Google Drive so that you can view and edit it later from a computer that does not have Word installed.

Notes:

• You will use a Google account, which you can create at no cost, to complete this assignment. If you do not have a Google account and do not want to create one, read this assignment without performing the instructions.

• To complete this assignment, you will be required to use the Data Files for Students. Visit www.cengage.com/ct/studentdownload for detailed instructions or contact your instructor for information about accessing the required files.

Instructions: Perform the following tasks:

1. In Word, open the document, Lab 3-3 Compliment Letter in Word, from the Data Files for Students. Look through the letter so that you are familiar with its contents and formats. If desired, print the letter so that you easily can compare it to the Google Docs converted file. Close the document.

2. Run a browser. Search for the text, google docs, using a search engine. Visit several websites to learn about Google Docs and Google Drive. Navigate to the Google website. If you do not have a Google account and you want to create one, click the SIGN UP button and follow the instructions. If you do not have a Google account and you do not want to create one, read the remaining instructions without performing them. If you have a Google account, sign in to your account.

3. If necessary, click Drive to display Google Drive. Click the UPLOAD, or similar, button and then follow the instructions to navigate to the location of the file, Lab 3-3 Compliment Letter in Word, and then upload the file.

4. Rename the file on Google Drive to Lab 3-3 Compliment Letter in Google. Open the file in Google Docs (Figure 3–82 on the next page). What differences do you see between the Word document and the Google Docs converted document? Fix the document in Google Docs so

Continued >

In the Labs *continued*

that it looks appealing. Download the revised document to your local storage media, changing its format to Microsoft Word. Submit the document in the format requested by your instructor.

5. ✻ What is Google Drive? What is Google Docs? Answer the question posed in #4. Do you prefer using Google Docs or Word? Why?

Figure 3–82

✻ Consider This: Your Turn

Apply your creative thinking and problem solving skills to design and implement a solution.

Note: To complete these assignments, you may be required to use the Data Files for Students. Visit www.cengage.com/ct/studentdownload for detailed instructions or contact your instructor for information about accessing the required files.

1: Design and Create an Admissions Acceptance Letter

Personal

Part 1: As a part-time student in your school's office of admissions, you send acceptance letters to new students. You have been asked to design a new letterhead using this information: Frottingham College, Home of the Huskies, 77 Husky Lane, Graber, OK 74877; Phone: (439) 555-6899; website: www.frottinghamcollege.edu. Once the letterhead is designed, you then write an acceptance letter to this new student: Mr. Donald Dillenger at 13 Allison Avenue, Graber, OK 74877.

The draft wording for the letter is as follows. First paragraph: Congratulations on your admission to the School of Biological Sciences at Frottingham College for the Fall 2014 semester. We are excited to welcome you to Frottingham College. Our decision to admit you to our college is an acknowledgment of your potential and our confidence in you as a valuable addition to our student body. Second paragraph: We would like to inform you of important upcoming dates. Although not mandatory, we would advise you to attend each of these activities. The schedule is as follows:

New Student Guide Schedule		
Activity	Date & Time	Location
Get to Know Your School Campus Tour	August 14, 2014 8:00 a.m. to 5:00 p.m.	Conner Student Center, Room 134
Meet the Teachers and Advisors	August 15, 2014 9:00 a.m. to 3:00 p.m.	Milton Student Center, Room 222
Fun Night! Get to Know Your Fellow Classmates	August 19, 2014 6:00 p.m. to Midnight	Bowling & Billiards Center
What Is My Major? Learn about What Is Offered	August 20, 2014 9:00 a.m. to 7:00 p.m.	Leonardo Auditorium

Third paragraph: Before the first day of classes, you must do the following: Bulleted list: Make sure your campus email account works properly. If it does not, call (439) 555-2898 for technical support.; Verify that you can sign in online to all of your semester classes. If you cannot, call (439) 555-2898 for technical support.; Purchase all course materials from the campus bookstore. Last paragraph: Again, congratulations on your admission to Frottingham College. We look forward to your success on campus.

The letter should contain a letterhead that uses a shape and clip art, a table with an appropriate table style applied (unformatted table shown above), and a bulleted list (to present the items to complete before classes start). Insert nonbreaking spaces in the college name. Create a building block for the college name, edit the building block so that it has a ScreenTip, and insert the building block whenever you have to enter the college name.

Use the concepts and techniques presented in this chapter to create and format a letter according to a letter style, creating appropriate paragraph breaks and rewording the draft as necessary. The unformatted paragraphs in the letter are in a file called Your Turn 2-1 Letter Paragraphs, which is located on the Data Files for Students. If you prefer, you can copy and paste this text into your letter instead of typing the paragraphs yourself. If requested by your instructor, use your name in the signature line in the letter. Be sure to check the spelling and grammar of the finished letter. Submit your assignment in the format specified by your instructor.

Part 2: ✸ You made several decisions while creating the letter in this assignment: where to position elements in the letterhead, how to format elements in the letterhead, which graphic to use in the letterhead, which theme to use in the letter, which font size to use for the letter text, which table style to use, and which letter style to use. What was the rationale behind each of these decisions?

2: Design and Create a Confirmation Letter
Professional

Part 1: As a CEO of Addy Lane & Company, a retailer, you communicate the conditions of a revised business agreement with Turner Industries in a letter. You design a letterhead using this information: Addy Lane & Company, 121 Rapture Road, Harrust, NH 03891; Phone: (657) 555-7744; Email: carlosdiaz@addyemail.com. Then, you write a confirmation letter to this contact: Ms. Joyce Adams at Turner Industries, 356 Thorn Avenue, Vigil, CT 06802.

The draft wording for the letter is as follows. First paragraph: Per our phone conversation, yesterday I approved the new conditions of the business agreement with Turner Industries. The table below outlines the revised terms. Please review this list and confirm receipt either by return letter to me or email message at carlosdiaz@addyemail.com. If you have any revisions to these terms, please also include them in your reply.

Revised Business Agreement Terms		
Section	Title	Summary of Revision
2b	Materials	Addy Lane & Company will split the cost with Turner Industries for any materials used to manufacture products for Addy Lane & Company.
11a–c	Resources	Resources from each company shall be shared for mutual benefit.
33a	Communications	Addy Lane & Company and Turner Industries shall meet every other week for an assessment.
109b–d	Profits	The profits between the companies on shared merchandise now will be split 50/50.

© 2014 Cengage Learning

Second paragraph: Please also confirm these new employee names and positions at Turner Industries: Bulleted list: Doreen Liner, Administrative Assistant; Frank Cart, Manager; Anthony Boyd, Web Administrator. Last paragraph: Thank you in advance for your assistance with these details. I look forward to a long-term business relationship.

The letter should contain a letterhead that uses a shape and clip art, a table with an appropriate table style applied (unformatted table shown above), and a bulleted list (to present the new employees). Insert nonbreaking spaces in the company name, Turner Industries. Create a building

Continued >

Consider This: Your Turn *continued*

block for the company name, Turner Industries, edit the building block so that it has a ScreenTip, and insert the building block whenever you have to enter the company name.

Use the concepts and techniques presented in this chapter to create and format a letter according to a letter style, creating appropriate paragraph breaks and rewording the draft as necessary. The unformatted paragraphs in the letter are in a file called Your Turn 2-2 Letter Paragraphs, which is located on the Data Files for Students. If you prefer, you can copy and paste this text into your letter instead of typing the paragraphs yourself. If requested by your instructor, use your name in the signature line in the letter. Be sure to check the spelling and grammar of the finished letter. Submit your assignment in the format specified by your instructor.

Part 2: ✸ You made several decisions while creating the letter in this assignment: where to position elements in the letterhead, how to format elements in the letterhead, which graphic to use in the letterhead, which theme to use in the letter, which font size to use for the letter text, which table style to use, and which letter style to use. What was the rationale behind each of these decisions?

3: Design and Create a Letter to a Potential Employer
Research and Collaboration

Part 1: As assistants in the Office of Career Development at your school, you and two others have been asked to prepare a sample letter to a potential employer; students seeking employment will use this letter as a reference document when creating their own letters. Form a three-member team to research, compose, and create this letter. As a group, locate a job advertisement for which your team could write a sample letter. One team member should design a letterhead. Another team member should create a table of educational background that relates to the advertisement, and the third team member should compose a list of activities that would be important to the potential employer. As a group, compose the letter using the individual elements where appropriate.

Use the concepts and techniques presented in this chapter to create and format a letter according to a letter style. If requested by your instructor, use team members' names in the letter. Be sure to check the spelling and grammar of the finished letter. Submit your team assignment in the format specified by your instructor.

Part 2: ✸ You made several decisions while creating the letter in this assignment: text to use, where to position elements in the letterhead, how to format elements in the letterhead, which graphic to use in the letterhead, which theme to use in the letter, which font size to use for the letter text, which table style to use, and which letter style to use. What was the rationale behind each of these decisions?

Learn Online

Reinforce what you learned in this chapter with games, exercises, training, and many other online activities and resources.

Student Companion Site Reinforcement activities and resources are available at no additional cost on www.cengagebrain.com. Visit www.cengage.com/ct/studentdownload for detailed instructions about accessing the resources available at the Student Companion Site.

SAM Put your skills into practice with SAM! If you have a SAM account, go to www.cengage.com/sam2013 to access SAM assignments for this chapter.

4 Creating a Document with a Title Page, Lists, Tables, and a Watermark

Microsoft product screen shots used with permission from Microsoft Corporation.

Objectives

You will have mastered the material in this project when you can:

- Border a paragraph
- Change paragraph indentation
- Insert and format a SmartArt graphic
- Apply character effects
- Insert a section break
- Insert a Word document in an open document
- Insert formatted headers and footers

- Sort paragraphs and tables
- Use the format painter
- Add picture bullets to a list
- Create a multilevel list
- Modify and format Word tables
- Sum columns in a table
- Create a watermark
- Change theme fonts

4 | Creating a Document with a Title Page, Lists, Tables, and a Watermark

Introduction

During the course of your business and personal endeavors, you may want or need to provide a recommendation to a person or group of people for their consideration. You might suggest they purchase a product, such as a vehicle or books, or contract a service, such as designing their webpage or remodeling their house. Or, you might try to convince an audience to take an action, such as signing a petition, joining a club, visiting an establishment, or donating to a cause. You may be asked to request funds for a new program or activity or to promote an idea, such as a benefits package to company employees or a budget plan to upper management. To present these types of recommendations, you may find yourself writing a proposal.

A proposal generally is one of three types: sales, research, or planning. A **sales proposal** sells an idea, a product, or a service. A **research proposal** usually requests funding for a research project. A **planning proposal** offers solutions to a problem or improvement to a situation.

Project — Sales Proposal

Sales proposals describe the features and value of products and services being offered, with the intent of eliciting a positive response from the reader. Desired outcomes include the reader accepting ideas, purchasing products, contracting services, volunteering time, contributing to a cause, or taking an action. A well-written proposal can be the key to obtaining the desired results.

The project in this chapter follows generally accepted guidelines for writing short sales proposals and uses Word to create the sales proposal shown in Figure 4–1. The sales proposal in this chapter is designed to persuade readers to visit a state park. The proposal has a colorful title page to attract readers' attention. To add impact, the sales proposal has a watermark consisting of animal paw prints and tracks, positioned behind the content on each page. It also uses lists and tables to summarize and highlight important data.

paragraph border

paragraph border

watermark

SmartArt graphic

(a) Title Page

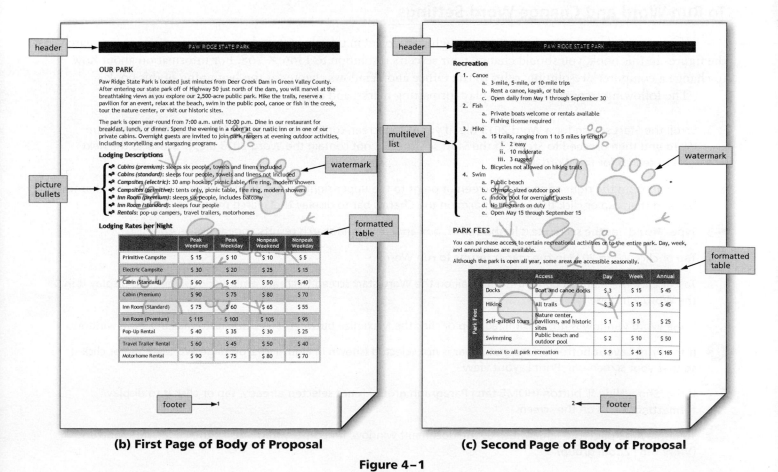

header

picture bullets

header

watermark

multilevel list

watermark

formatted table

formatted table

footer

footer

(b) First Page of Body of Proposal

(c) Second Page of Body of Proposal

Figure 4–1

Roadmap

In this chapter, you will learn how to create the sales proposal shown in Figure 4–1. The following roadmap identifies general activities you will perform as you progress through this chapter:

1. **CREATE** a **TITLE PAGE** for the proposal.
2. **INSERT** an **EXISTING** Word **DOCUMENT** in the proposal.
3. **CREATE** a **HEADER AND FOOTER** in the proposal.
4. **EDIT AND FORMAT LISTS** in the proposal.
5. **EDIT AND FORMAT TABLES** in the proposal.
6. **CREATE** a **WATERMARK** in the proposal.

At the beginning of step instructions throughout the chapter, you will see an abbreviated form of this roadmap. The abbreviated roadmap uses colors to indicate chapter progress: gray means the chapter is beyond that activity, blue means the task being shown is covered in that activity, and black means that activity is yet to be covered. For example, the following abbreviated roadmap indicates the chapter would be showing a task in the 2 INSERT EXISTING DOCUMENT activity.

1 CREATE TITLE PAGE | **2 INSERT EXISTING DOCUMENT** | 3 CREATE HEADER & FOOTER
3 EDIT & FORMAT LISTS | 4 EDIT & FORMAT TABLES | 5 CREATE WATERMARK

Use the abbreviated roadmap as a progress guide while you read or step through the instructions in this chapter.

One of the few differences between Windows 7 and Windows 8 occurs in the steps to run Word. If you are using Windows 7, click the Start button, type **Word** in the 'Search programs and files' box, click Word 2013, and then, if necessary, maximize the Word window. For a summary of the steps to run Word in Windows 7, refer to the Quick Reference located at the back of this book.

To Run Word and Change Word Settings

If you are using a computer to step through the project in this chapter and you want your screens to match the figures in this book, you should change your screen's resolution to 1366×768. For information about how to change a computer's resolution, refer to the Office and Windows chapter at the beginning of this book.

The following steps run Word, display formatting marks, and change the zoom to page width.

1 Scroll the Start screen for a Word 2013 tile. If your Start screen contains a Word 2013 tile, tap or click it to run Word and then proceed to Step 5; if the Start screen does not contain the Word 2013 tile, proceed to the next step to search for the Word app.

2 Swipe in from the right edge of the screen or point to the upper-right corner of the screen to display the Charms bar and then tap or click the Search charm on the Charms bar to display the Search menu.

3 Type **Word** as the search text in the Search box and watch the search results appear in the Apps list.

4 Tap or click Word 2013 in the search results to run Word.

5 Tap or click the Blank document thumbnail on the Word start screen to create a blank document and display it in the Word window.

6 If the Word window is not maximized, tap or click the Maximize button on its title bar to maximize the window.

7 If the Print Layout button on the status bar is not selected (shown in Figure 4–2 on page WD 206), tap or click it so that your screen is in Print Layout view.

8 If the 'Show/Hide ¶' button (HOME tab | Paragraph group) is not selected already, tap or click it to display formatting marks on the screen.

9 To display the page the same width as the document window, if necessary, tap or click the Page Width button (VIEW tab | Zoom group).

10 If the rulers are not displayed already, tap or click the View Ruler check box (VIEW tab | Show group), because you will use the rulers for several tasks in the creation of this project.

To Change Theme Colors

Recall that Word provides document themes, which contain a variety of color schemes and other effects. You should select a theme that includes colors that reflect the goals of a sales proposal. This proposal uses the Wisp document theme. The following steps the document theme.

1 Tap or click DESIGN on the ribbon to display the DESIGN tab.

2 Tap or click the Themes button (DESIGN tab | Document Formatting group) to display the Themes gallery.

3 Tap or click Wisp in the Themes gallery to change the document theme to the selected theme.

Creating a Title Page

A **title page** is a separate cover page that contains, at a minimum, the title of a document. For a sales proposal, the title page usually is the first page of the document. Solicited proposals often have a specific format for the title page. Guidelines for the title page of a solicited proposal may stipulate the margins, spacing, layout, and required contents, such as title, sponsor name, author name, date, etc. With an unsolicited proposal, by contrast, you can design the title page in a way that best presents its message.

How do you design an eye-catching title page?

The title page is the first section a reader sees on a sales proposal. Thus, it is important that the title page appropriately reflects the goal of the sales proposal. When designing the title page, consider its text and graphics.

• **Use concise, descriptive text.** The title page should contain a short, descriptive title that accurately reflects the message of the sales proposal. The title page also may include a theme or slogan. Do not place a page number on the title page.

• **Identify appropriate fonts, font sizes, and colors for the text.** Use fonts that are easy to read. Avoid using more than three different fonts because too many fonts can make the title page visually confusing. Use larger font sizes to add impact to the title page. To give the title more emphasis, its font size should be larger than any other text on the title page. Use colors that complement one another and convey the meaning of the proposal.

• **Use graphics to reinforce the goal.** Select simple graphics that clearly communicate the fundamental nature of the proposal. Possible graphics include shapes, pictures, and logos.

• **Use colors that complement text colors.** Be aware that too many graphics and colors can be distracting. Arrange graphics with the text so that the title page is attractive and uncluttered.

The title page of the sales proposal in this chapter (Figure 4–1a on page WD 203) contains a colorful title that is surrounded by a border with some shading, an artistic graphic with text, a colorful slogan, and the faded paw prints image in the background. The steps on the next several pages create this title page. The faded image of the paw prints is added to all pages at the end of the chapter.

To Format Characters

The title in the sales proposal should use a large font size and an easy-to-read font, and should be the focal point on the page. *Why? To give the title more emphasis, its font size should be larger than any other text on the title page.* The steps on the next page enter the title, Paw Ridge State Park, with the first two words centered on the first line and the second two words centered on the second line.

If you are using your finger on a touch screen and are having difficulty completing the steps in this chapter, consider using a stylus. Many people find it easier to be precise with a stylus than with a finger. In addition, with a stylus you see the pointer. If you still are having trouble completing the steps with a stylus, try using a mouse.

1 Tap or click HOME on the ribbon to display the HOME tab.

2 Tap or click the Center button (HOME tab | Paragraph group) to center the paragraph that will contain the title.

3 Tap or click the Font arrow (HOME tab | Font group). Scroll to and then tap or click Britannic Bold (or a similar font) in the Font gallery, so that the text you type will use the selected font.

4 Tap or click the Font Size arrow (HOME tab | Font group) and then tap or click 72 in the Font Size gallery, so that the text you type will use the selected font size.

5 Type **Paw Ridge** and then press the ENTER key to enter the first line of the title.

6 Tap or click the Font Color arrow (HOME tab | Font group) and then tap or click Brown, Accent 3 (seventh color, first row) in the Font Color gallery, so that the text you type will use the selected font color.

7 Type **State Park** as the second line of the title (shown in Figure 4–2).

To Border a Paragraph

1 CREATE TITLE PAGE | 2 INSERT EXISTING DOCUMENT | 3 CREATE HEADER & FOOTER
4 EDIT & FORMAT LISTS | 5 EDIT & FORMAT TABLES | 6 CREATE WATERMARK

If you are using a mouse and you click the Borders button (HOME tab | Paragraph group), Word applies the most recently defined border, or, if one has not been defined, it applies the default border to the current paragraph. To specify a border different from the most recently defined border, you click the Borders arrow (HOME tab | Paragraph group). If you are using a touch screen, recall that touch screens may not have a separate Borders button and Borders arrow.

In this project, the first line of the title in the sales proposal (Paw Ridge) has a 6-point brown border around it. *Why? You want the title to stand out more than the rest of the text on the title page.* The following steps add a border to all edges of a paragraph.

1
- Position the insertion point in the paragraph to border, in this case, the first line of the document.
- Tap or click the Borders arrow (HOME tab | Paragraph group) to display the Borders gallery (Figure 4–2).

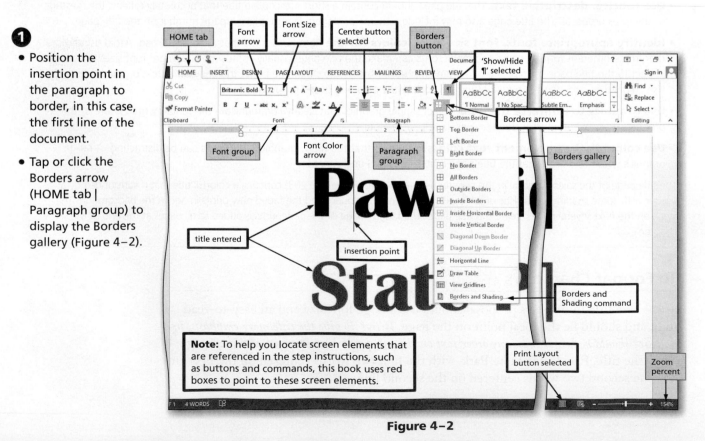

Figure 4–2

2

- Tap or click Borders and Shading in the Borders gallery to display the Borders and Shading dialog box.

- Tap or click Box in the Setting area (Borders and Shading dialog box), which will place a border on each edge of the current paragraph.

- Tap or click the Color arrow and then tap or click Brown, Accent 3 (seventh color, first row) in the Color palette to specify the border color.

- Tap or click the Width arrow and then tap or click 6 pt to specify the thickness of the border (Figure 4–3).

Q&A For what purpose are the buttons in the Preview area used?

They are toggles that display and remove the top, bottom, left, and right borders from the diagram in the Preview area.

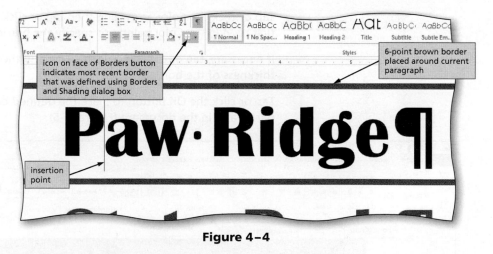

Figure 4–3

3

- Tap or click the OK button (Borders and Shading dialog box) to place the border shown in the preview area of the dialog box around the current paragraph in the document (Figure 4–4).

Q&A How would I remove an existing border from a paragraph?

Tap or click the Borders arrow (HOME tab | Paragraph group) and then tap or click the border in the Borders gallery that identifies the border you wish to remove, or tap or click No Border to remove all borders.

Figure 4–4

Other Ways

1. Tap or click 'Borders and Shading' button (DESIGN tab | Page Background group), tap or click Borders tab (Borders and Shading dialog box), select desired border, tap or click OK button

---

To Shade a Paragraph and Change Font Color

To make the first line of the title of the sales proposal more eye-catching, it is shaded in dark red. When you shade a paragraph, Word shades the rectangular area behind any text or graphics in the paragraph from the left margin of the paragraph to the right margin. If the paragraph is surrounded by a border, Word shades inside the border. The following steps shade a paragraph and change font color.

1 With the insertion point in the paragraph to shade, the first line in this case (shown in Figure 4–4), tap or click the Shading arrow (HOME tab | Paragraph group) to display the Shading gallery.

BTW

Normal Style
If your screen settings differ from Figure 4-2, it is possible the default settings in your Normal style have been changed. Normal style settings are saved in a file called normal.dotm file. To restore the original Normal style settings, exit Word and use File Explorer to locate the normal.dotm file (be sure that hidden files and folders are displayed, and include system and hidden files in your search — you may need to use Help to assist you with these tasks). Rename the normal.dotm file as oldnormal.dotm. After renaming the normal.dotm file, it no longer will exist as normal.dotm. The next time you start Word, it will recreate a normal.dotm file using the original default settings.

2 Tap or click 'Dark Red, Accent 1' (fifth color, first row) in the Shading gallery to shade the current paragraph (shown in Figure 4–5).

3 Drag through the words, Paw Ridge, in the first line of the title to select the text.

4 Tap or click the Font Color arrow (HOME tab | Font group) to display the Font Color gallery and then tap or click 'White, Background 1' (first color, first row) to change the color of the selected text (shown in Figure 4–5).

To Border Another Paragraph

To make the second line of the title of the sales proposal (State Park) more eye-catching, it has a 6-point olive green border around it. The following steps add a border to all edges of a paragraph.

1 Position the insertion point in the paragraph to border (in this case, the second paragraph containing the text, State Park).

2 Tap or click the Borders arrow (HOME tab | Paragraph group) to display the Borders gallery and then tap or click Borders and Shading in the Border gallery to display the Borders and Shading dialog box.

3 Tap or click Box in the Setting area (Borders and Shading dialog box), which will place a border on each edge of the current paragraph.

4 Tap or click the Color arrow and then tap or click 'Olive Green, Accent 4' (eighth color, first row) in the Color palette to specify the border color.

5 If necessary, tap or click the Width arrow and then tap or click 6 pt to specify the thickness of the border.

6 Tap or click the OK button to place the defined border shown around the current paragraph in the document (Figure 4–5).

Figure 4–5

To Change Spacing after a Paragraph

Currently, a small amount of blank space exists between the two paragraph borders because Word automatically places 8 points of blank space below paragraphs (shown in Figure 4–5). The following steps remove the blank space below the first paragraph.

1 Position the insertion point in the paragraph to be adjusted (in this case, the paragraph containing the text, Paw Ridge).

2 Display the PAGE LAYOUT tab. If you are using a touch screen, tap the Spacing After box (PAGE LAYOUT tab | Paragraph group) and then type   0   to change the spacing below the paragraph; if you are using a mouse, click the Spacing After down arrow (PAGE LAYOUT tab | Paragraph group) as many times as necessary until 0 pt is displayed in the Spacing After box to remove the space below the current paragraph (shown in Figure 4–6).

To Change Left and Right Paragraph Indent

1 CREATE TITLE PAGE | 2 INSERT EXISTING DOCUMENT | 3 CREATE HEADER & FOOTER
4 EDIT & FORMAT LISTS | 5 EDIT & FORMAT TABLES | 6 CREATE WATERMARK

The borders around the first and second paragraphs and the shading in the first paragraph currently extend from the left margin to the right margin (shown in Figure 4–5). In this project, the edges of the border and shading are closer to the text in the title. *Why? You do not want such a large gap between the edge of the text and the border.* If you want the border and shading to start and end at a location different from the margin, you change the left and right paragraph indent.

The Increase Indent and Decrease Indent buttons (HOME tab | Paragraph group) change the left indent by ½-inch, respectively. In this case, however, you cannot use these buttons because you want to change both the left and right indent. The following steps change the left and right paragraph indent.

1

- Be sure the insertion point is positioned in the paragraph to indent (the first paragraph in this case). If you are using a touch screen, tap the Indent Left box (PAGE LAYOUT tab | Paragraph group) and then type   0.5   to change the left indent; if you are using a mouse, click the Indent Left up arrow (PAGE LAYOUT tab | Paragraph group) five times so that 0.5" is displayed in the Indent Left box because you want to adjust the paragraph left indent by this amount.

- If you are using a touch screen, tap the Indent Right box (PAGE LAYOUT tab | Paragraph group) and then type   0.5   to change the right indent; if you are using a mouse, click the Indent Right up arrow (PAGE LAYOUT tab | Paragraph group) five times so that 0.5" is displayed in the Indent Right box because you want to adjust the paragraph right indent by this amount (Figure 4–6).

Figure 4–6

⌕ Experiment

- If you are using a mouse, repeatedly click the Indent Right and Indent Left up and down scroll arrows (PAGE LAYOUT tab | Paragraph group) and watch the left and right edges of the current paragraph change in the document window. When you have finished experimenting, set the left and right indent each to 0.5".

2

- Repeat Step 1 for the second paragraph, so that the paragraph containing the words, State Park, also has a left and right indent of 0.5" (shown in Figure 4–7).

Other Ways		
1. Drag Left Indent and Right Indent markers on ruler	2. Tap or click Paragraph Settings Dialog Box Launcher (HOME tab | Paragraph group), tap or click Indents and Spacing tab (Paragraph dialog box), set indentation values, tap or click OK button	3. Tap 'Show Context Menu' button on mini toolbar or right-click paragraph, tap or click Paragraph on shortcut menu, tap or click Indents and Spacing tab (Paragraph dialog box), set indentation values, tap or click OK button

To Clear Formatting

The title is finished. When you press the ENTER key to advance the insertion point from the end of the second line to the beginning of the third line on the title page, the border will be carried forward to line 3, and any text you type will be a 72-point Britannic Bold Brown, Accent 3 font. The paragraphs and characters on line 3 should not have the same paragraph and character formatting as line 2. Instead, they should be formatted using the Normal style. The following steps clear formatting, which applies the Normal style formats to the location of the insertion point.

BTW

The Ribbon and Screen Resolution
Word may change how the groups and buttons within the groups appear on the ribbon, depending on the computer's screen resolution. Thus, your ribbon may look different from the ones in this book if you are using a screen resolution other than 1366 × 768.

1 If necessary, press the END key to position the insertion point at the end of line 2, that is, after the k in Park.

2 Press the ENTER key.

3 Display the HOME tab. Tap or click the 'Clear All Formatting' button (HOME tab | Font group) to apply the Normal style to the location of the insertion point (Figure 4–7).

Q&A Could I have tapped or clicked Normal in the Styles gallery instead of the Clear All Formatting button?
Yes.

Figure 4–7

To Save a Document

BTW

Touch Screen Differences
The Office and Windows interfaces may vary if you are using a touch screen. For this reason, you might notice that the function or appearance of your touch screen differs slightly from this chapter's presentation.

You have performed many tasks while creating this title page and do not want to risk losing work completed thus far. Accordingly, you should save the document. The following steps assume you already have created folders for storing your files, for example, a CIS 101 folder (for your class) that contains a Word folder (for your assignments). Thus, these steps save the document in the Word folder in the CIS 101 folder using the file name, Paw Ridge Title Page.

1 Tap or click the Save button on the Quick Access Toolbar, which depending on settings, will display either the Save As gallery in the Backstage view or the Save As dialog box.

2 To save on a hard disk or other storage media on your computer, proceed to Step 2a. To save on SkyDrive, proceed to Step 2b.

2a If your screen opens the Backstage view and you want to save on storage media on your computer, tap or click Computer in the left pane, if necessary, to display options in the right pane related to saving on your computer. If your screen already displays the Save As dialog box, proceed to Step 4.

2b If your screen opens the Backstage view and you want to save on SkyDrive, tap or click SkyDrive in the left pane to display SkyDrive saving options or a Sign In button. If your screen displays a Sign In button, tap or click it and then sign in to SkyDrive.

3 Tap or click the Browse button in the right pane to display the Save As dialog box associated with the selected save location (i.e., Computer or SkyDrive).

4 Type **Paw Ridge Title Page** in the File name box to change the file name. Do not press the ENTER key after typing the file name because you do not want to close the dialog box at this time.

5 Navigate to the desired save location (in this case, the Word folder in the CIS 101 folder [or your class folder] on your computer or SkyDrive).

6 Tap or click the Save button (Save As dialog box) to save the title page in the selected folder on the selected save location with the entered file name.

SmartArt Graphics

Microsoft Office 2013 includes **SmartArt graphics**, which are visual representations of information. Many different types of SmartArt graphics are available, allowing you to choose one that illustrates your message best. Table 4–1 identifies the purpose of some of the more popular types of SmartArt graphics. Within each type, Office provides numerous layouts. For example, you can select from 40 different layouts of the list type.

Table 4–1 SmartArt Graphic Types	
Type	**Purpose**
List	Shows nonsequential or grouped blocks of information.
Process	Shows progression, timeline, or sequential steps in a process or workflow.
Cycle	Shows continuous sequence of steps or events.
Hierarchy	Illustrates organization charts, decision trees, and hierarchical relationships.
Relationship	Compares or contrasts connections between concepts.
Matrix	Shows relationships of parts to a whole.
Picture	Uses images to present a message.
Pyramid	Shows proportional or interconnected relationships with the largest component at the top or bottom.

© 2014 Cengage Learning

SmartArt graphics contain shapes. You can add text or pictures to shapes, add more shapes, or delete shapes. You also can modify the appearance of a SmartArt graphic by applying styles and changing its colors. The next several pages demonstrate the following general tasks to create the SmartArt graphic on the title page in this project:

1. Insert a SmartArt graphic.
2. Delete unneeded shapes from the SmartArt graphic.
3. Add shapes to the SmartArt graphic.
4. Add text to the shapes in the SmartArt graphic.
5. Change colors of the SmartArt graphic.
6. Apply a style to the SmartArt graphic.

To Insert a SmartArt Graphic

1 CREATE TITLE PAGE | 2 INSERT EXISTING DOCUMENT | 3 CREATE HEADER & FOOTER
4 EDIT & FORMAT LISTS | 5 EDIT & FORMAT TABLES | 6 CREATE WATERMARK

Below the title on the title page is a grouped list SmartArt graphic. *Why? The Grouped List SmartArt graphic allows you to place multiple lists side by side on the document, which works well for the content on this title page.* The following steps insert a SmartArt graphic centered below the title on the title page.

1

- With the insertion point on the blank paragraph below the title (shown in Figure 4–7), tap or click the Center button (HOME tab | Paragraph group) so that the inserted SmartArt graphic will be centered below the title.

- Display the INSERT tab.

- Tap or click the 'Insert a SmartArt Graphic' button (INSERT tab | Illustrations group) to display the Choose a SmartArt Graphic dialog box (Figure 4–8).

Figure 4–8

Experiment

- Tap or click various SmartArt graphic types in the left pane of the dialog box and watch the related layout choices appear in the middle pane.

- Tap or click various layouts in the list of layouts in the middle pane to see the preview and description of the layout appear in the right pane of the dialog box.

2

- Tap or click List in the left pane (Choose a SmartArt Graphic dialog box) to display the layout choices related to the selected SmartArt graphic type.

- Tap or click Grouped List in the middle pane, which displays a preview and description of the selected layout in the right pane (Figure 4–9).

Figure 4–9

3

- Tap or click the OK button to insert the selected SmartArt graphic in the document at the location of the insertion point (Figure 4–10).

Figure 4–10

Q&A What if the Text Pane appears next to the SmartArt graphic?

Close the Text Pane by tapping or clicking its Close button or tapping or clicking the Text Pane button (SMARTART TOOLS DESIGN tab | Create Graphic group).

Can I change the layout of the inserted SmartArt graphic?

Yes. Tap or click the More button in the Layouts gallery (SMARTART TOOLS DESIGN tab | Layouts group) to display the list of layouts and then select the desired layout.

To Delete Shapes from a SmartArt Graphic

The Grouped List SmartArt graphic initially has three outer groups that consist of nine different shapes (shown in Figure 4–10). Notice that each shape in the SmartArt graphic initially shows **placeholder text**, which indicates where text can be typed in a shape. The next step in this project is to delete one entire group. *Why? The SmartArt graphic in this project consists of only two major groups (Lodging and Recreation).* The following step deletes one entire group, or three shapes, in the SmartArt graphic.

1

- Be sure a shape is selected in the SmartArt graphic. If you are using a touch screen, tap the Cut button (HOME tab | Clipboard group) three times; if you are using a mouse, press the DELETE key three times to delete the three vertical shapes from the graphic (which is an entire group) and notice the other shapes resize and relocate in the graphic (Figure 4–11).

Q&A What if a shape is no longer selected?
Tap or click the edge of any shape to select the shape.

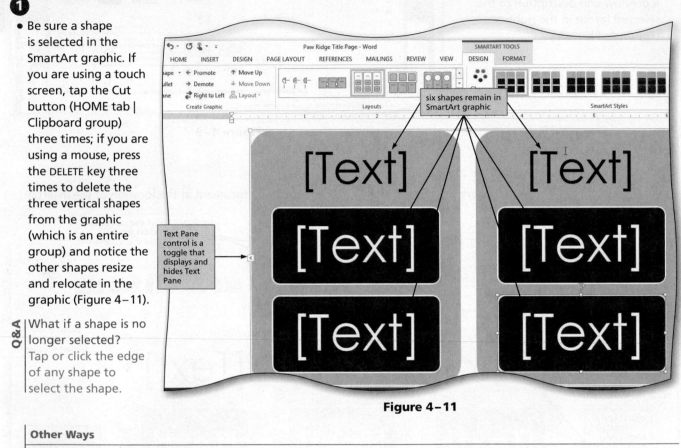

Figure 4–11

Other Ways

1. Tap or click Cut button (HOME tab | Clipboard group)

To Add Text to Shapes in a SmartArt Graphic

The placeholder text in a shape indicates where text can be typed in the shape. The following steps add text to the three shapes in the first group via their placeholder text. *Why? After entering the text in these three shapes, you will need to add two more shapes to finish the content in the group.*

1

- Tap or click the top-left shape to select it and then type `Lodging` to replace the placeholder text, [Text], with the entered text.

Q&A How do I edit placeholder text if I make a mistake?
Tap or click the placeholder text to select it and then correct the entry.

What if my typed text is longer than the shape?
The font size of the text may be adjusted or the text may wordwrap within the shape.

2
- Tap or click the middle-left shape to select it and then type `Cabins` as the new text.

- Tap or click the lower-left shape to select it and then type `Camp` as the new text (Figure 4–12).

Figure 4–12

Other Ways

1. Tap or click Text Pane control, enter text in Text Pane, close Text Pane

2. Tap or click Text Pane button (SMARTART TOOLS DESIGN tab | Create Graphic group), enter text in Text Pane, tap or click Text Pane button again

3. Tap Edit Text button on mini toolbar or right-click shape and then click Edit Text on shortcut menu, enter text

---

To Add Shapes to a SmartArt Graphic

1 CREATE TITLE PAGE | 2 INSERT EXISTING DOCUMENT | 3 CREATE HEADER & FOOTER
4 EDIT & FORMAT LISTS | 5 EDIT & FORMAT TABLES | 6 CREATE WATERMARK

The following steps add shapes to the SmartArt graphic. *Why? Each group has four subordinate items, which means two shapes need to be added to each group.*

1
- If you are using a touch screen, tap the Add Shape button (SMARTART TOOLS DESIGN tab | Create Graphic group) and then tap 'Add Shape After'; if you are using a mouse, click the Add Shape button (SMARTART TOOLS DESIGN tab | Create Graphic group) to add a shape to the SmartArt graphic.

2
- Repeat Step 1 to add the final shape to the group.

❸

- Tap or click a subordinate shape on the right (one of the brown shapes) to select it.
- Repeat Steps 1 and 2 so that the same number of shapes appear on the right and left sides of the SmartArt graphic.

❹

- Enter the text in the shapes shown in Figure 4–13.

Figure 4–13

Other Ways

1. If you are using a mouse, click Add Shape arrow (SMARTART TOOLS DESIGN tab), click desired shape position

2. Tap 'Show Context Menu' button on mini toolbar or right-click paragraph, tap or point to Add Shape on shortcut menu, tap or click desired shape position

To Change Colors of a SmartArt Graphic

1 CREATE TITLE PAGE | 2 INSERT EXISTING DOCUMENT | 3 CREATE HEADER & FOOTER
4 EDIT & FORMAT LISTS | 5 EDIT & FORMAT TABLES | 6 CREATE WATERMARK

Word provides a variety of colors for a SmartArt graphic and the shapes in the graphic. In this project, the inside shapes are tan, instead of red. *Why? The dark red color competes with the title, so you want a softer color for the shapes.* The following steps change the colors of a SmartArt graphic.

❶

- With the SmartArt graphic selected (shown in Figure 4–13), tap or click the Change Colors button (SMARTART TOOLS DESIGN tab | SmartArt Styles group) to display the Change Colors gallery.

Q&A | What if the SmartArt graphic is not selected?
Tap or click the SmartArt graphic to select it.

BTW
Resetting Graphics
If you want to remove all formats from a SmartArt graphic and start over, you would tap or click the Reset Graphic button (SMARTART TOOLS DESIGN tab | Reset group), which is shown in Figure 4-15 on page WD 217.

- If you are using a mouse, point to 'Colored Fill - Accent 3' in the Change Colors gallery to display a live preview of the selected color applied to the SmartArt graphic in the document (Figure 4–14).

Figure 4–14

Experiment

- If you are using a mouse, point to various colors in the Change Colors gallery and watch the colors of the graphic change in the document window.

2

- Tap or click 'Colored Fill - Accent 3' in the Change Colors gallery to apply the selected color to the SmartArt graphic.

To Apply a SmartArt Style

1 CREATE TITLE PAGE | 2 INSERT EXISTING DOCUMENT | 3 CREATE HEADER & FOOTER
4 EDIT & FORMAT LISTS | 5 EDIT & FORMAT TABLES | 6 CREATE WATERMARK

The next step is to apply a SmartArt style to the SmartArt graphic. *Why? Word provides a SmartArt Styles gallery, allowing you to change the SmartArt graphic's format to a more visually appealing style.* The following steps apply a SmartArt style to a SmartArt graphic.

1

- With the SmartArt graphic still selected, tap or click the More button in the SmartArt Styles gallery (shown in Figure 4–14) to expand the SmartArt Styles gallery.

- If you are using a mouse, point to Moderate Effect in the SmartArt Styles gallery to display a live preview of that style applied to the graphic in the document (Figure 4–15).

Experiment

- If you are using a mouse, point to various SmartArt styles in the SmartArt Styles gallery and watch the style of the graphic change in the document window.

Figure 4–15

2

- Tap or click Moderate Effect in the SmartArt Styles gallery to apply the selected style to the SmartArt graphic.

To Modify Character Spacing and Format Characters Using the Font Dialog Box

In this project, the next step is to enter and format the text at the bottom of the title page. This text is the theme of the proposal and is formatted so that it is noticeable. Its characters are 36-point, italic, dark red Britannic Bold. Each letter in this text is formatted in **small caps**, which are letters that look like capital letters but are not as tall as a typical capital letter. Also, you want extra space between each character so that the text spans the width of the page.

Thus, the next steps apply all of the formats mentioned above using the Font dialog box. *Why? Although you could use buttons on the HOME tab to apply some of these formats, the small caps effect and expanded spacing are applied using the Font dialog box. Thus, you apply all the formats using the Font dialog box.*

1

- Position the insertion point on the paragraph mark to the right of the SmartArt graphic and then press the ENTER key to position the insertion point centered below the SmartArt graphic.

- Type `Plan your next outing with us!`

- Select the sentence you just typed and then tap or click the Font Dialog Box Launcher (HOME tab | Font group) to display the Font dialog box. If necessary, tap or click the Font tab in the dialog box to display the Font sheet.

- Scroll to and then tap or click Britannic Bold in the Font list (Font dialog box) to change the font of the selected text.

- Tap or click Italic in the Font style list to italicize the selected text.

- Scroll through the Size list and then tap or click 36 to change the font size of the selected text.

- Tap or click the Font color arrow and then tap or click 'Dark Red, Accent 1' (fifth color, first row) in the Font color palette to change the color of the selected text.

- Tap or click the Small caps check box in the Effects area so that each character is displayed as a small capital letter (Figure 4–16).

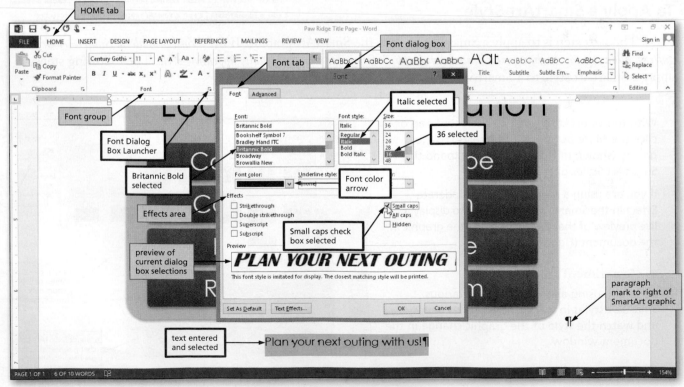

Figure 4–16

2

- Tap or click the Advanced tab (Font dialog box) to display the Advanced sheet in the Font dialog box.

- Tap or click the Spacing arrow and then tap or click Expanded to increase the amount of space between characters by 1 pt, which is the default.

- Double-tap or double-click the value in the Spacing By box to select it and then type 7 because you want this amount of blank space to be displayed between each character.

- Click in any box in the dialog box for the change to take effect and display a preview of the entered value in the Preview area (Figure 4–17).

Figure 4–17

Q&A | Can I tap or click the Spacing By arrows instead of typing a value in the box?
Yes.

3

- Tap or click the OK button to apply font changes to the selected text. If necessary, scroll so that the selected text is displayed completely in the document window.

- Tap or click to remove the selection from the text (Figure 4–18).

36-point italic dark red Britannic Bold font in small caps and expanded

PLAN · YOUR · NEXT · OUTING · WITH · US!¶

Figure 4–18

Other Ways

1. Tap 'Show Context Menu' button on mini toolbar or right-click selected text, tap or click Font on shortcut menu, select formats (Font dialog box), tap or click OK button

2. Press CTRL+D, select formats (Font dialog box), tap or click OK button

To Zoom One Page, Change Spacing before and after a Paragraph, and Set Zoom Level

The final step in creating the title page is to adjust spacing above and below the SmartArt graphic. You want to see the entire page while adjusting the spacing. Thus, the following steps zoom one page, increase spacing before and after the paragraph containing the SmartArt graphic, and then set the zoom level back to page width because you will be finished with the title page.

1 Display the VIEW tab. Tap or click the One Page button (VIEW tab | Zoom group) to display the entire page as large as possible centered in the document window.

2 Position the insertion point in the paragraph to adjust, in this case, on the paragraph mark to the right of the SmartArt graphic.

3 Display the PAGE LAYOUT tab. If you are using a touch screen, tap the Spacing After box (PAGE LAYOUT tab | Paragraph group) and then type 48 to change the spacing below the paragraph; if you are using a mouse, click the Spacing Before up arrow (PAGE LAYOUT tab | Paragraph group) as many times as necessary until 48 pt is displayed in the Spacing Before box because you want to increase the space above the graphic.

4 If you are using a touch screen, tap the Spacing After box (PAGE LAYOUT tab | Paragraph group) and then type 36 to change the spacing below the paragraph; if you are using a mouse, click the Spacing After up arrow (PAGE LAYOUT tab | Paragraph group) as many times as necessary until 36 pt is displayed in the Spacing After box because you want to increase the space below the graphic (Figure 4–19).

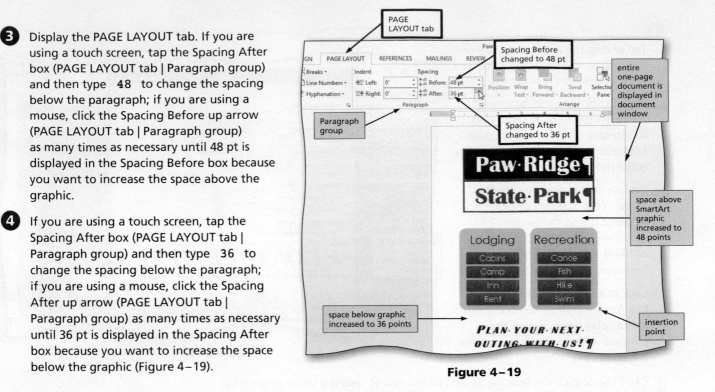

Figure 4–19

Q&A What if the document spills to two pages?
Decrease the spacing above or below the SmartArt graphic until the title page contents fit on a single page.

5 Display the VIEW tab. Tap or click the Page Width button (VIEW tab | Zoom group) to change the zoom to page width.

To Save an Existing Document with the Same File Name

You have made several modifications to the document since you last saved it. Thus, you should save it again. The following step saves the document again.

1 Tap or click the Save button on the Quick Access Toolbar to overwrite the previously saved file.

Break Point: If you wish to take a break, this is a good place to do so. You can exit Word now. To resume at a later time, run Word, open the file called Paw Ridge Title Page, and continue following the steps from this location forward.

Inserting an Existing Document in an Open Document

Assume you already have prepared a draft of the body of the proposal and saved it with the file name, Paw Ridge Draft. You would like the draft to be displayed on a separate page following the title page.

In the following pages, you will insert the draft of the proposal below the title page and then edit the draft by deleting a page break, changing theme fonts, and applying styles.

To Save an Active Document with a New File Name

BTW
Inserting Documents
When you insert a Word document in another Word document, the entire inserted document is placed at the location of the insertion point. If the insertion point, therefore, is positioned in the middle of the open document when you insert another Word document, the open document continues after the last character of the inserted document.

The current file name on the title bar is Paw Ridge Title Page, yet the document you will work on from this point forward in the chapter will contain both the title page and the body of the sales proposal. To keep the title page as a separate document called Paw Ridge Title Page, you should save the active document with a new file name. If you save the active document by using the Save button on the Quick Access Toolbar, Word will assign it the current file name. You want the active document to have a new file name. The following steps save the active document with a new file name.

1 Tap or click FILE on the ribbon to open the Backstage view and then tap or click the Save As tab to display the Save As gallery.

2 To save on a hard disk or other storage media on your computer, proceed to Step 2a. To save on SkyDrive, proceed to Step 2b.

2a Tap or click Computer in the left pane, if necessary, to display options in the right pane related to saving on your computer.

2b Tap or click SkyDrive in the left pane to display SkyDrive saving options or a Sign In button. If your screen displays a Sign In button, tap or click it and then sign in to SkyDrive.

3 Tap or click the Browse button in the right pane to display the Save As dialog box associated with the selected save location (i.e., Computer or SkyDrive).

4 Type `Paw Ridge Sales Proposal` in the File name box to change the file name. Do not press the ENTER key after typing the file name because you do not want to close the dialog box at this time.

5 Navigate to the desired save location (in this case, the Word folder in the CIS 101 folder [or your class folder] on your computer or SkyDrive).

6 Tap or click the Save button (Save As dialog box) to save the title page in the selected folder on the selected save location with the entered file name.

Sections

BTW
Section Numbers
If you want to display the current section number on the status bar, press and hold or right-click the status bar to display the Customize Status Bar menu and then tap or click Section on the Customize Status Bar menu. The section number appears at the left edge of the status bar. To remove the section number from the status bar, perform the same steps.

All Word documents have at least one section. A Word document can be divided into any number of sections. During the course of creating a document, you will create a new **section** if you need to change the top margin, bottom margin, page alignment, paper size, page orientation, page number position, or contents or position of headers, footers, or footnotes in just a portion of the document.

The pages in the body of the sales proposal require page formatting different from that of the title page. The title page will not have a header or footer; the next two pages will have a header and footer.

When you want to change page formatting for a portion of a document, you create a new section in the document. Each section then may be formatted differently from the others. Thus, the title page formatted with no header or footer will be in one section, and the next two pages of the proposal, which will have a header and footer, will be in another section.

To Insert a Next Page Section Break

When you insert a section break, you specify whether the new section should begin on a new page. *Why?* *Sometimes you want a page break to occur with a section break, as in this project. Other times, you do not want a page break to occur with a section break (which will be illustrated in a later chapter).* In this project, the title page is separate from the next two pages. Thus, the section break should contain a page break. The following steps insert a next page section break, which instructs Word to begin the new section on a new page in the document.

1

- Position the insertion point at the end of the title page (following the exclamation point), which is the location where you want to insert the next page section break.

- Display the PAGE LAYOUT tab. Tap or click the 'Insert Page and Section Breaks' button (PAGE LAYOUT tab | Page Setup group) to display the Insert Page and Section Breaks gallery (Figure 4–20).

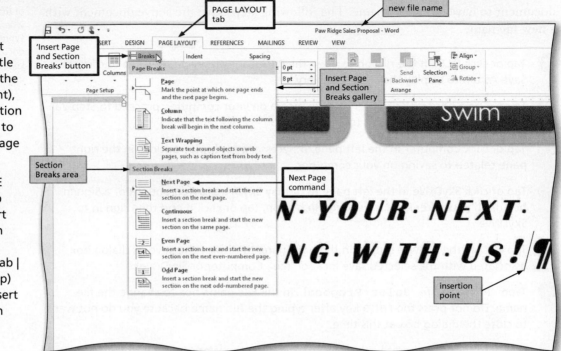

Figure 4–20

2

- Tap or click Next Page in the Section Breaks area of the Insert Page and Section Breaks gallery to insert a next page section break in the document at the location of the insertion point. If necessary, scroll so that your screen matches Figure 4–21.

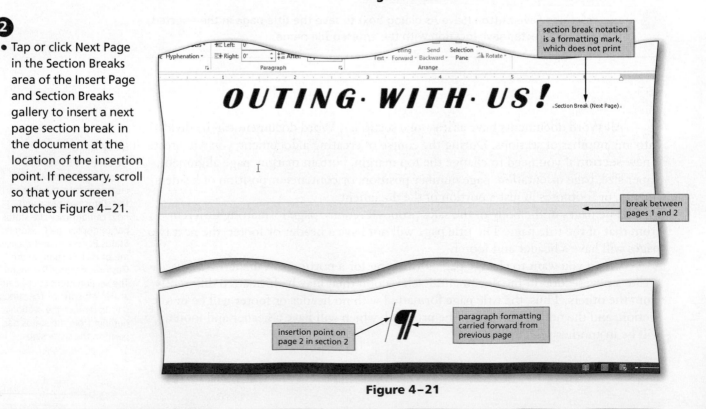

Figure 4–21

To Delete a Section Break

Word stores all section formatting in the section break. If you wanted to delete a section break and all associated section formatting, you would perform the following tasks.

1. Select the section break notation by dragging through it.
2. Press and hold or right-click the selection to display a mini toolbar or shortcut menu and then tap or click Cut on the mini toolbar or shortcut menu to delete the selection.

or

1. Position the insertion point immediately to the left or right of the section break notation.
2. Press the DELETE key to delete a section break to the right of the insertion point or press the BACKSPACE key to delete a section break to the left of the insertion point.

To Clear Formatting

When you create a section break, Word carries forward any formatting at the location of the insertion point to the next section. Thus, the current paragraph is formatted the same as the last line of the title page. In this project, the paragraphs and characters on the second page should be returned to the Normal style. Thus, the following step clears formatting.

1 Display the HOME tab. With the insertion point positioned on the paragraph mark on the second page (shown in Figure 4–21), tap or click the 'Clear All Formatting' button (HOME tab | Font group) to apply the Normal style to the location of the insertion point (shown in Figure 4–22).

To Insert a Word Document in an Open Document

1 CREATE TITLE PAGE | 2 INSERT EXISTING DOCUMENT | 3 CREATE HEADER & FOOTER
4 EDIT & FORMAT LISTS | 5 EDIT & FORMAT TABLES | 6 CREATE WATERMARK

The next step is to insert the draft of the sales proposal at the top of the second page of the document. *Why? You will modify a draft of the body of the proposal, which is located on the Data Files for Students. Visit www.cengage.com/ct/studentdownload for detailed instructions or contact your instructor for information about accessing the required files.* The following steps insert an existing Word document in an open document.

1

- Be sure the insertion point is positioned on the paragraph mark at the top of page 2, which is the location where you want to insert the contents of the Word document.
- Display the INSERT tab.
- Tap or click the Object arrow (INSERT tab | Text group) to display the Object menu (Figure 4–22).

Q&A
If I am using a mouse, what if I click the Object button by mistake?
Click the Cancel button (Object dialog box) and then repeat this step.

BTW

Sections
To see the formatting associated with a section, double-tap or double-click the section break notation or tap or click the Page Setup Dialog Box Launcher (PAGE LAYOUT tab | Page Setup group) to display the Page Setup dialog box. You can change margin settings and page orientation for a section in the Margins sheet. To change paper sizes for a section, tap or click the Paper tab. The Layout tab allows you to change header and footer specifications and vertical alignment for the section. To add a border to a section, tap or click the Borders button in the Layout sheet.

Figure 4–22

2

- Tap or click 'Text from File' on the Object menu to display the Insert File dialog box.

- Navigate to the location of the file to be inserted (in this case, the Chapter 04 folder in the Word folder in the Data Files for Students folder).

- Tap or click Paw Ridge Draft to select the file name (Figure 4–23).

Figure 4–23

3

- Tap or click the Insert button (Insert File dialog box) to insert the file, Paw Ridge Draft, in the open document at the location of the insertion point.

Q&A
Where is the insertion point now?
When you insert a file in an open document, Word positions the insertion point at the end of the inserted document.

- Press SHIFT+F5 to position the insertion point on line 1 of page 2, which was its location prior to inserting the new Word document (Figure 4–24).

Q&A
What is the purpose of SHIFT+F5?
The keyboard shortcut, SHIFT+F5, positions the insertion point at your last editing location. Word remembers your last three editing locations, which means you can press this keyboard shortcut repeatedly to return to one of your three most recent editing locations.

What if my keyboard does not have function keys?
Scroll to display the top of page 2 in the document window.

Figure 4–24

Other Ways

1. Tap or click Object button (INSERT tab | Text group), tap or click 'Create from File' tab (Object dialog box), tap or click Browse button, locate file, tap or click Insert button (Browse dialog box), tap or click OK button (Object dialog box)

To Print Specific Pages in a Document

The title page is the first page of the proposal. The body of the proposal spans the second and third pages. The following steps print a hard copy of only the body of the proposal, that is, pages 2 and 3. *Why? You would like to see the contents of the body of the proposal before you begin modifying it.*

1

- Tap or click FILE on the ribbon to open the Backstage view and then tap or click the Print tab in the Backstage view to display the Print gallery.

- Verify that the printer listed on the Printer Status button will print a hard copy of the document. If necessary, tap or click the Printer Status button to display a list of available printer options and then tap or click the desired printer to change the selected printer.

- Type 2–3 in the Pages text box in the Settings area of the Print gallery (Figure 4–25).

2

- Tap or click the Print button to print the inserted draft of the sales proposal (Figure 4–26).

Q&A

How would I print pages from a certain point to the end of a document?

You would enter the page number followed by a dash in the Pages text box. For example, 5- will print from page 5 to the end of the document. To print up to a certain page, put the dash first (e.g., -5 will print pages 1 through 5).

Why does my document wrap on different words than Figure 4–26?

Differences in wordwrap may be related to the printer used by your computer.

Why does my screen show the document has four pages?

You may have an extra blank page at the end of the document. This blank page will be deleted later in the chapter.

Figure 4–25

Other Ways

1. Press CTRL+P; press ENTER

CONSIDER THIS

What elements should the body of a sales proposal contain?

Be sure to include basic elements in your sales proposals:

- **Include an introduction, body, and conclusion.** The introduction could contain the subject, purpose, statement of problem, need, background, or scope. The body may include costs, benefits, supporting documentation, available or required facilities, feasibility, methods, timetable, materials, or equipment. The conclusion summarizes key points or requests an action.

- **Use headers and footers.** Headers and footers help to identify every page. A page number should be in either the header or footer. If the sales proposal should become disassembled, the reader can use the headers and footers to determine the order and pieces of your proposal.

---

1 CREATE TITLE PAGE | 2 INSERT EXISTING DOCUMENT | 3 CREATE HEADER & FOOTER
4 EDIT & FORMAT LISTS | 5 EDIT & FORMAT TABLES | 6 CREATE WATERMARK

To Delete a Page Break

After reviewing the draft in Figure 4–26, you notice it contains a page break below the bulleted list. The following steps delete a page break. *Why? This page break below the bulleted list should not be in the proposal.*

1

- Scroll to display the page break notation.

- To select the page break notation, double-tap or double-click it (Figure 4–27).

2

- Press and hold and then tap the Cut button on the mini toolbar or press the DELETE key to remove the page break from the document.

Figure 4–27

Other Ways
1. With page break notation selected, tap or click Cut button (HOME tab | Clipboard group)	2. With page break notation selected, press and hold or right-click selection and then tap or click Cut on mini toolbar or shortcut menu	3. With the insertion point to the left or right of the page break notation, press DELETE or BACKSPACE, respectively

To Apply Heading Styles

Word has many built-in, or predefined, styles that you can use to format text. Three of the Styles shown in the Styles gallery in Figure 4–28 are for headings: Heading 1 for the major headings and Heading 2 and Heading 3 for minor headings. In the Paw Ridge Draft, all headings except for the first two were formatted using heading styles.

The following steps apply the Heading 1 style to the paragraph containing the text, OUR PARK, and the Heading 2 style to the paragraph containing the text, Lodging Descriptions.

BTW

Q&As

For a complete list of the Q&As found in many of the step-by-step sequences in this book, visit the Q&A resource on the Student Companion Site located on www.cengagebrain.com. For detailed instructions about accessing available resources, visit www.cengage.com/ct/studentdownload or contact your instructor for information about accessing the required files.

1 Position the insertion point in the paragraph to be formatted to the Heading 1 style, in this case, the first line on the second page with the text, OUR PARK.

2 Tap or click Heading 1 in the Style gallery (HOME tab | Styles group) to apply the selected style to the paragraph containing the insertion point.

Q&A Why did a square appear on the screen near the left edge of the paragraph formatted with the Heading 1 style?

The square is a nonprinting character, like the paragraph mark, that indicates text to its right has a special paragraph format applied to it.

3 Position the insertion point in the paragraph to be formatted to the Heading 2 style, in this case, the line above the bulleted list with the text, Lodging Descriptions.

Tap or click Heading 2 in the Style gallery (HOME tab | Styles group) to apply the selected style to the paragraph containing the insertion point (Figure 4–28).

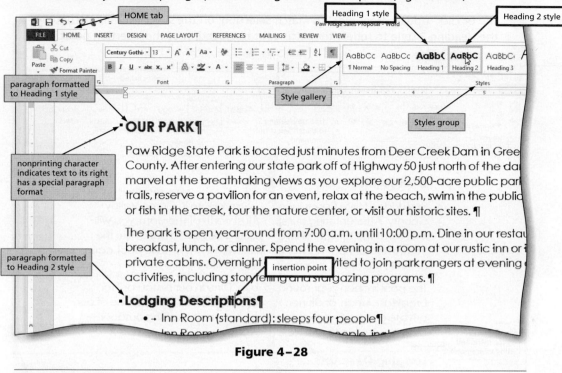

Figure 4–28

To Change Spacing before and after a Paragraph

The next step is to adjust spacing above and below the current paragraph, that is, the heading above the bulleted list. This paragraph is formatted using the Heading 2 style, which places no space above the paragraph and 8 points below the paragraph. You would like this paragraph, and all other paragraphs formatted using the Heading 2 style, to have 12 points of space above them and 6 points of space below them. Thus, the following steps adjust the spacing before and after a paragraph.

1 Display the PAGE LAYOUT tab. Position the insertion point as shown in Figure 4–29 on the next page. If you are using a touch screen, tap the Spacing Before box (PAGE LAYOUT tab | Paragraph group) and then type 12 to change the spacing above the paragraph; if you are using a mouse, tap or click the Spacing Before up arrow (PAGE LAYOUT tab | Paragraph group) as many times as necessary so that 12 pt is displayed in the Spacing Before box.

2 If you are using a touch screen, tap the Spacing After box (PAGE LAYOUT tab | Paragraph group) and then type 6 to change the spacing below the paragraph; if you are using a mouse, tap or click the Spacing After up arrow (PAGE LAYOUT tab | Paragraph group) so that 6 pt is displayed in the Spacing After box.

To Update a Style to Match a Selection

You want all paragraphs formatted in the Heading 2 style in the proposal to use this adjusted spacing. Thus, the steps on the next page update the Heading 2 style so that this adjusted spacing is applied to all Heading 2 paragraphs in the document.

1 If necessary, position the insertion point in the paragraph containing the style to be updated.

② Display the HOME tab. Press and hold or right-click Heading 2 in the Styles gallery (HOME tab | Styles group) to display a shortcut menu (Figure 4–29).

③ Tap or click 'Update Heading 2 to Match Selection' on the shortcut menu to update the Heading 2 style to reflect the settings at the location of the insertion point.

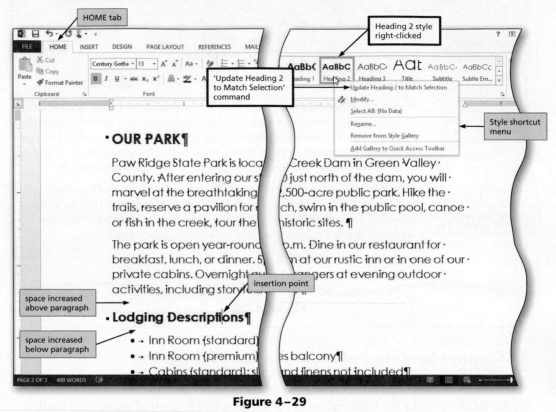

Figure 4–29

BTW

Headers and Footers

If a portion of a header or footer does not print, it may be in a nonprintable area. Check the printer user instructions to see how close the printer can print to the edge of the paper. Then, tap or click the Page Setup Dialog Box Launcher (PAGE LAYOUT tab | Page Setup group), tap or click the Layout tab (Page Setup dialog box), adjust the From edge text box to a value that is larger than the printer's minimum margin setting, tap or click the OK button, and then print the document again.

Creating Headers and Footers

A header is text that prints at the top of each page in the document. A footer is text that prints at the bottom of each page. In this proposal, you want the header and footer to appear on each page after the title page; that is, you do not want the header and footer on the title page. Recall that the title page is in a separate section from the rest of the sales proposal. Thus, the header and footer should not be in section 1, but they should be in section 2. The steps on the following pages explain how to create a header and footer in section 2 only.

To Insert a Formatted Header Different from the Previous Header

1 CREATE TITLE PAGE | 2 INSERT EXISTING DOCUMENT | **3 CREATE HEADER & FOOTER**

4 EDIT & FORMAT LISTS | 5 EDIT & FORMAT TABLES | 6 CREATE WATERMARK

Word provides several built-in preformatted header designs for you to insert in documents. The following steps insert a formatted header in section 2 of the sales proposal that is different from the previous header. *Why? You do not want the header to appear on the title page, so you will instruct Word to not place the header in the previous section. Recall that the title page is in section 1 and the body of the proposal is in section 2.*

①

● Display the INSERT tab. Tap or click the 'Add a Header' button (INSERT tab | Header & Footer group) and then tap or click Edit Header in the Header gallery to switch to the header for section 2.

● If the 'Link to Previous' button (HEADER & FOOTER TOOLS DESIGN tab | Navigation group) is selected, tap or click it to deselect the button because you do not want the header in this section to be copied to the previous section (that is, the header should not be on the title page).

- Tap or click the 'Add a Header' button (HEADER & FOOTER TOOLS DESIGN tab | Header & Footer group) to display the Add a Header gallery (Figure 4–30).

🔍 **Experiment**

- Scroll through the list of built-in headers to see the variety of available formatted header designs.

'Add a Header' button

INSERT tab

Add a Header gallery contains list of built-in headers

HEADER & FOOTER TOOLS DESIGN tab automatically appears because you are editing header

'Link to Previous' button is not selected, which means headers and footers added to this section will not be added to previous section

section 2 header

Banded header design

Remove Header command deletes an existing header

Figure 4–30

2

- If necessary, scroll to and then tap or click the Banded header design in the Add a Header gallery to insert the formatted header in the header of section 2, which contains a content control (Figure 4–31).

content control

Banded header design inserted

[DOCUMENT TITLE]¶

Header -Section 2-

section 2 header

top of section 2

·OUR PARK¶

Paw Ridge State Park is located just minutes from Deer Creek Dam in Green V

Figure 4–31

Q&A | What is a content control?

A **content control** is an object that contains sample text or instructions for filling in text and graphics.

3

- Tap or click the content control, DOCUMENT TITLE, to select it and then type **Paw Ridge State Park** in the content control (Figure 4–32).

'Add a Footer' button

'Go to Footer' button

HEADER & FOOTER TOOLS DESIGN tab

Header & Footer group

text entered in content control

Title

PAW RIDGE STATE PARK

Header -Section 2-

Figure 4–32

If requested by your instructor, enter your name instead of the state park name shown in Figure 4–31.

Q&A | How would I delete a header?
You would tap or click Remove Header in the Header gallery.

Other Ways

1. Tap or click 'Add a Header' button (INSERT tab | Header & Footer group), select desired header in list

2. Tap or click 'Explore Quick Parts' button (INSERT tab | Text group), tap or click 'Building Blocks Organizer' on Quick Parts menu, select desired header (Building Blocks Organizer dialog box), tap or click Insert button

---

To Insert a Formatted Footer

The next step is to insert the footer. Word provides the same built-in preformatted footer designs as header designs. The footer design that corresponds to the header just inserted contains a centered page number. The following steps insert a formatted footer in section 2 of the sales proposal that corresponds to the header just inserted.

BTW

Page Numbers

If Word displays {PAGE} instead of the actual page number, press ALT+F9 to turn off field codes. If Word prints {PAGE} instead of the page number, open the Backstage view, tap or click Options to display the Word Options dialog box, tap or click Advanced in the left pane (Word Options dialog box), scroll to the Print area, remove the check mark from the 'Print field codes instead of their values' check box, and then tap or click the OK button.

1 Tap or click the 'Go to Footer' button (shown in Figure 4–32) (HEADER & FOOTER TOOLS DESIGN tab | Header & Footer group) to display the Add a Footer gallery.

2 If the 'Link to Previous' button (HEADER & FOOTER TOOLS DESIGN tab | Navigation group) is selected, tap or click it to deselect the button because you do not want the footer in this section to be copied to the previous section (that is, the footer should not be on the title page).

3 Tap or click the 'Add a Footer' button (shown in Figure 4–32) (HEADER & FOOTER TOOLS DESIGN tab | Header & Footer group) to display the Add a Footer gallery.

4 Tap or click the Banded footer design to insert the formatted footer in the footer of section 2 (shown in Figure 4–33).

Q&A | Why is the page number a 2?
The page number is 2 because, by default, Word begins numbering pages from the beginning of the document.

To Format Page Numbers to Start at a Different Number

1 CREATE TITLE PAGE | 2 INSERT EXISTING DOCUMENT | 3 CREATE HEADER & FOOTER
4 EDIT & FORMAT LISTS | 5 EDIT & FORMAT TABLES | 6 CREATE WATERMARK

On the page after the title page in the proposal, you want to begin numbering with a number 1, instead of a 2 as shown in Figure 4–33. *Why? Word begins numbering pages from the beginning of the document and you want it to begin numbering on the body of the proposal.* Thus, you need to instruct Word to begin numbering the pages in section 2 with the number 1. The next steps format the page numbers so that they start at a different number.

1

• Tap or click the 'Add Page Numbers' button (HEADER & FOOTER TOOLS DESIGN tab | Header & Footer group) to display the Add Page Numbers menu (Figure 4–33).

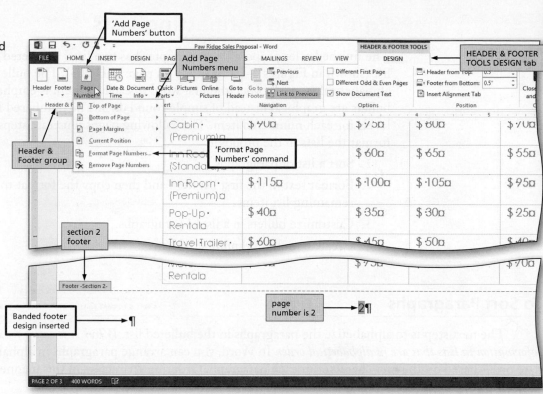

Figure 4–33

2

• Tap or click 'Format Page Numbers' on the Add Page Numbers menu to display the Page Number Format dialog box.

• Tap or click Start at in the Page numbering area (Page Number Format dialog box), which displays a 1 by default as the starting page number (Figure 4–34).

Q&A Can I also change the look of the page number?
Yes. Tap or click the Number format arrow (Page Number Format dialog box) for a list of page number variations.

Figure 4–34

3

• Tap or click the OK button to change the starting page number for section 2 to the number 1 (Figure 4–35).

• Tap or click the 'Close Header and Footer' button (HEADER & FOOTER TOOLS DESIGN tab | Close group) to close the header and footer.

Figure 4–35

Other Ways

1. Tap or click 'Add Page Numbers' button (INSERT tab | Header & Footer group), tap or click 'Format Page Numbers' on Add Page Numbers menu, set page formats (Page Number Format dialog box), tap or click OK button

Editing and Formatting Lists

The finished sales proposal in this chapter has two lists: a bulleted list and a numbered list (shown in Figures 4–1b and 4–1c on page WD 203). The bulleted list is in alphabetical (sorted) order, the first word of each list item is emphasized, and the bullets are graphical instead of simple round dots. The numbered listed has multiple levels for each numbered item. The following pages illustrate steps used to edit and format the lists in the proposal:

1. Sort a list of paragraphs.
2. Format text in the first list item and then copy the format to text in each of the remaining list items.
3. Customize bullets in a list of paragraphs.
4. Create a multilevel numbered list.

To Sort Paragraphs

1 CREATE TITLE PAGE | 2 INSERT EXISTING DOCUMENT | 3 CREATE HEADER & FOOTER
4 EDIT & FORMAT LISTS | 5 EDIT & FORMAT TABLES | 6 CREATE WATERMARK

The next step is to alphabetize the paragraphs in the bulleted list. *Why? It is easier for readers to locate information in lists that are in alphabetical order.* In Word, you can arrange paragraphs in alphabetic, numeric, or date order based on the first character in each paragraph. Ordering characters in this manner is called **sorting**. The following steps sort paragraphs.

1

- Scroll up to display the paragraphs to be sorted.

- Drag through the paragraphs to be sorted, in this case, the bulleted list.

- Tap or click the Sort button (HOME tab | Paragraph group) to display the Sort Text dialog box (Figure 4–36).

Q&A What does ascending mean?
Ascending means to sort in alphabetic, numeric, or earliest-to-latest date order.

2

- Tap or click the OK button (Sort Text dialog box) to instruct Word to alphabetize the selected paragraphs (shown in Figure 4–37).

- Tap or click anywhere to remove the selection from the text.

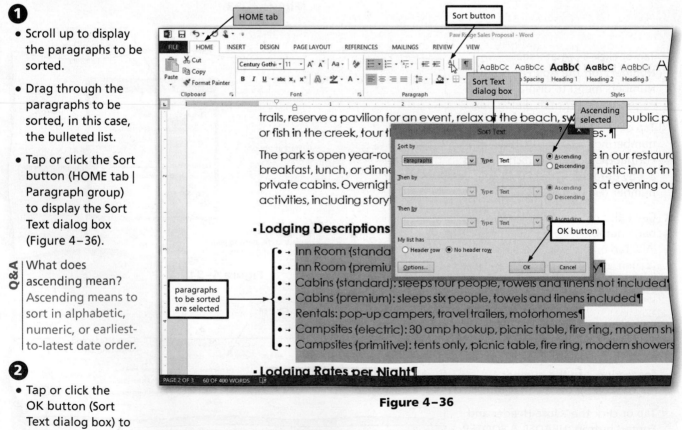

Figure 4–36

To Apply a Style Using the Mini Toolbar

The text up to the colon in each list item is to be formatted in bold, dark red, and italic. Although you could apply formatting using buttons in the Font group on the ribbon, it is more efficient to use the Intense Emphasis style. If you use a style and decide at a later time that you want to modify the formatting, you simply modify the style and Word will apply the changes to all text formatted with that style. Thus, the following steps format text using a style.

1 Drag through the text to be formatted (in this case, the text, Cabins (premium), in the first list item).

2 Tap or click the Styles button on the mini toolbar to display the Styles gallery (Figure 4–37).

3 Tap or click Intense Emphasis in the Styles gallery to apply the selected style to the selected text.

Q&A Could I use the Styles gallery on the HOME tab instead of the mini toolbar?
Yes.

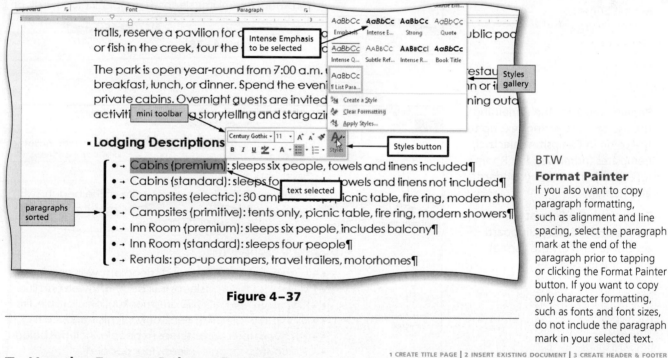

Figure 4–37

BTW

Format Painter
If you also want to copy paragraph formatting, such as alignment and line spacing, select the paragraph mark at the end of the paragraph prior to tapping or clicking the Format Painter button. If you want to copy only character formatting, such as fonts and font sizes, do not include the paragraph mark in your selected text.

To Use the Format Painter Button

1 CREATE TITLE PAGE | 2 INSERT EXISTING DOCUMENT | 3 CREATE HEADER & FOOTER
4 EDIT & FORMAT LISTS | 5 EDIT & FORMAT TABLES | 6 CREATE WATERMARK

The first words in each of the remaining list items is to be formatted the same as the first words in the first list item. *Why? You would like the lists to be formatted consistently.* Instead of selecting the text in each list item one at a time and then formatting it, you will copy the format from the first word to the remaining words. The following steps copy formatting.

1

- Position the insertion point in the text that contains the formatting you wish to copy (in this case, the text, Cabins (premium)).
- Double-tap or double-click the Format Painter button (HOME tab | Clipboard group) to turn on the format painter.

Q&A Why double-tap or double-click the Format Painter button?
To copy formats to only one other location, tap or click the Format Painter button (HOME tab | Clipboard group) once. If you want to copy formatting to multiple locations, however, double-tap or double-click the Format Painter button so that the format painter remains active until you turn it off.

- If you are using a mouse, move the pointer to where you want to copy the formatting (the text, Cabins (standard), in this case) and notice that the format painter is active (Figure 4–38).

Q&A How can I tell if the format painter is active?
The pointer has a paintbrush attached to it when the format painter is active.

2

- Drag through the text in the next list item (the text, Cabins (standard), in this case) to paste the copied format to the selected text.

Q&A What if the Format Painter button no longer is selected?
Repeat Step 1.

3

- Repeat Step 2 for the remaining the list items, selecting text up to the colon in Campsites (electric), Campsites (primitive), Inn Room (premium), Inn Room (standard), and Rentals.

- Tap or click the Format Painter button (HOME tab | Clipboard group) to turn off the format painter (Figure 4–39).

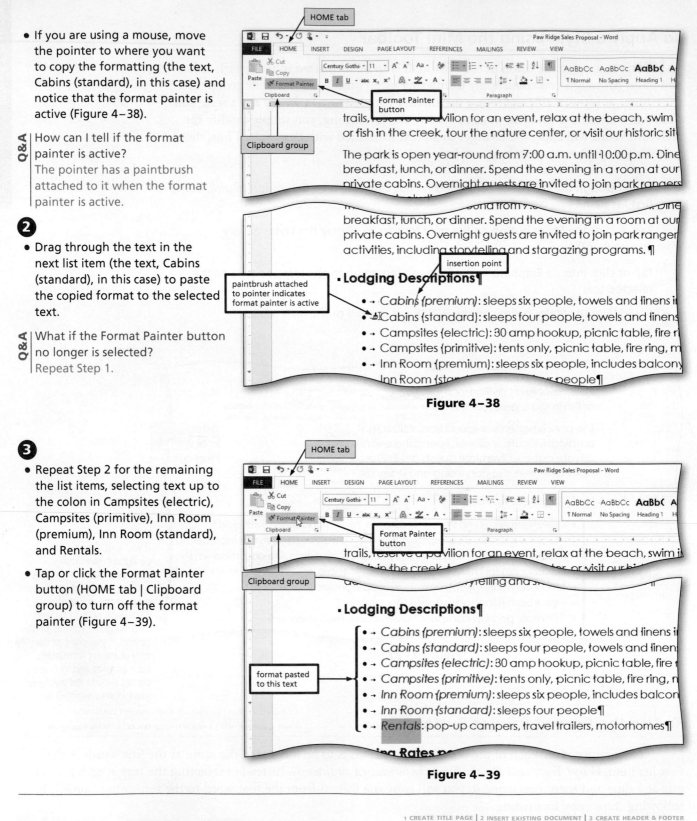

Figure 4–38

Figure 4–39

To Customize Bullets in a List

1 CREATE TITLE PAGE | 2 INSERT EXISTING DOCUMENT | 3 CREATE HEADER & FOOTER
4 EDIT & FORMAT LISTS | 5 EDIT & FORMAT TABLES | 6 CREATE WATERMARK

The bulleted list in the sales proposal draft uses default bullet characters, that is, the dot symbol. The following steps change the bullets in a list from the default to picture bullets. *Why? You want to use a more visually appealing bullet that looks like bed and pillow. Word refers to these graphical bullets as picture bullets.*

1

- Select all the paragraphs in the bulleted list.

- Tap or click the Bullets arrow (HOME tab | Paragraph group) to display the Bullets gallery (Figure 4–40).

Q&A Can I select any of the bullet characters in the Bullet Library area of the Bullets gallery?
Yes, but if you prefer a different bullet character, follow the rest of these steps.

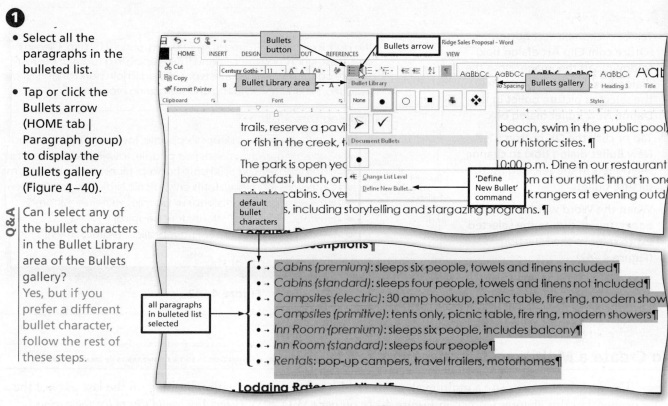

Figure 4–40

2

- Tap or click 'Define New Bullet' in the Bullets gallery to display the Define New Bullet dialog box.

- Tap or click the Picture button (Define New Bullet dialog box) to display the Insert Pictures dialog box.

Q&A Is this the same dialog box I use to locate clip art?
Yes.

- Type **pillow** in the Office.com Clip Art Search box (Insert Pictures dialog box) and then tap or click the Search button to display a list of clip art that matches the entered search text.

- Scroll through the list of clip art to locate the one shown in Figure 4–41 (or a similar image), if necessary, and then tap or click the clip art to select it.

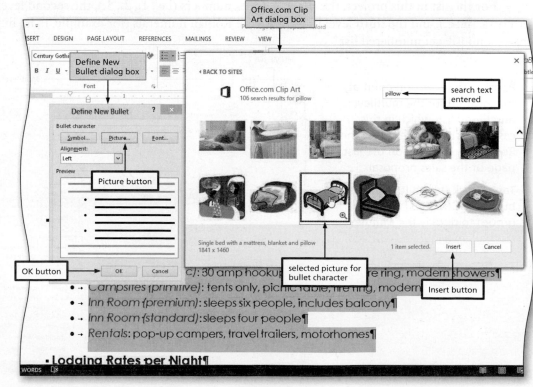

Figure 4–41

3

- Tap or click the Insert button (Office.com Clip Art dialog box) to download the image, close the dialog box, and show a preview of the selected picture bullet in the Define New Bullet dialog box.

- Tap or click the OK button (Define New Bullet dialog box) to change the bullets in the selected list to picture bullets.

- When the Word window is visible again, tap or click in the selected list to remove the selection (Figure 4–42).

The park is open year-round from 7:00 a.m. until 10:00 p.m. Dine in ou breakfast, lunch, or dinner. Spend the evening in a room at our rustic private cabins. Overnight guests are invited to join park rangers at e activities, including storytelling and stargazing programs. ¶

- **Lodging Descriptions**¶

changed to picture bullets

- *Cabins (premium)*: sleeps six people, towels and linens includ
- *Cabins (standard)*: sleeps four people, towels and linens not i
- *Campsites (electric)*: 30 amp hookup, picnic table, fire ring, m
- *Campsites (primitive)*: tents only, picnic table, fire ring, modern
- *Inn Room (premium)*: sleeps six people, [insertion point] lcony¶
- *Inn Room (standard)*: sleeps four people¶
- *Rentals*: pop-up campers, travel trailers, motorhomes¶ I

- **Lodging Rates per Night**¶

3   400 WORDS

Figure 4–42

To Create a Multilevel Numbered List

1 CREATE TITLE PAGE | 2 INSERT EXISTING DOCUMENT | 3 CREATE HEADER & FOOTER
4 EDIT & FORMAT LISTS | 5 EDIT & FORMAT TABLES | 6 CREATE WATERMARK

The next step is to create a multilevel numbered list below the Recreation heading on the last page of the sales proposal in this chapter (shown in Figure 4–1c on page WD 203). *Why? You would like to list the various types of recreation available at the state park.*

A **multilevel list** is a list that contains several levels of list items, with each lower level displaying a different numeric, alphabetic, or bullet character. In a multilevel list, the first level is displayed at the left edge of the list and subsequent levels are indented; that is, the second level is indented below the first, the third level is indented below the second level, and so on. The list is referred to as a numbered list if the first level contains numbers or letters and is referred to as a bulleted list if the first level contains a character other than a number or letter.

For the list in this project, the first level uses numbers (i.e., 1., 2., 3.), the second level uses lowercase letters (a., b., c.), and the third level uses lowercase Roman numerals (for example, i., ii., iii.). The following steps create a multilevel numbered list.

1

- Position the insertion point at the location for the multilevel numbered list, which in this case is the blank line below the Recreation heading on the last page of the sales proposal.

- Tap or click the Multilevel List button (HOME tab | Paragraph group) to display the Multilevel List gallery (Figure 4–43).

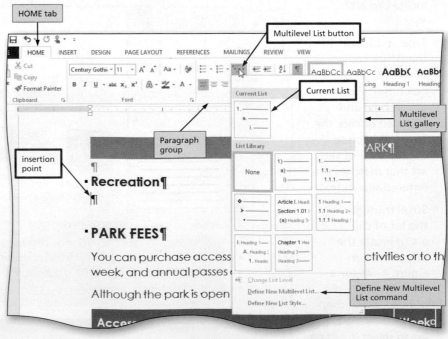

Figure 4–43

2

- Tap or click the Current List format in the Multilevel List gallery to display the current paragraph as a multilevel list item using the current number format, which in this case is an indented 1 followed by a period.

Q&A What if I wanted a different number format?
You would tap or click the Multilevel List button (HOME tab | Paragraph group) and then select the desired format in the Multilevel List gallery, or tap or click the Define New Multilevel List command in the Multilevel List gallery to define your own format.

- Type **Canoe** as a first-level list item and then press the ENTER key, which automatically places the next sequential number for the current level at the beginning of the next line (in this case, 2.) (Figure 4–44).

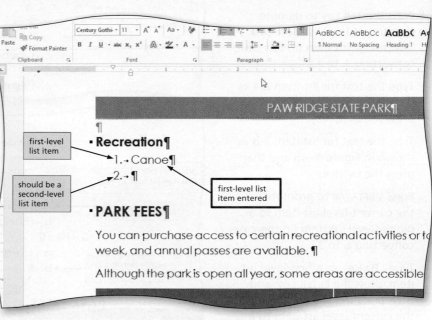

Figure 4–44

3

- Press the TAB key to demote the current list item (the 2.) to the next lower level, which is indented below the higher-level list item (in this case, converting 2. to a.).

4

- Type the text for list item 1-a as shown in Figure 4–45 and then press the ENTER key, which automatically places the next sequential list item for the current level on the next line (in this case, b.).

- Type the text for list item 1-b as shown in Figure 4–45 and then press the ENTER key, which automatically places the next sequential list item on the next line (in this case, c.).

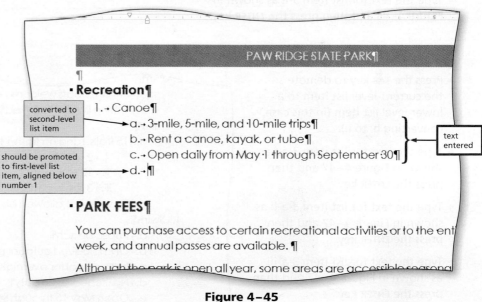

Figure 4–45

- Type the text for list item 1-c as shown in Figure 4–45 and then press the ENTER key, which automatically places the next sequential list item on the next line (Figure 4–45).

5

- Press SHIFT+TAB to promote the current-level list item to a higher-level list item (in this case, converting d. to 2.).

Q&A Can I use buttons on the ribbon instead of pressing TAB or SHIFT+TAB to promote and demote list items?
Yes. With the insertion point in the item to adjust, you can tap or click the Increase Indent or Decrease Indent button (HOME tab | Paragraph group) or press and hold or right-click the list item and then tap or click the desired command on the shortcut menu.

6

- Type **Fish** as a first-level list item and then press the ENTER key.

- Press the TAB key to demote the current level list item to a lower-level list item (in this case, converting 3. to a.).

- Type the text for list item 2-a as shown in Figure 4–46 and then press the ENTER key.

- Type the text for list item 2-b as shown in Figure 4–46 and then press the ENTER key.

- Press SHIFT+TAB to promote the current-level list item to a higher-level list item (in this case, converting c. to 3.).

- Type **Hike** as a first-level list item, press the ENTER key, and then press the TAB key to demote the current-level list item to a lower-level list item (in this case, converting 4. to a.).

- Type the text for list item 3-a as shown in Figure 4–46 and then press the ENTER key.

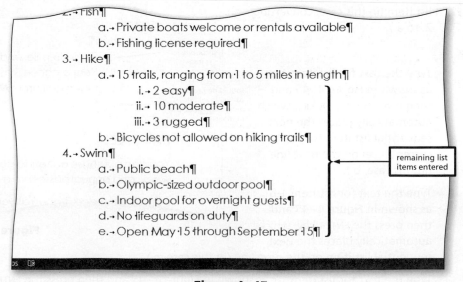

Figure 4–46

7

- Press the TAB key to demote the current-level list item to a lower-level list item (in this case, converting b. to i.).

- Type the text for list item 3-a-i as shown in Figure 4–47 and then press the ENTER key.

- Type the text for list item 3-a-ii as shown in Figure 4–47 and then press the ENTER key.

- Type the text for list item 3-a-iii as shown in Figure 4–47 and then press the ENTER key.

- Press SHIFT+TAB to promote the current-level list item to a higher-level list item (in this case, converting iii. to b.).

Figure 4–47

- Type the text for list item 3-b as shown in Figure 4–47 and then press the ENTER key.

- Press SHIFT+TAB to promote the current-level list item to a higher-level list item (in this case, converting c. to 4.).

- Finish entering the list as shown in Figure 4–47.

Other Ways

1. Type **1.**, press the SPACEBAR, and then type the numbered list

To Save an Existing Document with the Same File Name

You have made several modifications to the document since you last saved it. Thus, you should save it again. The following step saves the document again.

1 Tap or click the Save button on the Quick Access Toolbar to overwrite the previously saved file.

Break Point: If you wish to take a break, this is a good place to do so. You can exit Word now. To resume at a later time, run Word, open the file called Paw Ridge Title Page, and continue following the steps from this location forward.

Editing and Formatting Tables

The sales proposal draft contains two Word tables: the lodging rates table and the park fees table (shown in Figure 4–26 on page WD 227). The lodging rates table shows the rates for several types of overnight accommodations, and the park fees table shows the costs of accessing various areas in the park. In this section, you will make several modifications to these two tables so that they appear as shown in Figure 4–1 on page WD 203.

The following pages explain how to modify the tables in the sales proposal draft:

1. Lodging rates table
   a. Change the column width for the column containing the type of lodging.
   b. Change row heights so that they are not so tall.
   c. Shade table cells.
   d. Change cell spacing.
   e. Change the column width of columns containing costs.

2. Park fees table
   a. Delete the extra column on the right edge of the table.
   b. Sort the table contents by type of access.
   c. Split table cells so that the heading, Access, is above the second column.
   d. Display text in a cell vertically to the left of the table.
   e. Remove cell shading from the table.
   f. Add borders to the table.
   g. Sum columns in the table.

Why should you include visuals in a sales proposal?
Studies have shown that most people are visually oriented, preferring images to text. Use tables to clarify ideas and illustrate points. Be aware, however, that too many visuals can clutter a document.

CONSIDER THIS

---

1 CREATE TITLE PAGE | 2 INSERT EXISTING DOCUMENT | 3 CREATE HEADER & FOOTER
4 EDIT & FORMAT LISTS | 5 EDIT & FORMAT TABLES | 6 CREATE WATERMARK

To Show Gridlines

When a table contains no borders or light borders, it may be difficult to see the individual cells in the table. Thus, the step on the next page shows gridlines. *Why? To help identify the location of cells, you can display gridlines, which show cell outlines on the screen.* **Gridlines** are formatting marks, which means the gridlines do not print.

1

- Display the table to be edited in the document window (in this case, the lodging rates table).

- Position the insertion point in any cell in the table.

- Display the TABLE TOOLS LAYOUT tab.

- If gridlines are not displayed on the screen, tap or click the 'View Table Gridlines' button (TABLE TOOLS LAYOUT tab | Table group) to show gridlines in the table (Figure 4–48).

Q&A How do I turn off table gridlines?
Tap or click the 'View Table Gridlines' button again.

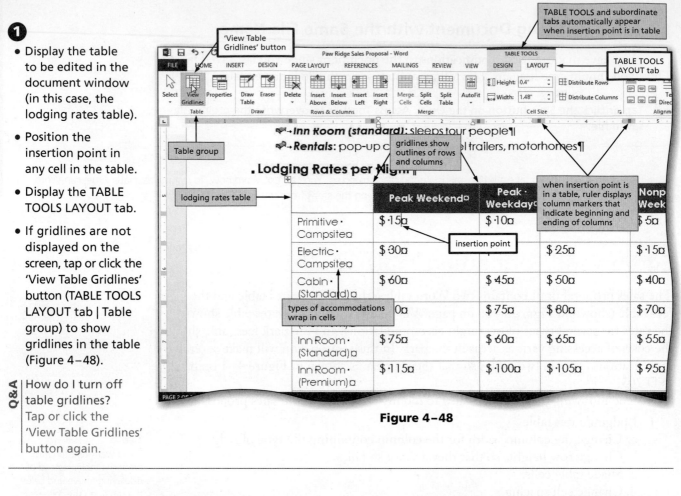

Figure 4–48

To Change Column Width

1 CREATE TITLE PAGE | 2 INSERT EXISTING DOCUMENT | 3 CREATE HEADER & FOOTER
4 EDIT & FORMAT LISTS | 5 EDIT & FORMAT TABLES | 6 CREATE WATERMARK

Notice in Figure 4–48 that the leftmost column containing the types of accommodations is not wide enough to fit the contents; that is, the accommodations wrap in the cells. Thus, you will change the column width of just this single column. *Why? In this proposal, the accommodations should appear on a single line that is just wide enough to accommodate the types of accommodations.*

You can change a column width by entering a specific value on the ribbon or in a dialog box, or by using a marker on the ruler or the column boundary. The following steps change column width by dragging a column's boundary.

1

- If you are using a mouse, position the pointer on the column boundary to the right of the column to adjust (in this case, to the right of the first column) so that the pointer changes to a double-headed arrow split by two vertical bars (Figure 4–49).

Figure 4–49

2

- If you are using a mouse, double-click the column boundary so that Word adjusts the column width according to the column contents. If all of the contents in the column still are not displayed on a single line, double-click the column boundary again so that all contents are displayed on a single line (Figure 4–50).

Q&A What if I am using a touch screen?
Position the insertion point In the column to adjust, tap the AutoFit button (TABLE TOOLS LAYOUT tab | Cell Size group), and then tap AutoFit Contents on the AutoFit menu.

Figure 4–50

Experiment

- Practice changing this column's width using other techniques: drag the 'Move Table Column' marker on the horizontal ruler to the right and then to the left. Tap or click the 'Table Column Width' box up and down arrows (TABLE TOOLS LAYOUT tab | Cell Size group). When you have finished experimenting, type **1.48** in the 'Table Column Width' box (TABLE TOOLS LAYOUT tab | Cell Size group).

Other Ways

1. Drag 'Move Table Column' marker on horizontal ruler to desired width

2. Enter desired value in 'Table Column Width' box (TABLE TOOLS LAYOUT tab | Cell Size group)

3. Tap or click Table Properties button (TABLE TOOLS LAYOUT tab | Table group), tap or click Column tab, enter width, tap or click OK button

---

To Change Row Height

1 CREATE TITLE PAGE | 2 INSERT EXISTING DOCUMENT | 3 CREATE HEADER & FOOTER
4 EDIT & FORMAT LISTS | 5 EDIT & FORMAT TABLES | 6 CREATE WATERMARK

The next step in this project is to narrow the height of the rows containing the accommodations and rates. *Why? This table extends close to the bottom of the page, and you want to ensure that it does not spill onto the next page. Note that it already may spill onto a second page.*

You change row height in the same ways you change column width. That is, you can change row height by entering a specific value on the ribbon or in a dialog box, or by using a marker on the ruler or the row boundary. The latter two methods, however, work only for a single row at a time. The following steps change row height by entering a value on the ribbon.

1

- Select the rows to change (in this case, all the rows below the first row).

Q&A How do I select rows?
If you are using a touch screen, drag through the rows; if you are using a mouse, point to the left of the first row and then drag downward when the pointer changes to a right-pointing arrow.

2

- If you are using a touch screen, enter `0.3` in the 'Table Row Height' box (TABLE TOOLS LAYOUT tab | Cell Size group); if you are using a mouse, click the 'Table Row Height' box up or down arrows (TABLE TOOLS LAYOUT tab | Cell Size group) as many times as necessary until the box displays 0.3" to change the row height to this value (Figure 4–51).

- Tap or click anywhere to remove the selection from the table.

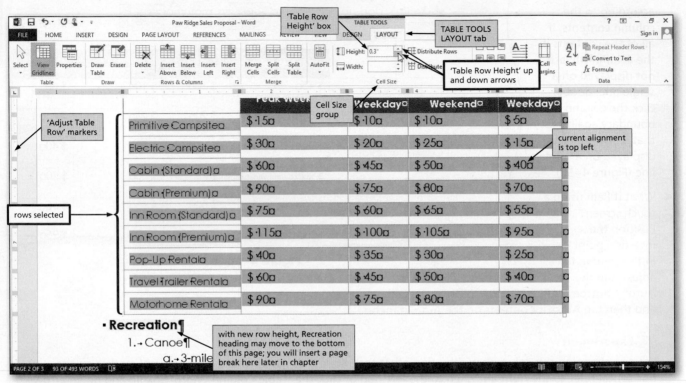

Figure 4–51

Other Ways

1. Tap or click Table Properties button (TABLE TOOLS LAYOUT tab | Table group), tap or click Row tab (Table Properties dialog box), enter row height, tap or click OK button

2. Tap 'Show Context Menu' button on mini toolbar or right-click selected row, tap or click Table Properties on shortcut menu, tap or click Row tab, enter row height (Table Properties dialog box), tap or click OK button

3. For a single row, drag row boundary (horizontal gridline at bottom of row in table) to desired height

4. Drag 'Adjust Table Row' marker on vertical ruler to desired height

To Align Data in Cells

The next step is to change the alignment of the data in cells that contain the dollar amounts. Recall that, in addition to aligning text horizontally in a cell (left, center, or right), you can align it vertically within a cell (top, center, or bottom). Currently, the dollar amounts have a top left alignment (shown in Figure 4–51). In this project, they should be aligned center so that they are more centered within the row height and width. The following steps change the alignment of data in cells.

1 Select the cells containing dollar amounts, as shown in Figure 4–52.

Q&A How do I select a series of cells?
Drag through the cells.

2 Tap or click the Align Center button (TABLE TOOLS LAYOUT tab | Alignment group) to center the contents of the selected cells (Figure 4–52).

3 Tap or click anywhere to remove the selection from the table.

Figure 4–52

To Shade a Table Cell

1 CREATE TITLE PAGE | 2 INSERT EXISTING DOCUMENT | 3 CREATE HEADER & FOOTER
4 EDIT & FORMAT LISTS | 5 EDIT & FORMAT TABLES | 6 CREATE WATERMARK

In this table, the cell in the upper-left corner of the table is to be shaded brown. *Why? You want all cells in the top row shaded the same color.* The following steps shade a cell.

1

- Position the insertion point in the cell to shade (in this case, the cell in the upper-left corner of the table).

- Display the TABLE TOOLS DESIGN tab.

- Tap or click the Shading arrow (TABLE TOOLS DESIGN tab | Table Styles group) to display the Shading gallery (Figure 4–53).

Figure 4–53

Experiment

- If you are using a mouse, point to various colors in the Shading gallery and watch the shading color of the current cell change.

2

- Tap or click 'Brown, Accent 3' (seventh color, first row) in the Shading gallery to apply the selected shading color to the current cell.

Q&A
How do I remove shading from a cell?
Tap or click the Shading arrow (TABLE TOOLS DESIGN tab | Table Styles group) and then tap or click No Color in the Shading gallery.

To Select Nonadjacent Items

1 CREATE TITLE PAGE | 2 INSERT EXISTING DOCUMENT | 3 CREATE HEADER & FOOTER
4 EDIT & FORMAT LISTS | 5 EDIT & FORMAT TABLES | 6 CREATE WATERMARK

The next step is to select every other row in the table and shade it light brown. *Why? You feel that using shading on alternating rows will make it easier to read across individual rows.* If you are using a mouse, Word provides a method of selecting nonadjacent items, which are items such as text, cells, or graphics that are not next to each other, that is, not to the immediate right, left, top, or bottom. When you select nonadjacent items, you can format all occurrences of the items at once. The following steps select nonadjacent cells.

1

- Select the first row to format (in this case, the row containing the Electric Campsite accommodation).

2

- While holding down the CTRL key, select the next row to format (in this case, the row containing Cabin (Premium) accommodation) to select the nonadjacent row.

- While holding down the CTRL key, select the remaining nonadjacent rows (that is, the rows containing the Inn Room (Premium) and Travel Trailer Rental accommodations), as shown in Figure 4–54.

Q&A
Do I follow the same procedure to select any nonadjacent item?
Yes. Select the first item and then hold down the CTRL key while selecting the remaining items.

What if my keyboard does not have a CTRL key?
You will need to format each row individually, one at a time.

Figure 4–54

To Shade Selected Cells

With the alternating rows selected, the next step is to shade them light brown. The following steps shade selected cells.

With the rows selected, tap or click the Shading arrow (TABLE TOOLS DESIGN tab | Table Styles group) to display the Shading gallery and then tap or click 'Brown, Accent 3, Lighter 80%' (seventh color, second row) in the Shading gallery to shade the selected rows with the selected color (Figure 4–55).

2 Tap or click anywhere to remove the selection from the table.

Figure 4–55

BTW

Table Headings

If a table continues on the next page, you can instruct Word to repeat the table headings at the top of the subsequent page(s) containing the table. To do this, select the first row in the table and then tap or click the 'Repeat Header Rows' button (TABLE TOOLS LAYOUT tab | Data group).

To Hide Gridlines

You no longer need to see the gridlines in the table. Thus, you can hide the gridlines. The following steps hide gridlines.

1 If necessary, position the insertion point in a table cell.

2 Display the TABLE TOOLS LAYOUT tab.

3 Tap or click the 'View Table Gridlines' button (TABLE TOOLS LAYOUT tab | Table group) to hide gridlines in the table on the screen.

To Change Cell Spacing

1 CREATE TITLE PAGE | 2 INSERT EXISTING DOCUMENT | 3 CREATE HEADER & FOOTER
4 EDIT & FORMAT LISTS | **5 EDIT & FORMAT TABLES** | **6 CREATE WATERMARK**

The next step in formatting the lodging rates table is to place a small amount of white space between every cell in the table. *Why? You feel the table would be easier to read with white space surrounding each cell.* The following steps change spacing between cells.

1

- With the insertion point somewhere in the table, tap or click the Cell Margins button (TABLE TOOLS LAYOUT tab | Alignment group) to display the Table Options dialog box.

• Place a check mark in the 'Allow spacing between cells' check box and then tap or click the up arrow once so that 0.02" is displayed in this box, because you want to increase space between cells by this value (Figure 4–56).

Figure 4–56

2

• Tap or click the OK button (Table Options dialog box) to apply the cell spacing changes to the current table (Figure 4–57).

Figure 4–57

Other Ways

1. Tap or click Table Properties button (TABLE TOOLS LAYOUT tab | Table group), tap or click Table tab (Table Properties dialog box), tap or click Options button, select desired options (Table Options dialog box), tap or click OK button in each dialog box

2. Tap 'Show Context Menu' button on mini toolbar or right-click table, tap or click Table Properties on shortcut menu, tap or click Table tab (Table Properties dialog box), tap or click Options button, select desired options (Table Options dialog box), tap or click OK button in each dialog box

---

To Change Column Width

In reviewing the lodging rates table, you notice that the columns containing the rates are different widths. Thus, the final step in formatting the lodging rates table is to change the column widths because you want the columns containing the rates to all be the same width, specifically .95". The following steps change column widths by specifying a value on the ribbon.

 Select the columns to be resized, in this case, all columns except the first.

2 Tap or click the 'Table Column Width' box (TABLE TOOLS LAYOUT tab | Cell Size group) to select it.

3 Type **.95** in the 'Table Column Width' box and then press the ENTER key to change the width of the selected table columns (Figure 4–58).

4 Tap or click anywhere to remove the selection from the table.

Figure 4–58

To Page Break Manually

If the Recreation heading appears below the lodging rates table, insert a page break immediately to its left so that this heading appears at the top of the last page of the proposal (as shown in Figure 4–1 on page WD 203). The following steps insert a manual page break, if necessary.

1 If the Recreation heading is not on the last page of the proposal, position the insertion point immediately to the left of the R in Recreation.

2 Display the INSERT tab.

3 Tap or click the 'Insert a Page Break' button (INSERT tab | Pages group) to insert a manual page break at the location of the insertion point, which will move the Recreation heading to the last page of the proposal.

BTW

BTWs
For a complete list of the BTWs found in the margins of this book, visit the BTW resource on the Student Companion Site located on www.cengagebrain.com. For detailed instructions about accessing available resources, visit www.cengage.com/ct/studentdownload or contact your instructor for information about accessing the required files.

To Delete a Column

1 CREATE TITLE PAGE | 2 INSERT EXISTING DOCUMENT | 3 CREATE HEADER & FOOTER
4 EDIT & FORMAT LISTS | 5 EDIT & FORMAT TABLES | 6 CREATE WATERMARK

With the lodging rates table finished, the next task is to format the park fees table. The following steps delete a column from a table. **Why?** *The table in the draft of the proposal contains a blank column that should be deleted.*

1

• Scroll to display the park fees table in the document window.

• Position the insertion point in the column to be deleted (in this case, the rightmost column).

- Tap or click the Delete Table button (TABLE TOOLS LAYOUT tab | Rows & Columns group) to display the Delete Table menu (Figure 4–59).

2

- Tap or click Delete Columns on the Delete Table menu to delete the column containing the insertion point (shown in Figure 4–60).

Figure 4–59

Other Ways

1. Press and hold column to delete, tap Delete Table button on mini toolbar, tap Delete Columns

2. Right-click column to delete, click Delete Cells on shortcut menu, click 'Delete entire column' (Delete Cells dialog box), click OK button

3. Select column, right-click selection, click Delete Columns on shortcut menu

TO DELETE A ROW

If you wanted to delete a row, you would perform the following tasks.

- Position the insertion point in the row to be deleted; tap or click the Delete Table button (TABLE TOOLS LAYOUT tab | Rows & Columns group) and then tap or click Delete Rows on the Delete Table menu.

or

- Press and hold row to delete, tap Delete Table button on mini toolbar, tap Delete Rows.

or

- Right-click the row to delete, click Delete Cells on the shortcut menu, click 'Delete entire row' (Delete Cells dialog box), and then click the OK button.

or

- Select the row to be deleted, right-click the selected row, and then click Delete Rows on the shortcut menu.

To Sort a Table

1 CREATE TITLE PAGE | 2 INSERT EXISTING DOCUMENT | 3 CREATE HEADER & FOOTER
4 EDIT & FORMAT LISTS | 5 EDIT & FORMAT TABLES | 6 CREATE WATERMARK

In the draft of this sales proposal, the access fees are grouped by category: self-guided tours, swimming, docks, and hiking. The next task is to sort rows in the table. *Why? The categories should be listed in alphabetical order: docks, hiking, self-guided tours, and then swimming.* The following steps sort rows in a table.

1

- Select the rows to be sorted (in this case, the four middle rows).

Q&A
What if I want to sort all rows in the table?
Place the insertion point anywhere in the table instead of selecting the rows.

- Tap or click the Sort button (TABLE TOOLS LAYOUT tab | Data group) to display the Sort dialog box (Figure 4–60).

Q&A What is the purpose of the Then by area (Sort dialog box)?
If you have multiple values for a particular column, you can sort by columns within columns. For example, if the table had a city column and a last name column, you could sort by last names within cities.

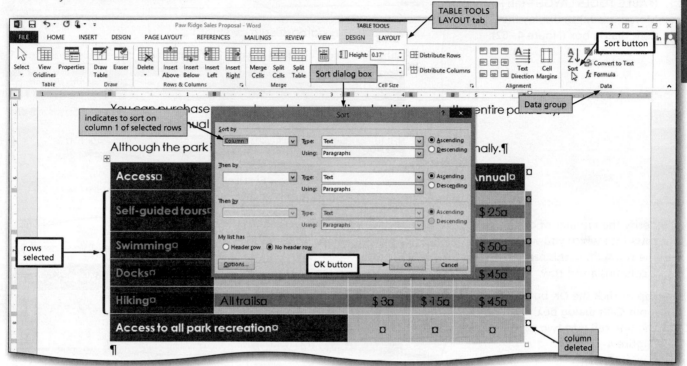

Figure 4–60

②

- Tap or click the OK button (Sort dialog box) to instruct Word to alphabetize the selected rows.

- Tap or click anywhere to remove the selection from the text (Figure 4–61).

Access□		Day□	Week□	Annual□
Docks□	Boat and canoe docks□	$ 3□	$ 15□	$ 45□
Hiking□	All trails□	$ 3□	$ 15□	$ 45□
Self-guided tours□	Nature center, · pavilions, and historic · sites□	$ 1□	$ 5□	$ 25□
Swimming□	Public beach and · outdoor pool□	$ 2□	$ 10□	$ 50□
Access to all park recreation□		□	□	□

Figure 4–61

1 CREATE TITLE PAGE | 2 INSERT EXISTING DOCUMENT | 3 CREATE HEADER & FOOTER
4 EDIT & FORMAT LISTS | 5 EDIT & FORMAT TABLES | 6 CREATE WATERMARK

To Split Cells

The top, left cell of the table contains the text, Access. In the draft of the sales proposal, this row is above the first two columns in the table (the categories and their descriptions). This heading, Access, should be above the descriptions of the facilities, that is, above the second column. Thus, you will split the cell into two cells. *Why? With the cell split, you can reposition the heading, Access, above the second column.* The steps on the next page split a single cell into two separate cells.

1

- Position the insertion point in the cell to split, in this case the top left cell as shown in Figure 4–61.
- Tap or click the Split Cells button (TABLE TOOLS LAYOUT tab | Merge group) to display the Split Cells dialog box (Figure 4–62).

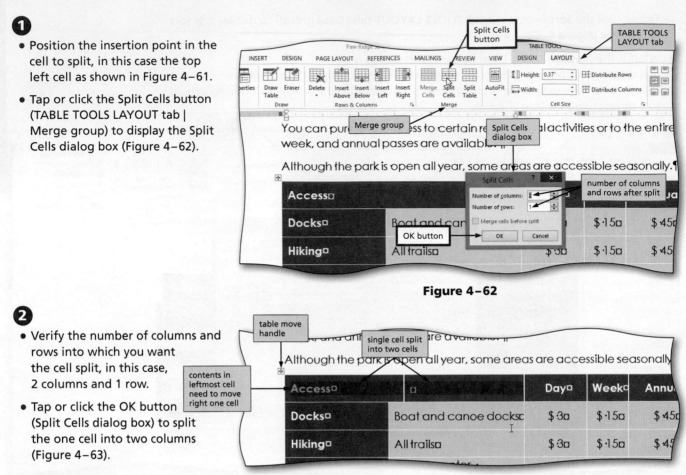

Figure 4–62

2

- Verify the number of columns and rows into which you want the cell split, in this case, 2 columns and 1 row.
- Tap or click the OK button (Split Cells dialog box) to split the one cell into two columns (Figure 4–63).

Figure 4–63

Other Ways

1. Tap 'Show Context Menu' button on mini toolbar or right-click cell, tap or click Split Cells on shortcut menu

---

BTW

Moving Tables

If you wanted to move a table to a new location, you would tap or click in the table to display the table move handle in the upper-left corner of the table (shown in Figure 4-63) and then drag the table move handle to move the entire table to a new location.

To Move Cell Contents

When you split a cell into two cells, Word places the contents of the original cell in the leftmost cell after the split. In this case, the contents (Access) should be in the right cell. Thus, the following steps move cell contents.

1 Select the cell contents to be moved (in this case, Access).

2 Drag the cell contents to the desired location (in this case, the second cell in the first row) (shown in Figure 4–64).

Q&A What if I cannot drag the cell contents properly?
Use the Cut and Paste commands.

---

1 CREATE TITLE PAGE | 2 INSERT EXISTING DOCUMENT | 3 CREATE HEADER & FOOTER
4 EDIT & FORMAT LISTS | 5 EDIT & FORMAT TABLES | 6 CREATE WATERMARK

To Move a Cell Boundary

Notice in Figure 4–64 that the cell boundary to the left of the Access label does not line up with the boundary to the right of the category types. *Why not? This is because when you split a cell, Word divides the cell into evenly sized cells.* If you want the boundary to line up with other column boundaries, drag it to the desired location. The next steps move a cell boundary.

1

- If you are using a mouse, position the pointer on the cell boundary you wish to move so that the pointer changes to a double-headed arrow split by two vertical bars (Figure 4–64).

Figure 4–64

2

- Drag the cell boundary to the desired new location, in this case, to line up with the column boundary to its left, as shown in Figure 4–65.

Q&A What if I am using a touch screen?
Position the insertion point in the upper-left cell, tap the Table Properties button (TABLE TOOLS LAYOUT tab | Table group), tap the Cell tab (Table Properties dialog box), type 1.44 in the Preferred width box, and then tap the OK button.

Figure 4–65

Other Ways

1. Drag 'Move Table Column' marker on horizontal ruler to desired width

To Distribute Columns

1 CREATE TITLE PAGE | 2 INSERT EXISTING DOCUMENT | 3 CREATE HEADER & FOOTER
4 EDIT & FORMAT LISTS | 5 EDIT & FORMAT TABLES | 6 CREATE WATERMARK

The next step in formatting the park fees table is to make the width of the day, week, and annual columns uniform, that is, the same width. The next step distributes selected columns. *Why? Instead of checking and adjusting the width of each column individually, you can make all columns uniform at the same time.*

1

- Select the columns to format, in this case, the three rightmost columns.

- Tap or click the Distribute Columns button (TABLE TOOLS LAYOUT tab | Cell Size group) to make the width of the selected columns uniform (Figure 4–66).

Q&A How would I make all columns in the table uniform?
Simply place the insertion point somewhere in the table before tapping or clicking the Distribute Columns button.

Figure 4–66

Other Ways

1. Tap 'Show Context Menu' button on mini toolbar or right-click selected columns, tap or click 'Distribute Columns Evenly' on shortcut menu

TO DISTRIBUTE ROWS

If you wanted to make rows the same height, you would perform the following tasks.

1. Select the rows to format.
2. Tap or click the Distribute Rows button (TABLE TOOLS LAYOUT tab | Cell Size group) to make the width of the selected rows uniform.

or

1. Tap the 'Show Context Menu' button on the mini toolbar or right-click selected columns and then tap or click 'Distribute Rows Evenly' on the shortcut menu.

To Insert a Column

In this project, the left edge of the park fees table has a column that displays the label, Park Fees. Thus, the following steps insert a column at the left edge of the table.

1 Position the insertion point somewhere in the first column of the table.

2 Tap or click the 'Insert Columns to the Left' button (TABLE TOOLS LAYOUT tab | Rows & Columns group) to insert a column to the left of the column containing the insertion point (Figure 4–67).

3 Tap or click anywhere in the table to remove the selection.

		Access	Day	Week	Annua
	Docks	Boat and canoe docks	$3	$15	$45
	Hiking	All trails	$3	$15	$45
	Self-guided tours	Nature center, pavilions, and historic sites	$1	$5	$25
	Swimming	Public beach and outdoor pool	$2	$10	$50
	Access to all park recreation				

Figure 4–67

To Merge Cells and Enter Text

The label, Park Fees, is to be displayed vertically to the left of the bottom five rows in the table. To display this text, the five cells should be merged into a single cell. The following steps merge cells and then enter text in the merged cell.

1 Select the cells to merge, in this case, the bottom five cells in the first column of the table.

2 Tap or click the Merge Cells button (TABLE TOOLS LAYOUT tab | Merge group) to merge the five selected cells into one cell.

③ Type **Park Fees** in the merged cell.

④ If necessary, center the entered text (Figure 4–68).

Figure 4–68

To Display Text in a Cell Vertically

1 CREATE TITLE PAGE | 2 INSERT EXISTING DOCUMENT | 3 CREATE HEADER & FOOTER
4 EDIT & FORMAT LISTS | 5 EDIT & FORMAT TABLES | 6 CREATE WATERMARK

The data you enter in cells is displayed horizontally by default. You can rotate the text so that it is displayed vertically. Changing the direction of text adds variety to your tables. The following step displays text vertically in a cell. *Why? The label, Park Fees, is displayed vertically at the left edge of the table.*

①

- Position the insertion point in the cell that contains the text to rotate (in this case, Park Fees).

- Tap or click the Text Direction button twice (TABLE TOOLS LAYOUT tab | Alignment group) so that the text reads from bottom to top in the cell (Figure 4–69).

Q&A | Why tap or click the Text Direction button twice?
The first time you tap or click the Text Direction button (TABLE TOOLS LAYOUT tab | Alignment group), the text in the cell reads from top to bottom. The second time you tap or click it, the text is displayed so that it reads from bottom to top (Figure 4–69). If you were to tap or click the button a third time, the text would be displayed horizontally again.

Figure 4–69

To Change Column Width

The cell containing the vertical text is too wide. Thus, the next step is to change the width of that column. The following step changes column width using the ruler.

1 If you are using a mouse, drag the column's boundary inward, as shown in Figure 4–70, to resize the column.

Q&A What if I am using a touch screen?
Position the insertion point in the column to adjust. Tap the 'Table Column Width' box (TABLE TOOLS LAYOUT tab | Cell Size group), type `.34` as the column width, and then press the ENTER key.

column resized

pointer on column boundary

Although the park is open all year, some areas are accessible seasonally.¶

□	□	Access□	Day□	Week□
Park Fees□	Docks□	Boat and canoe · docks□	$ 3□	$ ·15□
	Hiking□	All trails□	$ 3□	$ ·15□
	Self-guided · tours□	Nature center, · pavilions, and · historic sites□	$ ·1□	$ 5□
	Swimming□	Public beach and · outdoor pool□	$ 2□	$ ·10□

Figure 4–70

To Center a Table

The next step in formatting this table is to center it horizontally between the page margins. The following steps center a table.

1 Select the table.

2 Display the HOME tab. Tap or click the Center button (HOME tab | Paragraph group) to center the selected table between the left and right margins.

3 Tap or click anywhere to remove the selection from the table.

To Remove Cell Shading

In this table, only the first row and first column should have shading. Thus, the following steps remove shading from table cells.

1 Select the cells that should not contain shading (in this case, all of the cells below the first row and to the right of the first column).

2 Display the TABLE TOOLS DESIGN tab. Tap or click the Shading arrow (TABLE TOOLS DESIGN tab | Table Styles group) to display the Shading gallery (Figure 4–71).

3 Tap or click No Color in the Shading gallery to remove the shading from the selected cells (shown in Figure 4–72).

4 Tap or click anywhere in the table to remove the selection.

Figure 4–71

To Border a Table

1 CREATE TITLE PAGE | 2 INSERT EXISTING DOCUMENT | 3 CREATE HEADER & FOOTER
4 EDIT & FORMAT LISTS | **5 EDIT & FORMAT TABLES** | **6 CREATE WATERMARK**

The table in this project has a 1-point, olive green border around all cells. The following steps add a border to a table using the Borders and Shading dialog box. **Why?** *Earlier in this chapter when you created the title page, the border line weight was changed to 6 point. Because the table border should be ½ point, you will use the Borders and Shading dialog box to change the line weight before adding the border to the table.*

1

• Position the insertion point somewhere in the table.

• Tap or click the Borders arrow (TABLE TOOLS DESIGN tab | Table Styles group) to display the Borders gallery.

• Tap or click Borders and Shading in the Borders gallery to display the Borders and Shading dialog box.

• Tap or click All in the Setting area (Borders and Shading dialog box), which will place a border on every cell in the table.

• Tap or click the Color arrow and then tap or click 'Olive Green, Accent 4' (eighth color, first row) in the Color palette to specify the border color (Figure 4–72).

Figure 4–72

2

• Tap or click the OK button to place the border shown in the preview area of the dialog box around the table cells in the document (shown in Figure 4–73 on the next page).

To Sum Columns in a Table

Word can calculate the totals of rows and columns. You also can specify the format for how the totals will be displayed. The following steps sum the columns in a table. *Why? In this project, the last row should display the sum (total) of the values in the last two columns: Day, Week, and Annual.*

1

- Position the insertion point in the cell to contain the sum (last row, Day column).

2

- Type **$** (a dollar sign) and then press the SPACEBAR.

- Display the TABLE TOOLS LAYOUT tab.

- Tap or click the Formula button (TABLE TOOLS LAYOUT tab | Data group) to display the Formula dialog box (Figure 4–73).

Q&A What is the formula that shows in the Formula box, and can I change it?

Word places a default formula in the Formula box, depending on the location of the numbers in surrounding cells. In this case, because numbers are above the current cell, Word displays a formula that will add the numbers above the current cell. You can change the formula that Word proposes, or type a different formula. For example, instead of summing numbers you can multiply them.

Figure 4–73

3

- Tap or click the Number format arrow (Formula dialog box) and then tap or click the desired format for the result of the computation, in this case, the format with the numeral 0 (Figure 4–74).

Q&A Why select the format with the numeral 0?

You want the result to be displayed as a whole number so you select the numeral 0. If you wanted the result to display with cents, you would select the format #,##0.00 (the # symbol means to display a blank if the number has a value of zero).

Figure 4–74

4
- Tap or click the OK button (Formula dialog box) to place the sum of the numbers using the specified format in the current cell.

5
- Press the TAB key to move the insertion point to the next cell to sum.
- Repeat Steps 2, 3, and 4 for the next two cells (Figure 4–75).

Q&A
Can I sum a row instead of a column?
Yes. You would position the insertion point in an empty cell at the right edge of the row before tapping or clicking the Formula button.

If I make a change to a number in a table, does Word automatically recalculate the sum?
No. You will need to update the field by pressing and holding or right-clicking it and then tapping or clicking Update Field on the shortcut menu, or selecting the field and then pressing the F9 key.

Park Fees	Access	Day	Week	Annual
Docks	Boat and canoe docks	$3	$15	$45
Hiking	All trails	$3	$15	$45
Self-guided tours	Nature center, pavilions, and historic sites	$1	$5	$25
Swimming	Public beach and outdoor pool	$2	$10	$50
Access to all park recreation		$9	$45	$165

sums calculated and entered

Figure 4–75

To Delete a Blank Paragraph

If you notice an extra paragraph mark below the park fees table that it is causing an extra blank page in the document, you should delete the blank paragraph. If necessary, the following steps delete a blank paragraph.

1 Press CTRL+END to position the insertion point at the end of the document.

2 If necessary, press the BACKSPACE key to remove the extra blank paragraph and delete the blank page.

3 If text spills onto a fourth page, remove space above paragraphs in the sales proposal until the entire proposal fits on three pages, as shown in Figure 4–1 on page WD 203.

Creating a Watermark

The final task in this chapter is to create a watermark for the pages of the sales proposal. A **watermark** is text or a graphic that is displayed on top of or behind the text in a document. For example, a catalog may print the words, Sold Out, on top of sold-out items. The first draft of a five-year-plan may have the word, Draft, printed behind the text of the document. Some companies use their logos or other graphics as watermarks to add visual appeal to their documents.

BTW
Distributing a Document
Instead of printing and distributing a hard copy of a document, you can distribute the document electronically. Options include sending the document via email; posting it on cloud storage (such as SkyDrive) and sharing the file with others; posting it on a social networking site, blog, or other website; and sharing a link associated with an online location of the document. You also can create and share a PDF or XPS image of the document, so that users can view the file in Acrobat Reader or XPS Viewer instead of in Word.

To Zoom Multiple Pages

The following steps display multiple pages in their entirety in the document window as large as possible, so that you can see the position of the watermark as you create it.

1 Press CTRL+HOME to position the insertion point at the beginning of the document.

2 Display the VIEW tab. Tap or click the Multiple Pages button (VIEW tab | Zoom group) to display all three pages in the document window as large as possible.

To Create a Watermark

1 CREATE TITLE PAGE | 2 INSERT EXISTING DOCUMENT | 3 CREATE HEADER & FOOTER
4 EDIT & FORMAT LISTS | 5 EDIT & FORMAT TABLES | **6 CREATE WATERMARK**

In this project, the image of paw tracks is displayed behind all content in the proposal as a watermark. **Why?** *The graphic adds visual appeal to the document, enticing readers to look at its contents.* The following steps create a watermark.

- Display the DESIGN tab.
- Tap or click the Watermark button (DESIGN tab | Page Background group) to display the Watermark gallery (Figure 4–76).

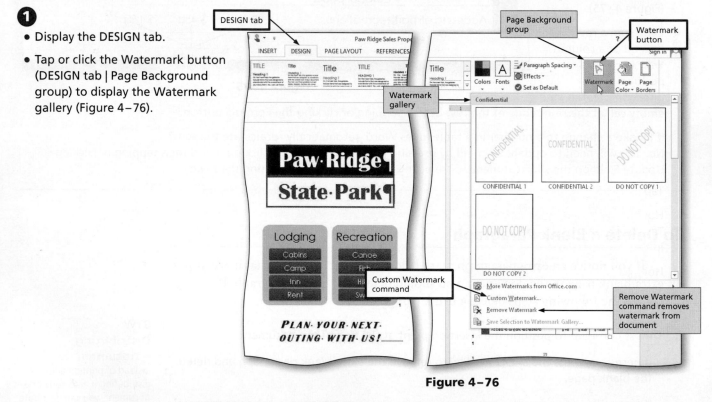

Figure 4–76

2

- Tap or click Custom Watermark in the Watermark gallery to display the Printed Watermark dialog box.
- Tap or click Picture watermark (Printed Watermark dialog box) so that you can select a clip art image for the watermark.
- Tap or click the Select Picture button to display the Insert Pictures dialog box.
- Type **paw prints** in the Search box and then tap or click the Search button. Tap or click the paw prints image shown in Figure 4–1 on page WD 203 (or a similar image) and then tap or click the Insert button to download the image and close the dialog box.

- Tap or click the Apply button to show a preview of the watermark on the pages in the document window (Figure 4–77).

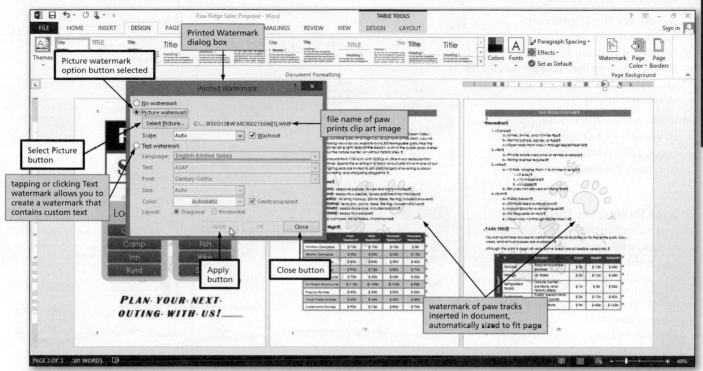

Figure 4–77

3

- Tap or click the Close button (Printed Watermark dialog box) to close the dialog box.

Q&A

How do I remove a watermark from a document?
Tap or click the Watermark button (DESIGN tab | Page Background group) and then tap or click Remove Watermark in the Watermark gallery.

How do I create a text watermark?
Tap or click Text watermark in the Printed Watermark dialog box, select or type the text for the watermark, select format options, and then tap or click the OK button.

Other Ways

1. Tap or click 'Explore Quick Parts' button (INSERT tab | Text group), tap or click 'Building Blocks Organizer' on Explore Quick Parts menu, select desired watermark (Building Blocks Organizer dialog box), tap or click Insert button

To Change Theme Fonts

1 CREATE TITLE PAGE | 2 INSERT EXISTING DOCUMENT | 3 CREATE HEADER & FOOTER
4 EDIT & FORMAT LISTS | 5 EDIT & FORMAT TABLES | 6 CREATE WATERMARK

The final step in formatting this project is to change the fonts used for text in the document. *Why? With the watermark, some of the text is difficult to read. You would prefer a bolder font.* If text is entered using the headings and body text fonts, you easily can change the font in the entire document by changing the theme fonts, or font set. A **font set** defines one font for headings and another for body text. The default font set is Office, which uses the Cambria font for headings and the Calibri font for body text. In Word, you can select from more than 20 predefined, coordinated font sets to give the document's text a new look.

If you previously changed a font using buttons on the ribbon or mini toolbar, Word will not alter those when you change the font set because changes to the font set are not applied to individually changed fonts. This means the font of the title on the title page will remain as Britannic Bold if you change the font set. The following steps change the theme fonts to TrebuchetMs for headings and for body text.

1

- Display the DESIGN tab.

- Tap or click the Theme Fonts button (DESIGN tab | Document Formatting group) to display the Theme Fonts gallery (Figure 4–78).

Experiment

- If you are using a mouse, point to various font sets in the Theme Fonts gallery and watch the fonts of text in the document change.

2

- Scroll through the Theme Fonts gallery and then tap or click TrebuchetMs in the Fonts gallery to set the document theme fonts to the selected font.

Q&A

What if I want to return to the default font set?

You would tap or click the Theme Fonts button and then tap or click Office in the Fonts gallery.

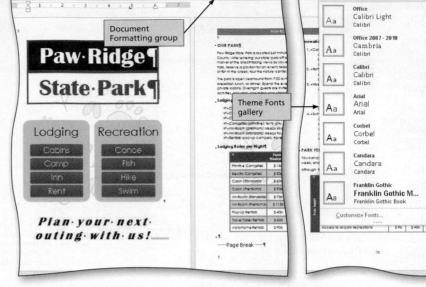

Figure 4–78

- If necessary, insert a page break before the Recreation heading (see instructions on page WD 247).

BTW

Conserving Ink and Toner

If you want to conserve ink or toner, you can instruct Word to print draft quality documents by tapping or clicking FILE on the ribbon to open the Backstage view, tapping or clicking Options in the Backstage view to display the Word Options dialog box, tapping or clicking Advanced in the left pane (Word Options dialog box), sliding or scrolling to the Print area in the right pane, placing a check mark in the 'Use draft quality' check box, and then tapping or clicking the OK button. Then, use the Backstage view to print the document as usual.

To Check Spelling, Save, Print, and Exit Word

The following steps check the spelling of the document, save and print the document, and then exit Word.

1 Display the REVIEW tab. Tap or click the 'Spelling & Grammar' button (REVIEW tab | Proofing group) to begin the spelling and grammar check. Correct any misspelled words.

2 Save the sales proposal again with the same file name.

3 Print the sales proposal (shown in Figure 4–1 on page WD 203).

4 Exit Word.

Chapter Summary

In this chapter, you learned how to add a border to a paragraph, change paragraph indentation, insert and format a SmartArt graphic, apply character effects, insert a section break, insert a Word document in an open document, change theme fonts, insert formatted headers and footers, sort lists and tables, modify and format existing Word tables, sum columns in a table, and insert a watermark. The items listed below include all the new Word skills you have learned in this chapter, with the tasks grouped by activity.

Enter and Edit Text
Insert a Word Document in an Open Document (WD 223)

Format a Page
Insert a Next Page Section Break (WD 222)
Delete a Section Break (WD 223)
Delete a Page Break (WD 226)
Insert a Formatted Header Different from the Previous Header (WD 230)
Insert a Formatted Footer (WD 230)
Format Page Numbers to Start at a Different Number (WD 230)
Create a Watermark (WD 258)
Change Theme Fonts (WD 259)

Format Text
Border a Paragraph (WD 206)
Change Left and Right Paragraph Indent (WD 209)
Modify Character Spacing and Format Characters Using the Font Dialog Box (WD 218)
Sort Paragraphs (WD 232)
Use the Format Painter Button (WD 233)
Customize Bullets in a List (WD 234)
Create a Multilevel Numbered List (WD 236)

Word Settings
Print Specific Pages in a Document (WD 225)

Work with Graphics
Insert a SmartArt Graphic (WD 212)
Delete Shapes from a SmartArt Graphic (WD 214)
Add Text to Shapes in a SmartArt Graphic (WD 214)
Add Shapes to a SmartArt Graphic (WD 215)
Change Colors of a SmartArt Graphic (WD 216)
Apply a SmartArt Style (WD 217)

Work with Tables
Show Gridlines (WD 239)
Change Column Width (WD 240)
Change Row Height (WD 241)
Shade a Table Cell (WD 243)
Select Nonadjacent Items (WD 244)
Change Cell Spacing (WD 245)
Delete a Column (WD 247)
Delete a Row (WD 248)
Sort a Table (WD 248)
Split Cells (WD 249)
Move a Cell Boundary (WD 250)
Distribute Columns (WD 251)
Distribute Rows (WD 252)
Display Text in a Cell Vertically (WD 253)
Border a Table (WD 255)
Sum Columns in a Table (WD 256)

What decisions will you need to make when creating your next proposal?

Use these guidelines as you complete the assignments in this chapter and create your own proposals outside of this class.

1. Identify the nature of the proposal.

   a) If someone else requests that you develop the proposal, it is solicited. Be sure to include all requested information in a **solicited proposal**.

   b) When you write a proposal because you recognize a need, the proposal is unsolicited. With an **unsolicited proposal**, you must gather information you believe will be relevant and of interest to the intended audience.

2. Design an eye-catching title page.

   a) The title page should convey the overall message of the sales proposal.

   b) Use text, graphics, formats, and colors that reflect the goals of the sales proposal.

   c) Be sure to include a title.

3. Compose the text of the sales proposal.

   a) Sales proposals vary in length, style, and formality, but all should be designed to elicit acceptance from the reader.

   b) The sales proposal should have a neat, organized appearance.

   c) A successful sales proposal uses succinct wording and includes lists for textual messages.

   d) Write text using active voice, instead of passive voice.

   e) Assume that readers of unsolicited sales proposals have no previous knowledge about the topic.

   f) Be sure the goal of the proposal is clear.

   g) Establish a theme and carry it throughout the proposal.

(Continued)

CONSIDER THIS: PLAN AHEAD

STUDENT ASSIGNMENTS

CONSIDER THIS

CONSIDER THIS: PLAN AHEAD *continued*

4. Enhance the sales proposal with appropriate visuals.

a) Use visuals to add interest, clarify ideas, and illustrate points.

b) Visuals include tables, charts, and graphical images (i.e., photos, clip art, etc.).

5. Proofread and edit the proposal.

a) Carefully review the sales proposal to be sure it contains no spelling, grammar, mathematical, or other errors.

b) Check that transitions between sentences and paragraphs are smooth. Ensure that the purpose of the proposal is stated clearly.

c) Ask others to review the proposal and give you suggestions for improvements.

How should you submit solutions to questions in the assignments identified with a ✳ symbol?

Every assignment in this book contains one or more questions identified with a ✳ symbol. These questions require you to think beyond the assigned document. Present your solutions to the questions in the format required by your instructor. Possible formats may include one or more of these options: write the answer; create a document that contains the answer; present your answer to the class; discuss your answer in a group; record the answer as audio or video using a webcam, smartphone, or portable media player; or post answers on a blog, wiki, or website.

Apply Your Knowledge

Reinforce the skills and apply the concepts you learned in this chapter.

Working with a Table

Note: To complete this assignment, you will be required to use the Data Files for Students. Visit www.cengage.com/ct/studentdownload for detailed instructions or contact your instructor for information about accessing the required files.

Instructions: Run Word. Open the document called Apply 4-1 Home Expenses Draft located the Data Files for Students. The document contains a Word table that you are to modify. The modified table is shown in Figure 4–79.

| Home Expenses | | | | | |
| Year-to-Date | | | | | |
	January	**February**	**March**	**April**	**Total**
Electric	55.38	52.22	40.28	33.18	$ 181.06
Gas	15.20	13.89	19.56	14.74	$ 63.39
Insurance	55.00	55.00	55.00	55.00	$ 220.00
Rent	525.00	525.00	525.00	525.00	$2,100.00
Water	48.74	48.74	43.25	43.25	$ 183.98
Total	$ 699.32	$ 694.85	$ 683.09	$ 671.17	$2,748.43

Figure 4–79

Perform the following tasks:

1. Show gridlines.

2. Delete the blank column between the March and April columns.

3. Use the Distribute Rows command to evenly space all the rows in the table.

4. Use the Distribute Columns command to make the January, February, March, April, and Total columns evenly spaced.

5. Change the width of the January, February, March, April, and Total columns to 1".

6. Use the Formula button (TABLE TOOLS LAYOUT tab | Data group) to place totals in the bottom row for the January, February, March, and April columns. The totals should be formatted to display dollar signs and cents.

7. Use the Formula button (TABLE TOOLS LAYOUT tab | Data group) to place totals in the right column using a dollars and cents format. Start in the bottom-right cell and work your way up the column.

8. Add a row to the top of the table. Merge all cells in the first row into a single cell. Enter the title, Home Expenses, as the table title. Align top center the title.

9. Split the cell in the first row into two rows (one column). In the new cell below the title, enter the text, Year-to-Date, as the subtitle.

10. Shade the first row Blue, Accent 1, Darker 50%. Change the font color of text in the first row to White, Background 1. Shade the second row Blue, Accent 1, Lighter 80%.

11. Add a 1 pt, White, Background 1, Darker 50% border to all cells in the table.

12. Hide gridlines.

13. Change the height of the row containing the month headings (row 3) to 0.1". Change the alignment of these headings to Align Top Center.

14. Change the height of all expense rows and the total row (rows 4 through 9) to 0.3".

15. Change the alignment of the cells in the first column to Align Center Left.

16. Change the alignment of the cells containing dollar amounts to Align Center Right.

17. Center the entire table across the width of the page.

18. Sort the rows containing the expenses.

19. If requested by your instructor, add your last name to the first row of the table before the words, Home Expenses.

20. Save the modified file with the file name, Apply 4-1 Home Expenses Modified, and submit it (shown in Figure 4–79) in the format specified by your instructor.

21. ✳ Which number format did you use in the Formula dialog box in #6 above? Why do some totals have a space after the dollar sign and others do not? Which Formula appeared in #7?

Extend Your Knowledge

Extend the skills you learned in this chapter and experiment with new skills. You may need to use Help to complete the assignment.

Modifying Multilevel List Formats, Drawing Tables, and Creating Text Watermarks

Note: To complete this assignment, you will be required to use the Data Files for Students. Visit www.cengage.com/ct/studentdownload for detailed instructions or contact your instructor for information about accessing the required files.

Instructions: Run Word. Open the document, Extend 4-1 Dog Training Classes Draft, from the Data Files for Students. You will define a new number format for the multilevel list, insert a text watermark, and use Word's Draw Table feature to draw a table.

Perform the following tasks:

1. Use Help to learn about defining multilevel list number formats, text watermarks, and Draw Table.

2. For each level in the multilevel list, define a new number format that is different from the format in the draft file. Be sure to change (at a minimum) the number style, font, font size, and font color of the number format.

Continued >

Extend Your Knowledge *continued*

3. Insert a text watermark using the text, TRAINING!, in a font, size, color, and layout that you feel works best on the page.

4. Below the multilevel list, draw the table shown in Figure 4–80. That is, use the Draw Table button to create the blank table.

Figure 4–80

5. In the leftmost column of the table, enter the text, Dog Training, so that it displays vertically in the cell.

6. In the second column of the table, enter these labels in the second, third, and fourth rows: Puppy Training, Beginner Obedience, and Advanced Obedience.

7. In the top row, enter these headings in the last three columns: Start Date, Times, and Cost.

8. For Puppy Training, use this data for the table: January 17 class times are 9:00 – 10:00 a.m. and 7:00 – 8:00 p.m.; January 31 class times are 1:00 – 2:00 p.m.; cost is $120.

9. For Beginner Obedience, use this data for the table: January 10 class times are 9:00 – 10:00 a.m. and 7:30 – 8:30 p.m.; January 24 class times are 1:30 – 2:30 p.m.; cost is $140.

10. For Advanced Obedience, use this data for the table: January 3 class times are 9:00 – 10:00 a.m. and 7:00 – 8:00 p.m.; January 10 class times are 2:00 – 3:00 p.m. and 5:00 – 6:00 p.m.; cost is $125.

11. Enter the text, Special Offer: Sign up in advance for all three classes, in the bottom row. The cost for the bottom, right cell is $350.

12. Enhance the table as you deem appropriate.

13. If requested by your instructor, change the phone number in the footer to your phone number.

14. Save the revised document using the file name, Extend 4-1 Dog Training Classes Modified, and then submit it in the format specified by your instructor.

15. ✳ For the text watermark, which font, font size, color, and layout did you choose and why?

Analyze, Correct, Improve

Analyze a document, correct all errors, and improve it.

Formatting a Title Page

Note: To complete this assignment, you will be required to use the Data Files for Students. Visit www.cengage.com/ct/studentdownload for detailed instructions or contact your instructor for information about accessing the required files.

Instructions: Run Word. Open the document, Analyze 4-1 Fitness Center Title Page Draft, from the Data Files for Students. The document is a title page that is missing elements and that is not formatted ideally (Figure 4–81). You are to remove the header and footer, edit the border, change paragraph indents, modify the SmartArt graphic, change the character spacing, and adjust the font sizes.

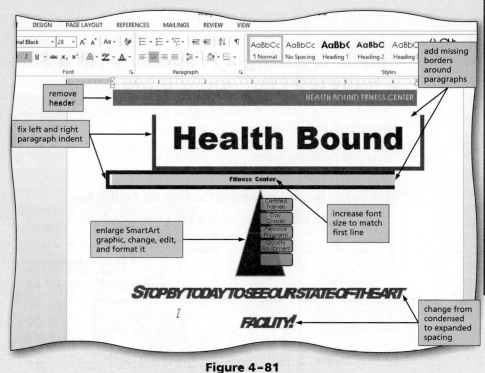

Figure 4–81

1. Correct On the title page, correct the following items:

a. Remove the header and footer from the title page.

b. Modify the borders on the first and second lines so that they surround all edges of each paragraph.

c. Change the left and right paragraph indent of the first two lines (paragraphs) so that they have a 0.5" left and right indent.

d. Increase the font size of the text in the second line to match the font size of the text in the first line.

e. Increase the size of the SmartArt graphic on the title page. Delete the shape that has no text in it. Change the word, Day, to Daily in the second shape.

f. Change the character spacing of the last two lines on the title page from condensed to expanded.

2. Improve Enhance the title page by changing the layout of the SmartArt graphic to one you feel is appropriate for the content. Then, change the colors and style of the SmartArt graphic to those that complement the rest of the content on the title page. Resize it appropriately. Increase the font size of the text in the shapes so that the text is easy to read. Add or remove space above or below paragraphs so that all contents of the title page fit on a single page and the contents are evenly spaced. If requested by your instructor, add a shape to the SmartArt graphic that contains your name. Save the modified document with the file name, Analyze 4-1 Fitness Center Title Page Modified, and then submit it in the format specified by your instructor.

3. ✳ In this assignment, you changed the layout of the SmartArt graphic. What layout did you select and why?

In the Labs

Design and/or create a document using the guidelines, concepts, and skills presented in this chapter. Labs 1 and 2, which increase in difficulty, require you to create solutions based on what you learned in the chapter; Lab 3 requires you to create a solution, which uses cloud and web technologies, by learning and investigating on your own from general guidance.

Lab 1: Creating a Proposal with a SmartArt Graphic, a Bulleted List, and a Table

Problem: The owner of Donna's Deli has hired you to prepare a sales proposal her menu and prices (Figure 4–82).

Perform the following tasks:
1. Change the document theme to Facet.
2. Change the theme fonts to the Century Gothic font set.
3. Create the title page as shown in Figure 4–82a. Be sure to do the following:

a. Insert the SmartArt graphic, add text to it, bold the text, and make all the shapes one size larger. (*Hint*: Use the Larger button (SMARTART TOOLS FORMAT tab | Shapes group).) Change the colors and style of the SmartArt graphic as shown. Change the spacing above the SmartArt graphic to 24 points and the spacing after the graphic to 54 points.

b. Change the fonts, font sizes, and font colors as specified in the figure. Add the paragraph border. Indent the left and right edges of the title paragraph by 0.25 inches and the left and right edges of the paragraph below the SmartArt graphic by 1 inch. Expand the characters in the sentence at the bottom of the page by 7 points.

4. At the bottom of the title page, insert a next page section break. Clear formatting.

Figure 4–82 (a)

5. Create the second page of the proposal as shown in Figure 4–82b.

   a. Insert the formatted header using the Retrospect design. The header should appear only on the second page (section) of the proposal. Enter the header text as shown.

   b. Enter the multilevel list as shown.

   c. Format the Heading 1 style as shown and update the Heading 1 style accordingly.

   d. Create the table as shown. Border the table as specified. Distribute rows so that they are all the same height. Change the row height to 0.21 inches. Center the table between the margins. Align top left the text in the first column, and align top center all other text in the table. Shade the table cells as specified. Change cell spacing to 0.04 inches between cells.

   e. Insert the formatted footer using the Retrospect design. The footer should appear only on the second page (section) of the proposal. Enter the footer text as shown. If requested by your instructor, change the phone number in the footer to your phone number.

6. Add a text watermark, RATED THE BEST!, using a 72-point Century Gothic font.

7. Adjust the spacing above and below paragraphs as necessary to fit all content as shown in the figure.

8. Check the spelling. Save the document with Lab 4-1 Deli Proposal as the file name.

9. ✻ This proposal contains a text watermark, which is semitransparent by default. For what type of text would you want to remove the check mark from the semitransparent check box?

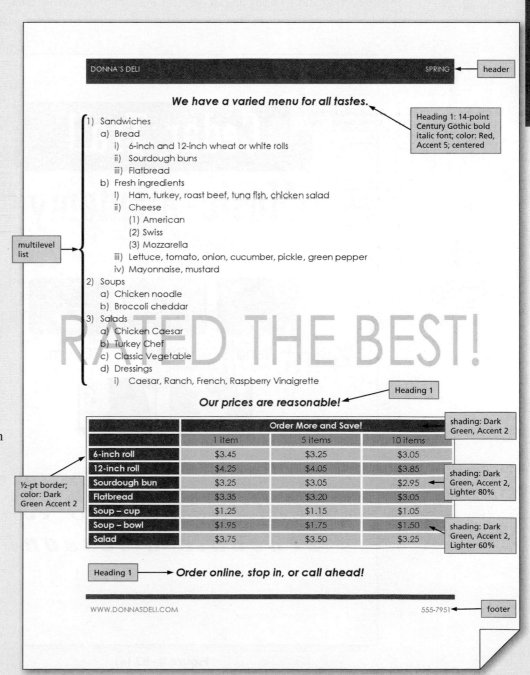

Figure 4–82 (b)

Continued >

Lab 2: Creating a Proposal with a SmartArt Graphic, a Complex Table, Picture Bullets, and a Numbered List

Problem: The owner of the Cedar Trail Music Academy has hired you to prepare a sales proposal that describes the academy's focus, class times, and costs (Figure 4–83).

Instructions: Perform the following tasks:

1. Change the document theme to the Slice theme.

2. Change the theme fonts to the Consolas-Verdana font set.

3. Create the title page as shown in Figure 4–83a. Be sure to do the following:

   a. Insert the Picture Caption List SmartArt graphic and add shapes as necessary; insert the pictures using this search text: piano notes, guitar notes, drum notes, trumpet notes, and song notes; and add text below each picture. (*Hint*: If you have difficulty adding text below the pictures, display the Text Pane and type the text in the Text Pane.) Resize the SmartArt graphic as necessary.

Figure 4–83 (a)

b. Change the fonts, font sizes, font colors, and shading as indicated in the figure. Indent the left and right edges of the title paragraph by 0.5 inches. Expand the characters in the sentence at the bottom of the page by 7 points.

4. At the bottom of the title page, insert a next page section break. Clear formatting.

5. Create the second page of the proposal as shown in Figure 4–83b.

a. Insert the formatted header using the Viewmaster design. The header should appear only on the second page of the proposal. Enter the header text as shown.

b. Format the headings using the heading styles specified. Adjust spacing before the Heading 1 style to 18 point and after to 6 point, and before the Heading 2 style to 12 point and after to 6 point. Update both heading styles.

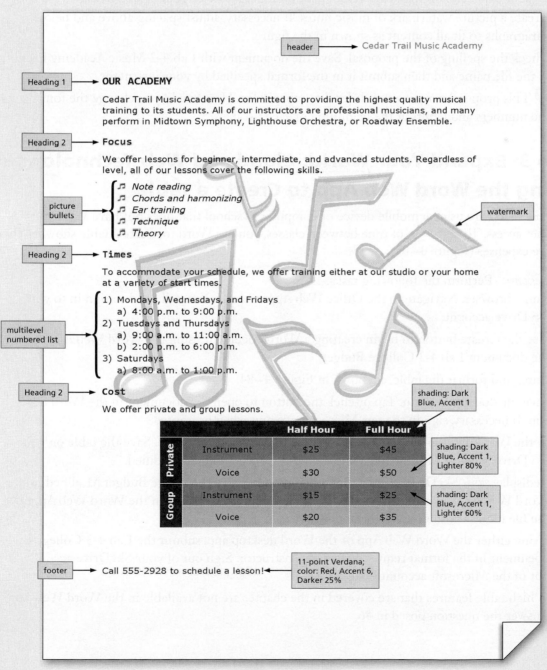

Figure 4–83 (b)

Continued >

In the Labs *continued*

    c. Create the bulleted list using the picture bullets shown (search for the text, music note). Apply the Emphasis style to the text in the first bulleted item. Use the format painter to copy the formatting to the text in the remaining bulleted items.

    d. Create the multilevel numbered list as shown.

    e. Create the table as shown. Distribute rows so that they are all the same height (about 0.42"). Distribute the last two columns so that they are the same width (about 1.30"). Align center all text. Center the table. Change the direction of the Group and Private headings. Shade the table cells as indicated in the figure.

    f. Insert the formatted footer using the Blank design. The footer should appear only on the second page of the proposal. Enter the footer text as shown in the figure. If requested by your instructor, change the phone number in the footer to your phone number.

6. Create a picture watermark of music notes. If necessary, adjust spacing above and below paragraphs to fit all content as shown in the figure.

7. Check the spelling of the proposal. Save the document with Lab 4-2 Music Academy Proposal as the file name and then submit it in the format specified by your instructor.

8. ✹ This proposal contains a multilevel numbered list. How would you change the font size of the numbers and letters at the beginning of each list item?

Lab 3: Expand Your World: Cloud and Web Technologies Using the Word Web App to Create a Table

Problem: You are using a mobile device or computer at school that does not have Word but has Internet access. To make use of time between classes, you use Word to create a table showing your college expenses (Figure 4–84).

Instructions: Perform the following tasks:

1. Run a browser. Navigate to the Office Web Apps website. You will need to sign in to your SkyDrive account.

2. Use the Create button to begin creating a Word document using the Word Web App. Name the document Lab 4-3 College Budget.

3. Enter and format the table, as shown in Figure 4–84.

4. Save the document again. Tap or click the button to open the document in the Word desktop app. If necessary, sign in to your Microsoft account when prompted.

5. In the Word desktop app, apply a table style to the table (any style). Save the table on your SkyDrive account with the file name, Lab 4-3 College Budget Modified.

6. Redisplay your SkyDrive account and open the file Lab 4-3 College Budget Modified in the Word Web App. Select the option to edit the modified document in the Word Web App. Did the file retain the table style you applied?

7. Using either the Word Web App or the Word desktop app, submit the Lab 4-3 College Budget document in the format requested by your instructor. Sign out of your SkyDrive account. Sign out of the Microsoft account in Word.

8. Which table features that are covered in the chapter are not available in the Word Web App? Answer the question posed in #6.

Figure 4–84

✳ Consider This: Your Turn

Apply your creative thinking and problem solving skills to design and implement a solution.

Note: To complete these assignments, you may be required to use the Data Files for Students. Visit www.cengage.com/ct/studentdownload for detailed instructions or contact your instructor for information about accessing the required files.

1: Create a Proposal for Tutoring

Personal

Part 1:   As a member of the investment club at your school, you have been asked to design a multipage sales proposal that can be distributed on campus to recruit new members. The proposal should contain a title page, followed by two pages of information about the club. The title page is to contain the club name, Moraine College Investment Club (MCIC), formatted with a border and shading. Include an appropriate SmartArt graphic that contains these words, at a minimum: finance, business, investing. Include this text on the title page: Make a difference by assisting with the management of our school's endowment fund!

The source for the text, tables, and lists in the body of the proposal is in a file called Your Turn 4-1 MCIC Draft. Use the concepts and techniques presented in this chapter to create and format the sales proposal. Include an appropriate watermark. Be sure to check the spelling and grammar of the finished document. Submit your assignment in the format specified by your instructor.

Part 2:   ✳ You made several decisions while creating the sales proposal in this assignment: how to organize and format the title page (fonts, font sizes, colors, shading, styles, etc.), which SmartArt graphic to use on the title page, and how to organize and format the tables and lists. What was the rationale behind each of these decisions? When you proofread the document, what further revisions did you make and why?

Continued >

Consider This: Your Turn *continued*

2: Create a Proposal for a Family Business

Professional

Part 1:   As a part-time employee at a local office supply store, you have been asked to design a multipage sales proposal that can be distributed to the local community. The proposal should contain a title page, followed by two pages of information about the store. The title page is to contain the store name, Malcom's Office Warehouse, formatted with a border and shading. Include an appropriate SmartArt graphic that contains these words, at a minimum: office supplies, technology, furniture. Include this text on the title page: Shop with us for all of your office needs!

The source for the text, tables, and lists in the body of the proposal is in a file called Your Turn 4-2 Office Draft. Use the concepts and techniques presented in this chapter to create and format the sales proposal. Include an appropriate watermark. Be sure to check the spelling and grammar of the finished document. Submit your assignment in the format specified by your instructor.

Part 2:   ✦ You made several decisions while creating the sales proposal in this assignment: how to organize and format the title page (fonts, font sizes, colors, shading, styles, etc.), which SmartArt graphic to use on the title page, and how to organize and format the tables and lists. What was the rationale behind each of these decisions? When you proofread the document, what further revisions did you make and why?

3: Create a Research Proposal

Research and Collaboration

Part 1:   You and two of your coworkers have been asked to prepare a multipage research proposal that recommends the type of vehicle your organization should purchase for its outside sales representatives this year. The proposal should provide comparisons and quotations on leasing, renting, and purchasing three different makes of vehicles, along with the suggested recommendation. The quotations must list the source from where the figures were obtained. Form a three-member team to research, compose, and create this proposal. Along with researching the makes of vehicles, also research how to write research proposals.

Use the concepts and techniques presented in this chapter to create and format the research proposal. The proposal should contain a title page, along with at least one table, at least one list, and an appropriate watermark. Be sure to check the spelling and grammar of the finished document. Submit your assignment in the format specified by your instructor.

Part 2:   ✦ You made several decisions while creating the research proposal in this assignment: text to use, sources to use, how to organize and format the title page (fonts, font sizes, colors, shading, styles, etc.), which SmartArt graphic to use on the title page, and how to organize and format the tables and lists. What was the rationale behind each of these decisions? When you proofread the document, what further revisions did you make and why?

Learn Online

Reinforce what you learned in this chapter with games, exercises, training, and many other online activities and resources.

Student Companion Site   Reinforcement activities and resources are available at no additional cost on www.cengagebrain.com. Visit www.cengage.com/ct/studentdownload for detailed instructions about accessing the resources available at the Student Companion Site.

SAM   Put your skills into practice with SAM! If you have a SAM account, go to www.cengage.com/sam2013 to access SAM assignments for this chapter.

5 | Using a Template to Create a Resume and Sharing a Finished Document

Objectives

You will have mastered the material in this chapter when you can:

- Use a template to create a document
- Change document margins
- Personalize a document template
- Indent a paragraph
- Customize theme fonts
- Create and modify a style
- Insert a building block
- Save a Word document as a PDF document and edit a PDF document

- Run the compatibility checker
- Enable others to access a document on SkyDrive or an online social network
- Send a Word document using email
- Save a Word document as a webpage
- Format text as a hyperlink
- Change a style set

5 | Using a Template to Create a Resume and Sharing a Finished Document

Introduction

Some people prefer to use their own creative skills to design and compose Word documents. Using Word, for example, you can develop the content and decide the location of each item in a document. On occasion, however, you may have difficulty composing a particular type of document. To assist with the task of creating certain types of documents, such as resumes and letters, Word provides templates. A **template** is similar to a form with prewritten text; that is, Word prepares the requested document with text and/or formatting common to all documents of this nature. After Word creates a document from a template, you fill in the blanks or replace prewritten words in the document.

Once you have created a document, such as a resume, you often share it with others electronically via email, links, online social networks, or webpages.

Project — Resume

At some time, you will prepare a resume to send to prospective employers. In addition to some personal information, a **resume** usually contains the applicant's educational background and job experience. Employers review many resumes for each vacant position. Thus, you should design your resume carefully so that it presents you as the best candidate for the job.

The project in this chapter follows generally accepted guidelines for creating resumes and uses Word to create the resume shown in Figure 5–1. The resume for Jordan Taylor Green, an upcoming graduate of a criminal justice program, uses a Word template to present relevant information to a potential employer.

Roadmap

In this chapter, you will learn how to create the resume shown in Figure 5–1. The following roadmap identifies general activities you will perform as you progress through this chapter:

1. CREATE a new resume DOCUMENT FROM a Word TEMPLATE.
2. MODIFY AND FORMAT the resume TEMPLATE.
3. SAVE the resume DOCUMENT IN OTHER FORMATS so that you can share it with others.
4. MAKE the resume DOCUMENT AVAILABLE ONLINE so that others can access it.
5. CREATE a WEBPAGE FROM the resume WORD DOCUMENT.
6. FORMAT the resume WEBPAGE.

1931 Elm Street
Beachcombe, FL 33115
583-555-2772 (cell)
jgreen@earth.com

JORDAN TAYLOR GREEN

OBJECTIVE   To obtain a full-time investigator position with a local or state law enforcement agency.

EDUCATION   **B.A. CRIMINAL JUSTICE – GROVE COLLEGE**
December 2014

- Dean's List, every semester
- Outstanding Student Award, May 2014
- *Justice Journal*, 1st Place, cross-cultural perspectives article
- Areas of concentration:
  Criminal law
  International justice systems
  Research methods
  Victims' rights

A.A. LEGAL STUDIES – PARKER COMMUNITY COLLEGE
December 2012, GPA 3.95/4.00

EXPERIENCE   **TEACHERS' ASSISTANT – GROVE COLLEGE**
August 2013 - Present

Research trends in course projects, grade student assignments, guide students with projects, manage student communications, present lectures when instructors are off campus.

MEMBERSHIPS
- Criminal Justice Club, Grove College
- Phi Kappa Sigma National Honor Society
- Student Government Association, Grove College

COMMUNITY SERVICE   **VICTIM ADVOCATE – GROVE COMMUNITY SERVICES**
October 2013 - Present

Volunteer eight hours a week at the call center. Offer emotional support and provide information on victims' legal rights and the criminal justice process.

Figure 5–1

At the beginning of step instructions throughout the chapter, you will see an abbreviated form of this roadmap. The abbreviated roadmap uses colors to indicate chapter progress: gray means the chapter is beyond that activity, blue means the task being shown is covered in that activity, and black means that activity is yet to be covered. For example, the following abbreviated roadmap indicates the chapter would be showing a task in the 2 MODIFY & FORMAT TEMPLATE activity.

1 CREATE DOCUMENT FROM TEMPLATE | **2 MODIFY & FORMAT TEMPLATE** | **3 SAVE DOCUMENT IN OTHER FORMATS**
4 MAKE DOCUMENT AVAILABLE ONLINE | **5 CREATE WEBPAGE FROM WORD DOCUMENT** | **6 FORMAT WEBPAGE**

Use the abbreviated roadmap as a progress guide while you read or step through the instructions in this chapter.

To Run Word and Change Word Settings

If you are using a computer to step through the project in this chapter and you want your screens to match the figures in this book, you should change your screen's resolution to 1366×768. The following steps run Word, display formatting marks, and change the zoom to page width.

One of the few differences between Windows 7 and Windows 8 occurs in the steps to run Word. If you are using Windows 7, click the Start button, type **Word** in the 'Search programs and files' box, click Word 2013, and then, if necessary, maximize the Word window. For a summary of the steps to run Word in Windows 7, refer to the Quick Reference located at the back of this book.

1 Run Word and create a blank document in the Word window. If necessary, maximize the Word window.

2 If the Print Layout button on the status bar is not selected (shown in Figure 5–4 on page WD 278), tap or click it so that your screen is in Print Layout view.

3 If the 'Show/Hide ¶' button (HOME tab | Paragraph group) is not selected already, tap or click it to display formatting marks on the screen.

4 To display the page the same width as the document window, if necessary, tap or click the Page Width button (VIEW tab | Zoom group).

Using a Template to Create a Resume

Although you could compose a resume in a blank document window, this chapter shows how to use a template instead, where Word formats the resume with appropriate headings and spacing. You then customize the resume that the template generated by filling in blanks and by selecting and replacing text.

To Create a New Document from an Online Template

1 CREATE DOCUMENT FROM TEMPLATE | 2 MODIFY & FORMAT TEMPLATE | 3 SAVE DOCUMENT IN OTHER FORMATS
4 MAKE DOCUMENT AVAILABLE ONLINE | 5 CREATE WEBPAGE FROM WORD DOCUMENT | 6 FORMAT WEBPAGE

Word has a variety of templates available online to assist you with creating documents. Available online templates include agendas, award certificates, calendars, expense reports, greeting cards, invitations, invoices, letters, meeting minutes, memos, resumes, and statements. When you select an online template, Word downloads (or copies) it from the Office.com website to your computer or mobile device. Many of the templates use the same design or style. *Why? If you create related documents, such as a resume and a letter, you can use the same template design or style so that the documents complement one another.* The next steps create a resume using the Basic resume (Timeless design) template.

1

- Tap or click FILE on the ribbon to open the Backstage view and then tap or click the New tab in the Backstage view to display the New gallery, which initially lists several featured templates.

- Type **resume** in the 'Search for online templates' box and then tap or click the Start searching button to display a list of online resume templates (Figure 5–2).

 Can I select a template from the Word start screen that appears when I initially run Word?
Yes, instead of selecting Blank document from the Word start screen, you can select any of the available templates.

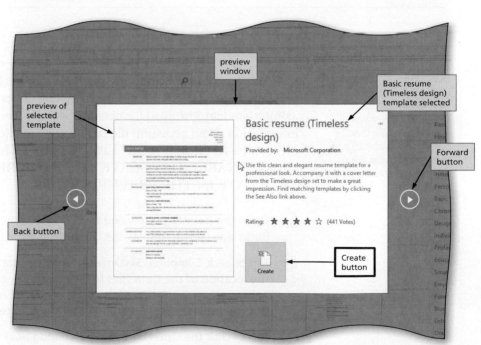

Figure 5–2

2

- If necessary, scroll through the list of templates to display the Basic resume (Timeless design) thumbnail.

- Tap or click the Basic resume (Timeless design) thumbnail to select the template and display it in a preview window (Figure 5–3).

🔍 **Experiment**

- Tap or click the Back and Forward buttons on the sides of the preview window to view previews of other templates. When finished, display the Basic resume (Timeless design) thumbnail in the preview window.

Q&A What if I cannot locate the Basic resume (Timeless design) template?
Exit the Backstage view and then proceed to the steps called To Open a Document Created from a Template that are shaded yellow and immediately follow these steps.

Figure 5–3

3

- Tap or click the Create button to create a new document based on the selected template (Figure 5–4).

Figure 5–4

BTW

Touch Screen Differences

The Office and Windows interfaces may vary if you are using a touch screen. For this reason, you might notice that the function or appearance of your touch screen differs slightly from this chapter's presentation.

To Open a Document Created from a Template

If you are unable to locate the Basic resume (Timeless design) template in the previous steps, you can open it from the Data Files for Students. Visit www.cengage.com/ct/studentdownload for detailed instructions or contact your instructor for information about accessing the required files. The following steps open a document. NOTE: PERFORM THE STEPS IN THIS YELLOW BOX ONLY IF YOU WERE UNABLE TO LOCATE THE BASIC RESUME (TIMELESS DESIGN) TEMPLATE IN THE PREVIOUS STEPS.

1 Open the Backstage view and then, if necessary, tap or click the Open tab in the Backstage view to display the Open gallery.

2 Tap or click Computer, SkyDrive, or another location in the left pane that references the location of the Data Files for Students, tap or click the Browse button, and then navigate to the location of the Basic resume (Timeless design) file to be opened (in this case, the Chapter 5 folder in the Word folder in the CIS 101 folder).

3 Tap or click the Open button (Open dialog box) to open the file.

To Print the Resume

To see the entire resume created by the resume template using the Basic resume (Timeless design), print the document shown in the Word window. The following steps print a document.

1 Tap or click FILE on the ribbon to open the Backstage view and then tap or click the Print tab in the Backstage view to display the Print gallery.

2 Verify that the printer listed on the Printer Status button will print a hard copy of the document. If necessary, change the selected printer.

3 Tap or click the Print button in the Print gallery to print the current document (Figure 5–5).

table consists of many rows and columns

content controls

[Street Address]
[City, ST ZIP Code]
[Telephone]
[Website]
[Email]

WINDOWS USER

table row

OBJECTIVE   Check out the few quick tips below to help you get started. To replace any tip text with your own, just click it and start typing.

table row

SKILLS & ABILITIES   On the Design tab of the ribbon, check out the Themes, Colors, and Fonts galleries to get a custom look with just a click.

Need another experience, education, or reference entry? You got it. Just click in the sample entries below and then click the plus sign that appears.

Looking for a matching cover letter? All you had to do was ask! On the Insert tab, select Cover Page.

table row

EXPERIENCE   **[JOB TITLE, COMPANY NAME]**
[Dates From – To]
This is the place for a brief summary of your key responsibilities and most stellar accomplishments.

[JOB TITLE, COMPANY NAME]
[Dates From – To]
This is the place for a brief summary of your key responsibilities and most stellar accomplishments.

content controls

table row

EDUCATION   **[SCHOOL NAME—LOCATION—DEGREE]**
You might want to include your GPA here and a brief summary of relevant coursework, awards, and honors.

COMMUNICATION   You delivered that big presentation to rave reviews. Don't be shy about it now! This is the place to show how well you work and play with others.

these three rows will be deleted

LEADERSHIP   Are you president of your fraternity, head of the condo board, or a team lead for your favorite charity? You're a natural leader—tell it like it is!

REFERENCES   **[REFERENCE NAME]**
[Title, Company]
[Contact Information]

table consists of three columns, one for section headings, one for content controls, and one to add blank space between the headings and the resume text

Figure 5–5

CONSIDER THIS

How do you craft a successful resume?

Two types of resumes are the chronological resume and the functional resume. A chronological resume sequences information by time, with the most recent listed first. This type of resume highlights a job seeker's job continuity and growth. A functional resume groups information by skills and accomplishments. This resume emphasizes a job seeker's experience and qualifications in specialized areas. Some resumes use a combination of the two formats. For an entry-level job search, experts recommend a chronological resume or a combination of the two types of resumes.

When creating a resume, be sure to include necessary information and present it appropriately. Keep descriptions concise, using action words and bulleted lists.

- **Include necessary information.** Your resume should include contact information, a clearly written objective, educational background, and experience. Use your legal name and mailing address, along with your phone number and email address, if you have one. Other sections you might consider including are memberships, skills, recognitions and awards, and/or community service. Do not include your Social Security number, marital status, age, height, weight, gender, physical appearance, health, citizenship, previous pay rates, reasons for leaving a prior job, current date, high-school information (if you are a college graduate), and references. Employers assume you will provide references, if asked, and this information simply clutters a resume.

- **Present your resume appropriately.** For printed resumes, use a high-quality ink-jet or laser printer to print your resume on standard letter-sized white or ivory paper. Consider using paper that contains cotton fibers for a professional look.

If you are using your finger on a touch screen and are having difficulty completing the steps in this chapter, consider using a stylus. Many people find it easier to be precise with a stylus than with a finger. In addition, with a stylus you see the pointer. If you still are having trouble completing the steps with a stylus, try using a mouse.

Resume Template

The resume created from the template, shown in Figure 5–5 on the previous page, contains several content controls and a table. A **content control** is an object that contains instructions for filling in text and graphics. To select a content control, you tap or click it. As soon as you begin typing in the selected content control, your typing replaces the instructions in the control. Thus, you do not need to delete the selected instructions before you begin typing.

The table below the name in the document consists of seven rows and three columns. Each resume section is contained in one row (i.e., objective, skills & abilities, experience, etc.) The section headings are in the first column, followed by a blank column, followed by the third column that contains the content controls.

The following pages personalize the resume created by the resume template using these general steps:

1. Change the name at the top of the resume.
2. Fill in the contact information at the top of the resume.
3. Fill in the Objective section.
4. Move the Education and Experience sections above the Skills & Abilities section.
5. Fill in the Education and Experience sections.
6. Change the Skills & Abilities heading to Memberships and fill in this section.
7. Add a row for the Community Service section and fill in this section.
8. Delete the last three unused rows.

To Set Custom Margins

1 CREATE DOCUMENT FROM TEMPLATE | 2 MODIFY & FORMAT TEMPLATE | 3 SAVE DOCUMENT IN OTHER FORMATS
4 MAKE DOCUMENT AVAILABLE ONLINE | 5 CREATE WEBPAGE FROM WORD DOCUMENT | 6 FORMAT WEBPAGE

The resume template selected in this project uses .75-inch top, bottom, left, and right margins. You prefer slightly wider margins for the top, left, and right edges of the resume and a smaller bottom margin. *Why? You do not want the text to run so close to the top edge and sides of the page and do not want the resume to spill to a second page.* In earlier chapters, you changed the margins by selecting predefined settings in the Margins gallery. The margins you will use for the resume in this chapter, however, are not predefined. Thus, the next steps set custom margins.

1

- Display the PAGE LAYOUT tab.

- Tap or click the Adjust Margins button (PAGE LAYOUT tab | Page Setup group) to display the Margins gallery (Figure 5–6).

Figure 5–6

2

- Tap or click Custom Margins in the Margins gallery to display the Page Setup dialog box. If necessary, tap or click the Margins tab (Page Setup dialog box) to display the Margins sheet.

- Type 1 in the Top box to change the top margin setting and then press the TAB key to position the insertion point in the Bottom box.

- Type .5 in the Bottom box to change the bottom margin setting and then press the TAB key to position the insertion point in the Left box.

- Type 1 in the Left box to change the left margin setting and then press the TAB key to position the insertion point in the Right box.

- Type 1 in the Right box to change the right margin setting (Figure 5–7).

3

- Tap or click the OK button to set the custom margins for this document.

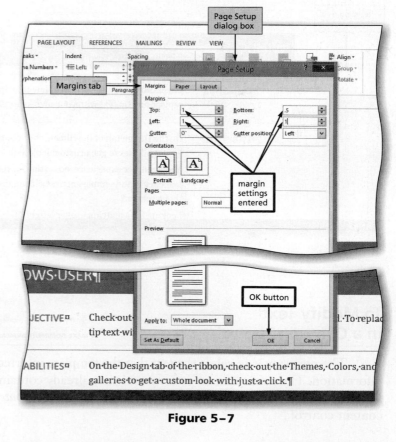

Figure 5–7

Other Ways

1. Drag margin boundaries on ruler

To View Gridlines

When tables contain no borders, such as those in this resume, it can be difficult to see the individual cells in the table. To help identify the location of cells, you can display gridlines, which show cell outlines on the screen. The following steps show gridlines.

1 Position the insertion point in any table cell (in this case, the cell containing the OBJECTIVE heading).

2 Display the TABLE TOOLS LAYOUT tab.

3 If it is not selected already, tap or click the 'View Table Gridlines' button (TABLE TOOLS LAYOUT tab | Table group) to show gridlines in the table (Figure 5–8).

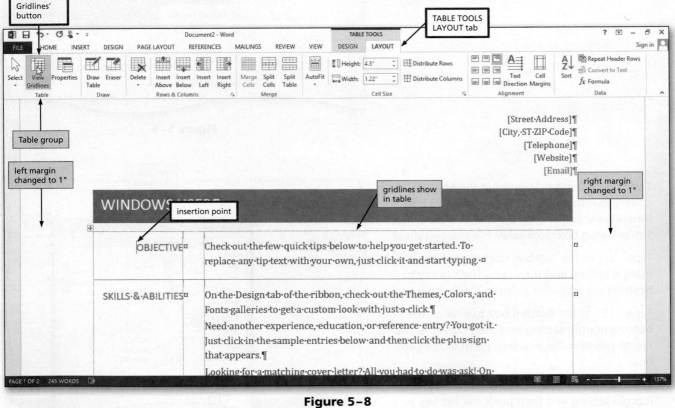

Figure 5–8

To Modify Text in a Content Control

1 CREATE DOCUMENT FROM TEMPLATE | 2 MODIFY & FORMAT TEMPLATE | 3 SAVE DOCUMENT IN OTHER FORMATS
4 MAKE DOCUMENT AVAILABLE ONLINE | 5 CREATE WEBPAGE FROM WORD DOCUMENT | 6 FORMAT WEBPAGE

The next step is to select the text that the template inserted in the resume and replace it with personal information. The name area on your resume may already contain your name. *Why? Word copies the user name from the Word Options dialog box and places it in the Your Name content control.* The next steps modify the text in a content control.

1

- Tap or click the content control to be modified (in this case, the Your Name content control) to select it.

Q&A

How can I tell if a content control is selected?
The appearance of selected content controls varies. When you select some content controls, they are surrounded by a rectangle. Selected content controls also may have a name that is attached to the top, and/or a tag that appears to the left. With others, the text inside the content control appears selected.

- If necessary, tap or click the content control name (in this case, the words Your Name) to select the contents of the content control (Figure 5–9).

Figure 5–9

2

- Type **Jordan Taylor Green** as the name (Figure 5–10).

If requested by your instructor, enter your name instead of the job seeker's name shown in Figure 5–10.

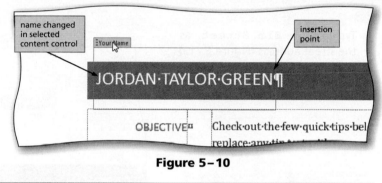

Figure 5–10

To Format a Content Control

1 CREATE DOCUMENT FROM TEMPLATE | 2 MODIFY & FORMAT TEMPLATE | 3 SAVE DOCUMENT IN OTHER FORMATS
4 MAKE DOCUMENT AVAILABLE ONLINE | 5 CREATE WEBPAGE FROM WORD DOCUMENT | 6 FORMAT WEBPAGE

The next step is to format the text in the name content control. *Why? You want the name slightly larger so that is stands out more.* To modify text in a content control, select the content control and then modify the formats. That is, you do not need to select the text in the content control. The following step formats the name content control.

1

- If the Your Name content control is not selected, tap or click it.

- Tap or click the 'Increase Font Size' button (HOME tab | Font group) to increase the font size of the text in the selected content control to the next font size (Figure 5–11).

Figure 5–11

To Replace Placeholder Text

The next step is to select the Street Address content control and replace its placeholder text with a street address. Word uses **placeholder text** to indicate where text can be typed. To replace placeholder text in a content control, you select the content control and then type. *Why? The typed text automatically replaces the selected placeholder text.* The following steps replace the placeholder text in the Street Address content control.

1

- Tap or click the Street Address content control to select it (Figure 5–12).

Figure 5–12

2

- Type **1931 Elm Street** as the street address (Figure 5–13).

Figure 5–13

To Replace Placeholder Text in Content Controls

The next step is to select the placeholder text in the remaining content controls for your contact information and replace their instructions with personal information. You will enter city, state, and ZIP code; cell phone number; and email address in the respective content controls. Because you do not have a website, you will leave the website contact control as is and delete it in later steps. The following steps replace placeholder text in content controls.

BTW
Remove Content Control
If you discover that Word ignores entries in placeholder text due to certain settings, you can use the 'Remove Content Control' command illustrated in the steps beside Figure 5–14 to convert values entered in placeholder text to regular text.

1 Tap or click the Category content control (with the placeholder text: City, ST ZIP Code) to select it.

2 Type **Beachcombe, FL 33115** as the city, state, and ZIP code.

3 Tap or click the Telephone content control to select it.

4 Type **583-555-2772 (cell)** as the cell phone number.

5 Tap or click the Email content control to select it.

6 Type **jgreen@earth.com** as the email address.

To Delete a Content Control

1 CREATE DOCUMENT FROM TEMPLATE | 2 MODIFY & FORMAT TEMPLATE | 3 SAVE DOCUMENT IN OTHER FORMATS
4 MAKE DOCUMENT AVAILABLE ONLINE | 5 CREATE WEBPAGE FROM WORD DOCUMENT | 6 FORMAT WEBPAGE

The following steps delete the Website content control. *Why? You do not have a website.*

1

- Tap or click the Website content control to select it.

- Press and hold and then tap the 'Show Context Menu' button on the mini toolbar or right-click the selected content control to display a shortcut menu (Figure 5–14).

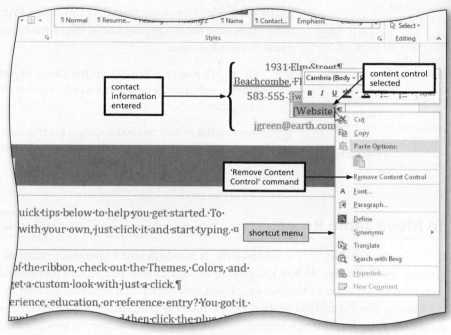

contact information entered

content control selected

'Remove Content Control' command

shortcut menu

Figure 5–14

2

- Tap or click 'Remove Content Control' on the shortcut menu to delete the selected content control, which also deletes the placeholder text contained in the content control.

- Press the DELETE key to remove the blank line between the phone number and the email address (Figure 5–15).

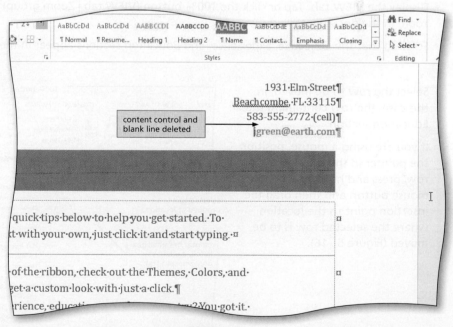

content control and blank line deleted

1931·Elm·Street¶
Beachcombe,·FL·33115¶
583-555-2772·(cell)¶
jgreen@earth.com¶

Figure 5–15

Other Ways

1. With content control selected, tap or click Cut button (HOME tab | Clipboard group)

2. With content control selected, press CTRL+X or DELETE or BACKSPACE

To Save a Document

You have performed several tasks while creating this resume and do not want to risk losing work completed thus far. Accordingly, you should save the document. The following steps assume you already have created folders for storing your files, for example, a CIS 101 folder (for your class) that contains a Word folder (for your assignments). Thus, these steps save the document in the Word folder in the CIS 101 folder using the file name, Green Resume.

1 Tap or click the Save button on the Quick Access Toolbar, which depending on settings, will display either the Save As gallery in the Backstage view or the Save As dialog box.

2 Save the file in the desired location (in this case, Word folder in the CIS 101 folder [or your class folder]) using the file name, Green Resume.

To Move Table Rows

1 CREATE DOCUMENT FROM TEMPLATE | 2 MODIFY & FORMAT TEMPLATE | 3 SAVE DOCUMENT IN OTHER FORMATS
4 MAKE DOCUMENT AVAILABLE ONLINE | 5 CREATE WEBPAGE FROM WORD DOCUMENT | 6 FORMAT WEBPAGE

In the resume, you would like the Education and Experience sections immediately below the Objective section, in that order. **Why?** *You want to emphasize your educational background and experience.* Thus, the next step is to move rows in the resume. Each row contains a separate section in the resume. You will move the row containing the Education section below the row containing the Objective section. Then, you will move the row containing the Experience section so that it is below the moved row containing the Education section.

You use the same procedure to move table rows as to move text. That is, select the rows to move and then drag them to the desired location. The following steps use drag-and-drop editing to move table rows.

1
- Display the VIEW tab. Tap or click the 100% button (VIEW tab | Zoom group) to display the resume at 100 percent zoom in the document window.
- Scroll so that the Objective, Experience, and Education sections appear in the document window at the same time.

2
- Select the row to be moved, in this case, the row containing the Education section.
- If you are using a mouse, position the pointer in the selected row, press and hold down the mouse button and then drag the insertion point to the location where the selected row is to be moved (Figure 5–16).

Figure 5–16

3

- If you are using a mouse, release the mouse button to move the selected row to the location of the insertion point (Figure 5–17).

Q&A What if I accidentally drag text to the wrong location?
Tap or click the Undo button on the Quick Access Toolbar and try again.

What if I am using a touch screen?
If you have a stylus, you can follow Steps 1 through 3 using the stylus. If you are using your finger, you will need to use the cut-and-paste technique: tap to position the insertion point in the row to be moved, tap the Select Table button (TABLE TOOLS LAYOUT tab | Table group), and then tap Select Row; press the selection to display the mini toolbar and then tap the Cut button on the mini toolbar to remove the row; tap to position the insertion point at the location where you want to move the row; display the HOME tab and then tap the Paste button (HOME tab | Clipboard group) to place the row at the location of the insertion point.

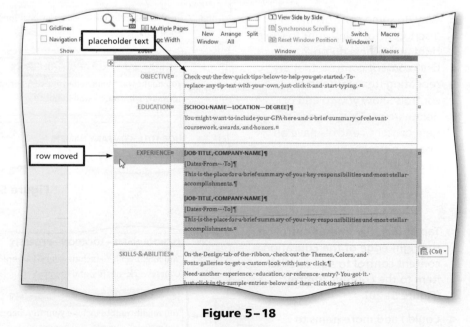

Figure 5–17

4

- Repeat Steps 2 and 3 to move the row containing the Experience section so that it is positioned below the row containing the Education section (Figure 5–18).

5

- Tap or click anywhere to remove the selection.
- Change the zoom to page width.

Figure 5–18

To Modify Text in a Content Control

The following steps select the placeholder text in the Objective content control in the resume and then replaces with personal information.

1 If necessary, scroll to display the Objective section of the resume in the document window.

2 In the Objective section of the resume, tap or click the placeholder text that begins, 'Check out the few…', in the Objective content control (shown in Figure 5–18 on the previous page) to select it.

3 Type the objective: `To obtain a full-time investigator position with a local or state law enforcement agency.`

To Add an Item to a Content Control

1 CREATE DOCUMENT FROM TEMPLATE | 2 MODIFY & FORMAT TEMPLATE | 3 SAVE DOCUMENT IN OTHER FORMATS
4 MAKE DOCUMENT AVAILABLE ONLINE | 5 CREATE WEBPAGE FROM WORD DOCUMENT | 6 FORMAT WEBPAGE

Some content controls contain repeating items. For example, the Experience section currently contains two identical items, for two separate job entries. You can add items or delete items from repeating item content controls. The following steps add an item to the Education content control. **Why?** *You would like to add two degrees to the resume.*

1

- Tap or click the Education content control to select it (Figure 5–19).

Q&A Why do some controls have an Insert Control (plus sign) to their right and others do not?
Only content controls that are repeating item content controls allow you to add or delete items. Thus, repeating item content controls have an Insert Control, which enables you to add items.

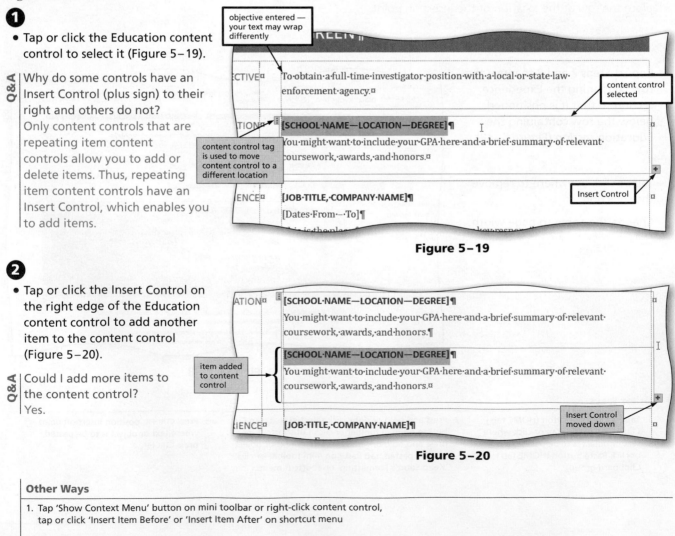

Figure 5–19

2

- Tap or click the Insert Control on the right edge of the Education content control to add another item to the content control (Figure 5–20).

Q&A Could I add more items to the content control?
Yes.

Figure 5–20

Other Ways

1. Tap 'Show Context Menu' button on mini toolbar or right-click content control, tap or click 'Insert Item Before' or 'Insert Item After' on shortcut menu

To Replace Placeholder Text in a Content Control

The next step is to begin to enter text in the Education section of the resume. The following step replaces placeholder text.

1 In the Education section of the resume, select the placeholder text, [SCHOOL NAME–LOCATION–DEGREE], in the first content control and then type `B.A. CRIMINAL JUSTICE - GROVE COLLEGE` as the degree and school name.

To Use AutoComplete

1 CREATE DOCUMENT FROM TEMPLATE | 2 MODIFY & FORMAT TEMPLATE | 3 SAVE DOCUMENT IN OTHER FORMATS | 4 MAKE DOCUMENT AVAILABLE ONLINE | 5 CREATE WEBPAGE FROM WORD DOCUMENT | 6 FORMAT WEBPAGE

As you begin typing, Word may display a ScreenTip that presents a suggestion for the rest of the word or phrase you are typing. *Why? With its **AutoComplete** feature, Word predicts the word or phrase you are typing and displays its prediction in a ScreenTip.* If the AutoComplete prediction is correct, you can instruct Word to finish your typing with its prediction, or you can ignore Word's prediction. Word draws its AutoComplete suggestions from its dictionary and from AutoText entries you create and save in the Normal template.

The following steps use the AutoComplete feature as you type the graduation date in the Education section of the resume.

1

- In the Education section of the resume, tap or click the placeholder text that begins, 'You might want to…', in the first content control and then type `Dece` and notice the AutoComplete ScreenTip that appears on the screen (Figure 5–21).

Q&A Why would my screen not display the AutoComplete ScreenTip?
Depending on previous Word entries, you may need to type more characters in order for Word to predict a particular word or phrase accurately. Or, you may need to turn on AutoComplete by tapping or clicking FILE on the ribbon to open the Backstage view, tapping or clicking Options in the Backstage view to display the Word Options dialog box, tapping or clicking Advanced in the left pane (Word Options dialog box), placing a check mark in the 'Show AutoComplete suggestions' check box, and then tapping or clicking the OK button.

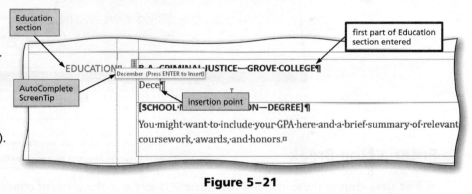

Figure 5–21

2

- Tap the ScreenTip or press the ENTER key to instruct Word to finish your typing with the word or phrase that appeared in the AutoComplete ScreenTip.

Q&A What if I do not want to use the text proposed in the AutoComplete ScreenTip?
Simply continue typing and the AutoComplete ScreenTip will disappear from the screen.

3

- Press the SPACEBAR. Type `2014` and then press the ENTER key (Figure 5–22).

Figure 5–22

BTW

AutoFormat
Word automatically formats quotation marks, dashes, lists, fractions, ordinals, and other items depending on your typing and settings. To check if an AutoFormat option is enabled, tap or click FILE on the ribbon to open the Backstage view, tap or click Options in the Backstage view, tap or click Proofing in the left pane (Word Options dialog box), tap or click the AutoCorrect Options button, tap or click the 'AutoFormat As You Type' tab (AutoCorrect dialog box), select the appropriate check boxes, and then tap or click the OK button in each open dialog box.

To Enter More Text

The following steps continue entering text in the Education section of the resume.

1 Type **Dean's List, every semester** and then press the ENTER key.

2 Type **Outstanding Student Award, May 2014** and then press the ENTER key.

3 Type **Justice Journal, 1st Place, cross-cultural perspectives article** and then italicize the journal title.

4 Bullet the three paragraphs just entered (Figure 5–23).

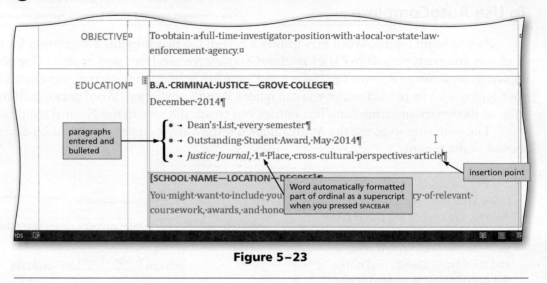

Figure 5–23

1 CREATE DOCUMENT FROM TEMPLATE | 2 MODIFY & FORMAT TEMPLATE | 3 SAVE DOCUMENT IN OTHER FORMATS
4 MAKE DOCUMENT AVAILABLE ONLINE | 5 CREATE WEBPAGE FROM WORD DOCUMENT | 6 FORMAT WEBPAGE

To Enter a Line Break

The next step in personalizing the resume is to enter the areas of concentration in the Education section. You want only the first line, which says, Areas of concentration:, to begin with a bullet. If you press the ENTER key on subsequent lines, Word automatically will carry forward the paragraph formatting, which includes the bullet. Thus, you will not press the ENTER key between each line. Instead, you will create a line break. **Why?** *A line break advances the insertion point to the beginning of the next physical line, ignoring any paragraph formatting.* The following steps enter the areas of concentration using a line break, instead of a paragraph break, between each line.

1

- With the insertion point positioned as shown in Figure 5–23, press the ENTER key.

- If necessary, turn off italics. Type **Areas of concentration:** and then press SHIFT+ENTER to insert a line break character and move the insertion point to the beginning of the next physical line (Figure 5–24).

Figure 5–24

- Type **Criminal law** and then press SHIFT+ENTER.

- Type **International justice systems** and then press SHIFT+ENTER.

- Type **Research methods** and then press SHIFT+ENTER.

- Type **Victims' rights** as the last entry. Do not press SHIFT+ENTER at the end of this line (Figure 5–25).

JORDAN·TAYLOR·GREEN¶

OBJECTIVE¤   To·obtain·a·full-time·investigator·position·with·a·local·or·state·law-enforcement·agency.¤

EDUCATION¤   **B.A.·CRIMINAL·JUSTICE—GROVE·COLLEGE**¶

December·2014¶

- → Dean's·List,·every·semester¶
- → Outstanding·Student·Award,·May·2014¶
- → *Justice·Journal*,·1ˢᵗ·Place,·cross-cultural·perspectives·article¶
- → Areas·of·concentration:↵

Criminal·law↵
International·justice·systems↵   **text entered**
Research·methods↵
Victims'·rights¶

all five entered lines considered one paragraph

insertion point   —LOCATION—DEGREE]¶   **line break characters**

Figure 5–25

To Replace Placeholder Text in Content Controls

The next step is to enter the information for the second degree in the Education section of the resume. The following steps replace placeholder text.

1. In the Education section of the resume, select the placeholder text, [SCHOOL NAME–LOCATION–DEGREE], in the second content control and then type **A.A. LEGAL STUDIES - PARKER COMMUNITY COLLEGE** as the degree and school name.

2. Select the placeholder text that begins, 'You might want to…', in the second content control and then type **December 2012, GPA 3.95/4.00** (Figure 5–26).

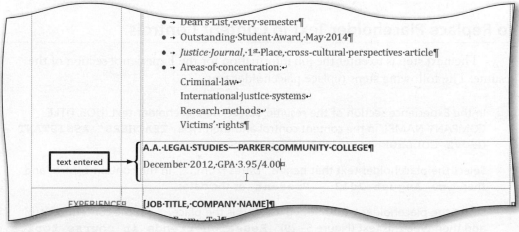

- → Dean's·List,·every·semester¶
- → Outstanding·Student·Award,·May·2014¶
- → *Justice·Journal*,·1ˢᵗ·Place,·cross-cultural·perspectives·article¶
- → Areas·of·concentration:↵

Criminal·law↵
International·justice·systems↵
Research·methods↵
Victims'·rights¶

A.A.·LEGAL·STUDIES—PARKER·COMMUNITY·COLLEGE¶

text entered   December·2012,·GPA·3.95/4.00¤

EXPERIENCE¤   [JOB·TITLE,·COMPANY·NAME]¶

Figure 5–26

To Delete an Item from a Content Control

You can delete items from repeating item content controls. The following steps delete an item from the Experience content control. *Why? You only have one job experience entry for the resume.*

1

- Tap or click the second item in the Experience content control to select it.

- Press and hold and then tap the 'Show Context Menu' button or right-click the selected item to display a shortcut menu (Figure 5–27).

Q&A | What is the difference between the Delete Item command and the Remove Content Control command?

The Delete Item command deletes one item from a repeating item content control, whereas the Remove Content Control deletes the entire content control (all items). If you personalized text in the content control, the Remove Content Control removes the content control but leaves your personalized text.

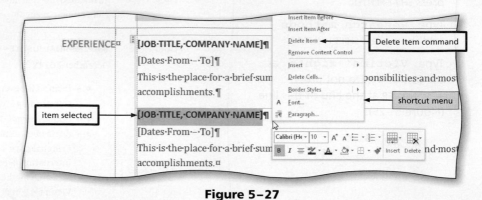

Figure 5–27

2

- Tap or click Delete Item on the shortcut menu to delete the second item from the content control.

- Press the BACKSPACE key to remove the blank line below the remaining item in the content control (Figure 5–28).

Figure 5–28

To Replace Placeholder Text in Content Controls

The next step is to enter the job information for the Experience section of the resume. The following steps replace placeholder text.

1 In the Experience section of the resume, select the placeholder text, [JOB TITLE, COMPANY NAME], in the content control and then type `TEACHERS' ASSISTANT – GROVE COLLEGE` as the job title and company name.

2 Select the placeholder text that begins, 'Dates From…', in the content control and then type `August 2013 – Present` as the dates.

3 Select the placeholder text that begins, 'This is the place…', in the content control and then type this text (Figure 5–29): `Research trends in course topics, grade student assignments, guide students with projects, manage student communications, present lectures when instructors are off campus.`

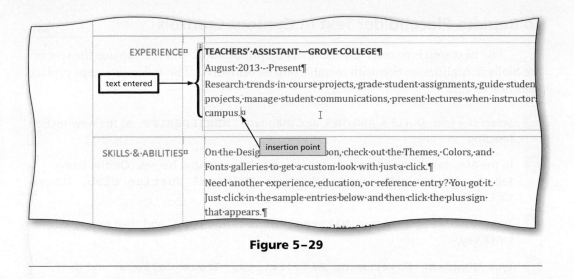

Figure 5–29

To Indent a Paragraph

In the resume, the lines below the job start date and end date that contain the job responsibilities are to be indented. *Why? You feel the responsibilities would be easier to read if they are indented.* The following step indents the left edge of a paragraph.

1

- With the insertion point in the paragraph to indent, tap or click the Increase Indent button (HOME tab | Paragraph group) to indent the current paragraph one-half inch (Figure 5–30).

Experiment

- Repeatedly tap or click the Increase Indent and Decrease Indent buttons (HOME

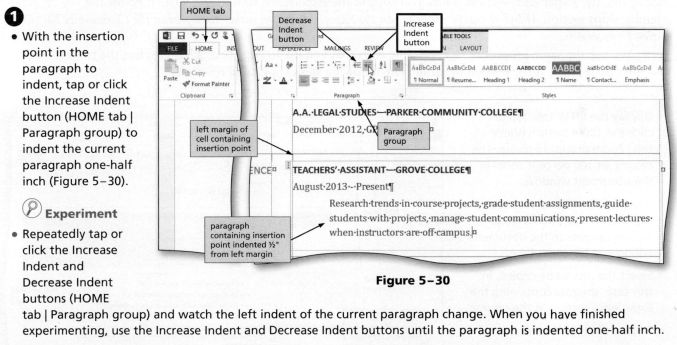

Figure 5–30

tab | Paragraph group) and watch the left indent of the current paragraph change. When you have finished experimenting, use the Increase Indent and Decrease Indent buttons until the paragraph is indented one-half inch.

Q&A Why is the paragraph indented one-half inch?

Each time you tap or click the Increase Indent button (HOME tab | Paragraph group), the current paragraph is indented one-half inch. Similarly, tapping or clicking the Decrease Indent button (HOME tab | Paragraph group) decreases the paragraph indent by one-half inch.

Other Ways				
1. Drag Left Indent marker on horizontal ruler	2. Enter value in Indent Left box (PAGE LAYOUT tab | Paragraph group)	3. Tap or click Paragraph Dialog Box Launcher (HOME tab | Paragraph group), tap or click Indents and Spacing tab (Paragraph dialog box), set indentation in Left box, tap or click OK button	4. Tap 'Show Context Menu' button on mini toolbar or right-click text, tap or click Paragraph on shortcut menu, tap or click Indents and Spacing tab (Paragraph dialog box), set indentation in Left box, tap or click OK button	5. Press CTRL+M

To Replace Placeholder Text in Content Controls

The next step is to enter the membership information. You will replace the text in the Skills & Abilities section with membership information. The following steps replace placeholder text.

1 Select the text, SKILLS & ABILITIES, and then type `MEMBERSHIPS` as the new section heading.

2 In the Memberships section, select the placeholder text that begins, 'On the Design tab…', in the content control and then type `Criminal Justice Club, Grove College` and then press the ENTER key.

3 Type `Phi Kappa Sigma National Honor Society` and then press the ENTER key.

4 Type `Student Government Association, Grove College` and then bullet the three paragraphs just entered (shown in Figure 5–31).

To Copy and Paste a Table Item

1 CREATE DOCUMENT FROM TEMPLATE | 2 MODIFY & FORMAT TEMPLATE | 3 SAVE DOCUMENT IN OTHER FORMATS
4 MAKE DOCUMENT AVAILABLE ONLINE | 5 CREATE WEBPAGE FROM WORD DOCUMENT | 6 FORMAT WEBPAGE

The next section of the resume in this chapter is the Community Service section, which is organized exactly like the Experience section. Thus, you copy of the Experience section and paste it below the Memberships section. *Why? It will be easier to edit the Experience section rather than format the Community Service section from scratch.*

You use the same procedure to copy table rows that you use to copy text. That is, select the rows to copy and then paste them at the desired location. The following steps copy table rows.

1

- Display the VIEW tab. Tap or click the 100% button (VIEW tab | Zoom group) to display the resume at 100 percent zoom in the document window.

- If necessary, scroll so that the Experience and Memberships sections appear in the document window at the same time.

- Select the row to be copied, in this case, the row containing the Experience section in the resume.

- Display the HOME tab.

- Tap or click the Copy button (HOME tab | Clipboard group) to copy the selected rows in the document to the Office Clipboard (Figure 5–31).

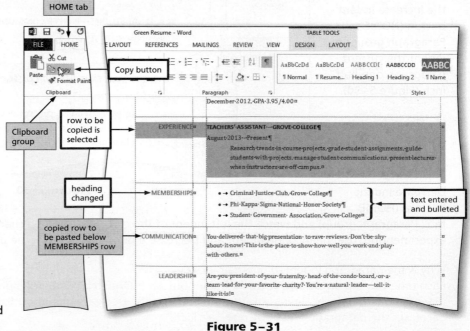

Figure 5–31

2

- Position the insertion point at the location where the copied row should be pasted, in this case, to the left of the M in the MEMBERSHIPS heading.

- Tap or click the Paste arrow (HOME tab | Clipboard group) to display the Paste gallery.

Q&A What if I tap or click the Paste button by mistake?
Tap or click the Undo button on the Quick Access Toolbar and then try again.

- If you are using a mouse, point to the Merge Table button in the Paste gallery to display a live preview of that paste option applied to the row in the table (Figure 5–32).

 Experiment

- Point to the four options in the Paste gallery and watch the format of the pasted row change in the document window.

- Tap or click the Merge Table button in the Paste gallery to apply the selected option to the pasted table row because you want the pasted row to use the same formatting as the copied row.

- Tap or click anywhere to remove the selection.

- Change the zoom to page width.

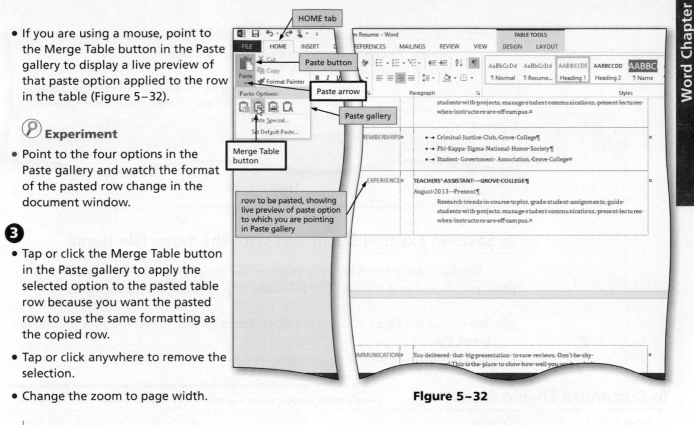

Figure 5–32

Other Ways	
1. Press and hold or right-click selected item, tap or click Copy on mini toolbar or shortcut menu, press and hold or right-click where item is to be pasted, tap or click desired option in Paste Options area on shortcut menu	2. Select item, press CTRL+C, position insertion point at paste location, press CTRL+V

To Delete Rows and Edit Text

Because you will not be using the last three rows of the resume template, the next step is to delete them and then enter the remainder of the text in the resume, that is, the Community Service section. The following steps delete rows and edit text.

1 If necessary, display the TABLE TOOLS LAYOUT tab.

2 Select the last three rows of the table (COMMUNICATION, LEADERSHIP, and REFERENCES), which might appear on a second page, tap or click the Delete Table button (TABLE TOOLS LAYOUT tab | Rows & Columns group), and then tap or click Delete Rows on the Delete Table menu.

3 Below the MEMBERSHIPS heading, select the text, EXPERIENCE, and then type `COMMUNITY SERVICE` as the new section heading.

4 In the Community Service section of the resume, replace the text that begins, TEACHERS' ASSISTANT..., with the text `VICTIM ADVOCATE - GROVE COMMUNITY SERVICES` as the title and organization name.

5 Replace the month of August with the text `October` as the month.

6 Select the indented paragraph of text and then type this text (Figure 5–33 on the next page): `Volunteer eight hours a week at the call center. Offer emotional support and provide information on victims' legal rights and the criminal justice process.`

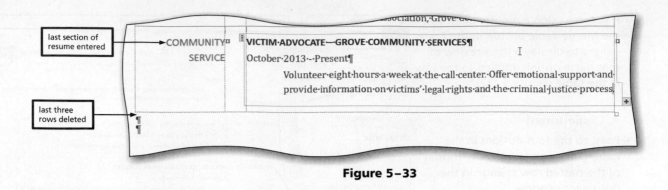

Figure 5-33

To Save an Existing Document with the Same File Name

You have made several modifications to the document since you last saved it. Thus, you should save it again. The following step saves the document again.

1 Tap or click the Save button on the Quick Access Toolbar to overwrite the previously saved file.

To Customize Theme Fonts

1 CREATE DOCUMENT FROM TEMPLATE | 2 MODIFY & FORMAT TEMPLATE | 3 SAVE DOCUMENT IN OTHER FORMATS
4 MAKE DOCUMENT AVAILABLE ONLINE | 5 CREATE WEBPAGE FROM WORD DOCUMENT | 6 FORMAT WEBPAGE

Recall that a font set defines one font for headings in a document and another font for body text. This resume currently uses the Calibri-Cambria font set, which specifies the Calibri font for the headings and the Cambria font for body text. The resume in this chapter creates a customized font set (theme font). *Why?* *You want the headings to use the Berlin Sans FB Demi font and the body text to use the Bookman Old Style font.* The following steps create a customized theme font set with the name Resume Text.

1

- Display the DESIGN tab.

- Tap or click the Theme Fonts button (DESIGN tab | Document Formatting group) to display the Theme Fonts gallery (Figure 5-34).

Figure 5-34

2

- Tap or click Customize Fonts in the Theme Fonts gallery to display the Create New Theme Fonts dialog box.

- Tap or click the Heading font arrow (Create New Theme Fonts dialog box); scroll to and then tap or click 'Berlin Sans FB Demi' (or a similar font).

- Tap or click the Body font arrow; scroll to and then tap or click Bookman Old Style (or a similar font).

- Type **Resume Text** in the Name text box as the name for the new theme font (Figure 5-35).

Figure 5-35

3

- Tap or click the Save button (Create New Theme Fonts dialog box) to create the customized theme font with the entered name (Resume Text, in this case) and apply the new heading fonts to the current document (Figure 5–36).

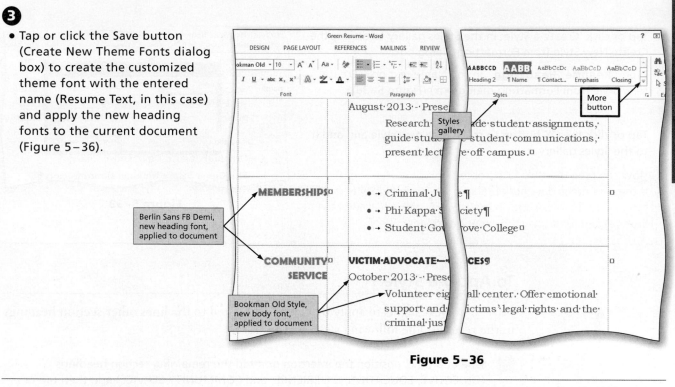

Figure 5–36

To Create a Style

1 CREATE DOCUMENT FROM TEMPLATE | 2 MODIFY & FORMAT TEMPLATE | 3 SAVE DOCUMENT IN OTHER FORMATS
4 MAKE DOCUMENT AVAILABLE ONLINE | 5 CREATE WEBPAGE FROM WORD DOCUMENT | 6 FORMAT WEBPAGE

Recall that a style is a predefined style that appears in the Styles gallery. You have used styles in the Styles gallery to apply defined formats to text and have updated existing styles. You also can create your own styles.

The next task in this project is to create a style for the section headings in the resume. *Why? To illustrate creating a style, you will increase the font size of a section heading and save the new format as a style. Then, you will apply the newly defined style to the remaining section headings.* The following steps format text and then create a style based on the formats in the selected paragraph.

1

- Position the insertion point in the MEMBERSHIPS heading, display the HOME tab, and then tap or click the 'Increase Font Size' button (HOME tab | Font group).

- Tap or click the More button (shown in Figure 5–36) in the Styles gallery (HOME tab | Styles group) to expand the gallery (Figure 5–37).

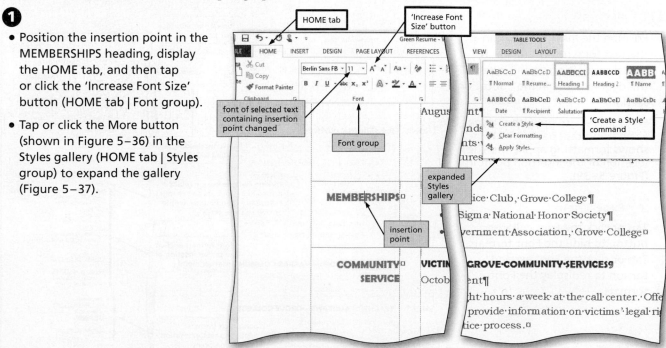

Figure 5–37

2

- Tap or click 'Create a Style' in the Styles gallery to display the Create New Style from Formatting dialog box.

- Type **Resume Headings** in the Name text box (Create New Style from Formatting dialog box) (Figure 5–38).

3

- Tap or click the OK button to create the new style and add it to the Styles gallery.

Q&A | How can I see the style just created?
If the style name does not appear in the in-ribbon Styles gallery, tap or click the More button in the Styles gallery (HOME tab | Styles group) to display the expanded Styles gallery.

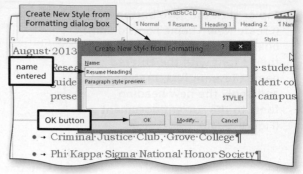

Figure 5–38

To Apply a Style

The next step is to apply the style just created to the lines other section headings in the resume. The following step applies a style.

1 One at a time, position the insertion point in the remaining section headings (OBJECTIVE, EDUCATION, EXPERIENCE, and COMMUNITY SERVICE) and then tap or click Resume Headings in the Styles gallery.

To Reveal Formatting

1 CREATE DOCUMENT FROM TEMPLATE | 2 MODIFY & FORMAT TEMPLATE | 3 SAVE DOCUMENT IN OTHER FORMATS
4 MAKE DOCUMENT AVAILABLE ONLINE | 5 CREATE WEBPAGE FROM WORD DOCUMENT | 6 FORMAT WEBPAGE

Sometimes, you want to know what formats were applied to certain text items in a document. *Why? For example, you may wonder what font, font size, font color, and other effects were applied to the degree and job titles in the resume.* To display formatting applied to text, use the Reveal Formatting task pane. The following steps open and then close the Reveal Formatting task pane.

1

- Position the insertion point in the text for which you want to reveal formatting (in this case, the degree name in the Education section).

- Press SHIFT+F1 to open the Reveal Formatting task pane, which shows formatting applied to the location of the insertion point in (Figure 5–39).

Experiment

- Tap or click the Font collapse button to hide the Font formats. Tap or click the Font expand button to redisplay the Font formats.

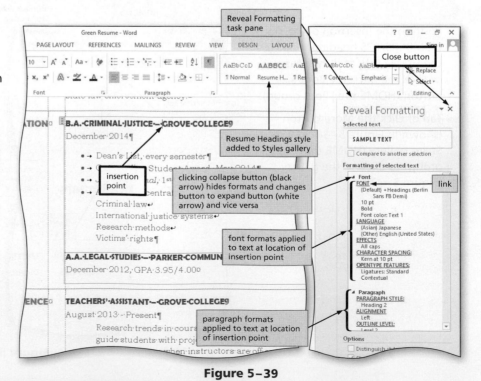

Figure 5–39

Q&A Why do some of the formats in the Reveal Formatting task pane appear as links?
Tapping or clicking a link in the Reveal Formatting task pane displays an associated dialog box, allowing you to change the format of the current text. For example, tapping or clicking the Font link in the Reveal Formatting task pane would display the Font dialog box. If you made changes in the Font dialog box and then tapped or clicked the OK button, Word would change the format of the current text.

2

- Close the Reveal Formatting task pane by tapping or clicking its Close button.

To Modify a Style Using the Styles Dialog Box

1 CREATE DOCUMENT FROM TEMPLATE | 2 MODIFY & FORMAT TEMPLATE | 3 SAVE DOCUMENT IN OTHER FORMATS
4 MAKE DOCUMENT AVAILABLE ONLINE | 5 CREATE WEBPAGE FROM WORD DOCUMENT | 6 FORMAT WEBPAGE

The next step is to modify the Heading 2 style. *Why? The degree and job names in the resume currently have a different font than the other text in the resume. You prefer that all text in the resume use the same font.* Thus, the following steps modify a style.

1

- Press and hold or right-click the style name to modify in the Styles gallery (Heading 2, in this case) to display a shortcut menu (Figure 5–40).

Figure 5–40

2

- Tap or click Modify on the shortcut menu to display the Modify Style dialog box.

- Tap or click the Font arrow (Modify Style dialog box) and then tap or click Bookman Old Style in the Font gallery to change the font of the current style.

- Place a check mark in the Automatically update check box so that any future changes you make to the style in the document will update the current style automatically (Figure 5–41).

Q&A What is the purpose of the Format button in the Modify Style dialog box?
If the formatting you wish to change for the style is not available in the Modify Style dialog box, you can tap or click the Format button and then select the desired command after you tap or click the Format button to display a dialog box that contains additional formatting options.

Figure 5–41

3

- Tap or click the OK button to close the dialog box and apply the style changes to the paragraphs in the document (Figure 5–42).

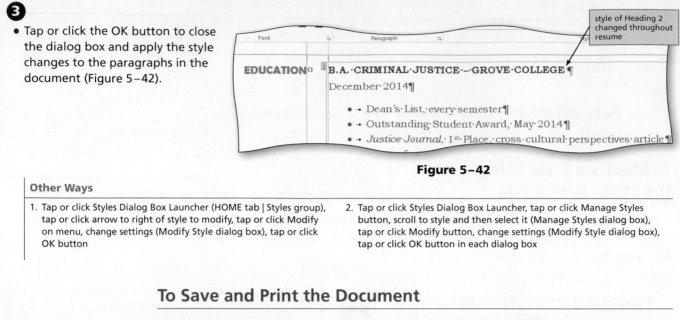

Figure 5–42

Other Ways

1. Tap or click Styles Dialog Box Launcher (HOME tab | Styles group), tap or click arrow to right of style to modify, tap or click Modify on menu, change settings (Modify Style dialog box), tap or click OK button

2. Tap or click Styles Dialog Box Launcher, tap or click Manage Styles button, scroll to style and then select it (Manage Styles dialog box), tap or click Modify button, change settings (Modify Style dialog box), tap or click OK button in each dialog box

---

To Save and Print the Document

The resume is complete. Thus, you should save it again. The following steps save the document again and print it.

1 Tap or click the Save button on the Quick Access Toolbar to overwrite the previously saved file.

2 Print the resume (shown in Figure 5–1 on page WD 275).

Break Point: If you wish to take a break, this is a good place to do so. You can exit Word now. To resume at a later time, run Word, open the file called Green Resume, and continue following the steps from this location forward.

Sharing a Document with Others

You may want to share Word documents with others electronically, such as via email, USB flash drive, or cloud storage. To ensure that others can read and/or open the files successfully, Word provides a variety of formats and tools to assist with sharing documents. This section uses the Green Resume created in this chapter to present a variety of these formats and tools.

To Insert a Building Block Using the Building Blocks Organizer

1 CREATE DOCUMENT FROM TEMPLATE | 2 MODIFY & FORMAT TEMPLATE | 3 SAVE DOCUMENT IN OTHER FORMATS
4 MAKE DOCUMENT AVAILABLE ONLINE | 5 CREATE WEBPAGE FROM WORD DOCUMENT | 6 FORMAT WEBPAGE

You would like to place the text, DRAFT, as a watermark on the resume before you share it, so that others are aware you might be making additional changes to the document. In an earlier chapter, you inserted a watermark using the ribbon. Because watermarks are a type of building block, you also can use the Building Blocks Organizer to insert them.

A **building block** is a reusable formatted object that is stored in a gallery. Examples of building blocks include cover pages, headers, footers, page numbers, watermarks, and text boxes. You can see a list of every available building block in the **Building Blocks Organizer**. From the Building Blocks Organizer, you can sort building blocks, change their properties, or insert them in a document.

The next steps sort the Building Blocks Organizer by gallery and then insert the Draft 1 building block in the document. *Why? Sorting the building blocks by gallery makes it easier to locate them.*

1

- Display the VIEW tab. Tap or click the One Page button (VIEW tab | Zoom group) to display the resume in its entirety in the document window.

- Display the INSERT tab.

- Tap or click the 'Explore Quick Parts' button (INSERT tab | Text group) to display the Explore Quick Parts menu (Figure 5–43).

Figure 5–43

2

- Tap or click 'Building Blocks Organizer' on the Explore Quick Parts menu to display the Building Blocks Organizer dialog box.

Experiment

- Drag the scroll bars in the Building Blocks Organizer so that you can look at all the columns and rows in the dialog box.

- Tap or click the Gallery heading (Building Blocks Organizer dialog box) in the building blocks list to sort the building blocks by gallery (Figure 5–44).

Experiment

- Tap or click various names in the building blocks list and notice that a preview of the selected building block appears in the dialog box.

Figure 5–44

3

- Scroll through the building blocks list to the Watermarks group in the Gallery column and then tap or click DRAFT 1 to select this building block (Figure 5–45).

Figure 5–45

4

- Tap or click the Insert button to insert the selected building block in the document (Figure 5–46).

Figure 5–46

TO EDIT PROPERTIES OF BUILDING BLOCK ELEMENTS

Properties of a building block include its name, gallery, category, description, location where it is saved, and how it is inserted in the document. If you wanted to change any of these building block properties for a particular building block, you would perform these steps.

1. Tap or click the 'Explore Quick Parts' button (INSERT tab | Text group) to display the Explore Quick Parts menu.
2. Tap or click 'Building Blocks Organizer' on the Explore Quick Parts menu to display the Building Blocks Organizer dialog box.
3. Select the building block you wish to edit (Building Blocks Organizer dialog box).
4. Tap or click the Edit Properties button (shown in Figure 5–45) to display the Modify Building Block dialog box.
5. Edit any property (Modify Building Block dialog box) and then tap or click the OK button. Close the Building Blocks Organizer dialog box.

CONSIDER THIS

Will a document look the same on another computer when you share it electronically?

When sharing a Word document with others, you cannot be certain that it will look or print the same on their computers or mobile devices as on your computer or mobile device. For example, the document may wordwrap text differently on others' computers and mobile devices. If others do not need to edit the document, that is, they need only to view and/or print the document, you could save the file in a format that allows others to view the document as you see it. Two popular such formats are PDF and XPS.

To Save a Word Document as a PDF Document and View the PDF Document in Adobe Reader

1 CREATE DOCUMENT FROM TEMPLATE | 2 MODIFY & FORMAT TEMPLATE | **3 SAVE DOCUMENT IN OTHER FORMATS**
4 MAKE DOCUMENT AVAILABLE ONLINE | 5 CREATE WEBPAGE FROM WORD DOCUMENT | 6 FORMAT WEBPAGE

PDF, which stands for Portable Document Format, is a file format created by Adobe Systems that shows all elements of a printed document as an electronic image. Users can view a PDF document without the software that created the original document. Thus, the PDF format enables users to share documents with others easily.

To view, navigate, and print a PDF file, you use an application called **Adobe Reader**, which can be downloaded free from Adobe's website.

When you save a Word document as a PDF document, the original Word document remains intact; that is, Word creates a copy of the file in the PDF format. The following steps save the Green Resume Word document as a PDF document and then open the Green Resume PDF document in Adobe Reader. *Why? You want to share the resume with others but want to ensure it looks the same on their computer or mobile device as it does on yours.*

1
- Open the Backstage view and then tap or click the Export tab in the Backstage view to display the Export gallery.

- If necessary, tap or click 'Create PDF/XPS Document' in the Export gallery to display information about creating PDF/XPS documents in the right pane (Figure 5–47).

Figure 5–47

2
- Tap or click the 'Create PDF/XPS' button in the right pane to display the Publish as PDF or XPS dialog box.

- Navigate to the desired save location (in this case, the Word folder in the CIS 101 folder [or your class folder] on the USB flash drive) (Publish as PDF or XPS dialog box).

Q&A Can the file name be the same for the Word document and the PDF document?
Yes. The file names can be the same because the file types are different: one is a Word document and the other is a PDF document.

- If necessary, tap or click the 'Save as type' arrow and then tap or click PDF.

- If necessary, place a check mark in the 'Open file after publishing' check box so that Word will display the resulting PDF document in Adobe Reader (Figure 5–48).

Q&A Why is my 'Open file after publishing' check box dimmed?
You do not have Adobe Reader installed on your computer. Use a search engine, such as Google, to search for the text, get adobe reader. Then, tap or click the link in the search results to download Adobe Reader and follow the on-screen instructions to install the program. After installing Adobe Reader, repeat these steps.

Figure 5–48

3

- Tap or click the Publish button to create the PDF document from the Word document and then, because the check box was selected, open the resulting PDF document in Adobe Reader.

- If necessary, tap or click the Maximize button in the Adobe Reader window to maximize the window (Figure 5–49).

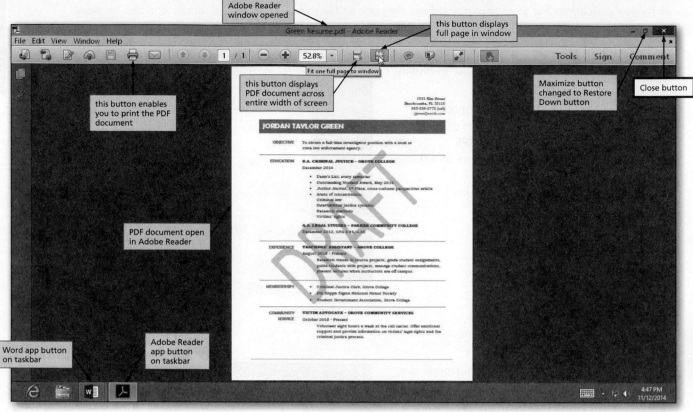

Figure 5–49

Q&A Do I have to display the resulting PDF document in Adobe Reader?

No. If you do not want to display the document in Adobe Reader, you would not place a check mark in the 'Open file after publishing' check box in the Publish as PDF or XPS dialog box (shown in Figure 5-48 on the previous page).

Is the Green Resume Word document still open?

Yes. Word still is running with the Green Resume document opened.

What if a blank screen appears instead of Adobe Reader?

You may not have Adobe reader installed. Press the Start key on the keyboard to redisplay the Start screen and then navigate back to Word.

4

- Tap or click the Close button on the Adobe Reader title bar to close the Green Resume.pdf document and exit Adobe Reader.

Q&A Can I edit documents in Adobe Reader?

No, you need Adobe Acrobat or some other program that enables editing of PDF files.

Other Ways

1. Press F12, tap or click 'Save as type' box arrow (Save As dialog box), select PDF in list, tap or click Save button

To Open a PDF Document from Word

1 CREATE DOCUMENT FROM TEMPLATE | 2 MODIFY & FORMAT TEMPLATE | 3 SAVE DOCUMENT IN OTHER FORMATS
4 MAKE DOCUMENT AVAILABLE ONLINE | 5 CREATE WEBPAGE FROM WORD DOCUMENT | 6 FORMAT WEBPAGE

When you use Word to open a PDF file, Word converts it to an editable document. *Why? You may want to change the contents of a PDF file.* The editable PDF document that Word creates from the PDF document may appear slightly different from the PDF due to the conversion process. To illustrate this feature, the next steps open the PDF document just saved.

1

- Open the Backstage view and then tap or click the Open tab in the Backstage view to display the Open gallery.

- Tap or click Computer, SkyDrive, or another location in the left pane that references the location of the saved PDF file, tap or click the Browse button, and then navigate to the location of the PDF file to be opened (in this case, the Word folder in the CIS 101 folder).

- If necessary, tap or click the File Types arrow to display a list of file types that can be opened by Word (Figure 5–50).

Q&A Why does the PDF file already appear in my list?
If the file type is All Word Documents, Word displays all file types that it can open in the file list.

Figure 5–50

2

- Tap or click PDF Files in the File Types list, so that Word displays PDF file names in the dialog box.

- Tap or click Green Resume to select the PDF file to be opened (Figure 5–51).

3

- Tap or click the Open button (Open dialog box) to open the selected file and display the opened document in the Word window.

- If Word displays a dialog box indicating it will begin converting the document, tap or click its OK button.

Figure 5–51

4

- If necessary, click the Print Layout button on the status bar to switch to print layout view.

Experiment

- Scroll through the PDF that Word converted, noticing any differences between it and the original resume created in this chapter.

- Close the Word window and do not save this converted PDF document.

TO SAVE A WORD DOCUMENT AS AN XPS DOCUMENT

XPS, which stands for XML Paper Specification, is a file format created by Microsoft that shows all elements of a printed document as an electronic image. As with the PDF format, users can view an XPS document without the software that created the original document. Thus, the XPS format also enables users to share documents with others easily. Windows includes an XPS Viewer, which enables you to view, navigate, and print XPS files.

When you save a Word document as an XPS document, the original Word document remains intact; that is, Word creates a copy of the file in the XPS format. If you wanted to save a Word document as an XPS document, you would perform the following steps.

1. Open the Backstage view and then tap or click the Export tab in the Backstage view to display the Export gallery.

2. Tap or click 'Create PDF/XPS Document' in the Export gallery to display information about PDF/XPS documents in the right pane and then tap or click the 'Create PDF/XPS' button to display the Publish as PDF or XPS dialog box.

or

BTW

Q&As
For a complete list of the Q&As found in many of the step-by-step sequences in this book, visit the Q&A resource on the Student Companion Site located on www.cengagebrain.com. For detailed instructions about accessing available resources, visit www.cengage.com/ct/studentdownload or contact your instructor for information about accessing the required files.

1. Press F12 to display the Save As dialog box.

2. If necessary, navigate to the desired save location.

3. If necessary, tap or click the 'Save as type' arrow and then tap or click XPS Document.

4. Tap or click the Publish or Save button to create the XPS document from the Word document and then, if the 'Open file after publishing' check box was selected, open the resulting XPS document in the XPS Viewer.

Q&A What if I do not have an XPS Viewer?
The document will open in a browser window.

5. If necessary, exit the XPS Viewer.

To Run the Compatibility Checker

Word 2013 enables you to determine if a document is compatible (will work with) with earlier versions of Microsoft Word. *Why? If you would like to save a document, such as your resume, in the Word 97-2003 format so that it can be opened by users with earlier versions of Microsoft Word, you want to ensure that all of its elements (such as building blocks, content controls, and graphics) are compatible with earlier versions of Word.* The following steps run the compatibility checker.

1

• Open the Backstage view and then, if necessary, tap or click the Info tab in the Backstage view to display the Info gallery.

• Tap or click the 'Check for Issues' button in the Info gallery to display the Check for Issues menu (Figure 5–52).

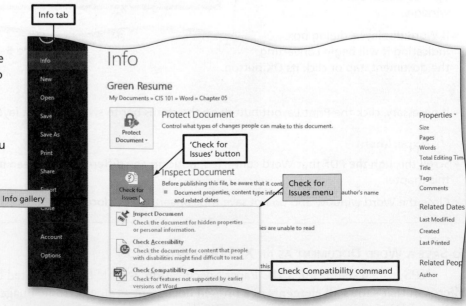

Figure 5–52

②

- Tap or click Check Compatibility on the Check for Issues menu to display the Microsoft Word Compatibility Checker dialog box, which shows any content that may not be supported by earlier versions of Word (Figure 5–53).

③

- Tap or click the OK button (Microsoft Word Compatibility Checker dialog box) to close the dialog box.

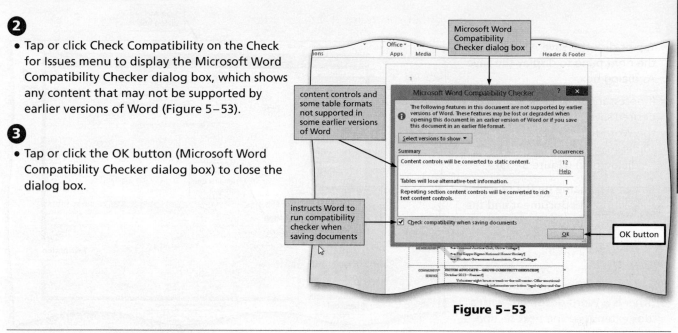

Figure 5–53

To Save a Word 2013 Document in an Earlier Word Format

1 CREATE DOCUMENT FROM TEMPLATE | 2 MODIFY & FORMAT TEMPLATE | 3 SAVE DOCUMENT IN OTHER FORMATS
4 MAKE DOCUMENT AVAILABLE ONLINE | 5 CREATE WEBPAGE FROM WORD DOCUMENT | 6 FORMAT WEBPAGE

If you send a document created in Word 2013 to users who have a version of Word earlier than Word 2007, they will not be able to open the Word 2013 document. *Why? Word 2013 saves documents in a format that is not backward compatible with versions earlier than Word 2007. Word 2013 documents have a file type of .docx, and versions prior to Word 2007 have a .doc file type.* To ensure that all Word users can open your Word 2013 document, you should save the document in a Word 97-2003 format. The following steps save the Word 2013 format of the Green Resume document in the Word 97-2003 format.

①

- Open the Backstage view and then tap or click the Export tab in the Backstage view to display the Export gallery.

- Tap or click 'Change File Type' in the Export gallery to display information in the right pane about various Word file types.

- Tap or click 'Word 97-2003' in the right pane to specify the new file type (Figure 5–54).

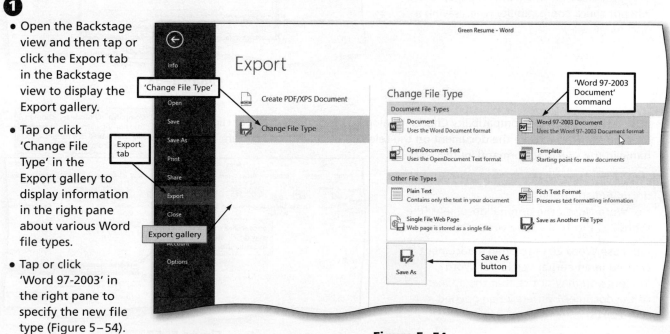

Figure 5–54

2

- Tap or click the Save As button in the right pane to display the Save As dialog box.

- If necessary, navigate to the desired save location (in this case, the Word folder in the CIS 101 folder [or your class folder]) (Save As dialog box) (Figure 5–55).

Q&A Can the file name be the same for the Word 2013 document and the Word 97-2003 document?
Yes. The file names can be the same because the file types are different: one is a Word document with a .docx extension, and the other is a Word document with a .doc extension. The next section discusses file types and extensions.

Figure 5–55

3

- Tap or click the Save button, which may display the Microsoft Word Compatibility Checker dialog box before saving the document (Figure 5–56).

Q&A My screen did not display the Microsoft Word Compatibility Checker dialog box. Why not?
If the 'Check compatibility when saving documents' check box is not selected (as shown in Figure 5–53 on the previous page), Word will not check compatibility when saving a document.

Figure 5–56

4

- If the Microsoft Word Compatibility Checker dialog box is displayed, tap or click its Continue button to save the document on the selected drive with the current file name in the specified format (Figure 5–57).

Q&A Is the Word 2013 format of the Green Resume document still open?
No. Word closed the original document (the Word 2013 format of the Green Resume).

Can I use Word 2013 to open a document created in an earlier version of Word?
Yes, but you may notice that the appearance of the document differs when opened in Word 2013.

Figure 5–57

Other Ways

1. Press F12, tap or click 'Save as type' arrow (Save As dialog box), select 'Word 97-2003 Document' in list, tap or click Save button

File Types

When saving documents in Word, you can select from a variety of file types that can be opened in Word using the Export gallery in the Backstage view (shown in Figure 5–54 on page WD 307) or by tapping or clicking the 'Save as type' arrow in the Save As dialog box. To save in these varied formats (Table 5–1), you follow the same basic steps as just illustrated.

Table 5–1 File Types

File Type	File Extension	File Explorer Image	Description
OpenDocument Text	.odt		Format used by other word processing programs, such as Google Docs and OpenOffice.org
PDF	.pdf		Portable Document Format, which can be opened in Adobe Reader
Plain Text	.txt		Format where all or most formatting is removed from the document
Rich Text Format	.rtf		Format designed to ensure file can be opened and read in many programs; some formatting may be lost to ensure compatibility
Single File Web Page	.mht		HTML (Hypertext Markup Language) format that can be opened in a browser; all elements of the webpage are saved in a single file
Web Page	.htm		HTML format that can be opened in a browser; various elements of the webpage, such as graphics, saved in separate files and folders
Word 97-2003 Document	.doc		Format used for documents created in versions of Word from Word 97 to Word 2003
Word 97-2003 Template	.dot		Format used for templates created in versions of Word from Word 97 and Word 2003
Word Document	.docx		Format used for Word 2013, Word 2010, or Word 2007 documents
Word Template	.dotx		Format used for Word 2010 or Word 2007 templates
XPS	.xps		XML (Extensible Markup Language) Paper Specification, which can be opened in the XPS Viewer

© 2014 Cengage Learning

TO SAVE A WORD 2013 DOCUMENT AS A DIFFERENT FILE TYPE

To save a Word 2013 document as a different file type, you would follow these steps.

1. Open the Backstage view and then tap or click the Export tab in the Backstage view to display the Export gallery.

2. Tap or click 'Change File Type' in the Export gallery to display information in the right pane about various file types that can be opened in Word.

3. Tap or click the desired file type in the right pane to display the Save As dialog box.

4. Navigate to the desired save location (in this case, the Word folder in the CIS 101 folder [or your class folder]) (Save As dialog box) and then tap or click the Save button in the dialog box.

5. If the Microsoft Word Compatibility Checker dialog box appears and you agree with the changes that will be made to the document, tap or click the Continue button (Microsoft Word Compatibility Checker dialog box) to save the document on the selected drive with the current file name in the specified format.

To Close a Document

You are finished with the Word 97-2003 format of the Green Resume. Thus, the next step is to close this document. The following steps close a document.

1 Open the Backstage view.

2 Tap or click Close in the Backstage view to close the current open document.

To Open a Recent Document

You would like to reopen the Word 2013 format of the Green Resume. Thus, the next step is to open this document. Because it recently was open, the following steps open a document from Recent Documents.

1 Open the Backstage view and then, if necessary, tap or click the Open tab in the Backstage view to display the Open gallery.

2 If necessary, tap or click Recent Documents in the Open gallery to display the list of recent documents.

3 To be sure you open the Word 2013 format of the Green Resume, if you are using a mouse, point to the file name and verify the file name is Green Resume.docx in the ScreenTip.

4 Tap or click the desired file name (in this case, Green Resume [the Word 2013 format]) in the list of recent documents in the Recent gallery to open the document in the Word document window.

BTW
Distributing a Document
Instead of printing and distributing a hard copy of a document, you can distribute the document electronically. Options include sending the document via email; posting it on cloud storage (such as SkyDrive) and sharing the file with others; posting it on a social networking site, blog, or other website; and sharing a link associated with an online location of the document. You also can create and share a PDF or XPS image of the document, so that users can view the file in Acrobat Reader or XPS Viewer instead of in Word.

To Save a File on SkyDrive

The steps on the next several pages require that you have a Microsoft account and an Internet connection. If you do not have a Microsoft account or an Internet connection, read these steps without performing them. The following steps save a file on SkyDrive so that you can share it online with others.

1 Open the Backstage view and then, if necessary, tap or click the Save As tab in the Backstage view to display the Save As gallery.

2 Tap or click SkyDrive to display SkyDrive saving options or a Sign In button, if you are not signed in already to your Microsoft account. If your screen displays a Sign In button, tap or click it and then follow the instructions to sign in to your account.

3 Tap or click your SkyDrive, if necessary, and then tap or click the Browse button to contact the SkyDrive server and then display the Save As dialog box.

4 Navigate to the desired save location on your SkyDrive and then tap or click the Save button (Save As dialog box) to save the file on SkyDrive.

To Invite Others to View or Edit a Document

1 CREATE DOCUMENT FROM TEMPLATE | 2 MODIFY & FORMAT TEMPLATE | 3 SAVE DOCUMENT IN OTHER FORMATS
4 MAKE DOCUMENT AVAILABLE ONLINE | 5 CREATE WEBPAGE FROM WORD DOCUMENT | 6 FORMAT WEBPAGE

If you have a SkyDrive account, you can share a Word document saved on your SkyDrive with others through email message invitations. *Why? Invited users can tap or click a link in an email message that displays a webpage enabling them to view or edit the document on SkyDrive.* The next steps invite a user to view the resume document. If you do not have a Microsoft account or an Internet connection, read these steps without performing them.

1

- Open the Backstage view and then tap or click the Share tab in the Backstage view to display the Share gallery.

- If necessary, tap or click Invite People in the Share gallery to display text boxes for entering email addresses and a message in the right pane.

- Type the email address(es) of the person(s) with whom you want to share the document, tap or click the box arrow so that you can specify Can view, and then type a message to the recipient(s) (Figure 5–58).

Q&A Why does my screen display a 'Save To Cloud' button in the right pane?

The document has not been saved on SkyDrive and/or you are not signed in to your Microsoft account.

Figure 5–58

2

- Tap or click the Share button in the right pane to send the message along with a link to the document on SkyDrive to the listed recipients.

How does a recipient access the shared document?

The recipient receives an email message that indicates it contains a link to a shared document (Figure 5–59). When the recipient taps or clicks the link in the email message, the document opens in the Word Web App on SkyDrive (Figure 5–60 on the next page).

Figure 5–59

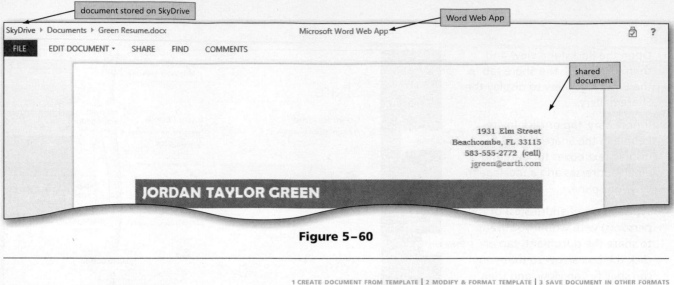

Figure 5–60

To Get a Sharing Link

1 CREATE DOCUMENT FROM TEMPLATE | 2 MODIFY & FORMAT TEMPLATE | 3 SAVE DOCUMENT IN OTHER FORMATS

4 MAKE DOCUMENT AVAILABLE ONLINE | 5 CREATE WEBPAGE FROM WORD DOCUMENT | 6 FORMAT WEBPAGE

Why share a link? Instead of inviting people to view or edit a document, you can create a link to the document's location on SkyDrive and then send others the link via an email message or text message, post it on a website, or communicate it via some other means. The following steps get a sharing link. If you do not have a Microsoft account or an Internet connection, read these steps without performing them.

1

- If necessary, open the Backstage view and then tap or click the Share tab in the Backstage view to display the Share gallery.

- Tap or click 'Get a Sharing Link' in the Share gallery to display options for obtaining a link to a document on SkyDrive in the right pane (Figure 5–61).

Q&A Why does my screen display a 'Save To Cloud' button in the right pane?
The document has not been saved on SkyDrive and/or you are not signed in to your Microsoft account.

Figure 5–61

2

- Tap or click the Create Link button in the View Link area in the right pane to create the link associated with the file on SkyDrive (Figure 5–62).

Q&A What do I do with the link?
You can copy and paste the link in an email or text message, on a webpage, or some other location.

What is the difference between a view link and an edit link?
A view link enables others to read the document but not modify it, while an edit link enables others to both view and edit the document.

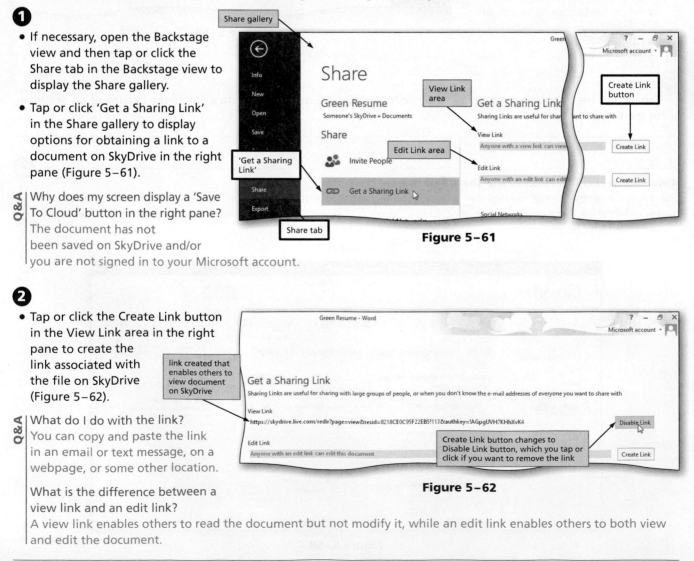

Figure 5–62

To Post a Document to a Social Network

If you belong to an online social network such as Facebook, Twitter, or LinkedIn, and you have connected that social network service to your Microsoft account, you can post a document directly to your online social network. The following steps post the resume document to Facebook, which is connected to the Microsoft account. *Why? You want your Facebook friends to review your resume.* If you do not have a Microsoft account connected to an online social network or do not have an Internet connection, read these steps without performing them.

❶

- If necessary, open the Backstage view and then tap or click the Share tab in the Backstage view to display the Share gallery.

- If necessary, tap or click 'Post to Social Networks' in the Share gallery to display online social networks connected to your Microsoft account, along with text boxes for a post, in the right pane.

- Type the post content (Figure 5–63).

Q&A Why does my screen display a 'Save To Cloud' button in the right pane?
The document has not been saved on SkyDrive and/or you are not signed in to your Microsoft account.

Figure 5–63

❷

- Tap or click the Post button in the right pane to post the document on the social network(s) connected to your Microsoft account.

❸

- If necessary, tap or click the Back button to return to the document window.

How do you see the resume post on Facebook?
Display your Facebook newsfeed to see the message and post (Figure 5–64).

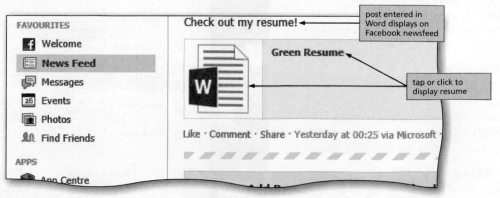

Figure 5–64

To Remove a Watermark

The following steps remove the DRAFT watermark from the resume in the document window, if it was saved with the document, because you now consider the document final and would like to distribute it to potential employers.

1 If necessary, open the Green Resume (Word 2013 format).

2 Display the DESIGN tab.

3 Tap or click the Watermark button (DESIGN tab | Page Background group) to display the Watermark gallery.

4 Tap or click Remove Watermark in the Watermark gallery to remove the watermark.

5 Save the document again with the same file name.

What file type should you use when emailing documents?

If you email a document, such as your resume, consider that the recipient, such as a potential employer, may not have the same software you used to create the resume and, thus, may not be able to open the file. As an alternative, you could save the file in a format, such as a PDF or XPS, that can be viewed with a reader program. Many job seekers also post their resumes on the web.

To Send a Document Using Email

1 CREATE DOCUMENT FROM TEMPLATE | 2 MODIFY & FORMAT TEMPLATE | 3 SAVE DOCUMENT IN OTHER FORMATS
4 MAKE DOCUMENT AVAILABLE ONLINE | 5 CREATE WEBPAGE FROM WORD DOCUMENT | 6 FORMAT WEBPAGE

In Word, you can include the current document as an attachment to an email message. An attachment is a file included with an email message. The following steps send the Green Resume as an email attachment, assuming you use Outlook as your default email program. *Why? When you attach an email document from within Word, it automatically uses the default email program, which is Outlook in this case.*

1

- Open the Backstage view and then tap or click the Share tab in the Backstage view to display the Share gallery.

- If necessary, tap or click Email in the Share gallery to display information in the right pane about various ways to send a document via email from within Word (Figure 5–65).

Q&A

Why is my list of share options in the Share gallery shorter?
You have not saved the document previously on SkyDrive.

What are the purpose of the 'Send as PDF' and 'Send as XPS' buttons?
Depending on which button you tap or click, Word converts the current document either to the PDF or XPS format and then attaches the PDF or XPS document to the email message.

Why is my 'Send a Link' button dimmed?
You have not saved the document previously on SkyDrive.

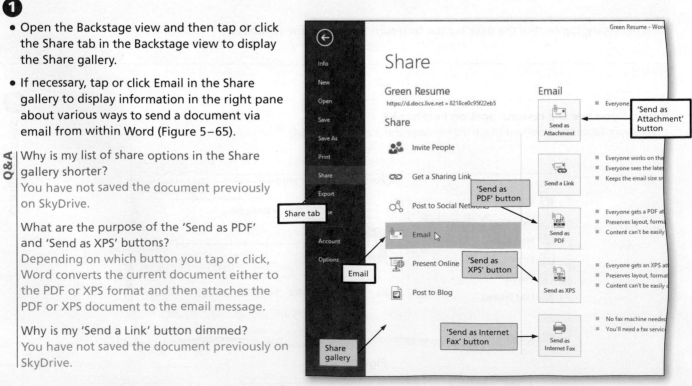

Figure 5–65

2

- Tap or click the 'Send as Attachment' button to start your default email program (Outlook, in this case), which automatically attaches the active Word document to the email message.

- Fill in the To text box with the recipient's email address.

- Fill in the message text (Figure 5–66).

3

- Tap or click the Send button to send the email message along with its attachment to the recipient named in the To text box and then close the email window.

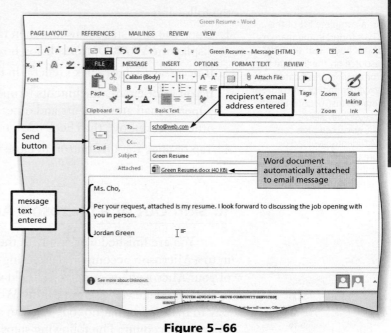

Figure 5–66

To Use the Document Inspector

Word includes a Document Inspector that checks a document for content you might not want to share with others, such as personal information. Before sharing a document with others, you may want to check for this type of content. If you wanted to use the Document Inspector, you would do the following:

1. Open the Backstage view and then tap or click the Info tab in the Backstage view to display the Info gallery.

2. Tap or click the 'Check for Issues' button in the Info gallery to display the Check for Issues menu.

3. Tap or click Inspect Document on the Check for Issues menu to display the Document Inspector dialog box.

4. Tap or click the Inspect button (Document Inspector dialog box) to instruct Word to inspect the document.

5. Review the results (Document Inspector dialog box) and then tap or click the Remove All button(s) for any item that you do not want to be saved with the document.

6. When finished removing information, tap or click the Close button to close the dialog box.

To Customize How Word Opens Email Attachments

When a user sends you an email message that contains a Word document as an attachment, Word may display the document in Read mode. This view is designed to increase the readability and legibility of an on-screen document. Read mode, however, does not represent how the document will look when it is printed. For this reason, many users prefer working in Print Layout view to read documents. To exit Read mode, press the ESC key.

BTW

Internet Fax
If you do not have a stand-alone fax machine, you can send and receive faxes in Word by tapping or clicking the 'Send as Internet Fax' button in the Backstage view (shown in Figure 5–65). To send or receive faxes using Word, you first must sign up with a fax service provider by tapping or clicking the OK button in the Microsoft Office dialog box that appears the first time you tap or click the 'Send as Internet Fax' button, which displays an Available Fax Services webpage. You also may need to install either the Windows Fax printer driver or Windows Fax Services component on your computer. When sending a fax, Word converts the document to an image file and attaches it to an email message where you enter the recipient's fax number, name, subject, and message for the cover sheet, and then tap or click a Send button to deliver the fax.

BTW
BTWs
For a complete list of the BTWs found in the margins of this book, visit the BTW resource on the Student Companion Site located on www.cengagebrain.com. For detailed instructions about accessing available resources, visit www.cengage.com/ct/studentdownload or contact your instructor for information about accessing the required files.

If you wanted to customize how Word opens email attachments, you would do the following.

1. Open the Backstage view and then tap or click Options in the Backstage view to display the Word Options dialog box.

2. If necessary, tap or click General in the left pane (Word Options dialog box).

3. If you want email attachments to open in Read mode, place a check mark in the 'Open e-mail attachments and other uneditable files in reading view' check box; otherwise, remove the check mark to open email attachments in Print Layout view.

4. Tap or click the OK button to close the dialog box.

To Sign Out of a Microsoft Account

You are finished working with the Green Resume on SkyDrive. If you are signed in to a Microsoft account and are using a public computer or otherwise wish to sign out of your Microsoft account, you should sign out of the account from the Account gallery in the Backstage view before exiting Word. Signing out of the account is the safest way to make sure that nobody else can access SkyDrive files or settings stored in your Microsoft account. The following steps sign out of a Microsoft account from Word.

1 If you wish to sign out of your Microsoft account, open the Backstage view and then tap or click the Account tab to display the Account gallery.

2 Tap or click the Sign out link, which displays the Remove Account dialog box. If a Can't remove Windows accounts dialog box appears instead of the Remove Account dialog box, tap or click the OK button and skip the remaining steps.

Q&A Why does a Can't remove Windows accounts dialog box appear?
If you signed in to Windows using your Microsoft account, then you also must sign out from Windows, rather than signing out from within the Word. When you are finished using Windows, be sure to sign out at that time.

3 Tap or click the Yes button (Remove Account dialog box) to sign out of your Microsoft account on this computer.

Q&A Should I sign out of Windows after signing out of my Microsoft account?
When you are finished using the computer, you should sign out of your account for maximum security.

4 Tap or click the Back button in the upper-left corner of the Backstage view to return to the document.

5 To be certain that the connection with SkyDrive no longer is active, exit Word, run Word, and then open the Green Resume document again.

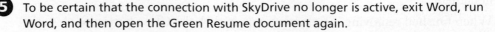

Creating a Webpage from a Word Document

If you have created a document, such as a resume, using Word, you can save it in a format that can be opened by a browser, such as Internet Explorer. When you save a file as a webpage, Word converts the contents of the document into **HTML** (Hypertext Markup Language), which is a set of codes that browsers can interpret. Some of Word's formatting features are not supported by webpages. Thus, your webpage may look slightly different from the original Word document.

When saving a document as a webpage, Word provides you with three choices:

- The **single file Web page format** saves all of the components of the webpage in a single file that has a **.mht** extension. This format is particularly useful for sending documents via email in HTML format.
- The **Web Page format** saves some of the components of the webpage in a folder, separate from the webpage. This format is useful if you need access to the individual components, such as images, that make up the webpage.
- The **filtered Web Page format** saves the file in webpage format and then reduces the size of the file by removing specific Microsoft Office formats. This format is useful if you want to speed up the time it takes to download a webpage that contains graphics, video, audio, or animations.

The webpage created in this section uses the single file Web page format.

BTW

Saving as a Webpage
Because you might not have access to SkyDrive or a web server, the webpage you create in this feature is saved in your class folder rather than on SkyDrive or a web server.

To Save a Word Document as a Webpage

1 CREATE DOCUMENT FROM TEMPLATE | 2 MODIFY & FORMAT TEMPLATE | 3 SAVE DOCUMENT IN OTHER FORMATS
4 MAKE DOCUMENT AVAILABLE ONLINE | 5 CREATE WEBPAGE FROM WORD DOCUMENT | 6 FORMAT WEBPAGE

The following steps save the Green Resume created earlier in this chapter as a webpage. *Why? You intend to post your resume online.*

1

- With the Word 2013 format of the resume file open in the document window, open the Backstage view and then tap or click the Export tab in the Backstage view to display the Export gallery.

- Tap or click 'Change File Type' in the Export gallery to display information in the right pane about various file types that are supported by Word.

- Tap or click 'Single File Web Page' in the right pane to specify a new file type (Figure 5–67).

Q&A

What if I wanted to save the document as a Web Page instead of a Single File Web Page?
You would tap or click 'Save as Another File Type' in the Change File Type area, tap or click the Save As button, tap or click the 'Save as type' arrow in the Save As dialog box, and then tap or click Web Page in the Save as type list.

Figure 5–67

2

- Tap or click the Save As button in the right pane to display the Save As dialog box.

- If necessary, navigate to the desired save location (in this case, the Word folder in the CIS 101 folder [or your class folder]) (Save As dialog box).

- If necessary, type `Green Resume` in the File name box to change the file name.

- Tap or click the Change Title button to display the Enter Text dialog box.

- Type **Green Resume** in the Page title text box (Enter Text dialog box) (Figure 5–68).

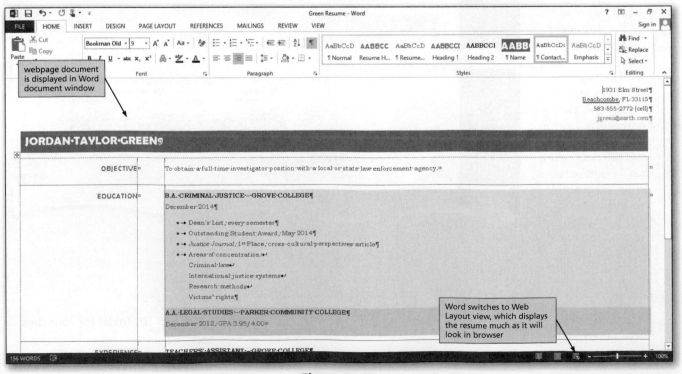

Figure 5–68

❸

- Tap or click the OK button (Enter Text dialog box) to close the dialog box.

- Tap or click the Save button (Save As dialog box) to save the resume as a webpage and then display it in the document window in Web Layout view.

- If necessary, change the zoom to 100% (Figure 5–69).

- If the Microsoft Word Compatibility Checker dialog box appears, tap or click its Continue button.

Q&A | Can I switch to Web Layout view at any time by tapping or clicking the Web Layout button?
Yes.

Can I save the webpage to a web server?
If you have access to a web server, you can save the webpage from Word directly to the web server.

Figure 5–69

TO SET A DEFAULT SAVE LOCATION

If you wanted to change the default location that Word uses when it saves a document, you would do the following.

1. Open the Backstage view and then tap or click the Options in the Backstage view to display the Word Options dialog box.
2. Tap or click Save in the left pane (Word Options dialog box) to display options for saving documents in the right pane.
3. In the 'Default file location' text box, type the new desired save location.
4. Tap or click the OK button to close the dialog box.

To Delete a Content Control

Recall that the email address is a content control. In the next step, you will format the email address as a hyperlink. To do this, you first must delete the content control. The following steps delete a content control.

1 Tap or click the Email content control to select it.

2 Press and hold and then tap the 'Show Context Menu' button on the mini toolbar or right-click the selected content control to display a shortcut menu and then tap or click 'Remove Content Control' on the shortcut menu to delete the selected content control.

To Format Text as a Hyperlink

1 CREATE DOCUMENT FROM TEMPLATE | 2 MODIFY & FORMAT TEMPLATE | 3 SAVE DOCUMENT IN OTHER FORMATS
4 MAKE DOCUMENT AVAILABLE ONLINE | 5 CREATE WEBPAGE FROM WORD DOCUMENT | **6 FORMAT WEBPAGE**

The email address in the resume webpage should be formatted as a hyperlink. *Why? When webpage visitors tap or click the hyperlink-formatted email address, you want their email program to run automatically and open an email window with the email address already filled in.* The following steps format the email address as a hyperlink.

1

- Select the email address in the resume webpage (jgreen@earth.com, in this case).
- Display the INSERT tab.
- Tap or click the 'Add a Hyperlink' button (INSERT tab | Links group) to display the Insert Hyperlink dialog box (Figure 5–70).

Figure 5–70

BTW

Certification
The Microsoft Office Specialist (MOS) program provides an opportunity for you to obtain a valuable industry credential — proof that you have the Word 2013 skills required by employers. For more information, visit the Certification resource on the Student Companion Site located on www .cengagebrain.com. For detailed instructions about accessing available resources, visit www.cengage.com/ct/studentdownload or contact your instructor for information about accessing the required files.

2

- Tap or click E-mail Address in the Link to bar (Insert Hyperlink dialog box) so that the dialog box displays email address settings instead of webpage settings.

- In the E-mail address text box, type `jgreen@earth.com` to specify the email address that the browser uses when a user taps or clicks the hyperlink.

Q&A Can I change the text that automatically appeared in the 'Text to display' text box?
Yes. Word assumes that the hyperlink text should be the same as the email address, so as soon as you enter the email address, the same text is entered in the 'Text to display' text box.

- If the email address in the 'Text to display' text box is preceded by the text, mailto:, delete this leading text because you want only the email address to appear in the document.

- Tap or click the ScreenTip button to display the Set Hyperlink ScreenTip dialog box.

- Type `Send email message to Jordan Green.` in the 'ScreenTip text' text box (Set Hyperlink ScreenTip dialog box) to specify the text that will be displayed when a user points to the hyperlink (Figure 5–71).

Figure 5–71

3

- Tap or click the OK button in each dialog box to format the email address as a hyperlink (Figure 5–72).

Q&A How do I know if the hyperlink works?
In Word, if you are using a mouse, you can test the hyperlink by holding down the CTRL key while clicking the hyperlink. In this case, CTRL+clicking the email address should open an email window.

Figure 5–72

Other Ways

1. Tap 'Show Context Menu' on mini toolbar or right-click selected text, tap or click Hyperlink on shortcut menu

2. Select text, press CTRL+K

To Edit a Hyperlink

If you needed to edit a hyperlink, for example, to change its ScreenTip or its link, you would follow these steps.

1. Position the insertion point in the hyperlink.
2. Tap or click the 'Add a Hyperlink' button (INSERT tab | Links group) or press CTRL+K to display the Edit Hyperlink dialog box.

or

1. Tap 'Show Context Menu' on mini toolbar or right-click the hyperlink to display a shortcut menu.
2. Tap or click Edit Hyperlink on the shortcut menu to display the Edit Hyperlink dialog box.

BTW

Quick Reference
For a table that lists how to complete the tasks covered in this book using touch gestures, the mouse, ribbon, shortcut menu, and keyboard, see the Quick Reference Summary at the back of this book, or visit the Quick Reference resource on the Student Companion Site located on www.cengagebrain .com. For detailed instructions about accessing available resources, visit www.cengage .com/ct/studentdownload or contact your instructor for information about accessing the required files.

To Change the Style Set

1 CREATE DOCUMENT FROM TEMPLATE | 2 MODIFY & FORMAT TEMPLATE | 3 SAVE DOCUMENT IN OTHER FORMATS
4 MAKE DOCUMENT AVAILABLE ONLINE | 5 CREATE WEBPAGE FROM WORD DOCUMENT | 6 FORMAT WEBPAGE

Word provides several built-in style sets to help you quickly change the look of an entire document. *Why? A style set contains formats for fonts and paragraphs.* The following steps change the style set to the Shaded style set.

1
- Display the DESIGN tab.
- Tap or click the More button (DESIGN tab | Document Formatting group) (shown in Figure 5–74 on the next page) to display the expanded Style Set gallery (Figure 5–73).

Experiment
- If you are using a mouse, point to various style sets in the Style Set gallery and watch the font and paragraph formatting change in the document window.

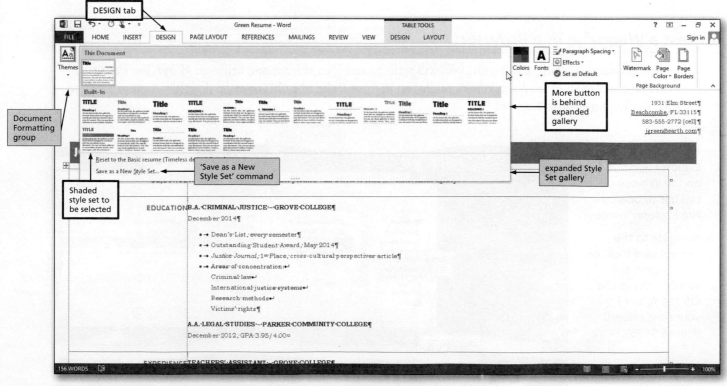

Figure 5–73

②

- Tap or click Shaded to change the style set to the selected style set (Figure 5–74).

Q&A

Can I create my own style sets?
Yes. Modify the fonts and other formats as desired, tap or click 'Save as a New Style Set' on the expanded Style Set gallery (shown in Figure 5–73 on the previous page), enter the name for the style set (Save as a New Style Set dialog box), and then click the Save button to create the custom style set. You then can access the custom style set through the Style Set gallery.

Figure 5–74

To Save an Existing Document and Exit Word

The webpage document now is complete. The following steps save the document again and exit Word.

① Tap or click the Save button on the Quick Access Toolbar to overwrite the previously saved file.

② Exit Word.

To Test a Webpage in a Browser

1 CREATE DOCUMENT FROM TEMPLATE | 2 MODIFY & FORMAT TEMPLATE | 3 SAVE DOCUMENT IN OTHER FORMATS
4 MAKE DOCUMENT AVAILABLE ONLINE | 5 CREATE WEBPAGE FROM WORD DOCUMENT | **6 FORMAT WEBPAGE**

After creating and saving a webpage, you will want to test it in at least one browser. *Why? You want to be sure it looks and works the way you intended.* The following steps use File Explorer to display the resume webpage in the Internet Explorer browser.

①

- Tap or click the File Explorer app button on the Windows taskbar to open the File Explorer window.

- Navigate to the desired save location (in this case, the Word folder in the CIS 101 folder [or your class folder]) (Figure 5–75).

Figure 5–75

2

- Double-tap or double-click the webpage file name, Green Resume, to run Internet Explorer and display the webpage file in the browser window (Figure 5–76).

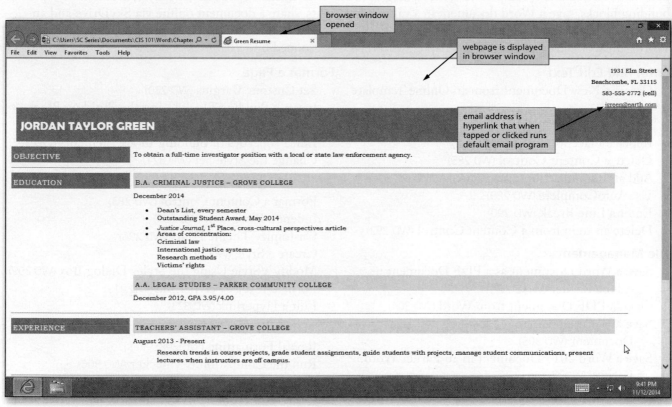

Figure 5–76

3

- With the webpage document displayed in the browser, tap or click the email address link to run the email program with the email address displayed in the email window (Figure 5–77).

- If Internet Explorer displays a security dialog box, tap or click its Allow button.

4

- Close all open windows.

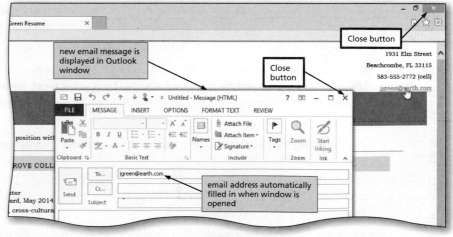

Figure 5–77

How do you publish a webpage?

Once you have created a webpage, you can publish it. **Publishing** is the process of making a webpage available to others on a network, such as the Internet or a company's intranet. Many Internet service providers (ISPs) offer storage space on their web servers at no cost to their subscribers.

Chapter Summary

In this chapter, you learned how to use Word to use a template to create a document, set custom margins, personalize a document template, indent a paragraph, customize theme fonts, create a style, modify a style, insert building blocks, save a Word document in a variety of formats, share a document online via SkyDrive and an online social network, insert a hyperlink, and change the style set. The items listed below include all the new Word skills you have learned in this chapter, with the tasks grouped by activity.

Enter and Edit Text

Create a New Document from an Online Template (WD 276)

Modify Text in a Content Control (WD 282)

Replace Placeholder Text (WD 284)

Delete a Content Control (WD 285)

Add an Item to a Content Control (WD 288)

Use AutoComplete (WD 289)

Enter a Line Break (WD 290)

Delete an Item from a Content Control (WD 292)

File Management

Save a Word Document as a PDF Document in Adobe Reader (WD 302)

Open a PDF Document from Word (WD 304)

Save a Word Document as an XPS Document (WD 305)

Save a Word 2013 Document in an Earlier Word Format (WD 307)

Save a Word 2013 Document as a Different File Type (WD 309)

Invite Others to View or Edit a Document (WD 310)

Get a Sharing Link (WD 312)

Post a Document to a Social Network (WD 313)

Send a Document Using Email (WD 314)

Save a Word Document as a Webpage (WD 317)

Format a Page

Set Custom Margins (WD 280)

Insert a Building Block Using the Building Block Organizer (WD 300)

Edit Properties of Building Block Elements (WD 302)

Change the Style Set (WD 321)

Format Text

Format a Content Control (WD 283)

Indent a Paragraph (WD 293)

Customize Theme Fonts (WD 296)

Create a Style (WD 297)

Modify a Style Using the Styles Dialog Box (WD 299)

Format Text as a Hyperlink (WD 319)

Edit a Hyperlink (WD 321)

Word Settings

Reveal Formatting (WD 298)

Run the Compatibility Checker (WD 306)

Use the Document Inspector (WD 315)

Customize How Word Opens Email Attachments (WD 315)

Set a Default Save Location (WD 319)

Work with Tables

Move Table Rows (WD 286)

Copy and Paste a Table Item (WD 294)

CONSIDER THIS: PLAN AHEAD

What decisions will you need to make when creating your next resume?

Use these guidelines as you complete the assignments in this chapter and create your own resumes outside of this class.

1. Craft a successful resume.

   a) Include necessary information (at a minimum, your contact information, objective, educational background, and work experience).

   b) Honestly present all your positive points.

   c) Organize information appropriately.

   d) Ensure the resume is error free.

2. For electronic distribution, such as email or online social media, ensure the document is in the proper format.

   a) Save the resume in a format that can be shared with others.

   b) Ensure that others will be able to open the resume using software on their computers and that the look of the resume will remain intact when recipients open the resume.

3. If desired, create a resume webpage from your resume Word document.

   a) Improve the usability of the resume webpage by making your email address a link to an email program.

   b) Enhance the look of the webpage by adding, for example, a background color.

   c) Test your finished webpage document in at least one browser to be sure it looks and works as intended.

   d) Publish your resume webpage.

CONSIDER THIS

How should you submit solutions to questions in the assignments identified with a ✳ symbol?

Every assignment in this book contains one or more questions identified with a ✳ symbol. These questions require you to think beyond the assigned document. Present your solutions to the questions in the format required by your instructor. Possible formats may include one or more of these options: write the answer; create a document that contains the answer; present your answer to the class; discuss your answer in a group; record the answer as audio or video using a webcam, smartphone, or portable media player; or post answers on a blog, wiki, or website.

Apply Your Knowledge

Reinforce the skills and apply the concepts you learned in this chapter.

Saving a Word Document in a Variety of Formats

Note: To complete this assignment, you will be required to use the Data Files for Students. Visit www.cengage.com/ct/studentdownload for detailed instructions or contact your instructor for information about accessing the required files.

Instructions: Run Word. Open the document, Apply 5-1 Online Job Searching, from the Data Files for Students. You are to save the document as a Single File Web Page (Figure 5–78), a PDF document, an XPS document, and in the Word 97-2003 format.

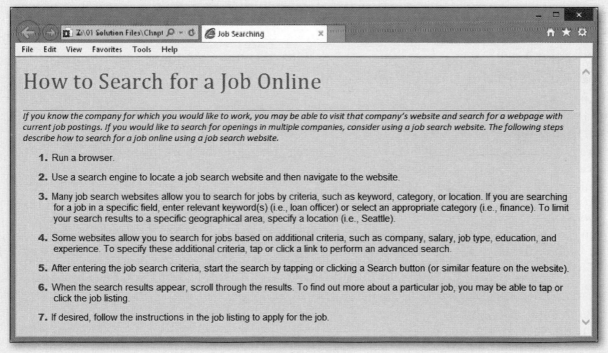

Figure 5–78

Perform the following tasks:

1. Save the document as a Single File Web Page using the file name, Apply 5-1 Online Job Searching Webpage. In the Save As dialog box, tap or click the Change Title button change the webpage title to Job Searching. If requested by your instructor, change the text, finance, in the third list item in the resume to your major.

2. Add the background color Tan, Background 2 to the webpage document. Save the file again.

Continued >

Apply Your Knowledge *continued*

3. Use Internet Explorer, or another browser, to view the webpage (shown in Figure 5–78). What differences do you notice between the Word document format and the Single File Web Page format? Exit Internet Explorer and then close the webpage document in Word.

4. Open the original Apply 5-1 Online Job Searching document. If requested by your instructor, change the text, finance, in the third list item in the resume to your major. Save the document as a PDF document and then view the PDF document in Adobe Reader. Submit the document as specified by your instructor. Exit Adobe Reader. In Word, open the PDF document just created. What differences do you notice between the Word document format and the PDF format? Close the converted PDF document without saving it.

5. If necessary, open the original Apply 5-1 Online Job Searching document. If requested by your instructor, change the text, finance, in the third list item in the resume to your major. Save the document as an XPS Document and then view the XPS document in the XPS Viewer. What differences do you notice between the Word document format and the XPS format? Exit the XPS Viewer.

6. If necessary, open the original Apply 5-1 Online Job Searching document. Run the compatibility checker. What issue(s) were identified by the compatibility checker? Save the document in the Word 97-2003 format.

7. If your instructor allows, email the document saved in #6 to his or her email account.

8. ✸ Answer the questions posed in #3, #4, #5, and #6. If you wanted to email this document to others, which format would you choose and why?

Extend Your Knowledge

Extend the skills you learned in this chapter and experiment with new skills. You may need to use Help to complete the assignment.

Creating a Multi-File Webpage, Applying a Fill Effect and Highlights, and Inserting Screen Shots

Note: To complete this assignment, you will be required to use the Data Files for Students. Visit www.cengage.com/ct/studentdownload for detailed instructions or contact your instructor for information about accessing the required files.

Instructions: Run Word. Open the document called Extend 5-1 Online Social Network located on the Data Files for Students. You will save a Word document as a multi-file webpage and format it by inserting links, adding a pattern fill effect as the background, and applying highlights to text. Then, you will create a new document that contains screen shots of the webpage and files created for the webpage.

Perform the following tasks:

1. Use Help to learn about saving as a webpage (not a Single File Web Page), hyperlinks, pattern fill effects, text highlight color, and screen shots.

2. If requested by your instructor, add your name on a separate line at the end of the document. Save the Extend 5-1 Online Social Networks file in the Web Page format (not as a Single File Web Page) using the file name, Extend 5-1 Online Social Networks Webpage.

3. Determine the web address of your favorite social network. At the end of the document, type a line of text that directs the reader to that web address for more information. Format the web address in the document as a hyperlink so that when a user clicks the web address, the associated webpage is displayed in the browser window.

4. Add a page color of your choice to the document. Add a pattern fill effect of your choice to the page color.

5. Apply a text highlight color of your choice to at least five words in the document.

6. Save the document again. Test the webpage by tapping or clicking its name in File Explorer. Test the web address link on the webpage. Leave this window open so that you can include its screenshot in the next step.

7. Redisplay the Word window. Create a new Word document. Insert a screen shot of the webpage displaying in the File Explorer window. Below the screen shot of the webpage, insert a screen shot(s) of File Explorer that shows all the files and folders created by saving the document as a webpage. Insert callout shapes with text that points to and identifies the files and folders created by saving the document as a webpage (Figure 5–79). Save the document with the file name, Extend 5-1 Online Social Networks Screen Shots.

8. Close all open windows. Submit the files in the format specified by your instructor.

9. ❀ Why would you add a pattern fill effect to a background?

Figure 5–79

Analyze, Correct, Improve

Analyze a document, correct all errors, and improve it.

Formatting a Resume Created from a Template

Note: To complete this assignment, you will be required to use the Data Files for Students. Visit www.cengage.com/ct/studentdownload for detailed instructions or contact your instructor for information about accessing the required files.

Instructions: Run Word. Open the document, Analyze 5-1 Ames Resume Draft, located on the Data Files for Students. The document is a resume created from a template that is formatted incorrectly (Figure 5–80 on the next page). You are to change the margins, delete table rows, move table rows, modify styles, adjust the paragraph indent, modify a content control, remove a hyperlink format, and change the document theme.

Continued >

STUDENT ASSIGNMENTS

Analyze, Correct, Improve *continued*

Perform the following tasks:

1. Correct In the resume, correct the following items:

a. Change the margins so that the resume text does not run off the page and its contents are centered (Figure 5–80).

b. Modify the Normal style so that the text is a color other than red.

c. Delete the SKILLS & ABILITIES, LEADERSHIP, and REFERENCES rows.

d. Move the EDUCATION row above the EXPERIENCE row.

e. Decrease the indent of the objective text so it is aligned at the left edge of the cell.

f. Increase the indent of items in the activities section so that they all line up with each other.

g. Increase the font size of the name content control so that it is predominant on the page.

h. Use the Reveal Formatting task pane to determine the font size of the section headings (i.e., OBJECTIVE) and section text (i.e., To secure a nursing…). Modify the Heading 1 style so that it uses a font size that is greater than the font size of the section text.

i. Remove the hyperlink format from the email address.

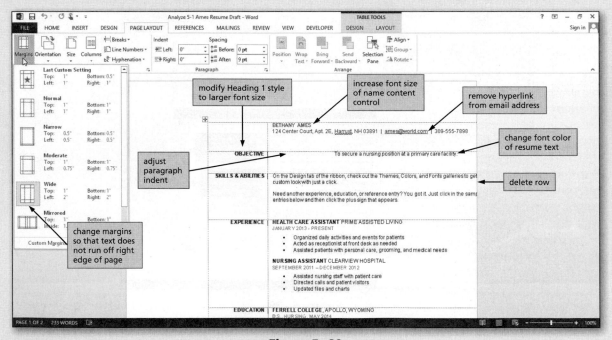

Figure 5–80

2. Improve Enhance the resume by customizing theme fonts, name the theme fonts. If necessary, edit the theme fonts until you are satisfied with the look of the resume. Adjust the font size of the contact line, if necessary, so that it all fits on a single line. If requested by your instructor, change the name at the top of the resume to your name. Save the modified document with the file name, Analyze 5-1 Ames Resume Modified, and then submit it in the format specified by your instructor.

3. ✹ In this assignment, you customized theme fonts. Which fonts did you select for the headings and body text and why?

In the Labs

Design and/or create a document using the guidelines, concepts, and skills presented in this chapter. Labs 1 and 2, which increase in difficulty, require you to create solutions based on what you learned in the chapter; Lab 3 requires you to create a solution, which uses cloud and web technologies, by learning and investigating on your own from general guidance.

Lab 1: Creating a Resume from a Template

Problem: You are hospitality management student at California College. As graduation quickly is approaching, you prepare the resume shown in Figure 5–81 on the next page using one of Word's resume templates.

Perform the following tasks:

1. Use the Basic resume (Timeless design) template to create a resume. If you cannot locate this template, open the file called Basic resume (Timeless design) from the Data Files for Students.

2. Change the document theme to Wisp.

3. Personalize the resume as shown in Figure 5–81. Following are some guidelines for some sections of the resume:

   a. Change the margins to 1" on the top, left, and right, and .5" on the bottom.

   b. If requested by your instructor, use your own name and contact information in the content controls. Delete the line containing the Website content control.

   c. Move the Education and Experience rows so that they appear as shown in Figure 5–81. Insert line breaks in the areas of concentration section of the education information.

   d. Add an item to the Education content control so that you can enter both degrees.

   e. Delete the second item from the Experience content control because the resume lists only one job.

   f. In the Experience section, indent the job responsibilities paragraphs one-half inch.

   g. Change the heading, SKILLS & ABILITIES, to MEMBERSHIPS.

   h. Copy the Experience section to below the Memberships section. Change the added row to show the community service information.

   i. Customize the theme fonts so that the headings are Arial Black and the body text is Verdana. Name the customized font Lab 1 Resume.

   j. Modify the Heading 2 style to the Verdana font.

   k. Change the Style Set to Shaded.

   l. Delete any unused rows in the resume.

4. The entire resume should fit on a single page. If it flows to two pages, decrease spacing before and after paragraphs until the entire resume text fits on a single page.

5. Check the spelling of the resume. Save the resume with Lab 5-1 Garlapati Resume as the file name and submit it in the format specified by your instructor.

6. ✳ Look through the other resume templates available. Which would work best for your resume? Why?

Continued >

In the Labs *continued*

1535 Casper Boulevard

Dilton, NH 03324

217-555-5381 (cell)

VIDYA@SKY.NET

16-point

VIDYA GARLAPATI

OBJECTIVE

To obtain a restaurant management position for a restaurant specializing in Mediterranean cuisine.

EDUCATION

B.S. HOSPITALITY MANAGEMENT – CALIFORNIA COLLEGE

December 2014
- Dean's List, six semesters
- Tanner Nutrition Award, May 2014
- Food Preparation Competition, 1st Place, February 2014
- Areas of concentration:
  Food preparation and service
  Marketing
  Nutrition

A.S. NUTRITION – ROSEWOOD COMMUNITY COLLEGE

December 2012, GPA 3.87/4.00

EXPERIENCE

CAFETERIA DIRECTOR ASSISTANT – CALIFORNIA COLLEGE

September 2013 - Present

paragraph indented

Organize work schedules, assist with meal catering for events and ceremonies, plan meals for staff and students on campus, prepare food, and serve dining patrons.

MEMBERSHIPS

- National Restaurant Management Association
- Nutrition Services of America
- Student Government Association, Secretary

COMMUNITY SERVICE

VOLUNTEER – HOPE MISSION

May 2012 - Present

paragraph indented

Prepare food and serve meals six hours a week.

Figure 5–81

Lab 2: **Creating a Resume from a Template**

Problem: You are an industrial engineering technology student at Alamo College. As graduation is approaching quickly, you prepare the resume shown in Figure 5–82 on the next page using one of Word's resume templates.

Perform the following tasks:

1. Use the Resume template to create a resume. If you cannot locate this template, open the file called Resume from the Data Files for Students.

2. Personalize and format the resume as shown in Figure 5–82. Remove and insert content controls and items as necessary so that the resume appears as in the figure. If requested by your instructor, use your own name and contact information in the content controls. Following are some guidelines for some sections of the resume:

   a. Create a customized theme font set that uses Rockwell for headings and Arial for body text. Save the theme font with the name Lab 2 Resume.

   b. Modify the Section style to contain paragraph shading of White, Background 1, Darker 5%. Reduce spacing to 24 point before paragraphs. Update the style so that it applies to the entire resume.

   c. Increase the font size of the name to 28 point and the Address content control to 10 point. Create a style called Contact Info using the format in the Address content control. Apply the Contact Info style to the phone and email content controls.

3. The entire resume should fit on a single page. If it flows to two pages, decrease spacing before and after paragraphs until the entire resume text fits on a single page.

4. Check the spelling of the resume. Save the resume with Lab 5-2 Chung Resume as the file name and submit it in the format specified by your instructor.

5. ✳ Look through the templates available besides resumes. Which ones might you find useful? Why?

Continued >

In the Labs *continued*

Kim Chung

5056 East Fourth Street, Blackburg, TX 77490 | 584-555-8052 | chung@world.com

Objective

· To obtain an entry-level engineering position, specializing in renewable energy, with a major firm in the Dallas area.

Education

B.S. INDUSTRIAL ENGINEERING TECHNOLOGY | MAY 2015 | ALAMO COLLEGE

· Major: Renewable Energy
· Minor: Economics and Public Policy
· GPA: 3.8/4.0

Skills & Accomplishments

INDUSTRIAL TECHNOLOGY COURSEWORK

· Electrical Circuits
· Fluid Power Systems
· Industrial Plastics
· Manufacturing Processes
· Technical Drawing

RENEWABLE ENERGY COURSEWORK

· Dynamic Weather
· Economics of Energy
· Energy and Climate Change
· Power Technology
· Renewable Energy and Agriculture

AWARDS RECEIVED

· Dean's List, seven semesters
· 2014 Engineering Student of the Year
· Top CAD Design Award, 2013

MEMBERSHIPS

· International Association of Industrial Engineers
· Engineering Management Association

Experience

TECHNICAL SUPPORT | BOWER ELECTRONICS | JANUARY 2013 – MAY 2015

· Offer phone assistance to customers with electronics problems.

paragraph shading

Figure 5–82

Lab 3: Expand Your World: Cloud and Web Technologies
Sharing a Resume Online

Problem: You are a technical writing graduate from Midway College. You have prepared a resume and are ready to share it with potential employers. You will save it on your SkyDrive account, invite others to view it, get a sharing link, post it on your online social network, send it via email, and post it on a job sharing website (Figure 5-83 on the next page).

Notes:
- You will use a SkyDrive, online social network, and job sharing website accounts, all of which you can create at no cost, to complete this assignment. If you do not have these accounts and do not want to create them, read this assignment without performing the instructions.

- To complete this assignment, you will be required to use the Data Files for Students. Visit www.cengage.com/ct/studentdownload for detailed instructions or contact your instructor for information about accessing the required files.

Instructions: Perform the following tasks:
1. In Word, open the document, Lab 5-3 Mendez Resume, from the Data Files for Students. Look through the resume so that you are familiar with its contents and formats.

2. Save the resume to your SkyDrive account.

3. In Word, invite at least one of your classmates to view your resume document. If requested, include your instructor in the invitation.

4. In Word, get a sharing link for the resume. Email the sharing link to at least one of your classmates. If requested, email the sharing link to your instructor.

5. If your Microsoft account is not connected to an online social network, connect it to one and then, in Word, post your resume document to the connected social network. Submit the posting in the format requested by your instructor.

6. Save the resume as a PDF file. Search for the text, post resume online, using a search engine. Visit several of the job search websites and determine on which one you would like to post a resume. If requested, create an account or profile, fill in the requested information, and then upload the PDF format of the resume (Figure 5–83). Submit the posting in the format requested by your instructor. Delete the posted resume from the job search website.

7. ✿ Which job search websites did you evaluate? Which one did you select to use and why? What would cause the file size of your resume to be too large to upload (post)? How can you reduce the file size?

Continued >

In the Labs *continued*

Figure 5–83

✷ Consider This: Your Turn

Apply your creative thinking and problem solving skills to design and implement a solution.

1: Create a Graduation Invitation and a Calendar

Personal

Part 1: To help organize your appointments and important dates, you use a calendar template. While filling in the calendar, you decide to schedule your graduation party for which you will need to send out invitations. Browse through Word's online templates and download appropriate invitation and calendar templates and then use the text in the next two paragraphs for content. Use the concepts and techniques presented in this chapter to create and format the invitation and calendar. Be sure to check the spelling and grammar of the finished documents. Submit your assignment in the format specified by your instructor.

Calendar information: May 1 – send out graduation party invitations; May 2 – Golf tournament at 3:00 p.m., May 5 – capstone project due, May 7 – internship presentation at 2:00 p.m., May 10 – call mom (Mother's Day); May 11 – Kristina's birthday and Psychology final at 10:00 a.m., May 12 – Literature final term paper due by 11:59 p.m., May 15 – Grandpa's birthday, May 16 – volunteer at Community Center from 6:00 to 9:00 p.m., May 19 – Dentist appointment at 9:00 a.m., May 23 – My Graduation Party! from noon to ?? p.m., May 26 – First day of work!, and May 31 – Mom and Dad's anniversary (28th). If the template requires, insert appropriate clip art or an image of your own. If requested by your instructor, insert a personal event in the calendar.

Invitation information: Congratulations Marianne!; Graduation Party!; Saturday, May 30, Noon - ??; 143 Baker Avenue, Donner Grove, NH; Come hungry!; Bring your swimsuit and towel!; Hope you can join us! If the template requires, insert appropriate clip art or an image of your own. If requested by your instructor, use your name and contact information instead of the information listed here.

Part 2: ✹ You made several decisions while creating the calendar and invitation in this assignment: which template to use, where to position elements, how to format elements, and which graphic(s) to use. What was the rationale behind each of these decisions?

2: Create Business Cards and a Sales Receipt

Professional

Part 1: As a part-time employee at Annika's Flowers, your boss has asked you to create business cards and a sales receipt form. Browse through Word's online templates and download appropriate business cards and sales receipts templates and then use the information in the next two paragraphs for content. Use the concepts and techniques presented in this chapter to create and format the business cards and sales receipt form. Be sure to check the spelling and grammar of the finished documents. Submit your assignment in the format specified by your instructor.

　　Business card information: business name: Annika's Flowers; owner: Annika Lundsteen; address: 76 Main Street, Mitcheltown, DE 19722; phone: 555-907-9400; fax: 555-908-9400; web address: www.annikasflowers.com; email: annika@earth.net; slogan: Celebrating all special occasions! Insert an appropriate clip art or photo on the business card. If requested by your instructor, use your name and contact information instead of the information listed here.

　　Sales receipt information: business name: Annika's Flowers; address: 76 Main Street, Mitcheltown, DE 19722; phone: 555-907-9400; fax: 555-908-9400; web address: www .annikasflowers.com; email: annika@earth.net; slogan: Celebrating all special occasions! Insert an appropriate clip art or photo as the logo on the sales receipt. Sales tax rate is 5.5 percent. Delete all placeholder text that will be handwritten by sales clerks. If requested by your instructor, use your name and contact information instead of the information listed here. Print out the sales receipt form and fill in a sample with this information: customer name: Scarlett Winters; customer address: 882 Elm Street, Micheltown, DE 19722; phone: 555-272-2653; payment method: cash; purchased one vase for $9.99 and a dozen tulips for $4.99.

Part 2: ✹ You made several decisions while creating the business cards and sales receipt in this assignment: which template to use, where to position elements, how to format elements, and which graphic(s) to use. What was the rationale behind each of these decisions?

3: Create a Meeting Agenda, Invoice, and Travel Expense Report

Research and Collaboration

Part 1: As partners in a new business venture, you and two others have been developing documents needed in the business. Documents yet to be created include meeting agenda forms, travel expense report forms, and invoice forms. Form a three-member team to research, create, and fill in sample data for these forms. Decide on a business name, slogan, logo, mailing address, web address, and email address as a group. One team member should design the meeting agenda forms, another should design the travel expense forms, and a third should design the invoice forms using Word's online templates. In addition to the form, each also should create a sample filled-in form.

　　Use the concepts and techniques presented in this chapter to create and format the forms. If requested by your instructor, use team members' names in the forms. Be sure to check the spelling and grammar of the finished forms. Submit your team assignment in the format specified by your instructor.

Part 2: ✹ You made several decisions while creating the forms in this assignment: text to use, graphic(s) to use, which template to use, where to position elements, and how to format elements. What was the rationale behind each of these decisions?

Learn Online

Reinforce what you learned in this chapter with games, exercises, training, and many other online activities and resources.

Student Companion Site Reinforcement activities and resources are available at no additional cost on www.cengagebrain.com. Visit www.cengage.com/ct/studentdownload for detailed instructions about accessing the resources available at the Student Companion Site.

 SAM Put your skills into practice with SAM! If you have a SAM account, go to www.cengage .com/sam2013 to access SAM assignments for this chapter.

6 | Generating Form Letters, Mailing Labels, and a Directory

Microsoft product screen shots used with permission from Microsoft Corporation.

Objectives

You will have mastered the material in this chapter when you can:

- Explain the merge process
- Use the Mail Merge task pane and the MAILINGS tab on the ribbon
- Use a letter template as the main document for a mail merge
- Create and edit a data source
- Insert merge fields in a main document
- Use an IF field in a main document

- Merge form letters
- Select records to merge
- Sort data records
- Address and print mailing labels and envelopes
- Change page orientation
- Merge all data records to a directory
- Convert text to a table

6 | Generating Form Letters, Mailing Labels, and a Directory

Introduction

People are more likely to open and read a personalized letter than a letter addressed as Dear Sir, Dear Madam, or To Whom It May Concern. Creating individual personalized letters, though, can be a time-consuming task. Thus, Word provides the capability of creating a form letter, which is an easy way to generate mass mailings of personalized letters. The basic content of a group of form letters is similar. Items such as name and address, however, vary from one letter to the next. With Word, you easily can address and print mailing labels or envelopes for the form letters.

Project — Form Letters, Mailing Labels, and a Directory

Both businesses and individuals regularly use form letters to communicate with groups of people via the postal service or email. Types of form letter correspondence include announcements of sales to customers, notices of benefits to employees, invitations to the public to participate in a sweepstakes giveaway, and job application letters to potential employers.

The project in this chapter follows generally accepted guidelines for writing form letters and uses Word to create the form letters shown in Figure 6–1. The form letters inform potential employers of your interest in a job opening at their organization. Each form letter states the potential employer's name and address, available job position, and location of the job fair they attended.

To generate form letters, such as the ones shown in Figure 6–1, you create a main document for the form letter (Figure 6–1a), create or specify a data source (Figure 6–1b), and then merge, or **blend**, the main document with the data source to generate a series of individual letters (Figure 6–1c). In Figure 6–1a, the main document represents the portion of the form letter that is repeated from one merged letter to the next. In Figure 6–1b, the data source contains the name, address, available position, and job fair attended for various potential employers. To personalize each letter, you merge the potential employer data in the data source with the main document for the form letter, which generates or prints an individual letter for each potential employer listed in the data source.

Word provides two methods of merging documents: the Mail Merge task pane and the MAILINGS tab on the ribbon. The Mail Merge task pane displays a wizard, which is a step-by-step progression that guides you through the merging process. The MAILINGS tab provides buttons and boxes you use to merge documents. This chapter illustrates both techniques.

If you are using your finger on a touch screen and are having difficulty completing the steps in this chapter, consider using a stylus. Many people find it easier to be precise with a stylus than with a finger. In addition, with a stylus you see the pointer. If you still are having trouble completing the steps with a stylus, try using a mouse.

(a) Main Document for the Form Letter

(b) Data Source

Title	First Name	Last Name	Organization Name	Address Line 1	Address Line 2	City	State	ZIP Code	Position	Job Fair
Mr.	Leo	Moretti	Armour Investigations	224 First Street		Beachcombe	FL	33115	Investigator	Fisher
Detective	Kristina	Cole	Windham City	10 Main Street	P.O. Box 2010	Windham	FL	33223	Associate Investigator	Pontiac
Lieutenant	Adelbert	Ruiz	Delavan County	32 Center Street	Room 4580	Beachcombe	FL	33115	Detective	Fisher
Ms.	Michelle	Stein	Granger Investigative Services	3879 Bailey Avenue		Waterton	FL	33879	Field Investigator	Fisher
Sergeant	Cam	Lin	Waterton Police Department	156 Cedar Lane	P.O. Box 229	Waterton	FL	33879	Investigator	Pontiac

(c) Form Letters

Figure 6–1

Roadmap

In this chapter, you will learn how to create the form letters shown in Figure 6–1 on the previous page. The following roadmap identifies general activities you will perform as you progress through this chapter:

1. IDENTIFY the MAIN DOCUMENT for the form letters.
2. CREATE a DATA SOURCE.
3. COMPOSE the MAIN DOCUMENT for the form letters.
4. MERGE the DATA SOURCE with the main document.
5. ADDRESS the MAILING LABELS.
6. MERGE all data records TO a DIRECTORY.

At the beginning of step instructions throughout the chapter, you will see an abbreviated form of this roadmap. The abbreviated roadmap uses colors to indicate chapter progress: gray means the chapter is beyond that activity, blue means the task being shown is covered in that activity, and black means that activity is yet to be covered. For example, the following abbreviated roadmap indicates the chapter would be showing a task in the 2 CREATE DATA SOURCE activity.

1 IDENTIFY MAIN DOCUMENT | **2 CREATE DATA SOURCE** | 3 COMPOSE MAIN DOCUMENT

4 MERGE DATA SOURCE | 5 ADDRESS MAILING LABELS | 6 MERGE TO DIRECTORY

Use the abbreviated roadmap as a progress guide while you read or step through the instructions in this chapter.

To Run Word and Change Word Settings

One of the few differences between Windows 7 and Windows 8 occurs in the steps to run Word. If you are using Windows 7, click the Start button, type Word in the 'Search programs and files' box, click Word 2013, and then, if necessary, maximize the Word window. For a summary of the steps to run Word in Windows 7, refer to the Quick Reference located at the back of this book.

If you are using a computer to step through the project in this chapter and you want your screens to match the figures in this book, you should change your screen's resolution to 1366 × 768. The following steps run Word, display formatting marks, and change the zoom to page width.

❶ Run Word and create a blank document in the Word window. If necessary, maximize the Word window.

❷ If the Print Layout button on the status bar is not selected, tap or click it so that your screen is in Print Layout view.

❸ If the 'Show/Hide ¶' button (HOME tab | Paragraph group) is not selected already, tap or click it to display formatting marks on the screen.

❹ To display the page the same width as the document window, if necessary, tap or click the Page Width button (VIEW tab | Zoom group).

Identifying the Main Document for Form Letters

The first step in the mail merge process is to identify the type of document you are creating for the main document. Typical installations of Word support five types of main documents: letters, email messages, envelopes, labels, and a directory. In this section of the chapter, you create letters as the main document. Later in this chapter, you will specify labels and a directory as the main document.

How should you create the letter for the main document?

When creating form letters, you either can type the letter for the main document from scratch in a blank document window or use a letter template. If you enter the contents of the main document from scratch, you can compose it according to the block, modified block, or semi-block letter style, formatted appropriately with business letter spacing. Alternatively, you can use a letter template to save time because Word prepares a letter with text and/or formatting common to all letters. Then, you customize the resulting letter by selecting and replacing prewritten text.

To Identify the Main Document for the Form Letter Using the Mail Merge Task Pane

1 IDENTIFY MAIN DOCUMENT | 2 CREATE DATA SOURCE | 3 COMPOSE MAIN DOCUMENT
4 MERGE DATA SOURCE | 5 ADDRESS MAILING LABELS | 6 MERGE TO DIRECTORY

This chapter uses a template for the main document for the form letter, where you select predefined content controls and replace them with personalized content, adjusting formats as necessary. *Why? You use the same style that you used with the resume in the previous chapter so that the two documents complement one another.* The following steps use the Mail Merge task pane to identify the Timeless letter template as the main document for a form letter.

1

- Tap or click MAILINGS on the ribbon to display the MAILINGS tab.

- Tap or click the 'Start Mail Merge' button (MAILINGS tab | Start Mail Merge group) to display the Start Mail Merge menu (Figure 6–2).

Q&A What is the function of the E-mail Messages command?

Instead of sending individual letters, you can send individual email messages using email addresses in the data source or using a Microsoft Outlook Contacts list.

Figure 6–2

2

- Tap or click 'Step-by-Step Mail Merge Wizard' on the Start Mail Merge menu to display Step 1 of the Mail Merge wizard in the Mail Merge task pane (Figure 6–3).

Figure 6–3

❸

- Tap or click the 'Next wizard step' link at the bottom of the Mail Merge task pane to display Step 2 of the Mail Merge wizard, which requests you select a starting document.

- Tap or click 'Start from a template' in the Select starting document area and then tap or click the 'Select mail merge template' link to display the Select Template dialog box.

Q&A

Why does the link name in the step differ from the name displayed in the Mail Merge task pane?

As with buttons and boxes, the text that appears on the screen may vary, depending on your screen resolution. The name that appears in the ScreenTip (when you point to the link), however, never changes. For this reason, this book uses the name that appears in the ScreenTip to identify links, buttons, boxes, and other on-screen elements.

- Tap or click the Letters tab (Select Template dialog box) to display the Letters sheet and then tap or click Timeless letter, which shows a preview of the selected template in the Preview area (Figure 6–4).

Figure 6–4

🔑 Experiment

- Tap or click various Letter templates in the Letters sheet and watch the preview change in the right pane of the dialog box. When you are finished experimenting, tap or click the Timeless letter template to select it.

Q&A

What if I cannot locate the Timeless letter template?

Skip the remainder of these steps and proceed to the steps called To Start a Mail Merge from an Existing Document that are shaded yellow at the top of the next page.

❹

- Tap or click the OK button to display a letter in the document window that is based on the Timeless letter template (Figure 6–5).

Q&A

Can I close the Mail Merge task pane?

Yes, you can close the Mail Merge task pane at any time by tapping or clicking its Close button. When you want to continue with the merge process, you repeat these steps and Word will resume the merge process at the correct step in the Mail Merge wizard.

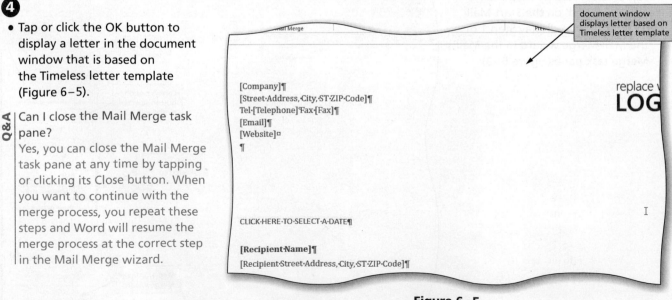

Figure 6–5

Other Ways

1. Open Backstage view, tap or click New, type `letters` in the 'Search for online templates' box, tap or click Start searching button, tap or click desired letter template, tap or click Create button

To Start a Mail Merge from an Existing Document

If you are unable to locate the Timeless letter template in the previous steps, you can open it from the Data Files for Students. Visit www.cengage.com/ct/studentdownload for detailed instructions or contact your instructor for information about accessing the required files. The following steps open a document. NOTE: PERFORM THE STEPS IN THIS YELLOW BOX ONLY IF YOU WERE UNABLE TO LOCATE THE TIMELESS LETTER TEMPLATE IN THE PREVIOUS STEPS.

1 Tap or click the 'Start from existing document' link in the Mail Merge task pane to display options for opening a document In the task pane.

2 Tap or click the Open button that appears in the Mail Merge task pane to display the Open dialog box.

3 Navigate to the location of the Timeless letter file to be opened (in this case, the Chapter 6 folder in the Word folder in the Data Files for Students folder).

4 Tap or click the Open button (Open dialog box) to open the file.

To Print the Document

The next step is to print the letter that Word generated, which is based on the Timeless letter template, so that you easily can see the entire letter contents.

1 Ready the printer. Open the Backstage view and then tap or click the Print tab. If necessary, select the desired printer, and then tap or click the Print button to print the document (Figure 6–6).

Q&A

What are the content controls in the document? Recall that a content control contains instructions for filling in areas of the document. To select a content control, tap or click it. Later in this chapter, you will personalize the content controls.

Why is Windows User displayed in the signature block? Word places the user name associated with your copy of Microsoft Word as the sender name. Windows User is the user name associated with this copy of Word.

BTW

Conserving Ink and Toner

If you want to conserve ink or toner, you can instruct Word to print draft quality documents by tapping or clicking FILE on the ribbon to open the Backstage view, tapping or clicking Options in the Backstage view to display the Word Options dialog box, tapping or clicking Advanced in the left pane (Word Options dialog box), sliding or scrolling to the Print area in the right pane, placing a check mark in the 'Use draft quality' check box, and then tapping or clicking the OK button. Then, use the Backstage view to print the document as usual.

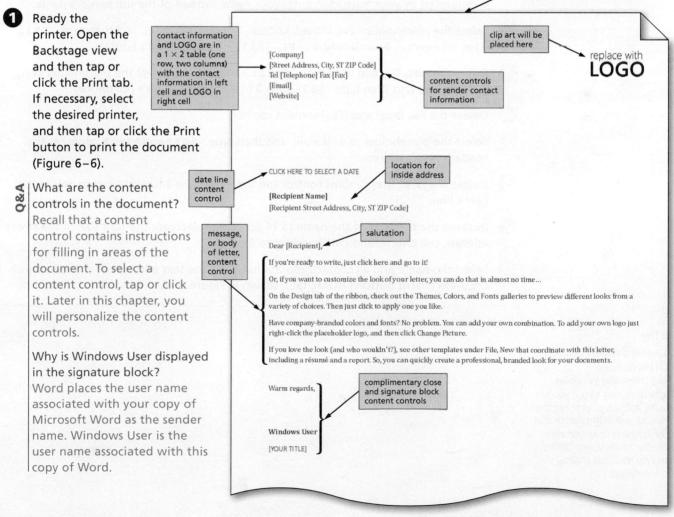

Figure 6–6

To Change the User Name and Initials

If you wanted to change the user name and initials associated with your copy of Microsoft Word, you would perform the following steps.

1. Open the Backstage view and then tap or click Options to display the Word Options dialog box.
2. If necessary, tap or click General in the left pane (Word Options dialog box).
3. Enter your name in the User name text box.
4. Enter your initials in the Initials text box.
5. Tap or click the OK button.

To Enter and Format the Sender Information

The next step is to enter the sender's contact information at the top of the letter. You will use the Company content control for the sender's name. You will delete the Fax and Website content controls because this sender does not have a fax or website. Then, you will change the font size of the text and indent the paragraphs one-half inch. The following steps enter and format the sender information.

1 Select the placeholder text, [Company], and then type **Jordan Taylor Green** as the sender name.
If requested by your instructor, enter your name instead of the job seeker's name.

2 Select the placeholder text, [Street Address, City, ST ZIP Code], and then type **1931 Elm Street, Beachcombe, FL 33115** as the sender's address.

3 Select the text, Tel, and then type **Cell:** as the label. Select the placeholder text, [Telephone], and then type **583-555-2772** as the sender's cell phone.

4 Delete the Fax label and [Fax] content control.

5 Select the placeholder text, [Email], and then type **jgreen@earth.com** as the sender's email address.

6 Delete the [Website] content control and then press the BACKSPACE key to delete the blank line.

7 Increase the font size of the name to 14 point, and decrease the font size of the street address, cell phone, and email address to 9 point.

8 Select the name and all contact information. Bold the text and indent it one-half inch (Increase Indent button | HOME tab), shown in Figure 6–7.

BTW
Touch Screen Differences
The Office and Windows interfaces may vary if you are using a touch screen. For this reason, you might notice that the function or appearance of your touch screen differs slightly from this chapter's presentation.

To Change a Picture and Format It

The current picture in the letter contains the text, replace the LOGO, which is a placeholder for a picture. The following steps change a picture.

1 Press and hold and then tap the 'Show Context Menu' button on the mini toolbar or right-click the picture to be changed (in this case, the picture placeholder with the text, replace the LOGO) to display a shortcut menu (Figure 6–7).

2 Tap or click Change Picture on the shortcut menu to display the Insert Pictures dialog box.

Q&A Can I use the Change Picture button (PICTURE TOOLS FORMAT tab | Adjust group) instead of the shortcut menu to display the Insert Pictures dialog box?
Yes.

3 Type **scales of justice** in the Office.com Clip Art Search box (Insert Pictures dialog box) and then tap or click the Search button to display a list of clip art that matches the entered search text.

4 Scroll through the list of clip art to locate the one shown in Figure 6–8 (or a similar image), tap or click the clip art to select it, and then tap or click the Insert button (Office.com Clip Art dialog box) to download the image, close the dialog box, and replace the selected placeholder with the new picture file (shown in Figure 6–8 on the next page).

Q&A What if I cannot locate the same clip art?
Tap or click the Cancel button and then tap or click the Browse button (Insert Pictures dialog box), navigate to the scales of justice file on the Data Files for Students, and then tap or click the Insert button (Insert Picture dialog box) to insert the picture.

5 Use the Shape Height and Shape Width boxes (PICTURE TOOLS FORMAT tab | Size group) to change the picture height to .75" and width to .8", respectively.

Tap or click the Center button (HOME tab | Paragraph group) to center the picture in the cell.

Q&A Why center the picture?
Currently, the picture is right-aligned in the cell. To balance the indent of the contact information, you center the picture.

BTW
The Ribbon and Screen Resolution
Word may change how the groups and buttons within the groups appear on the ribbon, depending on the computer's screen resolution. Thus, your ribbon may look different from the ones in this book if you are using a screen resolution other than 1366 × 768.

Figure 6–7

To Shade Cells and a Shape

In the letter in this chapter, the left and right cells of the table containing the contact information and picture are shaded different colors. The one-row table is contained in a rectangular shape that extends below the table. By shading the shape a different color, you create a letterhead with three different colors. The following steps shade table cells and a shape.

BTW

Q&As

For a complete list of the Q&As found in many of the step-by-step sequences in this book, visit the Q&A resource on the Student Companion Site located on www.cengagebrain.com. For detailed instructions about accessing available resources, visit www.cengage.com/ct/studentdownload or contact your instructor for information about accessing the required files.

1 Position the insertion point in the contact information (left cell of the one-row table). Display the TABLE TOOLS LAYOUT tab and then, if necessary, tap or click the 'View Table Gridlines' button (TABLE TOOLS LAYOUT tab | Table group) to show table gridlines.

Q&A | Why show table gridlines?
With table gridlines showing, the cells are easier to see.

2 Display the TABLE TOOLS DESIGN tab. With the insertion point in the left cell, tap or click the Shading arrow (TABLE TOOLS DESIGN tab | Table Styles group) and then tap or click 'Blue-Gray, Accent 1' (fifth color, first row) to shade the current cell with the selected color.

3 Select the contact information in the left cell and change its font color to 'White, Background 1' (first color, first row).

4 Position the insertion point in the cell with the picture, tap or click the Shading arrow (TABLE TOOLS DESIGN tab | Table Styles group) and then tap or click 'Brown, Accent 3, Lighter 80%' (seventh color, second row) to shade the current cell with the selected color.

5 Position the insertion point on the paragraph mark below the table to select the rectangle drawing object. Display the DRAWING TOOLS FORMAT tab. Tap or click the Shape Fill arrow (DRAWING TOOLS FORMAT tab | Shape Styles group) to display the Shape Fill gallery (Figure 6–8) and then tap or click 'Tan, Accent 2, Darker 25%' (sixth color, fifth row) to shade the selected shape with the selected color.

6 Hide table gridlines.

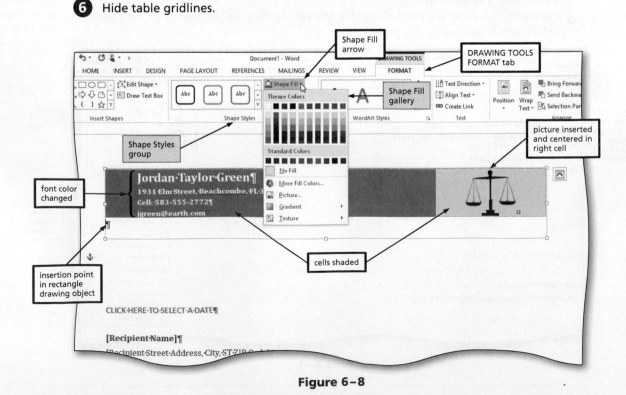

Figure 6–8

To Change Spacing above and below Paragraphs and Margin Settings

You would like to increase the space below the email address slightly, and decrease the space above the date line. Also, the Timeless letter template uses 0.9-inch top and .75-inch bottom, left, and right margins. You want the form letter to use 1-inch top and bottom margins and 1.25-inch left and right margins. The following steps change paragraph and margin settings.

1 Position the insertion point in the email address. Display the PAGE LAYOUT tab. Adjust the Spacing After box to 2 pt (PAGE LAYOUT tab | Paragraph group).

2 Tap or click the Date content control to select it. Adjust the Spacing Before box to 36 pt (PAGE LAYOUT tab | Paragraph group)

3 Tap or click the Adjust Margins button (PAGE LAYOUT tab | Page Setup group) to display the Margins gallery and then tap or click Custom Margins to display the Page Setup dialog box.

4 Change the values in the Top, Bottom, Left, and Right boxes (Page Setup dialog box) to 1", 1", 1.25", and 1.25", respectively (Figure 6–9).

5 Tap or click the OK button to change the margin values.

Q&A Why is the top margin unchanged?
The template specifies that the rectangle shape be positioned a certain distance from the top of the page, regardless of margin settings. The next steps change the position of the shape.

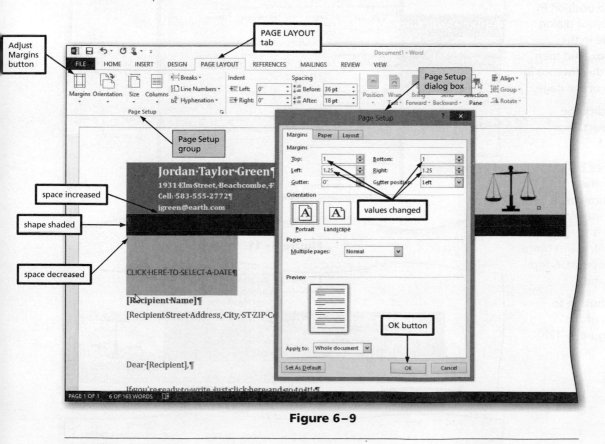

Figure 6–9

To Specify the Position of a Graphic

The next step is to change the distance between the shape and the top of the page. *Why? You want a one-inch space above the shape.* The following steps specify the position of a graphic.

1

• Tap or click the rectangle shape to select it.

• Tap or click the Layout Options button attached to the shape to display the Layout Options gallery (Figure 6–10).

Figure 6–10

2

• Tap or click the See more link (Layout Options gallery) to display the Position tab in the Layout dialog box.

• Tap or click Absolute position in the Vertical area (Layout dialog box), select the value in the Absolute position box, and then type 1 to specify the distance in inches from the top of the page.

• If necessary, tap or click the below arrow and select Page (Figure 6–11).

Q&A

What is the difference between the specifications in the Horizontal and Vertical areas? Horizontal settings specify the graphic's position left to right on the page, whereas vertical settings specify the graphic's position top to bottom on the page.

• Tap or click the OK button to change the position of the selected graphic (Figure 6–12).

Figure 6–11

Figure 6–12

To Create a Folder while Saving

You have performed several tasks while creating this project and, thus, should save it. The following steps assume you already have created folders for storing files, for example, a CIS 101 folder (for your class) that contains a Word folder and chapter folders. You want to save this and all other documents created in this chapter in a folder called Job Hunting in the Word folder. The following steps create a folder during the process of saving a document. *Why? This folder does not exist, so you must create it. Rather than creating the folder in Windows, you can create folders in Word.*

1

- Tap or click the Save button on the Quick Access Toolbar, which depending on settings, will display either the Save As gallery in the Backstage view or the Save As dialog box. If necessary, select the save location (i.e., Computer or SkyDrive) and then tap or click the Browse button to display the Save As dialog box associated with the selected save location.

- Type **Green Cover Letter** in the File name box (Save As dialog box) to change the file name. Do not press the ENTER key after typing the file name because you do not want to close the dialog box at this time.

- Navigate to the desired save location for the new folder (in this case, the Word folder in the CIS 101 folder [or your class folder]).

- Tap or click the 'Create a new folder' button to display a new folder icon with the name, New folder, selected in the dialog box (Figure 6–13).

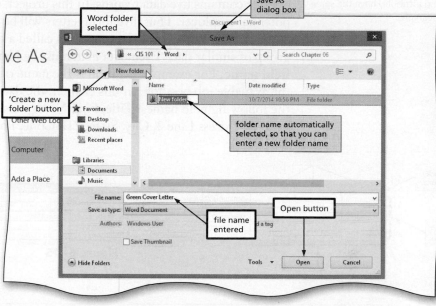

Figure 6–13

2

- Type **Job Hunting** as the new folder name and then press the ENTER key to create the new folder.

- Tap or click the Open button to open the selected folder, in this case, the Job Hunting folder (Figure 6–14).

3

- Tap or click the Save button (Save As dialog box) to save the current document in the selected folder on the selected drive.

Q&A

Can I create a folder in any other dialog box?

Yes. Any dialog box that displays a File list, such as the Open and Insert File dialog boxes, also has the 'Create a new folder' button, allowing you to create a new folder in Word instead of using Windows for this task.

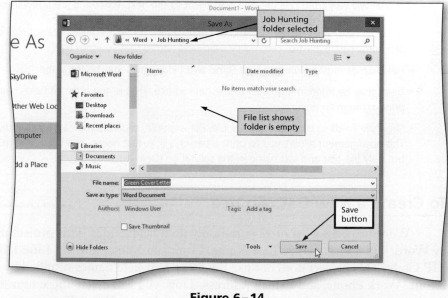

Figure 6–14

Creating a Data Source

The **data source** is a file that contains the variable, or changing, values from one merged document to the next. A data source can be an Access database table, an Outlook contacts list, or an Excel worksheet. If the necessary and properly organized data already exists in one of these Office programs, you can instruct Word to use the existing file as the data source for the mail merge. Otherwise, you can create a new data source using one of these programs.

As shown in Figure 6–15, a data source often is shown as a table that consists of a series of rows and columns. Each row is called a **record**. The first row of a data source is called the **header record** because it identifies the name of each column. Each row below the header row is called a **data record**. Data records contain the text that varies in each occurrence of the merged document. The data source for the project in this chapter contains five data records. In this project, each data record identifies a different potential employer. Thus, five form letters will be generated from this data source.

Each column in the data source is called a **data field**. A data field represents a group of similar data. Each data field must be identified uniquely with a name, called a **field name**. For example, Position is the name of the data field (column) that contains the available job position. In this chapter, the data source contains 11 data fields with the following field names: Title, First Name, Last Name, Organization Name, Address Line 1, Address Line 2, City, State, ZIP Code, Position, and Job Fair.

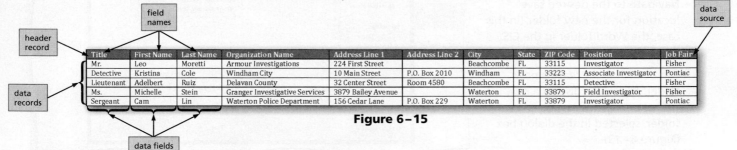

Title	First Name	Last Name	Organization Name	Address Line 1	Address Line 2	City	State	ZIP Code	Position	Job Fair
Mr.	Leo	Moretti	Armour Investigations	224 First Street		Beachcombe	FL	33115	Investigator	Fisher
Detective	Kristina	Cole	Windham City	10 Main Street	P.O. Box 2010	Windham	FL	33223	Associate Investigator	Pontiac
Lieutenant	Adelbert	Ruiz	Delavan County	32 Center Street	Room 4580	Beachcombe	FL	33115	Detective	Fisher
Ms.	Michelle	Stein	Granger Investigative Services	3879 Bailey Avenue		Waterton	FL	33879	Field Investigator	Fisher
Sergeant	Cam	Lin	Waterton Police Department	156 Cedar Lane	P.O. Box 229	Waterton	FL	33879	Investigator	Pontiac

Figure 6–15

CONSIDER THIS

What guidelines should you follow when creating a data source?
When you create a data source, you will need to determine the fields it should contain. That is, you will need to identify the data that will vary from one merged document to the next. Following are a few important points about fields:

- For each field, you may be required to create a field name. Because data sources often contain the same fields, some programs create a list of commonly used field names that you may use.

- Field names must be unique; that is, no two field names may be the same.

- Fields may be listed in any order in the data source. That is, the order of fields has no effect on the order in which they will print in the main document.

- Organize fields so that they are flexible. For example, separate the name into individual fields: title, first name, and last name. This arrangement allows you to print a person's title, first name, and last name (e.g., Mr. Leo Moretti) in the inside address but only the title and last name in the salutation (Dear Mr. Moretti).

To Create a New Data Source

1 IDENTIFY MAIN DOCUMENT | **2 CREATE DATA SOURCE** | 3 COMPOSE MAIN DOCUMENT
4 MERGE DATA SOURCE | 5 ADDRESS MAILING LABELS | 6 MERGE TO DIRECTORY

Word provides a list of 13 commonly used field names. This project uses 9 of the 13 field names supplied by Word: Title, First Name, Last Name, Company Name, Address Line 1, Address Line 2, City, State, and ZIP Code. This project does not use the other four field names supplied by Word: Country or Region, Home Phone, Work Phone, and E-mail Address. Thus, you will delete these four field names. Then, you will change the Company Name field name to Organization Name. *Why? The term, organization, better describes the potential employers in this project.* You also will add two new field names (Position and Job Fair) to the data source. *Why? You want to reference the available position, as well as the job fair at which you met with the potential employer.* The next steps create a new data source for a mail merge.

1

• Tap or click the 'Next wizard step' link at the bottom of the Mail Merge task pane (shown in Figure 6–12 on page WD 348) to display Step 3 of the Mail Merge wizard, which requests you select recipients.

• Tap or click 'Type a new list' in the Select recipients area, which displays the Type a new list area.

• Tap or click the 'Create new recipient list' link to display the New Address List dialog box (Figure 6–16).

Q&A When would I use the other two option buttons in the Select recipients area?

If a data source already was created, you would use the first option: Use an existing list. If you wanted to use your Outlook contacts list as the data source, you would choose the second option.

Figure 6–16

2

• Tap or click the Customize Columns button (New Address List dialog box) to display the Customize Address List dialog box (Figure 6–17).

Figure 6–17

3

• Tap or click 'Country or Region' in the Field Names list (Customize Address List dialog box) to select the field to be deleted and then tap or click the Delete button to display a dialog box asking if you are sure you want to delete the selected field (Figure 6–18).

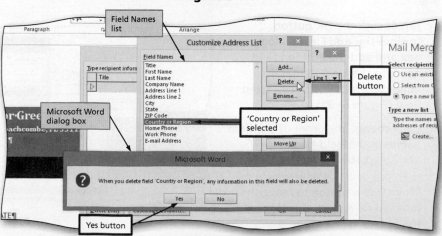

Figure 6–18

4

- Tap or click the Yes button (Microsoft Word dialog box) to delete the field.

- Tap or click Home Phone in the Field Names list to select the field. Tap or click the Delete button (Customize Address List dialog box) and then tap or click the Yes button (Microsoft Word dialog box) to delete the field.

- Use this same procedure to delete the Work Phone and E-mail Address fields.

5

- Tap or click Company Name in the Field Names list to select the field to be renamed.

- Tap or click the Rename button to display the Rename Field dialog box.

- Type **Organization Name** in the To text box (Rename Field dialog box) (Figure 6–19).

6

- Tap or click the OK button to close the Rename Field dialog box and rename the selected field.

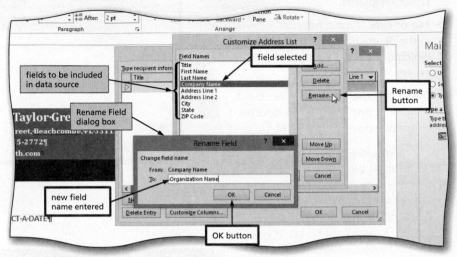

Figure 6–19

7

- Tap or click the Add button to display the Add Field dialog box.

- Type **Position** in the 'Type a name for your field' text box (Add Field dialog box) (Figure 6–20).

Figure 6–20

8

- Tap or click the OK button to close the Add Field dialog box and add the Position field name to the Field Names list immediately below the selected field (Figure 6–21).

Q&A Can I change the order of the field names in the Field Names list?
Yes. Select the field name and then tap or click the Move Up or Move Down button to move the selected field in the direction of the button name.

Figure 6–21

9

- With the Position field selected, tap or click the Move Down button five times to position the selected field at the end of the Field Names list.

- Tap or click the Add button to display the Add Field dialog box.

- Type `Job Fair` (Add Field dialog box) in the 'Type a name for your field' text box and then tap or click the OK button to close the Add Field dialog box and add the Job Fair field name to the bottom of the Field Names list (Figure 6–22).

Q&A Could I add more field names to the list?

Yes. You would tap or click the Add button for each field name you want to add.

Figure 6–22

10

- Tap or click the OK button to close the Customize Address List dialog box, which positions the insertion point in the Title text box for the first record (row) in the New Address List dialog box (Figure 6–23).

Figure 6–23

11

- Type `Mr.` and then press the TAB key to enter the title for the first data record.

- Type `Leo` and then press the TAB key to enter the first name.

- Type `Moretti` and then press the TAB key to enter the last name.

- Type `Armour Investigations` and then press the TAB key to enter the organization name.

- Type `224 First Street` to enter the first address line (Figure 6–24).

Q&A What if I notice an error in an entry?

Tap or click the entry and then correct the error as you would in the document window.

What happened to the rest of the Organization Name entry?

It is stored in the field, but you cannot see the entire entry because it is longer than the display area.

Figure 6–24

⓬

- Press the TAB key twice to leave the second address line empty.

- Type **Beachcombe** and then press the TAB key to enter the city.

- Type **FL** and then press the TAB key to enter the state code.

- Type **33115** and then press the TAB key to enter the ZIP code.

- Type **Investigator** and then press the TAB key to enter the Position.

- Type **Fisher** to enter the job fair (Figure 6–25).

Figure 6–25

⓭

- Press the TAB key to add a new blank record and position the insertion point in the Title field of the new record (Figure 6–26).

Figure 6–26

Other Ways

1. Tap or click Select Recipients button (MAILINGS tab | Start Mail Merge group)

To Enter More Records

The following steps enter the remaining four records in the New Address List dialog box.

❶ Type **Detective** and then press the TAB key. Type **Kristina** and then press the TAB key. Type **Cole** and then press the TAB key. Type **Windham City** and then press the TAB key.

❷ Type **10 Main Street** and then press the TAB key. Type **P.O. Box 2010** and then press the TAB key.

❸ Type **Windham** and then press the TAB key. Type **FL** and then press the TAB key. Type **33223** and then press the TAB key.

❹ Type **Associate Investigator** and then press the TAB key. Type **Pontiac** and then press the TAB key.

Q&A Instead of pressing the TAB key, can I tap or click the New Entry button at the end of one row to add a new blank record?

Yes. Tapping or clicking the New Entry button at the end of a row has the same effect as pressing the TAB key.

5 Type `Lieutenant` and then press the TAB key. Type `Adelbert` and then press the TAB key. Type `Ruiz` and then press the TAB key. Type `Delavan County` and then press the TAB key.

6 Type `32 Center Street` and then press the TAB key. Type `Room 4580` and then press the TAB key.

7 Type `Beachcombe` and then press the TAB key. Type `FL` and then press the TAB key. Type `33115` and then press the TAB key.

8 Type `Detective` and then press the TAB key. Type `Fisher` and then press the TAB key.

9 Type `Ms.` and then press the TAB key. Type `Michelle` and then press the TAB key. Type `Stein` and then press the TAB key. Type `Granger Investigative Services` and then press the TAB key.

10 Type `3879 Bailey Avenue` and then press the TAB key twice. Type `Waterton` and then press the TAB key. Type `FL` and then press the TAB key. Type `33879` and then press the TAB key.

11 Type `Field Investigator` and then press the TAB key. Type `Fisher` and then press the TAB key.

12 Type `Sergeant` and then press the TAB key. Type `Cam` and then press the TAB key. Type `Lin` and then press the TAB key. Type `Waterton Police Department` and then press the TAB key.

13 Type `156 Cedar Lane` and then press the TAB key. Type `P.O. Box 229` and then press the TAB key.

14 Type `Waterton` and then press the TAB key. Type `FL` and then press the TAB key. Type `33879` and then press the TAB key.

15 Type `Investigator` and then press the TAB key. Type `Pontiac` and then tap or click the OK button (shown in Figure 6–26), which displays the Save Address List dialog box (shown in Figure 6–27).

To Save a Data Source when Prompted by Word

1 IDENTIFY MAIN DOCUMENT | 2 CREATE DATA SOURCE | 3 COMPOSE MAIN DOCUMENT
4 MERGE DATA SOURCE | 5 ADDRESS MAILING LABELS | 6 MERGE TO DIRECTORY

When you tap or click the OK button in the New Address List dialog box, Word displays the Save Address List dialog box. *Why? You immediately save the data source so that you do not lose any entered information.* By default, the save location is the My Data Sources folder on your computer's hard drive. In this chapter, you save the data source to the Job Hunting folder created earlier in this chapter. The following steps save the data source.

1

• Type `Green Prospective Employers` in the File name box (Save Address List dialog box) as the name for the data source. Do not press the ENTER key after typing the file name because you do not want to close the dialog box at this time.

• Navigate to the desired save location for the data source (for example, the Job Hunting folder in the Word folder in the CIS 101 folder [or your class folder]) (Figure 6–27).

Figure 6–27

Q&A What is a Microsoft Office Address Lists file type?

It is a Microsoft Access database file. If you are familiar with Microsoft Access, you can open the Green Prospective Employers file in Access. You do not have to be familiar with Access or have Access installed on your computer, however, to continue with this mail merge process. Word simply stores a data source as an Access table because it is an efficient method of storing a data source.

2

• Tap or click the Save button (Save Address List dialog box) to save the data source in the selected folder using the entered file name and then display the Mail Merge Recipients dialog box (Figure 6–28).

Q&A What if the fields in my Mail Merge Recipients list are in a different order?

The order of fields in the Mail Merge Recipients list has no effect on the mail merge process. If Word rearranges the order, you can leave them in the revised order.

3

• Tap or click the OK button to close the Mail Merge Recipients dialog box.

Figure 6–28

Editing Records in the Data Source

All of the data records have been entered in the data source and saved with the file name, Green Prospective Employers. To add or edit data records in the data source, you would tap or click the 'Edit Recipient List' button (MAILINGS tab | Start Mail Merge group) to display the Mail Merge Recipients dialog box (shown in Figure 6–28). Tap or click the data source name in the Data Source list and then tap or click the Edit button (Mail Merge Recipients dialog box) to display the data records in a dialog box similar to the one shown in Figure 6–26 on page WD 354. Then, add or edit records as described in the previous steps. If you want to edit a particular record and the list of data records is long, you can tap or click the Find button to locate an item, such as a last name, quickly in the list.

To delete a record, select it using the same procedure described in the previous paragraph. Then, tap or click the Delete Entry button in the dialog box (Figure 6–26).

Using an Existing Data Source

Instead of creating a new data source, you can use an existing Microsoft Outlook Contacts list, an Access database table, an Excel table, or a Word table as a data source in a mail merge. To use an existing data source, select the appropriate option in the Select recipients area in the Mail Merge task pane or tap or click the Select Recipients button (MAILINGS tab | Start Mail Merge group) and then tap or click the desired option on the Select Recipients menu.

For a Microsoft Outlook Contacts list, tap or click 'Select from Outlook contacts' in the Mail Merge task pane or 'Choose from Outlook Contacts' on the Select Recipients menu to display the Select Contacts dialog box. Next, select the contact folder you wish to import (Select Contacts dialog box) and then tap or click the OK button.

For other existing data source types such as an Access database table, an Excel worksheet, or a Word table, tap or click 'Use an existing list' in the Mail Merge task pane or on the Select Recipients menu to display the Select Data Source dialog box. Next, select the file name of the data source you wish to use and then tap or click the Open button.

With Access, you can use any field in the database in the main document. (Later in this chapter you use an existing Access database table as the data source.) For the merge to work correctly with an Excel table or a Word table, you must ensure data is arranged properly and that the table is the only element in the file. The first row of the table should contain unique field names, and the table cannot contain any blank rows.

BTW
BTWs
For a complete list of the BTWs found in the margins of this book, visit the BTW resource on the Student Companion Site located on www.cengagebrain.com. For detailed instructions about accessing available resources, visit www.cengage.com/ct/studentdownload or contact your instructor for information about accessing the required files.

Composing the Main Document for the Form Letters

The next step in this project is to enter and format the text and fields in the main document for the form letters (shown in Figure 6–1a on page WD 339). A **main document** contains the constant, or unchanging, text, punctuation, spaces, and graphics, as well as references to the data in the data source. You will follow these steps to compose the main document for the form letter.

1. Enter the date.
2. Enter the address block.
3. Enter the greeting line (salutation).
4. Enter text and insert a merge field.
5. Insert an IF field.
6. Enter the remainder of the text and merge fields.
7. Merge the letters.

What guidelines should you follow when composing the main document for a form letter?
The finished main document letter should look like a symmetrically framed picture with evenly spaced margins, all balanced below an attractive letterhead or return address. The content of the main document for the form letter should contain proper grammar, correct spelling, logically constructed sentences, flowing paragraphs, and sound ideas; it also should reference the data in the data source properly.

Be sure the main document for the form letter includes all essential business letter elements. All business letters should contain a date line, inside address, message, and signature block. Many business letters contain additional items such as a special mailing notation(s), an attention line, a salutation, a subject line, a complimentary close, reference initials, and an enclosure notation. When finished, proofread your letter carefully.

CONSIDER THIS

To Display the Next Step in the Mail Merge Wizard

The following step displays the next step in the Mail Merge wizard, which is to write the letter.

 Tap or click the 'Next wizard step' link at the bottom of the Mail Merge task pane (shown in Figure 6–28) to display Step 4 of the Mail Merge wizard in the Mail Merge task pane (shown in Figure 6–29 on the next page).

To Enter the Date

The next step is to enter the date in the letter. *Why? All business letters should contain a date, which usually is positioned below the letterhead or return address.* You can tap or click the date content control and type the correct date, or you can tap or click the arrow and select the date from a calendar. The following steps use the calendar to select the date.

1
- Tap or click the Date content control to select it and then tap or click its arrow to display a calendar.
- Scroll through the calendar months until the desired month appears, October, 2014, in this case (Figure 6–29).

2
- Tap or click 7 in the calendar to display the selected month, day, and year in the date line of the form letter (shown in Figure 6–30).
- Tap or click outside the content control to deselect it.

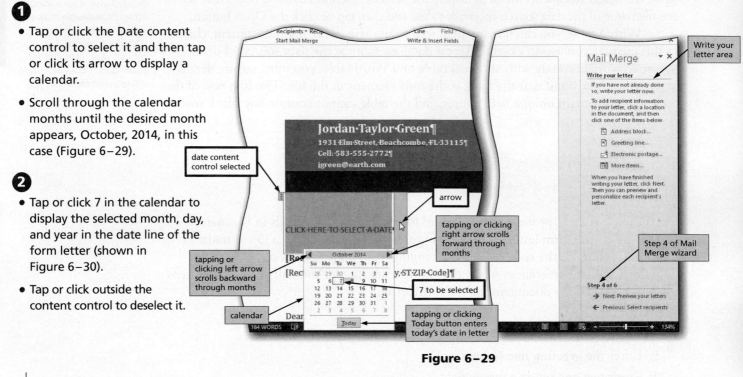

Figure 6–29

Other Ways

1. Type date in Date content control	2. Tap or click 'Insert Date & Time' button (INSERT tab | Text group)

Merge Fields

In this form letter, the inside address appears below the date line, and the salutation is placed below the inside address. The contents of the inside address and salutation are located in the data source. To link the data source to the main document, you insert the field names from the data source in the main document.

In the main document, field names linked to the data source are called **merge fields** because they merge, or combine, the main document with the contents of the data source. When a merge field is inserted in the main document, Word surrounds the field name with **merge field characters**, which are chevrons (« ») that mark the beginning and ending of a merge field. Merge field characters are not on the keyboard; therefore, you cannot type them directly in the document. Word automatically displays them when a merge field is inserted in the main document.

Most letters contain an address and salutation. For this reason, Word provides an AddressBlock merge field and a GreetingLine merge field. The **AddressBlock merge field** contains several fields related to an address: Title, First Name, Middle Name, Last Name, Suffix, Company, Street Address 1, Street Address 2, City, State, and ZIP Code. When Word uses the AddressBlock merge field, it automatically looks for any fields in the associated data source that are related to an address and then formats the address block properly when you merge the data source with the main document. For example, if your inside address does not use a middle name, suffix, or company, Word omits these items from the inside address and adjusts the spacing so that the address prints correctly.

To Insert the AddressBlock Merge Field

The default format for the AddressBlock merge field is the first name and last name on one line, followed by the street address on the next line, and then the city, state, and postal code on the next line. In this letter, you want the potential employer's title (i.e., Ms.) to appear to the left of the first name. **Why?** *You want to address the potential employers formally.* You also want the organization name to appear above the street address, if it does not already. The following steps insert the AddressBlock merge field in this format.

1

- Delete the content control that contains placeholder text for the recipient's address and then press the DELETE key to delete the blank paragraph.

- Delete the [Recipient Name] placeholder text but leave the paragraph mark; position the insertion point to the left of the paragraph mark because you will insert the AddressBlock merge field in that location.

- Tap or click the 'Insert formatted address' link in the Mail Merge task pane to display the Insert Address Block dialog box.

- Scroll through the list of recipient name formats (Insert Address Block dialog box) and then tap or click the format, Mr. Joshua Randall Jr., in this list, because that format places the title to the left of the first name and last name (Figure 6–30).

Experiment

- Tap or click various recipient name formats and watch the preview change in the dialog box. When finished experimenting, tap or click the format: Mr. Joshua Randall Jr.

- If necessary, tap or click the 'Insert company name' check box to select it, and notice the preview area shows the organization name in the sample formatted address (Figure 6–30).

Q&A
Why is my 'Insert company name' check box dimmed?
If your data source does not have a match to the Company Name in the AddressBlock merge field, this check box will be dimmed. Recall that earlier in this project the Company Name field was renamed as Organization Name, which may cause the fields to be unmatched. The next step shows how to match the fields.

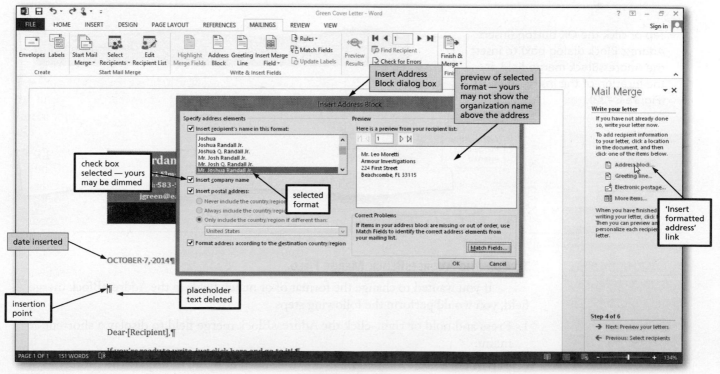

Figure 6–30

2

- If your AddressBlock merge field does not show the Organization Name above the address or if your 'Insert company name' check box is dimmed, tap or click the Match Fields button (Insert Address Block dialog box) to display the Match Fields dialog box; if the Organization Name already appears in your AddressBlock merge field, proceed to Step 4.

- If necessary, scroll through the Match Fields dialog box until Company appears.

- Tap or click the Company arrow (Match Fields dialog box) to display a list of fields in the data source and then tap or click Organization Name to place that selected field as the match field (Figure 6–31).

Figure 6–31

3

- Tap or click the OK button (Match Fields dialog box) to close the dialog box, and notice the 'Insert company name' check box no longer is dimmed because the Company field now has a matched field in the data source.

- If necessary, tap or click the 'Insert company name' check box to select it, and notice the preview area shows the organization name in the sample formatted address.

4

- Tap or click the OK button (Insert Address Block dialog box) to insert the AddressBlock merge field at the location of the insertion point (Figure 6–32).

OCTOBER·7,·2014¶

«AddressBlock»¶

Dear·[Recipient],¶

Figure 6–32

TO EDIT THE ADDRESSBLOCK MERGE FIELD

If you wanted to change the format of or match fields in the AddressBlock merge field, you would perform the following steps.

1. Press and hold or right-click the AddressBlock merge field to display a shortcut menu.

2. Tap or click 'Edit Address Block' on the shortcut menu to display the Modify Address Block dialog box.

3. Make necessary changes and then tap or click the OK button (Modify Address Block dialog box).

To View Merged Data in the Main Document

1 IDENTIFY MAIN DOCUMENT | 2 CREATE DATA SOURCE | 3 COMPOSE MAIN DOCUMENT
4 MERGE DATA SOURCE | 5 ADDRESS MAILING LABELS | 6 MERGE TO DIRECTORY

Instead of displaying merge fields, you can display merged data. *Why? One way to see how fields, such as the AddressBlock fields, will look in the merged letter, is to view merged data.* The following step views merged data.

1

- Tap or click the 'View Merged Data' button (MAILINGS tab | Preview Results group) to display the values in the current data record, instead of the merge fields (Figure 6–33).

Q&A How can I tell which record is showing?
The current record number is displayed in the Preview Results group.

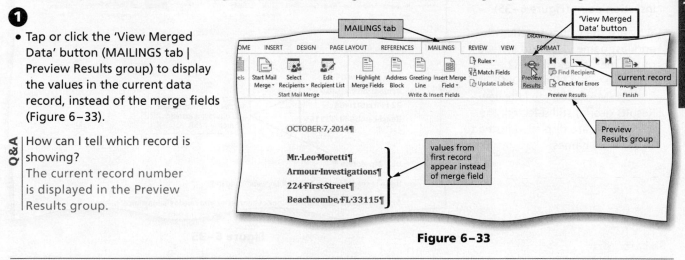

Figure 6–33

To Insert the GreetingLine Merge Field

1 IDENTIFY MAIN DOCUMENT | 2 CREATE DATA SOURCE | 3 COMPOSE MAIN DOCUMENT
4 MERGE DATA SOURCE | 5 ADDRESS MAILING LABELS | 6 MERGE TO DIRECTORY

The **GreetingLine merge field** contains text and fields related to a salutation. The default greeting for the salutation is in the format, Dear Leo, followed by a comma. In this letter, you want the salutation to be followed by a colon. *Why? Business letters use a more formal salutation (Dear Mr. Moretti:) in the cover letter.* The following steps insert the GreetingLine merge field.

1

- Delete the word, Dear, the [Recipient] placeholder text, and the comma in the salutation but leave the paragraph mark; position the insertion point to the left of the paragraph mark because you will insert the GreetingLine merge field in that location.

- Tap or click the 'Insert formatted salutation' link in the Mail Merge task pane to display the Insert Greeting Line dialog box.

- If necessary, tap or click the middle arrow in the Greeting line format area (Insert Greeting Line dialog box); scroll to and then tap or click the format, Mr. Randall, in this list because you want the title followed by the last name format.

- If necessary, tap or click the rightmost arrow in the Greeting line format area and then tap or click the colon (:) in the list (Figure 6–34).

Figure 6–34

2

- Tap or click the OK button to insert the GreetingLine merge field at the location of the insertion point (Figure 6–35).

Q&A Why are the values for the title and last name displayed instead of the merge field names?
With the 'View Merged Data' button (MAILINGS tab | Preview Results group) still selected, the field values are displayed instead of the field names.

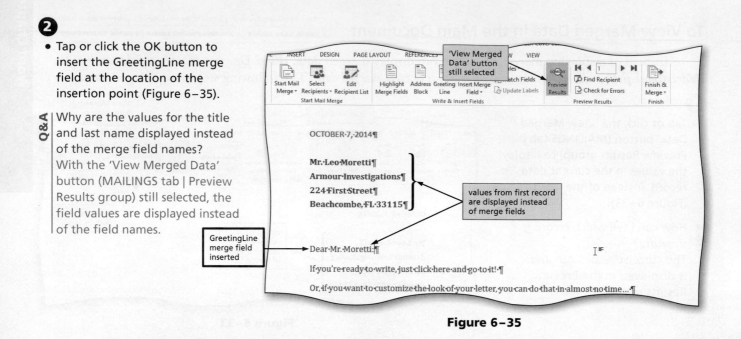

'View Merged Data' button still selected

OCTOBER·7,·2014¶

Mr.·Leo·Moretti¶
Armour·Investigations¶
224·First·Street¶
Beachcombe,·FL·33115¶

values from first record are displayed instead of merge fields

GreetingLine merge field inserted

Dear·Mr.·Moretti:¶

If·you're·ready·to·write,·just·click·here·and·go·to·it!·¶

Or,·if·you·want·to·customize·the·look·of·your·letter,·you·can·do·that·in·almost·no·time...¶

Figure 6–35

TO EDIT THE GREETINGLINE MERGE FIELD

If you wanted to change the format of or match fields in the GreetingLine merge field, you would perform the following steps.

1. Press and hold or right-click the GreetingLine merge field to display a shortcut menu.
2. Tap or click 'Edit Greeting Line' on the shortcut menu to display the Modify Greeting Line dialog box.
3. Make the necessary changes and then tap or click the OK button (Modify Greeting Line dialog box).

To View Merge Fields in the Main Document

Because you will be entering merge fields in the document next, you wish to display the merge fields instead of the merged data. The following step views merge fields instead of merged data.

1 Tap or click the 'View Merged Data' button (MAILINGS tab | Preview Results group) to display the merge fields instead of the values in the current data record (shown in Figure 6–36).

To Begin Typing the Body of the Form Letter

The next step is to begin typing the message, or body of the letter, which is located at the content control that begins with the placeholder text, If you're ready to write..., below the GreetingLine merge field. The following steps begin typing the letter in the location of the content control.

1 Tap or click the body of the letter to select the content control (Figure 6–36).

2 With the content control selected, type `I enjoyed meeting with you during the` and then press the SPACEBAR (shown in Figure 6–37).

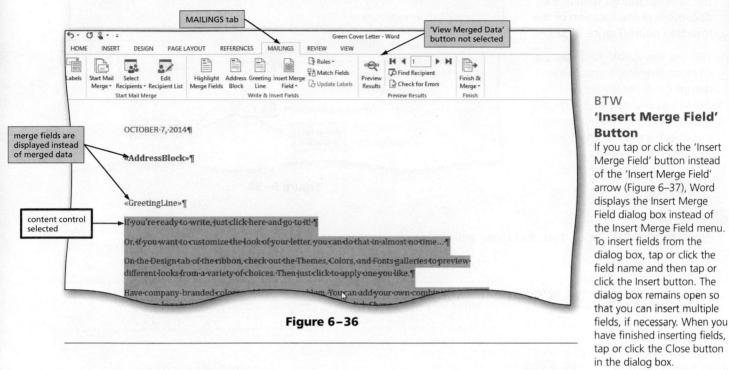

Figure 6–36

To Insert a Merge Field in the Main Document

1 IDENTIFY MAIN DOCUMENT | 2 CREATE DATA SOURCE | 3 COMPOSE MAIN DOCUMENT
4 MERGE DATA SOURCE | 5 ADDRESS MAILING LABELS | 6 MERGE TO DIRECTORY

The next step is to insert the Job Fair merge field into the main document. *Why? The first sentence in the first paragraph of the letter identifies the job fair, which is a merge field, at which the student met the prospective employer.* To instruct Word to use data fields from the data source, you insert merge fields in the main document for the form letter. The following steps insert a merge field at the location of the insertion point.

1

• Tap or click the 'Insert Merge Field' arrow (MAILINGS tab | Write & Insert Fields group) to display the Insert Merge Field menu (Figure 6–37).

Q&A What if I accidentally tap or click the 'Insert Merge Field' button instead of the arrow?
Tap or click the Cancel button in the Insert Merge Field dialog box and repeat Step 1.

Why is the underscore character in some of the field names?
Word places an underscore character in place of the space in merge fields.

BTW

'Insert Merge Field' Button

If you tap or click the 'Insert Merge Field' button instead of the 'Insert Merge Field' arrow (Figure 6–37), Word displays the Insert Merge Field dialog box instead of the Insert Merge Field menu. To insert fields from the dialog box, tap or click the field name and then tap or click the Insert button. The dialog box remains open so that you can insert multiple fields, if necessary. When you have finished inserting fields, tap or click the Close button in the dialog box.

Figure 6–37

2

- Tap or click Job_Fair on the Insert Merge Field menu to insert the selected merge field in the document at the location of the insertion point (Figure 6–38).

Q&A Will the word, Job_Fair, and the chevron characters print when I merge the form letters?
No. When you merge the data source with the main document, the value in the Job Fair field (e.g., Fisher) will print at the location of the merge field, Job_Fair.

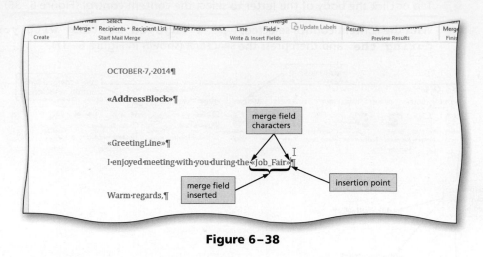

Figure 6–38

3

- Press the SPACEBAR. Type `job fair on` and then press the SPACEBAR again.

Other Ways

1. Tap or click 'Insert Merge Field' button (MAILINGS tab | Write & Insert fields group), tap or click desired field (Insert Merge Field dialog box), tap or click Insert button, tap or click Close button

---

BTW

Merge Fields
When you insert fields in a document, the displayed fields may be surrounded by braces instead of chevrons, and extra instructions may appear between the braces. If this occurs, then field codes have been turned on. To turn off field codes so that they are not displayed, press ALT+F9.

IF Fields

In addition to merge fields, you can insert Word fields that are designed specifically for a mail merge. An **IF field** is an example of a Word field. One form of the IF field is called an **If...Then:** If a condition is true, then perform an action. For example, If Mary owns a house, then send her information about homeowner's insurance. Another form of the IF field is called an **If...Then...Else:** If a condition is true, then perform an action; else perform a different action. For example, If John has an email address, then send him an email message; else send him the message via the postal service.

In this project, the form letter checks the job fair location and displays the corresponding date the job fair was held. If the job fair was held in Fisher, then the form letter should print the text, Friday, October 3; else if the job fair was held in Pontiac, then the form letter should print the text, Saturday, October 4. Thus, you will use an If...Then...Else: If the Job_Fair is equal to Fisher, then insert Friday, October 3; else insert Saturday, October 4.

The phrase that appears after the word If is called a rule, or condition. A **condition** consists of an expression, followed by a comparison operator, followed by a final expression.

Expression   The expression in a condition can be a merge field, a number, a series of characters, or a mathematical formula. Word surrounds a series of characters with quotation marks ("). To indicate an empty, or null, expression, Word places two quotation marks together ("").

Comparison operator   The comparison operator in a condition must be one of six characters: = (equal to or matches the text), <> (not equal to or does not match text), < (less than), <= (less than or equal to), > (greater than), or >= (greater than or equal to).

If the result of a condition is true, then Word evaluates the **true text**. If the result of the condition is false, Word evaluates the **false text** if it exists. In this project, the first expression in the condition is a merge field (Job_Fair); the comparison operator is equal to (=); and the second expression is the text "Fisher". The true text is "Friday, October 3". The false text is "Saturday, October 4". The complete IF field is as follows:

IF Job_Fair = "Fisher"   "Friday, October 3"   "Saturday, October 4"

            condition   true text   false text

To Insert an IF Field in the Main Document

1 IDENTIFY MAIN DOCUMENT | 2 CREATE DATA SOURCE | 3 COMPOSE MAIN DOCUMENT
4 MERGE DATA SOURCE | 5 ADDRESS MAILING LABELS | 6 MERGE TO DIRECTORY

The next step is to insert an IF field in the main document. *Why? You want to print the date of the job fair where you met the potential employer.* The following steps insert this IF field in the form letter: If the Job_Fair is equal to Fisher, then insert Friday, October 3, else insert Saturday, October 4.

1

- With the insertion point positioned as shown in Figure 6–39, tap or click the Rules button (MAILINGS tab | Write & Insert Fields group) to display the Rules menu (Figure 6–39).

Figure 6–39

2

- Tap or click 'If...Then...Else...' on the Rules menu to display the Insert Word Field: IF dialog box, which is where you enter the components of the IF field (Figure 6–40).

Figure 6–40

❸

- Tap or click the Field name arrow (Insert Word Field: IF dialog box) to display the list of fields in the data source.

- Scroll through the list of fields in the Field name list and then tap or click Job_Fair to select the field.

- Position the insertion point in the Compare to text box and then type **Fisher** as the comparison text.

- Press the TAB key and then type **Friday, October 3** as the true text.

- Press the TAB key and then type **Saturday, October 4** as the false text (Figure 6–41).

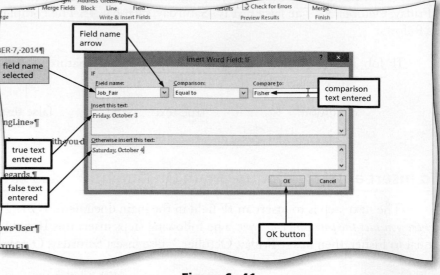

Figure 6–41

Q&A | Does the capitalization matter in the comparison text?
Yes. The text, Fisher, is different from the text, fisher, in a comparison. Be sure to enter the text exactly as you entered it in the data source.

❹

- Tap or click the OK button to insert the IF field at the location of the insertion point (Figure 6–42).

Q&A | Why does the main document display the text, Friday, October 3, instead of the IF field instructions?
The text, Friday, October 3, is displayed because the first record in the data source has a job fair equal to Fisher. Word, by default, evaluates the IF field using the current record and displays the results, called the **field results**, in the main document instead of displaying the IF field instructions. Later in the chapter, you will view the IF field instructions.

«GreetingLine»¶

I·enjoyed·meeting·with·you·during·the·«Job_Fair»·job·fair·on·Friday,·October·3¶

Warm·regards,¶

Figure 6–42

To Enter More Text and Merge Fields in the Main Document

The following steps enter the remainder of the text and merge fields into the form letter.

❶ With the insertion point at the location shown in Figure 6–42, press the PERIOD and then the SPACEBAR. Type **As you suggested, I have enclosed my resume for your review. I am interested in the** and then press the SPACEBAR.

❷ Tap or click the 'Insert Merge Field' arrow (MAILINGS tab | Write & Insert Fields group) and then tap or click Position on the Insert Merge Field menu to insert the selected merge field in the document.

❸ Press the SPACEBAR. Type **position we discussed and am confident I am an ideal candidate for this job.** Press the ENTER key. Type **I would appreciate the opportunity to meet with you to discuss my qualifications and potential employment with** and then press the SPACEBAR.

4 Tap or click the 'Insert Merge Field' arrow (MAILINGS tab | Write & Insert Fields group) and then tap or click Organization_Name on the Insert Merge Field menu to insert the selected merge field in the document.

5 Press the PERIOD key. Type **Thank you,** and then press the SPACEBAR. Insert the Title merge field, press the SPACEBAR, and then insert the Last Name merge field. Type **, for your time and consideration. I look forward to hearing from you soon.**

6 Change the closing to the word, Sincerely. Change the Your Name content control to Jordan Taylor Green, and change the Your Title content control to the word, ENCLOSURE, to complete the letter (Figure 6–43).

If requested by your instructor, enter your name instead of the job seeker's name.

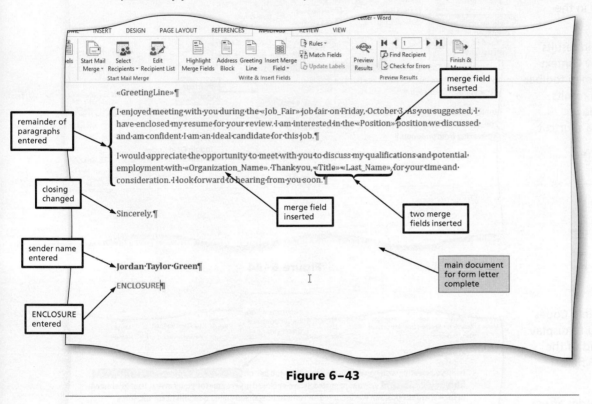

Figure 6–43

To Highlight Merge Fields

If you wanted to highlight all the merge fields in a document so that you could identify them quickly, you would perform the following steps.

1. Tap or click the 'Highlight Merge Fields' button (MAILINGS tab | Write & Insert Fields group) to highlight the merge fields in the document.

2. When finished viewing merge fields, tap or click the 'Highlight Merge Fields' button (MAILINGS tab | Write & Insert Fields group) again to remove the highlight from the merge fields in the document.

BTW

Word Fields

In addition to the IF field, Word provides other fields that may be used in form letters. For example, the ASK and FILLIN fields prompt the user to enter data for each record in the data source. The SKIP RECORD IF field instructs the mail merge not to generate a form letter for a data record if a specific condition is met.

To Display a Field Code

The instructions in the IF field are not displayed in the document; instead, the field results are displayed for the current record (Figure 6–42). The instructions of an IF field are called **field codes**, and the default for Word is for field codes not to be displayed. Thus, field codes do not print or show on the screen unless you turn them on. You use one procedure to show field codes on the screen and a different procedure to print them on a hard copy.

The following steps show a field code on the screen. *Why? You might want to turn on a field code to verify its accuracy or to modify it. Field codes tend to clutter the screen. Thus, most Word users turn them off after viewing them.*

❶

- If necessary, scroll to display the body of the letter in the document window.

- Press and hold the field results and then tap the 'Show Context Menu' button on the mini toolbar or right-click the field results showing the text, Friday, October 3, to display a shortcut menu (Figure 6–44).

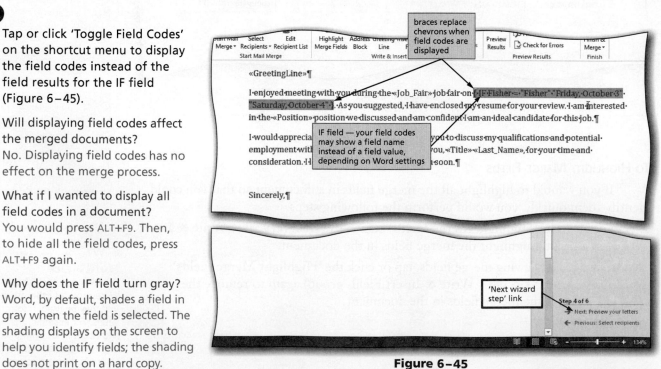

Figure 6–44

❷

- Tap or click 'Toggle Field Codes' on the shortcut menu to display the field codes instead of the field results for the IF field (Figure 6–45).

Q&A

Will displaying field codes affect the merged documents?
No. Displaying field codes has no effect on the merge process.

What if I wanted to display all field codes in a document?
You would press ALT+F9. Then, to hide all the field codes, press ALT+F9 again.

Why does the IF field turn gray?
Word, by default, shades a field in gray when the field is selected. The shading displays on the screen to help you identify fields; the shading does not print on a hard copy.

Figure 6–45

Other Ways

1. With insertion point in field, press SHIFT+F9

TO PRINT FIELD CODES IN THE MAIN DOCUMENT

When you merge or print a document, Word automatically converts field codes that show on the screen to field results. You may want to print the field codes version of the form letter, however, so that you have a hard copy of the field codes for future reference. When you print field codes, you must remember to turn off the field codes option so that merged documents print field results instead of field codes. If you wanted to print the field codes in the main document, you would perform the following steps.

1. Open the Backstage view and then tap or click Options to display the Word Options dialog box.
2. Tap or click Advanced in the left pane (Word Options dialog box) to display advanced options in the right pane and then scroll to the Print area in the right pane of the dialog box.
3. Place a check mark in the 'Print field codes instead of their values' check box.
4. Tap or click the OK button to instruct Word to show field codes when the document prints.
5. Open the Backstage view, tap or click the Print tab, and then tap or click the Print button to print the document with all field codes showing.
6. Open the Backstage view and then tap or click Options to display the Word Options dialog box.
7. Tap or click Advanced in the left pane (Word Options dialog box) to display advanced options in the right pane and then scroll to the Print area in the right pane of the dialog box.
8. Remove the check mark from the 'Print field codes instead of their values' check box.
9. Tap or click the OK button to instruct Word to show field results the next time you print the document.

To Save a Document Again

The main document for the form letter now is complete. Thus, you should save it again. The following step saves the document again.

1 Save the main document for the form letter again with the same file name, Green Cover Letter.

Opening a Main Document

You open a main document as you open any other Word document (i.e., tapping or clicking Open in the Backstage view). If Word displays a dialog box indicating it will run an SQL command, tap or click the Yes button (Figure 6–46).

When you open a main document, Word attempts to open the associated data source file, too. If the data source is not in exactly the same location (i.e., drive and folder)

BTW

Data Source and Main Document Files
When you open a main document, if Word cannot locate the associated data source file or it does not display a dialog box with the 'Find Data Source' button, then the data source may not be associated with the main document. To associate the data source with the main document, tap or click the Select Recipients button (MAILINGS tab | Start Mail Merge group), tap or click 'Use an Existing List' on the Select Recipients menu, and then locate the data source file. When you save the main document, Word will associate the data source with the main document.

Figure 6–46

Figure 6–47

as when it originally was saved, Word displays a dialog box indicating that it could not find the data source (Figure 6–47). When this occurs, tap or click the 'Find Data Source' button to display the Open Data Source dialog box, which allows you to locate the data source file. (Word may display several dialog boxes requiring you to tap or click an OK (or similar) button until the one shown in Figure 6–47 appears.)

Break Point: If you wish to take a break, this is a good place to do so. You can exit Word now. To resume at a later time, run Word, open the file called Green Cover Letter, and continue following the steps from this location forward.

BTW
Locking Fields
If you wanted to lock a field so that its field results cannot be changed, tap or click the field and then press CTRL+F11. To subsequently unlock a field so that it may be updated, tap or click the field and then press CTRL+SHIFT+F11.

Merging the Data Source with the Main Document to Generate Form Letters

The next step in this project is to merge the data source with the main document to generate the form letters (shown in Figure 6–1c on page WD 339). **Merging** is the process of combining the contents of a data source with a main document.

You can merge the form letters to a new document, which you can edit, or merge them directly to a printer. You also have the option of merging all data in a data source or merging just a portion of it. The following pages discuss various ways to merge.

To Preview the Merged Letters

1 IDENTIFY MAIN DOCUMENT | 2 CREATE DATA SOURCE | 3 COMPOSE MAIN DOCUMENT
4 MERGE DATA SOURCE | 5 ADDRESS MAILING LABELS | 6 MERGE TO DIRECTORY

Earlier in this chapter, you previewed the data in the letters using a button on the ribbon. The following step uses the Mail Merge wizard to preview the letters. *Why? The next wizard step previews the letters so that you can verify the content is accurate before performing the merge.*

1

• Tap or click the 'Next wizard step' link at the bottom of the Mail Merge task pane (shown in Figure 6–45) to display Step 5 of the Mail Merge wizard in the Mail Merge task pane (Figure 6–48).

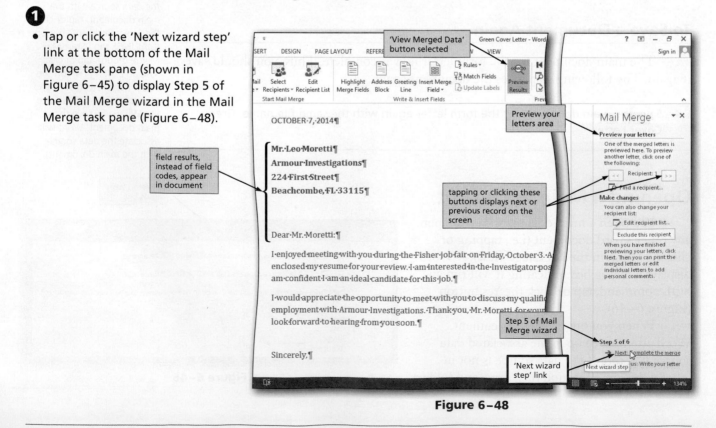

Figure 6–48

TO CHECK FOR ERRORS

Before merging documents, you can instruct Word to check for errors that might occur during the merge process. If you wanted to check for errors, you would perform the following steps.

1. Tap or click the 'Auto Check for Errors' button (MAILINGS tab | Preview Results group) or press ALT+SHIFT+K to display the Checking and Reporting Errors dialog box.

2. Select the desired option and then tap or click the OK button.

BTW

Converting Main Document Files

If you wanted to convert a mail merge main document to a regular Word document, you would open the main document, tap or click the 'Start Mail Merge' button (MAILINGS tab | Start Mail Merge group), and then tap or click 'Normal Word Document' on the Start Mail Merge menu.

To Merge the Form Letters to a New Document

1 IDENTIFY MAIN DOCUMENT | 2 CREATE DATA SOURCE | 3 COMPOSE MAIN DOCUMENT
4 MERGE DATA SOURCE | 5 ADDRESS MAILING LABELS | 6 MERGE TO DIRECTORY

With the data source and main document for the form letter complete, the next step is to merge them to generate the individual form letters. You can merge the letters to the printer or to a new document. *Why? If you merge the documents to a new document, you can save the merged documents in a file and then print them later, review the merged documents for accuracy and edit them as needed, or you can add personal messages to individual merged letters.* The following steps merge the form letters to a new document.

1

- Tap or click the 'Next wizard step' link at the bottom of the Mail Merge task pane (shown in Figure 6–48) to display Step 6 of the Mail Merge wizard in the Mail Merge task pane.

- Tap or click the 'Merge to new document' link in the Mail Merge task pane to display the Merge to New Document dialog box (Figure 6–49).

Q&A What if I wanted to print the merged letters immediately instead of reviewing them first in a new document window?
You would tap or click the 'Merge to printer' link instead of the 'Merge to new document' link.

Figure 6–49

2

- If necessary, tap or click All (Merge to New Document dialog box) so that all records in the data source are merged.

Q&A Do I have to merge all records?
No. Through this dialog box, you can merge the current record or a range of record numbers.

- Tap or click the OK button to merge the letters to a new document, in this case, five individual letters — one for each potential employer in the data source (Figure 6–50). (If Word displays a dialog box containing a message about locked fields, tap or click its OK button.)

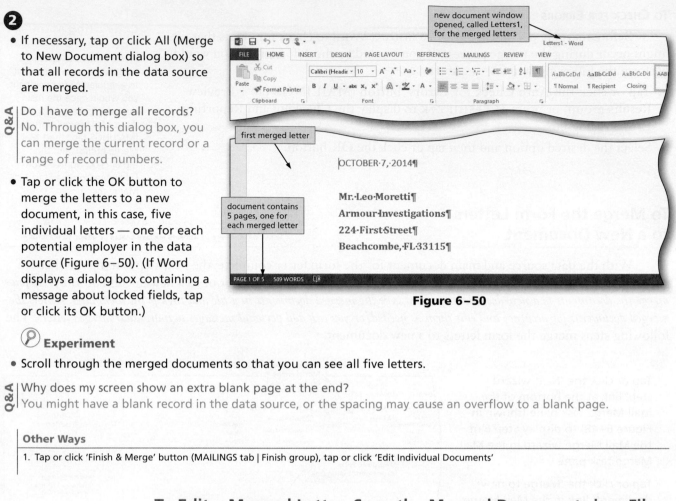

Figure 6–50

Experiment

- Scroll through the merged documents so that you can see all five letters.

Q&A Why does my screen show an extra blank page at the end?
You might have a blank record in the data source, or the spacing may cause an overflow to a blank page.

Other Ways

1. Tap or click 'Finish & Merge' button (MAILINGS tab | Finish group), tap or click 'Edit Individual Documents'

To Edit a Merged Letter, Save the Merged Documents in a File, and Close the Document Window

You should proofread the merged letters to be sure that the grammar and punctuation surrounding the merged fields is correct. After reviewing the merged letters, you notice a grammatical error in the last form letter. The word, the, should be inserted before the organization name. The following steps edit text in a form letter, save the merged letters in a file, and then close the document window containing the merged letters.

1 Scroll to the last form letter in the document and then insert the word, the, in front of the organization name, Waterton Police Department (Figure 6–51).

Figure 6–51

Q&A Is it common to edit the text in the merged letters?
Sentence structure may be awkward or incorrect for some field values following a merge. Always proofread the merged letters for accuracy before distributing them.

2 Tap or click the Save button on the Quick Access Toolbar, which depending on settings, will display either the Save As gallery in the Backstage view or the Save As dialog box.

3 Save the file in the desired location (in this case, the Job Hunting folder in the Word folder in the CIS 101 folder [or your class folder]) using the file name, Green Merged Letters.

Q&A Do I have to save the document containing the merged letters?
No. You can close the document without saving it.

4 Tap or click the Close button on the right side of the document window to close the document.

5 Tap or click the Close button on the Mail Merge task pane title bar (shown in Figure 6–49 on page WD 371) because you are finished with the Mail Merge wizard.

Correcting Merge Field Errors in Merged Documents

If the wrong field results appear, Word may be mapping the fields incorrectly. To view fields, tap or click the Match Fields button (MAILINGS tab | Write & Insert Fields group) (shown in Figure 6–49). Then, review the list of fields in the list. For example, Last Name should map to the Last Name field in the data source. If it does not, tap or click the arrow to change the name of the data source field.

If the fields are mapped correctly, the data in the data source may be incorrect. For a discussion about editing records in the data source, refer to page WD 356.

TO MERGE THE FORM LETTERS TO A PRINTER

If you are certain contents of the merged letters will be correct and do not need individual editing, you can perform the following steps to merge the form letters directly to the printer.

1. If necessary, display the MAILINGS tab.

2. Tap or click the 'Finish & Merge' button (MAILINGS tab | Finish group) and then tap or click Print Documents on the Finish & Merge menu, or tap or click the 'Merge to printer' link (Mail Merge task pane), to display the Merge to Printer dialog box.

3. If necessary, tap or click All (Merge to Printer dialog box) and then tap or click the OK button to display the Print dialog box.

4. Select desired printer settings. Tap or click the OK button (Print dialog box) to print five separate letters, one for each potential employer in the data source, as shown in Figure 6–1c on page WD 339. (If Word displays a message about locked fields, tap or click its OK button.)

To Select Records to Merge

Instead of merging all of the records in the data source, you can choose which records to merge, based on a condition you specify. The dialog box in Figure 6–49 allows you to specify by record number which records to merge. Often, though, you want to merge based on the contents of a specific field. The following steps select records for a merge. **Why?** *You want to merge just those potential employers who were at the Pontiac job fair.*

1

• Tap or click the 'Edit Recipient List' button (MAILINGS tab | Start Mail Merge group) to display the Mail Merge Recipients dialog box (Figure 6–52).

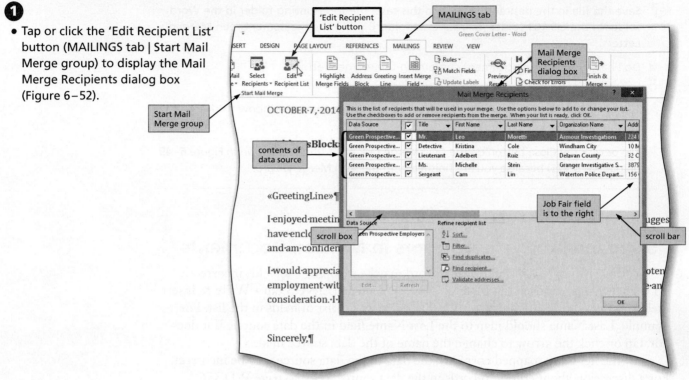

Figure 6–52

2

• Drag the scroll box to the right edge of the scroll bar (Mail Merge Recipients dialog box) so that the Job Fair field appears in the dialog box.

• Tap or click the arrow to the right of the field name, Job Fair, to display sort and filter criteria for the selected field (Figure 6–53).

Q&A
What are the filter criteria in the parentheses?
The (All) option clears any previously set filter criteria. The (Blanks) option selects records that contain blanks in that field, and the (Nonblanks) option selects records that do not contain blanks in that field. The (Advanced) option displays the Filter and Sort dialog box, which allows you to perform more advanced record selection operations.

Figure 6–53

3

- Tap or click Pontiac to reduce the number of data records displayed (Mail Merge Recipients dialog box) to two, because two potential employers attended the Pontiac job fair (Figure 6–54).

Q&A | What happened to the other three records that did not meet the criteria?
They still are part of the data source; they just are not appearing in the Mail Merge Recipients dialog box. When you clear the filter, all records will reappear.

4

- Tap or click the OK button to close the Mail Merge Recipients dialog box.

Figure 6–54

Other Ways

1. Tap or click Filter link (Mail Merge Recipients dialog box), tap or click Filter Records tab (Sort and Filter dialog box), enter filter criteria, tap or click OK button

---

To Merge the Form Letters to the New Document

The next step is to merge the selected records. To do this, you follow the same steps described earlier. The difference is that Word will merge only those records that meet the criteria specified, that is, just those with a job fair equal to Pontiac. The following steps merge the filtered records to a new document using the ribbon.

1 Tap or click the 'Finish & Merge' button (MAILINGS tab | Finish group) to display the Finish & Merge menu.

2 Tap or click 'Edit Individual Documents' to display the Merge to New Document dialog box. If necessary, tap or click All in the dialog box.

3 Tap or click the OK button (Merge to New Document dialog box) to display the merged documents in a new document window.

4 Change the zoom so that both documents, one for each potential employer whose job fair field equals Pontiac, appear in the document window at the same time (Figure 6–55 on the next page). (If Word displays a message about locked fields, tap or click its OK button.)

Q&A | Should I add the word, the, in these letters in front of the organization name of Waterton Police Department?
Because you are not saving this document, it is not necessary to edit its grammar.

5 Close the window. Do not save the merged documents.

two records meet criteria of Job Fair equals Pontiac

Figure 6–55

To Remove a Merge Condition

You should remove the merge condition. *Why? You do not want future merges be restricted to potential employers with a job fair equal to Pontiac.* The following steps remove a merge condition.

1
- Tap or click the 'Edit Recipient List' button (MAILINGS tab | Start Mail Merge group) to display the Mail Merge Recipients dialog box.

2
- Tap or click the Filter link (Mail Merge Recipients dialog box) to display the Filter and Sort dialog box.

- If necessary, tap or click the Filter Records tab to display the Filter Records sheet (Figure 6–56).

Figure 6–56

Q&A
Can I specify a merge condition in this dialog box instead of using the box arrow in the Mail Merge Recipients dialog box?
Yes.

3
- Tap or click the Clear All button (Filter and Sort dialog box).

- Tap or click the OK button in each of the two open dialog boxes to remove the merge condition.

To Sort the Data Records in a Data Source

The following steps sort the data records by ZIP code. **Why?** *You may want the form letters printed in a certain order. For example, if you mail the form letters using the U.S. Postal Service's bulk rate mailing service, the post office requires that you sort and group the form letters by ZIP code.*

1

- Tap or click the 'Edit Recipient List' button (MAILINGS tab | Start Mail Merge group) to display the Mail Merge Recipients dialog box.

- Scroll to the right until the ZIP Code field shows in the dialog box.

- Tap or click the arrow to the right of the field name, ZIP Code, to display a menu of sort and filter criteria (Figure 6–57).

Figure 6–57

2

- Tap or click Sort Ascending on the menu to sort the data source records in ascending (smallest to largest) order by ZIP Code (Figure 6–58).

3

- Tap or click the OK button to close the Mail Merge Recipients dialog box.

Q&A

In what order would the form letters print if I merged them again now?
Word would merge them in ZIP code order; that is, the records with ZIP code 33115 would appear first, and the records with ZIP code 33879 would appear last.

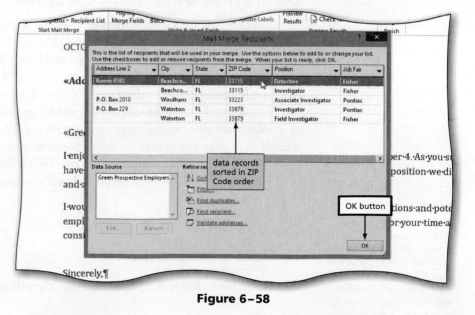

Figure 6–58

Other Ways

1. Tap or click Sort link (Mail Merge Recipients dialog box), enter sort criteria (Sort and Filter dialog box), tap or click OK button

To Find and Display Data

Why? *If you wanted to find a particular record in the data source and display that record's data in the main document on the screen, you can search for a field value.* The following steps find Stein, which is a last name in the data source, and display that record's values in the form letter currently displaying on the screen.

1

- If necessary, tap or click the 'View Merged Data' button (MAILINGS tab | Preview Results group) to show field results instead of merged fields on the screen.

- Tap or click the Find Recipient button (MAILINGS tab | Preview Results group) to display the Find Entry dialog box.

- Type **Stein** in the Find text box (Find Entry dialog box) as the search text.

- Tap or click the Find Next button to display the record containing the entered text (Figure 6–59).

2

- Tap or click the Cancel button (Find Entry dialog box) to close the dialog box.

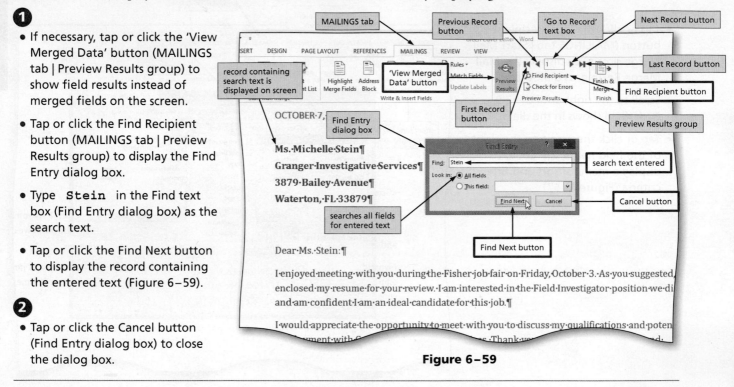

Figure 6–59

Displaying Data Source Records in the Main Document

When you are viewing merged data in the main document (Figure 6–59) — that is, the 'View Merged Data' button (MAILINGS tab | Preview Results group) is selected — you can tap or click buttons and boxes in the Preview Results group on the MAILINGS tab to display different results and values. For example, tap or click the Last Record button to display the values from the last record in the data source, the First Record button to display the values in record one, the Next Record button to display the values in the next consecutive record number, or the Previous Record button to display the values from the previous record number. You also can display a specific record by tapping or clicking the 'Go to Record' text box, typing the record number you would like to be displayed in the main document, and then pressing the ENTER key.

BTW

Closing Main Document Files

Word always asks if you want to save changes when you close a main document, even if you just saved the document. If you are sure that no additional changes were made to the document, tap or click the Don't Save button; otherwise, tap or click the Save button — just to be safe.

To Close a Document

The cover letter is complete. Thus, the following steps close the document.

1 Open the Backstage view and then tap or click Close.

2 If a Microsoft Word dialog box is displayed, tap or click the Save button to save the changes.

Addressing Mailing Labels and Envelopes

Now that you have merged and printed the form letters, the next step is to print addresses on mailing labels to be affixed to envelopes for the form letters. The mailing labels will use the same data source as the form letter, Green Prospective Employers. The format and content of the mailing labels will be exactly the same as the inside address in the main document for the form letter. That is, the first line will contain the title and first name followed by the last name. The second line will contain the organization name, and so on. Thus, you will use the AddressBlock merge field in the mailing labels.

You follow the same basic steps to create the main document for the mailing labels as you did to create the main document for the form letters. That is, determine the appropriate data source, create the label main document, and then merge the main document with the data source to generate the mailing labels and envelopes. The major difference here is that the data source already exists because you created it earlier in this project.

To Address and Print Mailing Labels Using an Existing Data Source

1 IDENTIFY MAIN DOCUMENT | 2 CREATE DATA SOURCE | 3 COMPOSE MAIN DOCUMENT
4 MERGE DATA SOURCE | 5 ADDRESS MAILING LABELS | 6 MERGE TO DIRECTORY

To address mailing labels, you specify the type of labels you intend to use. Word will request the label information, including the label vendor and product number. You can obtain this information from the box of labels. For illustration purposes in addressing these labels, the label vendor is Avery and the product number is J8158. The following steps address and print mailing labels using an existing data source. *Why? You already created the data source earlier in this chapter, so you will use that data source.*

Note: If your printer does not have the capability of printing mailing labels, read these steps without performing them. If you are in a laboratory environment, ask your instructor if you should perform these steps or read them without performing them.

1

- Open the Backstage view. Tap or click the New tab in the Backstage view to display the New gallery. Tap or click the Blank document thumbnail to open a new blank document window.

- If necessary, change the zoom to page width.

- Display the MAILINGS tab. Tap or click the 'Start Mail Merge' button (MAILINGS tab | Start Mail Merge group) and then tap or click 'Step-by-Step Mail Merge Wizard' on the Start Mail Merge menu to display Step 1 of the Mail Merge wizard in the Mail Merge task pane.

- Tap or click Labels in the Select document type area to specify labels as the main document type (Figure 6–60).

Figure 6–60

2

- Tap or click the 'Next wizard step' link at the bottom of the Mail Merge task pane to display Step 2 of the Mail Merge wizard.

- In the Mail Merge task pane, tap or click the 'Select label size' link to display the Label Options dialog box.

- Select the label vendor and product number (in this case, Avery A4/A5 and J8158), as shown in Figure 6–61.

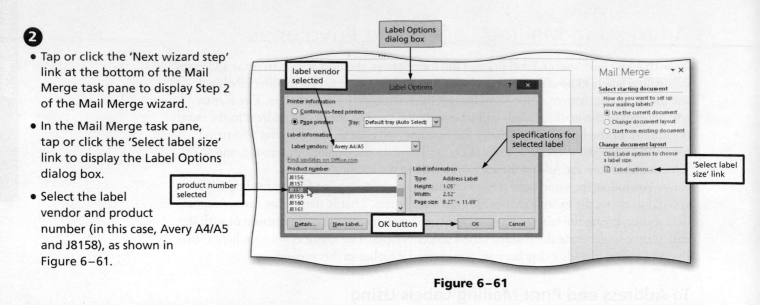

Figure 6–61

3

- Tap or click the OK button (Label Options dialog box) to display the selected label layout as the main document (Figure 6–62).

- If necessary, scroll to display the left edge of the main document in the window.

- If gridlines are not displayed, tap or click the 'View Table Gridlines' button (TABLE TOOLS LAYOUT tab | Table group) to show gridlines.

Figure 6–62

4

- Tap or click the 'Next wizard step' link at the bottom of the Mail Merge task pane to display Step 3 of the Mail Merge wizard, which allows you to select the data source.

- If necessary, tap or click 'Use an existing list' in the Select recipients area. Tap or click the 'Select recipient list file' link to display the Select Data Source dialog box.

- If necessary, navigate to the location of the data source (in this case, the Job Hunting folder in the Word folder in the CIS 101 folder [or your class folder]).

- Tap or click the file name, Green Prospective Employers, to select the data source you created earlier in the chapter (Figure 6–63).

Q&A What is the folder initially displayed in the Select Data Source dialog box?
It is the default folder for storing data source files. Word looks in that folder first for an existing data source.

Figure 6–63

5

- Tap or click the Open button (Select Data Source dialog box) to display the Mail Merge Recipients dialog box (Figure 6–64).

Figure 6–64

6

- Tap or click the OK button (Mail Merge Recipients dialog box) to close the dialog box.

- At the bottom of the Mail Merge task pane, tap or click the 'Next wizard step' link to display Step 4 of the Mail Merge wizard in the Mail Merge task pane.

- In the Mail Merge task pane, tap or click the 'Insert formatted address' link to display the Insert Address Block dialog box (Figure 6–65).

- If necessary, match the company name to the organization name (as shown on page WD 360).

Figure 6–65

7

- Tap or click the OK button to close the dialog box and insert the AddressBlock merge field in the first label of the main document (Figure 6–66).

Q&A

Do I have to use the AddressBlock merge field?

No. You can tap or click the Insert Merge Field button (MAILINGS tab | Write & Insert Fields group) and then select the preferred fields for the mailing labels, organizing the fields as desired.

Figure 6–66

8

- Tap or click the 'Update all labels' button in the Mail Merge task pane to copy the layout of the first label to the remaining label layouts in the main document (Figure 6–67).

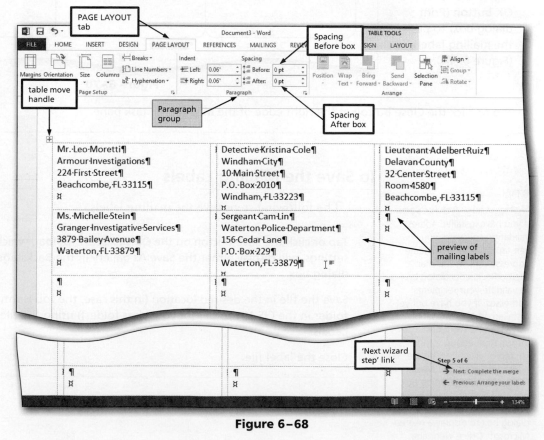

Figure 6–67

9

- Tap or click the 'Next wizard step' link at the bottom of the Mail Merge task pane to display Step 5 of the Mail Merge wizard, which shows a preview of the mailing labels in the document window.

- Because you do not want a blank space between each line in the printed mailing address, select the table containing the label layout (that is, tap or click the table move handle in the upper-left corner of the table), display the PAGE LAYOUT tab, change the Spacing Before and After boxes to 0 pt, and then tap or click anywhere to remove the selection (Figure 6–68).

Q&A What if the spacing does not change? Drag through the labels and try changing the Spacing Before and After boxes to 0 again.

Figure 6–68

10

- Tap or click the 'Next wizard step' link at the bottom of the Mail Merge task pane to display Step 6 of the Mail Merge wizard.

- In the Mail Merge task pane, if you want to print the mailing labels, tap or click the 'Merge to printer' link to display the Merge to Printer dialog box.

- If necessary, tap or click All (Merge to Printer dialog box) so that all records in the data source will be included in the merge (Figure 6–69).

Figure 6–69

11

- If necessary, insert a sheet of blank mailing labels in the printer.

- Tap or click the OK button (Merge to Printer dialog box) to display the Print dialog box.

- Tap or click the OK button (Print dialog box) to print the mailing labels (Figure 6–70).

Figure 6–70

12

- Tap or click the Close button at the right edge of the Mail Merge task pane.

To Save the Mailing Labels

BTW

Validating Addresses
If you have installed address validation software, you can tap or click the Validate addresses link in the Mail Merge Recipients dialog box to validate your recipients' addresses. If you have not yet installed address validation software and would like information about doing so, tap or click the Validate addresses link in the Mail Merge Recipients dialog box and then tap or click the Yes button in the Microsoft Word dialog box to display a related Microsoft Office webpage.

The following steps save the mailing labels.

1 Tap or click the Save button on the Quick Access Toolbar, which depending on settings, will display either the Save As gallery in the Backstage view or the Save As dialog box.

2 Save the file in the desired location (in this case, the Job Hunting folder in the Word folder in the CIS 101 folder [or your class folder]) using the file name, Green Mailing Labels.

3 Close the label file.

To Address and Print Envelopes

Instead of addressing mailing labels to affix to envelopes, your printer may have the capability of printing directly on envelopes. If you wanted to print address information directly on envelopes, you would perform the following steps to merge the form letters directly to the printer.

1. Open the Backstage view. Tap or click the New tab in the Backstage view to display the New gallery. Tap or click the Blank document thumbnail to open a new blank document window.

2. Display the MAILINGS tab. Tap or click the 'Start Mail Merge' button (MAILINGS tab | Start Mail Merge group) and then tap or click 'Step-by-Step Mail Merge Wizard' on the Start Mail Merge menu to display Step 1 of the Mail Merge wizard in the Mail Merge task pane. Specify envelopes as the main document type by tapping or clicking Envelopes in the Select document type area.

3. Tap or click the 'Next wizard step' link at the bottom of the Mail Merge task pane to display Step 2 of the Mail Merge wizard. In the Mail Merge task pane, tap or click the 'Set Envelope Options' link to display the Envelope Options dialog box.

4. Select the envelope size and then tap or click the OK button (Envelope Options dialog box), which displays the selected envelope layout as the main document.

5. If your envelope does not have a preprinted return address, position the insertion point in the upper-left corner of the envelope layout and then type a return address.

6. Tap or click the 'Next wizard step' link at the bottom of the Mail Merge task pane to display Step 3 of the Mail Merge wizard, which allows you to select the data source. Select an existing data source or create a new one. At the bottom of the Mail Merge task pane, tap or click the 'Next wizard step' link to display Step 4 of the Mail Merge wizard in the Mail Merge task pane.

7. Position the insertion point in the middle of the envelope. In the Mail Merge task pane, tap or click the 'Insert formatted address' link to display the Insert Address Block dialog box. Select desired settings and then tap or click the OK button to close the dialog box and insert the AddressBlock merge field in the envelope layout of the main document.

8. Tap or click the 'Next wizard step' link at the bottom of the Mail Merge task pane to display Step 5 of the Mail Merge wizard, which shows a preview of an envelope in the document window.

9. Tap or click the 'Next wizard step' link at the bottom of the Mail Merge task pane to display Step 6 of the Mail Merge wizard. In the Mail Merge task pane, tap or click the 'Merge to printer' link to display the Merge to Printer dialog box. If necessary, tap or click All (Merge to Printer dialog box) so that all records in the data source will be included in the merge.

10. If necessary, insert blank envelopes in the printer. Tap or click the OK button to display the Print dialog box. Tap or click the OK button (Print dialog box) to print the addresses on the envelopes. Close the Mail Merge task pane.

Note: Before printing address information directly on a printer, ensure your printer has the capability of printing on envelopes. If you are in a laboratory environment, ask your instructor if you should perform these steps.

BTW
AddressBlock Merge Field
Another way to insert the AddressBlock merge field in a document is to tap or click the Address Block button (MAILINGS tab | Write & Insert Fields group).

Merging All Data Records to a Directory

You may want to print the data records in the data source. Recall that the data source is saved as a Microsoft Access database table. Thus, you cannot open the data source in Word. To view the data source, you tap or click the 'Edit Recipient List' button (MAILINGS tab | Start Mail Merge group), which displays the Mail Merge Recipients dialog box. This dialog box, however, does not have a Print button.

One way to print the contents of the data source is to merge all data records in the data source into a single document, called a directory. A **directory** is a listing from the contents of the data source. A directory does not merge each data record to a separate document; instead, a directory lists all records together in a single document. When you merge to a directory, the default organization of a directory places each record one after the next, similar to the look of entries in a telephone book.

To create a directory, follow the same process as for the form letters. That is, determine the appropriate data source, create the directory main document, and then merge the main document with the data source to create the directory.

The directory in this chapter is more organized with the rows and columns divided and field names placed above each column (shown in Figure 6–83 on page WD 393). To accomplish this look, the following steps are required:

1. Change the page orientation from portrait to landscape, so that each record fits on a single row.
2. Create a directory layout, placing a separating character between each merge field.
3. Merge the directory to a new document, which creates a list of all records in the data source.
4. Convert the directory to a table, using the separator character as the identifier for each new column.
5. Format the table containing the directory.
6. Sort the table by organization name within city, so that it is easy to locate a particular record.

To Create a New Blank Document

The following steps create a new blank document.

1 Open the Backstage view.

2 Tap or click the New tab in the Backstage view to display the New gallery.

3 Tap or click the Blank document thumbnail to open a new blank document window (shown in Figure 6–71).

4 If necessary, change the zoom to page width.

BTW

Certification
The Microsoft Office Specialist (MOS) program provides an opportunity for you to obtain a valuable industry credential — proof that you have the Word 2013 skills required by employers. For more information, visit the Certification resource on the Student Companion Site located on www .cengagebrain.com. For detailed instructions about accessing available resources, visit www.cengage.com/ ct/studentdownload or contact your instructor for information about accessing the required files.

To Change Page Orientation

When a document is in **portrait orientation**, the short edge of the paper is the top of the document. You can instruct Word to lay out a document in **landscape orientation**, so that the long edge of the paper is the top of the document. The following steps change the orientation of the document from portrait to landscape. *Why? You want an entire record to fit on a single line in the directory.*

1

- Display the PAGE LAYOUT tab.

- Tap or click the 'Change Page Orientation' button (PAGE LAYOUT tab | Page Setup group) to display the Change Page Orientation gallery (Figure 6–71).

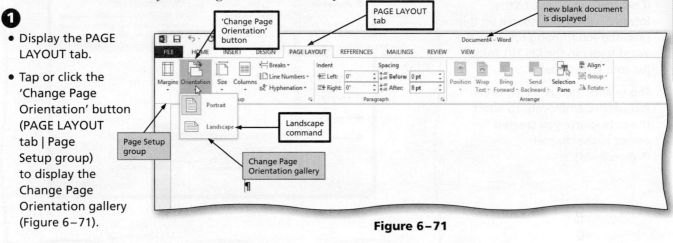

Figure 6–71

2

- Tap or click Landscape in the Change Page Orientation gallery to change the page orientation to landscape.

To Merge to a Directory

The next steps merge the data records in the data source to a directory. *Why? You would like a listing of all records in the data source.* For illustration purposes, the following steps use the buttons on the MAILINGS tab rather than using the Mail Merge task pane to merge to a directory.

1

- Display the MAILINGS tab.

- Tap or click the 'Start Mail Merge' button (MAILINGS tab | Start Mail Merge group) to display the Start Mail Merge menu (Figure 6–72).

Figure 6–72

2

- Tap or click Directory on the Start Mail Merge menu to select the main document type.

3

- Tap or click the Select Recipients button (MAILINGS tab | Start Mail Merge group) to display the Select Recipients menu (Figure 6–73).

Figure 6–73

4

- Tap or click 'Use an Existing List' on the Select Recipients menu to display the Select Data Source dialog box.

- If necessary, navigate to the location of the data source (in this case, the Job Hunting folder in the Word folder in the CIS 101 folder [or your class folder]).

- Tap or click the file name, Green Prospective Employers, to select the data source you created earlier in the chapter (Figure 6–74).

Figure 6–74

5

- Tap or click the Open button (Select Data Source dialog box) to associate the selected data source with the current main document.

6

- Tap or click the 'Insert Merge Field' arrow (MAILINGS tab | Write & Insert Fields group) to display the Insert Merge Field menu (Figure 6–75).

Figure 6–75

7

- Tap or click Title on the Insert Merge Field menu to insert the selected merge field in the document.

- Press the COMMA (,) key to place a comma after the inserted merge field.

Q&A Why insert a comma after the merge field?

In the next steps, you will convert the entered merge fields to a table format with the records in rows and the fields in columns. To do this, Word divides the columns based on a character separating each field. In this case, you use the comma to separate the merge fields.

8

• Repeat Steps 6 and 7 for the First_Name, Last_Name, Organization_Name, Address_Line_1, Address_Line_2, City, State, and ZIP_Code fields on the Insert Merge Field menu, so that these fields in the data source appear in the main document separated by a comma, except do not type a comma after the last field: ZIP_Code.

• Press the ENTER key (Figure 6–76).

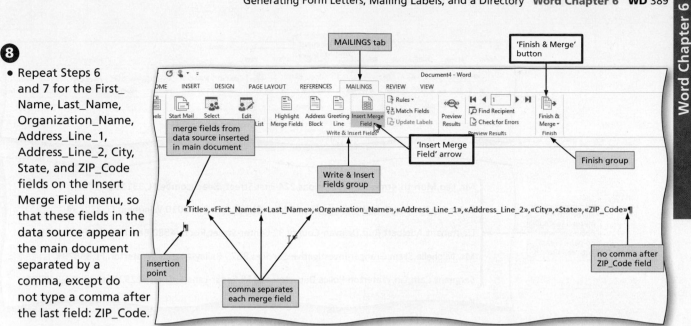

Figure 6–76

Q&A Why press the ENTER key after entering the merge fields names?
This will place the first field in each record at the beginning of a new line.

To Save the Directory

The following steps save the directory main document.

 Tap or click the Save button on the Quick Access Toolbar, which depending on settings, will display either the Save As gallery in the Backstage view or the Save As dialog box.

 Save the file in the desired location (in this case, the Job Hunting folder in the Word folder in the CIS 101 folder [or your class folder]) using the file name, Green Potential Employer Directory.

To Merge to a New Document

The next step is to merge the data source and the directory main document to a new document, so that you can edit the resulting document. The following steps merge to a new document.

 Tap or click the 'Finish & Merge' button (MAILINGS tab | Finish group) to display the Finish & Merge menu.

 Tap or click 'Edit Individual Documents' on the Finish & Merge menu to display the Merge to New Document dialog box.

 If necessary, tap or click All (Merge to New Document dialog box).

4 Tap or click the OK button to merge the data records to a directory in a new document window (Figure 6–77 on the next page).

BTW
Quick Reference
For a table that lists how to complete the tasks covered in this book using touch gestures, the mouse, ribbon, shortcut menu, and keyboard, see the Quick Reference Summary at the back of this book, or visit the Quick Reference resource on the Student Companion Site located on www.cengagebrain.com. For detailed instructions about accessing available resources, visit www.cengage.com/ct/studentdownload or contact your instructor for information about accessing the required files.

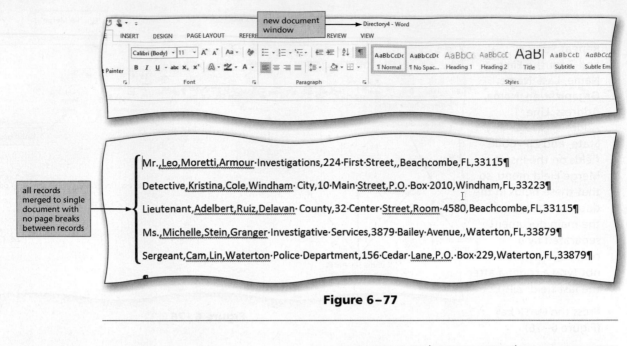

Figure 6–77

To Convert Text to a Table

1 IDENTIFY MAIN DOCUMENT | 2 CREATE DATA SOURCE | 3 COMPOSE MAIN DOCUMENT
4 MERGE DATA SOURCE | 5 ADDRESS MAILING LABELS | **6 MERGE TO DIRECTORY**

You want each data record to be in a single row and each merge field to be in a column. *Why? The directory will be easier to read if it is in table form.* The following steps convert the text containing the merge fields to a table.

1

- Press CTRL+A to select the entire document, because you want all document contents to be converted to a table.

- Display the INSERT tab.

- Tap or click the 'Add a Table' button (INSERT tab | Tables group) to display the Add a Table gallery (Figure 6–78).

Q&A
Can I convert a section of a document to a table?
Yes, simply select the characters, lines, or paragraphs to be converted before displaying the Convert Text to Table dialog box.

Figure 6–78

2

- Tap or click 'Convert Text to Table' in the Add a Table gallery to display the Convert Text to Table dialog box.

- If necessary, type 9 in the 'Number of columns' box (Convert Text to Table dialog box) to specify the number of columns for the resulting table.

- Tap or click 'AutoFit to window', which instructs Word to fit the table and its contents to the width of the window.

- If necessary, tap or click Commas to specify the character that separates the merge fields in the document (Figure 6–79).

Figure 6–79

3

- Tap or click the OK button to convert the selected text to a table and then, if necessary, tap or click to remove the selection from the table (Figure 6–80).

Q&A

Can I format the table?

Yes. You can use any of the commands on the TABLE TOOLS DESIGN and TABLE TOOLS LAYOUT tabs to change the look of the table.

merge fields converted to table

Mr.¤	Leo¤	Moretti¤	Armour·Investigations¤	224·First·Street¤	¤	Beachcombe¤	FL¤	33115¤	¤
Detective¤	Kristina¤	Cole¤	Windham·City¤	10·Main·Street¤	P.O.·Box·2010¤	Windham¤	FL¤	33223¤	¤
Lieutenant¤	Adelbert¤	Ruiz¤	Delavan·County¤	32·Center·Street¤	Room·4580¤	Beachcombe¤	FL¤	33115¤	¤
Ms.¤	Michelle¤	Stein¤	Granger·Investigative·Services¤	3879·Bailey·Avenue¤	¤	Waterton¤	FL¤	33879¤	¤
Sergeant¤	Cam¤	Lin¤	Waterton·Police·Department¤	156·Cedar·Lane¤	P.O.·Box·229¤	Waterton¤	FL¤	33879¤	¤

Figure 6–80

To Modify and Format a Table

The table would be more descriptive if the field names were displayed in a row above the actual data. The following steps add a row to the top of a table and format the data in the new row.

1 Add a row to the top of the table by positioning the insertion point in the first row of the table and then tapping or clicking the 'Insert Rows Above' button (TABLE TOOLS LAYOUT tab | Rows & Columns group).

2 Tap or click in the first (leftmost) cell of the new row. Type **Title** and then press the TAB key. Type **First Name** and then press the TAB key. Type **Last Name** and then press the tab key. Type **Organization Name** and then press the tab key. Type **Address Line 1** and then press the TAB key. Type **Address Line 2** and then press the TAB key. Type **City** and then press the TAB key. Type **State** and then press the TAB key. Type **ZIP Code** as the last entry in the row.

3 Bold the contents of the first row.

4 Change the page margins to Narrow.

5 Use the AutoFit Contents command on the ribbon or the shortcut menu to make all columns as wide as their contents (Figure 6–81).

header row added and bold

Title¤	First·Name¤	Last·Name¤	Organization·Name¤	Address·Line·1¤	Address·Line·2¤	City¤	State¤	ZIP·Code¤	¤
Mr.¤	Leo¤	Moretti¤	Armour·Investigations¤	224·First·Street¤	¤	Beachcombe¤	FL¤	33115¤	¤
Detective¤	Kristina¤	Cole¤	Windham·City¤	10·Main·Street¤	P.O.·Box·2010¤	Windham¤	FL¤	33223¤	¤
Lieutenant¤	Adelbert¤	Ruiz¤	Delavan·County¤	32·Center·Street¤	Room·4580¤	Beachcombe¤	FL¤	33115¤	¤
Ms.¤	Michelle¤	Stein¤	Granger·Investigative·Services¤	3879·Bailey·Avenue¤	¤	Waterton¤	FL¤	33879¤	¤
Sergeant¤	Cam¤	Lin¤	Waterton·Police·Department¤	156·Cedar·Lane¤	P.O.·Box·229¤	Waterton¤	FL¤	33879¤	¤

Figure 6–81

TO REPEAT HEADER ROWS

If you had a table that exceeded a page in length and you wanted the header row (the first row) to appear at the top of the table on each continued page, you would perform the following steps.

1. Position the insertion point in the header row.

2. Tap or click the 'Repeat Header Rows' button (TABLE TOOLS LAYOUT tab | Data group) to repeat the row containing the insertion point at the top of every page on which the table continues.

To Sort a Table by Multiple Columns

1 IDENTIFY MAIN DOCUMENT | 2 CREATE DATA SOURCE | 3 COMPOSE MAIN DOCUMENT
4 MERGE DATA SOURCE | 5 ADDRESS MAILING LABELS | 6 **MERGE TO DIRECTORY**

The next step is to sort the table. *Why? In this project, the table records are displayed by organization name within city.* The following steps sort a table by multiple columns.

1

• With the table selected or the insertion point in the table, tap or click the Sort button (TABLE TOOLS LAYOUT tab | Data group) to display the Sort dialog box.

• Tap or click the Sort by arrow (Sort dialog box); scroll to and then tap or click City in the list.

• Tap or click the first Then by arrow and then tap or click Organization Name in the list.

• If necessary, tap or click Header row so that the first row remains in its current location when the table is sorted (Figure 6–82).

Figure 6-82

2

- Tap or click the OK button to sort the records in the table in ascending Organization Name order within ascending City order (Figure 6-83).

- If necessary, tap or click to deselect the table.

Title¤	First Name¤	Last Name¤	Organization Name¤	Address Line 1¤	Address Line 2¤	City¤	State¤	ZIP Code¤	¤
Mr.¤	Leo¤	Moretti¤	Armour Investigations¤	224 First Street¤	¤	Beachcombe¤	FL¤	33115¤	¤
Lieutenant¤	Adelbert¤	Ruiz¤	Delavan County¤	32 Center Street¤	Room 4580¤	Beachcombe¤	FL¤	33115¤	¤
Ms.¤	Michelle¤	Stein¤	Granger Investigative Services¤	3879 Bailey Avenue¤	¤	Waterton¤	FL¤	33879¤	¤
Sergeant¤	Cam¤	Lin¤	Waterton Police Department¤	156 Cedar Lane¤	P.O. Box 229¤	Waterton¤	FL¤	33879¤	¤
Detective¤	Kristina¤	Cole¤	Windham City¤	10 Main Street¤	P.O. Box 2010¤	Windham¤	FL¤	33223¤	¤

Figure 6-83

To Save the Directory Listing and Exit Word

The following steps save and print the directory listing.

1 Tap or click the Save button on the Quick Access Toolbar, which depending on settings, will display either the Save As gallery in the Backstage view or the Save As dialog box.

2 Save the file in the desired location (in this case, the Job Hunting folder in the Word folder in the CIS 101 folder [or your class folder]) using the file name, Green Potential Employer Directory Listing.

3 If desired, print the directory file and then close all open files.

Q&A If Microsoft Access is installed on my computer, can I use that to print the data source? As an alternative to merging to a directory and printing the results, if you are familiar with Microsoft Access and it is installed on your computer, you can open and print the data source in Access.

4 Exit Word.

BTW
Distributing a Document
Instead of printing and distributing a hard copy of a document, you can distribute the document electronically. Options include sending the document via email; posting it on cloud storage (such as SkyDrive) and sharing the file with others; posting it on a social networking site, blog, or other website; and sharing a link associated with an online location of the document. You also can create and share a PDF or XPS image of the document, so that users can view the file in Acrobat Reader or XPS Viewer instead of in Word.

Chapter Summary

In this chapter, you have learned how to create and print form letters, create and edit a data source, address mailing labels and envelopes from a data source, and merge to a directory. The items listed below include all the new Word skills you have learned in this chapter, with the tasks grouped by activity.

Enter and Edit Text
Enter the Date (WD 358)

File Management
Create a Folder while Saving (WD 349)

Format a Page
Change Page Orientation (WD 387)

Word Settings
Change the User Name and Initials (WD 344)

Work with Graphics
Specify the Position of a Graphic (WD 348)

Work with Mail Merge
Identify the Main Document for the Form Letter Using the Mail Merge Task Pane (WD 341)
Create a New Data Source (WD 350)
Save a Data Source when Prompted by Word (WD 355)
Insert the AddressBlock Merge Field (WD 359)
Edit the AddressBlock Merge Field (WD 360)
View Merged Data in the Main Document (WD 361)
Insert the GreetingLine Merge Field (WD 361)
Edit the GreetingLine Merge Field (WD 362)

Insert a Merge Field in the Main Document (WD 363)
Insert an IF Field in the Main Document (WD 365)
Highlight Merge Fields (WD 367)
Display a Field Code (WD 368)
Print Field Codes in the Main Document (WD 369)
Preview the Merged Letters (WD 370)
Check for Errors (WD 371)
Merge the Form Letters to a New Document (WD 371)
Merge the Form Letters to a Printer (WD 373)
Select Records to Merge (WD 374)
Remove a Merge Condition (WD 376)
Sort the Data Records in a Data Source (WD 377)
Find and Display Data (WD 378)
Address and Print Mailing Labels Using an Existing Data Source (WD 379)
Address and Print Envelopes (WD 385)
Merge to a Directory (WD 387)

Work with Tables
Convert Text to a Table (WD 390)
Repeat Header Rows (WD 392)
Sort a Table by Multiple Columns (WD 392)

CONSIDER THIS: PLAN AHEAD

What decisions will you need to make when creating your next form letter?
Use these guidelines as you complete the assignments in this chapter and create your own form letters outside of this class.

1. Identify the main document for the form letter.

   a) Determine whether to type the letter from scratch in a blank document window or use a letter template.

2. Create or specify the data source.

   a) Determine if the data exists already in an Access database table, an Outlook contacts list, or an Excel worksheet.

   b) If you cannot use an existing data source, create a new one using appropriate field names.

3. Compose the main document for the form letter.

   a) Ensure the letter contains all essential business letter elements and is visually appealing.

   b) Be sure the letter contains proper grammar, correct spelling, logically constructed sentences, flowing paragraphs, and sound ideas.

   c) Properly reference the data in the data source.

4. Merge the main document with the data source to create the form letters.

   a) Determine the destination for the merge (i.e., a new document, the printer, etc.).

   b) Determine which records to merge (all of them or a portion of them).

5. Determine whether to generate mailing labels or envelopes.

    a) Create or specify the data source.

    b) Ensure the mailing label or envelope contains all necessary information.

6. Create a directory of the data source.

    a) Create or specify the data source.

    b) If necessary, format the directory appropriately.

Apply Your Knowledge

Reinforce the skills and apply the concepts you learned in this chapter.

Editing, Printing, and Merging a Form Letter and Its Data Source

Note: To complete this assignment, you will be required to use the Data Files for Students. Visit www.cengage.com/ct/studentdownload for detailed instructions or contact your instructor for information about accessing the required files.

Instructions: Run Word. Open the document, Apply 6-1 Fund-Raising Letter Draft, from the Data Files for Students. When you open the main document, if Word displays a dialog box about an SQL command, tap or click the Yes button. If Word prompts for the name of the data source, select Apply 6-1 Member List on the Data Files for Students.

    The document is a main document for the Valley View Golf Club form letter (Figure 6–84 on the next page). You are to edit the date content control and GreetingLine merge field, print the form letter, add a record to the data source, and merge the form letters to a file.

Perform the following tasks:

1. Edit the date content control so that it contains the date 8/26/2014.

2. Edit the GreetingLine merge field so that the salutation ends with a comma (,).

3. Save the modified main document for the form letter with the name Apply 6-1 Fund-Raising Letter Modified.

4. Highlight the merge fields in the document. How many are there? Remove the highlight from the merge fields.

5. View merged data in the document. Use the navigation buttons in the Preview Results group to display merged data from various records in the data source. What is the last name shown in the first record? The third record? The fifth record? View merge fields (that is, turn off the view merged data).

6. Print the main document for the form letter by opening the Backstage view, clicking the Print tab, and then clicking the Print button (Figure 6–84).

Continued >

Apply Your Knowledge *continued*

7. If requested by your instructor, add a record to the data source that contains your personal information. Type **student** in the Membership Type field.

8. In the data source, change Kim Chung's last name to Weavers.

9. Sort the data source by the Last Name field.

10. Save the main document for the form letter again.

11. Merge the form letters to a new document. Save the new document with the file name, Apply 6-1 Fund-Raising Merged Letters. Edit the merged letters by changing the word, a, to the word, an, before those members who are associate members.

12. If requested by your instructor, merge the form letters directly to the printer.

13. Submit the saved documents in the format specified by your instructor.

14. ✸ Answer the questions posed in #4 and #5. The form letter used in this assignment was based on one of Word's online mail merge letter templates called 'Mail merge letter (Apothecary design)'. What other online mail merge letter templates are available through Word? (*Hint*: In the New gallery, search for the text, mail merge template.) What merge fields are included in the mail merge letter templates? Which template do you like best and why?

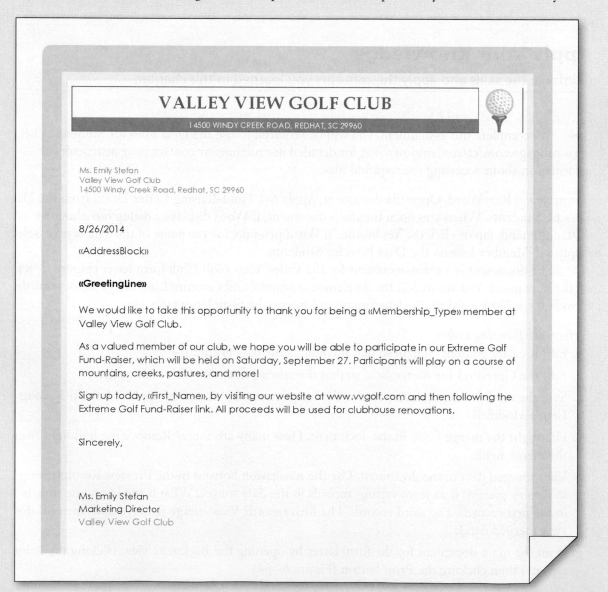

VALLEY VIEW GOLF CLUB

14500 WINDY CREEK ROAD, REDHAT, SC 29960

Ms. Emily Stefan
Valley View Golf Club
14500 Windy Creek Road, Redhat, SC 29960

8/26/2014

«AddressBlock»

«GreetingLine»

We would like to take this opportunity to thank you for being a «Membership_Type» member at Valley View Golf Club.

As a valued member of our club, we hope you will be able to participate in our Extreme Golf Fund-Raiser, which will be held on Saturday, September 27. Participants will play on a course of mountains, creeks, pastures, and more!

Sign up today, «First_Name», by visiting our website at www.vvgolf.com and then following the Extreme Golf Fund-Raiser link. All proceeds will be used for clubhouse renovations.

Sincerely,

Ms. Emily Stefan
Marketing Director
Valley View Golf Club

Figure 6–84

Extend Your Knowledge

Extend the skills you learned in this chapter and experiment with new skills. You may need to use Help to complete the assignment.

Editing an IF Field, Inserting a Fill-In Field, Formatting a Letter, and Merging Using Outlook and Access

Note: To complete this assignment, you will be required to use the Data Files for Students. Visit www.cengage.com/ct/studentdownload for detailed instructions or contact your instructor for information about accessing the required files.

Instructions: Run Word. Open the document called Extend 6-1 Vitamin Sale Letter Draft located on the Data Files for Students. When you open the main document, if Word displays a dialog box about an SQL command, tap or click the Yes button. If Word prompts for the name of the data source, select Extend 6-1 Customer List on the Data Files for Students.

The document is a main document for a form letter announcing a store moving (Figure 6–85). You will modify an IF field, and add a Fill-in field, print field codes, reformat the letter according to the block style for business letters, create envelopes for records in the data source, using an Access database file as a data source, and merge to email addresses.

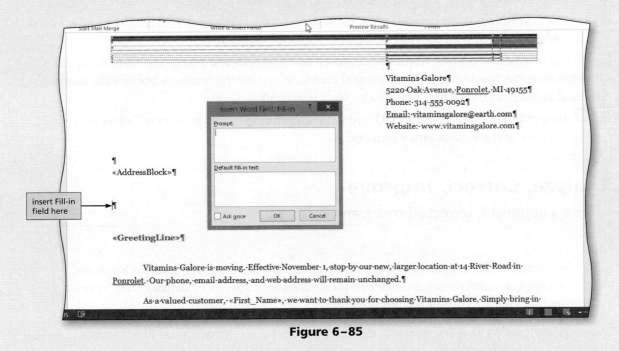

Figure 6–85

Perform the following tasks:

1. Use Help to learn about mail merge, IF fields, Fill-in fields, and merging to email addresses.

2. Edit the IF field so that the preferred customers receive a 20 percent discount and all others receive a 10 percent discount. (*Hint*: Use the 'Toggle Field Codes' command on the shortcut menu [press and hold or right-click the IF field code in the document window] and edit the IF field directly in the document.)

3. Below the AddressBlock merge field, insert a Fill-in field (Figure 6–85) that asks this question: What date will you be mailing these letters? Select the Ask once check box so that the question is asked only once, instead of for each letter. When merging the letters, use a date in September of 2014. What is the purpose of the Fill-in field?

Continued >

Extend Your Knowledge *continued*

4. If requested by your instructor, add a record to the data source that contains your personal information. Save the modified letter with the file name, Extend 6-1 Vitamin Sale Letter Modified.

5. Merge the letters to a new document. Save the merged letters using the file name, Extend 6-1 Vitamin Sale Merged Letters.

6. Print the main document for the form letter by opening the Backstage view, tapping or clicking the Print tab, and then tapping or clicking the Print button.

7. Print the form letter with field codes showing, that is, with the 'Print field codes instead of their values' check box selected in the Word Options dialog box. Be sure to deselect this check box after printing the field codes version of the letter. How does this printout differ from the one printed in #5?

8. Submit the merged letters in the format specified by your instructor.

9. If your instructor requests, create envelopes for each letter in the data source. Submit the merged envelopes in the format specified by your instructor.

10. Reformat the form letter so that it is properly spaced and sized according to the block style for business letters. Save the letter with the file name, Extend 6-1 Vitamin Sale Block Letter.

11. If you know Access and your instructor requests, create the data source in Access and then open the main document with the Access database file as the data source.

12. If your instructor requests, display your record on the screen and merge the form letter to an email message, specifying only the current record to receive the message. Submit the merged email message in the format specified by your instructor.

13. ✸ Answer the questions posed in #3 and #7. If you choose to merge to email addresses, what is the purpose of the various email formats?

Analyze, Correct, Improve

Analyze a document, correct all errors, and improve it.

Editing Merge Fields, Editing a Data Source, and Specifying Filter Conditions

Note: To complete this assignment, you will be required to use the Data Files for Students. Visit www.cengage.com/ct/studentdownload for detailed instructions or contact your instructor for information about accessing the required files.

Instructions: Run Word. Open the document, Analyze 6-1 Admissions Letter Draft, located on the Data Files for Students. When you open the main document, if Word displays a dialog box about an SQL command, tap or click the Yes button. If Word prompts for the name of the data source, select Analyze 6-1 Student List on the Data Files for Students.

The document is a form letter that is missing fields and requires editing (Figure 6–86). You are to insert an AddressBlock merge field and a GreetingLine merge field, insert and delete merge fields in the form letter, edit data source records, and filter and sort records.

Figure 6–86

Perform the following tasks:

1. Correct In the form letter, correct the following items:

a. Add a field to the data source called Major. Enter these majors in the five records: general engineering, biology, business, animal and poultry sciences, and psychology.

b. In the data source, find the record whose last name is Johnson. Fix the State entry so that it reads, NC, and ZIP Code entry so that it reads 38761.

c. In the data source, find the misspelled address, Bakr, and correct its spelling to Baker.

d. If requested by your instructor, add a record to the data source that contains your personal information.

e. In the main document, insert the AddressBlock merge field below the date.

f. In the main document, insert the GreetingLine merge field below the AddressBlock. Use an appropriate salutation and punctuation.

g. In the first sentence, delete the merge field, Last_Name, and the space that precedes it, so that just the First_Name merge field appears.

h. At the end of the second sentence in the second paragraph, insert the Major merge field.

i. Save the modified document with the file name, Analyze 6-1 Admissions Letter Modified, and then submit it in the format specified by your instructor.

2. Improve Enhance the letter specifying merge filters. Merge to a new document only those students who live in Georgia. Clear the filter. Identify another type of filter and merge those form letters to a new document. Clear the filter. Merge all records in last name order and merge to a new document. Clear the sort order. Identify another type of sort order and merge those form letters to a new document. Clear the sort order. If requested by your instructor, submit the filtered and sorted documents in the format specified.

3. ✹ This assignment contains only a few records in the data source. If it contained records for the entire school, what filters might be useful? Why?

In the Labs

Design and/or create a document using the guidelines, concepts, and skills presented in this chapter. Labs 1 and 2, which increase in difficulty, require you to create solutions based on what you learned in the chapter; Lab 3 requires you to create a solution, which uses cloud and web technologies, by learning and investigating on your own from general guidance.

Lab 1: Creating a Form Letter Using a Template, a Data Source, Mailing Labels, and a Directory

Problem: You are graduating this December and have prepared your resume (shown in Figure 5–81 on page WD 329 in Chapter 5). You decide to create a cover letter for your resume as a form letter that you will send to potential employers. The main document for the form letter is shown in Figure 6–87a.

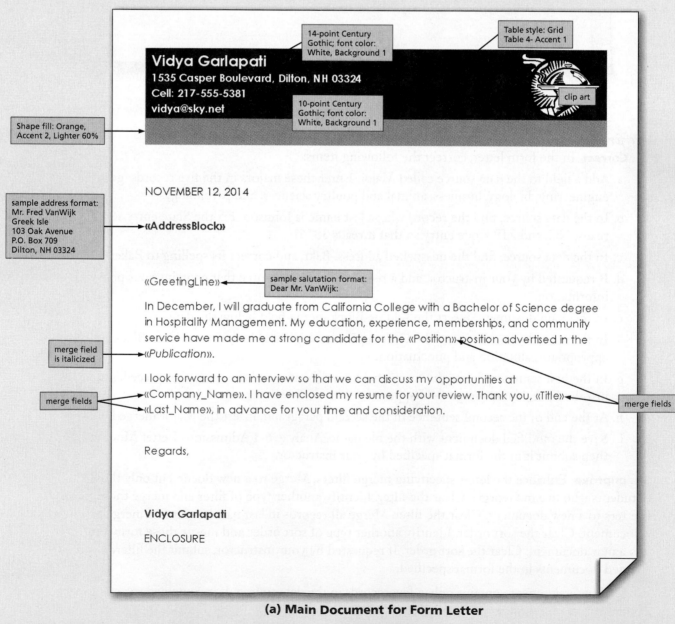

(a) Main Document for Form Letter

Figure 6–87

Perform the following tasks:

1. Use the Timeless letter template to begin creating the main document for the form letter. If you cannot locate this template, open the file called Basic resume (Timeless design) from the Data Files for Students. If necessary, change the document theme to Wisp (or a similar theme). Save the main document for the form letter with the file name, Lab 6-1 Garlapati Cover Letter.

2. Type a new data source using the data shown in Figure 6–87b. Delete the field names not used and add two field names: Position and Publication. If requested by your instructor, add a record to the data source that contains your personal information. Save the data source with the file name, Lab 6-1 Garlapati Potential Employers.

Title	First Name	Last Name	Company Name	Address Line 1	Address Line 2	City	State	ZIP Code	Position	Publication
Ms.	Dawn	Nitz	Garden Grill	145 Sunset Road		Dilton	NH	03324	Assistant Manager	Dilton Press
Mr.	Fred	VanWijk	Greek Isle	103 Oak Avenue	P.O. Box 709	Dilton	NH	03324	Restaurant Supervisor	Moraine Weekly
Ms.	Lynette	Galens	Lynette's Mediterranean Eatery	312 Center Street		Harrust	NH	03891	Manager	Weekly Gazette
Ms.	Latisha	Adams	Starlight Hotels	85 Cottage Grove Lane	P.O. Box 8722	Harrust	NH	03891	Associate Food Service Director	Tipton News
Mr.	Milton	Brewer	Paradise Cuisine	198 Shilling Boulevard	P.O. Box 239	Dilton	NH	03324	Management Trainee	Dilton Press

(b) Data Source

Figure 6–87 (continued)

3. Save the main document for the form letter again. Enter the text, clip art, merge fields, and formats as shown in the figure. Insert the AddressBlock and GreetingLine merge fields according to the sample formats shown in the figure. Italicize the Publication merge field. Change the top and bottom margins to 1 inch and the left and right margins to 1.25 inches. Specify the position of the rectangle graphic to 1 inch from the top of the page. Reduce the space above the paragraph containing the date to 36 point.

4. Merge the form letters to a new document. Save the merged letters in a file called Lab 6-1 Garlapati Merged Letters.

5. In a new document window, address mailing labels using the same data source you used for the form letters. Save the mailing label layout with the name, Lab 6-1 Garlapati Mailing Labels. If required by your instructor, merge the mailing labels to the printer.

6. In a new document window, specify the main document type as a directory. Change the page layout to landscape orientation. Change the margins to narrow. Insert all merge fields in the document, separating each with a comma. Merge the directory layout to a new document window. Convert the list of fields to a Word table (the table will have 11 columns). Add a row to the top of the table and insert field names in the empty cells. Change the font size of all text in the table to 8 point. Apply the List Table 3 - Accent 2 table style (remove formatting from the first column). Resize the table columns so that the table looks like Figure 6–87b. Center the table. Sort the table in the directory by the Last Name field. Save the merged directory with the file name, Lab 6-1 Garlapati Directory.

7. Submit all documents in the format specified by your instructor.

8. ✸ Why is the Publication merge field italicized in this letter?

Continued >

In the Labs *continued*

Lab 2: Designing a Data Source, Form Letter, and Directory from Sample Letters

Problem: You are graduating this May and have prepared your resume (shown in Figure 5–82 on page WD 331 in Chapter 5). You decide to create a cover letter for your resume as a form letter that you will send to potential employers. Sample drafted letters for the cover letter are shown in Figure 6–88a and Figure 6–88b.

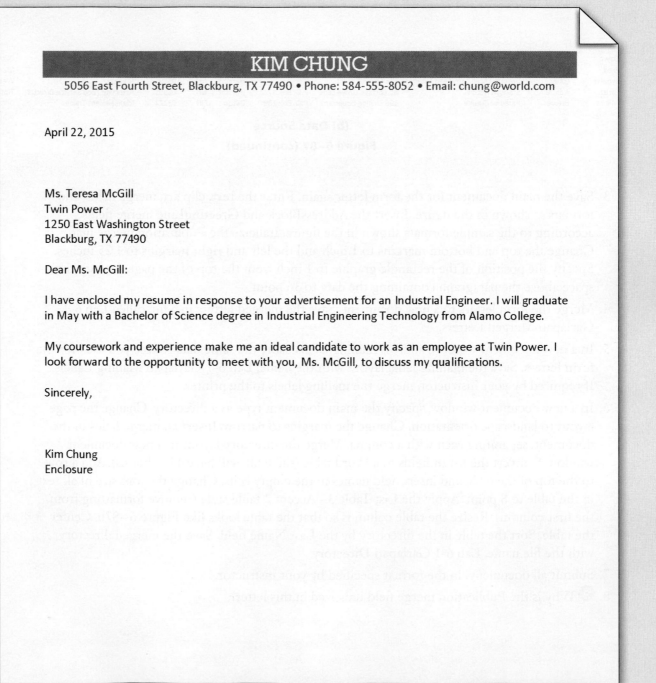

KIM CHUNG

5056 East Fourth Street, Blackburg, TX 77490 • Phone: 584-555-8052 • Email: chung@world.com

April 22, 2015

Ms. Teresa McGill
Twin Power
1250 East Washington Street
Blackburg, TX 77490

Dear Ms. McGill:

I have enclosed my resume in response to your advertisement for an Industrial Engineer. I will graduate in May with a Bachelor of Science degree in Industrial Engineering Technology from Alamo College.

My coursework and experience make me an ideal candidate to work as an employee at Twin Power. I look forward to the opportunity to meet with you, Ms. McGill, to discuss my qualifications.

Sincerely,

Kim Chung
Enclosure

(a) Sample First Letter

KIM CHUNG

5056 East Fourth Street, Blackburg, TX 77490 • Phone: 584-555-8052 • Email: chung@world.com

April 22, 2015

Mr. Ronald Hidalgo
Fluid Energy Corporation
7685 Independence Parkway
P.O. Box 2283
Gartner, TX 77399

Dear Mr. Hidalgo:

I have enclosed my resume in response to your advertisement for an Energy System Control Engineer. I will graduate in May with a Bachelor of Science degree in Industrial Engineering Technology from Alamo College.

My coursework and experience make me an ideal candidate to work as a contractor at Fluid Energy Corporation. I look forward to the opportunity to meet with you, Mr. Hidalgo, to discuss my qualifications.

Sincerely,

Kim Chung
Enclosure

(b) Sample Second Letter

Figure 6–88

Perform the following tasks:

1. Review the letters in Figure 6–88 and determine the fields that should be in the data source. Write the field names on a piece of paper.

2. Do not use a template to create this form letter. In Word, create a main document for the letters using the block letter style. Apply the No Spacing style to all paragraphs. Save the main document for the form letter with the file name, Lab 6-2 Chung Cover Letter.

3. Create a data source containing five records, consisting of data from the two letters shown in Figure 6–88 and then add three more records with your own data. If requested by your instructor, add a record to the data source that contains your personal information. Save the data source with the file name, Lab 6-2 Chung Potential Employers.

Continued >

In the Labs *continued*

4. Enter the text and merge fields into the letter. The letter requires one IF field that displays the words, an employee, if the available job position is for an employee; otherwise, it displays the words, a contractor, if the available job position is for a contractor. Merge the form letters to a new document. Save the merged letters with the file name, Lab 6-2 Chung Merged Letters. Submit the merged letters in the format specified by your instructor.

5. Merge the data source to a directory. Convert it to a Word table. Add an attractive border to the table and apply any other formatting you feel necessary. Submit the directory in the format specified by your instructor.

6. ✳ Which fields did you use in your data source?

Lab 3: Expand Your World: Cloud and Web Technologies
Exploring Apps for Office

Problem: You use apps on your phone and tablet regularly to look up a variety of information. You see that you can use apps not only in Word, but in other Office apps. You would like to investigate some of the apps available for Word to determine which ones would be helpful for you to use.

Note: You will be required to use your Microsoft Account to complete this assignment. If you do not have a Microsoft account and do not want to create one, read this assignment without performing the instructions.

Instructions: Perform the following tasks:

1. Use Help to learn about Apps for Office. If necessary, sign in to your Windows account.

2. If you are not signed in already, sign in to your Microsoft Account in Word.

3. Display the INSERT tab and then tap or click the 'Insert an App' button (INSERT tab | Apps group) to display the Apps for Office dialog box. (If a menu is displayed, tap or click the See All link to display the Apps for Office dialog box.) Tap or click the Office Store button to visit the online Office Store. Tap or click the 'What are apps?' link and read the information. Tap or click the Back button to return to the Office Store.

4. Scroll through the 'New Apps for Word', the 'Featured Apps for Word' (Figure 6–89), and the 'Top Downloaded Apps for Word'. Tap or click the More button in one of these categories to display more information about your selection. Locate a free app that you feel would be helpful to you while you use Word, tap or click the Add button, and then follow the instructions to add the app to Word.

5. In Word, tap or click the 'Insert an App' button (INSERT tab | Apps group) to display the Apps for Office dialog box. Tap or click the app you added and then tap or click the Insert button to add the app. Tap or click the 'Insert an App' arrow (INSERT tab | Apps group) to see the added app in the list.

6. Practice using the app. Does the app work as you intended? Would you recommend the app to others?

7. ✳ Which app did you download and why? Answer the questions in #6. If you download a dictionary app, how else in Word can you access that app?

your list of Featured
Apps for Word will differ

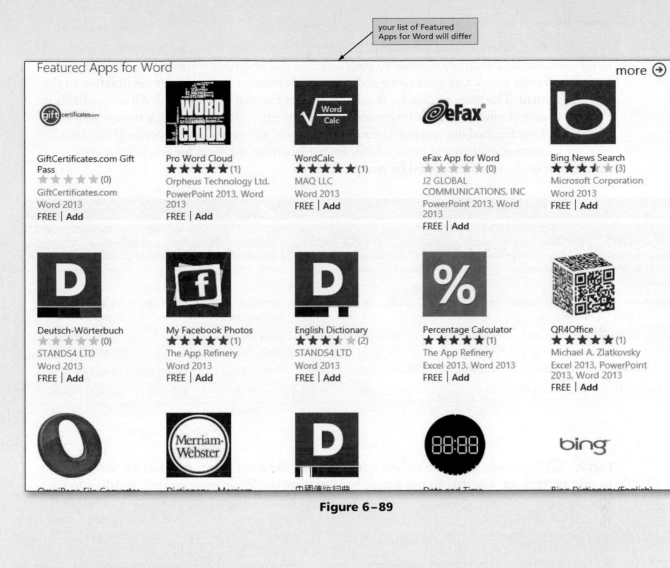

Figure 6–89

✺ Consider This: Your Turn

Apply your creative thinking and problem solving skills to design and implement a solution.

1: Create a Form Letter for a Family Reunion

Personal

Part 1: You are coordinating the 10th annual family reunion for all of your relatives. The reunion will be held in Wilmington Park in Graber on Saturday, September 6. The pavilion at the park has been reserved from 11:00 a.m. until 10:00 p.m. If anyone has a volleyball set, horseshoes, or other outdoor equipment, ask them to contact you. Anyone who wants to play baseball should bring bats and mitts. Everyone is being assigned a food and beverage item to bring, along with a table service such as plates, napkins, and condiments. Each person should bring enough of their assigned items to serve 20 people.

Continued >

STUDENT ASSIGNMENTS

Consider This: Your Turn *continued*

Use the concepts and techniques presented in this chapter to create and format a form letter announcing the family reunion to your relatives and assigning respective food, beverage, and table service items. Use your name and contact information as the sender information in the main document. The merge fields for the data source are shown in Table 6–1. All merge fields in the data source should be used at least once in the form letter. Be sure to check the spelling and grammar of the finished documents. Create a directory of the data source records. If required by your instructor, address and print accompanying labels for the form letters. Submit your assignment in the format specified by your instructor.

Table 6–1

Relative Name	Address Line 1	Address Line 2	City	State	ZIP Code	Assigned food	Assigned Beverage	Assigned Table Service
Tom and Betty Warner	32 Tipton Avenue		Graber	OK	74877	hamburgers	iced tea	plastic cups
George Peterson	127 First Placess	Apt. 52	Elwood	OK	74891	hamburger and hot dog buns	lemonade	paper plates and napkins
Henrietta Gilbert	58 Ohio Court	Unit 2B	Melville	OK	74770	brats and hot dogs	water	ketchup and mustard
The Carter Family	359 Hillside Lane	P.O. Box 17	Elwood	OK	74891	chips	regular soda	pickles and onions
The Wakefield Family	887 East Street		Graber	OK	74877	cookies	diet soda	salt and pepper

© 2014 Cengage Learning

Part 2: ✳ You made several decisions while creating the form letter, data source, and directory in this assignment: whether to use a template or create the letter from scratch, wording to use, where to position text and merge fields in the letter, how to format elements, how to set up the data source, and how to format the directory. What was the rationale behind each of these decisions?

2: Create a Form Letter for a Vehicle Service Center
Professional

Part 1: As office manager at Total Vehicle Care, you send reminder letters to customers for service to their vehicles. Your business is located at 983 Independence Parkway, Rocktown, AR 71672; phone number is (847) 555-3838; website is www.tvc.com. In the form letters, you inform customers of the month of their last vehicle service and the type of service performed on their vehicle. You ask them to call to schedule an appointment for a service appointment at their earliest convenience. If they bring their letter, they will receive a 10 percent discount on any service performed.

Use the concepts and techniques presented in this chapter to create and format a form letter reminding customers of service due on their vehicle. Use your name and contact information as the sender information in the main document. The merge fields for the data source are shown in Table 6–2. All merge fields in the data source should be used at least once in the form letter. Be sure to check the spelling and grammar of the finished documents. Create a directory of the data source records. If required by your instructor, address and print accompanying labels for the form letters. Submit your assignment in the format specified by your instructor.

Table 6–2

Title	First Name	Last Name	Address Line 1	Address Line 2	City	State	ZIP Code	Vehicle Type	Month of Last Service	Last Service Performed
Ms.	Lana	Canaan	202 Park Boulevard		Rocktown	AR	71672	pickup truck	January	oil change
Mr.	Raul	Ramos	22 Fifth Street	Apt. 2B	Hill City	AR	71630	SUV	May	oil change
Ms.	Laura	Ennis	74 MacEnroe Court	P.O. Box 77	Fairview	AR	71622	compact car	March	tune-up
Mr.	Max	Henreich	322 County Line Road		Rocktown	AR	71672	van	February	tire rotation and alignment
Ms.	Constance	Marsh	5421 Crestview Circle	Unit 10C	Horizon	AR	74642	sports car	March	inspection

© 2014 Cengage Learning

Part 2: ✹ You made several decisions while creating the form letter, data source, and directory in this assignment: whether to use a template or create the letter from scratch, wording to use, where to position text and merge fields in the letter, how to format elements, how to set up the data source, and how to format the directory. What was the rationale behind each of these decisions?

3: Create Form Letters Using Different Types of Data Sources
Research and Collaboration

Part 1:   This chapter illustrated using one type of data source for merging form letters. As mentioned in the chapter, however, other types of data sources can be used for a merge operation. As a starting point for this assignment, select the form letter created in this chapter, the Apply Your Knowledge letter, or any of the other assignments completed, along with the corresponding data source. Form a three-member team to research, create, and merge form letters as follows:

  a. If necessary, add an email field to the data source and then merge the contents of the data source to email addresses.

  b. Use Access 2013 to view and format the contents of a data source created in Word. It may be necessary to use Help in Access.

  c. Use Access 2013 to create a table and then use that table as the data source in the merge document. It may be necessary to use Help in both Word and Access for instructions about creating and saving an Access table in the proper format for a mail merge.

  d. Use Excel 2013 to create a table and then use that table as the data source in the merge document. It may be necessary to use Help in both Word and Excel for instructions about creating and saving an Excel table in the proper format for a mail merge.

  e. Use Outlook 2013 recipients as a data source in the merge document. It may be necessary to use Help in both Word and Outlook.

    Summarize the steps you followed for each of the above tasks. Submit your team assignment in the format specified by your instructor.

Part 2: ✹ Of the various data source types used in this assignment, which do you prefer and why? Do you prefer to create data sources in Word or to use one of the techniques in this assignment? Why?

Learn Online

Reinforce what you learned in this chapter with games, exercises, training, and many other online activities and resources.

Student Companion Site   Reinforcement activities and resources are available at no additional cost on www.cengagebrain.com. Visit www.cengage.com/ct/studentdownload for detailed instructions about accessing the resources available at the Student Companion Site.

SAM   Put your skills into practice with SAM! If you have a SAM account, go to www.cengage .com/sam2013 to access SAM assignments for this chapter.

7 Creating a Newsletter with a Pull-Quote and Graphics

Microsoft product screen shots used with permission from Microsoft Corporation.

Objectives

You will have mastered the material in this chapter when you can:

- Insert and format WordArt
- Set custom tab stops
- Crop a graphic
- Rotate a graphic
- Format a document in multiple columns
- Justify a paragraph
- Hyphenate a document
- Format a character as a drop cap

- Insert a column break
- Insert and format a text box
- Copy and paste using a split window
- Balance columns
- Modify and format a SmartArt graphic
- Copy and paste using the Office Clipboard
- Add an art page border

7 | Creating a Newsletter with a Pull-Quote and Graphics

Introduction

Professional-looking documents, such as newsletters and brochures, often are created using desktop publishing software. With desktop publishing software, you can divide a document in multiple columns, wrap text around diagrams and other graphical images, change fonts and font sizes, add color and lines, and so on, to create an attention-grabbing document. Desktop publishing software, such as Microsoft Publisher, Adobe PageMaker, or QuarkXpress, enables you to open an existing word processing document and enhance it through formatting tools not provided in your word processing software. Word, however, provides many of the formatting features that you would find in a desktop publishing program. Thus, you can use Word to create eye-catching newsletters and brochures.

Project — Newsletter

A newsletter is a publication geared for a specific audience that is created on a recurring basis, such as weekly, monthly, or quarterly. The audience may be subscribers, club members, employees, customers, patrons, students, etc.

The project in this chapter uses Word to produce the two-page newsletter shown in Figure 7–1. The newsletter is a monthly publication, called *Campus Post*. Each issue of *Campus Post* contains a feature article and announcements. This month's feature article discusses information literacy. The feature article spans the first two columns of the first page of the newsletter and then continues on the second page. The announcements, which are located in the third column of the first page, inform students about discounts and spirit wear and announce the topic of the next issue's feature article.

The *Campus Post* newsletter in this chapter incorporates the desktop publishing features of Word. The body of each page of the newsletter is divided in three columns. A variety of fonts, font sizes, and colors add visual appeal to the document. The first page has text wrapped around a pull-quote, and the second page has text wrapped around a graphic. Horizontal and vertical lines separate distinct areas of the newsletter, including a page border around the perimeter of each page.

The project in this chapter involves several steps requiring you to drag and drop. If you drag to the wrong location, you may want to cancel an action. Remember that you always can tap or click the Undo button on the Quick Access Toolbar to cancel your most recent action.

If you are using your finger on a touch screen and are having difficulty completing the steps in this chapter, consider using a stylus. Many people find it easier to be precise with a stylus than with a finger. In addition, with a stylus you see the pointer. If you still are having trouble completing the steps with a stylus, try using a mouse.

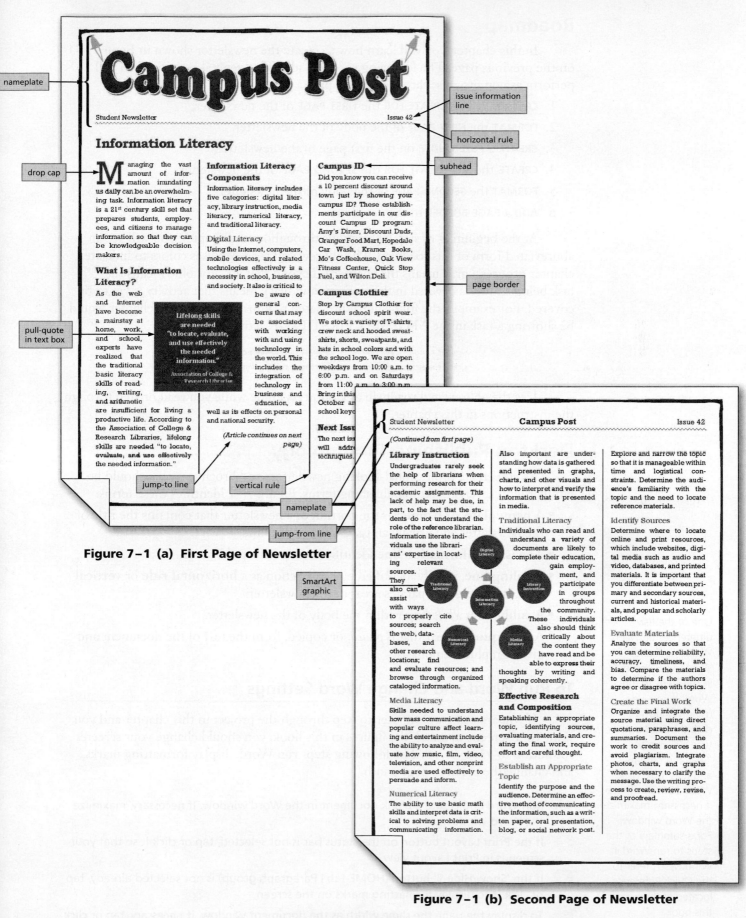

Figure 7–1 (a) First Page of Newsletter

Figure 7–1 (b) Second Page of Newsletter

Roadmap

In this chapter, you will learn how to create the newsletter shown in Figure 7–1 on the previous page. The following roadmap identifies general activities you will perform as you progress through this chapter:

1. CREATE the NAMEPLATE FOR the FIRST PAGE of the newsletter.
2. FORMAT the FIRST PAGE of the body of the newsletter.
3. CREATE a PULL-QUOTE on the first page of the newsletter.
4. CREATE the NAMEPLATE FOR the SECOND PAGE of the newsletter.
5. FORMAT the SECOND PAGE of the body of the newsletter.
6. ADD a PAGE BORDER to the newsletter.

At the beginning of step instructions throughout the chapter, you will see an abbreviated form of this roadmap. The abbreviated roadmap uses colors to indicate chapter progress: gray means the chapter is beyond that activity, blue means the task being shown is covered in that activity, and black means that activity is yet to be covered. For example, the following abbreviated roadmap indicates the chapter would be showing a task in the 2 FORMAT FIRST PAGE activity.

1 CREATE NAMEPLATE FOR FIRST PAGE | 2 FORMAT FIRST PAGE | 3 CREATE PULL-QUOTE

4 CREATE NAMEPLATE FOR SECOND PAGE | 5 FORMAT SECOND PAGE | 6 ADD PAGE BORDER

Use the abbreviated roadmap as a progress guide while you read or step through the instructions in this chapter.

Desktop Publishing Terminology

As you create professional-looking newsletters and brochures, you should be familiar with several desktop publishing terms. Figure 7–1 identifies these terms:

- A **nameplate**, or **banner**, is the portion of a newsletter that contains the title of the newsletter and usually an issue information line.
- The **issue information line** identifies the specific publication.
- A **ruling line**, usually identified by its direction as a **horizontal rule** or **vertical rule**, is a line that separates areas of the newsletter.
- A **subhead** is a heading within the body of the newsletter.
- A **pull-quote** is text that is *pulled*, or copied, from the text of the document and given graphical emphasis.

To Run Word and Change Word Settings

If you are using a computer to step through the project in this chapter and you want your screens to match the figures in this book, you should change your screen's resolution to 1366 × 768. The following steps run Word, display formatting marks, and change the zoom to page width.

1 Run Word and create a blank document in the Word window. If necessary, maximize the Word window.

2 If the Print Layout button on the status bar is not selected, tap or click it so that your screen is in Print Layout view.

3 If the 'Show/Hide ¶' button (HOME tab | Paragraph group) is not selected already, tap or click it to display formatting marks on the screen.

4 To display the page the same width as the document window, if necessary, tap or click the Page Width button (VIEW tab | Zoom group).

One of the few differences between Windows 7 and Windows 8 occurs in the steps to run Word. If you are using Windows 7, click the Start button, type Word in the 'Search programs and files' box, click Word 2013, and then, if necessary, maximize the Word window. For a summary of the steps to run Word in Windows 7, refer to the Quick Reference located at the back of this book.

To Change Spacing above and below Paragraphs and Margin Settings

Recall that Word is preset to use standard 8.5-by-11-inch paper, with 1-inch top, bottom, left, and right margins. In earlier chapters, you changed the margins by selecting predefined settings in the Margins gallery. For the newsletter in this chapter, all margins (left, right, top, and bottom) are .75 inches, which is not a predefined setting in the Margins gallery. Thus, the following steps set custom margins.

1 Display the PAGE LAYOUT tab.

2 Tap or click the Adjust Margins button (PAGE LAYOUT tab | Page Setup group) to display the Margins gallery and then tap or click Custom Margins to display the Page Setup dialog box.

3 Change each value in the Top, Bottom, Left, and Right boxes (Page Setup dialog box) to .75" (Figure 7–2).

4 Tap or click the OK button to change the margin values.

Figure 7–2

BTW

The Ribbon and Screen Resolution
Word may change how the groups and buttons within the groups appear on the ribbon, depending on the computer's screen resolution. Thus, your ribbon may look different from the ones in this book if you are using a screen resolution other than 1366 × 768.

To Change Theme Colors

The newsletter in this chapter uses the Damask theme. The following steps change the theme to Damask.

1 Display the DESIGN tab.

2 Tap or click the Themes button (DESIGN tab | Document Formatting group) and then tap or click Damask in the Themes gallery to change the document theme.

Creating the Nameplate

The nameplate on the first page of this newsletter consists of the information above the multiple columns (Figure 7–1a on page WD 411). In this project, the nameplate includes the newsletter title, Campus Post, images of thumbtacks, and the issue information line. The steps on the following pages create the nameplate for the first page of the newsletter in this chapter.

The following pages use the steps outlined below to create the nameplate for the newsletter in this chapter.

1. Enter and format the newsletter title using WordArt.
2. Set custom tab stops for the issue information line.
3. Enter text in the issue information line.
4. Add a horizontal rule below the issue information line.
5. Insert and format the clip art images.

How should you design a nameplate?

A nameplate visually identifies a newsletter. It should catch the attention of readers, enticing them to read a newsletter. Usually, the nameplate is positioned horizontally across the top of the newsletter, although some nameplates are vertical. The nameplate typically consists of the title of the newsletter and the issue information line. Some also include a subtitle, a slogan, and a graphical image or logo.

Guidelines for the newsletter title and other elements in the nameplate are as follows:

- Compose a title that is short, yet conveys the contents of the newsletter. In the newsletter title, eliminate unnecessary words such as these: the, newsletter. Use a decorative font in as large a font size as possible so that the title stands out on the page.

- Other elements on the nameplate should not compete in size with the title. Use colors that complement the title. Select easy-to-read fonts.

- Arrange the elements of the nameplate so that it does not have a cluttered appearance. If necessary, use ruling lines to visually separate areas of the nameplate.

To Insert WordArt

1 CREATE NAMEPLATE FOR FIRST PAGE | 2 FORMAT FIRST PAGE | 3 CREATE PULL-QUOTE
4 CREATE NAMEPLATE FOR SECOND PAGE | 5 FORMAT SECOND PAGE | 6 ADD PAGE BORDER

In Chapter 3, you inserted a shape drawing object in a document. Recall that a drawing object is a graphic you create using Word. Another type of drawing object, called **WordArt**, enables you to create text with special effects such as shadowed, rotated, stretched, skewed, and wavy effects.

This project uses WordArt for the newsletter title, Campus Post. *Why? A title created with WordArt is likely to draw the reader's attention.* The following steps insert WordArt.

1
- Display the INSERT tab.

- Tap or click the Insert WordArt button (INSERT tab | Text group) to display the Insert WordArt gallery (Figure 7–3).

Q&A Once I select a WordArt style, can I customize its appearance? Yes. The next steps customize the WordArt style selected here.

Figure 7–3

2

• Tap or click 'Fill - Pink, Accent 1, Outline - Background 1, Hard Shadow - Accent 1' in the WordArt gallery (third WordArt style in last row) to insert a drawing object in the document that is formatted according to the selected WordArt style, which contains the placeholder text, Your text here (Figure 7–4).

3

• Type `Campus Post` to replace the selected placeholder text in the WordArt drawing object (shown in Figure 7–5).

Q&A What if my placeholder text no longer is selected?
Drag through it to select it.

How do I correct a mistake in the WordArt text?
You correct WordArt text using the same techniques you use to correct document text.

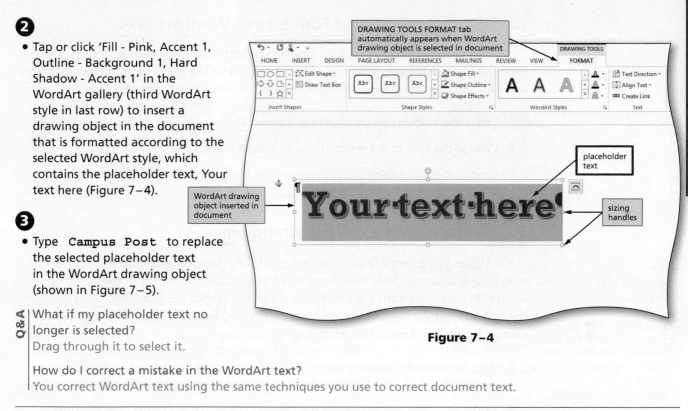

Figure 7–4

To Resize WordArt

You resize WordArt the same way you resize any other graphic. That is, you can drag its sizing handles or enter values in the Shape Height and Shape Width boxes. The next steps resize the WordArt drawing object.

1 With the WordArt drawing object selected, if necessary, display the DRAWING TOOLS FORMAT tab.

2 Change the value in the Shape Height box to 1.44 and the value in the Shape Width box to 7 (Figure 7–5).

BTW

Deleting WordArt
If you want to delete a WordArt drawing object, press and hold or right-click it and then tap Cut on the mini toolbar or click Cut on the shortcut menu, or select the WordArt drawing object and then tap or click the Cut button (HOME tab | Clipboard group).

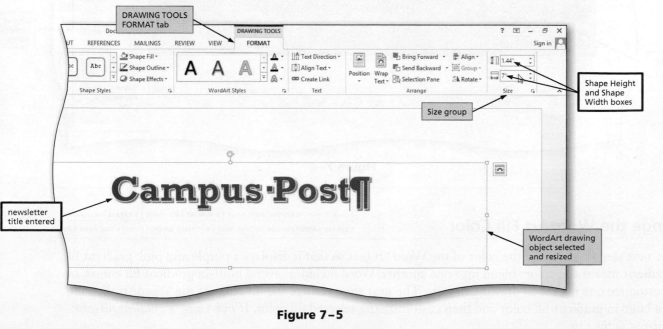

Figure 7–5

To Change the Font and Font Size of WordArt Text

You change the font and font size of WordArt text the same way you change the font and font size of any other text. That is, you select the text and then change its font and font size. The next steps change the font and font size of WordArt text.

1 Select the WordArt text, in this case, Campus Post.

2 Change the font of the selected text to Cooper Black.

3 Change the font size of the selected text to 72 point (shown in Figure 7–6).

To Change an Object's Text Wrapping

BTW

Touch Screen Differences

The Office and Windows interfaces may vary if you are using a touch screen. For this reason, you might notice that the function or appearance of your touch screen differs slightly from this chapter's presentation.

When you insert a drawing object in a Word document, the default text wrapping is Square, which means text will wrap around the object in the shape of a square. Because you want the nameplate above the rest of the newsletter, you change the text wrapping for the drawing object to Top and Bottom. The following steps change a drawing object's text wrapping.

1 With the WordArt drawing object selected, tap or click the Layout Options button that is attached to the WordArt drawing object to display the Layout Options gallery.

2 Tap or click 'Top and Bottom' in the Layout Options gallery so that the WordArt drawing object will not cover the document text; in this case, the paragraph mark moves below the WordArt drawing object (Figure 7–6).

3 Close the Layout Options gallery.

changed to 72-point Cooper Black font

WordArt text selected

WordArt drawing object selected

Layout Options button

LAYOUT OPTIONS

In Line with Text

With Text Wrapping

Layout Options gallery

'Top and Bottom' to be selected

Move with text
Fix position on page

See more...

Figure 7–6

To Change the WordArt Fill Color

1 CREATE NAMEPLATE FOR FIRST PAGE | 2 FORMAT FIRST PAGE | 3 CREATE PULL-QUOTE
4 CREATE NAMEPLATE FOR SECOND PAGE | 5 FORMAT SECOND PAGE | 6 ADD PAGE BORDER

The next step is to change the color of the WordArt text so that it displays a purple and pink gradient fill color. **Gradient** means the colors blend into one another. Word includes several built-in gradient fill colors, or you can customize one for use in drawing objects. The next steps change the fill color of the WordArt drawing object to a built-in gradient fill color and then customize the selected fill color. *Why? Using a gradient fill color will add interest to the title.*

1

- With the WordArt drawing object selected, tap or click the Text Fill arrow (DRAWING TOOLS FORMAT tab | WordArt Styles group) to display the Text Fill gallery.

Q&A

The Text Fill gallery did not appear. Why not?
If you are using a mouse, be sure you click the Text Fill arrow, which is to the right of the Text Fill button. If you mistakenly click the Text Fill button, Word places a default fill in the selected WordArt instead of displaying the Text Fill gallery.

2

- Tap or point to Gradient in the Text Fill gallery to display the Gradient gallery (Figure 7–7).

Figure 7–7

3

- Tap or click More Gradients in the Gradient gallery to display the Format Shape task pane. If necessary, tap or click the TEXT OPTIONS tab (Format Shape task pane) and then, if necessary, tap or click the 'Text Fill & Outline' button. If necessary, expand the TEXT FILL section.

- Tap or click Gradient fill in the TEXT FILL section to display options related to gradient colors in the task pane (Figure 7–8).

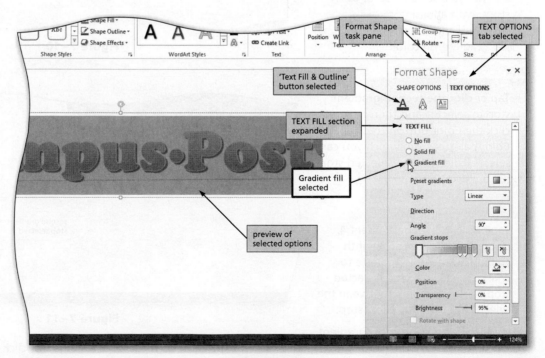

Figure 7–8

4

- Tap or click the Preset gradients button to display a palette of built-in gradient fill colors (Figure 7–9).

Figure 7–9

5

- Tap or click 'Radial Gradient - Accent 5' (bottom row, fifth column) in the Preset gradients palette to select the built-in gradient color, which shows a preview in the Gradient stops area (Figure 7–10).

Q&A What is a gradient stop?
A gradient stop is the location where two colors blend. You can change the color of a stop so that Word changes the color of the blend. You also can add or delete stops, with a minimum of two stops and a maximum of ten stops per gradient fill color.

Figure 7–10

6

- Tap or click the second gradient stop to select it and then tap or click the Color button to display a Color palette, from which you can select a color for the selected stop (Figure 7–11).

7

- Tap or click 'Lavender, Accent 4, Darker 25%' (fifth row, eighth column) in the Color palette to change the color of the selected stop and the gradient between the selected stop and the next stop.

Figure 7–11

- Tap or click the rightmost gradient stop to select it and then tap or click the Color button to display a Color palette. Tap or click 'Lavender, Accent 4, Darker 25%' (fifth row, eighth column) in the Color palette to change the color of the selected stop and the gradient between the selected stop and the previous stop.

Q&A Can I move a gradient stop?
Yes. You can drag a stop to any location along the color bar. You also can adjust the position, brightness, and transparency of any selected stop.

- Tap or click the Direction button to display a gallery that shows a variety of directions for the gradient colors (Figure 7–12).

Figure 7–12

- Tap or click 'From Top Left Corner' (rightmost direction) in the Direction gallery to specify the direction to blend the colors.

- Tap or click the Close button in the task pane.

- Tap or click the paragraph mark below the WordArt drawing object to deselect the text so that you can see its gradient fill colors (Figure 7–13).

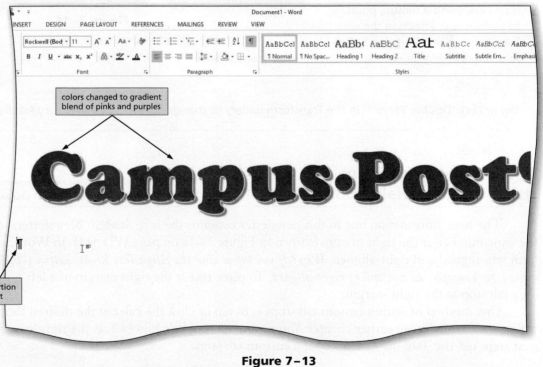

Figure 7–13

To Change the WordArt Shape

Word provides a variety of shapes to make your WordArt more interesting. The following steps change the WordArt shape. *Why? The WordArt in this newsletter has a wavy appearance.*

1

- Tap or click the WordArt drawing object to select it.

- If necessary, display the DRAWING TOOLS FORMAT tab.

- Tap or click the Text Effects button (DRAWING TOOLS FORMAT tab | WordArt Styles group) to display the Text Effects gallery.

- Tap or point to Transform in the Text Effects gallery to display the Transform gallery.

- If you are using a mouse, point to Double Wave 1 (third effect, fifth row in Warp area) in the Transform gallery to display a live preview of the selected transform effect applied to the selected drawing object (Figure 7–14).

Experiment

- If you are using a mouse, point to various text effects in the Transform gallery and watch the selected drawing object conform to that transform effect.

Figure 7–14

2

- Tap or click 'Double Wave 1' in the Transform gallery to change the shape of the WordArt drawing object.

To Set Custom Tab Stops
Using the Tabs Dialog Box

The issue information line in this newsletter contains the text, Student Newsletter, at the left margin and the issue number at the right margin (shown in Figure 7–1a on page WD 411). In Word, a paragraph cannot be both left-aligned and right-aligned. *Why? If you tap or click the 'Align Text Right' button (HOME tab | Paragraph group), for example, all text will be right-aligned.* To place text at the right margin of a left-aligned paragraph, you set a tab stop at the right margin.

One method of setting custom tab stops is to tap or click the ruler at the desired location of the tab stop, which you learned in an earlier chapter. You cannot tap or click, however, at the right margin location. Thus, the next steps use the Tabs dialog box to set a custom tab stop.

1

- If necessary, display the HOME tab.
- Position the insertion point on the paragraph mark below the WordArt drawing object, which is the paragraph to be formatted with the custom tab stops.
- Tap or click the Paragraph Settings Dialog Box Launcher to display the Paragraph dialog box (Figure 7–15).

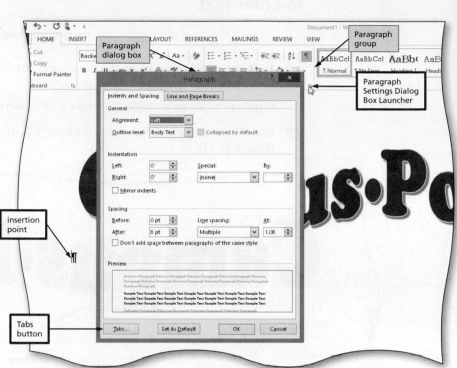

Figure 7–15

2

- Tap or click the Tabs button (Paragraph dialog box) to display the Tabs dialog box.
- Type 7 in the 'Tab stop position' text box (Tabs dialog box).
- Tap or click Right in the Alignment area to specify alignment for text at the tab stop (Figure 7–16).

3

- Tap or click the Set button (Tabs dialog box) to set a right-aligned custom tab stop at the specified position.
- Tap or click the OK button to set the defined tab stops.

Figure 7–16

Other Ways

1. Tap 'Show Context Menu' button on mini toolbar or right-click paragraph, tap or click Paragraph on shortcut menu, tap or click Tabs button (Paragraph dialog box), enter desired settings, tap or click OK button

To Enter Text

The following steps enter the issue information line text.

 With the insertion point on the paragraph below the WordArt, type **Student Newsletter** on line 2 of the newsletter.

If requested by your instructor, enter your name instead of the word, Student.

2 Press the TAB key and then type **Issue 42** to complete the issue information line (Figure 7–17).

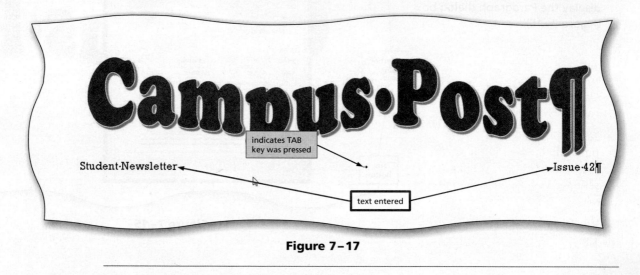

indicates TAB key was pressed

text entered

Student·Newsletter → → Issue·42¶

Figure 7–17

To Border One Edge of a Paragraph

1 CREATE NAMEPLATE FOR FIRST PAGE | 2 FORMAT FIRST PAGE | 3 CREATE PULL-QUOTE
4 CREATE NAMEPLATE FOR SECOND PAGE | 5 FORMAT SECOND PAGE | 6 ADD PAGE BORDER

In Word, you use borders to create ruling lines. As discussed in previous projects, Word can place borders on any edge of a paragraph; that is, Word can place a border on the top, bottom, left, and right edges of a paragraph.

One method of bordering paragraphs is by tapping or clicking the desired border in the Borders gallery, which you learned in an earlier chapter. If you want to specify a particular border, for example, one with color, you use the Borders and Shading dialog box. The following steps use the Borders and Shading dialog box to place a border below a paragraph. *Why? In this newsletter, the issue information line has a ¾-point wavy pink border below it.*

1

• Tap or click the Borders arrow (HOME tab | Paragraph group) to display the Borders gallery (Figure 7–18).

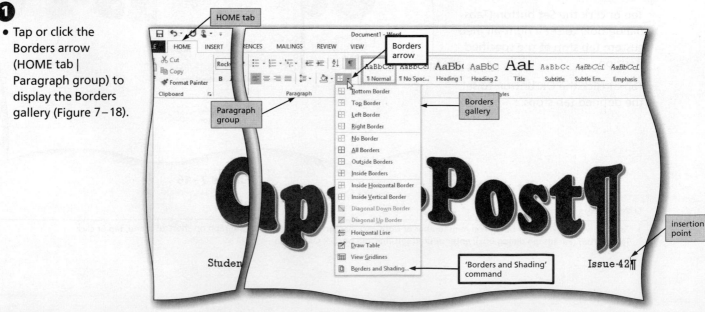

Figure 7–18

2

- Tap or click 'Borders and Shading' in the Borders gallery to display the Borders and Shading dialog box.

- Tap or click Custom in the Setting area (Borders and Shading dialog box) because you are setting just a bottom border.

- Scroll through the style list and tap or click the style shown in Figure 7–19, which has a wavy line as the border.

- Tap or click the Color button and then tap or click 'Pink, Accent 5, Darker 50%' (ninth column, sixth row) in the Color gallery.

- Tap or click the Bottom Border button in the Preview area of the dialog box to show a preview of the selected border style (Figure 7–19).

Figure 7–19

Q&A What is the purpose of the buttons in the Preview area?

They are toggles that display and remove the top, bottom, left, and right borders from the diagram in the Preview area.

3

- Tap or click the OK button to place the defined border on the paragraph containing the insertion point (Figure 7–20).

Q&A How would I change an existing border? You first remove the existing border by tapping or clicking the Borders arrow (HOME tab | Paragraph group) and then tapping or clicking the border in the Borders gallery that identifies the border you wish to remove. Then, add a new border as described in these steps.

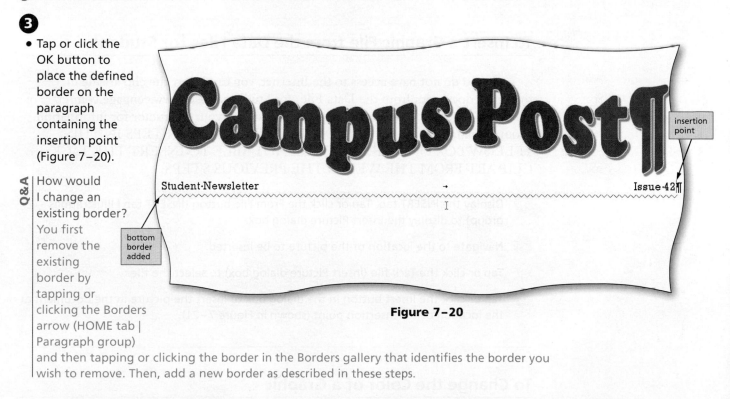

Figure 7–20

Other Ways

1. Tap or click 'Borders and Shading' button (DESIGN tab | Page Background group), tap or click Borders tab (Borders and Shading dialog box), select desired border, tap or click OK button

To Insert Clip Art

The next steps insert a clip art image of a thumbtack in the nameplate.

1 Display the INSERT tab.

2 Tap or click the Online Pictures button (INSERT tab | Illustrations group) to display the Insert Pictures dialog box.

3 Type `tack` in the Search box to specify the search text, which indicates the type of image you want to locate.

4 Tap or click the Search button to display a list of clip art that matches the entered search text.

5 Scroll through the list of clip art to locate the one shown in Figure 7–21 (or a similar image) and then tap or click the clip art to select it. (If the clip art image does not appear in the dialog box, tap or click the Cancel button in each dialog box and then proceed to the shaded steps immediately following these steps.)

6 Tap or click the Insert button to insert the selected clip art in the document at the location of the insertion point.

Q&A What if my clip art image is not in the same location as in Figure 7–21?
The clip art image may be in a different location, depending on the position of the insertion point when you inserted the image. In a later section, you will move the image to a different location.

BTW
Q&As
For a complete list of the Q&As found in many of the step-by-step sequences in this book, visit the Q&A resource on the Student Companion Site located on www.cengagebrain.com. For detailed instructions about accessing available resources, visit www.cengage.com/ct/studentdownload or contact your instructor for information about accessing the required files.

To Insert a Graphic File from the Data Files for Students

If you do not have access to the Internet, you can insert the clip art file in the Word document from the Data Files for Students. Visit www.cengage.com/ct/studentdownload for detailed instructions or contact your instructor for information about accessing the required files. NOTE: PERFORM THE STEPS IN THIS YELLOW BOX ONLY IF YOU WERE NOT ABLE TO INSERT THE TACK CLIP ART FROM THE WEB IN THE PREVIOUS STEPS.

1 Display the INSERT tab. Tap or click the From File button (INSERT tab | Illustrations group) to display the Insert Picture dialog box.

2 Navigate to the location of the picture to be inserted.

3 Tap or click the Tack file (Insert Picture dialog box) to select the file.

4 Tap or click the Insert button in the dialog box to insert the picture in the document at the location of the insertion point (shown in Figure 7–21).

To Change the Color of a Graphic

The next steps change the color of the graphic (the tack) to a lime green.

1 With the graphic still selected, tap or click the Color button (PICTURE TOOLS FORMAT tab | Adjust group) to display the Color gallery (Figure 7–21).

2 Tap or click 'Lime, Accent color 1 Light' (second color, third row) in the Recolor area in the Color gallery to change the color of the selected graphic.

Figure 7–21

To Crop a Graphic

1 CREATE NAMEPLATE FOR FIRST PAGE | 2 FORMAT FIRST PAGE | 3 CREATE PULL-QUOTE
4 CREATE NAMEPLATE FOR SECOND PAGE | 5 FORMAT SECOND PAGE | 6 ADD PAGE BORDER

The next step is to format the clip art image just inserted. You would like to remove the rounded frame from the perimeter of the image. **Why?** *You want just the tack to appear in the newsletter.* Word allows you to **crop**, or remove edges from, a graphic. The following steps crop a graphic.

1

- With the graphic selected, tap or click the Crop button (PICTURE TOOLS FORMAT tab | Size group), which places cropping handles on the image in the document.

Q&A What if I mistakenly tap or click the Crop arrow?
Tap or click the Crop button.

- If you are using a mouse, position the pointer on the top-middle cropping handle so that it looks like an upside-down letter T (Figure 7–22).

Figure 7–22

2

• Drag the top-middle cropping handle downward to the location of the shown in Figure 7–23 to remove the frame at the top of the image.

3

• If you are using a mouse, release the mouse button to crop the graphic to the location shown in Figure 7–23.

Figure 7–23

4

• Drag the left-middle cropping handle inward until the frame at the left edge of the image disappears, as shown in Figure 7–24.

• Drag the right-middle cropping handle inward until the frame at the right edge of the image disappears, as shown in Figure 7–24.

• Drag the bottom-middle cropping handle upward until the frame at the bottom edge of the image disappears, as shown in Figure 7–24.

5

• Tap or click the Crop button (PICTURE TOOLS FORMAT tab | Size group) to deactivate the cropping tool, which removes the cropping handles from the selected image.

Figure 7–24

Other Ways

1. Press and hold or right-click graphic, tap or click Crop button on mini toolbar, drag cropping handles, tap or click Crop button

To Change an Object's Text Wrapping and Size

When you insert clip art in a Word document, the default text wrapping is In Line with Text, which means the object is part of the current paragraph. Because you want the clip art images behind the newsletter title, you change the text wrapping for the clip art image to Behind Text. The next steps change a drawing object's text wrapping and also change its size.

1 With the clip art image selected, tap or click the Layout Options button attached to the graphic to display the Layout Options gallery.

2 Tap or click Behind Text in the Layout Options gallery so that the clip art image is positioned behind text in the document.

3 Close the Layout Options gallery.

4 Change the values in the Shape Height and Shape Width boxes (PICTURE TOOLS FORMAT tab | Size group) to .5" and .45", respectively.

To Move a Graphic

The clip art image needs to be moved up so that the tip of the tack is on the t in the word, Post, in the newsletter title. The following steps move a graphic.

1 Hide formatting marks so that you can see exactly where the letter t ends.

2 Drag the graphic to the location shown in Figure 7–25.

To Copy a Graphic, Flip It, and Move It

The next step is to copy the cropped thumbtack image, flip it so that it faces the opposite direction, and then move it so that it is positioned above the C in the word, Campus, in the nameplate. The following steps copy, flip, and move a graphic.

1 If necessary, tap or click the graphic (the tack) to select it.

2 If necessary, display the HOME tab.

3 Tap or click the Copy button (HOME tab | Clipboard group) to copy the selected item to the Office Clipboard.

4 Tap or click the Paste arrow (HOME tab | Clipboard group) to display the Paste gallery and then tap or click 'Keep Source Formatting' to paste the object using the same formatting as the original.

5 Display the PICTURE TOOLS FORMAT tab. With the graphic still selected, tap or click the Rotate Objects button (PICTURE TOOLS FORMAT tab | Arrange group) to display the Rotate Objects gallery and then tap or click Flip Horizontal in the Rotate Options gallery, so that Word flips the graphic to display its mirror image.

6 Drag the graphic to the location shown in Figure 7–25.

Figure 7–25

To Use the Selection Task Pane

The next step is to rotate the clip art images, but because they are positioned behind the text, it may be difficult to select them. The following step displays the Selection task pane. *Why? The Selection task pane enables you easily to select items on the screen that are layered behind other objects.*

1

- If necessary, tap or click in a graphic to display the PICTURE TOOLS FORMAT tab.

- Tap or click the 'Display the Selection Pane' button (PICTURE TOOLS FORMAT tab | Arrange group) to display the Selection task pane (Figure 7–26).

🔍 **Experiment**

- Tap or click Text Box 1 in the Selection task pane to select the WordArt drawing object. Tap or click Picture 3 in the Selection task pane to select the first tack image. Tap or click Picture 2 in the Selection task pane to select the second tack image.

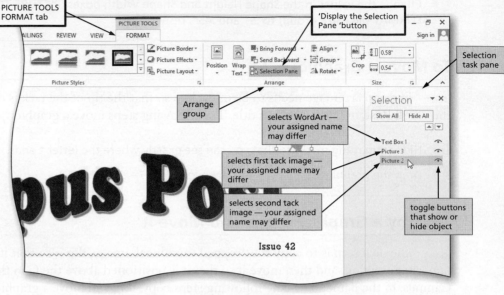

Figure 7–26

Q&A What are the displayed names in the Selection task pane?
Word assigns names to each object in the document. The names displayed on your screen may differ.

To Rotate a Graphic

The following steps rotate a graphic. *Why? You would like the tack images angled inward a bit more.*

1

- If necessary, tap or click Picture 2 in the Selection task pane to select the image of the tack on the right side of the screen.

- If you are using a mouse, position the pointer on the graphic's rotate handle (Figure 7–27).

Figure 7–27

2

- If you are using a mouse, drag the rotate handle leftward and downward to rotate the graphic slightly as shown in Figure 7–28.

Q&A Can I drag the rotate handle in any direction?
You can drag the rotate handle clockwise or counterclockwise.

Figure 7–28

3

- If you are using a mouse, release the mouse button to position the graphic at the location where you dragged the rotate handle (shown in Figure 7–28). (You may need to rotate the graphic a few times to position it in the desired location.)

Q&A What if I am using a touch screen?

Because the rotate handle is not available on a touch screen, you enter the degree of rotation in the Size dialog box. Tap the Rotate Objects button (PICTURE TOOLS FORMAT tab | Arrange group) to display the Rotate Objects menu, tap the More Rotation Options command on the Rotate Objects menu to display the Size tab in the Layout dialog box, change the Rotation value to 347, and then tap the OK button.

4

- Tap or click Picture 3 in the Selection task pane to select the tack image on the left side of the screen.

- If you are using a mouse, drag the rotate handle rightward and downward to rotate the graphic slightly as shown in Figure 7–29.

Q&A What if I am using a touch screen?

Follow the same steps outlined above, except change the rotation value to 14.

- If necessary, move the images or rotate them again or resize them so that they look the same as those shown in Figure 7–29 and then close the Selection task pane.

- Tap or click somewhere in the issue information to deselect the graphic (Figure 7–29).

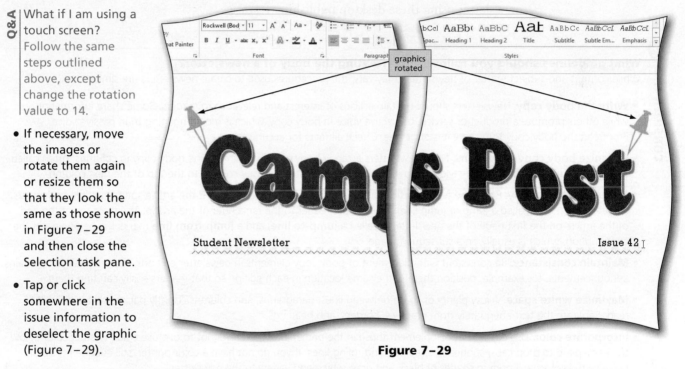

Figure 7–29

To Save a Document

You have performed several tasks while creating this resume and do not want to risk losing work completed thus far. Accordingly, you should save the document. The following steps assume you already have created folders for storing your files, for example, a CIS 101 folder (for your class) that contains a Word folder (for your assignments). Thus, these steps save the document in the Word folder in the CIS 101 folder using the file name, Campus Post Newsletter.

1 Tap or click the Save button on the Quick Access Toolbar, which depending on settings, will display either the Save As gallery in the Backstage view or the Save As dialog box.

2 Save the file in the desired location (in this case, Word folder in the CIS 101 folder [or your class folder]) using the file name, Campus Post Newsletter.

Break Point: If you wish to take a break, this is a good place to do so. You can exit Word now. To resume at a later time, run Word, open the file called Campus Post Newsletter, and continue following the steps from this location forward.

Formatting the First Page of the Body of the Newsletter

The next step is to format the first page of the body of the newsletter. The body of the newsletter in this chapter is divided in three columns (Figure 7–1a on page WD 411). The first two columns contain the feature article, and the third column contains announcements. The characters in the paragraphs are aligned on both the right and left edges — similar to newspaper columns. The first letter in the first paragraph is much larger than the rest of the characters in the paragraph. A vertical rule separates the columns. The steps on the following pages format the first page of the body of the newsletter using these desktop publishing features.

What guidelines should you follow when creating the body of a newsletter?
While content and subject matter of newsletters may vary, the procedures used to create newsletters are similar:

• **Write the body copy.** Newsletters should contain articles of interest and relevance to readers. Some share information, while others promote a product or service. Use active voice in body copy, which is more engaging than passive voice. Proofread the body copy to be sure it is error free. Check all facts for accuracy.

• **Organize body copy in columns.** Most newsletters arrange body copy in columns. The body copy in columns, often called **snaking columns** or newspaper-style columns, flows from the bottom of one column to the top of the next column.

• **Format the body copy.** Begin the feature article on the first page of the newsletter. If the article spans multiple pages, use a continuation line, called a jump or jump line, to guide the reader to the remainder of the article. The message at the end of the article on the first page of the newsletter is called a **jump-to line**, and a **jump-from line** marks the beginning of the continuation, which is usually on a subsequent page.

• **Maintain consistency.** Be consistent with placement of body copy elements in newsletter editions. If the newsletter contains announcements, for example, position them in the same location in each edition so that readers easily can find them.

• **Maximize white space.** Allow plenty of space between lines, paragraphs, and columns. Tightly packed text is difficult to read. Separate the text adequately from graphics, borders, and headings.

• **Incorporate color.** Use colors that complement those in the nameplate. Be careful not to overuse color. Restrict color below the nameplate to drop caps, subheads, graphics, and ruling lines. If you do not have a color printer, still change the colors because the colors will print in shades of black and gray, which add variety to the newsletter.

• **Select and format subheads.** Develop subheads with as few words as possible. Readers should be able to identify content of the next topic by glancing at a subhead. Subheads should be emphasized in the newsletter but should not compete with text in the nameplate. Use a larger, bold, or otherwise contrasting font for subheads so that they stand apart from the body copy. Use this same format for all subheads for consistency. Leave a space above subheads to visually separate their content from the previous topic. Be consistent with spacing above and below subheads throughout the newsletter.

• **Divide sections with vertical rules.** Use vertical rules to guide the reader through the newsletter.

• **Enhance the document with visuals.** Add energy to the newsletter and emphasis to important points with graphics, pull-quotes, and other visuals, such as drop caps, to mark beginning of an article. Use these elements sparingly, however, so that the newsletter does not have a crowded appearance. Fewer, large visuals are more effective than several smaller ones. If you use a graphic that you did not create, be sure to obtain permission to use it in the newsletter and give necessary credit to the creator of the graphic.

To Clear Formatting

The next step is to enter the title of the feature article below the horizontal rule. To do this, you position the insertion point at the end of the issue information line (after the 2 in Issue 42) and then press the ENTER key. Recall that the issue information line has a bottom border. When you press the ENTER key in a bordered paragraph, Word carries forward any borders to the next paragraph. Thus, after you press the ENTER key, you should clear formatting to format the new paragraph as the Normal style. The following steps clear formatting.

 Tap or click at the end of line 2 (the issue Information line) so that the insertion point is immediately after the 2 in Issue 42. Press the ENTER key to advance the insertion point to the next line, which also moves the border down one line.

2 If necessary, display the HOME tab. Tap or click the 'Clear All Formatting' button (HOME tab | Font group) to apply the Normal style to the location of the insertion point, which in this case moves the new paragraph below the border on the issue information line.

To Format Text as a Heading Style, Modify a Heading Style, and Adjust Spacing before and after the Paragraph

Below the bottom border in the nameplate is the title of the feature article, Information Literacy. The following steps apply the Heading 1 style to this paragraph, modify the style, and adjust the paragraph spacing.

 If necessary, display formatting marks.

2 With the insertion point on the paragraph mark below the border, tap or click Heading 1 (HOME tab | Styles group) to apply the Heading 1 style to the paragraph containing the insertion point.

3 Increase the font size 20 point. Bold the paragraph. Update the Heading 1 style to reflect these changes.

4 Type **Information Literacy** as the title of the feature article.

5 Display the PAGE LAYOUT tab. Change the Spacing Before box to 18 pt and the Spacing After box to 12 pt (Figure 7–30).

PAGE LAYOUT tab

Campus Post Newsletter – Word

ME   INSERT   DESIGN   PAGE LAYOUT   REFERENCES   MAILINGS   REVIEW

Breaks ▾
Line Numbers ▾
Hyphenation ▾
Indent
Left: 0"
Right: 0"
Spacing
Before: 18 pt
After: 12 pt

spacing before and after current paragraph changed

Align ▾
Group ▾
Rotate ▾

Page Setup   Paragraph   Arrange

feature article title entered and formatted

Student·Newsletter

·**Information·Literacy**¶

insertion point

Figure 7–30

Columns

When you begin a document in Word, it has one column. You can divide a portion of a document or the entire document in multiple columns. Within each column, you can type, modify, or format text.

To divide a portion of a document in multiple columns, you use section breaks. Word requires that a new section be created each time you alter the number of columns in a document. Thus, if a document has a nameplate (one column) followed by an article of three columns followed by an article of two columns, the document would be divided in three separate sections.

CONSIDER THIS

How should you organize the body copy in columns?

Be consistent from page to page with the number of columns. Narrow columns generally are easier to read than wide ones. Columns, however, can be too narrow. A two- or three-column layout generally is appealing and offers a flexible design. Try to have between five and fifteen words per line. To do this, you may need to adjust the column width, the font size, or the leading (line spacing). Font size of text in columns should be no larger than 12 point but not so small that readers must strain to read the text.

To Insert a Continuous Section Break

1 CREATE NAMEPLATE FOR FIRST PAGE | 2 FORMAT FIRST PAGE | 3 CREATE PULL-QUOTE
4 CREATE NAMEPLATE FOR SECOND PAGE | 5 FORMAT SECOND PAGE | 6 ADD PAGE BORDER

The next step is to insert a continuous section break below the nameplate. *Why? In this chapter, the nameplate is one column and the body of the newsletter is three columns.* The term, continuous, means the new section should be on the same page as the previous section, which, in this case, means that the three columns of body copy will be positioned directly below the nameplate on the first page of the newsletter. The following steps insert a continuous section break.

1

- With the insertion point at the end of the feature article title (shown in Figure 7–30), press the ENTER key to position the insertion point below the article title.

- Tap or click the 'Insert Page and Section Breaks' button (PAGE LAYOUT tab | Page Setup group) to display the Insert Page and Section Breaks gallery (Figure 7–31).

Figure 7–31

2

- Tap or click Continuous in the Insert Page and Section Breaks gallery to insert a continuous section break above the insertion point (Figure 7–32).

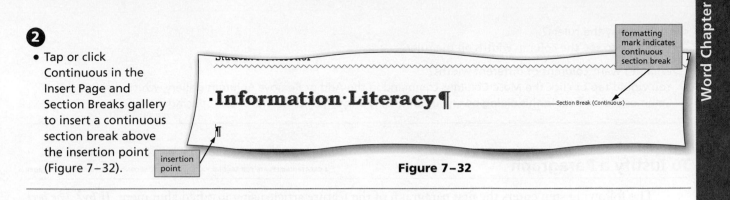

Figure 7–32

To Change the Number of Columns

1 CREATE NAMEPLATE FOR FIRST PAGE | 2 FORMAT FIRST PAGE | 3 CREATE PULL-QUOTE
4 CREATE NAMEPLATE FOR SECOND PAGE | 5 FORMAT SECOND PAGE | 6 ADD PAGE BORDER

The document now has two sections. The nameplate is in the first section, and the insertion point is in the second section. The second section should be formatted to three columns. *Why?* *The feature article and announcements appear in three columns that snake across the page.* Thus, the following steps format the second section in the document as three columns.

1

- Tap or click the 'Add or Remove Columns' button (PAGE LAYOUT tab | Page Setup group) to display the Add or Remove Columns gallery (Figure 7–33).

Figure 7–33

2

- Tap or click Three in the Add or Remove Columns gallery to divide the section containing the insertion point in three evenly sized and spaced columns

- Display the VIEW tab and then, if necessary, tap or click the View Ruler check box so that the rulers appear on the screen (Figure 7–34).

Figure 7–34

Q&A Why display the rulers?
You want to see the column widths on the ruler.

What if I want columns of different widths?
You would tap or click the More Columns command in the Add or Remove Columns gallery, which displays the Columns dialog box. In this dialog box, you can specify varying column widths and spacing.

To Justify a Paragraph

1 CREATE NAMEPLATE FOR FIRST PAGE | 2 FORMAT FIRST PAGE | 3 CREATE PULL-QUOTE
4 CREATE NAMEPLATE FOR SECOND PAGE | 5 FORMAT SECOND PAGE | 6 ADD PAGE BORDER

The following step enters the first paragraph of the feature article using justified alignment. *Why? The text in the paragraphs of the body of the newsletter is **justified**, which means that the left and right margins are aligned, like the edges of newspaper columns.*

1

- Display the HOME tab.

- Tap or click the Justify button (HOME tab | Paragraph group) so that Word aligns both the left and right margins of typed text.

- Type the first paragraph of the feature article (Figure 7–35):
`Managing the vast amount of information inundating us daily can be an overwhelming task. Information literacy is a 21st century skill set that prepares students, employees, and citizens to manage information so that they can be knowledgeable decision makers.` and then press the ENTER key.

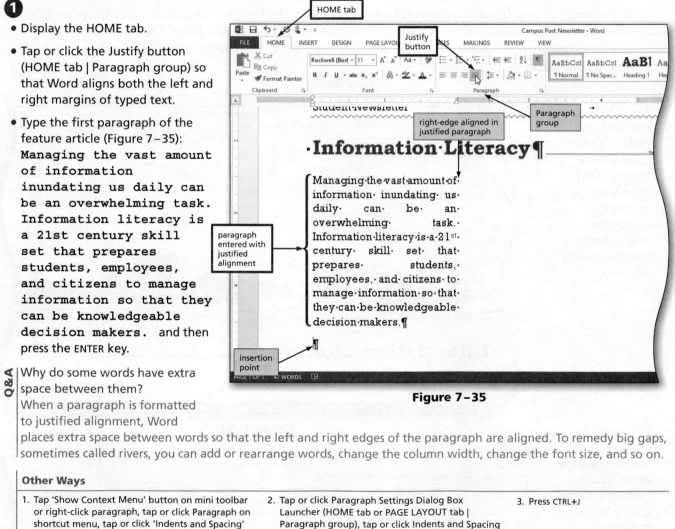

Figure 7–35

Q&A Why do some words have extra space between them?
When a paragraph is formatted to justified alignment, Word places extra space between words so that the left and right edges of the paragraph are aligned. To remedy big gaps, sometimes called rivers, you can add or rearrange words, change the column width, change the font size, and so on.

Other Ways

1. Tap 'Show Context Menu' button on mini toolbar or right-click paragraph, tap or click Paragraph on shortcut menu, tap or click 'Indents and Spacing' tab (Paragraph dialog box), tap or click Alignment arrow, tap or click Justified, tap or click OK button

2. Tap or click Paragraph Settings Dialog Box Launcher (HOME tab or PAGE LAYOUT tab | Paragraph group), tap or click Indents and Spacing tab (Paragraph dialog box), tap or click Alignment arrow, tap or click Justified, tap or click OK button

3. Press CTRL+J

To Insert a File in a Column of the Newsletter

1 CREATE NAMEPLATE FOR FIRST PAGE | 2 FORMAT FIRST PAGE | 3 CREATE PULL-QUOTE
4 CREATE NAMEPLATE FOR SECOND PAGE | 5 FORMAT SECOND PAGE | 6 ADD PAGE BORDER

The next step is to insert a file named Information Literacy Article in the newsletter. *Why? To save you time typing, the rest of the feature article is located on the Data Files for Students.* Visit www.cengage.com/ct/studentdownload for detailed instructions or contact your instructor for information about accessing the required files. The next steps insert the Information Literacy Article file in a column of the newsletter.

①

- Display the INSERT tab.

- With the insertion point positioned in the left column as shown in Figure 7–35, tap or click the Object arrow (INSERT tab | Text group) to display the Object menu.

- Tap or click 'Text from File' on the Object menu to display the Insert File dialog box.

- Navigate to the location of the file to be inserted (in this case, the Data Files for Students folder).

- Tap or click the file named, Information Literacy Article, to select the file (Figure 7–36).

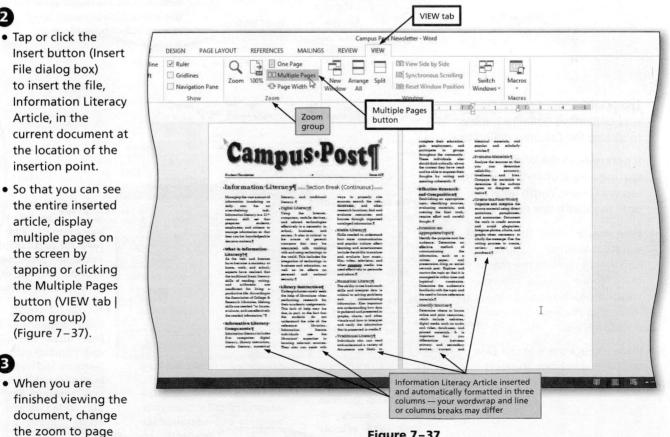

Figure 7–36

②

- Tap or click the Insert button (Insert File dialog box) to insert the file, Information Literacy Article, in the current document at the location of the insertion point.

- So that you can see the entire inserted article, display multiple pages on the screen by tapping or clicking the Multiple Pages button (VIEW tab | Zoom group) (Figure 7–37).

③

- When you are finished viewing the document, change the zoom to page width so that the newsletter content is larger on the screen.

Figure 7–37

To Increase Column Width and Place a Vertical Rule between Columns

The columns in the newsletter currently contain many rivers. *Why? The justified alignment in the narrow column width often causes large gaps between words.* To eliminate some of the rivers, you increase the size of the columns slightly in this newsletter. In newsletters, you often see a vertical rule separating columns. Through the Columns dialog box, you can change column width and add vertical rules. The following steps increase column widths and add vertical rules between columns.

1
- Position the insertion point somewhere in the feature article text.
- Display the PAGE LAYOUT tab.
- Tap or click the 'Add or Remove Columns' button (PAGE LAYOUT tab | Page Setup group) to display the Add or Remove Columns gallery (Figure 7–38).

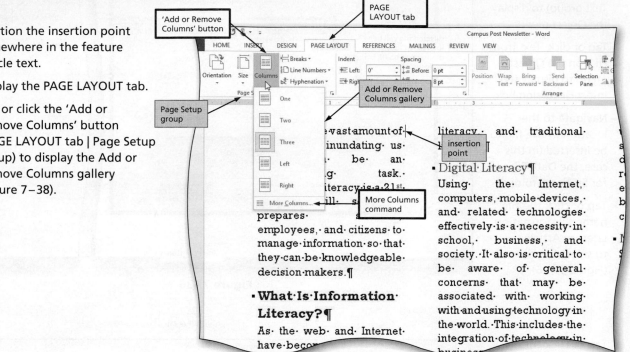

Figure 7–38

2
- Tap or click More Columns in the Add or Remove Columns gallery to display the Columns dialog box.
- If necessary, in the Width and spacing area (Columns dialog box), tap or click the Width up arrow until the Width box reads 2.1".

Q&A

How would I make the columns different widths?
You would remove the check mark from the 'Equal column width' check box and then set the individual column widths in the dialog box.

- Place a check mark in the Line between check box to select the check box (Figure 7–39).

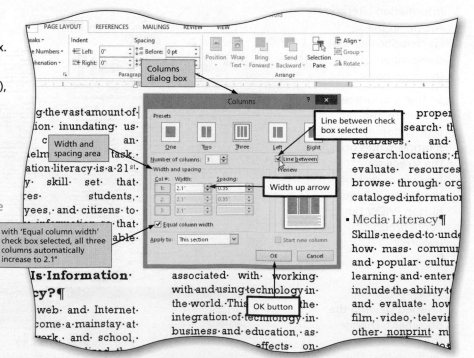

Figure 7–39

③

- Tap or click the OK button to make the columns slightly wider and place a line (vertical rule) between each column in the document (Figure 7–40).

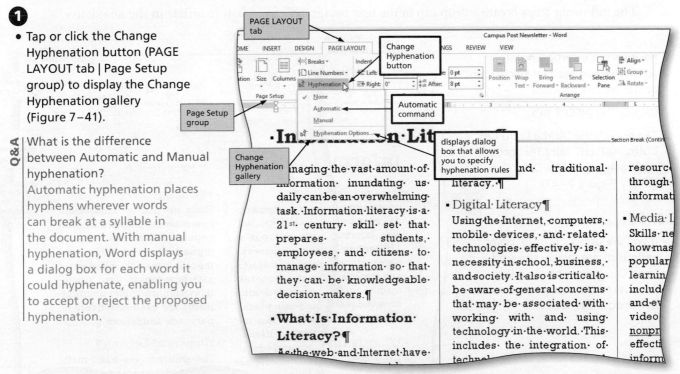

Figure 7–40

Other Ways

1. Double-tap or double-click shaded space between columns on ruler, enter settings (Columns dialog box), tap or click OK button

2. To adjust column widths, drag column boundaries on ruler

3. To insert single rule, tap or click Borders arrow (HOME tab | Paragraph group)

To Hyphenate a Document

1 CREATE NAMEPLATE FOR FIRST PAGE | 2 FORMAT FIRST PAGE | 3 CREATE PULL-QUOTE
4 CREATE NAMEPLATE FOR SECOND PAGE | 5 FORMAT SECOND PAGE | 6 ADD PAGE BORDER

The following steps turn on the hyphenation feature. *Why? To further eliminate some of the rivers in the columns of the newsletter, you turn on Word's hyphenation feature so that words with multiple syllables are hyphenated at the end of lines instead of wrapped in their entirety to the next line.*

①

- Tap or click the Change Hyphenation button (PAGE LAYOUT tab | Page Setup group) to display the Change Hyphenation gallery (Figure 7–41).

Q&A
What is the difference between Automatic and Manual hyphenation?
Automatic hyphenation places hyphens wherever words can break at a syllable in the document. With manual hyphenation, Word displays a dialog box for each word it could hyphenate, enabling you to accept or reject the proposed hyphenation.

Figure 7–41

2

- Tap or click Automatic in the Change Hyphenation gallery to hyphenate the document (Figure 7–42).

Q&A

What if I do not want a particular word hyphenated?

You can reword text, and Word will redo the hyphenation automatically.

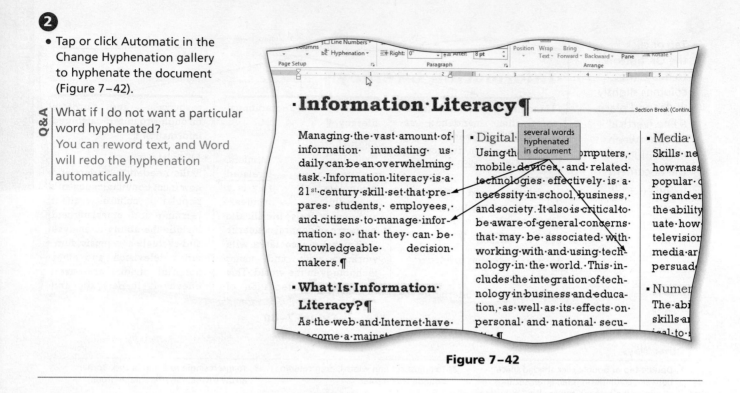

Figure 7–42

To Format a Character as a Drop Cap

1 CREATE NAMEPLATE FOR FIRST PAGE | 2 FORMAT FIRST PAGE | 3 CREATE PULL-QUOTE

4 CREATE NAMEPLATE FOR SECOND PAGE | 5 FORMAT SECOND PAGE | 6 ADD PAGE BORDER

The first character in the feature article in this newsletter, that is, the capital letter M, is formatted as a drop cap. **Why?** *To add interest to an article, you often see a **drop cap**, which is a capital letter whose font size is larger than the rest of the characters in the paragraph.* In Word, the drop cap can sink into the first few lines of text, or it can extend into the left margin, which often is called a stick-up cap. In this newsletter, the paragraph text wraps around the drop cap.

The following steps create a drop cap in the first paragraph of the feature article in the newsletter.

1

- Position the insertion point somewhere in the first paragraph of the feature article.

- Display the INSERT tab.

- Tap or click the 'Add a Drop Cap' button (INSERT tab | Text group) to display the Add a Drop Cap gallery (Figure 7–43).

Experiment

- If you are using a mouse, point to various commands in the Add a Drop Cap gallery to see a live preview of the drop cap formats in the document.

Figure 7–43

2

- Tap or click Dropped in the Add a Drop Cap gallery to format the first letter in the paragraph containing the insertion point (the M in Managing, in this case) as a drop cap and wrap subsequent text in the paragraph around the drop cap (Figure 7–44).

Q&A What is the outline around the drop cap in the document?
When you format a letter as a drop cap, Word places a frame around it. A **frame** is a container for text that allows you to position the text anywhere on the page. Word formats a frame for the drop cap so that text wraps around it. The frame also contains a paragraph mark nonprinting character to the right of the drop cap, which may or may not be visible on your screen.

Figure 7–44

To Format the Drop Cap

The following steps change the font color of the drop cap and make it slightly wider to eliminate the river near the end of the paragraph.

1 With the drop cap selected, display the HOME tab and then change the font color of the drop cap to 'Lime, Accent 1, Darker 25%' (fifth color, fifth row) in Font Color gallery.

Q&A What if my frame no longer is displayed?
Tap or click the drop cap to select it. Then, tap or click the blue selection rectangle to display the frame.

2 If necessary, drag the right-middle sizing handles on the frame until the drop cap and the text in the paragraph look like Figure 7–45. If necessary, reposition the drop cap again.

Figure 7–45

To Insert a Next Page Section Break

The third column on the first page of the newsletter is not a continuation of the feature article. *Why not? The third column, instead, contains several member announcements. The feature article continues on the second page of the newsletter (shown in Figure 7–1b on page WD 411).* Thus, you must insert a next page section break, which is a section break that also contains a page break, at the bottom of the second column so that the remainder of the feature article moves to the second page. The following steps insert a next page section break in the second column.

1

- Position the insertion point at the location for the section break, in this case, to the left of the L in the Library Instruction heading.

- Display the PAGE LAYOUT tab.

- Tap or click the 'Insert Page and Section Breaks' button (PAGE LAYOUT tab | Page Setup group) to display the Insert Page and Section Breaks gallery (Figure 7–46).

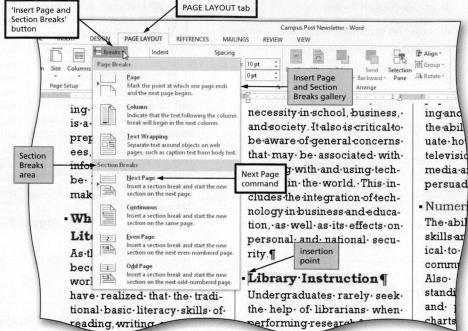

Figure 7–46

2

- In the Section Breaks area in the gallery, tap or click Next Page to insert a next page section break, which positions the insertion point on the next page.

- Scroll to the bottom of the first page so that you can see the moved text (Figure 7–47).

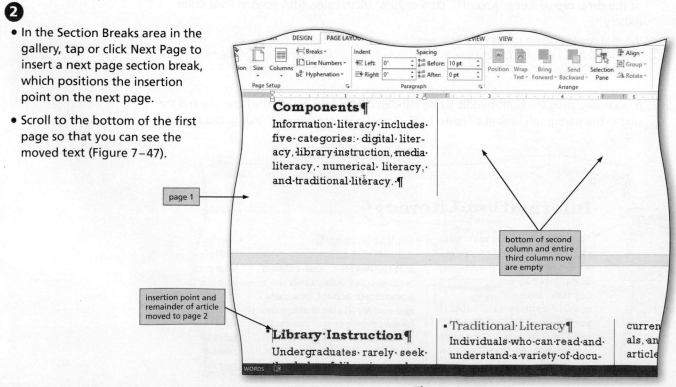

Figure 7–47

To Enter Text

The next step is to insert a jump-to line at the end of the second column, informing the reader where to look for the rest of the feature article. The following steps insert a jump-to line at the end of the text in the second column on the first page of the newsletter.

1 Scroll to display the end of the text in the second column of the first page of the newsletter and then position the insertion point between the paragraph mark and the section break notation.

2 Press the ENTER key twice to insert a blank line for the jump-to text above the section break notation.

3 Press the UP ARROW key to position the insertion point on the blank line. If the blank line is formatted in the Heading 1 style, tap or click the 'Clear All Formatting' button (HOME tab | Font group) so that the entered text follows the Normal style.

4 Press CTRL+R to right align the paragraph mark. Press CTRL+I to turn on the italic format. Type **(Article continues on next page)** as the jump-to text and then press CTRL+I again to turn off the italic format.

To Insert a Column Break

1 CREATE NAMEPLATE FOR FIRST PAGE | 2 FORMAT FIRST PAGE | 3 CREATE PULL-QUOTE
4 CREATE NAMEPLATE FOR SECOND PAGE | 5 FORMAT SECOND PAGE | 6 ADD PAGE BORDER

In the Campus Post newsletters, for consistency, the student announcements always begin at the top of the third column. If you insert the Campus Post Announcements at the current location of the insertion point, however, they will begin at the bottom of the second column. *Why? The insertion point currently is at the bottom of the second column.*

For the student announcements to be displayed in the third column, you insert a **column break** at the bottom of the second column, which places the insertion point at the top of the next column. Thus, the following steps insert a column break at the bottom of the second column.

1

- Position the insertion point to the left of the paragraph mark on the line containing the next page section break, which is the location where the column break should be inserted.

- Tap or click the 'Insert Page and Section Breaks' button (PAGE LAYOUT tab | Page Setup group) to display the Insert Page and Section Breaks gallery (Figure 7–48).

Figure 7–48

- Tap or click Column in the Insert Page and Section Breaks gallery to insert a column break at the location of the insertion point and move the insertion point to the top of the next column (Figure 7–49).

 What if I wanted to remove a column break?
You would double-tap or double-click it to select it and then tap or click the Cut button (HOME tab | Clipboard group) or press the DELETE key.

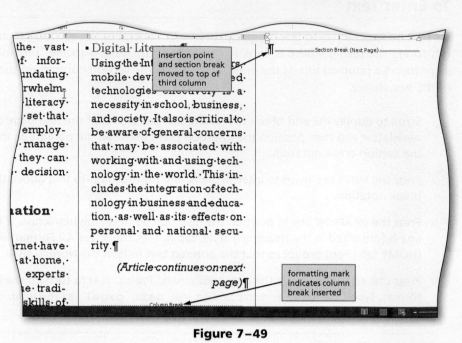

Figure 7–49

Other Ways

1. Press CTRL+SHIFT+ENTER

To Insert a File in a Column of the Newsletter

So that you do not have to enter the entire third column of announcements in the newsletter, the next step in the project is to insert the file named Campus Post Announcements in the third column of the newsletter. This file contains the three announcements: the first about student discounts, the second about spirit wear, and the third about the topic of the next newsletter issue.

The Campus Post Announcements file is located on the Data Files for Students. Visit www.cengage.com/ct/studentdownload for detailed instructions or contact your instructor for information about accessing the required files. The following steps insert a file in a column of the newsletter.

 With the insertion point at the top of the third column, display the INSERT tab.

2 Tap or click the Object arrow (INSERT tab | Text group) to display the Object menu and then tap or click 'Text from File' on the Object menu to display the Insert File dialog box.

3 Navigate to the location of the file to be inserted (in this case, the Data Files for Students folder).

4 Tap or click Campus Post Announcements to select the file.

5 Tap or click the Insert button (Insert File dialog box) to insert the file, Campus Post Announcements, in the document at the location of the insertion point.

 What if text from the announcements column spills onto the second page of the newsletter?
You will format text in the announcements column so that all of its text fits in the third column of the first page.

 Press SHIFT+F5 to return the insertion point to the last editing location, in this case, the top of the third column on the first page of the newsletter (Figure 7–50).

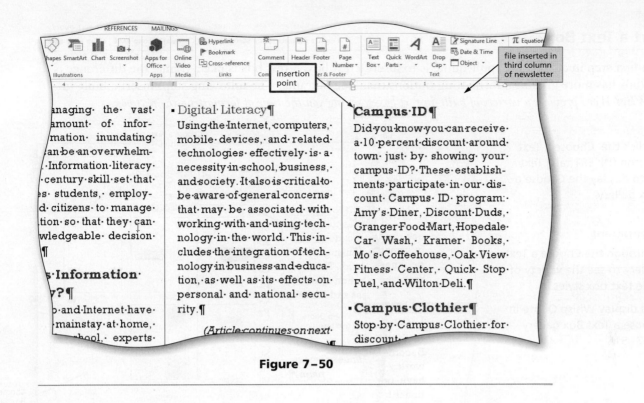

Figure 7–50

To Save a Document Again

You have performed several steps since the last save. Thus, you should save the newsletter again.

1 Save the newsletter again with the same file name, Campus Post Newsletter.

Creating a Pull-Quote

A pull-quote is text pulled, or copied, from the text of the document and given graphical emphasis so that it stands apart and commands the reader's attention. The newsletter in this project copies text from the second page of the newsletter and places it in a pull-quote on the first page between the first and second columns (Figure 7–1a on page WD 411).

What guidelines should you follow when using pull-quote?

Because of their bold emphasis, pull-quotes should be used sparingly in a newsletter. Pull-quotes are useful for breaking the monotony of long columns of text. Typically, quotation marks are used only if you are quoting someone directly. If you use quotation marks, use curly (or smart) quotation marks instead of straight quotation marks.

To create the pull-quote in this newsletter, follow this general procedure:

1. Create a **text box**, which is a container for text that allows you to position the text anywhere on the page.

2. Copy the text from the existing document to the Office Clipboard and then paste the text from the Office Clipboard to the text box.

3. Resize and format the text box.

4. Move the text box to the desired location.

To Insert a Text Box

The first step in creating the pull-quote is to insert a text box. A text box is like a frame; the difference is that a text box has more graphical formatting options than does a frame. The following steps insert a built-in text box. **Why?** *Word provides a variety of built-in text boxes, saving you the time of formatting the text box.*

①

- Tap or click the 'Choose a Text Box' button (INSERT tab | Text group) to display the Choose a Text Box gallery.

🔍 **Experiment**

- Scroll through the Choose a Text Box gallery to see the variety of available text box styles.

- Scroll to display Whisp Quote in the Choose a Text Box gallery (Figure 7–51).

Figure 7–51

②

- Tap or click Whisp Quote in the Text Box gallery to insert that style of text box in the document. If necessary, scroll to display the entire text box in the document window (Figure 7–52).

Q&A Does my text box need to be in the same location as in Figure 7–52?
No. You will move the text box later.

The layout of the first page is not correct because of the text box. What do I do?
You will enter text in the text box and then position it in the correct location. At that time, the layout of the first page will be fixed.

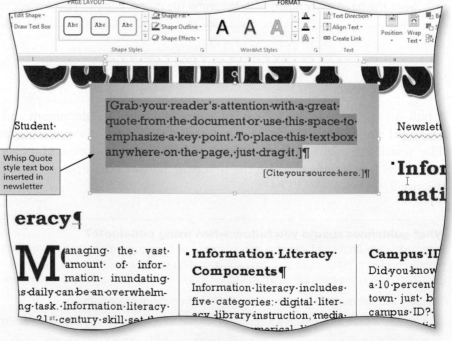

Figure 7–52

Other Ways

1. Tap or click 'Explore Quick Parts' button (INSERT tab | Text group), tap or click 'Building Blocks Organizer' on Explore Quick Parts menu, select desired text box name in Building blocks list, tap or click Insert button, tap or click OK button

To Split the Window

The text that you will copy for the pull-quote is at the bottom of the first page on the newsletter and the pull-quote (text box) is at the top of the first page of the newsletter. Thus, the next step is to copy the pull-quote text from the bottom of the first page and then paste it in the pull-quote at the top of the first page. You would like to view the pull-quote and the text to be copied on the screen at the same time. *Why? Viewing both simultaneously will simplify the copying and pasting process.*

Word allows you to split the window in two separate panes, each containing the current document and having its own scroll bar. This enables you to scroll to and view two different portions of the same document at the same time. The following step splits the Word window.

1

• Display the VIEW tab.

• Tap or click the Split Window button (VIEW tab | Windows group) to divide the document window in two separate panes — both the upper and lower panes display the current document (Figure 7–53).

Figure 7–53

Other Ways

1. Press ALT+CTRL+S, then ENTER

To Arrange All Open Word Documents on the Screen

If you have multiple Word documents open and want to view all of them at the same time on the screen, you can instruct Word to arrange all the open documents on the screen from top to bottom. If you wanted to arrange all open Word documents on the same screen, you would perform the following steps.

1. Tap or click the Arrange All button (VIEW tab | Window group) to display each open Word document on the screen.

2. To make one of the arranged documents fill the entire screen again, maximize the window by tapping or clicking its Maximize button or double-tapping or double-clicking its title bar.

BTW

Quick Reference

For a table that lists how to complete the tasks covered in this book using touch gestures, the mouse, ribbon, shortcut menu, and keyboard, see the Quick Reference Summary at the back of this book, or visit the Quick Reference resource on the Student Companion Site located on www.cengagebrain.com. For detailed instructions about accessing available resources, visit www.cengage.com/ct/ studentdownload or contact your instructor for information about accessing the required files.

To Copy and Paste Using Split Windows

The following steps copy text from bottom of the first page of the newsletter to the Clipboard (the source) and then paste the text into the text box (the destination). **Why?** *The item being copied is called the **source**. The location to which you are pasting is called the **destination**.*

❶

- In the lower pane, scroll to display text to be copied, as shown in Figure 7–54, and then select the text to be copied: lifelong skills are needed "to locate, evaluate, and use effectively the needed information."

- Tap or click the Copy button (HOME tab | Clipboard group) to copy the selected text to the Clipboard (Figure 7–54).

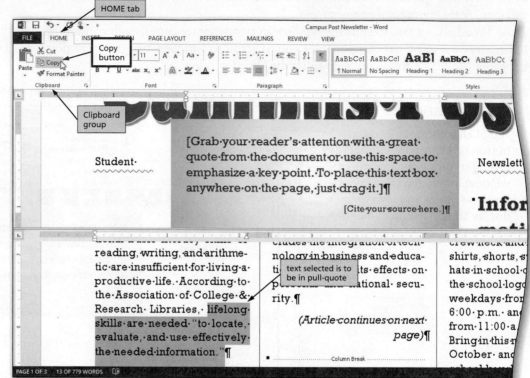

Figure 7–54

❷

- In the upper pane, if necessary, scroll to display a portion of the text box. Tap or click the text in the text box to select it.

- Tap or click the Paste arrow (HOME tab | Clipboard group) to display the Paste menu.

Q&A What if I tap or click the Paste button by mistake?
Tap or click the Paste Options button to the right of the pasted text in the text box to display the Paste Options menu.

- If you are using a mouse, point to the Merge Formatting button on the Paste menu and notice the text box shows a live preview of the selected paste option (Figure 7–55).

Q&A Why select the Merge Formatting button on the Paste menu?
You want the pasted text to use the formats that were in the text box (the destination) instead of the formats of the copied text (the source).

Figure 7–55

- Tap or click the Merge Formatting button on the Paste menu to paste the copied text into the text box.

- Repeat Steps 1, 2, and 3 for the source text, Association of College & Research Libraries, pasting it into the placeholder, [Cite your source here.].

Q&A | Why does a hyphen appear in the source?
Word may have hyphenated the word automatically. You will format the pull-quote text next.

Other Ways

1. Select text to copy, press CTRL+C; select destination for pasted text, press CTRL+V

To Remove a Split Window

The next step is to remove the split window so that you can position the pull-quote. The following step removes a split window.

 Double-click the split bar (shown in Figure 7–55), or tap or click the Split Window button again (VIEW tab | Window group), or press ALT+SHIFT+C, to remove the split window and return to a single Word window on the screen.

To Format Text in the Text Box

The next steps format text in the pull-quote.

❶ If necessary, scroll to display the text box in the document window.

❷ Capitalize the L in the word, Lifelong.

❸ Select all the text in the text box, change its font to Cambria, and bold the text.

❹ Select the first paragraph of text in the text box and change its font size to 11 point. Center this paragraph.

❺ Tap or click in the text box to deselect the text, but leave the text box selected.

BTW

Rotating Text Box Text
To rotate text in a text box, select the text box, tap or click the Text Direction button (DRAWING TOOLS FORMAT tab | Text group), and then tap or click the desired direction on the Text Direction menu.

To Resize a Text Box and Insert Line Break Characters

The next step in formatting the pull-quote is to resize the text box. You resize a text box the same way as any other object. That is, you drag its sizing handles or enter values in the height and width boxes through the Size button (DRAWING TOOLS FORMAT tab | Size group). You do not want any hyphenated words in the text box. Once the text box is resized, you insert line break characters to eliminate any hyphenated words. The following steps resize the text box and insert line break characters.

❶ Drag the sizing handles so that the pull-quote looks about the same size as Figure 7–56 on the next page.

❷ Verify the pull-quote dimensions in the Shape Height and Shape Width boxes (DRAWING TOOLS FORMAT tab | Size group) and, if necessary, change the value in the Shape Height box to 2 and the Shape Width box to 1.94.

❸ Position the insertion point to the left of the a in the word, are, and then press SHIFT+ENTER to insert a line break character, which places the word on the next line and removes the hyphen.

❹ Insert line break characters to the left of the first quotation mark and also to the left of the words, Information and Research. If necessary, delete the hyphen in the word, Research (Figure 7–56).

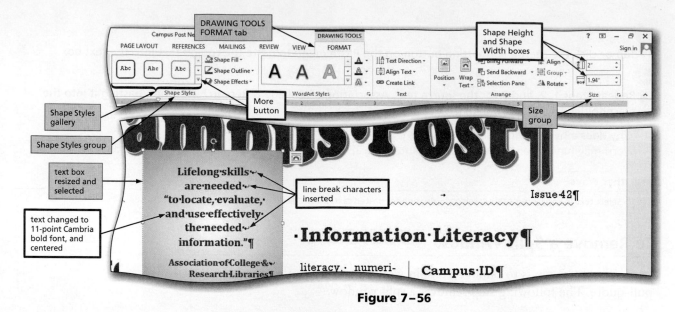

Figure 7–56

BTW

Text Box Styles
Like other drawing objects or pictures, text boxes can be formatted or have styles applied. You can change the fill in a text box by tapping or clicking the Shape Fill button (DRAWING TOOLS FORMAT tab | Shape Styles group), add an outline to a text box by clicking the Shape Outline button (DRAWING TOOLS FORMAT tab | Shape Styles group), and apply an effect such as shadow or 3-D effects by tapping or clicking the Shape Effects button (DRAWING TOOLS FORMAT tab | Shape Styles group).

To Apply a Shape Style to a Text Box

The next step in formatting the pull-quote is to apply a shape style to the text box to coordinate its colors with the rest of the newsletter. The following steps apply a shape style to a text box.

1 With the text box still selected, tap or click the More button (shown in Figure 7–56) in the Shape Styles gallery (DRAWING TOOLS FORMAT tab | Shape Styles group) to expand the gallery (Figure 7–57).

2 If you are using a mouse, point to 'Light 1 Outline, Colored Fill - Orange, Accent 6' (rightmost style, third row) in the Shape Styles gallery to display a live preview of that style applied to the text box.

3 Tap or click 'Light 1 Outline, Colored Fill - Orange, Accent 6' in the Shape Styles gallery to apply the selected style to the shape.

4 If the text in the text box did not change to white, select the text, tap or click the Font Color arrow (HOME tab | Font group), and then tap or click 'White, Background 1' to change the text color.

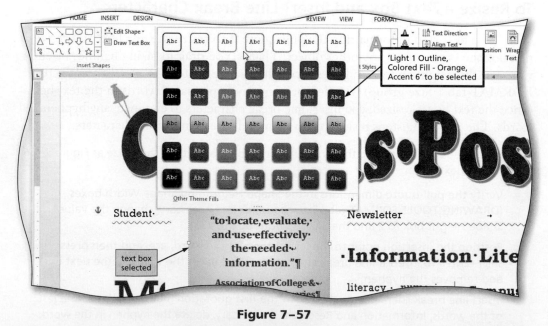

Figure 7–57

To Position a Text Box

The following step moves the text box to the desired location. *Why? The pull-quote text box should be positioned between the first and second columns of the newsletter.*

1

- With the text box still selected, drag the text box to its new location (Figure 7–58). You may need to drag and/or resize the text box a couple of times so that it looks similar to this figure.

- Tap or click outside the text box to remove the selection.

Q&A

Why does my text wrap differently around the text box?
Differences in wordwrap often relate to the printer used by your computer. Thus, your document may wordwrap around the text box differently.

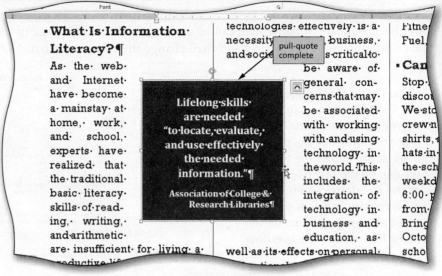

Figure 7–58

To Save a Document Again

You have performed several steps since the last save. You should save the newsletter again.

1 Save the newsletter again with the same file name, Campus Post Newsletter.

BTW

Moving Text Boxes
To move a text box using the keyboard, select the text box and then press the arrow keys on the keyboard. For example, each time you press the DOWN ARROW key, the selected text box moves down one line.

Break Point: If you wish to take a break, this is a good place to do so. You can exit Word now. To resume at a later time, run Word, open the file called Campus Post Newsletter, and continue following the steps from this location forward.

Formatting the Second Page of the Newsletter

The second page of the newsletter (Figure 7–1b on page WD 411) continues the feature article that began in the first two columns on the first page. The nameplate on the second page is less elaborate than the one on the first page of the newsletter. In addition to the text in the feature article, page two contains a graphic. The following pages format the second page of the newsletter in this project.

How do you create a nameplate for inner pages of a newsletter?

The top of the inner pages of a newsletter may or may not have a nameplate. If you choose to create one for your inner pages, it should not be the same as, or compete with, the one on the first page. Inner page nameplates usually contain only a portion of the nameplate from the first page of a newsletter.

CONSIDER THIS

To Change Column Formatting

The document currently is formatted in three columns. The nameplate at the top of the second page, however, should be in a single column. *Why? The nameplate should span across the top of the three columns below it.* The next step, then, is to change the number of columns at the top of the second page from three to one.

As discussed earlier in this project, Word requires a new section each time you change the number of columns in a document. Thus, you first must insert a continuous section break and then format the section to one column so that the nameplate can be entered on the second page of the newsletter. The following steps insert a continuous section break and then change the column format.

1

- If you have a blank page between the first and second pages of the newsletter, position the insertion point to the left of the paragraph mark at the end of the third column on the first page of the newsletter and then press the DELETE key as many times as necessary to delete the blank line causing the overflow.

- Position the insertion point at the upper-left corner of the second page of the newsletter (to the left of L in Library).

- Display the PAGE LAYOUT tab.

- Tap or click the 'Insert Page and Section Breaks' button (PAGE LAYOUT tab | Page Setup group) to display the Insert Page and Section Breaks gallery (Figure 7–59).

Figure 7–59

2

- Tap or click Continuous in the Insert Page and Section Breaks gallery to insert a continuous section break above the insertion point.

- Press the UP ARROW key to position the insertion point to the left of the continuous section break just inserted.

- Tap or click the 'Add or Remove Columns' button (PAGE LAYOUT tab | Page Setup group) to display the Add or Remove Columns gallery (Figure 7–60).

Figure 7–60

3

- Tap or click One in the Add or Remove Columns gallery to format the current section to one column, which now is ready for the second page nameplate.

- If necessary, scroll to display the bottom of the first page and the top of the second page, so that you can see the varying columns in the newsletter (Figure 7–61).

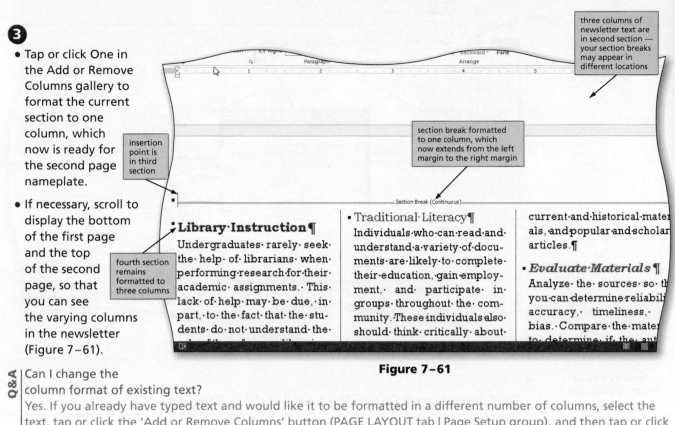

three columns of newsletter text are in second section — your section breaks may appear in different locations

insertion point is in third section

section break formatted to one column, which now extends from the left margin to the right margin

fourth section remains formatted to three columns

Library Instruction¶
Undergraduates· rarely· seek· the· help· of· librarians· when· performing·research·for·their· academic· assignments.· This· lack· of· help· may· be· due,· in· part,· to· the· fact· that· the· stu- dents· do· not· understand· the·

- Traditional· Literacy¶
Individuals·who·can·read·and· understand·a·variety·of·docu- ments·are·likely·to·complete· their·education,·gain·employ- ment,· and· participate· in· groups· throughout· the· com- munity.·These·individuals·also· should· think· critically· about·

current·and·historical·mater- als,·and·popular·and·scholar· articles.¶

- *Evaluate·Materials*¶
Analyze· the· sources· so· th you·can·determine·reliabili accuracy,· timeliness,· bias.· Compare· the· mater to· determine· if· the· au

Figure 7–61

Q&A
Can I change the column format of existing text?
Yes. If you already have typed text and would like it to be formatted in a different number of columns, select the text, tap or click the 'Add or Remove Columns' button (PAGE LAYOUT tab | Page Setup group), and then tap or click the number of columns desired in the Add or Remove Columns gallery. Word automatically creates a new section for the newly formatted columns.

To Set Custom Tab Stops Using the Tabs Dialog Box

The nameplate on the second page of the newsletter contains the text, Student Newsletter, at the left margin, the newsletter title in the center, and the issue number at the right margin (shown in Figure 7–1a on page WD 411). To properly align the text in the center and at the right margin, you will set custom tab stops at these locations. The following steps set custom tab stops.

1 Press the ENTER key twice and then position the insertion point on the first line of the second page of the newsletter, which is the paragraph to be formatted with the custom tab stops.

2 Tap or click the 'Clear All Formatting' button (HOME tab | Font group) to apply the Normal style to the first line on the second page of the newsletter.

3 Tap or click the Paragraph Settings Dialog Box Launcher (PAGE LAYOUT tab | Paragraph group) to display the Paragraph dialog box and then tap or click the Tabs button (Paragraph dialog box) to display the Tabs dialog box.

4 Type 3.5 in the Tab stop position text box (Tabs dialog box), tap or click Center in the Alignment area to specify the tab stop alignment, and then tap or click the Set button to set the custom tab stop.

5 Type 7 in the Tab stop position text box (Tabs dialog box), tap or click Right in the Alignment area to specify the tab stop alignment, and then tap or click the Set button to set the custom tab stop (Figure 7–62 on the next page).

6 Tap or click the OK button to set custom tab stops using the specified alignments.

Figure 7–62

BTW

Leader Characters
Leader characters, such as a series of dots, often are used in a table of contents to precede page numbers. Four types of leader characters, which Word places in the space occupied by a tab character, are available in the Leader area of the Tabs dialog box (shown in Figure 7-62).

To Format and Enter Text and Add a Border

The following steps enter the newsletter title at the top of the second page in the third section.

1 With the insertion point on the first line of the second page of the newsletter, tap or click the Font Color arrow and then change the font of the current text to 'Pink, Accent 5, Darker 50%' (ninth column, sixth row). Increase the font size to 12 point. Type **Student Newsletter** at the left margin.

If requested by your instructor, enter your name instead of the word, Student.

2 Press the TAB key to advance the insertion point to the centered tab stop. Increase the font size to 14 point and then tap or click the Bold button (HOME tab | Font group) to bold the text. Type **Campus Post** at the centered tab stop.

3 Press the TAB key to advance the insertion point to the right-aligned tab stop. Reduce the font size to 12 point and then tap or click the Bold button (HOME tab | Font group) to turn off the bold format. Type **Issue 42** at the right-aligned tab stop.

4 Tap or click the Borders button (HOME tab | Paragraph group) to add a bottom border (shown in Figure 7–63).

Q&A Why is the border formatted already?
When you define a custom border, Word uses that custom border the next time you tap or click the Borders button in the Borders gallery.

To Enter Text

The second page of the feature article on the second page of this newsletter begins with a jump-from line (the continued message) immediately below the nameplate. The next steps enter the jump-from line.

1 Position the insertion point on the blank line above the heading, Library Instruction, to the left of the paragraph mark.

2 Tap or click the 'Clear All Formatting' button (HOME tab | Font group) to apply the Normal style to the location of the insertion point.

3 Press CTRL+I to turn on the italic format.

4 Type (Continued from first page) and then press CTRL+I to turn off the italic format (Figure 7–63).

nameplate on second page entered

jump-from text entered

Student Newsletter → **Campus Post** → Issue 42

(Continued·from·first·page)¶ ―――――――Section Break (Continuous)―――――――

Library·Instruction¶
Undergraduates· rarely· seek·
the· help· of· librarians· when·
performing·research·for·their·
academic· assignments. · This·
lack· of· help· may· be· due, · in·

• Traditional· Literacy¶
Individuals·who·can·read·and·
understand·a·variety·of·docu-
ments·are·likely·to·complete·
their·education, ·gain·employ-
ment, · and· participate· in-

you·differentiate·between·pri-
mary·and·secondary·source
current·and·historical·mater-
als, ·and·popular·and·scholar
articles.¶

•Evaluate· Materials· ¶

Figure 7–63

To Balance Columns

1 CREATE NAMEPLATE FOR FIRST PAGE | 2 FORMAT FIRST PAGE | 3 CREATE PULL-QUOTE | 4 CREATE NAMEPLATE FOR SECOND PAGE | 5 FORMAT SECOND PAGE | 6 ADD PAGE BORDER

Currently, the text on the second page of the newsletter completely fills up the first and second columns and almost fills the third column. The text in the three columns should consume the same amount of vertical space. *Why? Typically, the text in columns of a newsletter is balanced.* To balance columns, you insert a continuous section break at the end of the text. The following steps balance columns.

1
- Scroll to the bottom of the text in the third column on the second page of the newsletter and then position the insertion point at the end of the text.
- If an extra paragraph mark is below the last line of text, press the DELETE key to remove the extra paragraph mark.
- Display the PAGE LAYOUT tab.
- Tap or click the 'Insert Page and Section Breaks' button (PAGE LAYOUT tab | Page Setup group) to display the Insert Page and Section Breaks gallery (Figure 7–64).

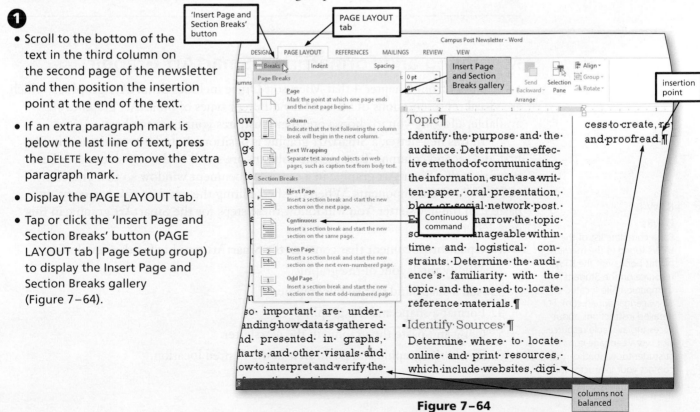

Figure 7–64

2

- Tap or click Continuous in the Insert Page and Section Breaks gallery to insert a continuous section break, which balances the columns on the second page of the newsletter (Figure 7–65).

how·mass·communication·and· popular·culture·affect·learn-ing·and·entertainment·include· the·ability·to·analyze·and·eval-uate·how·music,·film,·video,· television,·and·other·<u>nonprint</u>· media·are·used·effectively·to· persuade·and·inform.¶

▪ Numerical·Literacy¶
The·ability·to·use·basic·math· skills·and·interpret·data·is·crit-ical·to·solving·problems·and· communicating· information.· Also· important· are· under-standing·how·data·is·gathered· ¶

topic,· identifying· sources,· evaluating·materials,·and·cre-ating·the·final·work,·require· effort·and·careful·thought.·¶

▪ Establish·an·Appropriate· Topic¶
Identify·the·purpose·and·the· audience.·Determine·an·effec-tive·method·of·communicating· the·information,·such·as·a·writ-ten·paper,·oral·presentation,· blog,·or·social·network·post.· Explore·and·narrow·the·topic· so·that·it·is·manageable·within·

to· determine· if· the· authors· agree·or·disagree·with·topics.·¶

▪ Create·the·Final·Work¶
Organize· and· integrate· the· source· material· using· direct· quotations,·paraphrases,·and· summaries.· Document· the· work· to· credit· sources· and· avoid· plagiarism.· Integrate· photos,· charts,· and· graphs· when·necessary·to·clarify·the· message.·Use·the·writing·pro-cess·to·create,·review,·revise,· and·proofread. ···Section Break (Continuous)···

columns balanced

Figure 7–65

To Save a Document Again

You have performed several steps since the last save. Thus, you should save the newsletter again. The following step saves the newsletter again.

1 Save the newsletter again with the same file name, Campus Post Newsletter.

Modifying and Formatting a SmartArt Graphic

Recall from Chapter 4 that Microsoft Office includes **SmartArt graphics**, which are visual representations of ideas. Many different types of SmartArt graphics are available, allowing you to choose one that illustrates your message best.

In this newsletter, a SmartArt graphic is positioned on the second page, in the first and second columns. Because the columns are small in the newsletter, it is best to work with a SmartArt graphic in a separate document window so that you easily can see all of its components. When finished editing the graphic, you can copy and paste it in the newsletter. You will follow these steps for the SmartArt graphic in this newsletter:

1. Open the document that contains the SmartArt graphic for the newsletter.
2. Modify the layout of the graphic.
3. Add a shape and text to the graphic.
4. Format a shape and the graphic.
5. Copy and paste the graphic in the newsletter.
6. Resize the graphic and position it in the desired location.

BTW

BTWs
For a complete list of the BTWs found in the margins of this book, visit the BTW resource on the Student Companion Site located on www.cengagebrain.com. For detailed instructions about accessing available resources, visit www.cengage.com/ct/studentdownload or contact your instructor for information about accessing the required files.

To Open a Document from Word

The first draft of the SmartArt graphic is in a file called Information Literacy Diagram on the Data Files for Students. Visit www.cengage.com/ct/studentdownload for detailed instructions or contact your instructor for information about accessing the required files. The following steps open the Information Literacy Diagram file.

1 Open the Backstage view and then tap or click the Open tab to display the Open gallery.

2 Navigate to the location of the file to be opened (in this case, the Data Files for Students folder).

3 Tap or click Information Literacy Diagram to select the file name.

4 Tap or click the Open button (Open dialog box) to open the selected file.

5 Tap or click the graphic to select it and display the SMARTART TOOLS DESIGN and FORMAT tabs (Figure 7–66).

Q&A Is the Campus Post Newsletter file still open?
Yes. Leave it open because you will copy the modified diagram to the second page of the newsletter.

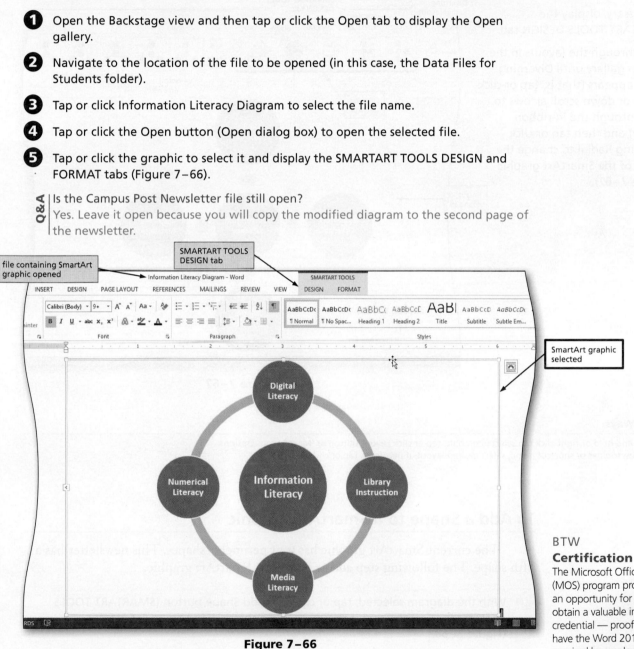

Figure 7–66

BTW

Certification

The Microsoft Office Specialist (MOS) program provides an opportunity for you to obtain a valuable industry credential — proof that you have the Word 2013 skills required by employers. For more information, visit the Certification resource on the Student Companion Site located on www.cengagebrain .com. For detailed instructions about accessing available resources, visit www.cengage .com/ct/studentdownload or contact your instructor for information about accessing the required files.

To Change the Layout of a SmartArt Graphic

The following step changes the layout of an existing SmartArt graphic. *Why? The SmartArt graphic currently uses the Radial Cycle layout, and this newsletter uses the Diverging Radial layout.*

1

- If necessary, display the SMARTART TOOLS DESIGN tab.

- Scroll through the layouts in the Layouts gallery until Diverging Radial appears (that is, tap or click the up or down scroll arrows to scroll through the in-ribbon gallery) and then tap or click Diverging Radial to change the layout of the SmartArt graphic (Figure 7–67).

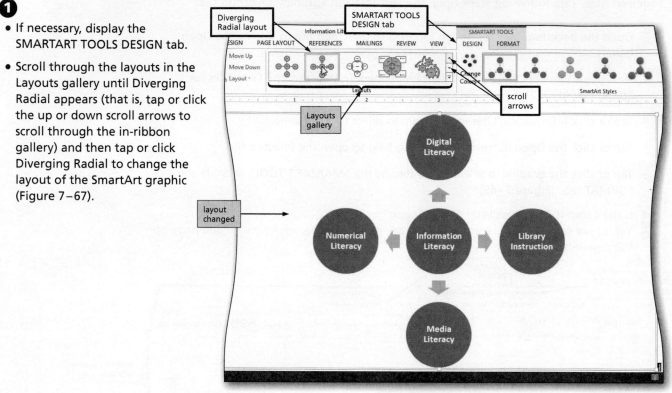

Figure 7–67

Other Ways

1. Press and hold or right-click the selected graphic, tap or click Layout button or 'More Layout Options' on mini toolbar or shortcut menu, select desired layout, if necessary, tap or click OK button

---

To Add a Shape to a SmartArt Graphic

The current SmartArt graphic has four perimeter shapes. This newsletter has a fifth shape. The following step adds a shape to a SmartArt graphic.

1 With the diagram selected, tap or click the Add Shape button (SMARTART TOOLS DESIGN tab | Create Graphic group) to add a shape to the SmartArt graphic (Figure 7–68).

Q&A Why did my screen display a menu instead of adding a shape?
You tapped or clicked the Add Shape arrow instead of the Add Shape button. Tapping or clicking the Add Shape button adds the shape automatically; tapping or clicking the Add Shape arrow displays a menu allowing you to specify the location of the shape.

How do I delete a shape?
Select the shape by tapping or clicking it and then press the DELETE key, or press and hold or right-click the shape and then tap or click Cut on the mini toolbar or shortcut menu.

Figure 7–68

BTW
Demoting Text
Pane Text
Instead of pressing the TAB key in the Text Pane, you could tap or click the Demote Selection button (SMARTART TOOLS DESIGN tab | Create Graphic group) to increase (or move to the right) the indent for a bulleted item. You also can tap or click the Promote Selection button (SMARTART TOOLS DESIGN tab | Create Graphic group) to decrease (or move to the left) the indent for a bulleted item.

To Add Text to a SmartArt Graphic through the Text Pane

1 CREATE NAMEPLATE FOR FIRST PAGE | 2 FORMAT FIRST PAGE | 3 CREATE PULL-QUOTE
4 CREATE NAMEPLATE FOR SECOND PAGE | 5 FORMAT SECOND PAGE | 6 ADD PAGE BORDER

In Chapter 4, you added text directly to the shapes in a SmartArt graphic. In this project, you enter the text through the Text Pane. *Why? Some users prefer to enter text in the Text Pane instead of in the shape.* The following steps use the Text Pane to add text to a shape.

1
- Tap or click the Text Pane control, which is on the left side of the SmartArt graphic, to display the Text Pane to the left of the SmartArt graphic.

2
- In the Text Pane, if necessary, position the insertion point to the right of the bullet that has no text to its right.
- Type **Traditional Literacy** as the text for the shape (Figure 7–69).

3
- Tap or click the Close button in the Text Pane to close the Text Pane.

Q&A Can I instead close the Text Pane by tapping or clicking the Text Pane button (SMARTART TOOLS DESIGN tab | Create Graphic group)?
Yes.

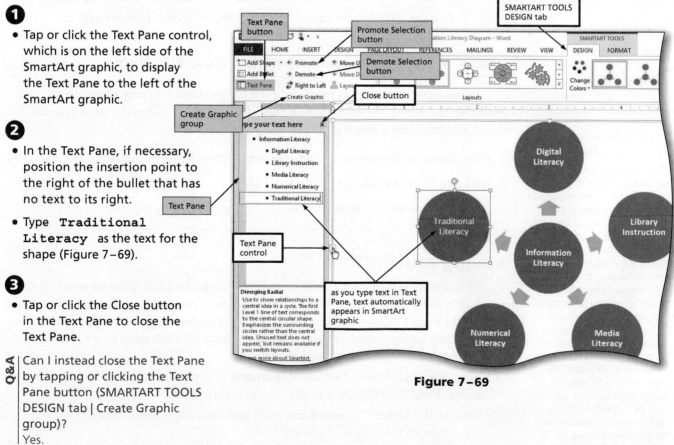

Figure 7–69

To Format SmartArt Graphic Text

To format text in an entire SmartArt graphic, select the graphic and then apply the format. The following steps bold the text in the SmartArt graphic.

1 If necessary, double-tap or double-click the shape just added to select it.

2 Display the HOME tab. Tap or click the Bold button (HOME tab | Font group) to bold the text in the SmartArt graphic (shown in Figure 7–70).

TO MODIFY THEME EFFECTS

If you wanted to change the look of graphics such as SmartArt graphics, you could perform the following steps to change the theme effects.

1. Tap or click the Theme Effects button (DESIGN tab | Document Formatting group).
2. Tap or click the desired effect in the Theme Effects gallery.

TO SAVE CUSTOMIZED THEMES

When you modify the theme effects, theme colors, or theme fonts, you can save the modified theme for future use. If you wanted to save a customized theme, you would perform the following steps.

1. Tap or click the Themes button (DESIGN tab | Document Formatting group) to display the Themes gallery.
2. Tap or click 'Save Current Theme' in the Themes gallery.
3. Enter a theme name in the File name box (Save Current Theme dialog box).
4. Tap or click the Save button to add the saved theme to the Themes gallery.

To Save an Active Document with a New File Name

To preserve the contents of the original Information Literacy Diagram file, you should save the active document with a new file name. The following steps save the active document with a new file name.

1 Open the Backstage view and then tap or click the Save As tab to display the Save As gallery.

2 Navigate to the location of the file to be saved.

3 Save the document with the file name, Information Literacy Diagram Modified.

Copying and Pasting

The next step is to copy the SmartArt graphic from this document window and then paste it in the newsletter. To copy from one document and paste into another, you can use the Office Clipboard. Through the Office Clipboard, you can copy multiple items from any Office document and then paste them into the same or another Office document by following these general guidelines:

1. Items are copied *from* a **source document**. If the source document is not the active document, display it in the document window.
2. Display the Office Clipboard task pane and then copy items from the source document to the Office Clipboard.
3. Items are copied *to* a **destination document**. If the destination document is not the active document, display the destination document in the document window.
4. Paste items from the Office Clipboard to the destination document.

To Copy a SmartArt Graphic Using the Office Clipboard

The following step copies the SmartArt graphic to the Office Clipboard. *Why? Sometimes you want to copy multiple items to the Office Clipboard through the Clipboard task pane and then paste them later.*

1

- Tap or click the Clipboard Dialog Box Launcher (HOME tab | Clipboard group) to display the Clipboard task pane.

- If the Office Clipboard in the Clipboard task pane is not empty, tap or click the Clear All button in the Clipboard task pane.

- With the SmartArt graphic selected in the document window, tap or click the Copy button (HOME tab | Clipboard group) to copy the selected text to the Clipboard (Figure 7–70).

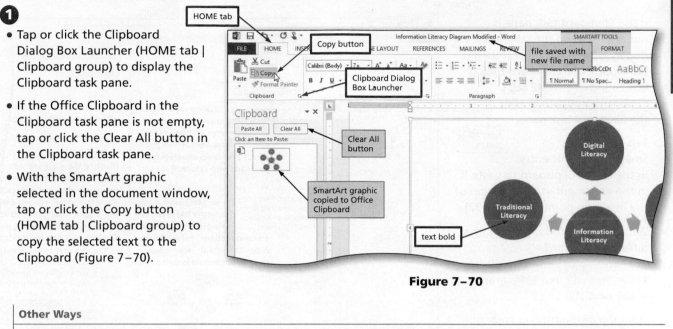

Figure 7–70

Other Ways

1. With Clipboard task pane displayed, press and hold or right-click selected item, tap or click Copy on mini toolbar or shortcut menu

2. With Clipboard task pane displayed and item to copy selected, press CTRL+C

To Switch from One Open Document to Another

The steps below switch from the open Information Literacy Diagram Modified document (the source document) to the open Campus Post Newsletter document (the destination document). *Why? You want to paste the copied diagram into the newsletter document.*

1

- If you are using a touch screen, tap the Word app button on the taskbar; if you are using a mouse, point to the Word app button on the taskbar to display a live preview of the open documents or window titles of the open documents, depending on your computer's configuration (Figure 7–71).

Figure 7–71

2

- Tap or click the live preview of the Campus Post Newsletter on the Windows taskbar to display the selected document in the document window (shown in Figure 7–72 on the next page).

Other Ways

1. Tap or click Switch Windows button (VIEW tab | Window group), tap or click document name

2. Press ALT+TAB

To Paste from the Office Clipboard

The following steps paste from the Office Clipboard. *Why? You want to paste the copied SmartArt graphic into the destination document, in this case, the newsletter document.*

1

- If the Clipboard task pane is not displayed on the screen, display the HOME tab and then tap or click the Clipboard Dialog Box Launcher (HOME tab | Clipboard group) to display the Clipboard task pane.

- Tap or click the SmartArt graphic entry in the Office Clipboard to paste it in the document at the location of the insertion point (Figure 7–72).

Q&A

What if my pasted graphic is in a different location?
The location of your graphic may differ. You will move the graphic in the next steps.

Does the destination document have to be a different document?
No. The source and destination documents can be the same document.

What is the function of the Paste All button?
If you have multiple items in the Office Clipboard, it pastes all items in a row, without any characters between them, at the location of the insertion point or selection.

Figure 7–72

2

- Tap or click the Close button in the Clipboard task pane.

Other Ways

1. With Clipboard task pane displayed, press and hold or right-click selected item, tap or click Paste on shortcut menu

2. With Clipboard task pane displayed, press CTRL+V

To Format a Graphic as Floating

The text in the newsletter should wrap tightly around the graphic; that is, the text should conform to the graphic's shape. Thus, the next step is to change the graphic from inline to floating with a wrapping style of tight. The following steps format the graphic as floating with tight wrapping.

 Tap or click the SmartArt graphic to select it.

 With the SmartArt graphic selected, tap or click the Layout Options button that is attached to the graphic to display the Layout Options gallery.

3 Tap or click Tight in the Layout Options gallery to change the graphic from inline to floating with tight wrapping.

4 Close the Layout Options gallery.

To Resize and Position the SmartArt Graphic

The next task is to increase the size of the SmartArt graphic and then position it in the first and second columns on the second page. The following steps resize and then position the graphic.

 Drag the sizing handles outward until the graphic is approximately the same size as shown in Figure 7–73, which has a height of 2.74" and a width of 4.26".

 Drag the edge of the graphic to the location shown in Figure 7–73. You may have to drag the graphic a couple of times to position it similarly to the figure.

3 If the newsletter spills onto a third page, reduce the size of the SmartArt graphic. You may need to delete an extra paragraph mark at the end of the document, as well.

BTW
Space around Graphics
The space between a graphic and the text, which sometimes is called the run-around, should be at least 1/8" and should be the same for all graphics in a document. Adjust the run-around of a selected floating graphic by doing the following: tap or click the Wrap Text button (SMARTART TOOLS FORMAT tab | Arrange group), tap or click 'More Layout Options' on the Wrap Text menu, tap or click the Position tab (Layout dialog box), adjust the values in the Horizontal and Vertical boxes, and then tap or click the OK button.

To Layer the SmartArt Graphic in Front of Text

1 CREATE NAMEPLATE FOR FIRST PAGE | 2 FORMAT FIRST PAGE | 3 CREATE PULL-QUOTE

4 CREATE NAMEPLATE FOR SECOND PAGE | 5 FORMAT SECOND PAGE | 6 ADD PAGE BORDER

In Word, you can layer objects on top of or behind other objects. The following steps layer the SmartArt graphic on top of all text. *Why? You want to ensure that the ruling line is positioned behind the SmartArt graphic.*

1

- If necessary, tap or click the SmartArt graphic to select it. Tap or click the Bring Forward arrow (SMARTART TOOLS FORMAT tab | Arrange group) to display the Bring Forward menu (Figure 7–73).

2

- Tap or click 'Bring in Front of Text' on the Bring Forward menu to position the selected object on top of all text.
- Tap or click outside the graphic so that it no longer is selected.

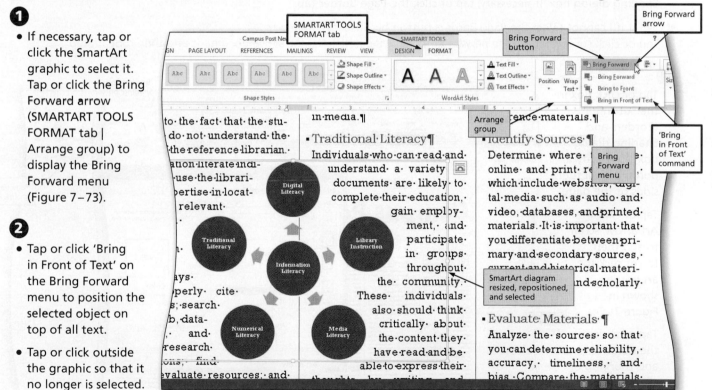

Figure 7–73

Finishing the Newsletter

With the text and graphics in the newsletter entered and formatted, the next step is to view the newsletter as a whole and determine if it looks finished in its current state. To give the newsletter a finished appearance, you will add a border to its edges.

To Turn Off Formatting Marks and Zoom Multiple Pages

The last step in formatting the newsletter is to place a border around its edges. First, you turn off formatting marks to remove the clutter from the screen. Then, you place both pages in the document window at once so that you can see all the page borders applied. The following steps turn off formatting marks and zoom multiple pages.

1 If necessary, display the HOME tab and then turn off formatting marks.

2 Display the VIEW tab and then display multiple pages on the screen.

To Add an Art Page Border

1 CREATE NAMEPLATE FOR FIRST PAGE | 2 FORMAT FIRST PAGE | 3 CREATE PULL-QUOTE
4 CREATE NAMEPLATE FOR SECOND PAGE | 5 FORMAT SECOND PAGE | **6 ADD PAGE BORDER**

The following steps add a page border around the pages of the newsletter. *Why? This newsletter has a purple art border around the perimeter of each page.*

1
- Display the DESIGN tab.
- Tap or click the 'Borders and Shading' button (DESIGN tab | Page Background group) to display the Borders and Shading dialog box. If necessary, tap or click the Page Border tab.

Q&A What if I cannot select the Page Borders button because it is dimmed?
Tap or click somewhere in the newsletter to make the newsletter the active document and then repeat Step 1.

2
- Tap or click Box in the Setting area (Borders and Shading dialog box) to specify a border on all four sides of the page.
- Tap or click the Art arrow, scroll to and then tap or click the art border shown in Figure 7–74.
- Tap or click the Color arrow and then tap or click 'Lavender, Accent 4, Darker 50%' (sixth row, eighth column) on the palette (Figure 7–74).

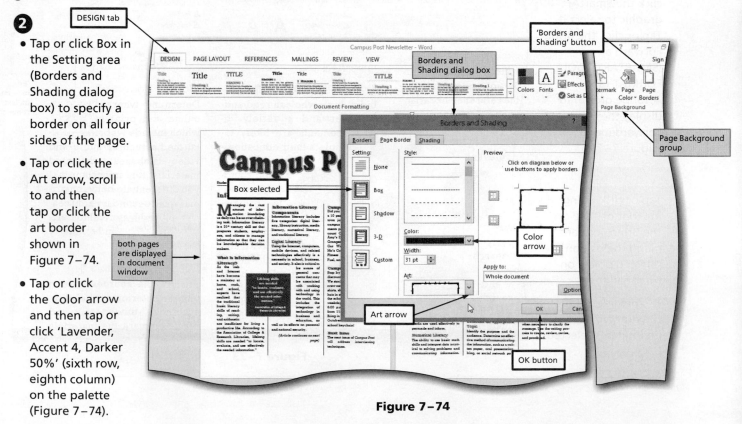

Figure 7–74

3

- Tap or click the OK button to place the defined border on each page of the newsletter (Figure 7–75).

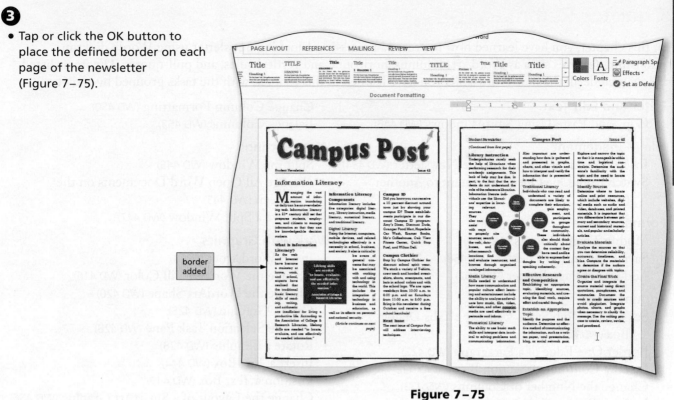

Figure 7–75

To Save and Print the Document, Then Exit Word

The newsletter now is complete. You should save the document, print it, and then exit Word.

1 Save the newsletter again with the same file name.

2 If desired, print the newsletter (shown in Figure 7–1 on page WD 411).

Q&A What if an error message appears about margins?
Depending on the printer you are using, you may need to set the margins differently for this project.

What if one or more of the borders do not print?
Tap or click the 'Borders and Shading' button (DESIGN tab | Page Background group), tap or click the Options button (Borders and Shading dialog box), tap or click the Measure from arrow and tap or click Text, change the four text boxes to 15 pt, and then tap or click the OK button in each dialog box. Try printing the document again. If the borders still do not print, adjust the text boxes in the dialog box to a number smaller than 15 pt.

3 Exit Word, closing all open documents.

BTW

Conserving Ink and Toner
If you want to conserve ink or toner, you can instruct Word to print draft quality documents by tapping or clicking FILE on the ribbon to open the Backstage view, tapping or clicking Options in the Backstage view to display the Word Options dialog box, tapping or clicking Advanced in the left pane (Word Options dialog box), sliding or scrolling to the Print area in the right pane, placing a check mark in the 'Use draft quality' check box, and then tapping or clicking the OK button. Then, use the Backstage view to print the document as usual.

BTW

Distributing a Document
Instead of printing and distributing a hard copy of a document, you can distribute the document electronically. Options include sending the document via email; posting it on cloud storage (such as SkyDrive) and sharing the file with others; posting it on a social networking site, blog, or other website; and sharing a link associated with an online location of the document. You also can create and share a PDF or XPS image of the document, so that users can view the file in Acrobat Reader or XPS Viewer instead of in Word.

Chapter Summary

In this chapter, you have learned how to create a professional-looking newsletter using Word's desktop publishing features such as WordArt, columns, horizontal and vertical rules, and pull-quotes. The items listed below include all the new Word skills you have learned in this chapter, with the tasks grouped by activity.

Enter and Edit Text
Copy and Paste Using Split Windows (WD 446)

File Management
Insert a File in a Column of the Newsletter (WD 434)
Switch from One Open Document to Another (WD 459)

Format a Page
Modify Theme Effects (WD 458)
Save Customized Themes (WD 458)
Add an Art Page Border (WD 462)

Format Text
Set Custom Tab Stops Using the Tabs Dialog Box (WD 420)
Border One Edge of a Paragraph (WD 422)
Insert a Continuous Section Break (WD 432)
Change the Number of Columns (WD 433)
Justify a Paragraph (WD 434)
Increase Column Width and Place a Vertical Rule between Columns (WD 436)
Hyphenate a Document (WD 437)
Format a Character as a Drop Cap (WD 438)
Insert a Next Page Section Break (WD 440)
Insert a Column Break (WD 441)

Change Column Formatting (WD 450)
Balance Columns (WD 453)

Word Settings
Split the Window (WD 445)
Arrange All Open Word Documents on the Screen (WD 445)
Remove a Split Window (WD 447)

Work with Graphics
Insert WordArt (WD 414)
Change the WordArt Fill Color (WD 416)
Change the WordArt Shape (WD 420)
Crop a Graphic (WD 425)
Use the Selection Task Pane (WD 428)
Rotate a Graphic (WD 428)
Insert a Text Box (WD 444)
Position a Text Box (WD 449)
Change the Layout of a SmartArt Graphic (WD 456)
Add Text to a SmartArt Graphic through the Text Pane (WD 457)
Copy a SmartArt Graphic Using the Office Clipboard (WD 459)
Paste from the Office Clipboard (WD 460)
Layer the SmartArt Graphic in Front of Text (WD 461)

CONSIDER THIS: PLAN AHEAD

What decisions will you need to make when creating your next newsletter?
Use these guidelines as you complete the assignments in this chapter and create your own newsletters outside of this class.

1. Create the nameplate.
   a) Determine the location of the nameplate.
   b) Determine content, formats, and arrangement of text and graphics.
   c) If appropriate, use ruling lines.

2. Determine content for the body of the newsletter.
   a) Write the body copy.
   b) Organize the body copy in columns.
   c) Format the body copy and subheads.
   d) Incorporate color.
   e) Divide sections with vertical rules.
   f) Enhance with visuals.

3. Bind and distribute the newsletter.
   a) Determine if newsletters should be printed, posted on bulletin boards, sent as an email message, or posted on websites.
   b) For multipage newsletters that will be printed, determine the appropriate method of binding the pages.
   c) For online newsletters, select a format that most users will be able to open.

How should you submit solutions to questions in the assignments identified with a ✸ symbol?
Every assignment in this book contains one or more questions identified with a ✸ symbol. These questions require you to think beyond the assigned document. Present your solutions to the questions in the format required by your instructor. Possible formats may include one or more of these options: write the answer; create a document that contains the answer; present your answer to the class; discuss your answer in a group; record the answer as audio or video using a webcam, smartphone, or portable media player; or post answers on a blog, wiki, or website.

Apply Your Knowledge

Reinforce the skills and apply the concepts you learned in this chapter.

Working with Desktop Publishing Elements of a Newsletter

Note: To complete this assignment, you will be required to use the Data Files for Students. Visit www.cengage.com/ct/studentdownload for detailed instructions or contact your instructor for information about accessing the required files.

Instructions: Run Word. Open the document, Apply 7-1 Meteor Shower Newsletter Draft, from the Data Files for Students. The document contains a newsletter that you are to modify (Figure 7–76).

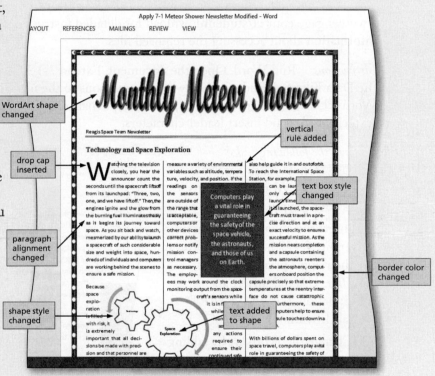

Figure 7–76

Perform the following tasks:

1. Change the WordArt shape to Inflate.

2. Turn on automatic hyphenation.

3. Change the column width of the columns in the body of the newsletter to 2.2".

4. Add a vertical rule (line) between each column.

5. Change the style of the pull-quote (text box) to 'Colored Fill - Tan, Accent 6' (DRAWING TOOLS FORMAT tab | Shape Styles group).

6. Format the first paragraph with a drop cap.

7. Change the alignment of the paragraph containing the drop cap from left-aligned to justified.

8. Change the layout of the SmartArt graphic to Gear.

9. Use the Text Pane to add the text, Space Exploration, to the right shape in the SmartArt graphic.

10. If necessary, move the SmartArt graphic and the pull-quote so that they are positioned similarly to the ones in Figure 7–76.

11. Change the color of the page border to Dark Blue, Accent 3.

12. If requested by your instructor, change the name Reagis in the issue information line to your name.

13. If the newsletter flows to two pages, reduce the size of elements such as WordArt or pull-quote, or adjust spacing above or below paragraphs so that the newsletter fits on a single page. Make any other necessary adjustments to the newsletter.

14. Save the modified file with the file name, Apply 7-1 Meteor Shower Newsletter Modified.

Continued >

Apply Your Knowledge *continued*

15. Submit the revised newsletter in the format specified by your instructor.

16. ✸ When you use hyphenation to divide words at the end of a line, what are the accepted guidelines for dividing the words? (*Hint:* Use a search engine to search the text, end of line hyphenation.)

Extend Your Knowledge

Extend the skills you learned in this chapter and experiment with new skills. You may need to use Help to complete the assignment.

Adding a Equations to a Newsletter and Enhancing a Nameplate

Note: To complete this assignment, you will be required to use the Data Files for Students. Visit www.cengage.com/ct/studentdownload for detailed instructions or contact your instructor for information about accessing the required files.

Instructions: Run Word. Open the document, Extend 7-1 Mathletes Newsletter Draft, from the Data Files for Students. You will add equations to the newsletter, change the format of the WordArt, format the drop cap, adjust the hyphenation rules, move the page border closer to the text, clear tabs, and insert leader characters.

Perform the following tasks:

1. Use Help to learn about equations, WordArt options, borders, hyphenation, and tabs.

2. Insert the equations shown in Figure 7–77 in the newsletter in their appropriate locations. *Hint:* Use the 'Insert an Equation' button (INSERT tab | Symbols group).

3. Change the WordArt by adding at least two WordArt style text effects. Change the color of the WordArt text outline. Change the color of the WordArt text fill color.

4. Add a shape fill color to the text box surrounding the WordArt.

5. Add a drop cap to the first paragraph in the body of the newsletter. Change the number of lines to drop from three to two lines.

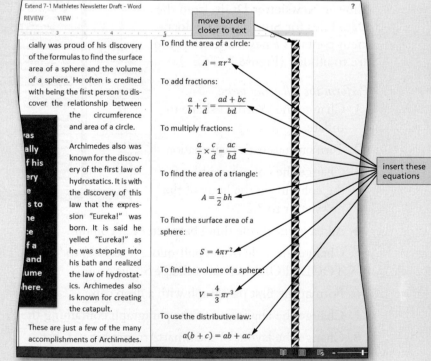

Figure 7–77

6. Change the hyphenation rules to limit consecutive hyphens to two.

7. Change the page border so that the border is closer to the text.

8. If the newsletter flows to two pages, reduce the size of elements such as WordArt or the pull-quote or the table, or adjust spacing above or below paragraphs so that the newsletter fits on a single page. Make any other necessary adjustments to the newsletter.

9. Clear the tabs in the issue information line in the nameplate. Use the Tabs dialog box to insert a right-aligned tab stop at the 6.5" mark. Fill the tab space with a leader character of your choice.

10. If requested by your instructor, change the name, Juniper, in the issue information line to your last name.

11. Submit the revised newsletter in the format specified by your instructor.

12. ✳ Which equations are predefined in Word? Which structures are available on the EQUATION TOOLS DESIGN tab? How do you change the alignment of an equation?

Analyze, Correct, Improve

Analyze a document, correct all errors, and improve it.

Formatting a Newsletter

Note: To complete this assignment, you will be required to use the Data Files for Students. Visit www.cengage.com/ct/studentdownload for detailed instructions or contact your instructor for information about accessing the required files.

Instructions: Run Word. Open the document, Analyze 7-1 Saddle Bits Newsletter Draft, from the Data Files for Students. The document is a newsletter whose elements are not formatted properly (Figure 7–78). You are to edit and format the WordArt, format the clip art image and columns, change tab stop alignment, change paragraph alignment, add a drop cap, format the pull-quote (text box), and add a border.

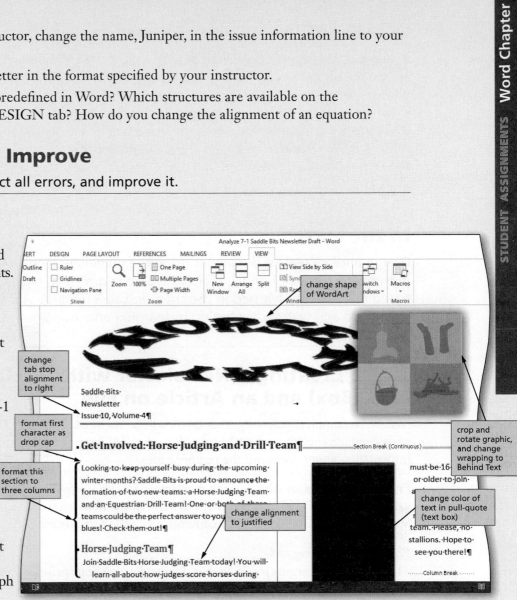

Figure 7–78

Perform the following tasks:

1. Correct In the newsletter, correct the following items:

a. Change the shape of the WordArt so that the text is more readable.

b. Format the clip art image in the nameplate to Behind Text.

c. Rotate the clip art image so it is upright and angled so that it fits the space. Adjust the location and size of the clip art image so that it has a pleasing appearance in the nameplate.

d. Crop the clip art image so that just the horse and boots show.

e. Change the alignment of the custom tab stop at the 7" mark in the issue information line from left-aligned to right-aligned.

f. Change the number of columns in the body of the newsletter from two to three.

g. Change the paragraphs in the Horse Judging Team and Equestrian Drill Team sections from centered to justified paragraph alignment.

h. Format the first letter in the first paragraph of text as a drop cap.

i. Change the color of the text in the pull-quote (text box) so that it is easier to read. Position the pull-quote between the first and second columns.

Continued >

Analyze, Correct, Improve *continued*

2. Improve Enhance the newsletter by adding color to the drop cap. Add an attractive art border around the edge of the newsletter. Do not use the default single line, black border. If the newsletter flows to two pages, reduce the size of elements such as WordArt or clip art or the pull-quote, or adjust spacing above or below paragraphs so that the newsletter fits on a single page. Make any other adjustments you deem appropriate to the newsletter. If requested by your instructor, change the stable name in the newsletter to your name. Save the modified document with the file name, Analyze 7-1 Saddle Bits Newsletter Modified, and then submit it in the format specified by your instructor.

3. ✺ In this assignment, you added an art border. Which border did you select and why?

In the Labs

Design and/or create a document using the guidelines, concepts, and skills presented in this chapter. Labs 1 and 2, which increase in difficulty, require you to create solutions based on what you learned in the chapter; Lab 3 requires you to create a solution, which uses cloud and web technologies, by learning and investigating on your own from general guidance.

Lab 1: Creating a Newsletter with a Pull-Quote (Text Box) and an Article on File

Note: To complete this assignment, you will be required to use the Data Files for Students. Visit www.cengage.com/ct/studentdownload for detailed instructions or contact your instructor for information about accessing the required files.

Problem: You are an editor of the newsletter, *Weekly Woofer*. The next edition is due out in one week (Figure 7–79). The text for the articles in the newsletter is in a file on the Data Files for Students. You need to create the nameplate and the text box for the pull-quote.

Perform the following tasks:
1. Change all margins to .75 inches. Depending on your printer, you may need different margin settings. Change the theme to Parallax.
2. Create the nameplate using the formats identified in Figure 7–79. Create the title using WordArt. Set the WordArt wrapping to Top and Bottom. If necessary, drag the bottom of the Word Art up to shorten the image. Set a right-aligned custom tab stop at the right margin. Search for and insert the clip art image (or a similar image). Resize the image to the size shown in the figure and apply the Beveled Oval, Black picture style to the image. Copy the image and flip the copied image horizontally. Format the images as Behind Text, rotate them, and then position them as shown.
3. Below the nameplate, enter the heading, Upcoming Events: Training, Shows, and More, as shown in the figure. Format the heading using the Heading 1 style. Change the spacing above this paragraph to 24 pt and the spacing after to 12 pt.
4. Create a continuous section break below the heading, Upcoming Events: Training, Shows, and More.
5. Format section 2 to three columns.
6. Insert the Lab 7-1 PAWS Article file, which is located on the Data Files for Students, in section 2 below the nameplate.
7. Format the newsletter according to Figure 7–79. Insert a column break before these headings: Shows and Dog of the Week. Columns should have a width of 2.1" with spacing of 0.35". Place a vertical rule between the columns.
8. If necessary, insert a continuous section break at the end of the document to balance the columns.

Figure 7–79

9. Format the subheads using the Heading 2 style.

10. Insert a text box using the Simple Text Box built-in text box. The text for the pull-quote is in the first paragraph of the article. Split the window. Use the split window to copy the text and then paste it in the text box. Remove the split window. Change the fill color (shape fill) of the text box to Black, Text 1, Lighter 15%. Resize the text box so that it is similar in size to Figure 7–79. Position the text box as shown in Figure 7–79.

11. Add the page border as shown in the figure.

12. If the document does not fit on a single page, adjust spacing above and below paragraphs.

13. If requested by your instructor, change the trainer name from Leonard Ortz to your name.

14. Save the document with Lab 7-1 PAWS Newsletter as the file name and then submit it in the format specified by your instructor.

15. ✹ This newsletter used a pull-quote. What other text in the newsletter could appear in the pull-quote?

Lab 2: **Creating a Newsletter with a SmartArt Graphic and an Article on File**

Note: To complete this assignment, you will be required to use the Data Files for Students. Visit www.cengage.com/ct/studentdownload for detailed instructions or contact your instructor for information about accessing the required files.

Problem: You are responsible for the weekly preparation of *Help Desk!*, a newsletter for college students. The next edition discusses how to search for a job online (Figure 7–80 on the next page). This article already has been prepared and is on the Data Files for Students. You need to create the nameplate, the SmartArt graphic, and the section at the bottom of the newsletter.

Perform the following tasks:

1. Change all margins to .75 inches. Depending on your printer, you may need different margin settings. Change the document theme to Slice.

2. Create the nameplate using the formats identified in Figure 7–80. Create the title using WordArt. Set a right-aligned custom tab stop at the right margin. Set the WordArt wrapping to Top and Bottom. If necessary, drag the bottom of the Word Art up to shorten the image.

Continued >

In the Labs *continued*

Search for and insert the clip art image (or a similar image). Resize the image as shown in the figure. Format the image as Behind Text and position the images as shown.

3. Below the nameplate, enter the heading, Search for a Job Online, as shown in the figure.

4. Create a continuous section break below the heading.

5. Format section 2 to two columns.

6. Insert the Lab 7-2 Help Desk Article file, which is located on the Data Files for Students, in section 2 below the nameplate.

7. Format the newsletter according to Figure 7–80. Columns should have a width of 3.33" with spacing of 0.35". Place a vertical rule between the columns.

8. Use Word's automatic hyphenation feature to hyphenate the document.

9. Insert a continuous section break at the end of the document to balance the columns.

10. In the next section, change the number of columns from two to one. Enter the text shown at the bottom of the newsletter.

11. Add the page border as shown in the figure.

12. Open a new document window and create the SmartArt graphic shown in Figure 7–80. Use the Radial Venn layout. Add the text shown in the figure (you will need to add shapes). Use the Office Clipboard to copy and paste the SmartArt graphic from the current window to the newsletter. Resize the pasted graphic as shown in the figure. Change the colors to Colorful Range - Accent Colors 2 to 3. Note that your graphic may look slightly different from the figure due to variations in the shape size.

13. If the document does not fit on a single page, adjust spacing above and below paragraphs.

14. If requested by your instructor, change the hall name from Bantam to your last name.

15. Save the newsletter using Lab 7-2 Help Desk Newsletter as the file name and submit it in the format specified by your instructor.

16. ✹ How many sections are in this newsletter? How many columns are in each section? If you wanted to add a second page to this newsletter, what type of section break would appear at the end of the first page?

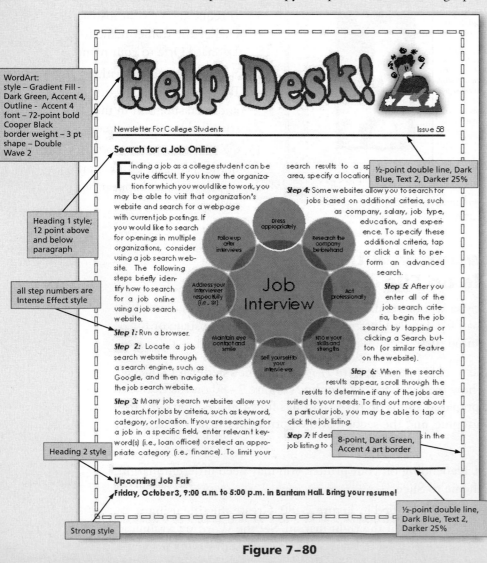

Figure 7–80

Lab 3: Expand Your World: Cloud and Web Technologies
Using Windows Essentials

Problem: You have heard that Windows Essentials includes some useful programs, so you decide to learn about it, download it, and use its programs.

Note: You may be required to use your Microsoft account to complete this assignment. If you do not have a Microsoft account and do not want to create one, read the assignment without performing the instructions.

Instructions: Perform the following tasks:

1. Run a browser. Search for the text, Windows Essentials, using a search engine. Tap or click a link to learn about Windows Essentials.

2. Navigate to the website to download Windows Essentials (Figure 7–81) and then follow the instructions to download Windows Essentials.

3. One at a time, run each program included with Windows Essentials. Browse through the features and functions of each program.

4. ✸ What programs are included with Windows Essentials? What is the purpose of each program? Which programs will you use and why? Which programs required you to sign in to your Microsoft account?

Figure 7–81

✸ Consider This: Your Turn

Apply your creative thinking and problem solving skills to design and implement a solution.

Note: To complete these assignments, you may be required to use the Data Files for Students. Visit www.cengage.com/ct/studentdownload for detailed instructions or contact your instructor for information about accessing the required files.

1: Create a Newsletter about E-Books
Personal

Part 1:   As a part-time assistant in the library at your school, you have been assigned the task of creating a newsletter called Bookmark It, which will be distributed to all enrolled students. The article in Issue 54 of the Library Newsletter covers e-books. The text for the article is in a file called Your Turn 7-1 E-Books Draft on the Data Files for Students.

The newsletter should contain at least two of these graphical elements: a clip art image, a SmartArt graphic, a pull-quote, or a table. Enhance the newsletter with a drop cap, WordArt, color, ruling lines, and a page border. Be sure to use appropriate desktop publishing elements, including a nameplate, columns of text, balanced columns, and a variety of font sizes, font colors, and shading. Use the concepts and techniques presented in this chapter to create and format the newsletter. Be sure to check spelling and grammar of the finished newsletter. Submit your assignment in the format specified by your instructor.

Part 2:   ✸ You made several decisions while creating the newsletter in this assignment: how to organize and format the nameplate (location, content, formats, arrangement of text and graphics, ruling lines, etc.), which two graphics to use (clip art, SmartArt graphic, text box, or table), and how to organize and format the body copy (columns, formats, headings and subheads, color, vertical rules, etc.). What was the rationale behind each of these decisions? When you proofread the document, what further revisions did you make and why?

Continued >

STUDENT ASSIGNMENTS

Consider This: Your Turn *continued*

2: Create a Newsletter about Safe Web Browsing
Professional

Part 1: As a part-time employee at JD Systems Technology, you have been asked to create a newsletter called Megabits, which is placed in the office lobby and on the company's website. The article in Issue 11 of the Technology Center Newsletter covers web browsing safety tips. The text for the article is in a file called Your Turn 7-2 Web Browsing Draft on the Data Files for Students.

The newsletter should contain at least two of these graphical elements: a clip art image, a SmartArt graphic, a pull-quote, or a table. Enhance the newsletter with a drop cap, WordArt, color, ruling lines, and a page border. Be sure to use appropriate desktop publishing elements, including a nameplate, columns of text, balanced columns, and a variety of font sizes, font colors, and shading. Use the concepts and techniques presented in this chapter to create and format the newsletter. Be sure to check spelling and grammar of the finished newsletter. Submit your assignment in the format specified by your instructor.

Part 2: ✸ You made several decisions while creating the newsletter in this assignment: how to organize and format the nameplate (location, content, formats, arrangement of text and graphics, ruling lines, etc.), which two graphics to use (clip art, SmartArt graphic, text box, or table), and how to organize and format the body copy (columns, formats, headings and subheads, color, vertical rules, etc.). What was the rationale behind each of these decisions? When you proofread the document, what further revisions did you make and why?

3: Create a Review Newsletter
Research and Collaboration

Part 1: The local newspaper has a two-page newsletter in its Wednesday edition each week that reviews current movies, live performances, books, restaurants, and local events. You and two other team members have been assigned the task of designing and writing the next newsletter. The newsletter should have a feature article that contains at least three separate reviews. One column of the newsletter should contain community calendar announcements.

Each team member should independently see or rent a current movie, watch a live performance, read a book, dine at a local restaurant, or attend a local event and then write at least a three paragraph review. Then, the team should meet as a group to combine all the reviews into a single article. As a team, compose the newsletter. The newsletter should contain at least one of each of these graphical elements: a clip art image, a SmartArt graphic, and a pull-quote. Enhance the newsletter with a drop cap, WordArt, color, ruling lines, and a page border. Be sure to use appropriate desktop publishing elements, including a nameplate, columns of text, balanced columns, and a variety of font sizes, font colors, and shading. Use the concepts and techniques presented in this chapter to create and format the newsletter. Be sure to check spelling and grammar of the finished newsletter. Submit your assignment in the format specified by your instructor.

Part 2: ✸ You made several decisions while creating the newsletter in this assignment: text to use, how to organize and format the nameplate (location, content, formats, arrangement of text and graphics, ruling lines, etc.), which graphics to use, and how to organize and format the body copy (columns, formats, headings and subheads, color, vertical rules, etc.). What was the rationale behind each of these decisions? When you proofread the document, what further revisions did you make and why?

Learn Online

Reinforce what you learned in this chapter with games, exercises, training, and many other online activities and resources.

Student Companion Site Reinforcement activities and resources are available at no additional cost on www.cengagebrain.com. Visit www.cengage.com/ct/studentdownload for detailed instructions about accessing the resources available at the Student Companion Site.

SAM Put your skills into practice with SAM! If you have a SAM account, go to www.cengage .com/sam2013 to access SAM assignments for this chapter.

Appendix

APA Research Paper — Chapter 2 Supplement

Project — Research Paper Based on APA Documentation Style

As described in Chapter 2, two popular documentation styles for research papers are the Modern Language Association of America (MLA) and American Psychological Association (APA). This appendix creates the same research paper shown in Chapter 2, except it uses the APA documentation style instead of the MLA documentation style (Figure 1 on the next page).

This appendix is intended as a supplement for Chapter 2. It assumes you have completed the Chapter 2 project and, thus, presents only the steps required to create the research paper following the APA guidelines. That is, this appendix does not repeat background, explanations, boxes, or steps from Chapter 2 that are not required specifically to create this APA research paper. For example, this appendix does not present proofing tools, citation placeholders, footnotes, copy and paste, Research task pane, etc. It does not contain the roadmap, Q&As, or BTWs. You should know the material presented in Chapter 2 because it will help you to complete later chapters in the book successfully and can help you prepare if you intend to take the Word Certification exam.

APA Documentation Style

The research paper in this appendix follows the guidelines presented by the APA. To follow the APA documentation style, format the text with a 12-point Times New Roman or a similar font. Double-space text on all pages of the paper using one-inch top, bottom, left, and right margins. Indent the first word of each paragraph in the body of the paper, and in footnotes if they are used, one-half inch from the left margin. At the top of each page, place a left-aligned running head and a right-aligned page number. The **running head** consists of the text, Running head:, followed by an abbreviated paper title (no more than 50 characters) in all uppercase letters.

The APA documentation style requires a title page. In addition to the running head and page number at the top of the page, the title page contains the complete paper title, author name, and institutional affiliation, all centered on separate lines in the upper half of the page. The paper title should not exceed 12 words and should be written so that it easily can be shortened to an abbreviated title for the running head. The author name,

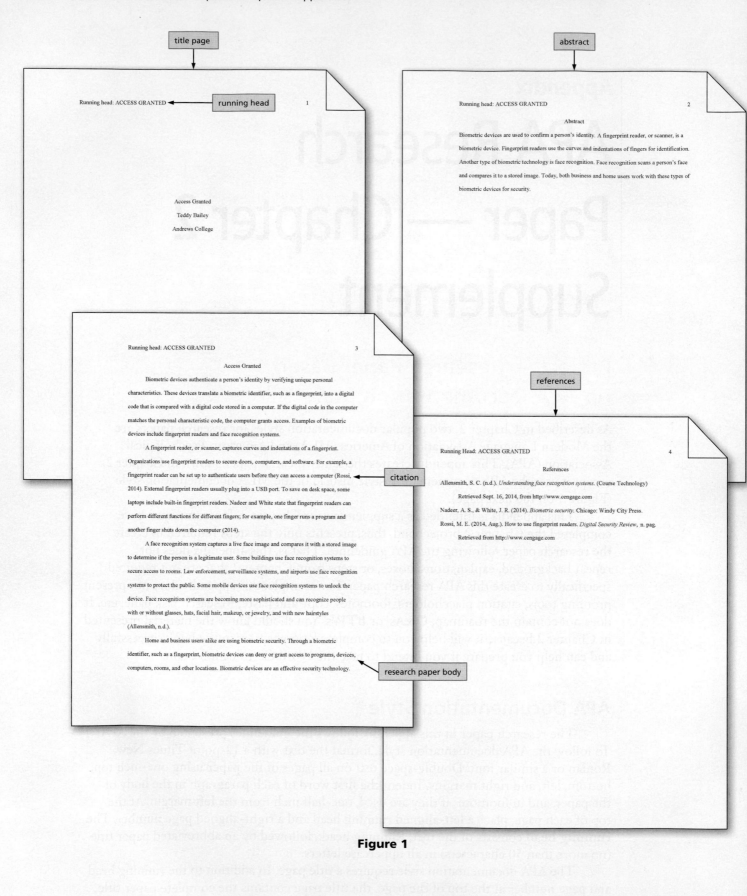

Figure 1

also called an author byline, should not contain any title (e.g., Professor) or degrees (e.g., PhD). If the author is not affiliated with an institution, list the author's city and state of residence. The title page also can include an author note centered at the bottom of the page, which can contain separate paragraphs identifying the author's departmental affiliation, changes in affiliation during research, acknowledgments, and contact information. If the title page contains an author note, the text, Author Note, should be centered above the notes.

Research papers that follow the APA documentation style include an abstract. The **abstract** is a one-paragraph summary (usually 250 words or less) of the most important topics in the paper. The abstract appears after the title page on its own numbered page, which includes the running head. The title, Abstract, is centered above a single paragraph that is double-spaced and not indented.

The APA documentation style cites references in the text of the paper, called **citations**, instead of noting each source at the bottom of the page or at the end of the paper. This documentation style also uses the term, **references,** to refer to the bibliographic list of sources at the end of the paper. The references page alphabetically lists sources that are cited in the paper. Place the list of sources on a separate numbered page. Center the title, References, one inch from the top margin. Double-space all entries and format them with a **hanging indent**, in which the first line of a paragraph begins at the left margin and subsequent lines in the same paragraph are indented. The APA guidelines specify the hanging indent should be one-half inch from the left margin. List each source by the author's last name, or, if the author's name is not available, by the title of the source. Capitalize only the first letter of the first word in a title, along with any proper nouns.

To Start Word

If you are using a computer to step through the project in this chapter and you want your screens to match the figures in this book, you should change your screen's resolution to 1366 × 768. For information about how to change a computer's resolution, refer to the Office and Windows chapter at the beginning of this book.

The following steps, which assume Windows 8 is running, use the Start screen or the Search box to run Word based on a typical installation. You may need to ask your instructor how to run Word on your computer. For a detailed example of the procedure summarized below, refer to the Office and Windows chapter.

1 Scroll the Start screen for a Word 2013 tile. If your Start screen contains a Word 2013 tile, tap or click it to run Word and then proceed to Step 5; if the Start screen does not contain the Word 2013 tile, proceed to the next step to search for the Word app.

2 Swipe in from the right edge of the screen or point to the upper-right corner of the screen to display the Charms bar and then tap or click the Search charm on the Charms bar to display the Search menu.

3 Type `Word` as the search text in the Search box and watch the search results appear in the Apps list.

4 Tap or click Word 2013 in the search results to run Word.

5 Tap or click the Blank document thumbnail on the Word start screen to create a blank document and display it in the Word window.

6 If the Word window is not maximized, tap or click the Maximize button on its title bar to maximize the window.

7 If the Print Layout button on the status bar is not selected (shown in Figure 2), tap or click it so that your screen is in Print Layout view.

8 If Normal (HOME tab | Styles group) is not selected in the Styles gallery (shown in Figure 2), tap or click it so that your document uses the Normal style.

9 To display the page the same width as the document window, if necessary, tap or click the Page Width button (VIEW tab | Zoom group).

10 If the 'Show/Hide ¶' button (HOME tab | Paragraph group) is not selected already, tap or click it to display formatting marks on the screen.

To Modify the Normal Style for the Current Document

The APA documentation style requires that all text in the research paper use a 12-point Times New Roman or similar font. If you change the font and font size using buttons on the ribbon, you will need to make the change many times during the course of creating the paper. *Why? Word formats various areas of a document based on the Normal style, which uses an 11-point Calibri font. For example, body text, headers, and bibliographies all display text based on the Normal style.*

Thus, instead of changing the font and font size for various document elements, a more efficient technique is to change the Normal style for this document to use a 12-point Times New Roman font. *Why? By changing the Normal style, you ensure that all text in the document will use the format required by the APA.* The following steps change the Normal style.

1
- Press and hold or right-click Normal in the Styles gallery (HOME tab | Styles group) to display a shortcut menu related to styles (Figure 2).

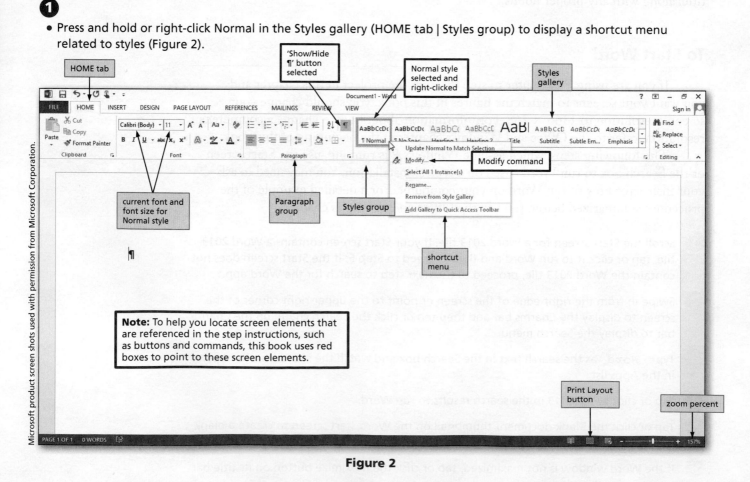

HOME tab

'Show/Hide ¶' button selected

Normal style selected and right-clicked

Styles gallery

Modify command

current font and font size for Normal style

Paragraph group

Styles group

shortcut menu

Note: To help you locate screen elements that are referenced in the step instructions, such as buttons and commands, this book uses red boxes to point to these screen elements.

Print Layout button

zoom percent

Microsoft product screen shots used with permission from Microsoft Corporation.

Figure 2

2

- Tap or click Modify on the shortcut menu to display the Modify Style dialog box.

3

- Tap or click the Font arrow (Modify Style dialog box) to display the Font list. Scroll to and then click Times New Roman in the list to change the font for the style being modified.

- Tap or click the Font Size arrow (Modify Style dialog box) and then tap or click 12 in the Font Size list to change the font size for the style being modified.

- Ensure that the 'Only in this document' option button is selected (Figure 3).

4

- Tap or click the OK button (Modify Style dialog box) to update the Normal style to the specified settings.

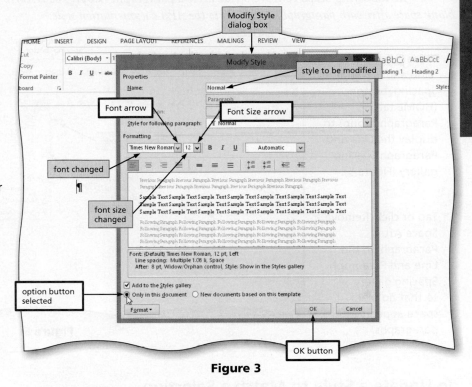

Figure 3

To Change Line Spacing to Double

The following steps change the line spacing to 2.0 to double-space lines in a paragraph. *Why? The lines of the research paper should be double-spaced, according to the APA documentation style.*

1

- Tap or click the 'Line and Paragraph Spacing' button (HOME tab | Paragraph group) to display the Line and Paragraph Spacing gallery (Figure 4).

2

- Tap or click 2.0 in the Line and Paragraph Spacing gallery to change the line spacing at the location of the insertion point.

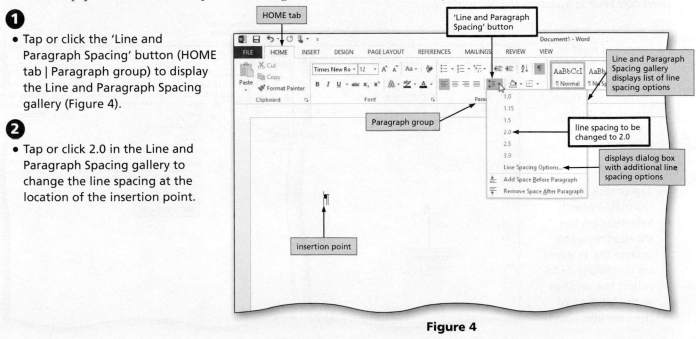

Figure 4

To Remove Space after a Paragraph

The following steps remove space after a paragraph. *Why? The research paper should not have additional blank space after each paragraph, according to the APA documentation style.*

1
- Tap or click the 'Line and Paragraph Spacing' button (HOME tab | Paragraph group) to display the Line and Paragraph Spacing gallery (Figure 5).

2
- Tap or click 'Remove Space After Paragraph' in the Line and Paragraph Spacing gallery so that no blank space appears after paragraphs.

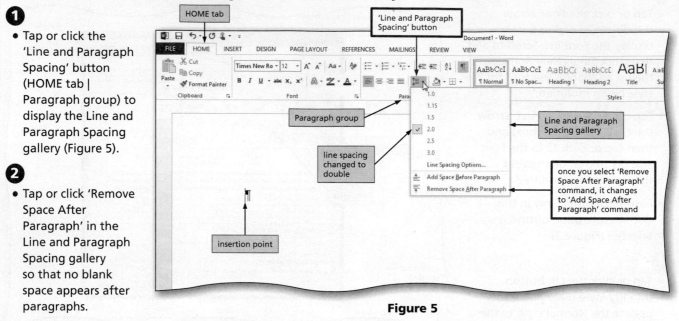

Figure 5

To Update a Style to Match a Selection

To ensure that all paragraphs in the paper will be double-spaced and do not have space after the paragraphs, you want the Normal style to include the line and paragraph spacing changes made in the previous two sets of steps. The following steps update the Normal style. *Why? You can update a style to reflect the settings of the location of the insertion point or selected text. Because no text has yet been typed in the research paper, you do not need to select text prior to updating the Normal style.*

1
- Press and hold or right-click Normal in the Styles gallery (HOME tab | Styles group) to display a shortcut menu (Figure 6).

2
- Tap or click 'Update Normal to Match Selection' on the shortcut menu to update the selected (or current) style to reflect the settings at the location of the insertion point.

Figure 6

To Insert a Formatted Header and Switch to the Header

In this research paper, the running head is to be placed at the left margin and the page number at the right margin, both on the same line one-half inch from the top of each page. You can insert a formatted header that contains placeholders for text at the left, center, and right locations of the header. *Why? The APA documentation style requires text at both the left and right margins.* The following steps insert a formatted header and then switch from editing the document text to editing the header.

1

- Tap or click INSERT on the ribbon to display the INSERT tab.

- Tap or click the 'Add a Header' button (INSERT tab | Header & Footer group) to display the Add a Header gallery (Figure 7).

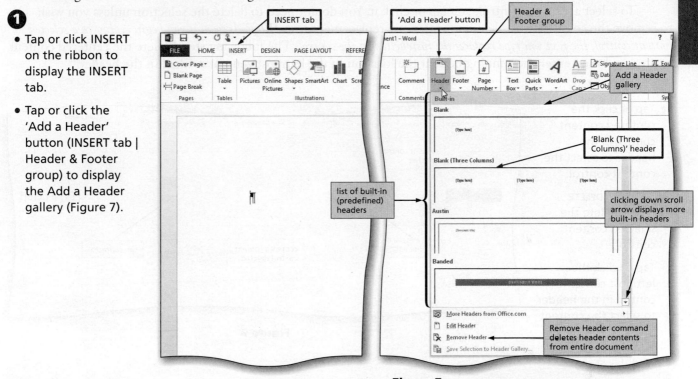

Figure 7

2

- Tap or click 'Blank (Three Columns)' in the Add a Header gallery to insert the selected header design in the document and switch from the document text to the header, which allows you to edit the contents of the header (Figure 8).

Figure 8

To Enter Text in a Header Content Control

The formatted header contains three content controls (one at the left margin, one centered, and one at the right margin) with a tab character between each content control. A **content control** contains instructions for filling areas of text or graphics. The tab characters, which are formatting marks that indicate the TAB key has been pressed, are displayed because Word uses tab stops to align these content controls. Chapter 3 discusses tab stops in more depth.

To select a content control, you tap or click it. You do not need to delete the selection unless you wish to remove the content control and not enter any replacement text. *Why? As soon as you begin typing in a selected content control, the text you type replaces the instruction in the control.* The following steps delete the centered content control and then enter the running head at the location of the leftmost content control in the header.

1

- Tap or click the centered content control in the header to select the content control.

- Press the DELETE key to delete the selected content control.

- Tap or click the leftmost content control in the header to select the content control (Figure 9).

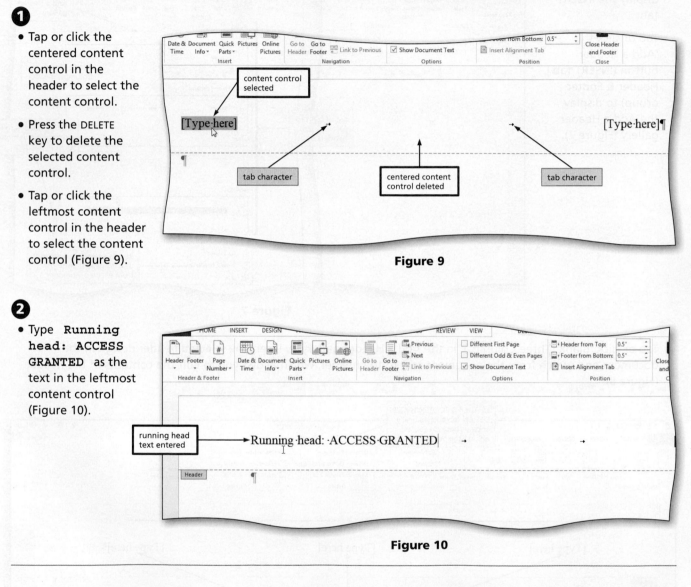

Figure 9

2

- Type **Running head: ACCESS GRANTED** as the text in the leftmost content control (Figure 10).

Figure 10

To Count Characters

The next steps count the characters in the running head. *Why? The running head should be no more than 50 characters, according to the APA documentation style.*

①

- Drag through the running head text, ACCESS GRANTED, to select the text.

- With the running head selected, tap or click the Word Count indicator on the status bar to display the Word Count dialog box (Figure 11).

②

- Tap or click the Close button (Word Count dialog box) to close the dialog box.

Running head: ACCESS·GRANTED

selected text contains 14 characters, including spaces

word flagged as a potential grammar error is correct as written

statistics about selected text

Word Count dialog box

Word Count indicator

Close button

PAGE 1 OF 1   2 WORDS

Figure 11

To Insert a Page Number in a Header Content Control

The next task is to insert the current page number in the header. *Why? The APA documentation style requires a page number in the upper-right corner of each page in the paper.* The following steps insert a page number at the location of the rightmost content control in the header.

①

- Tap or click the rightmost content control in the header to select the content control.

- Tap or click the 'Add Page Numbers' button (HEADER & FOOTER TOOLS DESIGN tab | Header & Footer group) to display the Add Page Numbers menu.

- Tap or point to Current Position on the Add Page Numbers menu to display the Current Position gallery (Figure 12).

'Add Page Numbers' button

Add Page Numbers menu

HEADER & FOOTER TOOLS DESIGN tab

Current Position gallery

Header & Footer group

content control selected

[Type·here]¶

Current Position command

Plain Number to be selected

clicking down scroll arrow displays more page number formats

Figure 12

2

- Tap or click Plain Number in the Current Position gallery to insert an unformatted page number at the location of the selected content control in the header (Figure 13).

Figure 13

To Close the Header

The next task is to switch back to the document text. *Why? You are finished entering text in the header.* The following step closes the header.

1

- Tap or click the 'Close Header and Footer' button (HEADER & FOOTER TOOLS DESIGN tab | Close group) (shown in Figure 13) to close the header and switch back to the document text (Figure 14).

Figure 14

To Type the Title Page Text

In addition to the header, which appears on every page in the paper, the title page for this research paper should contain the complete paper title, author name, and institutional affiliation, all centered on separate lines in the upper-half of the page. The next steps type the title page text.

1 With the insertion point at the top of the document, press the ENTER key six times.

2 Tap or click the Center button (HOME tab | Paragraph group) to center the insertion point.

3 Type **Access Granted** and then press the ENTER key.

4 Type **Teddy Bailey** and then press the ENTER key.

5 Type **Andrews College** and then press the ENTER key (Figure 15).

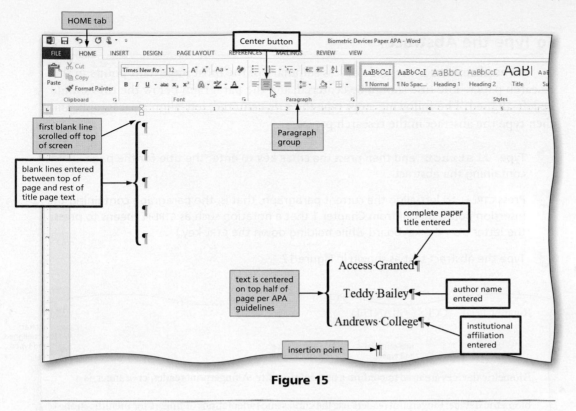

Figure 15

To Page Break Manually

To move the insertion point to the next page, you insert a manual page break. **Why?** *According to the APA documentation style, the abstract page is to be displayed on a separate numbered page.*

A **manual page break**, or **hard page break**, is one that you force into the document at a specific location. Word never moves or adjusts manual page breaks. Word, however, does adjust any automatic page breaks that follow a manual page break. Word inserts manual page breaks immediately above or to the left of the location of the insertion point. The following step inserts a manual page break after the title page text of the research paper.

1

- Verify that the insertion point is positioned below the name of the college on the title page, as shown in Figure 15.

- Tap or click INSERT on the ribbon to display the INSERT tab.

- Tap or click the 'Insert a Page Break' button (INSERT tab | Pages group) to insert a manual page break immediately to the left of the insertion point and position the insertion point immediately below the manual page break (Figure 16).

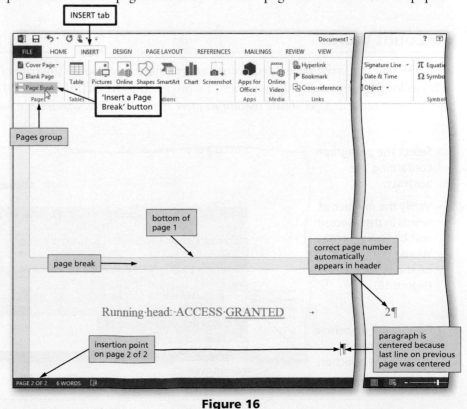

Figure 16

To Type the Abstract

The abstract is a one-page or less summary of the most important points in the research paper. The title should be centered, and the paragraph below the title should be left-aligned. The following steps type the title centered, left-align a paragraph, and then type the abstract in the research paper.

1 Type **Abstract** and then press the ENTER key to enter the title for the page containing the abstract.

2 Press CTRL+L to left-align the current paragraph, that is, the paragraph containing the insertion point. (Recall from Chapter 1 that a notation such as CTRL+L means to press the letter L on the keyboard while holding down the CTRL key.)

3 Type the abstract text as shown in Figure 17.

Running head: ·ACCESS·GRANTED → → 2¶

title centered and typed → ►Abstract¶

abstract left-aligned and typed

Biometric·devices·are·used·to·confirm·a·person's·identity.·A·fingerprint·reader,·or·scanner,·is·a·

biometric·device.·Fingerprint·readers·use·the·curves·and·indentations·of·fingers·for·identification.·

Another·type·of·biometric·technology·is·face·recognition.·Face·recognition·scans·a·person's·face·

and·compares·it·to·a·stored·image.·Today,·both·business·and·home·users·work·with·these·types·of·

biometric·devices·for·security.¶

Figure 17

To Count Words

When you write papers, you often are required to compose the papers with a minimum number of words. The following steps verify the number of words in the abstract. *Why? The APA documentation style specifies that the abstract in a research paper should contain no more than 250 words, sometimes no more than 150 words.*

1

• Select the paragraph containing the abstract.

• Verify the number of words in the selected text by looking at the Word Count indicator on the status bar (Figure 18).

2

• Tap or click anywhere in the abstract to remove the selection from the text.

Running head: ACCESS GRANTED →

Abstract¶

Biometric·devices·are·used·to·confirm·a·person's·identity.·A·fingerprint·reader,·or·scanner,·is·a·

biometric·device.·Fingerprint·readers·use·the·curves·and·indentations·of·fingers·for·identification

Another·type·of·biometric·technology·is·face·recognition.·Face·recognition·scans·a·person's·fac

selected text contains 65 words

ompares·it·to·a·stored·image.·Today,·both·business·and·home·users·work·with·these·types·

biometric·devices·for·security.¶

paragraph selected

65 OF 72 WORDS

document contains a total of 72 words

Figure 18

To Page Break Manually

The abstract is complete, and the text for the research paper should begin on a new page. The following steps insert a manual page break after the abstract.

 Press CTRL+END to position the insertion point at the end of the document, which is the end of the abstract in this case.

2 Tap or click the 'Insert a Page Break' button (INSERT tab | Pages group) to insert a manual page break immediately to the left of the insertion point and position the insertion point immediately below the manual page break.

To Enter the Paper Title

The following steps enter the title of the research paper centered between the page margins.

1 Center the paragraph containing the insertion point.

2 Type **Access Granted** and then press the ENTER key to enter the title of the paper (Figure 19).

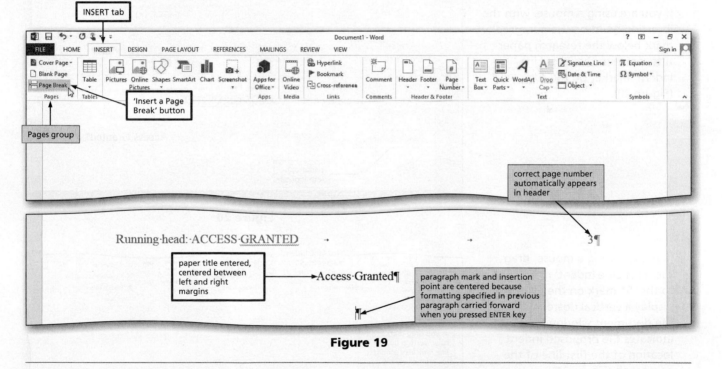

Figure 19

To Format Text

The paragraphs below the paper title should be left-aligned, instead of centered. Thus, the following step left-aligns the paragraph below the paper title.

1 Press CTRL+L to left-align the current paragraph, that is, the paragraph containing the insertion point.

To Display Rulers and First-Line Indent Paragraphs

If you are using a mouse, you can use the horizontal ruler, usually simply called the **ruler**, to indent just the first line of a paragraph, which is called a **first-line indent**. The left margin on the ruler contains two triangles above a square. The **First Line Indent marker** is the top triangle at the 0" mark on the ruler (Figure 20). The bottom triangle is discussed later in this appendix. The small square at the 0" mark is the Left Indent marker. The **Left Indent marker** allows you to change the entire left margin, whereas the First Line Indent marker indents only the first line of the paragraph.

The following steps first-line indent paragraphs in the research paper. *Why? The first line of each paragraph in the research paper is to be indented one-half inch from the left margin, according to the APA documentation style.*

❶

- Tap or click VIEW on the ribbon to display the VIEW tab.

- If the rulers are not displayed, tap or click the View Ruler check box (VIEW tab | Show group) to place a check mark in the check box and display the horizontal and vertical rulers on the screen.

❷

- If you are using a mouse, with the insertion point on the paragraph mark below the research paper title, point to the 'First Line Indent' marker on the ruler (Figure 20).

Figure 20

❸

- If you are using a mouse, drag the 'First Line Indent' marker to the .5" mark on the ruler to display a vertical dotted line in the document window, which indicates the proposed indent location of the first line of the paragraph (Figure 21).

Figure 21

❹

- If you are using a mouse, release the mouse button to place the 'First Line Indent' marker at the .5" mark on the ruler, or one-half inch from the left margin.

- If you are using a touch screen, you cannot drag the 'First Line Indent' marker and must follow these steps instead: tap the Paragraph Settings Dialog Box Launcher (HOME tab or PAGE LAYOUT tab | Paragraph group) to display the Paragraph dialog box, tap the Indents and Spacing tab (Paragraph dialog box), tap the Special arrow, tap First line, and then tap the OK button.

5
- Type **Biometric devices authenticate a person's identity by verifying unique personal characteristics.** and notice that Word automatically indented the first line of the paragraph by one-half inch (Figure 22).

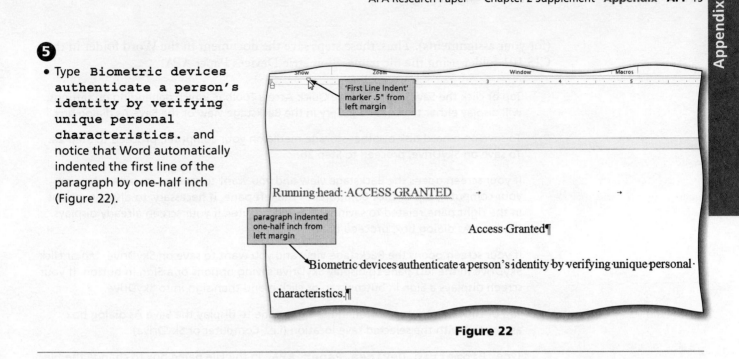

Figure 22

To Type the First and Second Paragraphs

The following steps type the remainder of the first paragraph and the second paragraph in the research paper.

1 Press the SPACEBAR. Type the remainder of the first paragraph of the research paper as shown in Figure 23 and then press the ENTER key.

2 Type the second paragraph of the research paper as shown in Figure 23.

Figure 23

To Save a Document

You have performed many tasks while creating this research paper and do not want to risk losing work completed thus far. Accordingly, you should save the document. The following steps assume you already have created folders for storing your files, for example, a CIS 101 folder (for your class) that contains a Word folder (for your assignments). Thus, these steps save the document in the Word folder in the CIS 101 folder using the file name, Biometric Devices Paper APA.

1 Tap or click the Save button on the Quick Access Toolbar, which depending on settings, will display either the Save As gallery in the Backstage view or the Save As dialog box.

2 To save on a hard disk or other storage media on your computer, proceed to Step 2a. To save on SkyDrive, proceed to Step 2b.

2a If your screen opens the Backstage view and you want to save on storage media on your computer, tap or click Computer in the left pane, if necessary, to display options in the right pane related to saving on your computer. If your screen already displays the Save As dialog box, proceed to Step 4.

2b If your screen opens the Backstage view and you want to save on SkyDrive, tap or click SkyDrive in the left pane to display SkyDrive saving options or a Sign In button. If your screen displays a Sign In button, tap or click it and then sign in to SkyDrive.

3 Tap or click the Browse button in the right pane to display the Save As dialog box associated with the selected save location (i.e., Computer or SkyDrive).

4 Type **Biometric Devices Paper APA** in the File name box to change the file name. Do not press the ENTER key after typing the file name because you do not want to close the dialog box at this time.

5 Navigate to the desired save location (in this case, the Word folder in the CIS 101 folder [or your class folder] on your computer or SkyDrive).

6 Tap or click the Save button (Save As dialog box) to save the research paper in the selected folder on the selected save location with the entered file name.

To Change the Bibliography Style

The APA guidelines suggest the use of in-text citations instead of footnoting each source of material in a paper. These parenthetical acknowledgments guide the reader to the end of the paper for complete information about the source.

The first step in inserting a citation is to be sure the citations and sources will be formatted using the correct documentation style, called the bibliography style in Word. **Why?** *You want to ensure that Word is using the APA documentation style for this paper.* The following steps change the specified documentation style.

1
- Tap or click REFERENCES on the ribbon to display the REFERENCES tab.

- Tap or click the Bibliography Style arrow (REFERENCES tab | Citations & Bibliography group) to display the Bibliography Style gallery, which lists predefined documentation styles (Figure 24).

2
- Tap or click 'APA Sixth Edition' in the Bibliography Style gallery to change the documentation style to APA.

Figure 24

To Insert a Citation and Create Its Source

With the documentation style selected, the next task is to insert a citation at the location of the insertion point and enter the source information for the citation. You can accomplish these steps at once by instructing Word to add a new source. The following steps add a new source for a magazine (periodical) article on the web. *Why? The material preceding the insertion point was summarized from a magazine article on the web.*

1

- Position the insertion point at the location for the citation (in this case, after the word, computer, in the third sentence of the second paragraph before the period) and then press the SPACEBAR.

2

- Tap or click the Insert Citation button (REFERENCES tab | Citations & Bibliography group) to display the Insert Citation menu (Figure 25).

Figure 25

3

- Tap or click 'Add New Source' on the Insert Citation menu to display the Create Source dialog box (Figure 26).

Figure 26

4

- If necessary, tap or click the 'Type of Source' arrow (Create Source dialog box) and then tap or click 'Article in a Periodical', so that the list shows fields required for a magazine (periodical).

- Tap or click the Author text box. Type **Rossi, M. E.** as the author.

- Tap or click the Title text box. Type **How to use fingerprint readers** as the article title.

- Press the TAB key and then type **Digital Security Review** as the periodical title.

- Press the TAB key and then type **2014** as the year.

- Press the TAB key and then type **Aug.** as the month.

- Press the TAB key twice and then type **n. pag.** as the number of pages (Figure 27).

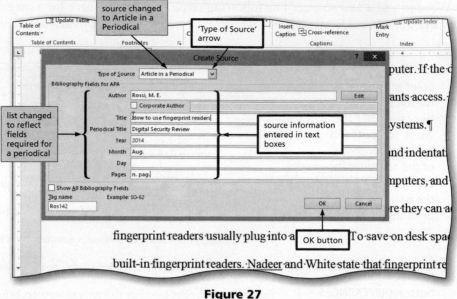

Figure 27

5

- Place a check mark in the 'Show All Bibliography Fields' check box so that Word displays all fields available for the selected source, including the date viewed (accessed) fields.

- If necessary, scroll to the bottom of the Bibliography Fields list to display the URL field.

- Tap or click the URL text box and then type **http://www.cengage.com** (Figure 28).

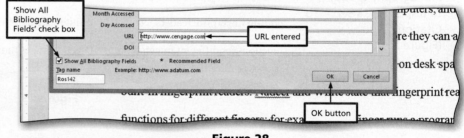

Figure 28

6

- Tap or click the OK button to close the dialog box, create the source, and insert the citation in the document at the location of the insertion point (Figure 29).

Figure 29

To Insert Another Citation and Create Its Source

The following steps add a new source for a book.

1 Position the insertion point at the location for the citation (in this case, after the word, computer, in the last sentence of the second paragraph) and then press the SPACEBAR.

2 If necessary, display the REFERENCES tab. Tap or click the Insert Citation button (REFERENCES tab | Citations & Bibliography group) to display the Insert Citation menu.

3 Tap or click 'Add New Source' on the Insert Citation menu to display the Create Source dialog box.

4 If necessary, tap or click the 'Type of Source' arrow (Create Source dialog box) and then tap or click Book, so that the list shows fields required for a Book.

5 Type `Nadeer, A. S.; White, J. R.` in the Author text box.

6 Type `Biometric security` the Title text box.

7 Type `2014` in the Year text box.

8 Type `Chicago` in the City text box.

9 Type `Windy City Press` in the Publisher text box (Figure 30).

10 Click the OK button to close the dialog box, create the source, and insert the citation in the document at the location of the insertion point.

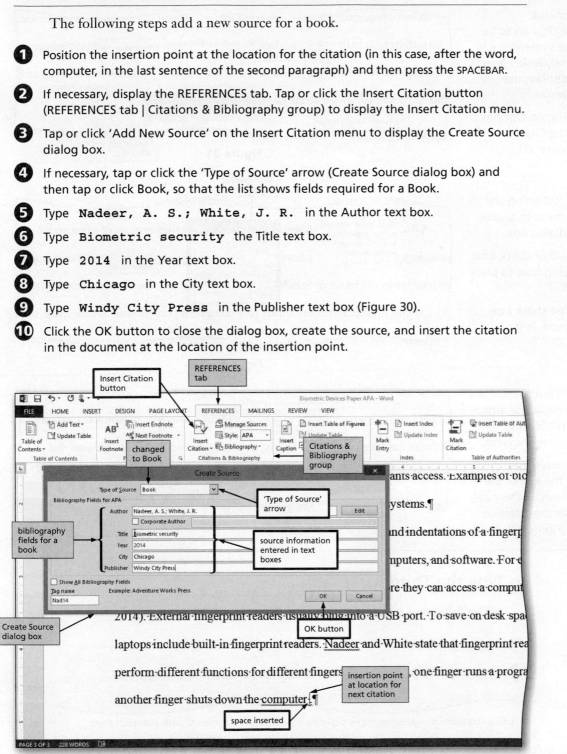

Figure 30

To Edit a Citation

In the APA documentation style, if you reference the author's name in the text, you should not list it again in the citation. Instead, just list the publication year in the citation. To do this, instruct Word to suppress the author and title. *Why? If you suppress the author, Word automatically displays the title, so you need to suppress both the author and title if you want just the page number(s) to be displayed.* The steps on the next page edit the citation, suppressing the author and title but displaying the year.

❶

- If necessary, tap or click somewhere in the citation to be edited, in this case somewhere in (Nadeer and White), which selects the citation and displays the Citation Options arrow.

- Tap or click the Citation Options arrow to display the Citation Options menu (Figure 31).

Figure 31

❷

- Tap or click Edit Citation on the Citation Options menu to display the Edit Citation dialog box.

- Tap or click the Author check box (Edit Citations dialog box) to place a check mark in it.

- Tap or click the Title check box to place a check mark in it (Figure 32).

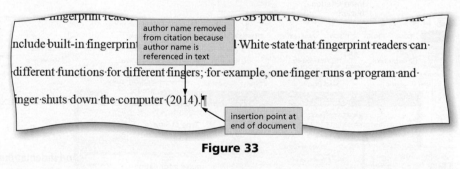

Figure 32

❸

- Tap or click the OK button to close the dialog box, remove the author name from the citation, and suppress the title from showing.

- Press CTRL+END to move the insertion point to the end of the document (paragraph, in this case), which also removes the selection from the citation (Figure 33).

Figure 33

To Type the Third Paragraph

The following steps continue typing text in the research paper.

❶ Press the ENTER key.

❷ Type the third paragraph of the research paper as shown in Figure 34.

A face recognition system captures a live face image and compares it with a stored image to determine if the person is a legitimate user. Some buildings use face recognition systems to secure access to rooms. Law enforcement, surveillance systems, and airports use face recognition systems to protect the public. Some mobile devices use face recognition systems to unlock the device. Face recognition systems are becoming more sophisticated and can recognize people with or without glasses, hats, facial hair, makeup, or jewelry, and with new hairstyles.

third paragraph entered

Figure 34

To Insert Another Citation and Create Its Source

The following steps add a new source for a Web site.

1 Position the insertion point at the location for the citation (in this case, after the word, hairstyles, in the last sentence of the third paragraph but before the period) and then press the SPACEBAR to insert a space.

2 Tap or click the Insert Citation button (REFERENCES tab | Citations & Bibliography group) to display the Insert Citation menu.

3 Tap or click 'Add New Source' on the Insert Citation menu to display the Create Source dialog box.

4 If necessary, tap or click the 'Type of Source' arrow (Create Source dialog box) and then tap or click Web site, so that the list shows fields required for a Web site.

5 Place a check mark in the 'Show All Bibliography Fields' check box so that Word displays all fields available for the selected source, including the date viewed (accessed) fields.

6 Type `Allensmith, S. C.` in the Author text box.

7 Type `Understanding face recognition systems` in the 'Name of Web Page' text box.

8 Type `2014` in the Year Accessed text box.

9 Type `Sept.` in the Month Accessed text box.

10 Type `16` in the Day Accessed text box.

11 Type `http://www.cengage.com` in the URL text box (Figure 35).

12 Tap or click the OK button to close the dialog box, create the source, and insert the citation in the document at the location of the insertion point.

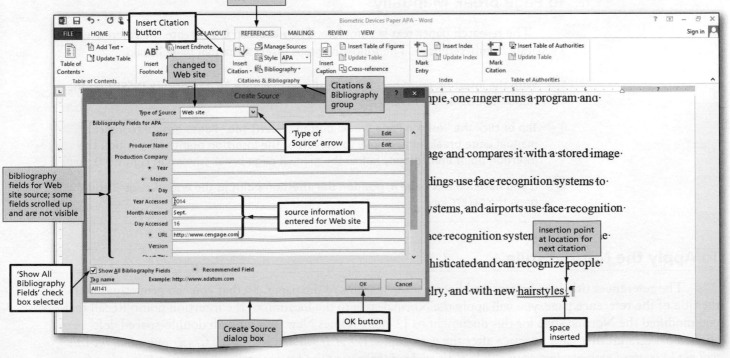

Figure 35

To Type the Fourth Paragraph

The following steps type the last paragraph in the research paper.

1 Press CTRL+END to move the insertion point to the end of the last paragraph and then press the ENTER key.

2 Type the fourth paragraph of the research paper as shown in Figure 36.

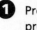

(Allensmith, n.d.).¶

Home and business users alike are using biometric security. Through a biometric identifier, such as a fingerprint, biometric devices can deny or grant access to programs, devices, computers, rooms, and other locations. Biometric devices are an effective security technology.¶

fourth paragraph entered

insertion point

Figure 36

To Save an Existing Document with the Same File Name

You have made several modifications to the document since you last saved it. Thus, you should save it again. The following step saves the document again. For an example of the step listed below, refer to the Office and Windows chapter at the beginning of this book.

1 Tap or click the Save button on the Quick Access Toolbar to overwrite the previously saved file.

To Page Break Manually

The research paper text is complete. The next step is to create the references on a separate numbered page. The following steps insert a manual page break.

1 With the insertion point positioned as shown in Figure 36, tap or click INSERT on the ribbon to display the INSERT tab.

2 Tap or click the 'Insert a Page Break' button (INSERT tab | Pages group) to insert a manual page break immediately to the left of the insertion point and position the insertion point immediately below the manual page break (shown in Figure 37).

3 If you have a blank page 4, position the insertion point at the end of page 3 and then press the DELETE key.

To Apply the Normal Style

The references title is to be centered between the margins of the paper. So that you can properly center the title of the reference page, you will apply the Normal style to the location of the insertion point. Recall that you modified the Normal style for this document to 12-point Times New Roman with double-spaced, left-aligned paragraphs that have no space after the paragraphs. *Why? If you simply issue the Center command, the title will not be centered properly. Instead, it will be to the right of the center point because earlier you set first-line indent for paragraphs to one-half inch from the left margin.*

To apply a style to a paragraph, first position the insertion point in the paragraph and then apply the style. The following step applies the modified Normal style to the location of the insertion point.

1

- Tap or click HOME on the ribbon to display the HOME tab.

- With the insertion point on the paragraph mark at the top of page 4, as shown in Figure 37, even if Normal is selected, tap or click Normal in the Styles gallery (HOME tab | Styles group) to apply the selected style to the paragraph containing the insertion point (Figure 37).

Figure 37

To Enter the References Page Title

The next step is to enter the title, References, centered between the margins of the paper. The following steps use shortcut keys to format the title.

1 Press CTRL+E to center the paragraph mark.

2 Type **References** as the title.

3 Press the ENTER key.

4 Press CTRL+L to left-align the paragraph mark (shown in Figure 38 on the next page).

To Create the Bibliographical List

While typing the research paper, you created several citations and their sources. The next task is to use Word to format the list of sources and alphabetize them in a **bibliographical list**. *Why? Word can create a bibliographical list with each element of the source placed in its correct position with proper punctuation, according to the specified style, saving you time looking up style guidelines. For example, in this research paper, the book source will list, in this order, the author name(s), publication year, book title, publisher city, and publishing company name with the correct punctuation between each element according to the APA documentation style.* The steps on the next page create an APA-styled bibliographical list from the sources previously entered.

①

- Tap or click REFERENCES on the ribbon to display the References tab.

- With the insertion point positioned as shown in Figure 38, tap or click the Bibliography button (REFERENCES tab | Citations & Bibliography group) to display the Bibliography gallery (Figure 38).

Figure 38

②

- Tap or click Insert Bibliography in the Bibliography gallery to insert a list of sources at the location of the insertion point.

- If necessary, scroll to display the entire list of sources in the document window (Figure 39).

Figure 39

To Convert a Field to Regular Text

If, for some reason, you wanted to convert a field, such as the bibliography field, to regular text, you would perform the following steps. Keep in mind, though, once you convert the field to regular text, it no longer is a field that can be updated. For example, the latest guidelines for the APA documentation style state that the page number in magazine articles should not be preceded with the p. notation.

① Tap or click somewhere in the field to select it, in this case, somewhere in the bibliography.

② Press CTRL+SHIFT+F9 to convert the selected field to regular text.

③ Tap or click anywhere in the document to remove the selection from the text.

④ Drag through the p. notation in the magazine entry to select it and press the DELETE key to delete the selected text (Figure 40).

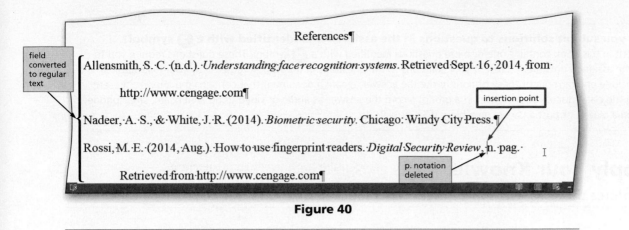

Figure 40

To Save an Existing Document, Print the Document, and Exit Word

The document now is complete. You should save the research paper again before exiting Word. The following steps save the document again, print the document, and then exit Word. For a detailed example of the procedure summarized below, refer to the Office and Windows chapter at the beginning of this book.

1 Tap or click the Save button on the Quick Access Toolbar to overwrite the previously saved file.

2 Tap or click FILE on the ribbon to open the Backstage view.

3 Tap or click the Print tab in the Backstage view to display the Print gallery.

4 Verify that the printer listed on the Printer Status button will print a hard copy of the document. If necessary, tap or click the Printer Status button to display a list of available printer options and then tap or click the desired printer to change the currently selected printer.

5 Tap or click the Print button in the Print gallery to print the document on the currently selected printer.

6 When the printer stops, retrieve the hard copy.

7a If you have one Word document open, tap or click the Close button on the right side of the title bar to close the open document and exit Word.

7b If you have multiple Word documents open, press and hold or right-click the Word app button on the taskbar and then tap or click 'Close all windows' on the shortcut menu to close all open documents and exit Word.

8 If a Microsoft Word dialog box appears, tap or click the Save button to save any changes made to the document since the last save.

Appendix Summary

In this appendix, you have learned how to create the same research paper as the one shown in Chapter 2, except you used the APA documentation style instead of the MLA documentation style. This appendix presented only the steps required to create this APA-styled research paper.

How should you submit solutions to questions in the assignments identified with a ✷ symbol?
Every assignment in this book contains one or more questions identified with a ✷ symbol. These questions require you to think beyond the assigned document. Present your solutions to the questions in the format required by your instructor. Possible formats may include one or more of these options: write the answer; create a document that contains the answer; present your answer to the class; discuss your answer in a group; record the answer as audio or video using a webcam, smartphone, or portable media player; or post answers on a blog, wiki, or website.

Apply Your Knowledge

Reinforce the skills and apply the concepts you learned in this chapter.

Revising Text and Paragraphs in a Document

Note: To complete this assignment, you will be required to use the Data Files for Students. Visit www.cengage.com/ct/studentdownload for detailed instructions or contact your instructor for information about accessing the required files.

Instructions: Run Word. Open the document, Apply A-1 Virtual Reality Paragraph Draft, from the Data Files for Students. The document you open contains a paragraph of text. You are to revise the document as follows: move a word, move another word and change the format of the moved word, change paragraph indentation, change line spacing, find all occurrences of a word, replace all occurrences of a word with another word, locate a synonym, and edit the header. The modified document is shown in Figure 41.

Figure 41

Perform the following tasks:

1. Copy the text, VR, from the first sentence and paste it in the last sentence after the underlined word, potential.

2. Select the underlined word, potential, in the paragraph. If you are using a mouse, use drag-and-drop editing to move the selected word, potential, so that it is before the word, buyers, in the same sentence. If you are using a touch screen, use the cut and paste commands to move the word. Tap or click the Paste Options button that displays to the right of the moved word, potential. Remove the underline format from the moved sentence by tapping or clicking 'Keep Text Only' on the Paste Options menu.

3. Display the ruler, if necessary. If you are using a mouse, use the ruler to indent the first line of the paragraph one-half inch; otherwise, use the Paragraph dialog box.

4. Change the line spacing of the paragraph to double.

5. Use the Navigation Pane to find all occurrences of the word, VR. How many were found?

6. Use the Find and Replace dialog box to replace all occurrences of the word, 3D, with the word, 3-D. How many replacements were made?

7. Use the Navigation Pane to find the word, endless. Use Word's thesaurus to change the word, endless, to the word, infinite. What other words are in the list of synonyms?

8. Switch to the header so that you can edit it. In the first line of the header, change the word, Draft, to the word, Modified, so that it reads: VR Paragraph Modified.

9. In the second line of the header, insert the page number (with no formatting) one space after the word, Page.

10. Change the alignment of both lines of text in the header from left-aligned to right-aligned. Switch back to the document text.

11. If requested by your instructor, enter your first and last name on a separate line below the page number in the header.

12. Tap or click FILE on the ribbon and then tap or click Save As. Save the document using the file name, Apply A-1 Virtual Reality Paragraph Modified.

13. Submit the modified document, shown in Figure 41, in the format specified by your instructor.

14. Use the Research task pane to look up the definition of the word, simulate, in the paragraph. Which dictionary was used? If you have a Microsoft account and are signed into it, use the Define button (REVIEW tab | Proofing group) to look up a definition of the word.

15. Change the search location to All Research Sites. Submit an article from one of the sites.

16. Display the Research Options dialog box. How many currently active Reference Books and Research Sites are in the list? If your instructor approves, activate one of the services.

17. ✻ Answer the questions posed in #5, #6, #7, #14, and #16. How would you find and replace a special character, such as a paragraph mark?

Extend Your Knowledge

Extend the skills you learned in this chapter and experiment with new skills. You may need to use Help to complete the assignment.

Working with References and Proofing Tools

Note: To complete this assignment, you will be required to use the Data Files for Students. Visit www.cengage.com/ct/studentdownload for detailed instructions or contact your instructor for information about accessing the required files.

Instructions: Run Word. Open the document, Extend A-1 Cybercrime Paper Draft APA, from the Data Files for Students. You will add another footnote to the paper, convert the footnotes to endnotes, modify the Endnote Text style, change the format of the note reference marks, use Word's readability statistics, translate the document to another language, and convert the document from APA to MLA documentation style.

Perform the following tasks:
1. Use Help to learn more about footers, footnotes and endnotes, readability statistics, bibliography styles, AutoCorrect, and the Mini Translator.

2. Delete the footer from the document.

Continued >

STUDENT ASSIGNMENTS

Extend Your Knowledge continued

3. Determine the APA guidelines for footnotes. Insert the following footnote at an appropriate place in the research paper: According to Ross, any illegal act involving the use of a computer or related devices generally is referred to as a computer crime (2014).

4. Insert this second footnote at an appropriate place in the research paper: Both hackers and crackers have advanced computer and network skills.

5. Convert the footnotes to endnotes, so that the footnotes are on a separate numbered page after the references. Place the title, Footnotes, at the top of the page.

6. Modify the Endnote Text style to 12-point Times New Roman font, double-spaced with a hanging indent.

7. Change the format of the note reference marks to capital letters (A, B, etc.).

8. Use the Find and Replace dialog box to find the word, excellent, in the document and then replace it with the word of your choice.

9. Add an AutoCorrect entry that replaces the word, perpetraters, with the word, perpetrators. Add this sentence as the last sentence in the paper, misspelling the word, perpetrators, to test the AutoCorrect entry: These perpetraters present a growing threat to society. Delete the AutoCorrect entry that replaces perpetraters with the word, perpetrators.

10. Display the Word Count dialog box. How many words, characters without spaces, characters with spaces, paragraphs, and lines are in the document? Be sure to include footnote and endnote text in the statistics.

11. Check spelling of the document, displaying readability statistics. What are the Flesch-Kincaid Grade Level, the Flesch Reading Ease score, and the percent of passive sentences? Modify the paper to lower the grade level, increase the reading ease score, and lower the percentage of passive sentences. How did you modify the paper? What are the new statistics?

12. If requested by your instructor, change the student name at the top of the paper to your name.

13. Save the revised document with the file name, Extend A-1 Cybercrime Paper Modified APA, and then submit it in the format specified by your instructor.

14. If you have an Internet connection, translate the research paper into a language of your choice (Figure 42) using the Translate button (REVIEW tab | Language group). Submit the

research paper translated from English to French

Figure 42

translated document in the format specified by your instructor. Use the Mini Translator to hear how to pronounce three words in your paper.

15. Select the entire document and then change the documentation style from APA to MLA. Save the MLA version of the document with a new file name. Compare the APA version to the MLA version. If you have a hard copy of each and your instructor requests it, circle the differences between the two documents.

16. ✸ Answer the questions posed in #10 and #11. Where did you insert the second footnote and why?

Analyze, Correct, Improve

Analyze a document, correct all errors, and improve it.

Inserting Missing Elements in an APA-Styled Research Paper

Note: To complete this assignment, you will be required to use the Data Files for Students. Visit www.cengage.com/ct/studentdownload for detailed instructions or contact your instructor for information about accessing the required files.

Instructions: Run Word. Open the document, Analyze A-1 Internet Filters Paper Draft APA, from the Data Files for Students. The document is a research paper that is missing several elements. You are to insert these missing elements, all formatted according to the APA documentation style: header with a running head and page number, title page, paper title, footnote, and source information for a citation.

1. Correct In the research paper, correct the following items:

a. Insert a header with a running head (Running head: INTERNET FILTERS) and a page number, formatted according to the APA documentation style.

b. Insert a title page that contains the header, along with the paper title (Internet Filters), author name (use your name), and school affiliation (use your school). If necessary, insert a manual page break after the end of the title page.

c. On the Abstract page, center the title and then remove the first-line indent from the paragraph below the title.

d. The Clark citation placeholder is missing its source information (shown in Figure 43). Use the following information to edit the source: book titled *Internet protection* written by Addison Lee Clark, publication year is 2014, publication city is New York, and the publisher is Journey Press.

e. Modify the website author name to include his middle name (the APA documentation style will display only the initials for the first and middle name on the references page): Robert Timothy Lane.

f. Use the Navigation Pane to display page 4. Insert a page break before the References heading.

Figure 43

Continued >

Analyze, Correct, Improve *continued*

2. Improve Enhance the paper by finishing the contents of the abstract page and using Word to insert the bibliographical list (bibliography) below the References heading. Save the modified document with the file name, Analyze A-1 Internet Filters Paper Modified APA, and then submit it in the format specified by your instructor.

3. ✸ This assignment uses a web source. How can you determine if a web source is reliable?

In the Labs

Design and/or create a document using the guidelines, concepts, and skills presented in this chapter. Labs 1 and 2, which increase in difficulty, require you to create solutions based on what you learned in the chapter; Lab 3 requires you to create a solution, which uses cloud and web technologies, by learning and investigating on your own from general guidance.

Lab 1: Preparing a Short Research Paper

Problem: You are a college student currently enrolled in an introductory English class. Your assignment is to prepare a short research paper (400–500 words) in any area of interest to you. The requirements are that the paper be presented according to the APA documentation style and have three references. At least one of the three references must be from the web. You prepare the paper shown in Figure 44, which discusses health risks associated with technology.

Instructions: Perform the following tasks:
1. Run Word. If necessary, display formatting marks on the screen.
2. Modify the Normal style to the 12-point Times New Roman font.
3. Adjust line spacing to double.
4. Remove space below (after) paragraphs.
5. Update the Normal style to reflect the adjusted line and paragraph spacing.
6. Create a header that includes the running head (Running head: HEALTH RISKS) at the left margin and the page number at the right margin.
7. Insert the title page as shown in Figure 44a, ensuring that it includes a header, along with the complete paper title (Health Risks Associated with Technology), author name, and school affiliation. If requested by your instructor, use your name and course information instead of the information shown in Figure 44a. Insert a manual page break after the last line on the title page.
8. Type the Abstract as shown in Figure 44b. Insert a manual page break after the last line of the abstract.
9. Set a first-line indent to one-half inch for paragraphs in the body of the research paper.
10. Type the research paper as shown in Figure 44c (on page APP 32) and Figure 44d (on page APP 33). Change the bibliography style to APA. As you insert citations, enter their source information (shown in Figure 44e on page APP 33). If necessary, edit the citations so that they are displayed according to Figure 44c and 44d.
11. At the end of the research paper text, press the ENTER key and then insert a manual page break so that the References page begins on a new page. Enter and format the references title (Figure 44e). Use Word to insert the bibliographical list (bibliography). Convert the bibliography field to text. Remove the p. notion from the page numbers in the magazine article entry (shown in Figure 44e).
12. Check the spelling and grammar of the paper at once.

Running head: HEALTH RISKS   1

Health Risks Associated with Technology

Rajesh Delhi

Lowland College

(a) Page 1

Running head: HEALTH RISKS   2

Abstract

Technology has led to a rising number of important user health concerns. Repetitive strain injuries (RSI) are injuries or disorders of the muscles, nerves, tendons, ligaments, and joints. Computer vision syndrome (CVS) is a health concern that affects eyesight. Other complaints associated with technology use are lower back pain, muscle fatigue, and emotional fatigue.

(b) Page 2
Figure 44 (Continued)

Continued >

In the Labs *continued*

Running head: HEALTH RISKS   3

Health Risks Associated with Technology

The widespread use of technology has led to some important user health concerns. Some

of the more common physical health risks are repetitive strain injuries, computer vision

syndrome, and muscular pain. These injuries are on the rise for users of technology.

A repetitive strain injury (RSI) is an injury or disorder of the muscles, nerves, tendons,

ligaments, and joints. Technology-related RSIs include tendonitis and carpal tunnel syndrome

(CTS). Tendonitis is inflammation of a tendon due to repeated motion or stress on that tendon.

CTS is inflammation of the nerve that connects the forearm to the palm. Repeated or forceful

bending of the wrist can cause tendonitis or CTS of the wrist. Factors that cause these disorders

include prolonged typing or mouse usage and continual shifting between a mouse and keyboard

(Jones, 2014, pp. 45-48). If untreated, these disorders can lead to permanent physical damage.

Computer vision syndrome (CVS) affects eyesight. Symptoms of CVS are sore, tired,

burning, itching, or dry eyes; blurred or double vision; distance blurred vision after prolonged

staring at a display device; headache or sore neck; difficulty shifting focus between a display

device and documents; difficulty focusing on a screen image; color fringes or afterimages when

looking away from a display device; and increased sensitivity to light. Eyestrain associated with

CVS is not thought to have serious or long-term consequences (Anderson & Dean, 2014).

People who spend their workday using the computer sometimes complain of lower back

pain, muscle fatigue, and emotional fatigue. Lower back pain sometimes is caused from poor

posture. It is advisable to sit properly in a chair while working and take periodic breaks. Users

also should be sure their workplace is designed ergonomically. Ergonomic studies have shown

that using the correct type and configuration of chair, keyboard, display device, and work surface

helps users work comfortably and efficiently and helps protect their health (Sanchez, 2014).

(c) Page 3
Figure 44

Running head: HEALTH RISKS   4

        Many physical health risks are associated with using technology. These risks include

repetitive strain injuries, computer vision syndrome, and muscular pain. Users should take as

many preventive measures as possible to avoid these risks.

(d) Page 4

Running head: HEALTH RISKS   5

References

Anderson, C. F., & Dean, S. A. (2014, Aug.). Computer pains. *The Medical Update*, n. pag.

        Retrieved October 2, 2014, from http://www.cengage.com

Jones, J. L. (2014). *Medical concerns of the 21st century*. Chicago: Smiley Incorporated.

Sanchez, J. M. (2014, Sept. 30). *Aches and pains*. Retrieved Aug. 5, 2014, from The Tech Spot:

        http://www.cengage.com

(e) Page 5
Figure 44 (Continued)

Continued >

In the Labs *continued*

13. Save the document using Lab A-1 Technology Health Risks Paper APA as the file name. Submit the document, shown in Figure 44, in the format specified by your instructor.

14. ✺ Read the paper in Print Layout view. Switch to Read mode and scroll through the pages. Do you prefer reading in Print Layout view or Read mode? Why? In Read mode, which of the page colors do you like best and why?

Lab 2: **Preparing a Research Report**

Problem: You are a college student enrolled in an introductory technology class. Your assignment is to prepare a short research paper (400–500 words) in any area of interest to you. The requirements are that the paper be presented according to the APA documentation style and have three references. At least one of the three references must be from the Internet. You prepare a paper about protecting mobile devices (Figure 45).

Instructions: Perform the following tasks:

1. Run Word. Modify the Normal style to the 12-point Times New Roman font. Adjust line spacing to double and remove space below (after) paragraphs. Update the Normal style to include the adjusted line and paragraph spacing. Create a header that includes a running head at the left margin and the page number at the right margin. Create an appropriate title page, using your name and school affiliation (page 1). Create the abstract (page 2) as shown in Figure 45a. Center and type the title (page 3). Set a first-line indent for paragraphs in the body of the research paper.

Running head: MOBILE DEVICE PROTECTION   2

Abstract

Many techniques can be used to help protect mobile devices. Users should not follow unknown links. Users should check the details surrounding the seller, the app, and the requested permissions before downloading to avoid malware. GPS features should be kept disabled. Also, passwords and mobile security software should be used to help safeguard devices further.

(a) Abstract
Figure 45

Running head: MOBILE DEVICE PROTECTION   3

Mobile Device Protection

The consequences of losing a smartphone or other mobile device are significant because these devices store personal and business data. The goal, therefore, for mobile device users is to make their data as secure as possible. Techniques include avoiding unsafe links, using caution when downloading apps, turning off GPS tracking, and installing mobile security software.

A high percentage of users follow unknown links, which can lead to a malicious website. Malicious links can inject malware on a mobile device. The malware may steal personal information or create toll fraud, which secretly contacts wireless messaging services that impose steep fees on a monthly bill (Bao, 2014). Users should avoid tapping or clicking unknown links.

Any device that connects to the Internet is susceptible to mobile malware. According to Jameson and Bennett, cyberthieves target apps on popular devices (2014, p. 72). Popular games are likely candidates to house malware, and it often is difficult to distinguish the legitimate apps from the fake apps. Users should check the reliability of the seller, the descriptions and reviews of the app, and the requested permissions before downloading.

GPS technology can track the mobile device's location as long as it is transmitting and receiving signals to and from satellites. Although this feature may be helpful, serious privacy concerns can arise when the technology is used in malicious ways, such as to stalk individuals or trace their whereabouts (Fields, n.d.). It is best to keep this feature disabled until needed.

Users can enable the password feature on their mobile device as the first step in stopping prying eyes from viewing contents. More protection is necessary, however, to stop viruses and spyware and to safeguard personal and business data. Mobile security apps can lock a mobile device remotely, erase its memory, and activate its GPS function (Bao, 2014).

(b) Body of Paper
Figure 45 (Continued)

Continued >

In the Labs *continued*

Running head: MOBILE DEVICE PROTECTION   4

        Some techniques users can take to protect their mobile devices include avoiding unsafe

links, using caution when downloading, turning off GPS tracking, and using mobile security

software. Users should take these measures to protect their mobile devices.

(c) Body of Paper
Figure 45 (Continued)

2. Type the research paper (pages 3 and 4) as shown in Figure 45b (on page APP 35) and
   Figure 45c. Change the bibliography style to APA. As you insert citations, use the following
   source information, entering it according to the APA style:

   a. Type of Source: Article in a Periodical
      Author: H. G. Bao
      Article Title: Securing Mobile Devices
      Periodical Title: Technology Today
      Year: 2014
      Month: Sept.
      Pages: no pages used
      Year Accessed: 2014
      Month Accessed: Oct.
      Day Accessed: 1

   b. Type of Source: Web site
      Author: C. Fields
      Name of web page: Secure Your Mobile Device
      Year/Month/Date: none given
      Year Accessed: 2014
      Month Accessed: Sept.
      Day Accessed: 22

   c. Type of Source: Book

      Author: L. T. Jameson and K. L. Bennett

      Title: Mobile Technologies

      Year: 2014

      City: New York

      Publisher: Maxwell Press

3. At the end of the research paper text, press the ENTER key once and insert a manual page break so that the References page begins on a new page (page 5). Enter and format the references title. Use Word to insert the bibliographical list.

4. Check the spelling and grammar of the paper.

5. Save the document using Lab A-2 Mobile Devices Protection Paper APA as the file name. Submit the document in the format specified by your instructor.

6. ✳ This paper uses web sources. What factors should you consider when selecting web sources?

Lab 3: Expand Your World: Cloud and Web Technologies
Using an Online Bibliography Tool to Create a List of Sources

Problem: Assume you are using a mobile device or computer that does not have Word but has Internet access. To make use of time between classes, you will use an online bibliography tool to create a list of sources that you can copy and paste into the References page of a research paper due tomorrow.

Instructions: Perform the following tasks:

1. Run a browser. Search for the text, online bibliography tool, using a search engine. Visit several of the online bibliography tools and determine which you would like to use to create a list of sources formatted according to the APA documentation style. Navigate to the desired online bibliography tool.

2. Use the online bibliography tool (Figure 46 on the next page) to enter the following list of sources:

Dayton, L. M., & Walsh, S. L. (2014) The wireless revolution. New York: New Artists Press.

Dover, G. S. (2014) Communications of today. Los Angeles: Sunshine Works.

Howard, T. J. (2014, Aug.) The wireless era. Computers and networks, n. pag. Retrieved August 29, 2014, from http://www.cengage.com

Matthews, C. J. (2014, Aug.) Wireless trends. Retrieved September 8, 2014, from http://www. cengage.com

Newby, T. L., & Hopper, H. L. (2014, Aug.) Wireless communications. Communications News, n. pag. Retrieved October 4, 2014, from http://www.cengage.com

Newman, W. J. (2014, Sept.) The amazing wireless world. Retrieved September 28, 2014, from http://www.cengage.com

3. If requested by your instructor, replace the name in one of the sources above with your name.

4. Search for another source that discusses wireless communications. Add that source.

5. Copy and paste the list of sources into a Word document.

6. Save the document with the name Lab A-3 Wireless Communications Sources APA. Submit the document in the format specified by your instructor.

Continued >

In the Labs *continued*

1. Create your citations

| APA | MLA | Chicago |

APA sources for creating a new citation

Journal   Book   Television
Newspaper   Website   Online Video/Blog Post
Magazine   Film/DVD   Audio Podcast

Enter Information - APA Journal Citation

| Print | **Online** |

	First initial	MI	Last name/Organization
Author(s)	T	L	Newby
	H	L	Hopper

Add Another Author

Year published   2014

Article title   Wireless communications

Journal name   Communications News

Volume   Issue

Page(s)   n. pag.

DOI or URL   http://www.cengage.com

Save Citation

* Not always necessary

Figure 46

7. ❂ Which online bibliography tools did you evaluate? Which one did you select to use and why? Do you prefer using the online bibliography tool or Word to create sources? Why? What differences, if any, did you notice between the list of sources created with the online bibliography tool and the lists created when you use Word?

❂ Consider This: Your Turn

Apply your creative thinking and problem solving skills to design and implement a solution.

Note: To complete these assignments, you may be required to use the Data Files for Students. Visit www.cengage.com/ct/studentdownload for detailed instructions or contact your instructor for information about accessing the required files.

1: Create a Research Paper about Laptops, Tablets, and Desktops
Personal

Part 1: As a student in an introductory computer class, your instructor has assigned a brief research paper that discusses types of computers. The source for the text in your research paper is in a file called Your Turn A-1 Computers Notes APA, which is located on the Data Files for Students. If your instructor requests, use the Research task pane to obtain information from another source and include that information as a note positioned as a footnote in the paper, along with entering its corresponding source information as appropriate. Add an AutoCorrect entry to correct a word you commonly mistype. If necessary, set the default dictionary. Add one of the source last names to the dictionary.

Using the concepts and techniques presented in this chapter, organize the notes in the text in the file on the Data Files for Students, rewording as necessary, and then create and format this research paper according to the APA documentation style. Be sure to check spelling and grammar of the finished paper. Submit your assignment and answers to the critical thinking questions in the format specified by your instructor.

Part 2: ✺ You made several decisions while creating the research paper in this assignment: how to organize the notes, where to place citations, how to format sources, and which source on the web to use for the footnote text (if requested by your instructor). What was the rationale behind each of these decisions? When you proofread the document, what further revisions did you make and why?

2: Create a Research Paper about POS Terminals, ATMs, and Self-Service Kiosks
Professional

Part 1:   As a part-time employee at an advertising firm that specializes in marketing for technology, your boss has asked you to write a brief research paper that discusses types of terminals. The source for the text in your research paper is in a file called Your Turn A-2 Terminals Notes APA, which is located on the Data Files for Students. If your instructor requests, use the Research task pane to obtain information from another source and include that information as a note positioned as a footnote in the paper, and enter its corresponding source information as appropriate. Add an AutoCorrect entry to correct a word you commonly mistype. If necessary, set the default dictionary. Add one of the source last names to the dictionary.

Using the concepts and techniques presented in this chapter, organize the notes in the file on the Data Files for Students, rewording as necessary, and then create and format this research paper according to the APA documentation style. Be sure to check spelling and grammar of the finished paper. Submit your assignment and answers to the critical thinking questions in the format specified by your instructor.

Part 2:   ✺ You made several decisions while creating the research paper in this assignment: how to organize the notes, where to place citations, how to format sources, and which source on the web to use for the footnote text (if requested by your instructor). What was the rationale behind each of these decisions? When you proofread the document, what further revisions did you make and why?

3: Create a Research Paper about Social Media Sites
Research and Collaboration

Part 1:   Because all local youth groups will be creating a page on a social media site, you and two other leaders of local youth groups have been asked to prepare a research paper comparing and contrasting three different social media sites. Form a three-member team to research, compose, and create this paper. Research three separate social media sites: features, capabilities, typical uses, privacy settings, etc. Each team member should write the supporting paragraphs for the social media site he or she researched, including all citations and sources. As a group, write the introduction and conclusion. Be sure to include your team's recommendation in the conclusion.

Use the concepts and techniques presented in this chapter to create and format this paper according to the APA documentation style. Be sure to check spelling and grammar of the finished paper. Submit your team notes and research paper in the format specified by your instructor.

Part 2:   ✺ You made several decisions while creating the research paper in this assignment: the sources to use, which notes to take from the sources, how to organize the notes, how to organize each team member's submissions, what text to write for the introduction and conclusion, where to place citations, and how to format sources. What was the rationale behind each of these decisions? When you proofread the document, what further revisions did you make and why?

Learn Online

Reinforce what you learned in this chapter with games, exercises, training, and many other online activities and resources.

Student Companion Site   Reinforcement activities and resources are available at no additional cost on www.cengagebrain.com. Visit www.cengage.com/ct/studentdownload for detailed instructions about accessing the resources available at the Student Companion Site.

SAM   **SAM**   Put your skills into practice with SAM! If you have a SAM account, go to www.cengage.com/sam2013 to access SAM assignments for this chapter.

Index

Note: **Boldfaced** page numbers
indicate key terms.

Quick Reference Summary

Microsoft Word 2013 Quick Reference Summary

Task	Page Number	Ribbon	Other On-Screen Element	Shortcut Menu	Keyboard Shortcut
All Caps	WD 19	Change Case button (HOME tab | Font group), UPPERCASE			CTRL+SHIFT+A
AddressBlock Merge Field, Edlt	WD 360			'Edit Address Block'	
AddressBlock Merge Field, Insert	WD 359		'Insert formatted address' link in Mail Merge task pane		
Arrange All Open Word Documents on Screen	WD 445	Arrange All button (VIEW tab | Window group)			
Art Page Border	WD 462	'Borders and Shading' button (DESIGN tab | Page Background group), Page Border tab (Borders and Shading dialog box)			
AutoCorrect Entry, Create	WD 85	Options (FILE tab), Proofing (Word Options dialog box)			
AutoCorrect Options Button, Use	WD 85		Point to AutoCorrect Options button in flagged word		
AutoCorrect, Delete Entry	WD 86	Options (FILE tab), Proofing (Word Options dialog box), AutoCorrect Options button			
AutoCorrect, Set Exceptions	WD 87	Options (FILE tab), Proofing (Word Options dialog box), AutoCorrect Options button, Exceptions button (Auto Correction Exceptions dialog box)			
Bibliographical List, Create	WD 106	Bibliography button (REFERENCES tab | Citations & Bibliography group)			

Microsoft Word 2013 Quick Reference Summary *(continued)*

Task	Page Number	Ribbon	Other On-Screen Element	Shortcut Menu	Keyboard Shortcut
Bibliography Style, Change	WD 89	Bibliography Style arrow (REFERENCES tab | Citations & Bibliography group)			
Bold	WD 29	Bold button (HOME tab | Font group)	Bold button on mini toolbar	Font, Font tab (Font dialog box) Touch mode: 'Show Context Menu' button on mini toolbar, Font on shortcut menu, Font tab (Font dialog box)	CTRL+B
Border Paragraph, Default Border	WD 160	Borders arrow (HOME tab | Paragraph group)			
Border Paragraph	WD 206	Borders arrow (HOME tab | Paragraph group), 'Borders and Shading' in Borders gallery			
Border Paragraph, One Edge	WD 422	Borders arrow (HOME tab | Paragraph group), 'Borders and Shading' in Borders gallery, Custom (Borders and Shading dialog box)			
Building Block, Create	WD 170	'Explore Quick Parts' button (INSERT tab | Text group)			ALT+F3
Building Block, Edit Properties	WD 302	'Explore Quick Parts' button (INSERT tab | Text group), 'Building Blocks Organizer', select building block to edit, Edit Properties button (Building Blocks Organizer dialog box)			
Building Block, Insert	WD 172	'Explore Quick Parts' button (INSERT tab | Text group), 'Building Blocks Organizer'			F3
Building Block, Modify	WD 171	'Explore Quick Parts' button (INSERT tab | Text group), press and hold or right-click building block, Edit Properties			
Bullets, Apply	WD 23	Bullets button (HOME tab | Paragraph group)	Bullets button on mini toolbar		* (ASTERISK), SPACEBAR
Bullets, Custom	WD 234	Bullets arrow (HOME tab | Paragraph group), 'Define New Bullet' in Bullets gallery			
Center	WD 15	Center button (HOME tab | Paragraph group)	Center button on mini toolbar	Paragraph, Indents and Spacing tab (Paragraph dialog box)	CTRL+E
Center Page Vertically	WD 43	Page Setup Dialog Box Launcher (PAGE LAYOUT tab | Page Setup group), Layout tab (Page Setup dialog box)			
Change Case	WD 19	Change Case button (HOME tab | Font group)		Font, Font tab (Font dialog box) Touch mode: 'Show Context Menu' on mini toolbar, Font on shortcut menu, Font tab (Font dialog box)	SHIFT+F3

Microsoft Word 2013 Quick Reference Summary *(continued)*

Task	Page Number	Ribbon	Other On-Screen Element	Shortcut Menu	Keyboard Shortcut
Change Spacing before or after Paragraph	WD 42	Spacing Before or Spacing After box (PAGE LAYOUT tab | Paragraph group)		Paragraph, Indents and Spacing tab (Paragraph dialog box) Touch mode: 'Show Context Menu' button on mini toolbar, Paragraph on shortcut menu, Indents and Spacing tab (Paragraph dialog box)	
Character Spacing	WD 218	Font Dialog Box Launcher (HOME tab | Font group), Advanced tab (Font dialog box)		Font	CTRL+D
Citation Placeholder, Insert	WD 93	Insert Citation button (REFERENCES tab | Citations & Bibliography group), 'Add New Placeholder'			
Citation, Edit	WD 98		Tap or click citation, Citations Options arrow, Edit Citation		
Citation, Insert	WD 89	Insert Citation button (REFERENCES tab | Citations & Bibliography group), 'Add New Source'			
Clear Formatting	WD 161	'Clear All Formatting' button (HOME tab | Font group)			CTRL+SPACEBAR, CTRL+Q
Click and Type	WD 79		Position pointer until desired icon appears, then double-tap or double-click		
Clip Art, Insert	WD 148	Online Pictures button (INSERT tab | Illustrations group)			
Color Text	WD 26	Font Color arrow (HOME tab | Font group)	Font Color arrow on mini toolbar	Font, Font tab (Font dialog box) Touch mode: 'Show Context Menu' on mini toolbar, Font on shortcut menu	
Column Break, Insert	WD 441	'Insert Page and Section Breaks' button (PAGE LAYOUT tab | Page Setup group), Column			CTRL+SHIFT+ENTER
Column Break, Remove	WD 442	Select column break, Cut button (HOME tab | Clipboard group)			Select column break, DELETE
Columns, Balance	WD 453	'Insert Page and Section Breaks' button (PAGE LAYOUT tab | Page Setup group), Continuous			
Columns, Change Number	WD 450	'Add or Remove Columns' button (PAGE LAYOUT tab | Page Setup group)			
Columns, Change Width	WD 436	'Add or Remove Columns' button (PAGE LAYOUT tab | Page Setup group), More Columns in Add or Remove Columns gallery			

Microsoft Word 2013 Quick Reference Summary *(continued)*

Task	Page Number	Ribbon	Other On-Screen Element	Shortcut Menu	Keyboard Shortcut
Columns, Different Widths	WD 434	'Add or Remove Columns' button (PAGE LAYOUT tab | Page Setup group), More Columns in Add or Remove Columns gallery, clear 'Equal column width' check box (Columns dialog box)	Double-tap or double-click between columns, enter settings (Column dialog box) or drag column boundaries		
Compatibility Checker	WD 306	'Check for Issues' button (FILE tab | Info tab)			
Content Control, Add Item	WD 288		Select content control, Insert Control on right edge of content control	'Insert Item Before' or 'Insert Item After'	
Content Control, Delete	WD 285	Cut button (HOME tab | Clipboard group)		'Remove Content Control'	CTRL+X or DELETE or BACKSPACE
Content Control, Delete Item	WD 292			Delete Item	
Content Control, Modify Text	WD 282		Tap or click content control name, type new text		
Convert Text to Table	WD 390	'Add a Table' button (INSERT tab | Tables group), 'Convert Text to Table' in Add a Table gallery			
Copy	WD 112	Copy button (HOME tab | Clipboard group)		Copy	CTRL+C
Count Words	WD 100	Word Count button (REVIEW tab | Proofing group)	Word Count indicator on status bar		CTRL+SHIFT+G
Custom Dictionary, Set Default, View or Modify Entries	WD 118	Options (FILE tab), Proofing (Word Options dialog box), Custom Dictionaries button			
Customized Themes, Save	WD 458	Themes button (DESIGN tab | Document Formatting group) 'Save Current Theme' in Themes gallery			
Data Source, Create	WD 350		'Type a new list' in Mail Merge task pane, 'Create new recipient list' in Type a new list area, Customize Columns button (New Address List dialog box)		
Data Source, Save	WD 355		Enter file name in File name box (Save Address List dialog box)		
Data Source, Sort Records	WD 377	'Edit Recipient List' button (MAILINGS tab | Start Mail Merge group), arrow to right of field name on which to sort			

Microsoft Word 2013 Quick Reference Summary *(continued)*

Task	Page Number	Ribbon	Other On-Screen Element	Shortcut Menu	Keyboard Shortcut
Data Source, Use Outlook Contacts, Access Table, Excel Table or Word Table	WD 356	Select Recipients button (MAILINGS tab | Start Mail Merge group)	'Select from Outlook contacts' or 'Use an existing list' in Mail Merge task pane		
Data, Find and Display	WD 378	Find Recipient button (MAILINGS tab | Preview Results group)			
Date, Insert Current	WD 168	'Insert Date and Time' button (INSERT tab | Text group)			
Date, Insert from Calendar	WD 358	'Insert Date & Time' button (INSERT tab | Text group)	Tap or click content control, tap or click arrow		
Document Inspector	WD 315	'Check for Issues' button (FILE tab | Info tab), Inspect Document			
Document Properties, Change	WD 44	Properties button (FILE tab | Info tab)			
Document Properties, Print	WD 104	FILE tab | Print tab, first button in Settings area			
Document Theme, Change	WD 148	Themes button (DESIGN tab | Document Formatting group)			
Double-Space	WD 72	'Line and Paragraph Spacing' button (HOME tab | Paragraph group)		Paragraph, Indents and Spacing tab (Paragraph dialog box)	CTRL+2
Double-Underline	WD 80	Underline arrow (HOME tab | Font group)		Font, Font tab (Font dialog box)	CTRL+SHIFT+D
Drop Cap	WD 438	'Add a Drop Cap' button (INSERT tab | Text group)			
Email Attachments, Customize How Word Opens	WD 315	Options (FILE tab), General (Word Options dialog box)			
Email, Send Document Using	WD 314	Email (FILE tab | Share tab), 'Send as Attachment' button			
Envelope, Address and Print	WD 187	Create Envelopes button (MAILINGS tab | Create group), Envelopes tab (Envelopes and Labels dialog box)			
Envelopes, Mail Merge	WD 385	'Start Mail Merge' button (MAILINGS tab | Start Mail Merge group), 'Step-by-Step Mail Merge Wizard' on Start Mail Merge Menu, Envelopes in Mail Merge task pane			
Exit Word	WD 46		Close button on title bar		

Microsoft Word 2013 Quick Reference Summary *(continued)*

Task	Page Number	Ribbon	Other On-Screen Element	Shortcut Menu	Keyboard Shortcut
Field Code, Display	WD 368			'Toggle Field Codes'	SHIFT+F9
Field Codes, Display All	WD 368				ALT+F9
Field Codes, Print	WD 369	Options (FILE tab), Advanced (Word Options dialog box), Print area			
Field, Convert to Regular Text	WD 110				Tap or click field, CTRL+SHIFT+F9
Field, Update	WD 110			Update Field Touch mode: 'Show Context Menu' button on mini toolbar, Update Field on shortcut menu	Tap or click field, F9
Find Text	WD 113	Find button (HOME tab | Editing group)	Page Number indicator on status bar		CTRL+F
Folder, Create while Saving	WD 349		Save As button (Quick Access Toolbar), 'Create a new folder' button (Save As dialog box)		
Font Size, Change	WD 17	Font Size arrow (HOME tab | Font group)	Font Size arrow on mini toolbar	Font, Font tab (Font dialog box) Touch mode: 'Show Context Menu' button on mini toolbar, Font on shortcut menu, Font tab (Font dialog box)	CTRL+D
Font Size, Decrease	WD 147	'Decrease Font Size' button (HOME tab | Font group)	Font button on mini toolbar	Font	CTRL+SHIFT+<
Font Size, Decrease 1 point	WD 80				CTRL+[
Font Size, Increase	WD 147	'Increase Font Size' button (HOME tab | Font group)	Font button on mini toolbar	Font	CTRL+SHIFT+>
Font Size, Increase 1 point	WD 80				CTRL+]
Font, Change	WD 18	Font arrow (HOME tab | Font group)	Font arrow on mini toolbar Touch mode: 'Show Context Menu' on mini toolbar, Font on shortcut menu	Font, Font tab (Font dialog box)	CTRL+D
Footnote, Change Format	WD 99	Footnote & Endnote Dialog Box Launcher (REFERENCES tab | Footnotes group)			
Footnote, Delete	WD 99	Select note reference mark, Cut button (HOME tab | Clipboard group)			CTRL+X
Footnote, Insert	WD 92	Insert Footnote button (REFERENCES tab | Footnotes group)			ALT+CTRL+F

Microsoft Word 2013 Quick Reference Summary *(continued)*

Task	Page Number	Ribbon	Other On-Screen Element	Shortcut Menu	Keyboard Shortcut
Footnote, Move	WD 99	Select note reference mark, Cut button (HOME tab | Clipboard group); Paste button (HOME tab | Clipboard group)			CTRL+X; CTRL+V
Format Painter	WD 233	Format Painter button (HOME tab | Clipboard group)			
Formatting Marks	WD 6	'Show/Hide ¶' button (HOME tab | Paragraph group)			CTRL+SHIFT+*
Go to a Page	WD 111	'Open the Navigation Pane' check box (VIEW tab | Show group), PAGES tab	Page Number indicator on status bar, PAGES tab		CTRL+G
Graphic, Adjust Brightness and Contrast	WD 153	Corrections button (PICTURE TOOLS FORMAT tab | Adjust group)	Format Picture, Picture button in Format Picture task pane		
Graphic, Change Border Color	WD 154	Picture Border arrow (PICTURE TOOLS FORMAT tab | Picture Styles group)			
Graphic, Change Color	WD 151	Color button (PICTURE TOOLS FORMAT tab | Adjust group)		Format Picture or Format Object, Picture Color button (Format Picture dialog box)	
Graphic, Crop	WD 425	Crop button (PICTURE TOOLS FORMAT tab | Size group)	Crop button on mini toolbar		
Graphic, Flip	WD 157	Rotate Objects button (PICTURE TOOLS FORMAT tab | Arrange group)			
Graphic, Move	WD 155		Drag graphic		
Graphic, Resize	WD 36	Shape Height and Shape Width boxes (PICTURE TOOLS FORMAT tab | Size group)	Drag sizing handle	More Layout Options, Size tab (Layout dialog box)	
Graphic, Resize to % of Original	WD 150	Advanced Layout: Size Dialog Box Launcher (PICTURE TOOLS FORMAT tab | Size group), enter height and width (Layout dialog box)	Layout Options button attached to graphic, See more link in Layout Options gallery, Size tab (Layout dialog box)	'Size and Position'	
Graphic, Rotate	WD 428	Rotate Objects button (PICTURE TOOLS FORMAT tab | Arrange group), 'More Rotation Options' on Rotate Objects menu	Drag rotate handle		
Graphic, Set Transparent Color	WD 152	Color button (PICTURE TOOLS FORMAT tab | Adjust group), 'Set Transparent Color' in Color gallery			
Graphic, Specify Position	WD 348		Layout Options button attached to graphic, See more link in Layout Options gallery		
GreetingLine Merge Field, Edit	WD 362			'Edit Greeting Line'	

Microsoft Word 2013 Quick Reference Summary *(continued)*

Task	Page Number	Ribbon	Other On-Screen Element	Shortcut Menu	Keyboard Shortcut
GreetingLine Merge Field, Insert	WD 361		'Insert formatted salutation' link in Mail Merge task pane		
Hanging Indent, Create	WD 108	Paragraph Dialog Box Launcher (HOME tab | Paragraph group), Indents and Spacing tab (Paragraph dialog box)	Drag Hanging Indent marker on ruler	Paragraph, Indents and Spacing tab (Paragraph dialog box)	CTRL+T
Hanging Indent, Remove	WD 80	Paragraph Dialog Box Launcher (HOME tab | Paragraph group), Indents and Spacing tab (Paragraph dialog box)	Drag Hanging Indent marker on ruler	Paragraph, Indents and Spacing tab (Paragraph dialog box)	CTRL+SHIFT+T
Header and Footer, Close	WD 77	'Close Header and Footer' button (HEADER & FOOTER TOOLS DESIGN tab | Close group)	Double-tap or double-click dimmed document text		
Header, Switch to	WD 74	'Add a Header' button (INSERT tab | Header & Footer group)	Double-tap or double-click dimmed header	Edit Header	
Header, Delete	WD 230	'Add a Header' button (INSERT tab | Header & Footer group), Remove Header in Add a Header gallery			
Header, Different from Previous	WD 228	'Add a Header' button (INSERT tab | Header & Footer group), Edit Header, deselect 'Link to Previous' button (HEADER & FOOTERS TOOLS DESIGN tab | Navigation group)			
Hide/Show White Space	WD 102	Options (FILE tab), Display (Word Options dialog box)	Double-tap or double-click white space between pages		
Hyperlink, Convert to Regular Text	WD 163	'Add a Hyperlink' button (INSERT tab | Links group)	Undo Hyperlink (AutoCorrect Options menu)	Remove Hyperlink	
Hyperlink, Edit	WD 321	'Add a Hyperlink' button (INSERT tab | Links group)		Edit Hyperlink	CTRL+K
Hyperlink, Format Text As	WD 319	'Add a Hyperlink' button (INSERT tab | Links group)		Hyperlink	CTRL+K
Hyphenate	WD 437	Change Hyphenation button (PAGE LAYOUT tab | Page Setup group)			
IF Field, Insert	WD 365	Rules button (MAILINGS tab | Write & Insert Fields group)			
Indent Paragraph	WD 293	Increase Indent button (HOME tab | Paragraph group)	Drag Left Indent marker on horizontal ruler	Paragraph, Indents and Spacing tab (Paragraph dialog box)	CTRL+M
Indent, Decrease	WD 80	Decrease Indent button (HOME tab | Paragraph group)	Drag 'First Line Indent' marker on ruler	Paragraph, Indents and Spacing tab (Paragraph dialog box)	CTRL+SHIFT+M
Indent, First-Line	WD 82	Paragraph Settings Dialog Box Launcher (HOME tab | Paragraph group)	Drag 'First Line Indent' marker on ruler	Paragraph, Indents and Spacing tab (Paragraph dialog box)	TAB

Microsoft Word 2013 Quick Reference Summary *(continued)*

Task	Page Number	Ribbon	Other On-Screen Element	Shortcut Menu	Keyboard Shortcut
Indent, Increase	WD 80	Increase Indent button (HOME tab | Paragraph group)			CTRL+M
Insert File in Column	WD 434	Object arrow (INSERT tab | Text group), 'Text from File'			
Insert Word Document in Existing Document	WD 223	Object arrow (INSERT tab | Text group), 'Text from File'			
Insertion Point, Move Down/Up One Line	WD 12				DOWN ARROW/ UP ARROW
Insertion Point, Move Down/Up One Paragraph	WD 12				CTRL+DOWN ARROW/ CTRL+UP ARROW
Insertion Point, Move Down/Up One Screen	WD 12				PAGE DOWN/ PAGE UP
Insertion Point, Move Left/ Right One Character	WD 12				LEFT ARROW/ RIGHT ARROW
Insertion Point, Move Left/ Right One Word	WD 12				CTRL+LEFT ARROW/ CTRL+RIGHT ARROW
Insertion Point, Move to Beginning/ End of Line	WD 12				HOME/ END
Insertion Point, Move to Beginning/End of Document	WD 12				CTRL+HOME/ CTRL+END
Insertion Point, Move to Bottom of Document Window	WD 12				ALT+CTRL+PAGE DOWN/ ALT+CTRL+PAGE UP
Invite Others to View or Edit Document	WD 310	Invite People (FILE tab | Share tab)			
Italicize	WD 25	Italic button (HOME tab | Font group)	Italic button on mini toolbar	Font, Font tab (Font dialog box) Touch mode: 'Show Context Menu' on mini toolbar, Font on shortcut menu, Font tab (Font dialog box)	CTRL+I
Justify Paragraph	WD 80	Justify button (HOME tab | Paragraph group)		Paragraph, Indents and Spacing tab (Paragraph dialog box)	CTRL+J
Last Editing Location, Go To	WD 224				SHIFT+F5

Microsoft Word 2013 Quick Reference Summary *(continued)*

Task	Page Number	Ribbon	Other On-Screen Element	Shortcut Menu	Keyboard Shortcut
Left and Right Paragraph Indent	WD 209	Indent Left and Indent Right box (PAGE LAYOUT tab | Paragraph group)	Drag Left Indent or Right Indent markers on ruler	Paragraph, Indents and Spacing tab (Paragraph dialog box)	
Left-Align Paragraph	WD 80	Align Left button (HOME tab | Paragraph group)		Paragraph, Indents and Spacing tab (Paragraph dialog box)	CTRL+L
Line Break	WD 290				SHIFT+ENTER
Line Spacing, Change	WD 72	'Line and Paragraph Spacing' button (HOME tab | Paragraph group)	Touch mode: 'Show Context button' on mini toolbar, Paragraph	Paragraph, Indents and Spacing tab (Paragraph dialog box) Touch mode: 'Show Context button' on mini toolbar, Paragraph, Indents and Spacing tab (Paragraph dialog box)	CTRL+[number of desired line spacing, i.e., 2 for double-spacing]
Mailing Label, Print	WD 187	Create Labels button (MAILINGS tab | Create group)			
Mailing Labels, Print	WD 379	'Start Mail Merge' button (MAILINGS tab | Start Mail Merge group), 'Step-by-Step Mail Merge Wizard' on Start Mail Merge Menu, Labels in Mail Merge task pane			
Main Document, Identify for Form Letter	WD 341	'Start Mail Merge button (MAILINGS tab | Start Mail Merge group)			
Margin Settings, Change	WD 140	Adjust Margins button (PAGE LAYOUT tab | Page Setup group)	Drag margin boundary on ruler		
Margins, Custom	WD 280	Adjust Margins button (PAGE LAYOUT tab | Page Setup group), Custom Margins	Drag margin boundaries on ruler		
Merge Condition, Remove	WD 376	'Edit Recipient List' button (MAILINGS tab | Start Mail Merge group), Filter link (Mail Merge Recipients dialog box), Clear All button (Filter and Sort dialog box)			
Merge Field, Insert	WD 363	'Insert Merge Field' arrow (MAILINGS tab | Write & Insert Fields group)			
Merge Fields, Highlight	WD 367	'Highlight Merge Fields' button (MAILINGS tab | Write & Insert group)			
Merge Form Letters to New Document	WD 371	'Finish & Merge' button (MAILINGS tab | Finish group), 'Edit Individual Documents'	'Merge to new document' link in Mail Merge task pane		
Merge Form Letters to Printer	WD 373	'Finish & Merge' button (MAILINGS tab | Finish group), Print Documents	'Merge to printer' link in Mail Merge task pane		
Merge to Directory	WD 387	'Start Mail Merge' button (MAILINGS tab | Start Mail Merge group), Directory			

Microsoft Word 2013 Quick Reference Summary *(continued)*

Task	Page Number	Ribbon	Other On-Screen Element	Shortcut Menu	Keyboard Shortcut
Merge, Select Records	WD 374	'Edit Recipient List' button (MAILINGS tab | Start Mail Merge group)			
Merged Data, View in Main Document	WD 361	'View Merged Data' button (MAILINGS tab | Preview Results group)			
Merged Letters, Check for Errors	WD 371	'Auto Check for Errors' button (MAILINGS tab | Preview Results group)			ALT+SHIFT+K
Merged Letters, Preview	WD 370		'Next wizard step' link in Mail Merge task pane		
Microsoft Account, Sign Out Of	WD 45	Sign out link (FILE tab | Account tab)			
Modify Style Using Styles Dialog Box	WD 299	Styles Dialog Box Launcher (HOME tab | Styles group), Modify	Press and hold or right-click style name in Styles gallery, Modify		
Move Text	WD 49	Cut button (HOME tab | Clipboard group); Paste button (HOME tab | Clipboard group)	Drag and drop selected text	Cut, Paste	CTRL+X, CTRL+V
Multilevel Numbered List	WD 236	Multilevel List button (HOME tab | Paragraph group)			Type 1., SPACEBAR
New Document, Create from Online Template	WD 276	New (FILE tab), type file name in 'Search for online templates' box, Start searching button, select template, Create button			
Nonbreaking Hyphen, Insert	WD 173				CTRL+SHIFT+HYPHEN
Nonbreaking Space, Insert	WD 172	'Insert a Symbol' button (INSERT tab | Symbols group), More Symbols, Special Characters tab (Symbol dialog box)			CTRL+SHIFT+SPACEBAR
Normal Style, Apply	WD 165	No Spacing (HOME tab | Styles group)			CTRL+SHIFT+S
Normal Style, Modlfy	WD 70	Styles Dialog Box Launcher (HOME tab | Styles group), style arrow, Modify		Press and hold or right-click style (HOME tab | Styles group), Modify	
Object, Change Position	WD 144	Position Object button (DRAWING TOOLS FORMAT tab | Arrange group)	Layout Options button attached to graphic, See more link in Layout Options gallery		
On-Screen Keyboard, Display	WD 6		Touch mode: Touch Keyboard button on Windows taskbar		
Open a Document	WD 47	Open (FILE tab)			CTRL+O
Open Document Created from Template	WD 278	Open (FILE tab), select location, select file, Open button			

Microsoft Word 2013 Quick Reference Summary *(continued)*

Task	Page Number	Ribbon	Other On-Screen Element	Shortcut Menu	Keyboard Shortcut
Page Border, Add	WD 41	'Borders and Shading' button (DESIGN tab | Page Background group)			
Page Break, Delete	WD 226	Select notation, Cut button (HOME tab | Clipboard group)	Touch Mode: Select notation, Cut button on mini toolbar	Cut	Select notation, DELETE or BACKSPACE
Page Break, Insert	WD 105	'Insert a Page Break' button (INSERT tab | Pages group)			CTRL+ENTER
Page Number, Insert	WD 76	'Add Page Numbers' button (HEADER & FOOTER TOOLS DESIGN tab | Header & Footer group)			
Page Numbers, Start at Different	WD 230	'Add Page Numbers' button (HEADER & FOOTER TOOLS DESIGN tab | Header & Footer group), 'Format Page Numbers', Start at (Page Number Format dialog box)			
Page Orientation, Change	WD 387	'Change Page Orientation' button (PAGE LAYOUT tab | Page Setup group)			
Paragraph Indent, Decrease	WD 80				CTRL+SHIFT+M
Paste	WD 112	Paste arrow (HOME tab | Clipboard group)	Paste Options button by moved/copied text	Paste	CTRL+V
Paste Options	WD 156	Paste arrow (HOME tab | Clipboard group)	Paste Options button by moved/copied text		
Paste Options Menu, Display	WD 113		Paste Options button by moved/copied text		
PDF Document, Create	WD 302	'Create PDF/XPS Document' (FILE tab | Export tab)			
PDF Document, Open from Word	WD 304	FILE tab | Open tab, navigate to file location, File Types arrow, PDF Files in File Types list			F12
Picture Effects, Apply	WD 39	Picture Effects button (PICTURE TOOLS FORMAT tab | Picture Styles gallery)		Format Picture or Format Object Touch mode: 'Show Context Menu' button on mini toolbar, Format Object or Format Picture on shortcut menu	
Picture Style, Apply	WD 38	More button in Picture Styles gallery (PICTURE TOOLS FORMAT tab | Picture Styles group)		'Picture Quick Styles'	
Picture, Insert	WD 34	From File button (INSERT tab | Illustrations group)			
Placeholder Text, Replace	WD 284		Select content control, type new text		

Microsoft Word 2013 Quick Reference Summary *(continued)*

Task	Page Number	Ribbon	Other On-Screen Element	Shortcut Menu	Keyboard Shortcut
Post Document to Social Network	WD 313	'Post to Social Networks' (FILE tab | Share tab)			
Print Document	WD 51	Print button (FILE tab | Print tab)			CTRL+P
Print Layout View	WD 53	Print Layout button (VIEW tab | Views group)	Print Layout button on status bar		
Print Specific Pages	WD 225	FILE tab | Print tab, type page numbers in Pages text box			
Read Mode	WD 52	Read Mode button (VIEW tab | Views group)	Read Mode button on status bar		
Read Mode, Change Color	WD 121	Page Color on View menu	Read Mode button on status bar, Page Color on View menu		
Readability Statistics	WD 118	FILE tab | Print tab, Proofing (Word Options dialog box)			
Record, Display Specific	WD 378	First, Last, Next, or Previous buttons or 'Go to Record' text box (MAILINGS tab | Preview Results group)			
Redo	WD 24		Redo button on Quick Access Toolbar		CTRL+Y
Remove Character Formatting	WD 80				CTRL+SPACEBAR
Remove Paragraph Formatting	WD 80				CTRL+Q
Remove Space after Paragraph	WD 80	'Line and Paragraph Spacing' button (HOME tab | Paragraph group)		Paragraph, Indents and Spacing tab (Paragraph dialog box)	CTRL+0 (zero)
Replace Text	WD 114	Replace button (HOME tab | Editing group)			CTRL+H
Research Task Pane, Look Up Information	WD 119		ALT+click desired word		ALT+SHIFT+F7
Reveal Formatting	WD 298				SHIFT+F1
Right-Align	WD 75	Align Right button (HOME tab | Paragraph group)		Paragraph, Indents and Spacing tab (Paragraph dialog box) Touch mode: 'Show Context Menu' button on mini toolbar, Paragraph, Indents and Spacing tab (Paragraph dialog box)	CTRL+R
Rulers, Display	WD 82	View Ruler check box (VIEW tab | Show group)			
Save	WD 12	Save (FILE tab | Save tab)	Save button on Quick Access Toolbar		
Save Document, Same File Name	WD 33	Save (FILE tab | Save tab)	Save button on Quick Access toolbar		

Microsoft Word 2013 Quick Reference Summary *(continued)*

Task	Page Number	Ribbon	Other On-Screen Element	Shortcut Menu	Keyboard Shortcut
Save Location, Set Default	WD 319	Options (FILE tab), Save (Word Options dialog box)			
Save Word 2013 Document in Earlier Word Format	WD 307	'Change File Type' (FILE tab | Export tab), select new file format			F12
Save Word Document as Different File Type	WD 309	'Change File Type' (FILE tab | Export tab), select new file type			
Scroll, Up/Down One Line	WD 12		Tap or click scroll arrow at top/bottom of vertical scroll bar		
Scroll, Up/Down One Screen	WD 12		Tap or click above/below scroll box on vertical scroll bar		
Section Break, Continuous	WD 432	'Insert Page and Section Breaks' button (PAGE LAYOUT tab | Page Setup group), Continuous			
Section Break, Delete	WD 223			Select break notation, Cut	Select break notation, DELETE or BACKSPACE
Section Break, Next Page	WD 222	'Insert Page and Section Breaks' button (PAGE LAYOUT tab | Page Setup group), Next Page			
Select Block of Text	WD 32		Click beginning, SHIFT+click end Touch mode: Drag selection handle(s)		
Select Character(s)	WD 32		Drag pointer through characters Touch mode: Drag selection handle(s)		SHIFT+RIGHT ARROW or SHIFT+LEFT ARROW
Select Entire Document	WD 32	Select button arrow (HOME tab | Editing group)	In left margin, triple-click		CTRL+A
Select Graphic	WD 32		Tap or click graphic		
Select Group of Words	WD 28		Drag pointer through words Touch mode: Drag selection handle(s)		CTRL+SHIFT+RIGHT ARROW or CTRL+SHIFT+LEFT ARROW repeatedly
Select Line	WD 16		Click in left margin Touch mode: Double-tap to left of line		SHIFT+DOWN ARROW
Select Multiple Lines	WD 32		Drag pointer in left margin Touch mode: Drag selection handle(s)		HOME, then SHIFT+DOWN ARROW; or END, then SHIFT+UP ARROW
Select Multiple Paragraphs	WD 32		Drag pointer in left margin Touch mode: Drag selection handle(s)		SHIFT+DOWN ARROW
Select Nonadjacent Items	WD 32		Select first item, hold down CTRL key while selecting item(s)		

Microsoft Word 2013 Quick Reference Summary *(continued)*

Task	Page Number	Ribbon	Other On-Screen Element	Shortcut Menu	Keyboard Shortcut
Select Nonadjacent Items	WD 244				CTRL+select
Select Paragraph	WD 32		Triple-click paragraph		CTRL+SHIFT+DOWN ARROW or CTRL+SHIFT+UP ARROW
Select Sentence	WD 32		CTRL-click		
Select Word	WD 32		Double-tap or double-click word		CTRL+SHIFT+RIGHT ARROW or CTRL+SHIFT+LEFT ARROW
Select Words	WD 32		Drag pointer through words Touch mode: Drag selection handle(s)		CTRL+SHIFT+RIGHT ARROW or CTRL+SHIFT+LEFT ARROW repeatedly
Selection Pane	WD 428	'Display the Selection Pane' button (PICTURE TOOLS FORMAT tab | Arrange group)			
Shade Paragraph	WD 21	Shading arrow (HOME tab | Paragraph group)			
Shape, Add Text	WD 146			Add Text Edit Text button on mini toolbar	
Shape, Apply Style	WD 145	More button in Shape Styles gallery (DRAWING TOOLS FORMAT tab | Shape Styles group)	'Shape Quick Styles' on mini toolbar		
Shape, Insert	WD 142	'Draw a Shape' button (INSERT tab | Illustrations group)			
Sharing Link, Get	WD 312	'Get a Sharing Link' (FILE tab | Share tab)			
Single-Space Lines	WD 80	'Line and Paragraph Spacing' button (HOME tab | Paragraph group)		Paragraph, Indents and Spacing tab (Paragraph dialog box)	CTRL+1
Small Caps	WD 80	Font Dialog Box Launcher HOME Tab | Font group), Font tab (Font dialog box)			CTRL+SHIFT+K
SmartArt Graphic, Add Shapes To	WD 215	Add Shape button (SMARTART TOOLS DESIGN tab | Create Graphic group) Touch Mode: Add Shape button (SMARTART TOOLS DESIGN tab | Create Graphic group), 'Add Shape After'		Add Shape	
SmartArt Graphic, Add Text through Text Pane	WD 457		Text Pane control on left side of graphic		
SmartArt Graphic, Add Text To	WD 214		Select shape, type text	Edit Text	

Microsoft Word 2013 Quick Reference Summary *(continued)*

Task	Page Number	Ribbon	Other On-Screen Element	Shortcut Menu	Keyboard Shortcut
SmartArt Graphic, Change Colors	WD 216	Change Colors button (SMARTART TOOLS DESIGN tab | SmartArt Styles group)			
SmartArt Graphic, Change Layout	WD 456	SMARTART TOOLS DESIGN tab, Layouts gallery			
SmartArt Graphic, Copy Using Office Clipboard	WD 459	Clipboard Dialog Box Launcher (HOME tab | Clipboard group), Copy button (HOME tab | Clipboard group)		Copy	CTRL+C
SmartArt Graphic, Delete Shapes From	WD 214	Select shape, Cut button (HOME tab | Clipboard group)			
SmartArt Graphic, Insert	WD 212	'Insert a SmartArt Graphic' button (INSERT tab | Illustrations group)			
SmartArt Graphic, Layer in Front of Text	WD 461	Bring Forward arrow (SMARTART TOOLS FORMAT tab | Arrange group), 'Bring in Front on Text'			
SmartArt Graphic, Paste Using Office Clipboard	WD 459	Clipboard Dialog Box Launcher (HOME tab | Clipboard group), Paste graphic from Office Clipboard		Paste	CTRL+V
SmartArt Style, Apply	WD 217	More button (SMARTART TOOLS DESIGN tab | SmartArt Styles group)			
Sort Paragraphs	WD 232	Sort button (HOME tab | Paragraph group)			
Source, Edit	WD 96		Tap or click citation, Citation Options arrow, Edit Source		
Source, Modify	WD 109	Manage Sources button (REFERENCES tab | Citations & Bibliography group), Edit button			
Space after Paragraph, Remove	WD 80	'Line and Paragraph Spacing' button (HOME tab | Paragraph group)		Paragraph Touch mode: 'Show Context Menu' on mini toolbar, Paragraph	
Spelling and Grammar, Check at Once	WD 116	'Spelling & Grammar' button (REVIEW tab | Proofing group)	'Spelling and Grammar Check' icon on status bar, Spelling	Spelling	F7
Spelling, Check as You Type	WD 10		Tap or click word, 'Spelling and Grammar Check' icon on status bar	Press and hold or right-click error, tap or click correct word on shortcut menu	
Split Window	WD 445	Split Window button (VIEW tab | Windows group)			CTRL+ALT+S, ENTER
Style Set, Change	WD 321	More button (DESIGN tab | Document Formatting group)			

Microsoft Word 2013 Quick Reference Summary *(continued)*

Task	Page Number	Ribbon	Other On-Screen Element	Shortcut Menu	Keyboard Shortcut
Style, Apply	WD 105	Style name in Quick Styles gallery (HOME tab | Styles group)			CTRL+SHIFT+S, Style Name arrow
Style, Create	WD 297	More button (HOME tab | Styles group), 'Create a Style' (Styles gallery)			
Style, Modify	WD 70	Styles Dialog Box Launcher (HOME tab | Styles group), select [style name], Modify		Modify	ALT+CTRL+SHIFT+S
Style, Update to Match Selection	WD 73	Styles Dialog Box Launcher (HOME tab | Styles group), 'Update Normal to Match Selection'		'Update Normal to Match Selection'	ALT+CTRL+SHIFT+S
Subscript	WD 80	Subscript button (HOME tab | Font group)		Font, Font tab (Font dialog box)	CTRL+EQUAL SIGN
Superscript	WD 80	Superscript button (HOME tab | Font group)		Font, Font tab (Font dialog box)	CTRL+SHIFT+PLUS SIGN
Switch between Open Documents	WD 459	Switch Windows button (VIEW tab | Window group)	Tap or click app button on taskbar		ALT+TAB
Symbol, Insert	WD 158	'Insert a Symbol' button (INSERT tab | Symbols group)			
Synonym, Find and Insert	WD 116	Thesaurus button (REVIEW tab | Proofing group)		Tap or click desired synonym on Synonym submenu Touch Mode: 'Show Context Menu' button on mini toolbar, Synonyms on shortcut menu	SHIFT+F7
Tab Stops, Set Custom	WD 167	Paragraph Dialog Box Launcher (HOME tab | Paragraph group), Tabs button (Paragraph dialog box)	Click desired tab stop on ruler	Paragraph, Tabs button (Paragraph dialog box)	
Table Columns, Resize to Fit Table Contents	WD 178	AutoFit button (TABLE TOOLS LAYOUT tab | Cell Size group)	Double-click column boundary	AutoFit	
Table Gridlines, Show/Hide	WD 239	'View Table Gridlines' button (TABLE TOOLS LAYOUT tab | Table group)			
Table Item, Copy and Paste	WD 294	Copy button (HOME tab | Clipboard group), display new location, Paste arrow (HOME tab | Clipboard group), Merge Table button (Paste gallery)		Copy, Paste Options	CTRL+C; CTRL+V
Table, Align Data in Cells	WD 80	Align [location] button (TABLE TOOLS LAYOUT tab | Alignment group)			
Table, Apply Style	WD 177	More button in Table Styles gallery (TABLE TOOLS DESIGN tab | Table Styles group)			
Table, Border	WD 255	Borders arrow (TABLE TOOLS LAYOUT tab | Table Styles group), 'Borders and Shading' in Borders gallery			

Microsoft Word 2013 Quick Reference Summary *(continued)*

Task	Page Number	Ribbon	Other On-Screen Element	Shortcut Menu	Keyboard Shortcut
Table, Center	WD 180	Select table, Center button (HOME tab | Font group)	Select table, Center button on mini toolbar		
Table, Change Cell Spacing	WD 245	Cell Margins button (TABLE TOOLS LAYOUT tab | Alignment group)		Table Properties	
Table, Change Column Width	WD 240	'Table Column Width' box (TABLE TOOLS LAYOUT tab | Cell Size group) Touch Mode: AutoFit button (TABLE TOOLS LAYOUT tab | Cell Size group), Autofit Contents	Drag column boundary in table or 'Move Table Column' marker on horizontal ruler		
Table, Change Row Height	WD 241	'Table Row Height' box (TABLE TOOLS LAYOUT tab | Cell Size group)	Drag row boundary in table or 'Adjust Table Row' marker on vertical ruler	Table Properties, Row tab (Table Properties dialog box)	
Table, Delete Cell Contents	WD 184	Cut button (HOME tab | Clipboard group)			Select cell contents, DELETE or BACKSPACE
Table, Delete Column/Row	WD 247	Delete Table button (TABLE TOOLS LAYOUT tab | Rows & Columns group)	Touch Mode: Delete Table on mini toolbar	Select column/row, Delete Columns or Delete Rows	
Table, Delete Entire	WD 184	Delete Table button (TABLE TOOLS LAYOUT tab | Rows & Columns group)			
Table, Delete Row or Column	WD 184	Delete Table button (TABLE TOOLS LAYOUT tab | Rows & Columns group)		Select row/column, Delete Rows or Delete Columns	
Table, Distribute Columns	WD 251	Distribute Columns button (TABLE TOOLS LAYOUT tab | Cell Size group)		'Distribute Columns Evenly'	
Table, Distribute Rows	WD 252	Distribute Rows button (TABLE TOOLS LAYOUT tab | Cell Size group)		'Distribute Rows Evenly'	
Table, Insert	WD 174	'Add a Table' button (INSERT tab | Tables group)			
Table, Insert Column	WD 182	'Insert Columns to the Left/Right' button (TABLE TOOLS LAYOUT tab | Rows & Columns group)		Insert	
Table, Insert Row	WD 181	'Insert Rows Above/Below' button (TABLE TOOLS LAYOUT Tab | Rows & Columns group)	Tap or click desired Insert Control	Insert	
Table, Merge Cells	WD 182	Merge Cells button (TABLE TOOLS LAYOUT tab | Merge group)		Merge Cells	
Table, Move Cell Boundary	WD 250	Table Properties button (TABLE TOOLS LAYOUT tab | Table group), Cell tab (Table Properties dialog box)	Drag cell boundary or 'Move Table Column' marker on horizontal ruler		

Microsoft Word 2013 Quick Reference Summary *(continued)*

Task	Page Number	Ribbon	Other On-Screen Element	Shortcut Menu	Keyboard Shortcut
Table, Move Row	WD 286	Cut button (HOME tab | Clipboard group); Paste button (HOME tab | Clipboard group)	Drag selected row to new location Touch Mode: Use stylus to select and drag row to new location	Cut; Paste	CTRL+X; CTRL+V
Table, Remove Shading from Cell	WD 244	Shading arrow (TABLE TOOLS DESIGN tab | Table Styles group), No Color in Shading gallery			
Table, Repeat Header Rows	WD 392	'Repeat Header Rows' button (TABLE TOOLS LAYOUT tab | Data group)			
Table, Resize	WD 182	'Table Column Width' or 'Table Row Height' boxes (TABLE TOOLS LAYOUT tab | Cell Size group)	ALT-drag markers on ruler		
Table, Select Cell	WD 179	Select Table button (TABLE TOOLS LAYOUT tab | Table group)	Tap or click left edge of cell		
Table, Select Column	WD 178	Select Table button (TABLE TOOLS LAYOUT tab | Table group)	Click top border of column		
Table, Select Entire	WD 179	Select Table button (TABLE TOOLS LAYOUT tab | Table group)	Tap or click table move handle		
Table, Select Multiple Cells, Rows, or Columns, Adjacent	WD 179		Drag through cells, rows, or columns		
Table, Select Next Cell	WD 179				TAB
Table, Select Previous Cell	WD 179				SHIFT+TAB
Table, Select Row	WD 179	Select button (TABLE TOOLS LAYOUT tab | Table group)	Tap or click to left of row		
Table, Shade Cell	WD 243	Shading arrow (TABLE TOOLS DESIGN tab | Table Styles group)			
Table, Sort	WD 248	Sort button (TABLE TOOLS LAYOUT tab | Data group)			
Table, Sort by Multiple Columns	WD 392	Sort button (TABLE TOOLS LAYOUT tab | Data group), Sort by arrow (Sort dialog box), Then by arrow (Sort dialog box)			
Table, Split	WD 183	Split Table button (TABLE TOOLS LAYOUT tab | Merge group)			
Table, Split Cells	WD 183	Split Cells button (TABLE TOOLS LAYOUT tab | Merge group)		Split Cells	

Microsoft Word 2013 Quick Reference Summary *(continued)*

Task	Page Number	Ribbon	Other On-Screen Element	Shortcut Menu	Keyboard Shortcut
Table, Sum Columns/Rows	WD 256	Formula button (TABLE TOOLS LAYOUT tab | Data group)			
Text Box, Insert	WD 444	'Choose a Text Box' button (INSERT tab | Text group)			
Text Box, Position	WD 449		Drag text box		
Text Effect, Apply	WD 20	'Text Effects and Typography' button (HOME tab | Font group)		Font Touch mode: 'Show Context Menu' on mini toolbar, Font on shortcut menu	
Text Wrapping, Change	WD 145	Wrap Text button (DRAWING TOOLS FORMAT tab | Arrange group)	Tap or click Layout Options button on graphic	Wrap Text	
Theme Colors, Change	WD 31	Theme Colors button (DESIGN tab | Document Formatting group)			
Theme Effects, Modify	WD 458	Theme Effects button (DESIGN tab | Document Formatting group)			
Theme Fonts, Change	WD 259	Theme Fonts button (DESIGN tab | Document Formatting group)			
Theme Fonts, Customize	WD 296	Theme Fonts button (DESIGN tab | Document Formatting group), Customize Fonts			
Underline	WD 29	Underline button (HOME tab | Font group)	Underline button on mini toolbar	Font, Font tab (Font dialog box) Touch mode: 'Show Context Menu' button on mini toolbar, Font on shortcut menu, Font tab (Font dialog box)	CTRL+U
Underline Words, Not Spaces	WD 80	Font Dialog Box Launcher (HOME tab | Font group), Font tab (Font dialog box), Underline style arrow			CTRL+SHIFT+W
Undo	WD 24		Undo button on Quick Access Toolbar		CTRL+Z
User Name and Initials, Change	WD 334	Options (FILE tab), General (Word Options dialog box)			
Vertical Rule between Columns	WD 436	'Add or Remove Columns' button (PAGE LAYOUT tab | Page Setup group), More Columns in Add or Remove Columns gallery, Line between check box (Columns dialog box)			
Vertically, Display Text	WD 253	Text Direction button (TABLE TOOLS LAYOUT tab | Alignment group)			
Watermark, Create	WD 258	Watermark button (DESIGN tab | Page Background group)			

Microsoft Word 2013 Quick Reference Summary (continued)

Task	Page Number	Ribbon	Other On-Screen Element	Shortcut Menu	Keyboard Shortcut
Webpage, Save Word Document As	WD 317	'Change File Type' (FILE tab | Export tab), 'Single File Web Page'			
WordArt, Change Fill Color	WD 416	Text Fill arrow (DRAWING TOOLS FORMAT tab | WordArt Styles group)			
WordArt, Change Shape	WD 420	Text Effects button (DRAWING TOOLS FORMAT tab | WordArt Styles group)			
WordArt, Insert	WD 141	Insert WordArt button (INSERT tab | Text group)			
XPS Document, Create	WD 305	'Create PDF/XPS Document' (FILE tab | Export tab)			
Zoom 100%	WD 37	100% button (VIEW tab | Zoom group)			
Zoom Document	WD 35	Zoom button (VIEW tab | Zoom group)	Zoom Out or Zoom In button or Zoom level button on status bar. Touch mode: Pinch or stretch		
Zoom Multiple Pages	WD 120	Multiple Pages button (VIEW tab | Zoom group)			
Zoom One Page	WD 30	One Page button (VIEW tab | Zoom group)			
Zoom Page Width	WD 7	Page Width button (VIEW tab | Zoom group)			

Important Notes for Windows 7 Users

The screen shots in this book show Microsoft Office 2013 running in Windows 8. If you are using Microsoft Windows 7, however, you still can use this book because Office 2013 runs virtually the same way on both platforms. You will encounter only minor differences if you are using Windows 7. Read this section to understand the differences.

Dialog Boxes

If you are a Windows 7 user, the dialog boxes shown in this book will look slightly different than what you see on your screen. Dialog boxes for Windows 8 have a title bar with a solid color, and the dialog box name is centered on the title bar. Beyond these superficial differences in appearance, however, the options in the dialog boxes across both platforms are the same. For instance, Figures 1 and 2 show the Font dialog box in Windows 7 and the Font dialog box in Windows 8.

Figure 1   Font Dialog Box in Windows 7

Figure 2   Font Dialog Box in Windows 8

Alternate Steps for Running an App in Windows 7

Nearly all of the steps in this book work exactly the same way for Windows 7 users; however, running an app (or program/application) requires different steps for Windows 7. The following steps show how to run an app in Windows 7.

Running an App (or Program/Application) Using Windows 7

1. Click the Start button on the taskbar to display the Start menu.
2. Click All Programs and then click the Microsoft Office 2013 folder (Figure 3).
3. If necessary, click the name of the folder containing the app you want to run.
4. Click the name of the app you want to run (such as Excel 2013).

Figure 3   Running an App Using the Windows 7 Start Menu